Explorations In
MACROECONOMICS

THIRD EDITION

James F. Willis
Martin L. Primack
San Jose State University

C·A·T Publishing Company

Acknowledgements

Quotations in Chapter 1, Chapter 7, and Application 13 from John Maynard Keynes, *The General Theory of Employment, Interest, and Money,* Harcourt, Brace & World, New York, 1936. Reprinted by permission of Harcourt Brace Jovanovich, Inc., and Macmillan, London and Basingstoke.

Quotation in Application to Chapter 1 from John G. Gurley, "Maoist Economic Development" (from *America's Asia,* edited by Edward Friedman and Mark Selden, Random House, New York, 1971) in *Economics, Mainstream Readings and Radical Critiques,* 2nd ed., edited by David Mermelstein, Random House, New York, 1973. Reprinted by permission of the author and Random House, Inc.

Application to Chapter 10, "First Steps in Banking," from *Punch,* April 3, 1957, pp. 440-441. © 1972 by McGraw-Hill, Inc.

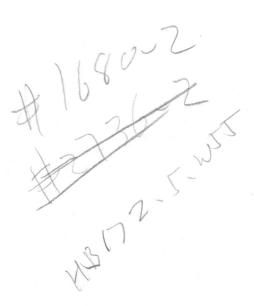

ISBN 0-929655-75-3

To Marianna, Jim, and my Mother.
J.F.W.

In memory of Marlene Primack.
M.L.P.

Table of Contents

Chapter 3: Supply and Demand:Price Determination in Competitive Markets

Application to Chapter 3: When Should We Let Supply and Demand Work?

Chapter 4: Components of an Economic Society: Households, Business Firms, Governments

Application to Chapter 4: The Social Responsibility of Business: The Invisible Hand Versus the Good Corporate Citizen

Chapter 5: Measuring National Income and Product

Chapter 6: Economic Fluctuations

Chapter 7: Aggregate Demand and Aggregate Supply

Chapter 8: Income and Employment: The Keynesian Beginnings

Chapter 9: Income and Employment Without Government

Chapter 10: Completing the Keynesian Model: Adding Government Expenditures and Fiscal Policy

Chapter 11: Automatic Stabilizers and the National Debt

Application to Chapter 11: The "Share Economy": Would it Create Full Employment?

Chapter 12: Money in the Modern Economy

Chapter 13: Commercial Banking and the Creation of M1 Money

Chapter 14: Monetary Policy: Central Banking in Deregulated Financial Markets

Chapter 15: Aggregate Supply, Supply-Side Economics, and the Role of Expectations

Chapter 16: Expansion and Growth

Application 1 to Chapter 16: Can We Have Growth Without Massive Military Spending?

Application 2 to Chapter 16: More Growth Versus a Clean Environment

Chapter 17: Patterns of International Trade

Chapter 18: Paying for International Trade

Chapter 19: Other Economic Systems in Theory

Chapter 20: The Former Soviet Union: Is it Moving from Planned Socialism to a Market Economy?

PREFACE

An educated person is one who has finally discovered that there are some questions to which nobody has the answers.

Anonymous

From our own observations as teachers and from recent developments in the field, two facts about the principles of economics course are apparent. First, enrollments are growing, and second, they are growing not just because students want to learn about economics, but also because they are *required* to take the course.

On the one hand, this boom gives those of us who teach economics a greater opportunity to expose students to our way of thinking, to economists' ideas on how to approach the understanding and solution of problems. On the other, it means that we have to provide students with some good reasons for learning about the subject, especially if we expect them to retain what they learn. It is our hope that this book will help students understand how economists think, and how applicable an economic perspective is to the problems of the real world. Furthermore, the basic questions facing our students, as political creatures in a democracy, are economic ones. This text should prepare them to understand policy debate in such areas as economic stabilization, the crisis of the cities; poverty, and agricultural policy. Obviously, an understanding of economics is also useful, if not necessary, for careers in such areas as business administration, sociology, psychology, history, and the administrative end of many types of engineering.

We have therefore tried to do two things. First, we have reduced the principles of economics in both volume and complexity to the point at which our students can grasp (and, we hope, *retain*) them. Second, we have applied the basic principles to problems that our students can recognize. We have tried to address particularly those students who are more concerned with a J.O.B. than a Ph.D. Many of the problems these students will face concern economics to some degree. And, although there are some questions in economics to which nobody knows the answers, there are even more for which there are *many* answers. Our students need to be able to analyze the alternatives, choose the most feasible one, and—perhaps most important—*know the basis on which the choice rests.*

Scope and Approach

In our experience, the greatest criticism of the principles of economics course is that we instructors try to do too much. Using the average textbook of 1,300-plus pages crammed with solid, valuable materials, the instructor naturally has to race in order to cover the ground. Furthermore, students tend to become swamped with the detail and diversity of the subject matter. They often become confused about what is most important. We have tried to avoid this situation.

Of necessity, we could not include in this text everything that our colleagues wanted us to—although we are grateful to them for their suggestions. We included those principles and problems that seemed most important *to us*, including what we did because both of us are teachers. In other words, we put in materials that work with our students. We have included the essential materials dealing with income determination, banking and money, government stabilization policy, supply and demand, the theory of the firm, and pricing of factors of production. In addition to this basic core, we have added materials on economic development, international trade, and other economic systems. We realize, however, that different instructors may wish to delve more deeply into an issue or expand on a problem in a particular chapter. Therefore, we have listed, at the end of chapters and applications, a number of additional sources.

We feel that this principles of economics text has several distinct advantages over many others in the field:

1. It is not an encyclopedia of economics but, rather, contains enough theory to equip the student with a permanent level of economic literacy.

2. Most theoretical chapters are immediately followed by applications that use the economic principles just covered in analyzing practical economic problems.

3. The use of mathematics has been limited to the practical minimum by avoiding complex algebraic manipulations and difficult derivations of relationships, and by using, instead, simple two-dimensional diagrams to illustrate principles.

4. Every attempt has been made to communicate in the everyday language of the student rather than in the technical language of the economic journal.

5. Special attention has been given to chapter summaries, end-of-chapter materials, and the glossary in order to help the student review and to reinforce the concepts presented in each chapter.

The Study Guide

To help students obtain some drill in economic problem solving and find out how well they are grasping the material, we have prepared a study guide. Each unit of this guide starts with a review of key terms and essay questions and problems that are designed to make students rethink the material just learned. It ends with a self-test consisting of true/false, multiple-choice, and matching questions. After the self-test are all self-test answers and occasional problem answers.

We regard the study guide as an important supplement to *Explorations in Macroeconomics*. Since economics requires a lot of concentration and going over material again and again, we strongly advise that students arm themselves with this learning aid.

Acknowledgments

We have benefited from the advice and assistance of many people in preparing the three editions of *Explorations in Macroeconomics*. While our indebtedness extends to too many economists to acknowledge each one individually, we would especially like to thank those who contributed formal reviews. In the first edition, we are indebted to four economists—James V. Koch of Illinois State University, R. D. Peterson of Colorado State University, Joseph M. Perry of the University of North Florida, and Joseph Domitrz of Western Illinois University. Each of these colleagues reviewed the entire manuscript. In the second edition, we wish to pay special thanks to Anthony L. Ostrosky of Illinois State University. For the same careful and professional review in the third edition, our thanks go to Kirk A. Blackerby of San Jose State University and, again, to Anthony L. Ostrosky. As is usual, we accept responsibility for any errors that remain.

The management and staff of C•A•T Publishing have been exceptionally accommodating and helpful in the lengthy process of preparing and polishing the new manuscript. While that has been true of all at C•A•T, we want to express our particular gratitude to our publisher, Leslie Winegar.

James F. Willis
Martin L. Primack

Chapter 1:
Breaking the Ice

The Aims of the Economist

Economics has had a bad press ever since the nineteenth-century Scottish essayist Thomas Carlyle referred to it as "the dismal science." Carlyle had in mind the gloomy predictions about the future welfare of the human race that many economists were making at the time. This was about a hundred years ago, when economists were still being referred to as "political economists"—an apt name for them, calling to mind Lenin's remark that "political institutions are a superstructure resting on an economic foundation."

Economics has changed in the hundred years since Carlyle called it a dismal science. It has become more scientific and less dismal. The subjects that economists deal with—for example, prices, jobs, the distribution of income, the growth of output and real income, the prevention of inflation—have remained the same, but what *has* changed are the methods we use to investigate them, and the amounts and kinds of information we have. Our view of the future has also changed: most economists today are optimistic about the *ability* of people to solve economic problems.

Frequently, we hear it said that economists seem unable to agree on solutions to economic problems. Since economics is a way of thinking about such problems, and is designed to identify *alternative* solutions, the disagreement is understandable. For long, it was common to find economists divided on ideological grounds between those who favored systems of private enterprise and individual initiative and those who favored systems of collective activity and public control. A major convergence among those concerned with economic policy in the late-twentieth century has occurred on the questions of which of these two systems should be given emphasis by society's seeking economic growth. Economists on the "left" now seem willing to grant the necessity for a society to appeal to human acquisitiveness and self-interest. Generating incentives to work, to take risks and to innovate seem to be an increasing priority in all parts of the world. We will have more to say about these developments not only in the application that follows this chapter but throughout the book.

Still, there is room for disagreement about specific measures to solve particular economic problems. Should government intervene to prevent mergers and takeovers of firms? Will the U.S. enter a recession this year and, if so, should interest rates be lowered? Are foreign manufacturers increasing their share of key U.S. markets and, if so, should the American government intervene? These are but a few of the many economic policy questions that arise constantly and about which economists may have different opinions. In short, when you complete your course in economics you will not have a set of policy conclusions to carry with you but a way of examining the alternatives and formulating your own views about policy questions as they arise. Nonetheless, certain tools and methodology, such as quantitative methods and model building, are widely accepted by nearly all economists. Most economists accept a basic procedure for looking at aggregate economic problems, like unemployment, and at nonaggregate market problems as well.

The fact that today's economists are, in the main, optimistic about the future, should not seem strange. Most of the increase in goods and services, the real income that improves the material well being of people, has occurred in the last century. While economic problems remain for all nations, we now know that improvement in economic organization combined with the enormous potential of further technological change make possible continued advance in standards of living. This is true not only for the relatively wealthy industrial nations but for the newly industrializing nations and less developed nations as well. Can economic problems, then, be eliminated? Few economists would go so far as to say yes. However, the most famous economist of this century, John Maynard Keynes (rhymes with *gains*), writing in 1930 and looking ahead to the next hundred years, put his view this way:

> I draw the conclusion that, assuming no important wars and no important increase in population, the *economic problem* may be solved, or at least be within sight of solution, within a hundred years. This means that the economic problem is not—if we look into the future—*the permanent problem of the human race.*

Keynes expressed this very optimistic view in the early years of the Great Depression of the 1930s. He was wrong, of course, in assuming that there would be no major wars after 1930, but his assumption about no major increase in population may turn out to be correct, at least for the more developed industrial countries. Keynes's statement illustrates two things: (1) economists of the twentieth century are no longer dismal about the future, and

(2) economists develop economic principles not for the sake of abstract exercise, but to be able to analyze and propose solutions to problems that plague the human race. Economists are, in short, deeply concerned with *people* and their material well being.

What Is Economics?

Economics
The social science that deals with the analysis of material problems, how societies allocate scarce resources to satisfy human wants.

Now let's define economics in terms of the "economic problem" to which Keynes referred.

      Economics is the social science that deals with the analysis of material problems. It identifies the various means by which people can satisfy their desires for goods and services by using the limited resources available to produce them. This is a very general definition, but a useful one, because it points out certain basic features of economics.

1. *Economics is a social science.* It deals with the actions of groups of people in relation to society. Economics differs from physical science, which has laws established in the laboratory, where conditions can be controlled. The laboratory of economists is the world, in which nothing is certain and nothing can be controlled with surety. Economists base their principles on what they observe about people—their willingness to spend money or to save it, for example, and on what they observe about the economic institutions that people have created, such as private property, government planning, and the banking system.

2. *Economics is analytical.* Economists use the principles of economics to diagnose various problems, such as unemployment and poverty, and propose solutions to them. Instead of choosing one solution and saying, "Here's what to do," economists set forth the available alternative solutions to a given problem and point out the costs and benefits of each.

3. *Economics is concerned with the material well-being of people.* Economists measure current economic activity and project figures for the future. This does not mean that they feel it is *only* material well-being that counts, but they do insist that it takes the use of limited material resources (land, labor, capital, and entrepreneurship) to solve social problems. Solving economic problems, thus, is closely tied to efforts to solve other kinds of problems.

Macroeconomics and Microeconomics: Economic Principles from Two Perspectives

Macroeconomics
The study of the forces that determine the level of income and employment in a society.

Macroeconomics is the study of the forces that determine the level of income and employment in a society. Macroeconomics gives us the big picture of a society, or what economists call its aggregate performance. That perspective focuses on the origins of economic scarcity, the problems of economic development, and how households and business firms make economic decisions. Going beyond that, we build a simple model of aggregate economics, gradually adding the components that make up our complex economic world: government spending, gross national product, business cycles, the level of employment, the level of income, the money supply, banking, and expansion and growth.

Microeconomics
The study of disaggregated economic activities or how a market economy allocates resources through prices.

Microeconomics is the study of disaggregated economic activities. Beginning with scarcity, economic development and basic decisions by households and firms, microeconomics seeks to provide an understanding of a market economy and, in particular, the role of prices in such an economy. It examines the various ways product and factor markets may be organized and how their performance may be understood both privately and socially.

While macroeconomics and microeconomics differ in focus, each deals with the same basic subject matter of economic activity. It is not surprising, therefore, that some areas of study are taught in both micro and macro, though from a different perspective. The two areas that may be included in both halves of this book are international trade and finance and comparative economic systems.

What Is the Economist's Method?

Even though economics is a social science, rather than a physical science, its method is scientific and based on facts and logic. An economist's starting point, like a chemist's or physicist's, is a hypothesis, or an assumption about a relationship between 2 things (or 10 or 20 things). At this point, however, the economist steps outside the safety of the laboratory into the unpredictable realm of people. We can best demonstrate the three stages of the economist's job with an example.

Suppose that you are a young economist, a consultant to the President's Council of Economic Advisors, and are called to a meeting of the council. Everyone looks grave. The chairman explains that the country's economy is showing some alarming tendencies. Personal incomes in the last year have risen, but for some reason, consumer spending has fallen. People just aren't buying, and business is beginning to hurt. The President is deeply concerned, and so is Congress. You are to find out what has happened and tell the government what to do about it.

Now you begin on stage 1 of the economist's 3-stage process (see Table 1-1). First you gather all the data you can that might explain what has happened. Exactly how much did incomes grow in this past year? Did spending on consumer goods change in any way, and if so, how? How do the figures for this past 3-month period compare with the figures for the same quarter a year ago? Has there been a change in the relationship between income and

Table 1-1
The Three Basic Stages in Economic Analysis

Stage 1	Stage 2	Stage 3
Gathering facts	*Formulating and testing theory*	*Making economic policy*
The economist gathers data that are relevant to the hypothesis or statement (this is called descriptive economics).	On the basis of the data, the economist sets forth a general theory about economic behavior and tests the theory (this is the theorizing stage).	The policy maker, who is not necessarily the same person as the economist, formulates measures to deal with economic behavior and its consequences (this is the policy-making stage).

spending? What have people been doing with all the money they haven't been spending? Have they been saving it? Have they been using it to pay taxes?

After you have finished this fact-finding or *descriptive* stage, you embark on stage 2, the *theorizing* stage. You try to formulate a theory that will explain the way behavior changes as income changes. You want to express not only what is happening now, but also what is likely to happen a year from now, 2 years, or 5 years from now, given certain incomes, populations, and supplies and prices of goods. The theory you evolve may be a simple one (people have lost faith in material things and are giving all their money to churches), or very complex (people are afraid of inflation and at the same time distrustful of anything modern, so they are putting all their money in gold, Renaissance paintings, and pre-1914 Rolls-Royces). In any event, you spend days writing up your version of the situation, using all the facts at your command and expressing your opinion in the clearest manner possible.

On the basis of the data you have collected, you form the hypothesis that short-term changes in consumer spending depend not only on changes in income but also on changes in other factors such as taxes and expectations about the future. You can use various statistical techniques to isolate the effect of one factor (short-term income changes) on another (consumer spending).

When you are setting up these theoretical interrelationships, you construct a model, a systematic analogy to real consumer behavior. This model enables you to interpret the statistical results.

Suppose you find that there is a weak (perhaps nearly zero) correlation, during any 6-month period, between changes in people's incomes and changes in their spending habits. In other words, even if their incomes go up, their spending changes little, or perhaps not at all. Then you must explain the decline in consumer spending in terms of changes in other factors.

Your model may include the expectations people have about future changes in prices and in taxes (income taxes, excise taxes). Suppose your data show that taxes (and other important factors that might offer some explanation) have not changed in the past 6 months. Then you conclude that the decline in spending must be due to *expectations* about the future. People are putting off buying things until later in the year. They're waiting for inventory-reduction sales, for the crops to come in, for an expected drop in the interest rate. For many reasons, they're just holding onto their money and waiting. You incorporate all these ideas in your report to the chairman of the President's Council of Economic Advisors.

The third stage is the *policy-making* stage. This stage is out of your hands, because the people who decide on the economic policy act on their own, although they may base their decisions on the economists' recommendations. The policy maker may be Congress, or the President, or the President and the Cabinet acting together. But bear in mind that a nation's economic policy is part of its overall social policy (including diplomatic, military, and political policies). Your role as an economist has been only to identify to the policy makers the nature of the problem, tell them how serious it is, and point out alternative solutions, with the costs and benefits of each.

(For a fascinating discussion of public policy decisions, read *America's Hidden Success*, by John E. Schwartz, published by Norton in 1988 as a paper back. This book provides a reassessment of public policy from Kennedy to Reagan.)

The Citizen and Economic Policy

The above example is fairly simple and clear-cut. The policy maker here may decide on the basis of reports prepared by you and others that no change in economic policy is required. It appears in this case that consumer spending is going to rise in the long term, as prices fall and as people adjust to their higher incomes.

From this illustration, you might conclude that economic investigation and policy making are processes reserved for experts in politics and economics. This is not so. Whether the issue is local or federal taxes, or local or national economic policies, the U.S. needs an enlightened public. The *non*economist, *non*politician, just plain citizen can review, criticize, and in the long run even change economic policy. People can do this by discussion and by the way they vote.

We write this book with the conviction that (1) the economic principles a person needs to know to make intelligent decisions on economic issues are simple, and that (2) such positions should be founded in fact and logic.

Applications: Concrete Examples of Abstract Ideas

Much of economics consists of abstractions, theories, and discussions of curves and trends. But, as we pointed out at the beginning of this chapter, it isn't all just theories; you already know a lot about economics. So we have tried to use the knowledge you already have to illustrate the theoretical part of economics. You will find sections called "applications" scattered throughout this book. They show you one or more practical applications of the theory or principle that has just been explained. For example, after the chapter that introduces the theory of supply and demand, there is an application that discusses a concrete example of supply and demand: rent controls and the price of housing. These applications can serve as beacons to help you fix your position in unfamiliar surroundings as you explore the economic way of thinking.

End-of-Chapter Summaries

At the end of each chapter, you'll find a section entitled "Summing Up." (Some applications carry these postscript sections too.) These sections repeat, in condensed form, what the chapter or application is about. Even if you feel you understand the chapter as you read it, read "Summing Up" carefully. The repetition will help to imprint the material in your mind. Also, after the "Summing Up" sections to each chapter, there is a list of "Key Terms," concepts that are important to understand and remember. These terms and their definition can be checked through (1) rereading the margin notes in that chapter as well as through (2) checking the glossary at the end of the book.

Mathematics De-emphasized

One reason why economics has a reputation for being a tough subject is that many people are afraid of mathematics, and they associate economics with it. However, as you work your way through this book, you will realize that it contains very little mathematics. When economists write articles in professional journals, they may use advanced mathematics, but you do not need to know advanced mathematics to learn the basic principles of economics.

Independent Variable In a set of relationships, this is the variable that changes first.

Dependent Variable In a set of relationships, the variable whose value depends on the value of the independent variable.

This book does contain a number of graphs and tables of data. The data serve to ensure that we are using facts as the basis for our discussions, and the graphs are simply devices to help you visualize abstract ideas. Figure 1-1 is an example of a graph.

All the graphs we use are two-dimensional. That is, they measure the relationships between two factors. They have *height* (measured along the vertical axis) and *length* (measured along the horizontal axis). The measure of the first factor to change (called the **independent variable**) comes from the vertical axis. The measure of the factor whose value depends on that of the first factor (the **dependent variable**) comes from the horizontal axis.[1]

As we go along, we will use graphs to chart the progress of a number of dependent and independent variables: prices of goods,

---

[1]Note that this is a convention adopted in economics with supply and demand diagrams. In mathematics, though, the reverse is usually the case with the dependent variable on the vertical axis and the independent variable on the horizontal axis.

Figure 1-1
An Illustration of Graphing

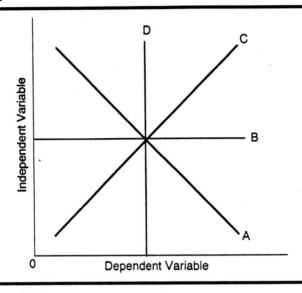

quantities sold, demand for goods and services, jobs, wages, and so forth. In each case, the rule about reading graphs will remain the same.

Now look at Figure 1-1 and we'll discuss some of the kinds of relationships that may occur between dependent and independent variables. The lines drawn on this diagram are called *curves*, even though in this case they are straight lines.

Inverse
The relation between independent and dependent variables is inverse if the dependent variable changes in the opposite direction from the independent variable.

1. Curve A is a case in which the relationship between independent and dependent variable is **inverse**. This means that as the independent variable increases (moves up the vertical axis), the dependent variable decreases (moves toward zero). As the independent variable decreases, the dependent variable increases. We say that curve A is *negatively sloped*, or that it *slopes downward*.

2. Curve B is a case in which the independent variable doesn't change at all. All change occurs in the dependent variable. The dependent variable responds almost without limit at the given value of the independent variable.

Direct
The relationship between the independent variable and the dependent variable is direct if the dependent variable changes in the same direction as the independent variable.

3. Curve C is a case in which the relationship between the independent and dependent variable is **direct**. As the independent variable increases, so does the dependent one. As the independent variable decreases, so does the dependent one. We say that curve C is *positively sloped*, or that it *slopes upward*.

4. Curve D is a case in which the dependent variable doesn't change at all. All change in D takes place in the *in*dependent variable. The independent variable responds almost without limit at the given value of the dependent variable.

If you keep these four cases in mind, you won't be confused by the graphs in this book. Indeed, the graphs will help you to visualize and understand relationships that might otherwise be hard to grasp.

Positive Versus Normative Economics

A person starting out in a first course in principles of physics or chemistry usually does so with no preconceived notions. Since we don't feel at home talking about subnuclear particles, we're willing to leave that subject to the physicists and take anything they say as the truth. However, most people approach economics with a considerable amount of built-in expertise. We have biases about economics, as we do about any social science. We cannot avoid having them, since from an early age we have all had considerable experience as members of the economic society. For example, we get jobs, spend income, pay taxes, and watch the government spend.

But we do not simply leave economic issues to the economists and the politicians. Citizens who are *not* economists, who are *not* politicians, are the ones who must in the long run make choices, through voting or in other ways. Citizens must choose among alternative solutions to economic problems, and they often have to approve or turn down choices that have already been made by some governing body. To be a good citizen, to make intelligent choices on voting day, one needs an understanding of economic principles, backed up by a knowledge of how those principles work out in actual application.

Normative Economics Consists of making judgments about what should be.

When you come to the point of choosing among alternative solutions, you enter the area of **normative economics**, or making judgments about what *should* be.

Positive Economics Consists of determining what is.

Positive economics, on the other hand, consists of determining what *is*. It involves stating facts. We have pointed out that when you gather facts and apply economic principles in an attempt to find a solution to a problem, you do not find just one answer, one unique "right" way; you find that there are several alternative solutions. Normative economics involves looking at these various solutions and applying personal or collective value judgments, to decide what *should* be. (Generalizing about economic behavior naturally has some normative aspects. Therefore, in writing a book about economics, we cannot avoid a few judgments here and there. We have tried to keep them to a minimum. When they do appear, we try to point them out and you're free to agree or disagree.)

To be sure that you understand the difference between positive and normative statements, let's take an example. You go to a party and find an economist who is talking about food stamps and their economic impact. The following conversation takes place:

Economist: The U.S. spent $4 billion in 1984 on the food stamp program. *(Positive)*

You: But a lot of people were still going hungry because they had to present the food stamps at stores in person, and many elderly or disabled people were too feeble to go to the store. It wasn't fair. *(Normative)*

Economist: A family of four with an income of $6,000 a year or less can qualify for $150 a month in food stamps. *(Positive)*

You: A family of four can't *live* on $6,000 a year—not what *I'd* call living. *(Normative)*

See how hard it is to keep from being normative? *(Normative)*

A Word About Words

Economists sometimes speak what seems to be a language all their own. In fact, someone once defined an economist as a person who states the obvious in terms of the incomprehensible. When economists speak of contrived versus natural scarcities, implicit factor returns, and maximum-profit monopoly equilibrium, you sometimes wonder if they're really speaking English. Throughout this book, we have tried to avoid speaking "economese," or what William F. Buckley calls "econospeak." However, we could not weed out *all* the economese, because economics is a complex subject, full of precise language. When we introduce a term, we put it in italics and define it. Boldface color means that you can find the word defined and highlighted in the margin of the text page on which it appears as well as in the Glossary at the back of the book. As you go along, whenever you are not certain of the meaning of something, don't look back through the book for the definition. Just turn to the Glossary and look it up. Definitions are important in economics, because often a word means one thing in everyday usage and another in the language of economists. This book is designed to help you learn economics, in the clearest and most painless way possible.

SUMMING UP

1. Economics has acquired the reputation of being difficult, abstract, and mathematical. This book attempts to make the difficult understandable, to give concrete examples to demonstrate the abstractions, and to de-emphasize the mathematics so that people without an extensive mathematics background can readily grasp the ideas.

2. In the nineteenth century, people referred to economists as "political economists." They also called economics "the dismal science," because of the pessimistic views of the future many economists held. We have come a long way in the past hundred years.

Technology and improved economic organization have caused many modern economists to have an optimistic view of the ability of people to improve their material well-being.

3. Economists differ greatly among themselves about how to *solve* economic problems, but less about how to *study* them. While there is room for disagreement about alternative solutions to specific economic problems, there is growing agreement that economic growth is enhanced by a system of incentives to individual initiative that encourages work, risk taking, and innovation.

4. *Economics* may be defined as the social science that deals with the analysis of material problems. Economists perform their functions by identifying alternative means through which people can provide for their material well-being.

5. Economics differs from physical science, in that physical science proves its principles by means of controlled and repeatable experiments. The laws of economics are derived from observations of human behavior. As behavior changes, so must economists' rules.

6. When economists identify the alternative solutions to economic problems, they also point out the costs and benefits of each.

7. Economists are not necessarily more materialistic than other people. They do, however, insist that solutions to noneconomic questions require material resources (land, labor, capital, and entrepreneurship). Thus, these solutions are based in economic reality.

8. An economist's work is in three stages: (a) gathering facts, (b) theorizing and testing theory, and (c) making economic policy.

9. Gathering of facts is necessary to ensure that concrete information (not hearsay or superstition) is the basis for economic investigation and decisions. Theorizing is necessary to enable the economist to construct a systematic analogy to real life (a *model*), since reality itself is too complex to be described fully. Policy making though frequently based on economic advice, is often out of the economist's hands.

10. This book is written with the following convictions: (a) people need to know economic principles in order to understand economic issues and these principles *can* be stated in a clear, understandable way; and (b) discussions about economic issues should be founded in logic and fact.

11. This book contains very little mathematics. However, it does use many graphs to help you visualize certain concepts. In a graph, the vertical line represents the *independent variable*. The horizontal line represents the *dependent variable* (it depends on the independent one).

12. Lines (called *curves*) come in four varieties: (a) the relationship between the dependent and the independent variable is inverse; (b) the independent variable does not change and only the dependent one changes; (c) the relationship between the dependent and the independent variable is direct; and (d) the independent variable changes, but the dependent variable does not.

13. In *normative economics*, value judgments form the basis for choosing solutions to economic problems. Normative economics states what *should be. Positive economics* states what *is*; no value judgments are made. This book tries to avoid making normative statements. When they do occur, we have identified them, and the reader is free to agree or disagree.

14. The book makes a strong effort to avoid the use of "economese," or complex ways of wording economic principles. When more technical terms first occur, they are defined at once and highlighted in margin notes. They are defined once again in the Glossary at the end of the book.

KEY TERMS

Economics
Independent variable
Dependent variable
Inverse relationship
Direct relationship
Normative economics
Positive economics

QUESTIONS

1. The President has proposed fighting a war on drug-related crime in the streets. Is this an economic question? If so, in what ways?

2. Is it possible to solve noneconomic problems without answering economic questions? Why or why not?

3. Consider the following statements and decide whether each is normative or positive:
    a. There are too many homeless in the U.S. today.
    b. Unemployment among black teenagers in the U.S. is almost 50 percent.
    c. A federally guaranteed annual income is a good idea.
    d. Federally guaranteed annual incomes involve a transfer of income from one group to another.
    e. The distribution of wealth in the U.S. is not equal.
    f. The distribution of wealth in the U.S. should be equal.

4. Why is it that economists cannot conduct their experiments in controlled laboratory surroundings the way physical scientists do?

5. Do you think Keynes was right in believing it possible to solve the economic problem? Why?

6. What is an economic model? Why do economists construct models rather than just trying to describe reality?

7. Why do economists differ on solutions to specific economic problems when they differ relatively little on the way to analyze these problems?

8. Suppose that you are the personal assistant to the President of the U.S. on economic matters. The President calls you in and says: "For my main campaign plank this year, I am going to promise to solve the nation's economic problems. I want your advice, though, on whether this is a realistic promise." What advice would you offer?

Application to Chapter 1: Self-interest: Endangered Motivation or the Key to the Future?

The public is merely a multiplied "me."
Mark Twain

There is only one class in the community that thinks more about money than the rich, and that is the poor. The poor can think of nothing else.
Oscar Wilde

These quotations illustrate two points: (1) what happens to the economy as a whole depends on the economic actions of individuals, and (2) economic forces vitally affect and concern each of us. Economists and noneconomists alike have long sought to understand the basic motivations that determine how we play our roles as consumers or producers on the economic stage. In this application we are going to examine some views on this subject.

Self-Interest: Key to All Characters

One of the first people to theorize about economic motivation was Smith, Adam Smith, author of *The Wealth of Nations* (1776), who is often considered the founder of modern economics. Smith contended that people were not moved primarily by love of their fellow humans; they ordinarily acted in their own self-interest. Smith said, "It is not from the benevolence of the butcher, the brewer, or the baker that we expect our dinner, but from their regard to their own interest." He said that he never knew business people to get together in the social interest. Rather, they sought some "nefarious purpose."

If Adam Smith were alive today and could see laborers banding together to form unions, co-ops, and consumer-protection societies or business executives getting together to discuss common concerns, he would probably attribute the same motives to these groups. Such ventures, he'd probably say, would result in conspiracies against the public interest. This view of human nature led Smith to argue that the economic role government should perform is to create conditions under which the individual's pursuit of self-interest results in maximizing the public welfare. But Smith did not make clear what *kind* of political system would do this. What would prevent public officials from acting in their own

"I wish all I had to worry about was the world—
not taxes, mortgages, rising prices, the cost of college..."

interest rather than in the public's? This problem of self-interested people making public choices comes up again and again.

Samuel Butler wrote in his notebooks: "The world will always be governed by self-interest. We should not try to stop this; we should try to make the self-interest of cads a little more coincident with that of decent people."

Homo Economicus

Hedonism
A philosophical school that argues that self-satisfaction is the primary goal of individuals.

Homo Economicus
A term meaning "economic man."

After Adam Smith, other philosophers continued to name self-interest as the dominant force moving people. Jeremy Bentham (founder of **hedonism**, or the philosophical school of self-satisfaction) carried this idea to new heights in his concept of **homo economicus,** or economic man, who was not only motivated by self-interest, but was literally a walking calculator of pain and pleasure. *Homo economicus* measured every action in terms of the amount of the self-satisfaction that could be derived from it, precisely maximizing personal pleasure or minimizing pain.

Private Citizens Want Private Profits

Economists today no longer hold such an extreme hedonist view. They no longer believe that people either can, or always try to, maximize their pleasure or minimize their pain with precision. However, they do still believe that all people are motivated by self-interest. Alfred Marshall, considered by many to be the originator of modern economic methods, put it this way in his pathbreaking book *Principles of Economics:*

> The steadiest motive to ordinary business work is the desire for the pay which is the material reward of work. The pay may be on its way to be spent selfishly or unselfishly, for noble or base ends; and here the variety of human nature comes into play. But the motive is supplied by a definite amount of money; and it is this definite and exact money measurement of the steadiest motives in business life, which has enabled economics far to outrun every other branch of the study of man.

In other words, Marshall, although admitting to a higher nature in humans, still argued that people's basic economic nature is one of self-interest, the desire for monetary gain. Keynes was quoted as saying that he foresaw an end to the economic problem. But Keynes, too, felt that an appeal to the acquisitive motives of people would be necessary, at least into the twenty-first century, in order to get them to save, invest, and assure economic growth.

Do Corporations Value Profits Above All Else?

Most orthodox economists today still accept the concept of the "economic man," especially as it relates to the decisions of business people. Some of them have attacked the idea that business firms seek to maximize profits. However, Nobel laureate Robert Solow defended it in these words:

> Does the modern industrial corporation maximize profits? Probably not rigorously and single-mindedly, and for much the same reason that Dr. Johnson did not become a philosopher—because cheerfulness keeps breaking in. Most large corporations are free enough from competitive pressure to offer a donation to the Community Chest or a fancy office building without a close calculation of its incremental contribution to profit. The received doctrine can survive if businesses merely *almost* maximize profits.

Solow also feels that consumers are more likely "almost" to maximize satisfaction than "almost" to do anything else and argues that the idea of firms maximizing profits comes closer to explaining and predicting their behavior than any other single assumption. His beliefs probably represent the position of most American economists.

Homo Economicus: Voices of Dissent

Several economists, however, have attacked the idea of *homo economicus*. John Kenneth Galbraith, for one, in his books *The New Industrial State* and *Economics and the Public Purpose* says that the view is outmoded. He feels the power of individuals has been eroded by a corporate system in which "technocrats" in big corporations control the system. These technocrats seek to maximize a larger set of *corporate* (not stockholder) interests (growth, security, their own salaries, and so on). Galbraith maintains that, through advertising, technocrats cause consumers to want what they (the technocrats) *wish* them to want.

Galbraith believes that government should use controls and planning to replace much of this "distorted" profit-maximizing behavior of the markets. But if this came about, public bureaucrats might replace market technocrats. One can imagine government agencies imposing their own ideas on what was socially correct on private decision makers. Galbraith's plan, in other words, would transfer the locus of *Homo economicus* to public agencies.

Arguments continue about who *should* make economic decisions and on what basis they are made. Advertising and its effects on the economy are a controversial area. Our purpose in mentioning the subject is simply to indicate that dissent remains about economic motivations.

The Radical View

A second attack on economic self-interest has come from radical economists, who say that, in an industrial or capitalist society, *homo economicus* is at best an endangered species and at worst a myth. Karl Marx argued that the concentration of power and ownership in private hands (which exists in a capitalist society) leads to alienation of workers and deprives consumers of their right to consume as they wish. It also deprives producers of their right to produce as they wish, because, according to the Marxists, it means that fewer and fewer people make decisions about production. Some radicals have argued that out of a marxist society will evolve **homo communista**, communist man, in place of *homo economicus*. John Gurley, in an essay entitled, "Maoist Economic Development," put it this way:

Homo Communista Communist man.

> The Maoists' disagreement with the capitalist view of economic development is profound.... The profit motive is officially discouraged from assuming an important role in the allocation of resources, and material incentives, while still prevalent, are downgraded.... Development is not likely to occur unless everyone rises together.... Selflessness and unity of purpose will release a huge reservoir of enthusiasm, energy and creativity. Maoists believe that each person should be devoted to "the masses" rather than to his own pots and pans.

As we noted earlier, it appears as we approach the twenty-first century that it is *homo communista* rather than *homo economicus* that is the endangered concept. Not only has "Maoism" been rejected in China, but in many other socialist societies as well, there are widespread pressures to reform economic institutions in ways that recognize the need to appeal to the economic self interests of individuals. We shall have much more to say about this in the final chapters of this book which deal with a comparison of economic systems.

SUMMING UP

1. Adam Smith, considered by many the founder of modern economics, argued that self-interest and acquisitiveness were the primary economic motivations of people. Smith thought that the appropriate economic role of government would be to provide a system within which individual self-interest could be harnessed to accomplish the public good.

2. The *hedonists* (Benthamites), or self-satisfiers, thought that people were walking calculators who measured every act in terms of the pain or pleasure it would bring. Benthamites thought that people would always precisely maximize the amount of pleasure they could achieve. This view is now discredited.

3. Most modern economists, beginning with Alfred Marshall, assume that people are motivated in their economic actions primarily by a desire for monetary gain and a desire to achieve maximum satisfaction. They are not able, however, to measure satisfaction or pain precisely, even though they can measure profit.

4. Although Keynes thought that the economic problem was on its way to being solved, he too believed that until this solution is reached, we must rely on the economic citizen's primary desire; that is, the desire for money.

5. Most orthodox economists (such as Robert Solow) regard the idea of the economic citizen (the profit- and satisfaction-maximizing person) as the most useful long-term view of human behavior, and believe that this view explains and predicts people's economic actions more accurately than any other single assumption.

6. John Kenneth Galbraith says "technocrats" (who hold the power in large corporations) maximize corporate interests and manipulate the tastes of consumers through advertising. He feels that the technocrats have replaced the old competitive economic citizen. Galbraith proposes a system of public controls and planning to replace these distorted (noncompetitive) market forces. Radical

economists have argued that individualism will be replaced by concern for collective well being but this view appears to be receding throughout much of the world.

QUESTIONS

1. Whether self-interest basically motivates people is a question of human behavior. Why can't we simply observe human behavior to answer the questions easily?

2. What is wrong with the hedonistic view of an individual as a walking calculator of pain and pleasure?

3. If people don't exactly maximize their satisfaction or their profit, how can assumptions that they do lead to a satisfactory basis for explaining and predicting economic events?

4. Was Keynes right in saying that, until the economic problem is solved, we need to rely on acquisitiveness of people? Why?

5. Which do you think is more likely to be the economic motivation of the future: self-interest or community interest? Why?

SUGGESTED READING

Dolan, Edwin G. and John C. Goodman. *Economics of Public Policy*. 4th Edition, Chapter 1, "Thinking about Public Issues and Policy." St. Paul, Minn., West Publishing Co. 1989.

Chapter 2:
Scarcity and Economic Development

We have previously defined economics, related it to other subject areas, and talked about its methods of investigation. Now let us look at the overall operation of an economic system. At the outset, let us assume that the economy we are discussing is basically a free, private-enterprise economy and that it is capitalist in organization. This means that most of the means of production—land, labor, capital, and entrepreneurship—are allocated as a result of many private decisions made by buyers and sellers in that economy's marketplaces.

Market System
A set of means by which buyer-seller exchanges are made.

Before moving on to look at this allocative process, let us define the term **market system**. All of us have had experience with markets. We tend to think of them as places such as stores or auction houses in which commodities are sold or exchanged. Although these places are markets, a market need not have a specific physical location. In fact, a market exists whenever buyers and sellers have means to make exchanges. Thus, a *market system* is the set of means by which buyer-seller exchanges are made. For example, today we can all make exchanges as readily by electronic means as by going to an auction house. Whatever form they may take, market transactions provide answers to vital economic questions in the capitalist society.

The Results of Market Exchanges:
The Invisible Hand

Market processes can be viewed as like games in some respects. Each team (buyers, sellers) is in the game to win. Each, in other words, is trying to maximize its own (self) interests. Buyers are presumably attempting to make choices that will yield them, individually, the greatest benefits possible. Sellers, likewise, are attempting to make choices about offering goods and services that will yield them, individually, the greatest return on their activities.

We often associate games with *both* winners *and* losers. In many games such as football, baseball, and the like, the association is correct since if one team wins the other must lose. A remarkable feature of "market games," however, is that *everyone* can be a winner. To see why, we need first to note that market transactions are voluntary rather than coercive. Buyers willingly exchange their income for the anticipated benefit or satisfaction of consuming goods and services. The fact that they do so voluntarily implies that these choices, as opposed to others, will make them better off. Sellers, too, voluntarily give up their ownership rights in these goods and services in the anticipation that the revenue they receive will make them (the firms) better off. Both parties, then, receive a net benefit. Viewed as a game, the market is a positive sum game, one in which all parties can improve their welfare.

It is important to note, however, that these net benefits are *not* created because buyers and sellers necessarily *intend* to make each other better off. Indeed, economists since Adam Smith (*The Wealth of Nations*, 1776) have assumed as a fundamental presumption, that individuals ordinarily act in ways that serve their own interests rather than those of others. Smith observed that by these actions, and, "as if by an invisible hand," the larger interests of an economic society and its members are served. This has come to be known as the **invisible hand argument** or that self-interest decisions that involve voluntary exchanges can make everyone better off even if those decisions were not intended to accomplish that result.

Invisible Hand Argument
The idea that self-interest based voluntary exchanges can make all those involved in the exchanges better off.

Market exchanges occur, therefore, because individuals place different values on the things that can be traded. Suppose you owned an automobile which you value at $5,000 in terms of the satisfaction it provides you. What would induce you to exchange (sell) the automobile for money offered you by someone else? Presumably, there would have to be an offer of more than $5,000 since that would be necessary to make you feel better off. If someone sees your automobile and offers you $6,000 for it, that person is placing a higher value on it than you because he or she expects a larger benefit from its ownership. If you exchange the automobile, however, both you and the buyer are better off. The key point here is that voluntary exchanges occur because individuals place *different* values on the exchangeable goods and services.

We will explore these benefit-creating results of market activities in more detail as we progress through the examination of a market economy and, in particular, will see how the structure of an economic society affects those benefits. This will be especially important in the chapters which deal with the effects of competitiveness on the operation of a market economy.

Scarcity: Source of Basic Economic Questions

Why do societies need to find answers to economic questions? For that matter, why do economic questions arise at all? To understand this, consider two important facts:

Resources
The inputs that are used to make consumer and producer goods.

1. At any given time, the resources available to a society are limited. There is only so much oil, gold, timber, or wheat, just so much capital, just so much labor. **Resources**—the inputs we use to make consumer and producer goods—are limited.

2. People—individuals, families, or larger groups—have needs, wants, and desires which have to be satisfied, as much as they can be, by the goods and services produced by employing the society's limited resources. However, wants and desires—unlike resources—appear to be virtually unlimited. History and psychology show us that they may never be satisfied, since satisfaction of some wants only seems to lead people to acquire new wants.

Scarcity
The relationship between limited resources and unlimited wants which results in the inability to satisfy all human wants for goods and services.

As we move along, we shall look at each of these considerations in greater detail. For now, let's stress the fact that resources are *limited,* human wants are *unlimited,* and this means that our society, and every other society, no matter how rich or how poor, has to face the problem of **scarcity,** the inability to satisfy all people's wants for goods and services. We can best see why this is so by considering the hypothetical case of a country without scarcity.

An Unreal World: No Scarcity

Free Goods
Those in such abundant supply that they have zero prices.

If there were no scarcity, there would be no need for social organizations (markets, planners, and the like) to allocate resources among competing potential users. But of course there always is scarcity, so assuming a world of nonscarcity would not be a satisfactory basis on which to learn about economic reality. If there were no scarcity, all wants could be satisfied. You and I would be able to choose among a vast number of **free goods,** goods in such abundant supply that they have zero prices, to satisfy ourselves. Free goods would exist in unlimited supply, and thus command no price. Air—under most conditions—is an example of a free good. We certainly would not buy anything that existed in unlimited quantities. If beef, for example, were available in unlimited quantities, we would not pay today's prices for it. Indeed, we would not pay for it at all, since our nation would be giving up nothing to produce enough beef to satisfy our wants. Buyers and sellers of beef would not have to organize a market system. And if there were unlimited supplies of labor, no one would pay a wage for labor. Indeed, labor, in the traditional sense of the word, would be a free good too.

Back to the Real World: Basic Questions

But in the real world that we all know there *is* scarcity, and social organizations are needed everywhere to allocate a society's limited resources. In the U.S., a system of markets, established over several centuries, is mainly responsible for arbitrating the problem of resource allocation

Consider the vast array of goods and services to be produced in the U.S. this year. Will there be 10 or 11 million automobiles? How many video cassette recorders (VCRs) and how many color television sets? Will automobile production be even more automated this year than last? Who will "consume" the automobiles and television sets? These are the kinds of questions each resource-using society must ask. The basic questions that result from scarcity are:

Scarcity results in the following basic questions: 1) what shall be produced, 2) how shall goods be produced, and 3) for whom shall output be produced.

1. *What* shall be produced? Out of all the combinations of goods that present technology makes possible, what combinations of cars, television sets, vacations, medical services, and so on, shall we choose?

2. *How* shall the goods be produced? There are many questions contained within this big question, which encompasses not only the technology of production, but also the *system* by which production is organized. Will markets be publicly or privately controlled? Will there be competition? How much consolidation of producers will there be? (That is, large firms, as opposed to small, mom-and-pop producer units.)

3. *For whom* shall output be produced? In other words, who is going to have the satisfaction of consuming the goods? This is the basic *distributive* question. Will the income of the society be distributed equally, or will there be a few who are rich and a majority who are poor? Or will there be some other distribution?

Are the solutions to these questions interdependent? Clearly they are. The technology and organizational structure of a society heavily influence who will receive satisfaction as consumers. When a society's industry tends toward large firms, the markets that result are likely to create a more unequal distribution of income. Why this is so will become clear later.

Is Scarcity Meaningful Today?

In many of the applications, we'll talk about debates in the U.S. that involve scarcity and its effects on choice making. As we will see, in many ways the debates have centered on differences in definitions and ideologies. In spite of these differences of opinion, it is clear that, in the sense of unlimited wants pursuing limited resources, scarcity exists even for supposedly well-off Americans, and that even this affluent society must make choices about how to use its limited resources.

Viewing the Choices: The Production-Possibilities Curve

At this point a numerical example will help. Suppose that a hypothetical society, Ruritania, must economize, that is, choose between producing 2 goods: beef and all-purpose machines. (These all-purpose machines produce television programs, build roads, churn ice cream, dry wet hair, dig wells, light buildings, type letters, sew shoe uppers to soles, and drive people to work.) Obviously, this is a great simplification of choice making. In the real world, two things are obvious: (1) choices are in *many* dimensions, with thousands of alternatives among which to choose, and (2) choices change almost continuously as technology changes. But in order to simplify the description of the process and make it easier to visualize what we mean by choices, we chose just 2 commodities. Let these 2 represent, in microcosm, the more complex process of choice making in the real world.

One way to visualize Ruritania's choices is to look at the *production-possibilities curve*, a useful device, derived from the *production-possibilities function*, which is defined as follows:

Production-Possibilities Function
Shows the combinations of goods that a society's resources can produce at full employment in a particular period of time (using the best technology).

The production-possibilities function shows those combinations of goods that the full-employment use of a society's resources can produce during a particular period of time (using the best available technology).

In other words, this represents for a society a kind of frontier, or outer limit to the capacity both to produce and to make choices among goods.

The Production-Possibilities Table
Suppose that Table 2-1 represents the various combinations of beef and all-purpose machines available to Ruritania at a given time, within the limitations set out above full employment and the best use of existing technology).

What does this table show? Let's look at it as a set of trade-offs; that is, it's like a menu, except that the diner can't buy *all* the items on it. Consider combination A. This shows that when Ruritania employs all its resources and the best technology, it can produce 20,000 machines, providing it produces no beef. Alternatively, if Ruritania chooses to produce 2,000 tons of beef, it can

Table 2-1
Production Possibilities for Beef Versus Machines, Ruritania, 1987

Product	Production Rates				
	A	**B**	**C**	**D**	**E**
Beef (thousands of tons)	0	2	4	6	8
Machines (thousands)	20	18	14	8	0
Marginal Rate of Transformation (MRT)		$=\frac{2}{2}\cdot 1$	$=\frac{2}{4}\cdot\frac{1}{2}$	$=\frac{2}{6}\cdot\frac{1}{3}$	$=\frac{2}{8}\cdot\frac{1}{4}$

produce only 18,000 machines. In the second case, it must give up 2,000 machines for 2,000 tons of beef. These tradeoffs may continue until the situation evolves into combination E. At this point, Ruritania can devote all its resources to producing 8,000 tons of beef, but then it can't manufacture any machines.

Which of these various combinations will (or should) Ruritania produce? There is no way for us to find out from this table. Answering this question is very complex, and the mechanisms by which societies make such choices vary greatly. Remember that we assumed that Ruritania is a private-enterprise capitalist society, and so the decision is largely made in its market places. But we don't know which decision its producers and consumers will make. The data in Table 2-1 simply indicate the possibilities. (In some societies, these decisions might be made by both markets and government. In others, the decision may be made only by government fiat.)

Graphing the Production-Possibilities Curve

Graphs, being pictures, not only adorn, but also tell stories. For many people, a graph—in this case a picture of certain economic relationships—can be worth a thousand words. For clarification, refer back to the basic data which it portrays. Figure 2-1 is a visual image of the data in Table 2-1.

Point C in Figure 2-1, for example, represents a combination that is a maximum attainable output: 4,000 tons of beef and 14,000 all-purpose machines. Each of the combinations, A, B, C, D, and E is possible for Ruritania. The curve that has been drawn through these points is the production-possibilities curve (PP curve).

Figure 2-1
Production-Possibilities Curve, Ruritania, 1987

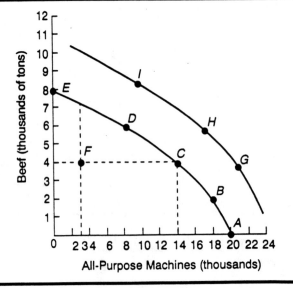

Why are points $F, G, H,$ and I not on the 1987 PP curve? Point F represents less production of *both* beef and machinery than some combinations that are on the curve. In other words, F does not represent a maximum attainable output. To see this, follow the dashed line that goes through point F. If Ruritania chose to produce 3,000 machines (possible at F), it could produce approximately 7,400 tons of beef, much more than the 4,000 indicated at F. In other words, if Ruritania picked combination F, it would not be maximizing output, and it would not be employing its resources fully.

We could apply the same logic to all such points (combinations) below or to the left of the PP curve. On the other hand, points such as $G, H,$ and I which lie beyond or to the right of the current PP curve, are by definition not attainable. They would involve Ruritania turning out more of *both* products than it possibly could, given its current technology and endowments of resources. Since we are assuming full employment and best use of existing technology, points $G, H,$ and I are clearly unattainable.

Economic Growth:
Shifting the Production-Possibilities Curve

While points $G, H,$ and I are not attainable for Ruritania in 1987, they may be reached if one or more of the following things happen:

1. Resources available to the nation (land, labor, capital, and entrepreneurship) increase, or

2. There is an improvement in the technology with which Ruritania employs its resources, or

3. Ruritania engages in trade with other nations, allocating its resources to their most productive uses and importing goods from Urbania and other nations who can produce them with greater efficiency. This means producing goods in which Ruritania has a comparative advantage and importing goods in which it does not have such an advantage. This very important source of growth will be explained more fully in the chapters which deal with international trade and finance.

Any one of all of these happenings will make it possible to produce more of both beef and machines. They will, in other words, shift the PP curve outward or to the right. We should note that although the two curves, (A, B, C, D, E) and (G, H, I) are parallel, it is by no means sure that the economic growth that the shift reflects, will involve the same mixture of output as before. As we shall see later in this chapter, economic growth is likely to change the composition of output (what is produced) since it is likely to change both the costs of production and the tastes and preference of those who consume it.

Employment, Full Employment, Unemployment, and Underemployment

Employment
The condition in which a resource is used to produce commodities or services.

In the section on economic development, we will use concepts of employment, including full employment and underemployment. Therefore, we must define some terms. The person in the street probably uses the word *employment* most often in connection with people's jobs. Here, however, we want to relate employment to all the resources available to a society. So for our purposes, we define **employment** as that condition in which a unit of resource (labor, land, capital, entrepreneurship) is used in some economic activity. In other words, as soon as a resource becomes an *input* in a process that results in the *output* of economic goods, it is considered *employed*.

Unemployment
The condition in which a resource is unable to find a use to produce economic goods.

Now this means that **unemployment**, on the other hand, is the condition in which a unit of resource that would otherwise become an input is unable to find use as such. In the case of labor, this means that a person can't find a job. Land, capital, and entrepreneurship can also be unemployed.

Today all societies—especially in developed nations—give high priority to achieving an employment goal. Frequently, this goal is full employment, or something near it. In other words, the society seeks to ensure that each person who is looking for a job can find one (provided that he or she abides by certain institutional and legal restrictions, such as acceptable age of entry into the labor force or not working longer hours than the maximum work week). When a society attains full employment, it is reaching the maximum on its PP curve. Each unit of resource is not only employed, but is employed in conjunction with other resources to create the greatest output of goods and services possible at that time, with existing technology.

Achieving a full-employment (maximum-output) position—that is, reaching any point on the PP curve—is extremely difficult and unlikely. We shall deal later with some of the reasons why. As we shall see, the PP curve is a *limit*, an ideal bench mark against which the deficiencies of *actual* economic performance can be assessed.

Underemployment
The condition in which some units of resources are not employed in their most productive uses.

What is likely to occur in any society is that there is always **underemployment**, which means that some units of the nation's resources are not employed in their most productive uses. For reasons we shall explore later in this chapter, physicists may be tending shops and journeyman carpenters may be mowing lawns for a living. Although they are employed, these people would be more productive if used in more appropriate job opportunities; therefore, underemployment exists even though the nation may attain full employment.

A Word of Caution

Resist the temptation to read too much into a picture or graph. When we look at a Picasso painting, we may each read into it something different if we wish. On the other hand, what one may legitimately see in a graph is determined by the definitions and assumptions underlying the graph. In Table 2-1, we can see what the production alternatives are (at full employment and using the best technology). We do not, however, know which choice Ruritania will make. There are social, political, moral, cultural, and legal aspects to be taken into account.

One thing is evident: What Ruritania produces today will influence what it can produce in the future. Let us assume that Ruritania is a less-developed (low-income) country. Ruritania, let us suppose, has a 10-year objective to increase productivity from point C (in 1987) to point H (in 1997). Refer again to Figure 2-1. This means that Ruritania has to shift its PP curve to the right. To do this, it must have more productive capacity, which means more all-purpose machines. Thus, politico-economic objectives in 1987 may dictate more machines (at the cost of less beef) to increase capacity for tomorrow's output. We say that movement from C to H is Ruritania's planned growth path.

What Is Economic Integration?

Full Economic Integration When all resources are employed and used in their most productive uses.

Perfect Economic Integration Exists when all resources are employed and each is paid the same in all uses.

We have built our model of Ruritania's development on the assumption that its economy has a single set of social and technological conditions—in other words, that Ruritania is a country with a single economic standard for all its people and that all its resources are allocated by the same process. We are implying that all people who own resources in Ruritania have the same information and the same objectives and that Ruritania's potential users of resources also have the same information and the same objectives. For Ruritania to reach the PP curve, both groups must want to use those resources with maximum efficiency. We are also implying that there is a set of known choices—reflected in the PP curve—open to all of them. If all these conditions were fulfilled, the economy would be operating under **full economic integration**. In other words, it would be using all its resources in the most efficient manner. (Technically speaking, one has **perfect integration** in a market society only when all units of resources are employed and a given resource is paid the same in all its uses. Can you imagine why?) Such a society would be one in which there was no significant resistance to the goal of maximum efficiency, given the full use of resources with the best available technology. (We shall discuss later the reasons why maximum efficiency might be opposed.)

In reality, however, many influences stand in the way of integration in an economy, influences that reduce the likelihood of

Economic Dualism
The coexistence with-
in a society of two or
more economies.

the economy's achieving full efficiency. Particularly in less developed countries, these influences may be so strong that the system becomes characterized by **economic dualism**, which means the coexistence within a society of two or more different economies. The two that most often exist together in a dualistic society are (1) a modern exchange economy and (2) an indigenous (or native) *non*exchange economy. In a number of poorer countries in the world (such as Pakistan) we can observe a cash economy with people buying and selling in (urban) market places. For others in the economy, especially in isolated rural areas, subsistence agriculture is practiced by families with only occasional barter exchanges occuring with others.

Coexistence of a modern economy and a (usually primitive) subsistence economy complicates any explanation of economic development in terms of the production-possibilities model. So let us introduce two modifications to the model:

1. In the modern sector of the economy, reaching the PP curve is no longer solely a question of increasing efficiency. Ruritania may now seek to make the indigenous nonexchange sector part of the modern exchange economy.

2. The resulting economy, which will be much larger, will have different resources from which to choose, and thus many more paths along which it can grow toward greater development.

Suppose that the nation making these choices is not Ruritania, but Urbania. Let's say that Urbania is a mature industrial economy whose chief problems include environmental pollution and hard-core unemployment. You can see that Urbanians would choose a different combination of alternatives on the PP curve in Figure 2-1. They might choose a combination of factors that would enable them to move from underemployment or unemployment (for instance, at point *F*) to full employment. Under these conditions, Urbania's equilibrium choice might be *D* rather than *B*, because Urbanians would give low priority to economic activities that would result in more machinery and thus more pollution.

Increasing Opportunity Costs: Why Is the Curve Shaped that Way?

Opportunity Cost
What is given up of
other goods in order
to produce more of
one particular good.

Refer again to Table 2-1. Each time Ruritania chose to produce more of one good (beef or machines) it had to produce less of the other (remember that it has no unemployed resources with which to produce more of the desired good). We define what the nation gives up of the one good to produce more of the other as its **opportunity cost**. This is a very fundamental concept that underlies the entire study of microeconomics. With all economic goods as opposed to free goods, there is a (positive) opportunity cost. Put another way, we shall assume that there is no "free lunch" (zero opportunity cost) in using resources. The real or opportunity cost of using any resource, thus, is what we give up of other things in order to do so.

What is the (Positive) "Cost of the Lunch"?

Increasing Opportunity Cost
The assumption that as a nation chooses to produce more of one good, it must (ultimately) give up increasing amounts of the other good.

You have of course noticed that the PP curve is concave to the origin of the diagram. This is so because there is a hidden assumption underlying the choosing of the numbers and the construction of the curve. The assumption is that of **increasing opportunity cost**. To define this concept, let us go back to Ruritania and its twin industries, beef and all-purpose machines. Figure 2-2 shows Ruritania's PP curve.

We can illustrate *opportunity cost* by referring to movements along the PP curve. Suppose that the Farmers Party gains power in Ruritania, and the government decides to produce fewer machines (producer goods) and more beef (consumer goods). It decides to move from the machine-beef ratio at point *C* on the PP curve to the ratio at point *D*. This means that Ruritania gives up 6,000 machines in order to get 2,000 more tons of beef. The machines it gives up (6,000) are the *real opportunity cost* of the additional beef (2,000).

Now suppose that Ruritania decides to produce *no* all-purpose machines and instead uses its resources to produce *only* beef. The effect is that Ruritania moves to point *E* from point *D* on the PP curve. What has Ruritania given up? As you can see, the 2,000 additional tons of beef cost 8,000 machines. In other words, the real opportunity cost—as measured by the increasing slope of the PP curve—is becoming larger. This would also be true if Ruritania chose to produce more machines instead of more beef. In

Figure 2-2
Production-Possibilities Curve, Ruritania

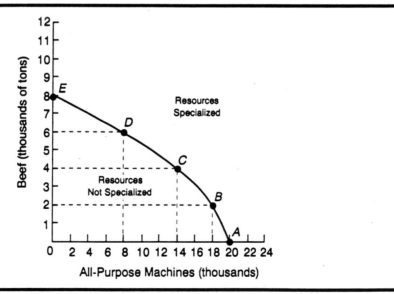

moving down the PP curve, Ruritania would be forced to give up more and more beef for each additional machine produced or would face *increasing opportunity cost.*

Resources are Specialized

The Ruritanian example we are considering is hypothetical. Consideration of opportunity cost as well as benefits is always important in reality in making private or public choices. Suppose that the U.S. is considering a public choice involving speed limits on its highways (as it did in the 1970s and has done again in the late 1980s). If a law is enacted lowering the speed limit to 55 mph, it will presumably have some social benefits, especially the saving of human lives as well as the saving of automotive fuels. What, though, are the (opportunity) costs? Some are obvious such as the added cost of law enforcement, but these are relatively small. The most significant cost to both individuals and to society is the cost of people's time. Driving more slowly, of course, results in more time being used in transportation; that additional time could have been used to produce goods and services and their value is the major real (opportunity cost) of lowering the speed limit.

Why does relative cost ultimately increase as a full-employment society chooses to reallocate its resources? Why aren't resources completely *substitutable* in all uses, so that the PP curve looks like the straight dashed line AE in Figure 2-2? There are complex factors involved. We shall examine some of these later in this chapter. Fundamentally, the reason is this:

Resources are relatively more productive in some uses than in others.

Imagine what would happen in Ruritania as it tried to produce more beef. Beyond some point, Ruritanian farmers would have to start turning their cows out into pasture land that is less well suited for cattle raising. Of course, if resources were equally adaptable to any use, all land could be used just as well for one thing as for another. In other words, it would be technically homogeneous in application. In such a case, the curve would be a straight line, such as the dashed line AE in Figure 2-2. But in real life this is not usually the case, though occasionally one does find either perfect substitutability or perfect lack of it. In fact, sometimes resources gain in efficiency as they are reallocated from one use to another. We want our economic models to clarify reality, therefore, if models are to help us analyze general economic problems, they must be based on valid assumptions. For this reason, we shall assume a **diminishing rate of transformation**, which means that the rate at which one good may be traded off or transformed into another *ultimately* decreases—for a single firm, for an enterprise, or for an industry. In our illustration, this rate is shown as always decreasing.

Obviously, increasing efficiency, tied to growth, is an important aspect of economic development. Nonetheless, for the

Rate of Transformation
The rate at which one good is traded off for another.

Diminishing Rate of Transformation
Means that the rate ultimately decreases or that the real opportunity cost ultimately rises.

society as a whole, with existing technology, moving resources from one activity or industry to another (moving along the PP curve) ultimately decreases efficiency. This is so because, beyond some point (and with given technology and resources), people use inputs that are less and less well adapted to the new employment. Thus, the industry will ultimately experience increasing relative cost. People will have to sacrifice more and more of one good to obtain a greater output of another.

Mental Reservations

You may have some mental opposition to these working assumptions about scarcity and increasing relative cost and may ask why you should accept them. In your own experience with producing something or your reading of economic history, you may have observed the following cases: (1) Sometimes, as a production process is speeded up or modernized—that is, as more inputs are used—output increases more rapidly than input. Consider automobile production after 1914 and the emergence of the assembly line. (2) In the twentieth century, U.S. resources have become much more productive, thus shifting the PP curve. Actually, both these observations may be correct, and yet neither invalidates the law of increasing opportunity costs. The reasons why both factors above do *not* invalidate the concept of increasing opportunity costs are: (1) larger scale activities require new plant and equipment which can only be accomplished in a long run time frame *within* an industry not in terms of moving resources from one industry to another, and (2) most of the increase in resource productivity in the twentieth century has resulted from changes (improvements) in technology which are not incorporated into a particular PP curve.

A Classical Explanation of Growth: Shifts in Production Possibilities

Consider case 1. Efficiency does increase as a result of specialization of resources and division of tasks, as markets expand and firms produce more and on a larger scale. This improvement of technique, which means more output from the same inputs, results in the shifting of the PP curve, not in movements along it. Economists have noted such growth in efficiency ever since Adam Smith, who published *The Wealth of Nations* in 1776. Smith wrote about a pin factory in England in which, as specialization increased, labor became much more productive and output increased accordingly, just as it has in twentieth-century automobile-assembly plants.

In the same way, steel output has increased. In the 1950s and 1960s the use of automation and improved techniques expanded greatly within the steel industry, resulting in increased production in the 1980s. Steel productivity throughout the world has grown in the 1970s and 1980s as the result of new technology such as the oxygen process and continuous rolling mill. This has enabled the steel industry in the U.S. to prove that it is more than cost-competitive with foreign producers in the late 1980s.

As for case 2, twentieth-century economic history does bear out this observation. Resources have indeed become much more productive since 1900. On the other hand, the static assumptions of the PP curve about fixed supplies of resources and given technology clearly do not hold true. Since 1900, the PP curve has shifted dramatically to the right. Except during depressions, such as that of the 1930s, the shifts have been fairly continuous. We can conclude from the assumptions of our production-possibilities model that the shifts have resulted from two factors:

1. Productivity has increased as a result of technological changes (new tools, new processes, and larger-scale activities). These changes have resulted, at least in part, from (a) increased economic integration, (b) market growth, and (c) specialization and division of use of resources.

2. Amounts and varieties of resources have increased. Our producers today possess many resources not even considered potential inputs in 1900 (including a labor force that is much more productive, partly as a result of investment in education).

Institutions Play a Very Important Part In Decision Making

Economic Institutions
The social arrangements through which economic decisions are made.

The *rate* at which productivity has grown has also been influenced by changes and refinements in **economic institutions**, the social arrangements through which economic decisions are made.

Property Rights
Rights of ownership to use, to transfer, and to benefit from the employment of factors of production.

At the heart of resource usage lies the question of **property rights**, the rights to use, transfer, and benefit from the employment of factors of production. Institutional arrangements that efficiently assign and permit the transfer of such rights obviously enhance the productivity of resources. In addition, institutional arrangements may create incentives to resource owners to assume risks and make innovative uses of resources. If so, not only are resources used efficiently in a static sense but they also are likely to be employed with increasing efficiency as time passes.

As an example of a private institution, consider the modern corporation. Corporations today come in all sizes and forms, including the big multinational ones that cut across national boundaries and reach their roots into capital markets throughout the world. As efficient devices for raising capital and spreading risk, such corporations have greatly enhanced the efficiency with which resources are used by business enterprises.

Let us sum up. Any changes in institutions such as these, whether for good or ill, can change the economic climate in which decisions are made. And naturally the pace of development—the shifting of the PP curve—can be altered as a result.

Economic development—such as that experienced by the U.S.—is a long-term, dynamic process, stemming from a complex set of economic, political, and social changes. Let's now look at that process.

Economic Development: How Do Poor Countries Become Rich?

Economic Development
The long-term process by which the material well-being of a society's people is significantly increased.

In this chapter, we have talked about scarcity and about the knottiest decision of all: How should one best use resources? Through the device of a PP curve, we have examined the impact that both factors—scarcity and allocation of resources—have on economic growth. Now we can employ these concepts to examine what is perhaps every nation's most basic economic problem: **economic development**. It is one topic on which nearly everyone—expert and layman—has an opinion. Interest in economic development was intense during the Industrial Revolution in the nineteenth century, when people were losing their jobs to machines, but interest waned in the early twentieth century. Since World War II, the subject has generated interest again—not only for economists and other academicians, but also for politicians and the person in the street. It's easy to see why if we examine the definition of economic development.

Economic development *is the long-term process by which the material well-being of a society's people is significantly increased.*

Why does the definition deal only with *material* well-being? Basically because, as students of economics, we are concerned with goods and services. We know that goods and services are necessary to satisfy people's needs and wants, although having more of them doesn't necessarily make people better off or happier. On the other hand, people who are very poor, unless they can create the potential to produce more, cannot choose among alternatives. Their lives are hemmed in by necessity. They cannot choose whether they prefer more automobiles to more leisure, prefer more coal furnaces to cleaner air, or anything else. It is the freedom to make such choices that is a great value of economic development, and the main reason why we are concerned with it. The person who must toil for 14 hours a day just in order to live and the society that can barely keep this year's output the same as last year's small output have very little economic freedom. Without economic freedom—the freedom to choose among many alternatives—can there ever be much social and political freedom?

The above definition of development raises questions as well as answering them! How do you measure well-being? How much increase is a significant increase? How long does the process of economic development take? Let us deal with each of the questions in turn. As a generalization, however, our definition is broad enough to permit the study of the characteristics of development.

1. *Economic development is an evolutionary process, a set of interdependent actions.* Economic development is associated with the creation of new products and processes. Consider the development of synthetic rubber. Prior to World War II, most developed countries had to import raw rubber from Malaysia and South America, because despite a hundred years of research, chemists had been unable to produce a synthetic rubber molecule. At the beginning of the war, enemy warships cut off U.S. supply lines of natural rubber, just as the U.S. was gearing up its war machine and desperately needed rubber for truck, plane, and tank tires, for waterproof clothing and footwear for soldiers, and for hundreds of civilian uses. The U.S. government stepped in and combined forces with industry to search for the optimum combination of ingredients and for improved technology for making synthetic rubber. (The same thing was happening in Germany.) Finally, chemists abandoned the search for chemical equivalence and concentrated on trying to find materials with the same physical properties as rubber. And they succeeded. Today the world uses more than *twice* as much synthetic as natural rubber, and the U.S. is the largest world producer. If it had not been for the war and for the incentive created by the government, chemical engineers might not have made that all-out effort, and still might not have developed synthetic rubber.

2. *Actions resulting in development have multiple origins, both economic and noneconomic.* For example, world food shortages and the population explosion led to the development of new strains of wheat, rice, and corn. Searching for a new wheat strain, Norman E. Borlaug, a plant breeder at the Rockefeller Foundation research station in Chapingo, Mexico, began in the 1950s to cross various strains of hybrid wheats until eventually he developed a new dwarf type that had much higher yields than the usual varieties and would flourish in many climates. This hybrid made possible year-round plantings in parts of the subtropics and tropics. Mexico was the first country to grow Borlaug's new wheat extensively, with astonishing results. Until the mid-1950s, Mexico had been importing a large percentage of its wheat, but with the new dwarf wheat, Mexico was able, by 1964, to export a sizable amount of wheat, although in the 1980s, it again became an importer due to serious declines in agricultural productivity. Borlaug won a Nobel Prize for his accomplishment, the results of which have been termed the "green revolution."

3. *The results of development are broad, and are both economic and noneconomic.* For example, the success of the dwarf wheat strains led rice researchers at the University of the Philippines College of Agriculture (founded jointly by the Ford and Rockefeller foundations in 1962) to try to increase rice production in Asia. They used the same crossbreeding techniques as the wheat growers, and found a new dwarf variety of rice—IR-8—which grows approximately 40 inches high (compared to 70 inches for the traditional Asian rices), yields 6,000 to 8,000 pounds of rice per acre (versus 4,600 for the older rices), and is ready to harvest only 4 months after it is sown (versus 5 to 6 months for the traditional rices). Where the weather is warm enough and water is plentiful, farmers can raise 2 or 3 crops of it a year. Thus, IR-8 has become known as the miracle rice, since it can double farmers' per-acre yields. Even tradition-bound Asian peasants were quickly won over to these new high-yielding varieties. By 1969 they were planting 34 million acres of the miracle rice.

However, this rapid switch brought about problems. More labor is needed for more frequent planting, and there must be continuous weeding, frequent irrigation, and vastly increased storage and transportation facilities to store and market the greatly increased crops. In many cases Asian farmers have had to store their grain in open fields or in public buildings such as schoolhouses which increased the demand for storage facilities that were in short supply. Another problem was consumer resistance. Many peasants didn't like the IR-8 rice because it doesn't stick together when cooked. Agronomists continuing their experiments in cross-breeding, managed to alter the grains to suit local preferences.

As a result of the development of IR-8 rice and Borlaug's dwarf wheat strain, many people who would have starved to death are now alive—and having more babies.

Economic Determinism

Pure Economic Determinism Involves assuming that the actions of people and institutions are mere reactions to changing economic reality or opportunities.

Our investigation of the problems of developing nations will naturally have to be very broad. We will emphasize people's economic motives, but also, of necessity, we will cover certain social and cultural factors bearing on the development process, factors that are not solely economic. If we were to examine the long-term evolution of a nation or people from a strictly economic standpoint, it would involve assuming **pure economic determinism**—in other words, assuming that the actions of people and institutions are mere reactions to changing economic reality, or economic opportunities. Not only is such a notion simplistic, but it ignores, for example, the relationship between social-cultural patterns and economic behavior.

Basic Questions About Economic Development

How Do You Measure Well-Being?

To some people, just having enough rice to fill their empty stomachs is material well-being. To someone else, owning a car that runs well enough to drive to work is material well-being. To a third person, having a chalet in a fashionable ski area is material well-being. Clearly there is no single number or index that is adequate for this measure. However, many economists feel that growth in *real per capita income* (Y/P + N, where Y = income and P = prices, and N = population) is the best approximation. To obtain this index, divide the total national income (Y) by the prices existing in the country in question. To get "real" income figures we must, in other words, be sure to leave out of our accounting mere price increases. For example, if prices go up 8 percent this year and national income rises by 8 percent, then for a given population there is *no* increase in real per capita income. The resulting "real" national income (Y/P) is divided by population (N) to obtain per capita real national income to obtain a measure of purchasing power by individuals.

To sum up:

1. Total national income + price increases = real national income.

2. Real national income + population = real per capita national income.

3. Growth in real per capita national income is the best single representation of development.

Thus, in order to estimate what is happening to an individual's ability to buy goods and services as national income grows, we must sort out both *population* increases, which reduce the per capita effect of income increases, and *price* increases, which do not represent more goods.

How Great is the Income Gap?

Table 2-2 shows something about the income gap between the developed and less developed nations.

We must be cautious in interpreting the differences too strictly. Biases are introduced when we convert figures in Indian rupees, for example, into dollars. Also, we don't know what the distribution of income in India is or what nonmarket services the Indian government provides for its people.

Having said this, however, we can conclude from the data the following:

1. The income gap between the "rich" nations (for example, the U.S. and Sweden) and the "poor" nations (for example, India and Haiti) is very great—so great that we must conclude that, whatever

Table 2-2
Estimates of Per Capita Gross National Income, 1988

Area	Per Capita National Income (U.S. dollars)
Africa	
Egypt	660
Ethiopia	120
Nigeria	290
Kenya	370
South Africa	2,290
North America	
United States	19,840
Canada	16,960
Caribbean and Latin America	
Brazil	2,160
Guatemala	900
Haiti	380
Mexico	1,760
Venezuela	3,250
Argentina	2,520
Asia	
China	330
India	340
Indonesia	440
Japan	21,000
Pakistan	350
Philippines	630
Taiwan	N/A
Singapore	9,070
Europe	
France	16,090
Germany (Federal Republic)	18,480
Italy	13,330
Portugal	3,650
Sweden	19,300
United Kingdom	12,810
Oceania	
Australia	12,340
New Zealand	10,000

Source: Adopted from The World Bank, World Development Report 1990.

the distribution of income and nonmarket services provided by government, the average citizen is much better off in the rich than in the poor nations.[1]

2. Many countries with low per capita income have very small total income bases, in relation to their national populations. Ethiopia, for example, has a population of about 35 million and a 1988 gross national income of $4.2 billion, with a resulting per capita national income in 1988 of only $120. Similar relationships can be found elsewhere in nations in Latin America, Africa, and Asia.

This is important because for even a well-integrated nation to adopt modern technology, it must have a market large enough to make specialization and division of resources economically feasible. With its small population and a per capita income of only $120, Ethiopians find it hard to build the modern plants and install the processes that would enable them to reap the benefits of specialization and division of labor. Unless countries like Ethiopia undergo economic integration (either internal or with other countries) to enlarge their markets, the large scale of modern industry may well remain beyond their reach. Imagine how few nations can afford the billion dollar plus investment necessary to build a fully efficient steel plant, or sell its output competitively if they do build it.

3. In almost every part of the world, there are wide income gaps between nations. Per capita income is highest in Europe, North America, Australia, and in certain parts of Asia (Japan, Singapore, Taiwan, etc.). Even in these areas, however, there are nations that are pockets of poverty. See, for example, the income data for Portugal in Europe and for Mexico in North America—where it belongs geographically, if not culturally.

A Nobel laureate in economics has said that poverty rather than plenty is the international human condition. And Jesus said 2,000 years ago, "The poor we have always with us." Even though the world has experienced 200 years of industrialization, real income growth and diffusion of technological information, all these advances have failed to raise significantly the economic well-being of at least half of the more than 5 billion people in the world today.

What is a Significant Increase in Real Per Capita National Income?

Will the percentage increase in $Y/P + N$ (real per capita national income) necessarily be the same, for example, in China as in India? This is unlikely because significant income growth is reached only when development becomes self-sustaining. In other words, the development process must build up a *permanent* momentum. For this to happen, the pace of development, reflected in the growth of per capita income, must be great enough to overcome whatever

---

[1]The average per capita income of developed countries in 1985 was over $9,000 while the average per capita income of less developed countries was about $750.

resistances there are to development in individual societies. These resistances, which often differ in kind and intensity from one society to another, fall into two categories.

Resistances to Growth and Development

Social and Cultural Resistances

Social and cultural resistances are those aspects of the social organization and cultural practice that influence the society's kinds and levels of economic activities. Such influences are too numerous to list, but some examples may help.

In India, the Hindus, who comprise the majority of the people, believe that it is sacrilege to slaughter cattle for beef. Even in the face of poverty, their bony cows wander the streets. Why is this important to India's development? Economists generally agree that an agricultural surplus—producing more than is consumed—is a necessary precondition for urbanization and industrial development. The Indians and their sacred cattle are an example of a poor nation deliberately, for religious or cultural reasons, depriving itself of a source of potential surplus.

Consider another example of cultural resistance to growth. In some Latin-American nations, middle-class families have for centuries clung to culturally ingrained biases against their sons getting jobs in commerce or industry. Families wanted sons to enter the legal profession, the clergy, and the military because these professions were—and to some extent still are—considered more prestigious than working in business or trade. The importance of this sort of social resistance is that it is likely to affect the supply of *effort* in a society. Because bright, energetic people raised in comfortable surroundings are needed to run a nation's businesses, the social stigma attached to commerce may downgrade both the amount and composition of entrepreneurial activity. Since **entrepreneurship**—the organization of diverse resources into producing units—is vital to technological change and development, such social foot dragging may retard growth in productivity or even prevent it entirely.

Entrepreneurship
The function of organizing resources into producing units.

Population Growth

Perhaps the greatest resistance to income growth in less developed countries is offered by hugely increasing populations. The facts that women begin in their early teens to bear children and the large size of families make development all the more difficult. (You may wonder why, since in the twentieth-century U.S., population growth has meant more prosperity because of dollars spent on everything from baby buggies to education.) Population growth that exceeds productivity growth makes almost impossible the creation of a surplus from which saving and investment may occur. If a country sets aside only enough to take care of what is used up (*depreciated*) in current production, future output is at best likely to be no greater than what it is now.

As Nobel Laureate W. Arthur Lewis has put it, the development of a nation depends on knowledge, capital, and the will to economize. A part of knowledge is that the future can be better than the present; this prospect induces people to save and form capital.

Remember, however, that the U.S., like other developed nations, has a large surplus. It does not consume everything it produces, while merely setting aside something to make up for depreciating plant and equipment. One of the basic economic questions is was how much of current output one should set aside to invest in machinery and other facilities with which to produce for the future. Now, suppose that a less developed country, because of foreign aid or some internal "bootstrap" operation (a feat achieved by its own efforts), generates a surplus and uses this surplus initially to increase productivity. It cannot necessarily maintain this surplus, or even expand it. Suppose that the higher productivity induces people to have larger families. Or suppose that the surplus is used to reduce the death rate. In either case there are more people of nonproductive (not in the labor force) ages to be fed, housed, and clothed. Supporting these people may literally eat up the surplus.

Therefore, the resistance to income growth may be so strong that development does not occur or is not self-sustaining. How serious is this kind of resistance? Table 2-3 indicates that is may be severe.

Several things stand out in these data. Population throughout the world has grown since 1920—even in the depression years of the 1930s. It has grown much more rapidly since 1930 in the developing (low-income) regions than in the more developed regions. This population boom has put heavier pressures on the ability to create and effectively use surpluses in the underdeveloped countries than in the developed nations. Forecasts are that this disparity will not only remain but widen to the year 2000. However, the economic backwardness of the less developed countries cannot be attributed to this population increase alone, or

Table 2-3
Percentage Annual Growth Rate of Population (1920-1985)

Year	World	More Developed Regions	Developing Regions
1920-1930	1.0	1.2	1.0
1930-1940	1.0	0.8	1.2
1940-1950	0.9	0.4	1.2
1950-1960	1.8	1.3	2.0
1960-1965	2.0	1.3	2.3
1965-1970	2.0	1.0	2.4
1970-1975	2.1	1.0	2.5
1975-1985	2.0	0.7	2.5

Source: Population Division, United Nations, New York (reprinted in Morgan and Betz, *Economic Development, Readings in Theory and Practice*; Wadsworth, Belmont, CA, 1970), and International Bank for Reconstruction and Development, *World Development Report*, 1986. More developed regions include North America, temperate South America, Europe, Japan, Australia and New Zealand. Developing regions include Africa, East Asia (except Japan), South Asia, Latin America (except temperate South America, Melanesia, Polynesia, and Micronesia.

even primarily to it. Indeed, not all such countries have high population-growth rates. And some, such as Mexico, have, until recent years, shown rapid income growth even while maintaining high rates of population growth. In most cases, however, a burgeoning population has exerted a negative effect on development.

Technological and Technical Resistances

Figure 2-3 shows the PP curve of two nations: one a developed country and the other a less developed country. Shown are trade-offs between present goods (such as beef in our earlier example) and future goods (such as the all-purpose machines used earlier). The curves in Figure 2-3 represent—for the same points in time—a country with a high per capita income (Sweden) and a country with a low per capita income (India). Note that both curves reflect, in their slopes, *increasing opportunity cost*. In other words, each country's development comes not from ability to substitute resources for various present uses, but from the ability to substitute future goods for present goods. If a country wants future capital, it has to forgo some consumption today. (This is hard to do if the country's populace is unable to read and write, and if many of them are half-starved.)

Clearly, the more a country moves out the future-goods axis—in other words, trades off present for future consumption—the greater its future stock of capital, including human capital, will be. More rapid diffusion of knowledge about technical change will shift the PP curve and development will take place. This is a major difference between the two curves.

The less developed country (India) runs into the resistances we mentioned above and finds it harder to use its surpluses productively. Notice in Figure 2-3 that the slope of India's supposed PP curve—in other words, the rate at which it may substitute future for present consumption—decreases quickly. This means that the

Figure 2-3
Production-Possibilities Curves for Developed and Underdeveloped Countries

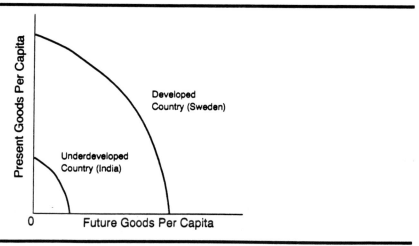

underdeveloped country quickly approaches a zero rate of transformation, or a point beyond which no amount of giving up present consumption increases future output. The rate of substitution, or of giving up present consumption, is shown by the slope of the PP curve. In other words, it is equal to the *rate of change in present goods per unit change in future goods* per capita.

The developed country (Sweden) is able to substitute future consumption for present consumption more effectively and in larger per capita amounts. The developed country generates a larger surplus and reinvests more of it in future growth in productivity. Thus, the rich get richer while the poor get (relatively) poorer.

What are the major technological barriers the underdeveloped countries must overcome? Indeed, is the argument for the existence of such barriers valid? Some students have argued that low-income countries actually have certain technological advantages over high-income parts of the world. Two of the principal building blocks of this argument are:

1. Progress is a matter of degree. Underdeveloped countries for the most part have relatively simple capital requirements. Introducing an inexpensive, manually operated irrigation pump may constitute a major technological leap forward in a low-income country, whereas to get the same degree of impact in an industrial nation, major changes in technology would have to be introduced. This amounts to saying that the underdeveloped countries have a relatively low ratio of additional capital needed to produce additional output **incremental capital-output ratio**).

Incremental Capital-Output Ratio
The ratio of the additional capital to additional output.

2. Less developed countries, unlike high-income nations, can import modern goods from the vast menu of technological choices developed in the industrial nations. They do not have to use their resources to develop sophisticated processes such as continuous-rolling steel mills, automated assembly plants, and the like. According to this reasoning, these less developed countries stand to inherit the benefits of the historic labors of the industrial nations.

We, however, specifically reject these two arguments, on grounds that the costs involved in realizing the benefits are likely to outweigh the benefits themselves. In many cases, the benefits are illusory; that is, they only seem to be benefits. Let us see why.

1. It may well be that underdeveloped countries need only (technically) simple changes in capital equipment. But how productive will these changes be? One economist estimated that in the U.S., between 1929 and 1957, about 43 percent of growth in real income was the result of (a) *increased education of labor* and (b) *advances in technical and managerial knowledge*. The study maintained that only 15 percent of such growth came from increased amounts of physical capital, such as factories and machines. Less developed

Human Capital
Consists of improvement in the skills and knowledge of people.

countries invest typically less in their **human capital**—that is, in the skills and knowledge of their people—than developed countries do. Poor countries spend much less than rich nations do on education, health care, and the like. The fact is that simple attainable capital improvements—such as the water pump—may not rapidly increase productivity, unless the country has already made major investments in its human capital.

Instances of such barriers abound in the underdeveloped countries. Some years ago, an American economist doing research in Central Mexico met a state planning official who told him of a program to distribute steel plows to the owners of small nonmarket farms in the region. The program was good in theory, but some time after the plows had been handed out, a team of officials, who had returned to assess the results, found that most of the steel plows were sitting in corners, unused. The native owners of the small plots said that they had not used the steel plows because the cold of the steel—as opposed to the warmth of the wooden plow—would offend the earth god. In other words, the steel plow—which had a strong positive effect on agricultural productivity growth in the U.S. in the nineteenth century—had no effect in this Mexican setting because there had been no prior investment in education. Nobody had come along before the plows were handed out and tried to overcome the peasants' religious-cultural bias. This is an example of *interdependency*, an important principle in economics.

Complementary Investment
One that increases the productivity of other investments.

In many cases, such **complementary investments**—those that increase the productivity of other investments—lie beyond the capacity of the underdeveloped countries, which often cannot substitute a present good (time and money spent on education) in favor of a future good (in the human capital form of a more educated populace).

2. In part, the impact of importing advanced technology depends on the complementary investments outlined in reason 1. Will a modern oxygen-process, continuous-rolling steel mill built in Egypt have the same productivity (output per hour of labor employed) as one built to the same engineering specifications, but designed and built in West Germany? Studies indicate that it will not, in the absence of the complementary investments discussed above—especially in education and social overhead capital such as roads, railroads, harbors, and the like. There are also other reasons to believe that the advantages that imported technology offer to the undeveloped countries are partly illusory. Modern technology is not completely divisible. Egypt cannot build *half* a modern steel mill. Even if it built a *whole* one, in order to use the mill's output to best advantage it would have to develop simultaneously metal-fabricating mills, a freight transport system, an automobile industry, and so forth. Thus, in order to internalize the efficiencies of modern technology, a nation must often adopt that technology in toto. So Egypt and other societies that are not *fully integrated* (using their resources in the most efficient manner) may not find

the appropriate technology in the industrial countries. The cost of adapting advanced technology to the skill levels, market sizes, and degrees of economic integration in the underdeveloped countries may outweigh the seeming benefits.

As a further point, consider that factor prices (wages, interest rates, land rents) differ throughout the world. The technological processes of industrial nations where wage rates are relatively high are almost always **capital-intensive**. That is, they use relatively more capital than labor or land. In most less developed countries, *labor* is the surplus factor. (Exceptions are the oil-rich sheikdoms, such as Kuwait, which we won't consider here because, although they have high per capita incomes, they have yet to demonstrate the kind of economic balance among agriculture, industry, and commerce that goes along with being developed countries.) In countries such as India, **labor-intensive processes**, those that use relatively more (relatively cheap) labor than capital or land, yield the greatest relative advantage.

Let us summarize: Technological advantages for poor nations are difficult to find. Transferring modern technology and adapting it to their peculiar problems and characteristics is likely to be a costly process and one that involves far more than merely using their surpluses to import technology.

Capital-Intensive Processes
Those that use relatively more capital than labor or land.

Labor-Intensive Processes
Those that use relatively more labor than capital or land.

What About Natural Resources?

Let us return to the production-possibilities model outlined in Figure 2-3. Remember that a shift factor—one that can move the curve to the right to reflect increased productive capacity—is an increase in the endowment of resources. Many poor nations are seemingly rich in resources. Why has the development of these natural resources not been effective as a device for accelerating their growth?

Basically, we must go back to the saying by the late Erich Zimmerman: "Resources are not, they *become*." Consider the example of oil. Prior to the late nineteenth century, oil was not a major resource for the U.S. It only became so with the rise of the automobile—a complementary development—and related changes in the American economy.

For Brazil, the riches of the Amazon basin fall into the same uncertain category. Without complementary investments in human capital and transportation, Brazil's rich mineral resources remain merely potential riches.

For most poor nations, exporting natural resources has failed to boost their economies to rapid growth. An exception would be the exports of cotton by the U.S. prior to 1860. However, in the case of the U.S., much internal integration and investment in human capital accompanied that increase in exports of cotton.

Is the Income Gap Widening or Closing?

An enormous income gap exists between the poor of the world's population and the affluent. As Simon Kuznets put it in his Nobel Prize address in 1971:

> At present, about two-thirds or more of the world population is in the economically less developed group. In 1965, the per capita gross domestic product (at market prices) of 1.72 billion out of a world total of 3.27 billion was less than $120, whereas 0.86 billion in economically developed countries had a per capita product of some $1,900.

Given this wide gap, we must ask a follow-up question. Is the gap closing or widening? In other words, is the development problem being solved, or is it growing more acute? The data in Table 2-4 shed some light on this.

Interpretation of these data unfortunately yields answers of only limited hope to our question. Except for the Near East, the "Asian Tigers" (South Korea, Taiwan, Hong Kong, Singapore), and some other countries such as Malaysia and Thailand—which contain a relatively small percentage of the population of the low-income areas—in the 1970s and 1980s the less developed countries grew less rapidly than the developed countries in terms of per capita GNP. It is too early yet to know whether the exporting of the oil riches of the Near and Middle East will result in long-term structural change and economic development for that part of the world. If if does, this region may join the ranks of the rich nations in the twentieth century. The other major success stories have, as noted, occurred in Asia among the export-oriented economies of Korea, Taiwan, Singapore, and Hong Kong. As a region, though, Asia continues to have both some of the world's poorest nations as well as some of its most rapidly growing ones.

Table 2-4
Percentage increase in GNP Per Capita, Less-developed and Developed Countries

	1970-75	1975-80	1984
Less-developed countries			
Africa	2.3	.6	−1.8
Caribbean & Latin America	3.5	2.5	1.0
Middle East	5.4	.6	−1.5
East & Southeast Asia	2.5	3.8	4.9
Developed Countries	4.0	3.2	1.3
North America	1.9	2.5	5.9
Europe	3.2	2.7	−2.8
Other developed countries	4.6	4.6	5.6

Source: *Gross National Product, Growth Rates and Trend Data,* Agency for International Development, Statistics and Reports Division, RCW-138.

Is there Hope for Less Developed Countries?

If by now you feel only mildly encouraged about the prospects of the poor nations, you have good reasons. We have argued that shifting the PP curve in the underdeveloped countries will require a combination of the following factors:

1. Basic structural or institutional change.

2. Economic integration.

3. Technological change through adaptation.

4. Specialization and division of resources.

Achieving these goals is obviously going to take a lot of doing. It will involve much more, as Simon Kuznets put it, than "merely borrowing existing tools, material and societal, or of directly applying past patterns of growth." The political and social changes the less developed countries will have to make to achieve these goals will be traumatic and, in some cases, probably violent. Economic development involves basic changes, and since it alters basic social, political, and economic power relationships, it destabilizes a society. Any student of American history knows that this has been the case in the U.S. Consider the redistribution of income away from landowners and in favor of owners of capital. This and many other changes in political and economic power create resistances and struggles. (Some believe that the American Civil War was the result of just such struggles.) It would be unrealistic of us to expect economic development to be otherwise in the less developed nations.

One thing is clear, however. Economic development in the less developed countries *is* possible, in spite of the disadvantages these countries face today in comparison with the way things were in Europe, the U.S., Japan, and Australia when those countries were on the verge of *their* big climb in economic development.

When will this climbing process begin? And in which less developed nations? Will it involve extensive economic planning, or will it involve reliance on the incentives of a market economy? And will industrialization bring in its wake the problems of urbanization? As we have noted, many economists now question the arguments for extensive central planning and industrialization as a basis for economic development. There can be no question that most of the world's people want improved material well-being. As they realize more and more the gap between their own economic reality and what is socially and technically possible, pressure for the above four aspects of change will increase. It may well be that this pressure for change, particularly in the face of the huge external debts of many less developed countries, will be a primary fact of our international future. If so, the impact on the economic and social positions of all the developed nations will be intense.

How Long Will It Take?

There is no clear answer to the question of how long it will take because development, at least in the way we have defined it, is an open-ended process. Any society, no matter how affluent, is capable of further economic development. The less developed countries must bring their population-growth rates down to at least the level of the developed countries. Then, assuming the debt problems can be solved and incentives to productive savings and investments created, the productivity in use of their surpluses will depend on the awesome power of compound interest. Assuming modern economic institutions to use it, a per capita income that has a 6 percent compound rate of growth will double in 12 years. In this sense, even supposing that the people in a given underdeveloped country begin with only $100 annual per capita income, that nation can significantly improve the material well-being of its people in a quarter of a century. And this, after all, represents but a brief moment in human history.

SUMMING UP

1. In a private-enterprise economy, owners and employers of *resources* determine the uses of resources. Thus, decision making about markets is a decentralized process.

2. A society has to decide which resources to use, and how to use them, because (a) At any given time, resources are limited, and (b) Human wants for economic goods are virtually unlimited. The conjunction of these two factors gives rise to *scarcity*. This (relative) scarcity forces an economic society to choose among alternative uses of its resources.

3. Deciding what to do about resources involves answering the fundamental questions facing all economies: (a) *What* shall be produced? (b) *How* shall it be produced? (c) *Who* shall consume the output? (d) We recognize that there are interdependencies among the first three questions and that answers to one heavily affect the answers to others.

4. A useful means of visualizing the resource dilemma is the *production-possibilities function and curve*, which reflect the maximum output choice and most productive technology of a society with full employment. In moving from one point (choice) to another on the curve, we incur an *opportunity cost*, what we give up of one good to obtain more of another. Drawing the curve

usually involves assuming *increasing opportunity cost*. This is another way of saying that resources are partially specialized in their uses, and beyond some point, become less efficient as they are reallocated to other uses.

5. The PP curve derives from static considerations. Nonetheless, if we understand the basis on which it is built, studying it can provide insight into the problems of economic development connected with *employment, unemployment, underemployment,* and related factors.

6. The PP function or curve can help one visualize the impact of *economic dualism* (or lack of *economic integration*) in a society. Dualism, which is the coexistence of multiple economies with different social and technological conditions, influences the way a society moves onto and shifts the PP curve to meet development objectives.

7. The PP curve shows that a nation must give up some thing(s) if it is to produce other things. What the society forgoes in order to do so is called the *real opportunity cost* of production. The PP curve naturally does not tell us which choice a nation will make in using its resources.

8. We can make the PP curve more useful as a device for explaining economic growth by bearing in mind the classical idea that as economic activities expand, growth depends on efficiency, which is tied to specialization and division of tasks.

9. To complete our model, we must recognize that changes in *economic institutions* engender more efficient decision making, which in turn leads to both economic integration and faster growth, or shifting of the PP curve.

10. *Economic development* is the process by which the material well-being of a society's people is significantly increased.

11. The concern for material well-being derives, at least in part, from its relation to social and political well-being and to *economic freedom*, which enables people to choose among growing numbers of alternatives.

12. *Pure economic determinism*, the idea that social and political decisions depend only on changing economic opportunities, fails to reflect the interdependence of these three kinds of influences.

13. The best single measure of economic development is growth in real per capita income. But this does not take into account public services and income redistribution, which also affect the material well-being of people.

14. Economic development in an underdeveloped country initially generates resistances, both sociocultural and technological. Sociocultural patterns affect the kinds and amount of effort needed to cause an economy to develop. Advanced technology is difficult to adapt to the peculiar conditions of the underdeveloped countries.

15. Population growth is a major impediment to economic development. The beginnings of development brought about through the use of surpluses may be eaten up by a larger population in the form of food, clothing, and housing. Data indicate that population growth is a greater disadvantage to the less developed than to the developed nations.

16. The developed nation can shift its PP curve by substituting future for present consumption much more effectively than the underdeveloped country can; that is, over a much wider range of its PP choices. This ensures that output will continue to grow in the future.

17. For a less developed country, importing advanced technology is difficult, not only because of its indivisibilities, but also because technology is not as productive in the less developed as in the developed countries. Statistics show that productivity brought about by technological improvements depends heavily on *complementary investments*, especially investments in *human capital*, achieved by education and health care. Also, many less developed countries, in the absence of economic integration, constitute markets that are too small for large-scale modern technology and the benefits due to specialization to be economically feasible.

18. Natural resources are potentially abundant in many less developed countries. The productivity of these investments, however, depends again on complementary investments, especially the formation of human capital.

19. Data suggest that recently the income gap between the less developed countries and the rich nations has grown rather than diminished. With the exception of the Middle and Near East and a number of Asian nations, most less developed countries are not growing rapidly (in terms of economic development). More than half of the world's population lives in less developed countries, in which the annual per capita income is very low.

20. Economic development for the less developed countries is possible, in spite of barriers against it. However, basic structural changes in society within these countries will be needed to bring it about. Where such development does take place, it will be the power of compound interest that will make its benefits possible.

KEY TERMS

Macroeconomics
Microeconomics
Market system
Resources
Scarcity
Free goods
Production-possibilities function
Employment, unemployment, underemployment
Economic integration
Perfect economic integration
Economic dualism
Opportunity cost
Rate of transformation
Diminishing rate of transformation
Economic institutions
Property rights
Economic development
Pure economic determinism
Entrepreneurship
Incremental capital/output rates
Human capital
Complementary investment
Labor intensive process
Capital intensive process

QUESTIONS

1. In what ways have modern communication and transportation changed the ways in which markets function?

2. Will scarcity, as economists define it, always be a part of the human condition? Why?

3. Why are resources not perfectly substitutable? Why, for example, can we not easily move resources from an industry that isn't employing them fully to an industry that is booming, and that needs them?

4. What are some of the economic institutions that have changed or come into being in recent years?

5. Does economic dualism exist at all in the U.S.? If so, where?

6. Suppose that the Secretary of Labor says to you, "We're having a lot of trouble getting people in areas such as Appalachia and the urban inner-cities to seek and find jobs in commerce and industry. It seems as though these people are part of a different economy." In

terms of economic integration, do you suppose that the Secretary's conclusion is correct?

7. What is the opportunity cost or real cost to the American economy of the present all volunteer armed forces of the U.S.? Would it be lower with a return to the military draft?

8. How does one define economic development? Would a broader definition be more useful? If so, what additional factors (or measures) do you think should be added?

9. Do you agree that pure economic determinism should not be used as the basis for explaining economic decisions and development patterns? Why?

10. Why is it important to subtract price increases from data on income growth in order to measure economic development in a given country?

11. What is an economic surplus? What factors do you think determine how large the surplus must be to permit economic development?

12. What are the basic resistances to economic development? Are they purely economic?

13. What role does the size of a nation's market play in the classical explanation of growth and development?

14. What are some of the countries that have had rapid economic growth in the 1970s and 1980s? What are some that remain very low income countries?

15. How would you explain the fact that, after 200 years of industrialization, more than half of the world's people are still very poor?

16. Construct an economic argument that industrialization is not necessary to the economic development of a country such as India, and that agricultural development may advance India's prospects just as well.

17. Why is investment in human capital so important to the economic development of a country such as Egypt?

18. What are the principal advantages of the developed nations in substituting future consumption for present consumption?

19. Given that many less developed countries, such as Zaire, are rich in natural resources, why have these nations not used them more effectively to bring about economic development?

SUGGESTED READINGS

Ahluwalia, M.S., N. Carter, and H. Chenery. "Growth and Poverty in Developing Countries." *Journal of Development Economics*. 6, September, 1979.

Easterlin, Richard. "Why Isn't the Whole World Developed?" *Journal of Economic History*. 61, March, 1981.

Gillis, Malcolm, Dwight Perkins, Michael Roemer, and Donald R. Snodgrass. *Economics of Development*. 2nd Ed. New York: W.W. Norton & Company, 1987.

Hailstones, Thomas and Frank Mastriana. *Contemporary Economic Problems and Issues*. Chapters 12, 13, 14, and 15. Cincinnati: South-Western Publishing Co., 1988.

Ranis, Gustav. *The United States and the Developing Economies*. New York: W.W. Norton and Co., 1973.

Schnitzer, Martin C. *Contemporary Economic Systems*. Cincinnati: South-Western Publishing Co., 1987.

Wilcox, Clair, Willis D. Weatherford, Jr., Holland Hunter, and Norton S. Baratz. *Economies of the World Today*. New York, Harcourt, Brace, Jovanovich, 1976.

World Bank. *World Development Report*. 1986.

Chapter 3:
Supply and Demand:
Price Determination in Competitive Markets

The operation of society necessarily involves making choices and that these choices derive from three basic queries common to all societies: (1) *What* should be produced? (2) *How* should output be produced? (3) *For whom* should it be produced?

Let us now examine the means by which such choices—implicit in the PP curve—are made in a competitive private-enterprise system.

Economic reality is so complex that it cannot be described completely. What we can do, though, is to establish principles and build models in order to draw analogies to reality. First we are going to set forth some building-block principles that will serve to explain a few things about a competitive market economy. Who is in control? Who or what sends out the signals that determine how we are going to use our resources?

Any economy, including one based on competition, is much more complex. For the moment, we will not discuss the influence that big institutions—government, business, labor—have on the making of economic decisions. We will focus on competition and then, as we go along, add in the complexities introduced by big institutions and measure their effects by comparing them to the effects of competition.

Competition
The market form in which no buyer or seller has influence over the price at which the product is sold.

What Is Competition?

A single word can have many different meanings. Take the word **competition**. If you think of competition as a contest between rivals (as the dictionary defines it), then it describes how the rivals interact. For economists, such a definition has two defects: (1) It is

Price Rivalry
The contest in which
sellers watch what
prices others charge
and then react to those
prices.

too general to use in analytical questions. (2) It contradicts real life, in which **price rivalry**—the contest in which sellers watch what prices others charge, and then react to those prices—*frequently is inversely related to the number of contestants.* If you are one seller among ten thousand others and you raise your prices, it affects the others little or not at all. If you are one seller among four and you raise your prices, the others may follow suit. Thus, for economists:

Competition *is the market form in which no individual buyer or seller has influence over the price at which the product is sold.*

Unorganized single buyers bid for the available goods, and this determines demand. Unorganized single sellers make offers to sell, and this determines supply. This general definition will permit us to set forth some basic concepts of supply and demand.

How are Prices Set? Supply and Demand

If no single seller can set prices and no single buyer can either, how do prices become set, and how are resources allocated in competitive markets? The answer is that there are two independent influences—supply and demand—that determine prices in a competitive market. Let's look at these two components separately.

DEMAND

Demand
A set of relationships showing the quantity of a good that consumers will buy at each of several prices within a specific period of time.

Demand is another word that has many meanings. For one thing, demand is not desire alone, but desire plus the purchasing power to back up that desire. The newspapers may say that the demand for cars is expected to reach 9 million cars. A worried business executive may say that demand for the firm's product is "not good" or is "weak." Both these statements mean something to the person making them. To economists, however, they lack one or both of the ingredients needed for analyzing markets: (1) the timing of the demand and (2) the range of prices for which the demand is expected to hold. The statement about automobile demand does not indicate the time period (this year) or the price range for which this estimate will hold. The worried executive, on the other hand, is summing up his or her judgment about the state of the market, rather than analyzing the general demand for the product. So let's define demand in a way that includes both necessary ingredients.

Demand *is a set of relationships showing the quantity of a good that consumers will buy at each of several prices within a specific period of time.*

Let's take as an example a good that most people consider desirable: T-bone steak. What will be the quantity you demand this year of T-bone steaks? You'll probably say, "That depends on what happens to the price of T-bones." Exactly! The price of a product—and changes in that price—are the main factors that determine how much of that product the public will buy. For example, an upswing in car sales followed the offer of price rebates by car manufacturers in 1988.

Of course, there are other factors that influence an individual's demand:

1. Income of buyers.

Complements
Products used in conjunction with each other.

2. Tastes and preferences of buyers.

3. Prices of other products, both **complements** (products used in conjunction with T-bone steaks, such as potatoes) and **substitutes** (products used in place of T-bone steaks, such as fish or chicken).

Substitutes
Products that may be consumed in place of each other.

4. Consumers' expectations about future prices and market conditions.

These factors determine how many T-bones you or any other individual will buy or numbers bought by all buyers, within any given price range. So when you say that your demand for T-bones depends on what happens to the price, you are saying that this is true for your income and tastes, given prices of other products and given your expectations about future prices and market conditions. In addition, there is a fifth factor that influences the total or market demand for a product, or for all products. That factor is *population*, or the number of consumers. (Remember that a problem of underdeveloped countries is that some have such small populations that there is inadequate demand to justify large-scale industries.) Let's hold these factors constant and establish demand for T-bone steaks in terms of the relationship between their price and quantity demanded. This amounts to the same thing as holding certain variables constant and permitting a *key* variable to change. This is called the **ceteris paribus** ("other things being equal") condition. It is an assumption that is common to much economic analysis, and in fact to analysis in other fields too.

Ceteris Paribus
The (other things being equal) assumption that involves holding other factors constant while permitting a key variable to change.

An Individual Demand Curve

Let's take a week as the time period for which we're going to analyze your demand for T-bone steaks. Table 3-1 is a demand schedule which shows the number you will buy at various prices (holding constant your income, tastes, prices of other products, and your expectations about the future).

Table 3-1
Demand Schedule for T-bone Steaks

Price Per Pound	Quantity Bought Per Week
$5.00	0
4.50	1
4.00	2
3.50	3
3.00	4
2.50	5
2.00	6
1.50	7

What do these data on demand tell us?

1. The quantity of T-bones you buy increases as the price falls and decreases as the price rises.

2. There is a price ($5.00) above which you will buy no T-bones; in other words, above that price you will be excluded from this market (or you will exclude yourself).

Demand Schedule
Indicates the quantity demanded at each of several prices.

Demand Curve
Represents that schedule when plotted on a two dimensional graph.

When we plot the **demand schedule** in Table 3-1, we obtain the **demand curve** shown in Figure 3-1, which shows price on the vertical axis and quantity on the horizontal axis. (Remember that economists call a diagonal line of this sort a curve, even though it is a straight line.)

Point *A* (price = $5.00, quantity = 0) is the upper limit to your demand. For you, $5.00 is the price at which (or above which) you will stop buying. Point *B* represents 3 T-bone steaks per week (price, $3.50); and point *C*, 7 T-bone steaks (price, $1.50). As price falls, quantity demanded increases.

Figure 3-1
Demand Curve for T-bone Steaks

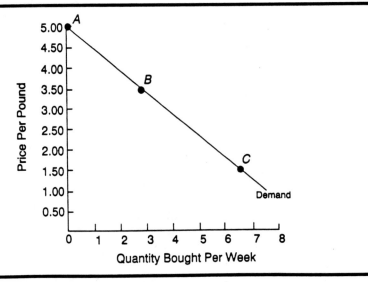

Law of Demand
Consumers buy more of a product at (relatively) low prices than at (relatively) high prices (ceteris paribus).

Income Effect
The change in quantity demanded of a good due to a change in real income caused by a change in the price of a good.

Substitution Effect
The change in quantity demanded of a good as its relative price changes and it becomes relatively less or more expensive leading to its substitution.

The fact that demand curve D in Figure 3-1 slopes down or to the right reflects the **law of demand**. *Consumers buy more at relatively low prices than at relatively high prices* (ceteris paribus). There are two reasons why:

1. As the price of a good falls, the purchasing power of your income increases, which ordinarily causes you to buy more of that good (the **income effect**). As the price of the good rises, your purchasing power declines which ordinarily causes you to buy less of the good.

2. As the price of a good falls (other prices being unchanged), the good becomes relatively cheaper than other goods and you substitute the good for other now more expensive goods (the **substitution effect**). As the price of the good rises, you substitute other now less expensive goods for the one in question.

Each effect tends to reinforce the other. Under normal conditions, both tend to cause consumer demand for a greater quantity of a desirable good as its price goes down.

There are exceptions to this normal pattern. There are some *Veblen goods* whose appeal to consumers increases with higher prices (perhaps Russian caviar, sable coats, large diamonds, and so on).

And then there are *income-inferior goods*, such as beans and rice, which people in poor countries eat because prices of these goods are very low and their cheapness permits people with low incomes to eat them. Compared to meat, milk, and other high-protein goods, beans and rice are very cheap. When the prices of these income-inferior goods drop sharply, people may eat less of them and use their greater purchasing power (income) to diversify their diet, by buying meat, for example.

Change in Quantity Demanded
A movement along a good's demand curve that can be caused only by a change in the price of that good.

Change in Demand
A shift of the demand curve for a good that may be caused by a change in any factor other than the price of that good.

Changes in Quantity Demanded Versus Changes in Demand

So far, we have been talking about a single demand curve, a curve charting the demand schedule for a desirable good and showing that *movements along* that curve are the result of changes in the price of that good. The only thing that can cause a **change in quantity demanded** (such as A to B in Figure 3-2), therefore, is a change in the price of the good. Remember that we are holding four factors constant: income, tastes of the consumer, prices of other goods, and consumers' expectations of the future (plus population, for total demand). If even one of these factors changes, the entire demand curve will *shift*. There will be a **change in demand** itself (such as B to C in Figure 3-2).

But people's incomes and tastes often do change, and so do the other factors. If we are to analyze the operations of markets and the pricing of goods and services, we must account for variations in

Figure 3-2
Demand for T-Bone Steaks

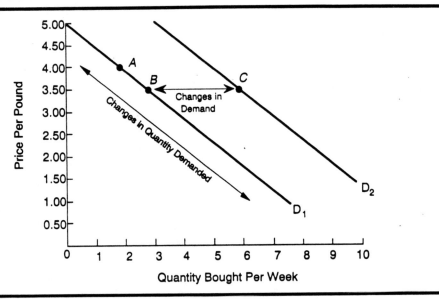

these aspects, in addition to variations in price. Figure 3-2 shows the difference between a change in quantity demanded and a change in demand. The movement from *A* to *B* along demand curve D_1 (caused by a reduction in price from $4.00 to $3.50) is called a *change in quantity demanded*. The movement from *B* to *C* is from demand curves D_1 to D_2 and may be caused by a change in consumers' incomes or tastes, prices of other goods, or consumers' expectations for the future (or all of these). This movement involves a shift in the entire demand schedule.

First let's see what effect a change in income will have on changing demand. In Figure 3-2, D_1 is a curve showing your original demand for T-bone steaks. All points on it represent the original price-quantity relations. Now suppose you receive a raise in pay. Since we are assuming that T-bone steaks are a good you want, your demand curve will shift to D_2. Now that you have more income, you buy approximately 3 more steaks per week, at any price per pound between $1.50 and $5.00. Of course, if you were to have a pay cut, your demand curve would shift to the left as your income decreased. If we now take your income increase away, we expect that you will buy approximately 3 fewer steaks per week. In other words, your demand curve will shift back to D_1—unless, at the same time, your tastes or your expectations of the future, or the prices of other goods, change to offset the decrease in income.

Change in Other Prices. Suppose that the price of chicken doubles. Since T-bone steaks and chicken are to some extent substitutes for each other, your demand for the now relatively cheaper T-bone steaks will increase, perhaps to D_2. But if the price of chicken falls, your demand for the now relatively more expensive T-bones will decrease, perhaps from D_2 to D_1. The same thing might happen if potatoes suddenly went up to $5.00 per pound: since potatoes are a complement to steak, you might consume less steak along with fewer potatoes.

Change in Tastes. Suppose that your demand for T-bone steaks is at D_2 and you develop a yen for pizza, which weakens your taste for T-bones. Your demand for T-bones will shift to the left (perhaps to D_1).

Changes in Expectations About Future Prices. Suppose that you read in the newspaper that there is a failure in the grain crop and that there will soon be big increases in the price of steak because of a jump in the price of feed grains. Your demand curve for T-bones may shift to the right (you may decide to buy a dozen steaks and freeze them). In other words, D_1 is your demand curve only as long as your current expectations about prices remain the same.

Demand: Summing Up

There are four main things to remember about demand:

1. Demand curves slope downward, to the right. In other words, consumers buy more of a good at (relatively) lower prices than they buy at (relatively) higher prices (the *law of demand*).

2. Only changes in the price of a good can cause changes in the *quantity demanded* of that good. Such changes result in *movements along* a demand curve.

3. The only demand factor that cannot cause a change in the demand for a good is a change in its own price.

4. Factors that may singly or jointly change the demand for a good are changes in income or tastes, changes in prices of other commodities, and changes in expectations about the future.

Market Demand

So far, we have looked only at one person's demand. But competitive markets are made up of many unorganized buyers expressing their individual demands. How, theoretically, do we figure the total market demand? We must add up the demand schedules of many individuals, assuming that there are no interdependencies of demand, such as a desire to keep up with the Joneses.

Figure 3-3 illustrates the principle involved, since it shows the sum of your and my demand curves at each price, which gives a picture of market demand. My demand schedule is plotted from the same kind of data as in Table 3-1. Thus, when T-bone steaks are selling at $4.00 a pound, you buy 3 and I buy 2. Let's assume for simplicity that we are the only 2 consumers who are buying them. Market demand at this price is then 5 T-bones per week.

Figure 3-3
Market Demand for T-Bone Steaks

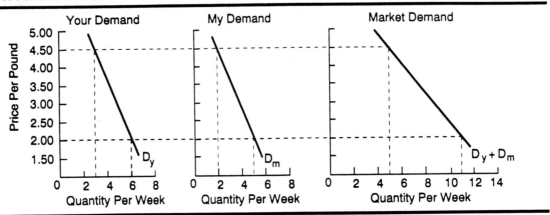

Similarly, when T-bones are selling at $2.00 a pound, you demand 6 per week and I demand 5, making market demand 11 T-bones per week.

Here are some general remarks about market demand:

1. People's demand curves are not the same, since individuals have different incomes, tastes, and expectations for the future.

2. Market demand curves, like the demand curves of individuals, slope downward or to the right, since they derive their slope from the slopes of the demand curves of individuals. Of course, the market demand curve represents a larger quantity of a given thing, because many people buy more than one person does.

3. *Number of buyers* (population) is a determinant of market demand. As the number of buyers increases, so does demand.

SUPPLY

Supply
The set of relationships showing the quantity of a product a firm will offer for sale at each of several prices within a specific period of time.

As we know, there are two sides to a market: demand and **supply**. Now we want to set up the same kind of concepts for supply as we did for demand. We can use the same techniques.

You may think that the wellspring of the world's supplies—the business firm—has no objectives in common with the consumer who demands the output of the firm, but each *maximizes* (that is, builds up to the maximum) some aspect of self-interest. Consumers maximize satisfaction and business firms maximize profit.

What Is Supply?

Supply *is the set of relationships showing the quantity of a product that a firm will offer for sale at each of several prices within a specific period of time.*

We set up the picture of the supply situation on the assumption that certain other factors are constant or unchanged—the *ceteris paribus* or other-things-being-equal assumption mentioned earlier. The other factors, which if they did change could affect the firm's supply curve, are:

1. The technology of production.

2. The prices of inputs or resources.

3. The prices of other goods.

4. The firm's expectations about future prices.

5. The objective of the firm. Will it maximize profit or does it have some other objective?

In addition, the *number of firms* in the industry will affect total or market supply.

Who is the source of supply? In our competitive market, many relatively small firms do the supplying. Enough firms participate in the market so that no one firm can influence the price of a good in the market as a whole.

To illustrate, let's go back to T-bone steaks. Table 3-2, the supply schedule of the ABC Meat Market, sums up the quantities supplied at each price for T-bone steaks. See what happens to quantity as price goes down. The firm offers more for sale at (relatively) high prices than at (relatively) low prices (the **law of supply**).

The **supply curve** of a firm or industry shows the relationships between the various prices of a product and the quantities of it the firm or industry offers for sale. A change in the price of a product is the only thing that can cause a change in the quantity supplied. Such changes are reflected in movements along the supply curve, as shown by the arrow parallel to S in Figure 3-4, which shows the relationship between price per pound and quantity supplied. Note that the supply curve goes up, to the right. The vertical bar at the upper right of the graph means that a given firm—here the ABC Meat Market—eventually reaches its capacity,

Law of Supply
A firm will offer more for sale at (relatively) higher prices than at (relatively) lower prices (ceteris paribus).

Supply Curve
Represents a firm's or industry's supply schedule plotted on a two dimensional graph.

Table 3-2
ABC Meat Market: Supply Schedule of T-bone Steaks

Price Per Pound	Quantity Supplied Per Week
$5.00	5
4.50	5
4.00	4
3.50	3
3.00	2
2.50	1
2.00	0
1.50	0

Figure 3-4
ABC Meat Market: Supply Curve

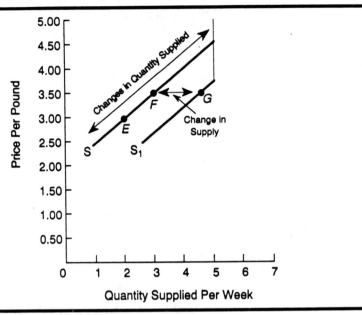

it runs out of storage space, counter space, or sales clerks to sell all those steaks. In other words, after a certain maximum is reached, it becomes impossible for the supplier to supply any more.

Suppose that the price of T-bone steaks goes up from $3.00 to $3.50 per pound. The ABC Meat Market will increase the quantity it supplies from 2 to 3 T-bone steaks per week. All such price changes are reflected in movements along a given supply curve, and are called **changes in quantity supplied**.

What happens when there is a change in one or more of those "other factors" we mentioned? An improvement in the technique of production (a new meat-slicing machine), a lower resource price (price of feed grains goes down), a change in the firm's expectation (a rumor that meat prices may go down), or a change in price of other goods (a drop in the price of chickens)—all these factors, or just one of them, can cause the *entire* supply curve to shift. For example, in Figure 3-4, the movement from F to G reflects an increase in supply from level S to level S_1. Such shifts are called **changes in supply**.

Changes in Quantity Supplied
Movements along a supply curve that are caused only by changes in the price of that product.

Changes in Supply
Shifts in a supply curve that may be caused by changes in any factor affecting supply other than a change in the price of that good.

What Do Supply Data and the Supply Curve Tell Us?

1. The number of steaks supplied per week rises as price rises and falls as price falls (the *law of supply*).

2. There is a price below which the firm will supply *nothing*. Reason: The firm that seeks to maximize profit likewise seeks to minimize losses. It will produce nothing if it cannot make a profit,

or at least cover production expenses that cease if it ceases to produce.

3. Although, for a given firm with given physical facilities, the number of steaks supplied rises as the price rises, it rises slowly. The number of steaks finally reaches a maximum, because the firm reaches its capacity.

Why Do Supply Curves Slope Upward?

There are two easily identifiable reasons why an individual firm's supply curve—unlike its demand curve—slopes upward or to the right. In the first place, a firm's resources can be used to produce more than one good. If, for instance, the price of beef increases (ceteris paribus), it becomes relatively more profitable to use resources to produce beef than to devote those resources to some other product such as pork. The reverse occurs with price decreases; as a good's price falls, relative profitability declines and the firm reduces quantity supplied and shifts resources to other products. In addition, a firm producing larger rates of output will ultimately experience decreasing efficiency as it utilizes existing plant and equipment more intensively (the effect of bottlenecks, and the like).

The supply curve of an industry, obtained by adding the supply curves of individual firms, also slopes upward. An additional reason for variations in quantities supplied is that firms have *different* costs of production. As product price falls, those with higher costs may stop offering it for sale at all (industry quantity supplied will decrease). And, as the price rises, such *firms* will again offer it for sale (industry quantity supplied will increase.

Why Do Supply Curves Shift?

The factors discussed above explain why a firm or industry will have an upward sloping supply curve and also what *can cause a shift in supply or, in other words, cause supply to increase.* Quantity supplied changes (such as the movement from E to F in Figure 3-4) vary directly with price. What, though, causes changes in supply, the shift from S to S_1 (such as the movement from F to G) in Figure 3-4. The factors that can cause such shift are:

1. *Improvements in Technology.* Technological changes increases productivity which reduces cost. Firms find it profitable to offer more of a product for sale at each price as a result.

2. *Reductions in factor prices.* As factor (labor, capital, land) prices fall, costs of firms are lowered and, again, firm's find it profitable to offer more of a product for sale at each price.

3. *Changes in the prices of other products.* These prices determine the opportunity costs of a firm's resources. If the price of alternative products falls, the opportunity costs to ABC Meat Market decrease and cause the firm to offer more meat for sale, at each price.

4. *Changes in price expectations.* If a firm expects its prices to fall in the future, it will offer more for sale at each present price. The reverse occurs for expected future price increases.

5. *Changes in the number of firms in an industry.* Industry supply, unlike the firm supply in Figure 3-4, depends on the number of firms. As new firms enter an industry, industry supply grows; as firms exit the industry, industry supply decreases or shifts to the left.

Market Supply

We can chart supply the same way we chart demand. Figure 3-5 shows the process of adding up, or *aggregation.*

For simplicity, we have assumed that there are only 2 firms operating in the market. But the adding-up process is the same, even if there are thousands of firms. When steak is selling at $3.00, the ABC Meat Market will supply 2 steaks per week and the XYZ Meat Market will supply 1. Total market quantity supplied at this price is 3 per week. At $4.00 per pound, ABC will supply 4 per week and XYZ, 3; total market quantity supplied at this price is 7 per week.

The market supply curve takes its shape from the curves of the individual firms, so it slopes upward to the right. Remember that the number of firms helps to determine market supply. Naturally, more firms make a greater supply.

Figure 3-5
Market Supply of T-bone Steaks

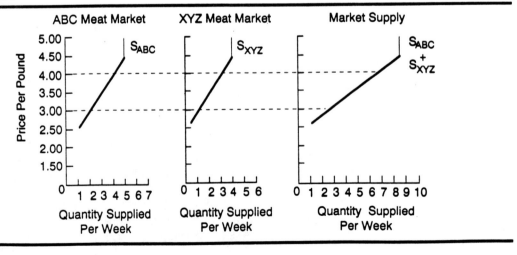

Before we go any further, let us sum up the distinctions between *movements along* demand and supply curves and *shifts in* them.

Difference Between Movements Along and Shifts In Curves

1. The only thing that can cause a *movement along* the demand curve for a product is a change in price of that product. Such movements are called changes in *quantity demanded*.

2. Factors that can cause a *change in demand* or *shift in* the individual's demand curve for a product are things other than the price of that product: (a) changes in consumers' incomes, (b) changes in prices of other products, (c) changes in consumers' tastes, and (d) changes in consumers' expectations about future prices.

3. The only thing that can cause a *movement along* the supply curve for a product is a change in the price of that product. Such movements are called changes in *quantity supplied*.

4. Factors that can cause a *change in supply* or *shift in* the individual firm's supply curve for a product are things other than the price of that product: (a) changes in techniques of production, (b) changes in prices of other products, (c) changes in prices of inputs or resources, and (d) changes in firms' expectations about future prices and market conditions.

5. Changes in the number of consumers can cause changes in market demand. Changes in the number of firms can cause changes in market supply.

EQUILIBRIUM PRICING

Equilibrium Price
The price at which quantity demanded equals quantity supplied. It is a market clearing price.

Now let's return to our original question: How is the price of T-bone steaks, or of any product, determined? The answer is that their price tends toward an equilibrium price, one that clears the market.

An **equilibrium price** is the price at which the quantity demanded is equal to the quantity supplied. It is the price that tends to prevail unless the factors (that is, supply and demand) operating in the market change.

Let's see how such an equilibrium price comes into being in a competitive market through the joint influences of supply and demand. Table 3-3, shows price versus demand and supply for our minimarket, which—just to keep things simple—consists of only 2 consumers and 2 meat markets.

Table 3-3 shows that the equilibrium price—the price that prevails in this market—is $3.60 per pound. It is at this price that

Table 3-3
Market Demand and Supply Schedules for T-bone Steaks

Price Per Pound	Quantity Demanded Per Week	Quantity Supplied Per Week
$5.00	0	9
4.80	1	9
4.20	3	7
3.60	5 = Equilibrium =	5
3.00	7	3
2.40	9	2
1.80	11	1
1.20	13	0

quantity demanded equals quantity supplied, or the market is cleared. Because it is sometimes easier to understand relationships visually, Figure 3-6 shows these demand and supply schedules combined on the same graph. (D represents columns (1) and (2) in Table 3-3, while S represents columns (1) and (3).

As you can see, $3.60 is the equilibrium price—the price that clears this competitive market. This is so because any other price would create either shortages or surpluses.

Suppose that for a while one of the meat markets cuts its price to $2.40 per pound. From Figure 3-6, we can see that the consumers would like to buy 9 steaks per week at that price, while the firms would supply only 2. The difference—7 steaks—is **excess demand**; or, from the consumer's point of view, a shortage of steaks. (Other examples of excess demand are long lines of drivers

Excess Demand
The amount consumers are unable to obtain of a good at a non-equilibrium price.

Figure 3-6
Market Demand and Supply: Equilibrium Pricing of T-bone Steaks

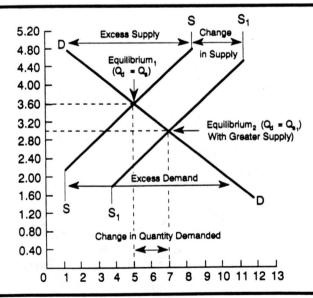

waiting for gas when a small gas station offers gas at cut-rate prices and the rush to get cheap balcony seats for a concert.)

Since the demand curve (D) reflects consumers' tastes, incomes, and the like, it indicates that the consumers are willing to pay more than $2.40 to obtain more than those 2 steaks they can buy at that price. As the consumers offer to pay more, the meat markets offer more steaks for sale. Only when steaks sell for $3.60 per pound is there no difference between the 2 sets of interests, quantity supplied and quantity demanded. Neither of the consumers is willing to pay more than $3.60 to buy the additional steaks that the meat markets would supply if the price were higher.

Excess Supply
The quantity of a good firms are unable to sell at a non-equilibrium price.

What's the matter with prices higher than $3.60? At a price of $4.80, the meat markets will gladly supply 9 steaks per week. But at that price, one consumer will not buy *any* steaks, and the other consumer will buy only *1*. The difference—8 steaks—is **excess supply** or the quantity of a good firms are unable to sell at a non-equilibrium price. In order to sell steaks and clear the market, the meat markets lower their prices—moving along their supply curves—until the market is cleared at $3.60. (Other examples of excess supply are new cars left on the showroom floor after a price increase and new textbooks left on a bookstore's shelves after a price hike.)

Equilibrium at a price of $3.60 lasts as long as the set of forces defining supply and demand holds. If supply changes, as in the shift to S_1 (more supplied at all prices), a new market-clearing price (or equilibrium price) comes into being, in this instance at $3.00, where $Q_d = Q_{s_1}$.

Note that a *change in supply cannot change demand, and a change in demand cannot change supply*. In a competitive market, demand and supply are independent of each other. Thus, a change in the supply from S to S_1 results in a change in quantity demanded (see the bottom of Figure 3-6 between 5 and 7 on the horizontal axis).

It follows that (1) any change in supply or demand changes price, (2) any change in supply changes the quantity demanded, and (3) any change in demand changes the quantity supplied. The only exception occurs when equal and offsetting changes (either increases or decreases) of supply and demand occur simultaneously. We see this illustrated in Figure 3-7.

In Figure 3-7, the competitive market initially tends toward price P_E with demand, D_1 and supply, S_1. A market clearing equilibrium quantity of Q_e is established and there is neither excess demand nor excess supply. If there are equal increases in both demand (D_1 to D_2) and supply (S_1 to S_2), there is a larger market with equilibrium quantity increases from Q_e to $Q_e{'}$ but the equilibriating price remains $\overline{P_E}$. The reverse can happen with a declining market size. Had demand and supply both decreased (D_2 to D_1, S_2 to S_1), the equilibrium quantity would have fallen ($Q_e{'}$ to Q_e) but the equilibriating price would have remained $\overline{P_E}$.

Figure 3-7
Competitive Market Equilibrium with Equal Changes in Supply and Demand

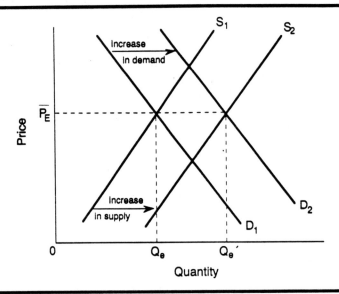

In Figure 3-7, the initial market equilibrium with demand, D, and supply, S_1, is with price, $\overline{P_E}$ and quantity, Q_e. When demand increases to D_2 and there is a proportional increase in supply to S_2, equilibrium price remains $\overline{P_E}$ and equilibrium quantity increases to Q_e'.

Conditions for Competitive Pricing

Let us summarize the conditions that are necessary for competitive pricing to exist.

1. *Completely flexible pricing.* If the government (or some other agency) had set the price of meat at $2.40, there would have been excess or unsatisfied demand. Black markets might have developed—as they did during World War II—to fill this unsatisfied demand at unregulated prices. In the application to this chapter, we will see a case of inflexible prices in the of price ceilings established by rent control laws.

2. *Full information.* In order for prices to be bid up or down to equilibrium, buyers and sellers obviously need to be aware of their alternatives, such as other prices.

3. *Expectation of constant prices.* If consumers think that today's $1.80 price will come down to $1.50 tomorrow, they may not buy any steak today. If producers think the same way, they may want to supply more steaks today than they would have otherwise.

4. *Free entry to and exit from markets.* Both buyers and sellers must be free to participate in the market or withdraw from it. In other words, there must be complete mobility of resources.

5. *Maximization of satisfaction and profits*. Buyers and sellers seek to maximize their satisfaction or profits, respectively, and always act to do so.

6. *Absence of collusion*. There must be no collusion between single buyers or sellers or between groups of buyers and sellers. Otherwise, prices might be pegged rather than being competitively flexible.

SUMMING UP

1. Studying the market system helps to answer three basic questions about the use of resources: (a) *what* goods are produced (composition), (b) *how* goods are produced (technique), and (c) *for whom* goods are produced (distribution).

2. To understand the market system, one needs to begin with conditions of *competition*: the market form in which no buyer or seller has influence over the price at which the product sells.

3. Since each participant in a competitive market acts independently, *prices*—the signals for action in the market—are determined by unrelated movements of demand and supply.

4. There are two sides to every market: the demand side and the supply side. *Demand* is a set of relationships showing the quantity of a good that consumers will buy at each of several prices within a specific period of time.

5. One draws a demand curve for a good on the assumption of *ceteris paribus* (other things being equal). In other words, one assumes that the price, and only the price, of that good changes, not any of the other factors of demand.

6. We expect a demand curve to slope downward to the right, which means that people buy more of a good at low prices than at high prices (the law of demand).

7. The *law of demand* is based on (a) the income effect and (b) the substitution effect. The *income effect*: As the price of a good falls, the consumer has more purchasing power and ordinarily buys more of that good as a result. The *substitution effect*: As the price of a good falls, it becomes relatively cheaper than those goods for which it is a substitute. Thus, people buy more of it because it is cheaper.

8. There are exceptions to the normal case, such as *Veblen goods* (perhaps diamonds, caviar, sable coats), and, in poor countries, certain basic staple goods *(income-inferior goods)* such as beans and rice.

9. For a given good, a *change in quantity demanded* is a movement along a demand curve. It can result only from a change in the price of the good. A *change in demand* is a shift of the demand curve, and can result from a change in any of the other factors affecting demand: income, tastes, the prices of substitutes and complements, and expectations.

10. Basic factors that can change demand are (a) consumers' incomes, (b) consumers' tastes and preferences, (c) prices of other products, (d) consumers' expectations about future market conditions and prices, and (e) number of consumers.

11. One can estimate the curve for market demand by adding individual curves, given that consumers buy independently of each other. Curves for market demand get their shapes from the demand curves of individuals, but measure larger quantities.

12. *Supply* is the set of relationships showing the quantity of a product that a firm will offer for sale at each possible price within a specific period of time.

13. Factors that can change supply are (a) changes in technology, (b) changes in prices of factors of production, (c) changes in prices of other goods, (d) changes in firms' expectations about future prices and (e) changes in the number of firms.

14. A *supply curve* shows that (a) firms supply more of a given product at higher prices than at lower prices, and (b) there is a price below which firms supply nothing to the market.

15. Supply curves that slope upward to the right are based on the assumption that ultimately firms run into decreasing efficiency and increasing costs as they expand output, either because of fixed physical facilities or difficulty in managing a larger operation. Also the relative profitability of supplying a product increases as its price increases.

16. One can estimate the curve for market supply by adding supply curves of individual firms, assuming that each firm behaves independently of the others. Changes in the number of firms cause changes in market supply.

17. Competitive prices are *equilibrium prices*. That is, they are market-clearing prices. When there are equilibrium prices, quantity demanded and quantity supplied are equal and there is neither excess demand nor excess supply.

18. If prices are *above* equilibrium, there is *excess supply*—a market surplus or excess. If prices are *below* equilibrium, there is *excess demand*—a market shortage. In either case, demand and supply are not in equilibrium.

19. Conditions necessary to ensure competitive prices are (a) completely flexible prices; (b) possession of full information by both buyers and sellers; (c) expectation of constant prices; (d) free entry into and exit from markets; (e) consistent effort of firms to maximize profits and of consumers to maximize satisfaction; and (f) no collusion between buyers and sellers; all must behave independently of each other.

KEY TERMS

Price rivalry
Competition
Demand
Complements, substitutes
Ceteris paribus assumption
Demand schedule
Demand curve
Law of demand
Income effect
Substitution effect
Changes in quantity demanded
Changes in demand
Supply
Law of supply
Supply curve
Changes in quantity supplied
Changes in supply
Equilibrium price
Excess demand
Excess supply

QUESTIONS

1. Review the basic questions about use of resources, questions that are common to all societies. Be sure that you not only understand these questions but also realize why we need answers.

2. Define *competition*, as economists use the word. How does the economist's way of looking at competition differ from your familiar usage of the word?

3. What is *demand*? Does the economist's meaning of demand differ from your usual meaning? If so, what do you think accounts for the differences? What is the *ceteris paribus* assumption?

4. Why do demand curves usually slope downward to the right? What would it mean if one sloped *up* to the right? List the five basic factors that influence demand. Which of these factors, in

addition to price, do you think will be more influential in determining the demand for (a) cars? (b) safety matches? Why?

5. Define the *income effect* and the *substitution effect*. For a small change in the price of a good, which of the two effects would you expect to be more important? What are *inferior* goods? Can you think of some possible examples beyond those given in the chapter?

6. What is the *law of demand*? How is it explained? What can cause a change in demand? A change in quantity demanded?

7. How does one derive curves for market demand? What assumption(s) does one use to do so?

8. What is the *supply curve*? How do competitive suppliers behave toward each other? Why do supply curves usually slope up to the right?

9. What factors determine supply? What can cause a change in supply? A change in quantity supplied?

10. How does one derive curves for market supply? What assumption(s) does one use to do so?

11. How is *price* determined in a competitive market? What does *equilibrium* mean, in relation to the operation of a market? What conditions must exist in a market for competitive prices to be established? Are they hard to establish? Do you know any markets in which these conditions exist, or are approximated?

12. Suppose that you are chief economist for an automobile industry council. You are asked to forecast industry sales for next year. You know that in the coming year personal income is expected to rise by 3 percent, that mass transit is going to be heavily subsidized by government, and that the population and its average age are expected to remain fairly constant. What influences will each of these factors have on your forecast?

Application to Chapter 3: When Should We Let Supply and Demand Work? Rent Controls and the Price of Housing

---

Friend and foe alike concede that market prices can be efficient devices for bringing the interests of buyers and sellers together and, ultimately, for making the two sets of interests consistent. The alternative in a world of scarcity, where resources must be allocated and products and services rationed, is for someone to set prices. The someone is *usually* (but not always) government.

We may presume that governments intentionally set prices at non-equilibrium, non-market clearing levels. There is no reason for governments to intervene in determining prices (other than an ideological reason) if prices are set at the same level as markets would tend to establish. As we have seen, actual prices can be above or below equilibrium levels and tend, *in free markets*, to create self-correcting responses to either excess demand (shortages) or excess supply (surpluses).

There are many examples of government intervention in price determination in the history of the U.S. Indeed, such controls go back as far as the American revolution. Sometimes, as in that instance, these controls have occurred during periods of grave crisis and have consisted of direct establishment of "ceiling" prices. Such ceilings, for example, were created for many products (sugar, flour, gasoline, etc.) during World War II by the Office of Price Administration (O.P.A.). At times, intervention has taken the form of "floors" or efforts to keep prices from moving below pre-established levels or targets. Since 1929, the federal government has established target prices for a broad range of agricultural products (wheat, corn, tobacco, etc.) and has undertaken various activities to achieve those prices.

Government-Determined Prices: The Arguments

Throughout history, governments have expressed their dissatisfaction with prices established in markets by either setting prices directly or by mandating the limits within which prices are permitted to (legally) move. As we indicated above, this has happened even in private enterprise economies such as that of the U.S. What is the main (non-ideological) argument for this kind of activity? Generally, governments, whether local or national, have assumed authority over prices because of concern that markets would price and ration goods in a manner that is "unfair" or "inequitable." Concern, in other words, is over the availability of the good at the market price or over the effect on real income distribution of buying (or selling) it at that price. In this application, we will concentrate on concerns of public officials that market prices would be "too high." As a result, price ceilings are imposed. For the sake of specific illustration, we will focus on the price of housing and efforts especially at local government levels, to impose rent controls through legislation. Such laws have been enacted in many American cities and the question about them is not *whether* they work; rather; it is *how* do they work, *who* they benefit, and *who* bears their costs. The question is especially meaningful given the numbers of people who can neither find nor afford housing and who show up in the data on homeless persons as the economy enters the 1990s.

Are Rent Controls Effective? (The Best Case)

Since we have argued that there is "no free lunch," you might suppose that the above question is needless. While that may be true, answering the question does illustrate the futility of trying to make resource allocation decisions without incurring opportunity costs.

In Figure A3-1, we see a hypothetical example of the imposition of rent controls in a situation in which the supply of housing (S) is $\overline{Q_m}$ and quantity supplied does not vary with housing prices. $\overline{Q_m}$ housing units, in other words, will be offered for rent

Figure A3-1
Rent Controls When the Housing Supply is Fixed

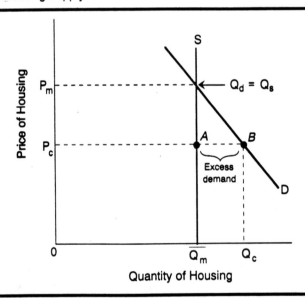

In Figure A3-1, the demand for housing (D) is downward sloping while the supply of housing (S) is represented by a vertical line (from $\overline{Q_m}$) parallel to the axis on which the price of housing is measured. A market equilibrium price would tend to be established at P_m where the quantity demanded of housing equals the quantity supplied of housing or $\overline{Q_m}$. If government sets a price below equilibrium such as P_c (ceiling price), the equilibrium will still be at $\overline{Q_m}$ but there will be excess demand of Q_c - $\overline{Q_m}$ or *AB*.

at any of the prices represented on the vertical axis. With demand for housing, D, a free housing market would tend to establish a market clearing price, P_m, and the quantity demanded of housing (Q_d) would equal the quantity supplied (Q_s). All those looking for housing at that price would find it. Now let us suppose that a local government (New York City or one of the numerous others with rent control laws) imposes a ceiling price of $\underline{P_c}$ on housing units. The number of housing units offered for rent ($\overline{Q_m}$) does not change but there is a cost imposed on would-be renters. The quantity of housing demanded at $\underline{P_c}$, $0Q_c$, is greater than the quantity supplied, $0\overline{Q_m}$. The difference ($0Q_c - 0\overline{Q_m}$), or the distance AB, represents excess demand—the number of units renters cannot find at the controlled price. The costs of searching for housing that is unavailable are a significant part of this burden.

The costs above are only a part of the reason why many economists are skeptical of the argument that rent controls are effective tools of public policy whose objectives (housing availability and equity) are accomplished at low cost. Still, cities such as New York, which has had rent controls since World War II, show little inclination to repeal such controls.

Are Rent Controls Effective? (The Worst Case)

In the hypothetical case illustrated in Figure A3-1, renters didn't suffer a reduction in the number of housing units available because of rent controls. Instead, they incurred costs because at a below-equilibrium price, they searched fruitlessly for more housing than was available. The crucial assumption upon which that conclusion rested, that housing units offered for rent do not vary with rental prices, seems unrealistic. In Figure A3-2, we see what economists would expect (and data suggest) is more likely, a housing market with an upward sloping supply. A free housing market would tend to create a market equilibrium in Figure A3-2 with price, P_m, and quantity, Q_m, ($Q_d = Q_s$). Government now sets ceiling price, P_c, with the following effects: (1) the quantity supplied of housing declines from $0Q_m$ to $0Q_{c_1}$, creating an excess demand of ($0Q_m - 0Q_{c_1}$), or the distance AB, (2) at the lower ceiling price, renters try to increase the quantity demanded of housing from $0Q_m$ to $0Q_{c_2}$ creating additional excess demand of $0Q_{c_2} - 0Q_m$ or the distance BC, (3) the total excess demand resulting from the rent control is the sum of the two effects or ($0Q_m - 0Q_{c_1}$) + ($0Q_{c_2} - 0Q_m$) or $AB + BC = AC$.

Are *any* renters made better off by the rent control (as city officials apparently intended)? *Yes.* Those who are able to rent housing ($0Q_{c_1}$) at the legislated price, P_c. They expend on housing, $0P_cAQ_1$, whereas to obtain that amount of housing at the market price (P_m), they would have had to spend $0P_mDQ_{c_1}$. The difference, P_mP_oAD, represents an income transfer to renters which political decision makers apparently intended.

Figure A3-2
Rent Controls With a Variable Supply of Housing

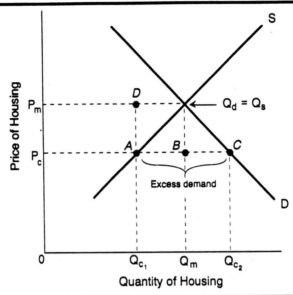

In Figure A3-2, the demand for housing (D) is downward sloping and the supply of housing (S) is upward sloping. A market equilibrium price would tend to be established at P_m where the quantity demanded of housing (Q_d) equals the quantity supplied (Q_s), or Q_m. If government sets a ceiling price such as P_c, the quantity supplied will be $0Q_{c_1}$, while the quantity demanded will be $0Q_{c_2}$; there will be excess demand of ($0Q_{c_1} - 0Q_{c_2}$) or AC.

Are renters as a *whole* made better off by the rent control? Economists are doubtful. Renters lose $0Q_m - 0Q_{c_1}$ of housing as a direct consequence of the price control because they have fewer units of housing that are offered for rent. Beyond this "supply effect," there is a "demand effect" as well; the quantity demanded of housing in Figure A3-2 increases from Q_m to Q_{c_2} as the legal price ceiling of P_c is imposed. The legally contrived shortage of housing, thus, at the controlled price is $0Q_{c_2} - 0Q_{c_1}$ or the distance AC. While some people are made better off, others are made worse off, and it is by no means clear that, on balance, rent controls improve the welfare of the general populace.

The Dynamics of Rent-Controlled Housing

The hypothetical housing market represented in Figure A3-2 is pictured at a point in time or in a static situation. Over time, or in a dynamic sense, the situation would likely get worse in terms of the costs of controlling housing prices. Since resources are required to maintain or expand housing, fixing its price lowers the returns on housing relative to the returns on other (non-controlled) uses of resources. In New York City, for instance, prices of coops, condominiums and expensive apartments are not controlled. Neither are the prices of most goods other than housing. As the (relative) rate of return on housing for low and middle income renters declines, buildings may no longer be maintained adequately. In fact, buildings may even be abandoned and/or converted to other uses. A leftward shift of the supply curve from S to S' in Figure A3-3 would normally result in housing prices rising from P_e to P_e'; since this cannot (legally) occur, the quantity supplied at P_c will continue to decline further. Whereas excess demand at the controlled price would have equalled *BC*, the excess (people searching and working for housing) increases to *ABC*.

New York City has seen all of these effects. Landlords sometimes do not pay taxes on or adequately maintain buildings. There are entire blocks of buildings that stand vacant (at least for *legal* activities) and are unfit for housing. The city has, through tax arrears, become the owner of thousands of apartment buildings but is unwilling or financially unable to provide the housing that private landlords find it unprofitable to provide. Finally, many buildings have been converted to condominiums or to other uses whose prices are uncontrolled.

Illegal or "Black Markets"

Faced with the shortage of housing shown in Figure A3-3, renters, who cannot wait for months or years to obtain housing at the

Figure A3-3
The Dynamics of Rent Controlled Housing With a Declining Supply

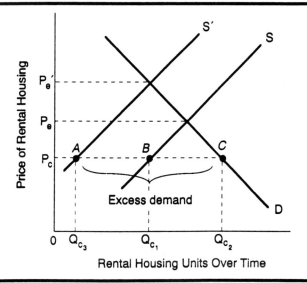

controlled price, resort to bribes or "side payments." People who have apartments at controlled prices sublet them out for higher prices or landlords accept non-rental payments in lieu of rents. New York City and other cities with stringent rent control laws have not only to spend resources enforcing the laws but also to revise them often in order to prevent the voluntary exchanges in which renters and landlords would otherwise engage.

The Future of Rent Controls

Economists, even those on opposite ends of the political spectrum, agree that rent control laws have perverse effects on those they seek to benefit. Assar Lindbeck characterizes them as "the most efficient technique so far known for destroying cities." Why are such efforts to stymie the operation of free housing markets (ones in which landlords and renters make voluntary and mutually beneficial exchanges) not repealed? It seems unlikely that their continuation results from ignorance of their effects. Robert Thomas suggests instead that it is because the benefits of control are concentrated in the hands of a relatively small group (those who occupy rent controlled housing) while the costs are spread over a much larger group (landlords who are few, but many who seek better housing or who are new to the housing market.). Says Thomas: "Politicians, attempting to win or to stay in office have found it necessary to pay attention to the private interests of tenants even at the cost of continued urban decay."

SUMMING UP

1. In a market economy, as long as resources are scarce, prices must be used to allocate resources and ration output. If markets are not permitted to establish equilibrium, prices must be set, usually by government, at non-equilibrium levels.

2. Non-equilibrium prices in markets set in motion self-correcting movements of price and quantity that eliminate excess demand or excess supply. Non-market determined disequilibrium prices have no corresponding mechanisms of self-correction.

3. Governmentally established non-equilibrium prices may consist of price floors or price ceilings. There have been numerous examples of both in American history and there are many such examples today.

4. Government intervention in market pricing is most often based on "fairness" in pricing, rationing and income distribution. In this application, the focus is on local government control over housing prices which usually leads to rent control ordinances.

5. Free housing markets will establish equilibrium through prices that equate quantity demanded and quantity supplied. Housing prices that are set below equilibrium will result in excess demand.

6. Even if the quantity supplied of housing does not vary as housing prices are lowered by rent controls, there will be an excess demand at the legal price ceiling. Those seeking housing will not be able to obtain all (including the quality of housing) they wish at the ceiling price (Figure A3-1).

7. Economists are skeptical of the argument that rent controls make housing available at equitable prices. This is especially the case with a downward sloping demand for housing combined with an upward sloping supply of housing (Figure A3-2).

8. When rent controls are imposed those who benefit are the individuals who obtain the amount and quality of housing desired at the controlled price. Those who lose include landlords but also renters who see a decline in the quantity supplied of housing (the direct effect of rent control) and renters who seek more housing at the lower price than they would have sought at the equilibrium price (the indirect effect of rent control).

9. The indirect effect plus the direct effect above constitute the total excess demand for housing at the controlled price.

10. Over time, stringent rent controls are likely to result in a decline in both the quantity and quality of rental housing available. Incentives are created (through changes in relative prices and returns on resource usage) to convert housing units to other uses, to decrease maintenance outlays and even to abandon buildings rather than pay taxes on them.

11. Rent controls continue in spite of the view of economists that they have unintended ill effects on those they seek to benefit. One explanation for their popularity is that their benefits are concentrated in politically active small groups, while their costs are spread over a much larger group (landlords but also those who suffer from urban decay and inability to find better housing.) One effect of rent controls is in the illegal housing markets they tend to create.

QUESTIONS

1. What determines the availability of housing to individuals in a free market?

2. What is meant in saying that there is no "free lunch" in imposing ceiling prices in housing markets?

3. Who benefits from rent control laws?

4. How is the supply of housing related to the costs of rent controls?

5. Does the area in which you live have a rent control ordinance? If so, what costs and benefits are created by its enforcement?

6. Why do rent control laws tend to foster the development of "black" (illegal) markets?

7. Is it likely, in a dynamic sense, that rent control laws accomplish their objectives of making housing generally available at "affordable" prices? Why or why not?

8. If your answer to (7) above is negative, why do we continue to see rent control laws passed and enforced?

SUGGESTED READINGS

Cheung, Stephen N.S. "The Stated Intents and Actual Effects of a Rents Ordinance." *Economic Inquiry*. March, 1975.

Egan, John J., John Carr, Andrew Mott, and John Roos. *Housing and Public Policy: A Role for Mediating Structures*. Washington, D.C. American Enterprise Institute, 1981.

Lindbeck, Assar. *The Political Economy of the New Left*. New York: Harper and Row, 1971.

Rand Corporation. "The Effects of Rent Control on Housing in New York City." In *Contemporary Issues in Economics: Selected Readings*. R.W. Crandall and R.S. Eckhaus, Eds. New York, Little Brown, 1972.

Schuettinger, Robert F. and Eamonn F. Butler. *Forty Centuries of Wage and Price Controls*. Chapter 19. Washington, D.C. The Heritage Foundation, 1979

Thomas, Robert Paul. *Microeconomic Applications: Understanding the American Economy*. Chapter 24. Belmont, CA: Wadsworth Publishing Co., 1981.

Chapter 4:
Components of an Economic Society:
Households, Business Firms, Governments

What are the basic parts of our economy, and how are they interrelated? One useful view is that the economy is made up of three basic sectors: (1) *households*, which provide all the factors of production and in return buy the output of the firms; (2) *business firms*, which employ these factors of production and produce goods and services; and (3) *governments*, which buy part of the output of firms, take away some of the income of householders in the form of taxes, and make transfer payments to individuals. Governments also provide various forms of goods and services. These three sectors mesh in a system of flows of income and production called the *circular-flow model* of economic activity. In this chapter we will see how this circular flow of economic activity works and then describe the characteristics of each of the three interrelated sectors.

The application that accompanies this chapter discusses the question of whether businesses are committed simply to competition and profits or whether they have a sense of social responsibility that transcends profits.

The Circular-Flow Model

The Simple Model
Let us begin by simplifying things, and assume for the moment that there are only two basic components of the economy: consumers and business firms. Consumers *own* all the factors of production; that is, the resources necessary for production to take place. Firms *hire* all the factors of production, produce the goods and services consumers use, and pay a return (income) to the factors.

Figure 4-1 illustrates this. Households provide factors of production to business firms. In return, business firms pay households income for the use of those factors of production. Labor, as a factor of production, receives its reward in the form of wages and salaries. Owners of land get theirs in the form of rent; owners of capital get interest; entrepreneurs get profits. Firms utilize the factors of production to produce goods and services for the use of the householders. Householders, with incomes obtained from firms' use of their factors of production, pay firms for goods and services. Firms now have incomes so they can pay the factors of production to produce more goods and services. And so the process continues.

The circular-flow model and the world of economic production have no beginning. You may start the analysis at any point. Only the amount of resources available (factors of production) limits the level of production—resources plus technology and efficiency of use of these resources, of course. Firms use these resources because householders use all the income they receive to buy the output firms produce by employing the resources.

The upper half of Figure 4-1, showing the flow of resources and the reverse flow of income, portrays the **factor markets**, in which the supply of and demand for factors of production interact to determine wages and other factor prices. The bottom half, which shows flows of product output and reverse flows of payments for goods and services, portrays the **product markets**. In these, the supply of goods and services—and the demand for them—interact to determine prices of goods.

The Complex Model
Figure 4-1 is a great oversimplification of our economic system. Let us now examine a more complex, more realistic circular-flow model.

Factor Markets
Those markets in which the supply of and demand for factors of production interact to determine wages and other factor prices.

Product Markets
Markets in which goods and services flows are established.

Figure 4-1
Simple Circular-Flow Model

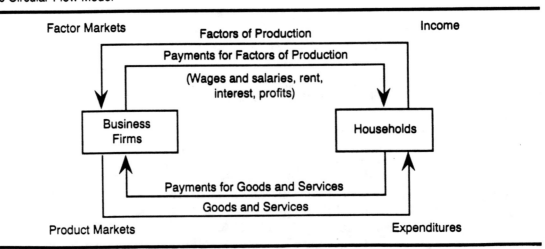

The flow of resources, products, and income between firms and households is circular in nature.

Figure 4-1 assumes that households spend all their income on buying the goods and services firms produce. This is not realistic, because people do manage to save some of their income, and also pay some of their income to the government in the form of taxes, both of which reduce the demand for goods and services (see Figure 4-2). Since saving and paying taxes both mean *not* consuming, these two factors reduce households' demand for firms' output.

Figure 4-1 also assumes that all output goes to households in the form of goods and services. Again this is unrealistic. The complete model includes two other sources of demand for firms' output:

1. *Other firms.* When firms demand output from other firms, this is not counted as part of the flows of goods and services to households, but as capital goods that aid in the production of other goods and services.

2. *Governments.* Federal, state, and local governments demand output from firms.

In both complex and simple circular-flow models of the economy, the flows of income to households consist of wages, rent, interest, and profits. However, in the complex model, households

Figure 4-2
Complex Circular-Flow Model

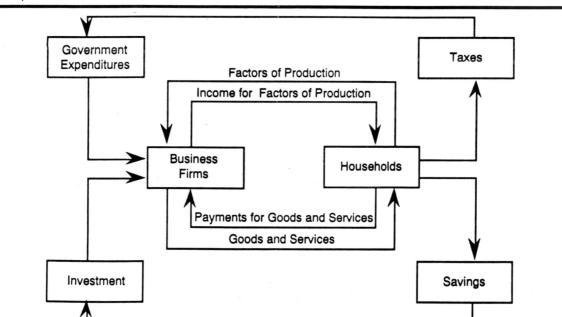

Savings and taxes drain off households' purchasing power and thus reduce their demand for consumer goods. Investment and government expenditures increase the demand for firms' output. These additions are also part of the flow, in that taxes become part of the government's purchasing power. And financial institutions such as banks make savings available for investment.

spend their incomes not only on consumption, but also on savings and taxes. Governments enter the picture with spending for goods and services, and so do business firms themselves, with expenditures for investment. So the flow of funds is still circular.

The money that taxes siphon from households' incomes becomes part of the purchasing power governments use for their expenditures. In addition, financial institutions make available for investment the money they get from people's savings. This keeps the money flowing. (By *financial institutions*, we usually mean savings banks and other financial institutions including stock exchanges, though there are many other kinds.)

It should be readily obvious to you that our economy is a great deal more complex than even the so-called complex model shows. Not only households, but also firms save. Firms also have to pay taxes to various governments, especially if the firms are incorporated and have, so to speak, a life of their own. Governments also provide goods and services to households (for example, public schools). Governments, furthermore, provide households with income. By this we don't mean just social security and welfare payments. Governments provide jobs; governments hire labor from households. And not only firms invest (demand capital from other firms); households also invest. The main form their investments take is home buying. (A house is considered an investment.) The list of activities that could be added to the model is endless. But the complex model gives us enough of a picture for us to approximate the vast complexity of reality.

What Does the Model Show?

The model in Figure 4-2 tells us that there are three sources of demand for the output of firms: households, other business firms, and governments. There are, therefore, as many different levels of demand as there are combinations of spending patterns by these three parts of society.

This more complex system of economic flows doesn't necessarily result in a socially desirable level of demand, one that includes full employment and a low rate of inflation. Yet households, because they have to set aside money for savings and for taxes, reduce their demand for consumer goods. Firms, by their investments, and governments by buying output of business firms, may take up some of the slack—but not all. So you may have a decrease in demand for goods and services and, eventually, unemployment. (The size of the circular flow decreases.) But if governments and business firms spend *more* than households have saved and have paid in taxes, then demand for products and services increases (the size of the circular flow increases) and inflation may result. While this is an oversimplification, you can get the general and important idea that as these flows change, the level of economic activity in a society increases or decreases with various effects on incomes, prices, and employment.

The rest of this chapter will deal with various aspects of the three sectors in order to show what determines their patterns of demand for goods and services.

HOUSEHOLDS

There are three basic questions about households: (1) Where do they get their income? (2) How do they use it? (3) What is their share of total income? Answers to these questions will give you an insight into the probable effects of the economic decisions of households on total output and income and on the level and composition of output.

The Sources of Income: Functional Distribution

Functional Distribution of Income
The distribution of income that shows how each factor of production derives income according to its economic function(s).

When we talk about sources of income, we speak of the distribution of income as a **functional distribution**. Households—in other words, people—receive their income from the wages and salaries they get from working; owners of land get theirs from rent; owners of capital get theirs from interest; businesses, both corporations and unincorporated firms, get theirs in the form of profits that are a result of their entrepreneurial activity. Economists look at these sources of income in terms of the functions they perform. It is convenient to view this functional distribution in relative terms, using percentage shares, as in Table 4-1.

Labor gets the largest portion of the money income, in the form of wages and salaries. Labor's share increased from 60 percent at the end of the 1920s to more than 70 percent at the beginning of the 1980s. Labor's increase is due mainly to the decline in the share that went to owners of unincorporated firms (proprietors' income), which fell by more than half during the same time span.

Corporate profits—which ran about 10 to 15 percent of total income during this period—vary according to the state of the economy. They go down in times of recession and go up when times are good. The share of income that comes from rent has been

Table 4-1
Percentage Functional Distribution of Income

	1929	1941	1950	1960	1974	1984
Wages and salaries	60	62	69	71	75	73
Proprietors' income	17	16	15	10	6	8
Corporate profits	12	15	15	11	10	9
Rental income	6	3	4	4	2	2
Interest income	5	3	1	2	6	8

Source: U.S. Department of Commerce, 1984.

fairly steady (between 2 and 4 percent), while the share of income that comes from interest declined between 1929 and 1970 because of falling interest rates. However, in the 1970s and the early 1980s the share of interest income went up to 8 percent and more because of the revival of high interest rates.

Many factors contributed to the changing ratios. Chief among them are changing market demand and supply for different resources, government's enlarged role in maintaining high levels of employment, efforts by unions to raise wages (at least for their members), growth in the number of corporations, and continued concentration of economic activity in corporate enterprise. You can see that both market and nonmarket forces play a role in determining the functional distribution of income.

The Way Households Allocate Their Income

How do people spend their money? A typical pattern is shown in Tables 4-2 and 4-3 in which 80 percent is spent on personal consumption, of which 14 percent is spent for consumer durables such as automobiles, furniture, and electrical equipment. The rest is divided between nondurable goods (doughnuts, shoes, 35 percent) and services (movies, haircuts, 51 percent).

Householders pay about 15 percent of their income in taxes to the various levels of government, a figure that has grown in both absolute and relative terms from only 3 percent of their income in 1929. A substantial part of this increase is due to the increase in government expenditures for military goods and services. There have also been big increases in government social services: social security, Medicare, aid to education and housing, welfare and unemployment relief, highway construction, expansion of the park service—the list is a long one.

Table 4-2
Households' Allocation of Income, 1985

	Billions of Dollars	Percent
Consumption	2582	80
Savings	129.1	5
Taxes	492.7	15

Source: Survey of Current Business

Table 4-3
Composition of Expenditures for Personal Consumption, 1985

	Billions of Dollars	Percent
Durable Goods	361.1	14
Nondurable Goods	912.3	35
Services	1308.8	51

Source: Ibid

The Way Personal Income Is Distributed

Lorenz Curve
The difference between the actual distribution of income and a perfectly proportional distribution as shown graphically.

How is money distributed throughout the U.S.? Who has much, and who has little? Table 4-4 gives us a general idea and shows the unequal nature of the distribution.

When you convert the data on income distribution in Table 4-4 into a graph, you get a curve of the inequality of income. This curve has a special shape, which is called a **Lorenz curve** (Figure 4-3). It shows the difference between the actual distribution of income and a perfectly proportional distribution. By comparing the Lorenz curves for various countries, you can also compare the relative inequality in the distribution of income between one country and another. However, before you draw any conclusions, remember that the Lorenz curve shows money income only and not noncash production, such as food that farmers grow for their own tables. Therefore comparisons between countries, especially when noncash incomes are significant, may be misleading.

Since 1935, there has been some trend toward a more equal distribution of income in the U.S., with the largest change between 1935 and 1945, mainly because of four factors: (1) The U.S. pulled out of the depression and wartime gave rise to full employment, which increased workers' income quickly. (2) During the war, excess-profits taxes and a more progressive income tax reduced the after-tax income of the rich more than that of the poor. (3) Wartime labor scarcity increased opportunities to blacks and other minorities that had been discriminated against before. (4) Labor unions quadrupled their membership and increased the relative income of their members.

Then, between 1945 and 1955, the trend toward more equality in distribution of income continued, but slowed. (1) After the war, the labor unions continued to increase the relative incomes of their members, but met greater resistance in their efforts to do

Table 4-4
Distribution of Family Income in the U.S., 1985

	Percent of Families in Class	Percent of Income Received in Class	Family Income by Rank	Percent of Total Income
Under 10,000	16	1	Lowest one-fifth	4.7
10,000 - 14,999	12	4	Second one-fifth	11.0
15,000 - 24,999	23	8	Third one-fifth	17.0
25,000 - 34,999	20	11	Fourth one-fifth	24.4
35,000 - 49,999	17	16	Highest one-fifth	42.9
50,000 - 74,999	9	14		
75,000 and up	3	16		

Source: U.S. Department of Commerce, 1984.

Figure 4-3
Lorenz Curve: Distribution of Family Income in the U.S., 1985.

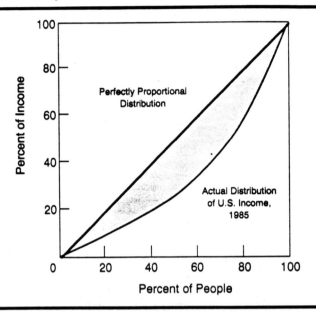

The straight diagonal line shows what a perfectly proportional distribution of income would look like. The shaded area, which is the difference between the actual (unequal) and the perfectly proportional distribution, represents the inequality of income.

so. (2) Continued prosperity meant continued good jobs for minorities and women. There were also increased educational opportunities for minorities. (3) The GI bill enabled millions of men who would not have attended college to do so and to achieve higher levels of skill than they would have otherwise. These factors, however, were not felt as strongly as the factors that influenced the period from 1935 to 1945.

Since 1955, the distribution of income has remained relatively constant, because governments, at all levels, have imposed taxes that are less progressive in nature than in former years. Also the number of families that economists call "economically irrelevant" has been increasing. (When we say that certain workers are economically irrelevant, we mean they do not have the skills necessary for employment. Employers aren't looking for people with their skills. The economy, in other words, doesn't need them.) The increases in taxes and in the number of economically irrelevant workers have slowed the trend toward greater equality in income.

It is important to note that the income distribution data shown in the Lorenz curve of Figure 4-3 reflect only cash incomes and do not reflect transfer payments from government. Should all such "welfare" payments be incorporated, it is quite likely that the distribution would be less unequal.

Economic Implications of Inequality in Income Distribution

Although the ethical implications of inequality in distribution of income are fascinating, we will restrict ourselves to the economic implications.

In underdeveloped countries, the main problem is to increase the economy's output so that all citizens can have a better standard of living. These countries need increased resources, especially capital, to shift the PP curve outward and increase economic growth. Forming new capital requires increased savings. Increasing savings withdraws resources from the production of consumer goods, thus making these resources available for investment, and the production of capital. So to increase the formation of capital and to foster more rapid economic growth, a higher rate of savings is needed. The rich save a larger percentage of their income than the poor because the poor spend all their income to maintain a low standard of living. Thus, a more *uneven* distribution of income would increase the income of the rich and might increase savings. Apart from other considerations, an underdeveloped country, in order to increase savings and the rate of formation of new capital, might require a less equal income distribution than it already has.

On the other hand, in a developed economy, the main problem is how to maintain full employment and keep the large industrial system growing. To do this, you want consumers to demand all the goods and services that business firms can produce. Here one may reverse the argument of the preceding paragraph and say that a developed country ought to have *its* income more evenly distributed. That way, the rich would get a smaller slice of the pie. Savings would be less and consumer demand higher. This view, prevalent in the 1950s, 60s, and 70s, was challenged by supply-side economists in the 1980s who argued that increased savings were needed in developed economies also.

Two qualifications are necessary to the above. The problems of economic growth and full employment are much more complex than the above brief sketch indicates. Second, economic *efficiency* (maximizing output with a given set of resources) is not the same thing as economic *equity* (what we think is right or wrong in a moral sense). The implications for distribution of income may differ, depending on whether our goal is efficiency or equity and on what weight we give to each.

BUSINESS FIRMS

Today there are more than 10 million companies in the U.S., from the corner grocery store to such corporate giants as AT&T. We can classify business firms primarily under three legal headings: (1) *Sole proprietorships*, (2) *partnerships*, and (3) *corporations*.

Sole Proprietorships

Sole Proprietorship
A business firm owned by one individual who has full responsibility for it.

The commonest form of business organization is the **sole proprietorship**, an enterprise owned by one person, who is solely responsible for it. There are more than 9 million sole proprietorships in the U.S., chiefly in agriculture, the retail trade, pharmacy, law, and medicine. They are usually small in scale and have an average life span of 5 to 7 years. Although hundreds of thousands cease production each year, even larger numbers begin each year.

Advantages of a Sole Proprietorship

1. You can easily form a sole proprietorship; it doesn't take much cash. In many areas, just the act of beginning production is all that is necessary.

2. The sole proprietor is the only one to receive benefits when the firm succeeds, and is the only one responsible for its activity, so there is a close correlation between effort expended and reward. Thus, the incentives for efficiency are great.

Disadvantages of a Sole Proprietorship

Unlimited Liability
In a sole proprietorship, the responsibility of its owner to pay all losses even from personal wealth.

1. The sole proprietorship has **unlimited liability**. This means that there is no differentiation between the assets of the business enterprise and the personal wealth of the proprietor. If the business incurs losses, the proprietor is responsible for them.

2. Sole proprietors must rely on themselves for all management skills, and since no one person can be a specialist in all managerial functions, the business may suffer. Inadequate management is the chief cause of failure in small, sole-proprietor businesses.

3. The sole proprietorship often has limited capital, since the proprietor has to depend primarily on his or her own resources, and an individual's borrowing capacity is limited. Sole proprietors also tend to have lower credit ratings than partnerships or corporations.

4. The sole proprietorship has *limited life*, in the sense that the lifetime of the business may be limited to the working lifetime of the proprietor.

Partnerships

Partnership
A form of business organization in which two or more individuals combine to operate an enterprise.

A second form of business organization is the **partnership**, in which two or more individuals combine to operate a business enterprise. There are several kinds of partnerships, but the following is a general description.

Advantages of a Partnership

1. Because there are two or more people involved in the ownership, the partner-owned business has access to more capital. The enterprise can draw on the wealth and borrowing power of its several partners.

2. A business with more than one owner can count on specialized skills in management. One partner can be in charge of production; another of accounting; a third, of sales; and so on. Specialization of management functions strengthens a business greatly.

Disadvantages of a Partnership

1. A partnership, like a sole proprietorship, has unlimited liability. Each individual partner's personal wealth can be tapped to pay debts. Each partner is responsible not only for his or her own mistakes, but also for the mistakes of all the rest of the partners.

2. Partnerships have limited life, which fosters instability. Partnership agreements are automatically dissolved whenever a partner dies, or whenever one withdraws from the partnership because of a disagreement. The remaining partners may draw up a new partnership agreement, or they may not.

3. Partnerships have limited access to capital. Various devices that the corporation can use to raise financial capital are not available to the partnership.

Corporations

Corporations
Business firms whose existence and function is apart from that of their owners.

Corporations are legal entities that function separately from their owners. There are fewer corporations by far than there are sole proprietorships or partnerships, but corporations produce more, employ more people, and have more assets than all other business forms combined.

Advantages of a Corporation

Limited Liability
In a corporation the fact that individual owners are responsible only for the value of their shares purchased and not other debts.

1. A corporation's owners have **limited liability**. This means that the people who own it—the stockholders—are not responsible for its debts. They can lose only the money they paid for their stock.

Obviously, the situation is not that simple. The owner-manager of a small corporation may very well have to pledge her or his own credit and take on a personal liability. For example, in order to raise additional funds, the manager may become personally liable by signing a personal note for a loan for the corporation. The discussion that follows, however, relates more to the larger corporation than the smaller.

2. Because a corporation is a legal entity, it can be sued (or it can sue) without the owners, the stockholders, becoming involved.

Unlimited Life
The fact that a corporation's existence continues no matter the composition of its ownership.

Bonds
Debt instruments issued by corporations.

Preferred Stock
Stock issued by a corporation that has no voting rights but has a preferred right to dividend payments.

Common Stock
Stock issued by a corporation that has voting rights but no preference in the distribution of dividends.

3. A corporation has **unlimited life**; it can continue to exist no matter who owns stock in it. Stockholders continually buy and sell their ownership instruments (shares of stock) with no effect on the company.

4. A corporation has access to greater amounts of money because of its ability to tap the market for financial capital, and has great flexibility in getting transfusions of capital because it can use a variety of financial instruments: bonds, preferred stock, and common stock. **Bonds** are instruments of debt; the corporatio has to pay interest on them regularly, and counts this as a cost of production. Stocks, on the other hand, are equities or instruments of ownership, and the company is not required to pay dividends on them regularly. **Preferred stock** is called preferred because the company has to pay dividends on it *before* it pays dividends to holders of **common stock**. Owners of preferred stock have no voting privileges, however, and usually there are limits on the amount of dividends the company can pay to them. Owners of common stock have full voting rights and no limitations on the amount of dividends that the company can pay them.

5. Because stockholders need not be managers of a corporation, and because the corporation can raise large amounts of financial capital, it can afford to hire efficient managers, capable of taking on very specialized management functions.

Disadvantages of a Corporation

1. Forming a corporation may take a long time and be very expensive, depending on the nature of the proposed firm. People involved in the formation of a new corporation have to follow state and federal laws, pay fees of incorporation, and pay lawyers' fees and other expenses.

Double Taxation
The fact that a corporation pays taxes on its gross earnings and its shareholders pay taxes again when corporate earnings are distributed as dividends.

2. A corporation has to pay taxes to both the state and federal governments corporate income taxes, property taxes, and so on). This leads to **double taxation**, which means that the corporation pays taxes on the gross income it earns, and distributes parts of the remaining income as dividends to stockholders; then the stockholders have to pay income taxes on the dividends, since this money constitutes personal income.

3. State and federal governments pass laws that restrict the behavior of corporations. These restrictions do not apply to sole proprietorships or partnerships.

4. The larger the corporation, the more ownership gets separated from control, and the greater the possibility of conflict of interest between managers and owners. Large corporations may have thousands of stockholders. The largest corporations, such as AT&T, have millions. Stockholders who hold only a few shares

have neither the time nor the incentive to take an active part in controlling the corporation by their votes.

When management sends out its annual report, containing a glowing description of what it has done for the stockholder this year, it includes a proxy card. This proxy card, if the stockholder signs and returns it, gives the company's management the right to vote his or her stock. If the corporation has paid the usual dividend, the stockholder generally mails the proxy card back. In this way management tends to become self-perpetuating and often may regard its stockholders as being, in a sense, the recipient of corporate welfare (after all, they get their regular dividend checks). Stockholders—busy people placated by regular payments of money—may become lethargic and uncritically accept the policies of management. Management may orient its policies first and foremost toward its own continued control of the corporation. In brief, we are implying that, in many large corporations, the stockholders may find it hard to control the management. If this occurs, the self-interest of these independent managers may conflict with the self-interest of the stockholders.

Big Business and the American Corporation

Americans have long worried about companies that get so big that they are able to dominate an industry, as evidenced by U.S. acceptance of the antimonopoly provisions of English Common Law and by the many antimonopoly or antitrust laws that Congress has passed since the Sherman Antitrust Act of 1890.

People have feared that large monopolistic firms would interfere in a competitive economy and even try to subvert the democratic political system, and that these firms would increase prices while reducing output, slow the rate of adoption of improved technology, and render the economic system more unstable and susceptible to business fluctuations. In addition, people have been afraid that firms of great size and wealth could encourage decisions by government that would be unduly favorable to them, and that would ignore the public good.

Corporations are the dominant form of business organization, except in number. Table 4-5 shows that the four largest

Table 4-5
Concentration of Manufacturing Production: Sales Ratio for Selected Industries

Industry	Percentage of Sales by Four Largest Firms
Motor vehicles	92
Malt beverages	77
Aircraft engines and parts	72
Soap and detergents	53
Metal cans	42
Food Preparation	32

Source: U.S. Bureau of the Census, Census of Manufactures, 1986 (data are for 1982).

automobile corporations had more than 90 percent of the sales of the industry, not including imports, in 1982 alone. Concentration, though, becomes much smaller in other industries such as food preparation in which the four largest firms made 32 percent of sales. We will consider the implications of such concentration in later sections of this book.

Figure 4-4 shows again how dominant the corporate form of business is in the modern American economy. In contrast with 20 percent of the number of firms, corporations in 1988 accounted for 90 percent of sales. On the other hand, single proprietorships dominated the number of firms (70 percent) but accounted for only 6 percent of sales. Partnerships made up the remainder in both categories (10 percent of firms, only 4 percent of sales).

Some critics have criticized corporations for their dominance of the economy and feared their ability to exert undue influence both politically and economically in American society. As we have seen, though, this form of business organization offers great advantages in its ability to raise capital and bring together the larger quantities of resources, including organization and management, that modern technology dictates for the sake of efficiency. It is a mistake to assume that bigness equates with the ability to restrict competition or to exercise monopolistic influences over both the economy and its political processes.

It is worth noting that many modern corporations have crossed national boundaries in this century. Indeed, since World War II, there has been a major growth of **multinational corporations**, those that buy resources as well as produce and sell products in many countries throughout the world. Though fear was

Multinational Corporations
Those that buy resources as well as produce and sell products in many countries and parts of the world.

Figure 4-4
Number of Firms and Percent of Sales by Types of Firms, 1988

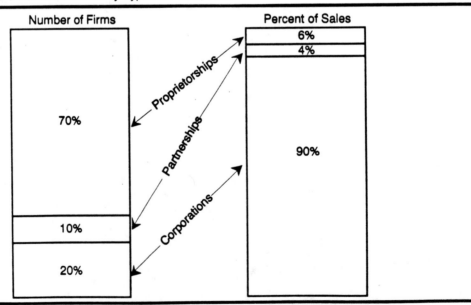

Source: Statistical Abstract of the United States, 1989.

expressed early on that such corporations would lie beyond the control or oversight of individual nations, and thus potentially destabilize economic relations, international competition and growth in market sizes seems to have greatly diminished that concern. Clearly, the multinationals have performed a useful role in enhancing the movement of resources as well as goods and services throughout the globe.

GOVERNMENTS

Governments—federal, state, and local—affect economic activities by four means: (1) expenditures, (2) taxation, (3) enactment of laws, and (4) regulatory agencies.

Expenditures: What Do They Spend All That Money On?

The expenditures of the federal government for all sorts of things, from guns to butter, stimulate output in the economy, both directly and indirectly. These expenditures stimulate output directly by creating a demand for goods and services; they stimulate it indirectly by income transfers that do not require an immediate good or service in return, such as educational grants, social security, and interest on the national debt.

When you look at Table 4-6, you will immediately notice the figure for "income security" that consists of social security and Medicare, which accounted for almost 38 percent of expenditures in 1989.

Defense expenditures came second, with 26.4 percent. The three categories that are listed after defense expenditures are payments for obligations incurred in the past—obligations caused by national defense (veteran's services, interest on the national debt). Or they are expenses for keeping foreign allies strong. When

Table 4-6
Expenditures of the Federal Government, 1989

Item on which Money is Spent	Billions of Dollars	Percent of Total
National defense and space research	316	26.4
Veterans' services	30	2.5
Interest on public debt	169	14.1
International affairs and finance	15	1.3
Natural resources, environment, and agriculture	33	2.8
Income security, Social Security & Medi Care	454	37.9
Health and education	85	7.1
Commerce and transportation	53	4.4
All other	42	3.5
Total	1197	100

Source: Economic Report of the President, 1984, 1989

you add them all up, they amounted to 43 percent of total federal expenditures.

Table 4-7 shows the way state and local governments generally spend their money. For states, the two major items in 1984 were education (24 percent) and public welfare (24 percent). These two added up to 48 percent of the states' budgets. For local governments, education expenditures ranked first, making up 43 percent of the total.

Taxation

Taxes drain off purchasing power that households (that is, people) could otherwise use to buy consumer goods. Thus, taxation reduces consumer demand. Let us look briefly at the way taxation affects this demand.

Principles of Taxation

Who should pay for government services? And how much should they pay? There are two ways of looking at this problem: (1) benefits received, and (2) ability to pay.

Benefits Received. According to the **benefits-received principle,** people should pay taxes commensurate with the benefits they receive from government services. School taxes are an example: a family with two children in public schools should pay twice as much as a family with only one in public school, and a family with no children in public school should pay no school taxes.

This view conceives of government services as services that the taxpayer buys, much as she or he buys shoes or tomatoes in the market. It reverses the old adage that "you get what you pay for" to "you pay for what you get." The people who receive government services pay for them with taxes. By this reasoning, the more services you get, the more taxes you should pay.

Benefits-Received Principle
That argument that tax payments should be commensurate with the benefits received from government services.

Table 4-7
Direct Expenditures of State and Local Governments, 1984

State			Local		
Item	Billions of Dollars	Percent	Item	Billions of Dollars	Percent
Education	48	24	Housing	33	12
Highways	22	11	Education	130	43
Public welfare	48	24	Police and fire	52	17
Health	22	11	Public welfare	15	5
Safety	15	17	Highways	15	5
Other	45	23	Health	25	8
			Other	30	10
Total	200	100	Total	300	100

Source: Bureau of the Census. Government Finances

In reality, there are two limitations to applying the benefits-received principle. First, it is practically impossible in many cases to figure out a fair basis for taxes by this principle. For example, how could national security expenditures be distributed on the basis of benefits received? Suppose you refused to pay for fire protection (or couldn't afford to), and your house caught fire. Even the distribution of school taxes is not simple, because a person who never has children benefits from living in a society of better-educated citizens. Second, if one applied the benefits-received principle strictly, it would place heavy burdens on the poor and disadvantaged members of our society, who would be denied access to most government services because they could not pay for them. Government would then become incapable of dealing with the problems of poverty. The point is that the benefits-received principle may be more appropriate in some areas than others, and in some areas it may not be appropriate at all.

Notwithstanding these two drawbacks, the government has two major sources of tax revenue based substantially on benefits received:

1. *State and federal excise taxes on gasoline.* These taxes are frequently earmarked for construction and maintenance of highways; the more you use the highways, the more gasoline you must buy and the more taxes you must pay to maintain the highways.

2. *Payroll taxes.* These are put into various insurance funds, out of which social security, Medicare, and other benefit payments are made. As the social security program is expanded, the government increases these taxes to pay for the added benefits, and to compensate for inflation. (Although social security benefits do vary somewhat, according to variations in how much one has paid into the program, these differences are fairly limited and thus weaken this example.)

Ability-to-Pay Principle
The argument that, as peoples' incomes grow, they can afford to pay a larger part of their incomes in taxes.

The Ability to Pay. The **ability-to-pay principle** of taxation assumes that those who have a larger income are capable of paying not only a larger tax, but also of paying a larger percentage of their income in taxes than those who have smaller incomes. According to this argument, when a person has a very low income, all of it goes to buy necessities just to keep the person alive. As the person's income increases, some of it can be devoted to non-necessities. The higher a family's income, the more it can afford to spend on nonessentials and the larger percentage of its income it can pay in taxes, while still being able to buy essentials.

One tax based on the ability-to-pay concept is the graduated income tax. The taxpayer, after deducting for size of family and for certain expenditures (health-care expenses, interest payments, charity, and so on), pays a percentage of net income in taxes. The higher the net income, the higher the percentage. The only real flaw in this system is the difficulty of enacting tax laws that are

Capital Gains Tax
A provision of the tax law that establishes the tax rate on assets held more than one year.

equitable to all and of arranging the deductions in such a way that families are taxed at a comparable rate. For a long time there has been controversy about these deductions and about other rules relating to what is considered taxable income. Many people charge that tax loopholes benefit higher-income groups. One big loophole which you have probably heard discussed, is the **capital gains tax**. It used to work this way: If you bought an asset and held it for at least 1 year and sold it for a gain, only 25 percent of the difference, or capital gain (that is, the increase in value of the asset), was considered taxable income. There is again discussion of reinstating the differential tax treatment of capital gains, a provision that was abolished by the Tax Reform Act of 1986. Proponents argue that it would lead to increased saving and investment while opponents say that it would simply reinstate a loophole that primarily benefits those with high incomes.

Types of Taxes

The **tax rate** is the percentage of income a person pays in taxes. We can classify taxes in relation to the tax rate and what happens to it as our income increases. From this point of view, taxes are either progressive, regressive, or proportional.

Tax Rate
The percentage of income paid in taxes.

A **progressive tax** is one with a rate (that is, percentage of income) that increases as income increases. The best example of it is federal income tax. As a person's taxable income gets bigger, the rate of taxation increases also.

Progressive Tax
A tax in which the rate increases as income increases.

A **regressive tax** is one with a rate (that is, percentage of income) that declines as income increases. A sales tax is an example: When you pay a sales tax on clothes, you pay it on the basis of how much you buy. The *rate* does not change as the amount you buy increases. However, the higher your income, the larger the percentage of income you put into savings, and the smaller the percentage of income you put into clothes. So the percentage of your income that the government takes for sales taxes declines as your income increases.

Regressive Tax
A tax in which the rate decreases as income increases.

Here is how this works in figures. Suppose that the sales tax is 5 percent. Adams has an income of $100 a week and spends all of it on taxable items. Thus, Adams spends 5 percent of income on sales tax. However, Bloggs makes $200 a week. Being "richer," Bloggs saves $50 and spends only $150 on sales-taxable items. The sales tax Bloggs pays, as a percentage of income, is only 3¾ percent. *Note:* Some sales taxes have a stronger impact on low-income groups than others. A sales tax on bread would be much more regressive than a sales tax on swimming pools. In fact, if a sales tax is properly selective, it need not be regressive at all.

Proportional Tax
A tax in which the rate remains constant as income changes.

A **proportional tax** is one with a rate that remains the same as the taxpayer's income changes. Property taxes are an example: The tax rate per $100 valuation of a piece of property generally remains constant as the value of the property increases. As a family's income increases, the family tends to continue to spend the same proportion of its income on housing. Since the rate of taxes on property and the percentage of family income spent on housing are both constant, as income varies, the *percentage* of income devoted to property taxes tends to remain constant. Some states have proportional taxes on incomes.

Figure 4-5 shows that the progressive curve slopes upward, so that the tax rate increases (up the vertical axis) as the tax-base income increases (out the horizontal axis). The regressive curve slopes downward, so the tax rate decreases (down the vertical axis) as the tax-base income increases (out the horizontal axis). The proportional curve is horizontal, since the tax rate remains unchanged as the tax-base income increases (out the horizontal axis).

Composition of Taxes

Table 4-8 shows where the federal government gets its taxes. As you would expect, personal income taxes are the most important source, bringing in 45 percent of the total in 1989. Payroll taxes, which mostly go to pay for social security and Medicare, are next, with 36 percent. These payroll taxes are regressive, since they apply to the first $51,000 of income a person earns. Corporate income taxes come third, with 11 percent of the 1989 total.

Table 4-9 gives the same information about state and local governments. Note that state governments tend to get the biggest percentage of their tax money from sales taxes: 49 percent. Only about 30 percent of state money comes from personal income taxes. The local governments collect most of theirs from property taxes: 75 percent of the total.

Who Pays the Tax?

Usually you cannot shift the responsibility for paying your personal income taxes to another person. Most of us lack the economic power to pass on these taxes by making others pay higher rates for our service or products. Property taxes are, in effect, paid by those who use the property. For example, renters usually pay the property tax, indirectly, as part of their rent unless their building

Figure 4-5
The Three Types of Taxes

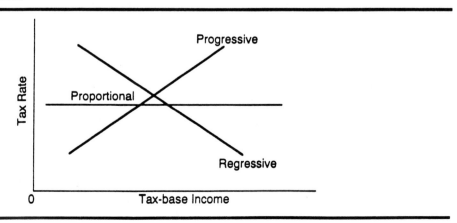

Table 4-8
Sources of Federal Taxes, 1989

Source	Billions of Dollars	Percent
Personal income taxes	446	45
Payroll taxes	359	36
Corporate income taxes	104	11
Excise taxes	34	3
Estate and gift taxes	9	1
Other	39	4

Source: Economic Report of the President, 1990.

Table 4-9
Sources of State and Local Taxes, 1984-85

State			Local		
Source	Billions of Dollars	Percent	Source	Billions of Dollars	Percent
Sales tax	106	49	Property tax	100	75
Personal income tax	64	30	Sales tax	21	15
Corporate income tax	18	8	Income tax	6	5
Property tax	4	2	Other	6	5
Other	25	11			
Total	217	100	Total	133	100

Source: Bureau of the Census. Government Finances in 1984-85.

has many vacancies, in which case the landlord may not be able to charge high enough rents to shift all the tax to the renters.

But what about corporate income taxes? Does the corporation pay them, or can they pass these taxes along to their customers through higher prices? If the corporation is operating in a field in which there is a lot of competition, the competition prevents it from passing the tax along to customers. If a corporation is in an industry in which there is little competition (for example, large firms that make a product for which there are few good substitutes), the firm may be able to shift the burden of the tax to the customer.

Is the tax structure as a whole—federal, state, and local—progressive or regressive? Federal income taxation, because of the large share coming from personal income taxes, is probably somewhat progressive. Tax loopholes (such as the exemption from taxes of the interest from tax-free municipal bonds) cancel some of the progressiveness of the personal income tax. State taxes, because of the predominance of sales taxes, are probably regressive, whereas local taxes are probably proportional, because of the predominance of property taxes.

Government and the Rules of the Game

Governments—by enacting and enforcing various laws—set the rules for economic activity. To begin with, the Constitution itself sets some of the rules, and the Supreme Court has backed it up by its interpretations of the Constitution. Also there have been many statutes passed, plus countless laws relating to contracts. Virtually every business transaction involving a contract is limited by these laws. The many antitrust laws indicate how anxious Congress is to keep large corporations from exercising monopoly power. Bear in mind that labor unions—and the government itself—also have monopoly power.

Government and Regulation

To set limits for the nation's industries, many federal and state commissions regulate economic activities to varying degrees. For example, in every state, there are public utility commissions that set prices and make other guidelines for telephone, electricity, gas, water, and transportation services. Some argue that these utility commissions are politically biased. Perhaps so, but their intended purpose is to prevent the utility companies from taking advantage of the public through their power over prices.

Some of the principal federal government agencies charged with economic regulations are:

1. *The Interstate Commerce Commission.* Established in 1886, responsible for overseeing rail, bus, and truck transportation; sets rate schedules, routes, and various conditions of competition.

2. *The Federal Trade Commission.* Established in 1914 to prevent unfair practices by firms (such as false and misleading advertising).

3. *The Federal Drug Administration.* Acts as watchdog against harmful or disease-carrying foods, cosmetics, and drugs; also checks the efficacy of drugs and the validity of drug advertising.

4. *The Federal Communications Commission.* Regulates TV and radio; grants, and revokes, licenses to broadcast.

5. *The Securities and Exchange Commission.* Supervises the stock exchanges, the over-the-counter stock market, and the issuance of new securities; tries to prevent manipulation of stock prices; tries to ensure truthful and adequate information on stocks to stockholders, both present and potential.

6. *The Departments of Agriculture; Housing; Transportation;* and *Health and Human Services* have branches that perform overseeing and regulatory functions.

With all these agencies to protect consumers and businesses, is the public well protected? There is doubt; many people feel that in spite of this network of regulatory agencies, the consumer is often short-changed. Some people charge that many of the people serving on the commissions, in fact, favor the industries they're supposed to regulate, a case of the wolves guarding the sheep. This may be true, at least in some cases, since many of them were executives in these very industries before they were appointed, and many of them, after their term of office, become executives in the same industries they have been regulating. Again, these are subjects that will be treated more extensively in the microeconomic principles of economics course in which the regulatory functions of governments are examined in detail.

SUMMING UP

1. In the simple circular-flow model of the national economy, households provide firms with all the factors of production. Firms, in turn, pay to employ these resources, which they use to produce goods and services for the households. To complete the circle, households use the income from selling their resources to pay for the goods and services. Firms using the income from the sale of goods and services pay for still more factors of production to produce still more goods and services. And so on.

2. The more complex model of the national economy takes into account the fact that people do not spend all of their incomes. They save some and pay some out as taxes. This reduces the public's demand for business firms' goods and services. The householder's savings go to financial institutions, which make them available for investments. The householder's tax dollars go to government, which uses them to buy goods and services, and thereby becomes industry's biggest customer. However, these flows of money from investment and from government to business firms, to buy industry's goods and services, are not always at a level that make possible full employment and stable prices.

3. The concept of *functional distribution of income* has to do with the sources of income. In 1984, 73 percent of income in the U.S. came from wages and salaries; 9 percent was corporate profits; 8 percent was proprietors' income; 8 percent was interest income; and 2 percent was rental income.

4. Americans spend about 80 percent of their income on personal consumption and 15 percent on taxes; they save 5 percent. Of the amounts spent on consumption, they spend about 14 percent on durable goods, 35 percent on nondurable goods, and 51 percent on services.

5. The distribution of cash income in the U.S. is unequal. The 20 percent of families receiving the lowest incomes get only about 4.7 percent of the total U.S. income, while the 20 percent receiving the highest incomes get about 42.9 percent of it. When one diagrams the data on income distribution for a given period, one sees that the resulting curve is called a *Lorenz curve*. The distribution after taxes and transfer payments, if drawn, would likely be less unequal.

6. The three main forms of business organization are the *sole proprietorship*, the *partnership*, and the *corporation*.

7. The advantages of a *sole proprietorship* are that (a) it is easy to form, and (b) there are high incentives to succeed. The disadvantages are that (a) its owner has *unlimited liability*, (b) it is difficult for a person working independently to specialize management functions, (c) access to capital is limited, and (d) it has limited life.

8. The advantages of a *partnership* are that (a) it has increased access to capital, and (b) it offers management more chances to specialize functions. The disadvantages are that (a) its owners have unlimited liability, (b) it has limited life, and (c) its access to capital is less than that of a corporation.

9. The advantages of a *corporation* are that (a) its owners have *limited liability*, (b) it constitutes a legal entity, (c) it has *unlimited life*, (d) it has greater access to capital than a sole proprietorship or a partnership, and (e) its management can specialize functions because of its larger size. The disadvantages are that (a) the process of forming a corporation takes a long time and is expensive, (b) corporate profits are double-taxed, (c) there are special laws directed at corporations, and (d) there is a danger of separation of ownership and control.

10. Many industries in the U.S., are dominated by corporations. Some people charge that these large firms prevent competition and bias political decision making though large firms, including multinational firms are an efficient means for raising capital and enhancing resource mobility.

11. The federal government spends more than 26 percent of its money on defense and defense-related activities and more than 40 percent on income security. States spend 35 percent of their money on education and highways. Local (city) governments spend 43 percent of theirs on education.

12. There are two main principles of taxation: (a) benefits received, and (b) ability to pay. According to the *benefits-received principle*, one should pay taxes on the basis of the amount of benefits one receives from government expenditures. According to the *ability-to-pay principle*, the tax rate should be higher for higher incomes.

13. A *tax rate*, the percentage of income one pays in taxes, can be either *progressive*, *regressive*, or *proportional*. When a tax is *progressive*, the tax rate increases as income increases (for example, the graduated federal income tax). When a tax is *regressive*, the tax rate decreases as income increases (for example, some sales taxes). When a tax is *proportional*, the tax rate remains unchanged as income increases (for example, property taxes).

14. Personal income taxes are most important at the federal level, since they account for 46 percent of the total. Sales taxes are most important at the state level, bringing in 49 percent of the state's monies. Property taxes are most important at the local level, because they are the source of 75 percent of the total.

15. Governments, by passing laws, set the rules for economic activity. Two important areas of law are those that deal with (a) contracts, and (b) antitrust legislation. Governments also affect economic activities through various regulatory commissions and agencies.

KEY TERMS

Factor markets
Product markets
Functional distribution of income
Lorenz curve
Sole proprietorship
Partnership
Corporation
Multinational Corporations
Benefits-received principle
Ability-to-pay principle
Progressive tax
Regressive tax
Proportional tax

QUESTIONS

1. Using the complex circular-flow model, show how changes in (a) efforts to save, (b) efforts to invest, (c) payments of tax, and (d) spending by government all affect total output and employment. Show these changes in factors one at a time.

2. How has the functional distribution of income changed since 1929?

3. How would one compare a number of countries in terms of the level of equality in their respective distributions of cash income?

What effect(s) could taxes and transfer payments have on the equality of income distribution?

4. If you were in charge of a firm, what would be the advantages and disadvantages of operating as a sole proprietorship, as a partnership, or as a corporation?

5. In general, which principle of taxation do you prefer: benefits received or ability to pay? Why?

6. Look at the taxes listed in Tables 4-9 and 4-10 and decide which are progressive, which regressive, and which proportional. What determines who ultimately pays each of the taxes?

7. "Economic activity is heavily influenced by the way governments define the rules of the game." Do you agree? Why?

8. "With all the government regulatory commissions and agencies, the consumer is amply protected from improper business activity." Do you agree? Why?

9. You are the economic adviser for a federal commission studying taxes. You have been given the task of recommending comprehensive changes in the composition of taxes. What recommendations on tax changes would you make? Since any changes in the composition of taxes would shift the incidence of taxes (change the people who would be paying taxes), clearly state what changes in the incidence of taxes would occur. Explain your recommended changes from an economic point of view; from a moral or ethical point of view.

Application to Chapter 4: The Social Responsibility of Business: The Invisible Hand Versus the Good Corporate Citizen

---

The Effect of Competition on Business Morals

In Western Europe in the Middle Ages, the moral prescriptions of the church affected the economic behavior of merchants. The church held God over their heads. "The laborer is worthy of his hire" (Luke 10:7). "Thou shalt not steal" (Exodus 20:15). "Charity suffereth long, and is kind" (I Corinthians 13:4). The concepts of just price and just wages—plus the widespread idea that anyone who charged interest on money was guilty of usury—was intended to limit employers and merchants in setting prices.

By the time Adam Smith wrote *The Wealth of Nations* in 1776, the dictates of the church that restrained economic "abuses" were replaced by the dictates of competition, which surprisingly enough exerted an even stronger effect, and in the same direction. Adam Smith's "invisible hand" was *competition*. According to Smith, businessmen (as well as consumers) were selfish and concerned only with their own personal gain. Greed ruled economic behavior, but competition restrained this greed, this desire to maximize one's own economic good, and channeled it into maximizing the public good. Not altogether, of course, but the effect of competition was noticeable, for the following reasons:

Each producer had such a small part of the total market that he or she could not control the price of a given product and thus gain an advantage over others. Each small producer seeking customers had to produce at the most efficient level, turn out the kinds of products and services the consumer wanted, and sell them at the lowest price commensurate with staying in business. The selfishness of these small producers was guided, as if by an invisible hand (competition), to maximize the welfare of society at large.

However, today, although many industries do have to cope with fierce competition, many others are dominated by a few giant firms (though even these may be restrained by foreign competition). So the tenets of the medieval church no longer exercise the force of law over the people, and monopoly power may have weakened Adam Smith's invisible hand of competition.

How should corporate producers behave? Should they produce goods and services and price them with only the goal of maximizing their own profits, using every advantage their size and market dominance affords? Or should the corporation, like a good citizen, consider the social and economic needs of the society as a whole? In other words, what are the social responsibilities of business?

Responsible to Whom?

Business decision makers, including corporate managers, have many responsibilities. Among these are responsibility to stockholders, to employees, and, of course, to their own self interests. An interesting and important question to ask is: Does the pursuit of profit (or sales) by firms, especially in a competitive market environment, necessarily lead to the serving the broader interests of society? Adam Smith clearly believed that this coincidence of interests (those of individuals and society) would occur through the invisible hand of competitive pressure even though it was through "no intent" of those making the business decisions. In more recent times, however, questions have been raised about whether and under what conditions the coincidence occurs. Further questions have arisen as to whether firms *should* act out of a sense of social responsibility as well as one of responsibility to shareholders. In a fundamental sense, these two sets of questions (*are* society's interests served by individual firm decisions, *should* firms try to serve social interests) are bound up together. Let's look at the arguments on both sides.

Maximizing Profits: Serving Private or Public Interests?

Corporate directors and the managers who report to them have a responsibility to the firm's owners, its stockholders. That responsibility to enhance the value of their shares is consistent with making decisions that maximize the firms profits (the difference between its revenues and costs). Critics of decisions made on this basis say that while it satisfies one narrow set of (stockholder) interests, it can result in actions that are socially irresponsible or

"I figure someone has to hold the line."

that impose costs on many others in society. While it may, for example, be possible to produce a passenger vehicle at lower costs by failing to make it "crash-safe," or to equip it with tires or other systems that are unsafe, the extra profit gained merely transfers costs to others and, in the judgment of such critics, is unethical or immoral. More to the point, say critics, it creates a need for government regulation to ensure that public health and safety standards are adequately represented where profit maximizing decisions do not lead to those results.

Critics of profit maximizing decisions, frequently argue, thus, that the public's representatives (government) should constraint profit maximizing decisions by (1) limiting how products can be produced (e.g., crash resistant construction of cars, non-polluting insecticides) and (2) What products can be marketed (e.g., banning such "noxious" products as marijuana, cocaine, asbestos, and the like). Also government has a responsibility, say critics, to regulate the behavior of the firm not only in producing its products, but also in marketing them. While deceptive advertising, for instance, *might* be profitable for a firm, government agencies (e.g., the Federal Trade Commission) should prevent consumers from being misled by narrowly focused profit seeking firms.

Of course, there are many others who say that business firms, while concerned with profits, also *do* act out of a sense of social responsibility. Why else, say proponents of this view, would corporations sponsor medical research or make donations to public broadcasting or voluntarily recall defective products. If nothing else, say those with this view, the "immoral" and abusive actions that profit maximizing firms might undertake would be deterred by the fear of a reaction from the public. Such corporate actions might lead to public insistence that governments strictly regulate firm behavior and do so in a way contradictory of the firm's and its stockholders' interests.

Maximizing Profits: Competition and the Invisible Hand
There is evidence that the American economy has become substantially more competitive in the last three decades. According to an important study by William Shephard, increased competitiveness was due to (1) deregulation (removal of government controls) of several industries, (2) increased competition from other countries (imports), and (3) antitrust (antimonopoly) legal actions by governments. Thus, although market power remains significant in some U.S. industries (e.g., computers, soups, cereals, drugs, and the like) there has been a major resurgence of competitive forces in almost all others. While these are subjects that you will explore more fully in the microeconomic principles course, for our purposes, it suffices to ask: How is competition related to socially responsible behavior by firms?

The answer to the above question turns heavily on the kind of business behavior considered. Firms in a competitive industry all sell at the same price. We would not, therefore, expect a single firm to make production decisions that raise its costs above those of other firms for to do so would lower the firm's profit. The market, in other words, would punish such behavior. On the other hand, the competitive market will also punish firms that produce inferior or unsafe products for such firms will lose customers to the many other firms whose (superior or safe) products are very good substitutes for those of the "greedy" firm.

Where monopoly exists, that is where consumers do not have good alternatives to buying from "greedy" firms or those that produce unsafe or inferior products, markets may not punish or at least may not punish as quickly or surely a firm's "profits at any cost" strategy. Under these market circumstances, many argue for government regulations that may take such forms as product safety standards or even government licensing of products. Even in many of these cases, however, it may be more advantageous for government policy to encourage competition than to engage in regulation.

When May Markets Punish Socially Responsible Behavior?

Even competitive markets will not necessarily encourage socially desirable behavior or punish undesirable behavior in all cases. One of the clearest examples is the case of environmental pollution. A firm that voluntarily undertook costly pollution reduction decisions (e.g., smokestack scrubbers) in producing its products while other firms did not would see its relative profit fall. The market, in other words, might well punish socially desirable behavior. To ensure that such behavior is forthcoming, therefore, may well require government action or intervention. As environmental problems have become more apparent and in many instances more severe, pressure for government intervention to cause firms to use scarce environment resources (e.g., air, water) in ways compatible with social goals has increased. As a result, air quality goals and standards have been developed in many areas. Emissions controls have been mandated and other actions taken that affect products produced and the techniques used to produce them. While these actions have not changed the basic nature of profit maximizing decisions by firms, they have altered the constraints within which those decisions are made.

Can or Should Firms Decide What is in Society's Interest?

The idea of Smith's invisible hand was not that business people either intended to promote the public's interest or, in fact, even *knew* necessarily what that interest was. Doubtless, there are instances in which decision makers realize that certain actions would even be counter to the interests of many other citizens. Selling products that are known to be harmful and deceiving consumers into believing them to be beneficial falls into this category. In other cases, though, firms may simply not have either the information or the perspective to judge what is or is not in society's interest as opposed to their own (profit maximizing) interest. A single competitive firm in Los Angeles, for example, may have no idea what *its* production technology contributes to the environmental pollution of that "air shed." As a result, it could make no rational choice, even if it chose to act in a socially responsible manner, about how much it should spend on modifying its plant. All firms acting in this same manner, though, may significantly pollute the air. A decision about socially desirable air purity standards, thus, must be made socially rather than privately. The main point here is that, in instances such as the hypothetical one above, it is not always greed or selfishness that creates the lack of correspondence between private and social interests; rather, it is at least sometimes the lack of information or perspective that creates the problem. Where those circumstances exist, society must, through some means, create the perspective and provide the information upon which firms are expected to act.

SUMMING UP

1. The dictates of the church, about just prices and wages, in the middle ages were intended to restrain business pricing. These dictates were replaced in recent centuries by the "invisible hand" of competition which caused the private pursuit of self-interest to result in socially desirable outcomes. Development of monopoly power in markets, though, may have limited the effect of the "invisible hand."

2. A firm's decision makers have responsibilities to the owners of the firm and profit maximization is consistent with serving the owners' interests. Adam Smith argued that competition would make selfish (profit maximizing) decisions by individuals consistent with the interests of society.

3. Arguably, efforts by firms to minimize cost and maximize profit may lead to the production of products that are harmful and that impose costs on many members of society. This has led critics of profit maximizing decisions to argue that government should constrain such decisions by limiting how some products may be produced and even, in some instances, *which* products may be marketed.

4. Some say that business firms *do* act with a sense of social responsibility which tempers their profit maximizing decisions. If nothing else, according to proponents of this view, strict profit maximizing decisions are not always undertaken because of a fear

that public insistence would lead to government strictly regulating firms' decisions.

5. Evidence suggests that the American economy has become substantially more competitive in recent decades though market power continues to exist in some industries. The way in which competition is related to firm behavior depends on the type of behavior considered.

6. Competitive markets will punish firms that incur costs not incurred by other firms since all sell at the same price. Competitive markets also will punish firms that produce inferior or unsafe products. Monopolistic markets are not as certain to punish the latter type of behavior.

7. Socially desirable behavior, such as reducing the environmental pollution effects of production will not likely be undertaken by competitive firms. To insure such behavior probably requires government intervention and constraining profit maximizing behavior.

8. In some instances, the invisible hand may not lead to socially desirable behavior by firms not because of greed, but because of lack of knowledge of what is socially desirable and also because of lack of social perspective.

QUESTIONS

1. What is meant by saying that the "invisible hand" leads self-interest serving private individuals to make decisions that are "through no intent of their own" consistent with society's interests?

2. What are some types of profit maximizing behavior by firms that may be socially irresponsible? Should governments intervene where such behavior takes place?

3. If governments do intervene to constrain private business decisions in (2) above, what types of constraints may be imposed?

4. Even if firms are tempted to engage in narrowly "greedy" behavior, what fear might cause them not to maximize their narrow self interests?

5. What has happened to the competitiveness of the American economy in recent decades? What factors contributed to this change?

6. What types of behavior by firms will competitive markets punish? Reward?

7. Can a society rely on the "invisible hand" to solve its environmental problems?

8. Why may it be difficult for firms that seek to behave in a socially responsible way to do so?

SUGGESTED READINGS

1. Arrow, Kenneth. "The Limitations of the Profit Motive." *Challenge*. September/October, 1979.

2. Berle, Adolf Jr. and Gardiner C. Means. *The Modern Corporation and Private Property*. New York: Harcourt, Brace and World, 1968.

3. Dolan, Edwin G. and John C. Goodman. "Regulating Safety, Autos, Drugs, and Consumer Sovereignty." In *Economics of Public Policy*. 4th Edition. St. Paul, West Publishing Co., 1989.

4. Greer, Douglas F. "Introduction: Functions and Values." In *Business, Government and Society*. New York: MacMillian Publishing Co., 1983.

5. Hessen, Robert. *In Defense of the Corporation*. Stanford, Calif: Hoover-Institute Press, 1979.

6. Johnson, M. Bruce (ed). *The Attack on Corporate America*. New York: McGraw-Hill, 1976.

7. Thomas, Robert. "Business Organization: Does Competition Control the Grant Corporation?" In *Microeconomic Applications*. Belmont, CA Wadsworth Publishing Co., 1981.

Chapter 5:
Measuring National Income and Product

For reasons you will examine closely in this course, it is extremely important to measure (or estimate) how much the American economy is producing in any particular period of time. The largest such measure is called the *Gross National Product (GNP)* or the value of final goods and services in any particular year (or quarter). Such measures by government, including the GNP, go back to the 1930s and are regarded not only as indicators of the nation's economic health but also as vital information in the making of national economic policy. They are, thus, useful *estimates*, but not as is illustrated in the following incident, to be taken with more precision than that.

Way back in 1971, President Nixon unveiled the GNP clock in the lobby of the Bureau of the Census building. The machine had been preset, according to the predictions of statisticians, to tick off the value of output produced. When the President showed the clock to reporters, it was recording a $1-trillion GNP. It didn't seem to bother anyone that (1) the machine had been running for some time, waiting for the proper moment to be revealed, (2) actual GNP was a good bit less than the $1 trillion predicted at the time, and (3) the $1-trillion GNP was in part achieved by increased prices rather than by increased output.

But despite the gadgetry and the "slight" distortions of politicians, GNP and the concept of national economic accounting are important to a better understanding of the economy. Changes in the amount of the output of an economy can affect the material levels of existence of everyone within that economy. In this chapter we shall discuss some of the most important such concepts and measures of economic performance.

An important question is: Even if the level of output in the economy increases, does it really mean that the individual member of the economy is better off? With all these urgings for increases in GNP, do such increases really improve material life? The application which follows this chapter, will discuss that question. But first we need some basic understanding of the national economic accounts.

Background: Why Is National Economic Accounting Important?

Although most of these concepts were, as indicated before, worked out before the war, economists greatly improved and expanded the national economic accounts during World War II to meet the government's needs for wartime planning. Government agencies had to have measures of economic performance in order to make the best allocation of output and to formulate policies that would keep the economy stable. A British economist, Richard Stone, who made a major contribution to this effort, was awarded the Nobel Prize in Economic Science for his efforts. A difficult problem for the U.S. was how to shift all those resources to fight the war and still minimize inflation. Data provided by the national economic accounts gave information about how much production could be used for consumption and how much income people would have for consumption. Now, knowing how much excess income people had, the government could estimate the size of government programs, taxes, savings, and government bond sales. The government needed to soak up consumers' excess income and reduce demand, so that prices could be kept down. Sales of government bonds were an important way to keep people from spending their incomes on consumer goods.

The national economic accounts—like a family's account books—give government policy makers the information necessary to formulate economic policies that are appropriate to prevailing economic conditions as well as those that are expected. This information is also important for business groups and consumers, who also have to make economic decisions. Do you buy your house now or next year? What you think the economy is going to do next year is important because—along with many other things—it not only affects your own income, but also the income of others, and *their* level of demand and prices. The totals of these accounts, especially when we compare one year with another, give us all indications as to whether the economy is changing, and if so, how.

The Expenditure and Income Approaches

People look at the national economic accounts from two points of view: (1) the **expenditure approach**, which concerns what kind of goods and services people buy, or the kinds of expenditures they make and (2) the **income approach**, which concerns what kinds of income are generated by the output of the economy. To sum it up,

Expenditure Approach
An approach to national income accounting that measures goods and services people buy or the expenditures they make.

Income Approach
An approach to national income accounting that measures the incomes generated in producing the national output.

the expenditure approach deals with kinds of output, while the income approach deals with kinds of income generated in the production of that output.

In effect the two approaches are two sides of the same coin, and the statistical results of each are equal. Suppose that the only output of an economy were one car, one machine to produce the car, and one schoolhouse. The expenditure approach to measuring economic performance would entail totaling the value of those three items of production. But the value of that output would be apportioned to the factors of production as income. The income approach would entail recording how much of that income is apportioned to each of the different factors of production. The two results—that obtained from the expenditure approach and that from the income approach—must be equal. The *value of what is produced is equal to the income distributed.*

We see how these two approaches lead to the same result in Table 5-1. The expenditure approach is concerned with what is produced. In Table 5-1, the total value (column (4)), the value of the labor and other costs, is $18,000. The income approach is concerned with the income generated. The total income, the sum of columns (1), (2), and (3), is $18,000. The two approaches lead to the same numerical results. In each case, the income generated must be equal to the value produced.

"Remember when one billion was such a frightening figure?"

Table 5-1
Income and Expenditure Approaches

| Income Approach | Expenditure Approach | | | (4) Total Value |
	(1) Car	(2) Machine	(3) Schoolhouse	
Labor	$1,000	$3,000	$6,000	$10,000
Interest	500	750	1,000	2,250
Rent	250	400	750	1,400
Profits	750	500	1,000	2,250
Depreciation	250	250	1,150	1,650
Indirect business taxes	250	100	100	450
	$3,000	$5,000	$10,000	$18,000

Gross National Product and Gross National Income

Gross National Product (GNP)
For a given economy, the total value of all final goods and services produced in a specific period.

Gross National Product (GNP)

Gross national product (GNP), as mentioned earlier, measures the total dollar value of all final goods and services produced in a given period, in a given economy. Two elements of that definition need explaining.

1. When we say that only the value of *final goods and services* is included in the GNP, we avoid the possibility of counting output more than once in the GNP statistic. Most manufactured products use materials from several firms. These intermediate products become part of the final product, so the value of the final product also covers the cost of these intermediate products. To include the intermediate products separately would mean that we would be counting them twice, once when we included them separately and again when we listed the final product.

For example, suppose that the intermediate products that go to make up our $3,000 car in Table 5-1 include $500 worth of steel and $100 worth of rubber, which the automobile producers buy and then incorporate into the car. When the manufacturer sells the car, the price must be high enough to cover the cost of all the intermediate products. Economists—to avoid counting a unit of output twice in the GNP—therefore list only the final value of the car, the price to the ultimate user.

This policy, however, creates a problem. Work in progress and inventory on hand at the end of the year represent output for that year, and should be included in the GNP for that year. At the same time, work that was in progress the year before and inventory that was produced the year before are also included in the final product, and they should not be included in the current year's output. Economists resolve this by subtracting from the GNP the inventory at the beginning of the year and adding to the GNP the inventory at the end of the year. Formally, this is accomplished by including in investment a net inventory figure (beginning inventory subtracted from ending inventory).

Let's look at our car again. At the beginning of the year, it was only partially completed and was worth about $1,000. That was output from last year, which should not be included in this year's GNP. But the car is completed this year, and sold to a consumer. Also, this year, more than just one car is produced. Half of the second car is made, say, $1,500 worth. That $1,500 in partially completed car should be counted as part of this year's output. Solution: Subtract the $1,000 work-in-progress car that was on hand at the beginning of the year (beginning inventory) from the $1,500 work-in-progress car that is on hand at the end of the year (ending inventory). Net inventory (part of the investment) is +$500.

2. The GNP contains the total dollar value of goods and services for a specific time period only, usually one year. Only output for that year is included, and none from any prior period.

The three major groupings of expenditures on goods and services that are counted in the GNP are (1) expenditures for private consumption, (2) expenditures for investment, and (3) expenditures by the government.

Private Consumption Expenditures
Expenditures by consumers for durable goods, nondurable goods, and for services.

When we talk about expenditures for **private consumption expenditures**, we're actually talking about three kinds of expenditures: (1) When you buy a refrigerator or a car, you're buying *durable goods* (durable because is takes a long time to use them up). (2) When you buy food or clothes, you're buying *nondurable goods* (they are used up quickly). (3) When a barber cuts your hair or a waiter brings you a pizza, you're buying *services* (somebody does something for you). But remember that although the waiter who brings you that pizza is giving you a service, the pizza itself is a nondurable good.

Gross Private Domestic Investment
Capital creating activities that are private (nongovernmental) in a domestic economy.

Investment expenditures is really a simplified way of referring to **gross private domestic investment** (G_{Inv}). *Gross* means all investment output is counted, including investment that replaced depreciated and obsolete capital. *Private* means that only *non*government investment is counted. *Domestic* means that only investment made within the U.S. is counted. So, when General Motors builds a new plant for its Chevrolets in Michigan, this is included in investment because it represents output of U.S. resources. However, when GM builds another assembly plant in Mexico, it is not part of our GNP. It may be owned by a company based in the U.S., but the employment generated and production capacity created benefit the Mexican economy, not the U.S. economy. *Investment* is the act of creating capital, manufactured producer goods that aid in the production of other goods and services.

Gross investment is divided into (1) equipment and machinery, (2) business and residential construction, and (3) net

Government
Expenditures
Purchases of goods
and services by all
levels of government.

changes in inventory. Remember that one subtracts beginning inventory from ending inventory. The balance is part of investment.

Government expenditures (G_X) include only government purchases of goods and services. These are divided into three types: services, goods, and investment. *Services* include the salaries the government pays to its employees, such as soldiers and county agents. *Goods* are products used up in the operation of the government (paper, gasoline used in government cars, and so on). Government *investment*, like private investment, is the creation of physical things that aid in the production of goods and services and exist for at least one year (typewriters, school buildings, and so on). Of course, when we say government, we mean *all* levels of government: local, state, and federal.

GNP measures only the output of the economy, and therefore, includes only those expenditures for goods and services (these are output of the economy) by the government. However, the government also spends money for things other than output that it buys, and these are not included in GNP. People receive these transfer payments without an immediate obligation to do something in return. The secretary taking dictation in the Department of Commerce provides a service (labor) for a paycheck. The secretary's salary *is* included in GNP. The family on welfare does not give goods or services in return for its check, nor does the jobless worker who receives unemployment compensation, nor does the wheat farmer from Kansas who receives agricultural subsidy payments. These government expenditures, since they do not involve concurrent production of either goods or services, are not included in GNP.

However, several adjustments still have to be made. Imports are included in these expenditures, and since imports were produced outside the U.S., we must subtract them from GNP. Also, the U.S. produces goods that are not included in our expenditures for consumption, investment, and government: our exports. Since exports represent output of the U.S. economy, we must add them to GNP. The plus exports and minus imports can be shortened to ± **net exports** (N_X). In other words, we subtract imports from exports. If exports are larger, net exports are positive; and if imports are larger, net exports are negative.

Net Exports
The difference for an
economy between its
exports and its
imports. Net exports
are positive when
exports > imports,
negative when exports
< imports.

For example, the U.S. imports Toyota Corollas from Japan. They are part of our consumption, because Americans buy them. But the Corollas are not part of our output. Therefore, they must be subtracted from our GNP. On the other hand, we export wheat to Japan. It is not part of our consumption, because we do not consume it—the Japanese do. But it *is* part of our output and must be added to our GNP. In other words, we subtract the imports (Toyota Corollas) and add the exports (wheat sold to Japan).

Table 5-2 contains a breakdown of the GNP for 1986. The formula for GNP is thus:

$$GNP = C + G_{Inv} + G_X \pm N_X.$$

Table 5-2
Gross National Product (GNP) and Gross National Income (GNI) for 1986 (billions of dollars)

Consumption (C)	2,819.9
Gross private domestic investments (G_{Inv})	674.5
Government expenditures (G_X)	889.7
Net exports (N_X)	-115.6
Gross National Product (GNP) equals $GNP = C + G_{Inv} + G_X \pm N_X$	4,268.5
Wages and salaries (W&S)	2,507.2
Rents (R)	62.5
Interest (I)	284.1
Proprietors' income (P_{Inc})	283.7
Corporate profits (CP)	302.0
Capital consumption allowances or depreciation (D)	462.5
Indirect business taxes (IBT)	353.1
Miscellaneous	12.9
Gross National Income (GNI) equals $GNI = W\&S + R + I + P_{Inc} + CP + D + IBT$	4,268.5

Note: GNP is equal to GNI.

Gross National Income (GNI)
For an economy, the total income at market prices generated in the production of all final goods and services.

Wages and Salares
The income payments to labor.

Rent
The income payments to owners of land.

Interest
The income payments to owners of capital.

Gross National Income (GNI)

Gross national income (GNI) measures the total income at market prices generated in the production of all final goods and services during a given period, in a given economy. The term *at market prices* simply indicates that we compute the measure at the market level for goods and services and that this measure must cover all costs incurred through that market. You can keep this straight if you remember that GNP shows total output, while GNI shows how the income generated by that output is distributed. The two must be equal for the same time period.

Table 5-2 shows the breakdown for GNI in 1986. Naturally this summation includes the income earned by the factors of production (labor, capital, land, and entrepreneurship). Wages and salaries encompass all income earned by labor, including social security taxes paid by employees and employers. **Wages and salaries** are the income payments to labor. **Rent** is the income payments to owners of land; this figure includes an estimated rent for homes occupied by their owners. **Interest** is the income paid to owners of capital. Only interest paid by private business is included; the interest on government debt and on consumer debt is not. Profit is the payment to entrepreneurship or the function of organizing and taking the risks of business. *Proprietors' income* is the return to entrepreneurship in firms that are *not* incorporated. (Another term for proprietors' income is *profits of unincorporated businesses*.) *Corporate profits* are the return to entrepreneurship in forms that *are* incorporated.

Besides the five income items listed for GNI in Table 5-2, there are two costs that must be covered by the final value of the

Capital Consumption Allowance (Depreciation)
A measure of the wearing out of capital through use or obsolescence.

Indirect Business Taxes
Taxes on goods and services that are passed on to consumers.

product, but cannot be apportioned to the factors of production. **Capital consumption allowance**, or **depreciation**, is a legitimate expense, since it measures the wearing out of capital each year, either through use or obsolescence. The other nonincome cost in **indirect business taxes**, or taxes on goods and services that are passed on the consumer. Two main forms of these are excise and sales taxes. The firm pays excise taxes (for example, cigarette and liquor taxes) and passes them on to the consumer in the form of higher prices. These taxes are covered by the final value and must be listed separately in GNI.

In brief, then, we see from Table 5-2 that the formula for GNI is:

$$GNI = W\&S + R + I + P_{Inc} + CP + D + IBT.$$

Net National Product and Net National Income

Net National Product (NNP)

Net National Product (NNP)
For an economy, the net value of all final goods and services produced in a particular period of time.

GNP includes depreciation or the amount of capital used up in producing output. Because economists find it useful to have a measure of output that does *not* include this depreciation, so that they can measure only net additions to total production, they use the expenditure approach to compute **net national product (NNP)**, which is the net dollar value of all final goods and services produced during a given period. We speak of GNP as being "total value," indicating that depreciation *is* included, while we speak of NNP as being "net value," indicating that depreciation is *not* included.

Your car is not considered an investment, but part of consumption. (A salesperson's car would be an investment.) However, to give you an understanding of what is meant by depreciation, let us think about your car as an investment. After your new car is one year old, it is less valuable than when it was new. Its value has gone down for the following reasons: (1) It has been driven, and there is only just so much mileage one can get out of the car. Let us say that you can get 100,000 miles of driving out of the car. If you drove 20,000 miles the first year, the car is one-fifth used up. (2) The car is no longer new, styles have changed, and—most important—manufacturers have made improvements in cars since this one was made. This aspect of depreciation is called *obsolescence.* Just as a car, a consumer durable, decreases in value over time, investment goods—the capital people produce to aid in production, such as machines and factory buildings—depreciate by being used up and becoming obsolete, unless they have the most up-to-date improvements. One can say that depreciation is excluded in calculating the NNP because to count the value of capital used up in the process of current production would be to count something made in previous income periods.

Net National Income (NNI)

Net National Income (NNI)
For an economy, the net income at market prices that is generated in producing all final goods and services in a particular period of time.

By the same token, economists use the income approach to compute **net national income** (NNI), which is the net income (at market prices) generated in the production of all final goods and services during a given period. Once again, we speak of GNI as being total income, indicating that depreciation *is* included and we speak of NNI as being net income, indicating that depreciation is *not* included.

Table 5-3 contains a breakdown of NNP and NNI for 1986. For NNI, the only change from GNI (Table 5-2) is that depreciation is not included. For NNP, gross private domestic investment becomes net private domestic investment. The difference between gross and net is measured by the amount of depreciation, or capital consumption allowance. Net investment, therefore, measures only the additions to the capital stock of the economy. If the value of gross investment is greater than depreciation, then more capital is being created than is being lost through depreciation. Net investment is then *positive*, and the economy generally expands because its stock of capital is expanding. Depreciation may be greater than the value of gross investment. If so, net investment is *negative*. In this case, the stock of capital is contracting because more capital is being lost than is currently produced. Capital stock, and thus the ability of the economy to produce, is contracting. This situation of a negative net investment has occurred during severe depressions (1930-1933) and during wars (World Wars I and II) when the need to produce war goods was greater than the need to produce investment. During the years 1917-1918, while the U.S. was fighting in World War I, total real output declined because the

Note: When gross investment exceeds depreciation, net investment is *positive*.

Note: When gross investment is less than depreciation, net investment is *negative*.

Table 5-3
Net National Product (NNP) and Net National Income (NNI) for 1986 (billions of dollars)

Consumption (C)	2,819.9
Net private investment (N_{Inv})	212.0
Government expenditures (G_X)	889.7
Net exports (N_X)	-115.6
Net National Product (NNP) equals $NNP = C + N_{Inv} + G_X \pm N_X$ $NNP = GNP - D$	3,806.0
Wages and salaries (W&S)	2,507.2
Rents (R)	62.5
Interest (I)	284.1
Proprietors' income (P_{Inc})	283.7
Corporate profits (CP)	302.0
Indirect business taxes (IBT)	353.1
Miscellaneous	12.9
Net National Income (NNI) equals $NNI = W\&S + R + I + P_{Inc} + CP + IBT$ $NNI = GNI - D$	3,806.0

Note: The difference between NNP/NNI and GNP/GNI is capital consumption allowances (depreciation).

U.S. was at full employment when it entered the war. But during World War II, in 1942, 1943, and 1944, real output increased substantially (despite a negative net investment) because of the large amounts of unemployed labor and unused plant capacity remaining from the depression of the 1930s, and because employers used both labor and plant more intensively by the device of overtime.

National Income (NI)

National Income (NI)
For an economy, the net income at factor prices generated in the production of all final goods and services.

The third major measure of the value of economic output is **national income (NI)**, which is a measure of income generated only by the factors of production (labor, land, capital, and entrepreneurship). NI is net income at factor prices generated in the production of all final goods and services in a given time period. As before, *net income* means that depreciation is not included. *At factor prices* means prices obtained in the factor market for the factors of production, and therefore we are excluding indirect business taxes, which are paid as a part of market prices. For example, an excise tax is levied on cigarettes by the federal government and is collected not at the retail level, as with a sales tax, but at the manufacturing level. The market value for cigarettes for inclusion in GNP and NNP includes the excise tax. The income generated by the production of cigarettes at the factor market does not include excise tax.

Table 5-4 shows the breakdown of NI for 1986. There is no comparable way to measure it using the expenditure approach.

Personal Income (PI)

Personal Income (PI)
For an economy, all incomes received by individuals in the production of final goods and services as well as from transfer payments.

Our first measure of economic performance was GNP-GNI, the second measure was NNP-NNI, and the third was NI. Our fourth measure of a nation's economic performance is **personal income (PI)**. PI consists of all income received by *individuals*, whether from production or by transfer payments. It is computed by deducting from NI those income flows that do not accrue to

Table 5-4
National Income (NI) for 1986 (billions of dollars)

Wages and salaries (W&S)	2,507.2
Rent (R)	62.5
Interest (I)	284.1
Proprietors income (P_{Inc})	283.7
Corporate profits (CP)	302.0
National income (NI) equals $$NI = W\&S + R + I + P_{Inc} + CP$$ $$NI = NNI - IBT$$	3,439.5

Note: NI includes only the income generated by the factors of production. The difference between NNI and NI is indirect business taxes.

individuals, as distinct from corporations and governments, and by adding those income flows to people that are not included in NI.

First, to compute PI (see Table 5-5), subtract that part of NI that does not accrue to people. Corporate profits consist of corporate taxes, the savings of corporations or retained earnings, and dividends. Dividends are distributed to the stockholders (people) and are retained in PI. Corporate taxes and retained earnings (undistributed corporate profits) are not income to people and are subtracted from NI. Social security taxes are included in wages and salaries. These are transfer payments to the government and must also be subtracted from NI to derive PI.

Second, add income people receive that is not included in NI. These are transfer payments *from* the government, such as unemployment compensation, welfare payments, social security payments, and interest on government debt. Although interest on government debt is not really a transfer payment, since it is a payment for the use of borrowed funds, we included it here by definition. (Remember that the accounts are definitional concepts, depending for their definition on the decisions of the authority responsible for computing the accounts.)

The computation can be condensed by deriving a figure for net transfer payments. Subtract the transfer payments *to* the government from the transfer payments *from* the government. If the latter is larger, it is a plus figure. If the former is larger, it is a negative figure.

Table 5-5 shows the breakdown of PI for 1986. Once again, there is no comparable measure using the expenditure approach.

Personal Disposable Income (PDI)

Personal Disposable Income (PDI)
For an economy, those personal incomes over which individuals have control as to their uses.

The fifth and last measure of economic performance is **personal disposable income (PDI)**. This is the portion of people's incomes that they have control over; that is, they can control where and how this portion is spent. (See Table 5-6.) People do not have control over the part of their income paid to the government in taxes, such as personal income and property taxes. So personal *disposable* income is PI less personal taxes.

Table 5-5
Personal Income (PI) for 1986 (billions of dollars)

National income (NI)	3,439.5
Less corporate taxes (CT)	104.4
Less undistributed corporate profits (UCP)	108.8
Less transfer payments to the government (TP to G)	190.5
Plus transfer payments from the government (TP from G)	497.6
Equals personal income (PI)	3,533.4
$PI = NI - CT - UCP \pm NTP$	

Note: One can compute PI by subtracting from NI that part that is not income to people, and by adding incomes accruing to people that are not part of NI. In Table 5-5, *NTP* represents all transfer payments.

Table 5-6
Personal Disposable Income (PDI) for 1986 (billions of dollars)

Personal income (PI)	3,533.4
Less personal taxes (PT)	(532.2)
Equals personal disposable income (PDI)	3,001.2
PDI = PI − PT	
or	
Consumption (C)	2,820.4
Personal savings (PS)	82.8
Interest on consumer loans (ICL)	98.0
Equals personal disposable income (PDI)	3,001.2
PDI = C + PS + ICL	

Note: One can compute PDI by subtracting personal taxes from PI, or by adding consumption, personal savings, and interest on consumer loans.

One can also look at disposable income from the point of view of how people apportion it. They can either spend it (consumption), save it (personal savings), or use it to pay interest on consumption loans.

PDI is an important measure in the national economic accounts. It is, in effect, the measure of purchasing power of the consuming public. Changes in PDI result in changes in total consumer demand. Government economic policy must keep a close eye on this measure. How would tax changes affect it? How would changes in government expenditures affect it? The federal government made tax cuts for the 1974 and 1975 tax years precisely for the purpose of increasing PDI to stimulate consumer demand.

Table 5-6 shows the breakdown of PDI for 1986. Table 5-7 summarizes the formulas for the national economic accounts.

Table 5-7
Summary of the National Economic Accounts

1	$GNP = C + G_{Inv} + G_X \pm N_X$
	$GNI = W\&S + R + I + P_{Inc} + CP + D + IBT$
2	$NNP = C + N_{Inv} + G_X \pm N_X$
	$\quad = GNP - D$
	$NNI = W\&S + R + I + P_{Inc} + CP + IBT$
	$\quad = GNI - D$
	$NI = W\&S + R + I + P_{Inc} + CP$
	$\quad = NNI - IBT$
4	$PI = NI - CT - UCP \pm NPT$
5	$PDI = PI - PT$
	$\quad = C + PS + ICL$

Note: This summary of the formulas for the national economic accounts uses the notations contained in Tables 5-2 through 5-6. If you have any problem in interpreting the notation, refer to the appropriate table.

Circular Flow: Another View

The use of a tabular step-by-step procedure to present the national economic accounts is a useful exercise. However, as we learned from the circular-flow model, the economy is a system of flows of income and production. Our understanding of the national economic accounts should be improved if we consider the accounts from a flow viewpoint. Figure 5-1 is such a flow presentation.

Output and income flow from GNP through the other four accounts to disposable income. Siphoned off from each account are savings of businesses and government receipts of taxes. Reverse flows of demand for consumption, investment, and government expenditures relate back from net receipts by people, businesses, and government.

Final-Value and Value-Added Methods

We have been defining the various national accounts and what goes to make them up. But how does one compute the values for

Figure 5-1
The Flow of the National Economic Accounts, 1986

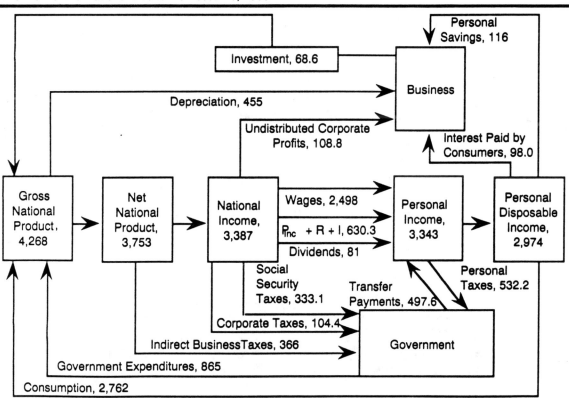

As income is circulated to the three sectors of the economy—the people (or households), business, and government—there are also reverse flows of demand for the output of the economy. These flows stress the interdependency of the various parts of the economy with each other and with the whole.

GNP? By two methods: the final-value method and the value-added method.

Final-Value Method
A method of computing the GNP in which only the prices of goods sold to final users are added.

Value-Added Method
A method of computing the GNP in which the values added at each stage of production are summed.

1. *The final-value method.* The sum of prices to the ultimate users of goods and services produced. These final values include all values added at substages of production. To avoid double counting, one does not list intermediate products.

2. *The value-added method.* Commodities go through many stages of production. As an unfinished product moves from one firm to another, it is changed in form, or location, or is stored. Each of these functions adds value. The sum of these additions to value equals the final value of the product.

Let us examine Table 5-8 where we have used a desk as an example. *Stage 1*: Lumbermen cut down a tree and transport it to the sawmill. By the time the tree arrives at the sawmill, it is worth more than when it stood in the forest. Value has been added to it—say, $2.50—because of the expenditure of labor, land, capital, and entrepreneurship. *Stage 2*: The sawmill cuts the tree into lumber. Again, value is added—say $2.00—and again it is equal to the cost of the factors of production used at that stage. At each succeeding stage (the furniture factory and the retailer) the expenditure of resources means that value is being added. The furniture factory takes $4.50 worth of materials, applies resources, and sells the resulting product for $10.00. Value added was $5.50. The values added at each stage are equal to the final value, or the price to the ultimate user ($20.00).

Table 5-9 shows how this value-added method of computation works. The left-hand side shows how the income produced by the added value was distributed during production by the furniture factory, Atlas Furniture Company. Labor (one factor of production) received wages plus social security taxes, or $865,000. Land ownership received rent, or $250,000. Corporate profits earned were $150,000. However, the factors of production are not the only contributors to value added. Depreciation and business taxes also contribute, $300,000 and $150,000 respectively,

Table 5-8
Stages of Production of a Desk

Stages	Value of Product Sold	Value Added
1. Lumbering	$2.50	$2.50
2. Sawmill	4.50	2.00
3. Furniture factory	10.00	5.50
4. Retailer (the final value)	20.00	10.00
Final value		$20.00

Note: The value added does not include values from prior stages. When one adds all of the values at each stage, the total equals the final value.

Table 5-9
The Atlas Furniture Company, Statement of Value Added

Income Generated by Value Added		Sources of Value Added	
Wages	$850,000	Net sales to U.S. government	$600,000
Social security taxes	15,000	To Smith Company	600,000
Rent	250,000	To Jones Company	800,000
Interest	200,000	To business firms	400,000
Depreciation	300,000	To exports	250,000
Taxes other than corporate income taxes	150,000	Inventory increase or decrease	
Corporate profits	150,000	Inventory decreased	−100,000
Income generated by value added	$1,915,000	Value of production	$2,550,000
		Cost of raw material	−635,000
		Value added	$1,915,000

because the company has to count these costs into the expense of making furniture.

The right-hand side of Table 5-9 shows how the production of furniture now embodying the value added at that stage was distributed. Two companies, the Smith Company and the Jones Company, bought furniture to sell at retail; together, they paid $1,400,000. Various firms bought office furniture directly from the Atlas Furniture Company for their own use: $400,000. This becomes part of gross investment. The government bought $600,000 worth and Atlas exported $250,000 worth. Because ending inventory was less than beginning inventory, the total production figure must be reduced by that difference (-$100,000). Last, and most important, not all the value was created at this stage of production (the fashioning of wood into furniture). The raw materials bought by the firm acquired their value at prior stages of production. Value added, according to both the final-value method and the value-added method, was thus $1,915,000.

The British (and several other European countries) use *value-added taxes* to raise tax money although the tax rates vary from one nation to another. The British call it the VAT. The French have a similar tax, which they call a *turnover tax*. Thus far the U.S. does not have a value-added tax, although a proposal to enact one was discussed in the Congress in 1989.

Current, Constant, and Per Capita GNP

Back in the 1960s a Republican Senator (Barry Goldwater) and a Democratic Secretary of Labor (Arthur Goldberg), debated on educational TV with each using extensive statistics concerning the national economic accounts. With these statistics, each of the speakers proved that the only time Americans were well off was when his own party was in power. Who was lying, the statistics or the statisticians? In a sense, neither, because the debaters were using different measures, sometimes including, sometimes excluding the effects of prices on GNP. It would have been "fairer" if they had made clear to the onlookers what measures they were using. When statistics are being bandied about, a healthy skepticism is needed, especially concerning whether prices are or are not included. As Disraeli said, "There are three kinds of lies: lies, damn lies, and statistics."

GNP may change because of changes in (1) prices and (2) level of real output. But only the changes in real output (that is, in number of products produced) affect material well-being. To obtain GNP data for comparative purposes, therefore, you must do away with price changes. Here's how you do it.

Money (Current) GNP
The value of final goods and services produced expressed in the prices of the period in which they are produced.

Statistics on GNP before the data are adjusted for price changes are called **money** or **current GNP**, which is the output of a given year valued in the prices of that year. (In 1940 you could buy a brand-new Oldsmobile for less than $1,000. But at that time many people were paid only $25 a week, and the best hamburger was 25 cents a pound.)

Real (Constant) GNP
The value of final goods and services produced expressed in terms of a base year's prices.

Real or **constant GNP** is the output of a given year adjusted for price changes. Converting money to real GNP involves the use of a *price index*, which is a measure of changes in the price levels.

There are various kinds of price indexes, depending on what you're measuring. Two well-known indexes are (1) the *consumer price index*, compiled and published by the Bureau of Labor Statistics, which measures price changes for a certain marketbasket of goods purchased by a family of four in an urban area, and (2) the *wholesale price index*, which measures changes in wholesale prices. In addition, the national income division of the Commerce Department has developed an index called (3) the *general price index* (or more formally the *GNP implicit price deflator*), by which you can convert current to constant GNP.

Now let's see how this works. Pick a specific year as the base year, and consider it as 100; then compare the prices that prevailed in all other years to the prices that prevailed during the base year. Let's say that in year 2, prices increased by 20 percent over the base year, so, the price index for year 2 is 120. Let's say that in year 3, prices were 10 percent lower on the average than prices in the base year. Then the price index for year 3 is 90. By the same token, a price index of 132 means that prices in general have increased by 32 percent over the base year. A price index of 84 would mean that prices had declined by 16 percent from the base year.

To convert money GNP to real GNP, divide money GNP by the price index and multiply by 100. For example, if you take 1967 as the base year (in other words, 1967 = 100), and if the price index today is 130, to find the real or constant GNP for the year, you divide this year's money GNP by 130 and multiply by 100. That gives you this year's GNP in terms of 1967 dollars; in other words, *real GNP*.

Real GNP does not account for changes in population, so when you divide real GNP by population, you have *per capita real GNP*. This, is the best-known statistic for comparing a nation's relative material well-being at one time with its material well-being at another time.

Table 5-10 gives a sampling of real GNP, with the accompanying price index. The year 1967 is the base year for this particular set of statistics. Therefore its price index is 100; money GNP in 1967 is equal to real GNP. You can see that the ratio of money GNP to the price index for that year multiplied by 100, equals real GNP.

Although prices dropped in some years before 1946, they have risen since.

If the price index is less than 100, this means that prices are lower than for the base year. So when you convert money GNP to constant GNP, the amount increases. This is known as *inflating current GNP* to obtain a real figure that compensates for lower prices. When the price index is greater than 100, it indicates that prices are higher than the base year, so money GNP is greater than constant. The conversion is known as *deflating current GNP* to account for increases in price.

Output Excluded from GNP

The national economic accounts are *definitional* concepts. The people responsible for computing the accounts define what will be considered output, and, for various reasons, they do not include everything produced. By definition, they exclude the following kinds of output from the national income accounts.

1. *Services by homemakers.* If one had to buy these services on the market—children's nurses, house cleaner, cook, chauffeur, companion—the cost would be high. The services of a homemaker, for example, would cost hundreds of dollars per week if bought in market. National income accountants, though, exclude these services when they are figuring the NI because homemakers don't get paid in money.

Table 5-10
U.S. Current GNP, Price Index, and Constant or Real GNP for Selected Years (billions of dollars; 1967 = 100)

Year	Money GNP	General Price Index	Real GNP
1946	212.4	58.5	363.1
1953	371.6	80.1	463.9
1962	574.6	90.6	634.2
1967	816.4	100.0	816.4
1974	1,472.8	147.7	997.2
1978	2,249.7	195.4	1,151.3
1981	3,052.6	272.4	1,120.6
1984	3,765.0	311.1	1,210.2
1986	4,208.0	331.1	1,289.2

Source: Economic Report of the President. 1986.

2. *Illegal goods and services.* These illegal activities involve production, supply, demand, and a price in a market. Economists exclude them, however, because it is impossible to estimate their monetary value. You can't ask the local pushers how much heroin or cocaine they sold last year, or the owners of gambling joints what their takings were. (Imagine a president analyzing the way GNP had increased in the nation because drug sales had increased 10 percent.)

3. *Labor of children in the household.* If your daughter or son mows the lawn, it doesn't add to the GNP. But if he or she mows the *neighbor's* lawn and is paid $2.00, economists count it in (or at least attempt to).

4. *The labor in do-it-yourself projects.* When you buy wood and brackets to build bookshelves in your living room, economists include the materials you bought in GNP. But the labor it takes you to build them doesn't count.

5. *Volunteer help to nonprofit organizations.* For example, the Red Cross has a paid staff; their wages *are* counted. But if you donate your services—even though you work very hard for long hours, this volunteer help isn't counted in the GNP.

Economic Transactions Excluded from GNP

Just as economists exclude certain types of production, they also exclude the following types of economic transactions:

1. *The buying and selling of intermediate products.* This is excluded because intermediate products are included in the final value of the products. This exclusion prevents counting them twice.

2. *The buying and selling of used items* such as cars and homes. This is excluded because the production of these items took place and was included in a prior time period. Their resale now constitutes only a change in ownership, not an increase in production of goods and services.

3. *The buying and selling of financial securities such as bonds and stocks.* This is excluded because production has not taken place, only the transfer of ownership of debt (though the value of the services involved in the transfers are counted).

SUMMING UP

1. The national economic accounts are measures of economic activity. They are definitional concepts, and in each country the economists who compute the accounts define what is to be included and what excluded.

2. The *expenditure approach* to economic accounts analyzes the kinds of output the economy produces. The *income approach* looks at the kinds of income generated by the economy's output.

3. There are five main kinds of yardsticks used to measure national economic accounts. The first consists of *gross national product (GNP)*, computed by the expenditure approach, and *gross national income (GNI)*, computed by the income approach.

4. *GNP* is the total value *at market prices* of all *final goods and services* produced during a given period. GNP is made up of *consumption, gross private domestic investment, government expenditures*, and *net exports*.

5. *Gross national income (GNI)* is the total income at market prices generated in the production of all final goods and services produced during a given period. GNI is made up of *wages and salaries, rents, interest, proprietors' income, corporate profits, capital consumption allowances,* and *indirect business taxes*.

6. The second measure of economic performance consists of *net national product (NNP)*, computed via the expenditure approach, and *net national income (NNI)*, computed via the income approach. Both exclude capital consumption allowances.

7. *NNP* is the net value of all final goods and services produced in a given period. NNP is made up of consumption, net private domestic investment, government expenditures, and net exports.

8. *NNI* is the net income at market prices generated by the production of all final goods and services produced in a given period. NNI is made up of wages and salaries, rent, interest, proprietors' income, corporate profits, and indirect business taxes.

9. The third measure of a nation's economic accounts is *national income (NI)*, which is the net income *at factor prices* generated in the production of all final goods and services in a given period. NI is made up of wages and salaries, rent, interest, proprietors' income, and corporate profits.

10. The fourth measure is *personal income (PI)*, which is all income received by private citizens. PI is made up of NI, less corporate taxes, less retained earnings, plus or minus net transfer payments.

11. The fifth measure, *personal disposable income (PDI)*, is the income that people can dispose of. PDI is made up of PI less personal taxes, or consumption, personal savings, and interest on consumer loans.

12. Economists use two methods, the *final-value method* and the *value-added method,* to compute the values of the GNP. When they

use the final-value method, they add all the prices paid by the ultimate consumers of all goods and services produced. When they use the value-added method (the second method), they first compute the value added at each stage of production, and second, total all the values added.

13. *Money* or *current GNP*, for a given year is GNP valued in the prices of that year. *Real* or *constant GNP* is the output of a given year adjusted for changes in prices. One computes real or constant GNP by dividing money GNP, by the *price index* and multiplying by 100. However, the best single measure of comparative well-being is *per capita real GNP*, which one finds by dividing the real or constant GNP by the total population.

14. The following output is excluded from GNP: (a) services by homemakers, (b) illegal goods and services, (c) labor of children in the household, (d) labor on do-it-yourself projects, and (e) volunteer help to nonprofit organizations.

15. The following transactions are excluded from GNP: (a) the buying and selling of intermediate products, (b) the buying and selling of used items, and (c) the buying and selling of financial securities.

KEY TERMS

Gross national product (GNP)
Expenditure approach
Income approach
Private consumption expenditure
Gross private domestic investment
Government expenditures
Net exports
Gross national income (GNI)
Wages and salaries
Rent
Interest
Capital consumption allowances
Indirect business taxes
Net national product (NNP)
Net national income (NNI)
National income (NI)
Personal income (PI)
Personal disposable income (PDI)
Final value method
Value added method
Money (current) GNP
Real (constant) GNP

QUESTIONS

1. Economists in the Soviet Union do not include services as output when they are computing national income accounts. If you were doing it, would you include services as part of the national income accounts?

2. From the following data for a hypothetical nation, compute:
   a. gross national product.
   b. net national product.
   c. national income.
   d. personal income.
   e. personal disposable income.

	Billions of Dollars
Consumption	300
Gross private domestic investment	150
Government expenditures	200
Imports	35
Exports	30
Capital consumption allowances (depreciation)	50
Indirect business taxes	25
Social security taxes	20
Transfer payments from the government	35
Corporate taxes	20
Retained earnings	10
Personal taxes	100

3. GNP must be equal to GNI, and NNP must be equal to NNI. Why?

4. Of the two methods of computing the national economic accounts, the final-value method and the value-added method, which do you think is easier to use? Why?

5. If you were listening to a politician quote income statistics, what role would price changes play in helping you to understand the statistics?

6. Compute real GNP of a hypothetical nation from the following data:

Year	Money GNP	Price Index
1929	103.1	50.6
1940	99.7	43.9
1950	284.8	80.2
1960	503.7	103.3
1970	974.1	135.3
1980	1075.0	150.7

7. The national economic accounts are definitional concepts and do not include all output or economic transactions. What kinds of output and transactions are excluded from the national economic accounts? Why?

Application to Chapter 5: Is GNP Growth a Measure of Human Well-Being?

There is a temptation to view the various measures of national income as measures also of material well-being. Many people, economists among them, view increases in per capita real GNP as evidence that everyone is better off. Until a few years ago, most people went along with this idea. But since then, we are less certain of the relationship between income growth and human welfare. You may well ask, "Am I *really* better off as GNP increases?" If the nation increases the annual output of cars and color television sets, will we all be happier for it?

The attack on the use of GNP as a measure of human well-being is threefold. First, since GNP doesn't include *all* output and costs, it is not an accurate measure of output contributing to well-being. Second, there is a large amount of counted output that does not contribute to material well-being, and may even detract from it by wasting resources. Third, the very process of increasing GNP may decrease well-being.

What GNP Does Not Include

When we discussed national economic accounting, we noted that not all output is included in GNP. Remember that the labor of homemakers, illegal production, labor on do-it-yourself projects, labor by children in the household, and volunteer labor are all excluded from GNP. But when comparing the change in output from one year to the next, one tends to think that these exclusions don't really matter.

The women's liberation movement has long argued for concrete recognition of work in the home by placing dollar values on household chores. However, the amount of housework as a percentage of GNP does not change much from one year to the next. Although the value of household services is estimated at about 25 percent of GNP, the distortion in GNP that results when some people hire housekeepers (included in the GNP) or some people marry their housekeepers (causing a slight decrease in GNP) is too slight to count.

As for illegal production, such as gambling, prostitution and dope peddling, who is going to convince anybody that this sort of thing adds to the well-being of the public or that the level of it changes from one year to the next?

As for the other excluded items—do-it-yourself work, children's work in the household, and volunteer work—no one can measure them accurately enough to give statistics, so they are excluded in the measurement of GNP for very practical reasons.

In addition, GNP statistics fail to take into account many costs outside the realm of the marketplace itself, such as pollution. The air, the rivers, the oceans, and the land are all free dumping grounds for the wastes that are by-products of the production and consumption of goods. This pollution, however, does cost society something, because pollution affects the aesthetic quality of the environment, causes physical discomfort, threatens health, disrupts the food chain, and unbalances the atmosphere. For example, in the U.S. we pollute the air with several hundred million tons of aerial garbage each year, even though we know dirty air is a major factor in such diseases as emphysema, bronchitis, and lung cancer, and contributes to colds, pneumonia, and asthma.

The cost of all this pollution is not borne by either the producers or consumers of the products that create the pollution, but by those who are hurt by the pollution. Since this kind of cost is not reflected in GNP or in the cost of the specific products, we cannot make completely intelligent choices in the marketplace about what to produce and how much to produce. If the costs of pollution were reflected in the price of the products we buy, the composition of our output would probably be quite different from what it is now.

The problems of estimating the costs of pollution are hard to overcome. It would be much like subtracting depreciation from gross investment to get net investment. After one had subtracted the external costs from the final value, one would have "net economic product," a phrase coined by Nobel Laureate Paul Samuelson.

If you measured the net economic value of production in these terms, some products would add less to the country's well-being than their value. In fact, some kinds of output might even detract from the country's well-being. How much do people benefit from the output of a chemical plant in Cincinnati after you deduct the destructive effects of the millions of gallons of waste the plant pours annually into the Ohio River? What is the contribution to public well-being of a new car after you deduct the car's pollution of the air with hydrocarbons and carbon monoxide? It is true that the chemicals farmers use substantially increase the per-acre yields of crops, but these chemical pesticides, weed killers, and fertilizers do not go away after they have done their work. The rains wash them down through the soil and into the water table, thence into the rivers and our drinking water, and into oceans, where they often disrupt the food chain. Fish and birds eat smaller creatures that have eaten pesticides, for example, and these poisons build up in the bodies of the fish and birds. Livestock eat feed containing the chemicals, so that every hamburger we eat contains traces of pesticides. Some people have even been unwilling to feed their children milk and liver because they are afraid of the hidden pesticide content.

What Does Contribute to Well-Being?

One can also attack GNP as a measure of well-being by challenging the contributions to social welfare of large parts of the output included in GNP figures. Does the flood of advertising to which we are all exposed make us healthier, happier, or wiser? We haven't space here to go into the pros and cons of advertising. There seems little doubt, however, that a lot of the money spent on advertising is wasted, as far as material improvement is concerned. Advertising that does not give information on which to base an economic decision or that actually gives wrong information does not benefit the consumer.

And then there are defense expenditures. While such expenditures do add to security, or the protection of our lives and property, there is an optimal outlay on this as well as other activities. Sometimes we exceed this level. For example, expenditures that make it possible for U.S. military forces to kill each human being on earth a hundred times over certainly do not increase security or well-being.

The forms of output that increase GNP but not human well-being—and certainly you can add many more to the few mentioned here—use up resources of the economy that could have been used to produce other things that do add to material well-being. In other words, the opportunity costs of these "wasted" resources are the goods we could have produced by using the resources in other ways.

Is Further GNP Growth Desirable?

In an article written in the 1970s, Robert Heilbroner, seemed to take the view that continued growth would lead not so much to the exhaustion of the earth's natural resources as to the destruction of it's environment. He said that the exponential curves of growth, human and industrial "would sooner or later overtake the finite capabilities of the biosphere," and bring about a terrible reduction in the quality of life. Heilbroner's recommended solution was public (government) control over family size and consumption habits and over the volume and composition of industrial and agricultural output.

There are probably few today, including few economists, who concur with this extreme or "doomsday" view. Our space here is too limited to permit us to survey the large amounts of literature on the economics of pollution. However, we do not believe that growth per se causes pollution. The problem lies in the way production and consumption take place. We believe that industry can control pollution by various devices and incorporate the cost of controlling it into the market price of the products. Or there could be government regulation of the matter. How to eliminate pollution or even *how much* of it to eliminate (the question of opportunity cost enters in) are the questions. But it is highly probable that we *can* control pollution and still maintain growth. In fact, we need continued growth to be able to create the resources necessary to control pollution.

To the claim of those who would slow growth in order not to use up nonreproducible resources, one could make at least two responses:

1. The normal workings of the market will slow down industry's use of scarce resources and encourage the shift to more plentiful ones, and will also encourage technological innovation that will lead to new resources. Figure A5-1 shows the situation. As resources become scarcer, normal supply s decreases to S_1. That is, the supply curve shifts up to the left. Prices increase and quantity demanded shrinks. The higher price causes users of the scarce resource (let's say it is oil) to use a more plentiful resource (coal). It also forces them to develop new resources (atomic energy).

2. Technology has developed during the past 250 years at an unbelievable pace. Scientists and engineers have brought forth many new resources. There is no reason to believe that this process will stop. Something not considered a resource today may become one tomorrow. On the other hand, today's resources may be old-fashioned and even useless tomorrow, because of technological change.

Again, let us emphasize that we are not trying to examine all the pros and cons of these economic positions. We just want you to be aware of some of the viewpoints, because these arguments force us to stop and think. Can society control pollution

Figure A5-1
Shift in Supply of a Scarce Resource

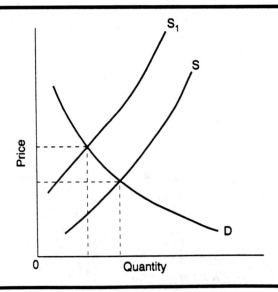

without stopping GNP growth? Can science solve the problem of the scarcity of resources? The problems are serious ones, but they do not justify the dire predictions set forth in the Club of Rome's 1972 book *The Limits to Growth*, which declared that we are all guilty of ruining the earth and making it uninhabitable for future generations.

Alternatives to Using GNP as a Welfare Yardstick

Two well-known macroeconomists, William Nordhaus and (Nobel Laureate) James Tobin of Yale University have undertaken a controversial and interesting attempt to construct a measure of economic welfare that improves on the straight GNP measure. Their concept, called *measured economic welfare* (MEW) consists of the following:

(A) NNP is taken as the "resource base" from which welfare improving goods and services must come. To this base is *added*.

(B) The value of leisure and nonmarket services which, though not necessarily priced in NNP, add to our material well being. From this (A) + (B) base, Nordhaus and Tobin subtract.

(C) Regrettable necessities and disamenities such as defense and pollution.

(D) MEW thus, is (A) + (B) - (C) = MEW.

The Nordhaus-Tobin argument has attractive elements. GNP measures for example, fail to include any value for leisure, although it is a "good" highly valued by individuals. Failing to include, for example, the decline in the average workweek over the last 150 years from 70 hours to about 40 hours understates the effect of NNP growth on well being. Absent also from NNP growth is improvement in product quality. New medical treatments, including new drugs, are incorporated into NNP only in terms of their prices. But what of the welfare effects, for instance, of reducing or eliminating whole diseases that have come about from penicillin or the Salk polio vaccine. Are these welfare effects fully incorporated in these drug's prices? Nordhaus and Tobin conclude that they are not.

An additional controversial element in the MEW calculation is what to subtract from the (A) + (B) base. The main such corrections for Nordhaus-Tobin are (1) environmental pollution and (2) defense expenditures. Many of the costly effects on the environment of operating the economy are not, as we noted earlier, reflected in market prices, yet, scarce resources must be employed to correct the damage. This social cost, according to MEW calculations, must be subtracted. In what some would see as a questionable assumption, the authors of MEW regard defense outlays as regrettable necessities (those that create no direct satisfaction) and choose to subtract these as well.

Making the above corrections (A + B - C), MEW calculations in 1958 dollars (corrected for price changes) may be summarized as follows:

1. NNP grew by 206 percent between 1929 and 1965.

2. MEW in the same period grew less slowly, by 128 percent.

Measures of Economic Welfare: A Caveat

There is likely no measure of economic welfare that will not be highly controversial. Nonetheless, such attempts are not only interesting but useful. If nothing else they focus our effort to relate economic production and human well-being. A noted economist, Arthur Okun once observed that caution is advisable in these regards. According to Okun:

> I know you will not ignore the GNP. I urge that you not try to "fix" it—to convert GNP into a purported measure of social welfare. You are doing your job so well that people are asking you to take on a different and bigger job. Resist at all costs, for you can't do that job; indeed, nobody can. Producing a summary measure of social welfare is a job for a philosopher-king, and there is no room for a philosopher-king in the federal government.

SUMMING UP

1. Arguments that GNP does not accurately measure people's well-being are as follows:

   a. GNP does not include all the output and costs of our society. Housework, illegal production, labor on do-it-yourself projects, volunteer labor and labor of children in the household are all excluded. GNP also fails to take into account the costs of pollution caused by production and consumption.

   b. Some output included in the GNP does not contribute to material well-being: for example, a great deal of advertising and many defense expenditures.

   c. Economic growth itself intensifies pollution and depletes the world's supply of nonreproducible resources.

2. Economists generally are skeptical of the argument that GNP growth leads to resource exhaustion. Price changes lead to both supply and demand effects that prevent that.

3. Alternative measures of well-being confront the problem of assigning values to nonmarket costs and benefits. The Nordhaus-Tobin effort to calculate an index of measured economic welfare (MEW) by adding leisure and nonmarket services to NNP and their subtracting regrettable necessities and disamenities is an interesting example.

KEY TERM

Measured economic welfare (MEW)

QUESTIONS

1. What is the basis for the argument that GNP measures fail to include many things that are part of human welfare?

2. Do GNP measurements correct for the social costs of environmental pollution?

3. Why are economists skeptical of the argument that continued GNP growth will lead to the exhaustion of nonreproducible resources?

4. How is the Nordhaus-Tobin calculation of *measured economic welfare* made? What is the fundamental problem with all such measures?

SUGGESTED READINGS

Andrews, Frederick. "Measuring Society." *Current*. March, 1972.

Cole, H.S.D., et al., eds. *Models of Doom*. Universe, New York, 1973.

Kendrick, John W. "Expanding Imputed Values in the National Income and Product Accounts." *Review of Income and Wealth*. December, 1979.

Meadows, Donella H., et al. *The Limits to Growth*. Universe, New York, 1972.

Nordhaus, William and James Tobin. "Is Growth Obsolete?" in National Bureau of Economic Research, *Fiftieth Anniversary Colloquium*. Columbia University Press, 1972.

Okun, Arthur. "Should GNP Measure Social Welfare?" *Survey of Current Business*. July, 1971.

Passell, Peter, and Leonard Ross. *The Retreat from Riches*. Viking, New York, 1972.

Chapter 6:
Economic Fluctuations

During the "Great Depression" of the 1930s, President Roosevelt said that one-fourth of America's people were "ill-fed, ill-clothed, and ill-housed." At that time one-fourth of the U.S. labor force was totally unemployed, and another one-fourth was only partially employed, that is, worked less than a full week. Even as late as January 1942, when we were already at war, more than 10 percent of the U.S. labor force was still unemployed.

Fifty years later, unemployment was between 5 and 6 percent and prices were growing at a modest rate of 2 to 4 percent per year.

The history of the U.S. is marked by these recurrent periods of unemployment and depression, followed by recovery, prosperity, and inflation. However, the long-term tendency has been toward economic growth of about 3 percent per year. The chief problem of economic policy still remains: In our affluent society, how can employment and prices be stabilized in the face of changes in business activity? The first section of this chapter explores the nature of business fluctuations, the second discusses employment, and the third discusses the effects of changes in prices.

It's easy to guess who pays the cost of unemployment: the unemployed, and the employers with idle equipment. But what can a society do to avoid these costs? In the following application we will examine this question.

Fluctuations: Characteristics and Clues

Types of Economic Fluctuations
Economists can identify four types of fluctuations in the economy.

Secular Trend
The very long-term expansion or contraction of an economy.

Business Cycles
Variations in economic activity that are irregular in length but average between six and eight years.

Seasonal Variations
Regular variations in economic activity that occur within a year.

Random Variations
Irregular variations in economic activity that cannot be accounted or planned for.

Contraction Phase
That downward part of the business cycle in which output and employment fall and prices tend to move downward.

Expansion Phase
That upward part of the business cycle in which output and employment rise and ultimately, as capacity approaches, prices tend to rise.

1. The **secular trend** is the expansion or contraction of an economy over very long periods of time, 50 to 100 years. Within these long-run trends, shorter fluctuations occur. These are called business cycles.

2. **Business cycles** are variations in general economic activity; that is, fluctuations in output, income, employment, and prices. They happen over and over again, but not necessarily in any regular or periodic way, and take place over a period of 6 to 8 years. These business cycles will be the main topic of this chapter. Within these business cycles, regular seasonal fluctuations occur.

3. **Seasonal variations** are fluctuations that occur regularly within each year. For example, employment in agriculture increases in the summer as harvest time approaches, and retail sales increase just before Christmas and Easter. To judge the significance of these seasonal increases or decreases in economic activity, you must compare them to the levels of activity at the same time in other years. In other words, to analyze various other influences on business activity, you must make allowances for seasonal activity and "filter out" the seasonal effects.

4. **Random variations** are irregular variations that one can't account or plan for, since they don't follow any regular pattern. Examples of random variations are the depressed agricultural output caused by the drought of 1936; the steel strike of 1959; and the stock market panic when President Kennedy was assassinated.

Phases of a Business Cycle
In the beginning of the **contraction phase** of a business cycle, the level of economic activity begins to fall. (See Figure 6-1.) Output and employment start to sag, and investment and consumption start to shrink. Prices tend to creep downward. As the contraction continues, unemployment may become high, investment and consumption low and sluggish. A great deal of plant capacity sits idle, and price drops may be very noticeable. Profits fall.

In the **expansion phase**, unemployment begins to diminish and unused plant capacity begins to be put into operation again, while income, output, and consumption rise. At this stage, prices may stay relatively stable. As the expansion continues, the nation approaches full employment and full utilization of capacity. Investment and consumption rise, and because of high levels of demand, so do prices. Profits rise.

Do Business Cycles Follow a Regular Pattern?
The very word *cycles*, the concept of phases, and diagrams such as Figure 6-1 seem to imply regularity or uniformity. However, history shows that although business cycles do recur, there is little or no regularity or uniformity to them. Because of this lack of uniformity, many economists say that the terms *business*

Figure 6-1
The Phases of a Business Cycle

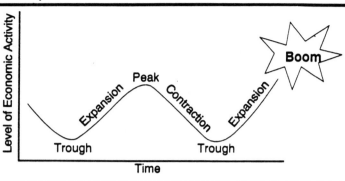

fluctuation or *economic instability* are more appropriate than *business cycle*.

For example, in Figure 6-2, there is no uniformity in the length of time from one peak to another. It took 9 years for the U.S. to go from the peak in 1960 to the next peak in 1969, but only 2 years to go from the peak in 1953 to the next peak in 1955. And there is no uniformity in the contraction phases, either. In the Great Depression, the contraction phase lasted from 1929 to 1933, about 3½ years. In the recession of 1949, the contraction phase was about 1 year. Similarly, there is no uniformity in the expansion phases. You can also see that there has been no uniformity in the *intensity* of the various phases of the business cycles.

Durable- Versus Nondurable-Goods Industries
Not only do the cycles differ from one to another, but also each cycle differs in the way it affects various kinds of economic activity. The biggest differences are those in price and output in industries that produce durable goods and industries that produce nondurable goods. Over the whole cycle, in the durable-goods industries, output varies widely. Prices vary much less. In the nondurable-goods industries, prices vary, but output tends to be more stable.

In the durable-goods industries (heavy equipment and machines, major appliances), the main effect of declining demand during the recession and depression phases is reduced output and employment. In the nondurable-goods industries (food, clothing, furniture), the main impact of declining demand is on prices. To learn why this variation occurs, let's think about the differences between durable and nondurable goods, and the differences between these industries in the nature of competition.

1. People can postpone buying new durable goods for a long time. When times are bad, the consumer repairs the old car or washing machine rather than buying a new one. A manufacturer faced with falling demand and dwindling profits repairs the machines on hand rather than buying new ones. And, with plenty of idle plant space

Figure 6-2
Business Activity in the United States

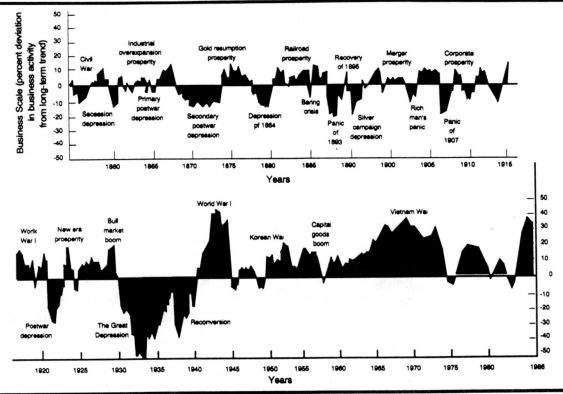

Here we see the ups and downs of business activity in the U.S. from before the Civil War until today. The prosperity during the 1960s and that during the 1980s were the longest periods of sustained rise in business activity that we have ever had. The ups and downs in business activity are measured as a *percentage change* compared with the long-range trend.

Source: Cleveland Trust Company

going begging, the manufacturer sees no point in building a new plant or a new wing on the old one.

2. The industries that make consumer and producer durables (cars, steel, electrical equipment) are highly concentrated industries, with just a few large companies and less competition than in other industries. Various forms of monopoly power are manifest, so the big firms tend to protect their prices. They react to decreases in demand by cutting back on the quantity they produce.

During a recession, when decreased consumer buying is combined with decreased production by the large durable-goods companies, supply decreases. Prices may also go down, but at a slow rate. In the recession of 1958 and the ones in 1969 and 1970, prices rose rather than fell. The likely reason is that the concentrated durable-goods industries prevented their own prices from falling, and even increased them in order to maintain profits.

3. People can't postpone buying nondurable goods (food, clothing, furniture) because there is a recession. Thus, the demand for the

output of these industries is more stable. But it still falls off in a recession.

4. In the nondurable-goods industries, there are many small companies and more competition. These firms can't stabilize prices by cutting supply, and because they lack power, their prices fluctuate more with the business cycle.

Leading Economic Indicators

The general level of economic activity moves with the business cycle. However, there are exceptions. In 1974, for example, real or constant GNP fell by about 5 percent. Inflation increased at a 2-digit rate and business profits in some industries were high, yet unemployment increased. In the recession phase, the general level of activity goes down. With the recovery phase, it goes up. Changes in output and price vary in degree as well as timing in different kinds of activity. Some kinds of economic activity, called **leading indicators**, lead the business cycle by decreasing or increasing before the rest do.

The Department of Commerce has put together an index called the *index of leading indicators (ILI)*, a list of 11 of these key statistics. They are (1) average work week, (2) percentage of companies reporting slower deliveries, (3) change in prices of so-called sensitive materials, (4) number of new businesses formed, (5) number of building permits issued, (6) stock prices, (7) new orders for consumer goods, (8) new orders for plant and equipment, (9) the nation's money supply, (10) change in total liquid assets, and (11) the layoff rate. Economic forecasters use these leading indicators to predict cyclical changes. Most economists wait for a trend to show up in the index of leading indicators. When the indicators move in the same direction for 3 months in a row, most economists agree that the economy is going to move in that direction.

There are many indicators that may be useful for predicting or forecasting the future of the economy but the ILI is one of the simplest and most widely used. The two problems with it are (1) it is difficult to know whether short-term movements will be sustained, and (2) many data are revised afterward and the future they predict is uncertain in length. Nonetheless, the ILI is useful to both firms, independent agencies; and to governments.

Unemployment

Full employment is a main goal of any country's national economic policy. But *full employment* must be defined and doesn't necessarily mean that every person in the nation has a job. The term refers to the labor force in general, which, by definition, includes anyone in the U.S. age 16 or over who has a job or is actively seeking one. Full employment doesn't even mean that all the labor force is employed. Allowances are made for people who are temporarily between jobs or are in the process of changing jobs.

Leading Indicators
A monthly index of eleven economic indicators which tends to lead changes in GNP. When a trend of several months appears, the economy tends later to move in that direction.

Full Employment
A concept of the employment goal to be attained in an economy.

"Merry Christmas, Staff!"

Kinds of Unemployment

Frictional Unemployment
The measure of unemployment of those who are moving from one job to another (also called transitional unemployment).

You may think that unemployment is unemployment, and that's that. But economists have identified three different *kinds* of unemployment:

Frictional or *transitional unemployment* are those people who are unemployed for a while as they move from one job to another. There are imperfections in the labor market that cause *frictional unemployment*:

1. Labor immobility of one kind or another, such as inability or unwillingness to commute or relocate.

2. Workers' inadequate knowledge of the job market.

3. The impossibility of instantly matching job-hunting people with job vacancies.

The amount of frictional unemployment depends on the degree of these imperfections. When everybody in the labor force is employed except for people who are frictionally unemployed, we say that full employment exists.

Unemployment due to lack of demand. During ecession and depression phases of a business cycle, the demand of the public for goods and services may not be enough to create a full-employment demand for members of the labor force. Although frictional unemployment is a fact of life in all phases of a business cycle, unemployment due to lack of demand is a direct result of the "down" phase of a business cycle. Consequently, a government, to get rid of this kind of unemployment, has to try to achieve

*Structural
Unemployment*
Unemployment due to
changes in technology
or the composition of
output.

economic growth or at least stability and to reduce business fluctuations.

Structural unemployment. Changes in the structure of the economy are what cause *structural unemployment*. These changes in structure may come about because of changes in technology or because of changes in the composition of output, which lead to shifts in the pattern of demand for labor. Such structural changes affect both skilled and unskilled workers. In the 1950s and early 1960s, the shift from coal to oil for heating homes left massive un-employment in the anthracite coal mines in eastern Pennsylvania. In Minnesota many workers became jobless when iron ore deposits in the Mesabi Range were exhausted. On the West Coast, in the late 1960s, large numbers of engineers who worked in the aerospace industries lost their jobs because of the government's cutback in its aerospace program when the Vietnam War caused reallocation of defense expenditures. All these events are examples of structural unemployment. In the 1990s, it will be interesting to see if reduced defense spending and the resulting changes in GNP composition create a new wave of structural unemployment.

Problems that Accompany Unemployment
A particularly disturbing aspect of structural unemployment involves unskilled workers, many of whom are members of minority groups. Since World War II, with the advent of computers and countless technologically sophisticated gadgets, the demand for unskilled labor, as a percentage of total demand for labor, has dropped greatly, even though the percentage of unskilled laborers in the labor force has remained constant. Many jobs for the unskilled have disappeared entirely. One tragedy of the last 40 years is that our educational system seems incapable of giving some students the skills they need to make them employable. The needs of minority groups, in particular, are not adequately met.

Unemployment due to lack of demand is a serious problem. However, if we can maintain economic growth or at least greater stability in the business cycle, we seem to have the tools to control it. Structural unemployment, though, is much more difficult to control. We must give the hard-core unemployed, particularly those in the inner cities, the new skills they need to survive in today's economy. Job-training programs in the last 30 years have, for the most part, failed. Minimum-wage laws, originally intro-duced to help unskilled workers and young people entering the job market for the first time, may actually be hurting them. These laws have caused wages to rise beyond the productive ability of the unskilled worker and the teenager. Some people argue that a reduction in these minimum-wages—at least for certain categories of workers, especially the young entering the labor force—would increase employment among teenagers. The minimum wage law in effect in 1990 provides for a training wage for several months and its effects will be interesting to observe.

We should also mention the discouraged-worker effect. Workers who have been rendered unemployed by so-called structural changes may eventually give up seeking work and just drop out of the labor force. Teenagers especially suffer from this discouragement. Those who never find jobs in the first place, disappear from the labor force and from our GNP statistics, as if they had become invisible and form a hidden cost of unemployment.

The continuous unemployment rate among minority groups, and among teenagers indicates the magnitude of our failure to deal with structural unemployment among those who are unskilled and discriminated against.

Economic Costs of Unemployment: The GNP Gap

The costs of unemployment to society are both economic and psychological. Obviously we can measure the economic costs in terms of goods and services the unemployed could have produced if they had had jobs. One economist, Sherman Maisel, in a book called *Fluctuations, Growth, and Forecasting*, estimated that unemployment in the depression of the 1930s cost the economy $650 billion in foregone product (using 1957 prices as a basis). This was more than enough to pay for World War II, to provide every family in the U.S. with a new home and two cars, or to give all who can use it a college education.

Tom Wicker, in an article in the *New York Times* in July of 1975, estimated that every 1 percent of unemployment adds $16 billion annually to the federal budget: $14 billion in lost tax revenue and $2 billion in government payments for unemployment and other benefits.

GNP Gap
The difference between full-employment GNP and actual GNP achieved.

We can also measure economic costs of unemployment as the difference between actual GNP achieved and potential GNP, or the GNP that could have been obtained with full employment. Figure 6-3 shows actual and potential GNP (assuming 4 percent unemployment). The difference between the two is called the **GNP gap**.

The GNP gap, the amount of output sacrificed when the economy does not fully use its existing resources, was marked between 1957 and 1965. Between 1965 and 1968, unemployment fell below 4 percent and actual GNP exceeded the 4 percent potential. This GNP surplus occurred because of the 1965 tax cut, plus high government expenditures for the war on poverty and the escalation in Vietnam. This period of full employment was brief, and the gap reappeared by the end of 1969. You can see that it is extremely difficult to utilize the labor force fully and hold unemployment down to the 4 percent level. In the late 1980s, we approached this potential with an unemployment rate between 5 and 6 percent.

Psychological and Social Costs of Unemployment

In a society basically still ruled by the work ethic, to be out of work—especially to be unemployed for a long time—causes people acute mental suffering. An extreme example, which appeared in the newspapers in the mid-1980s, is the case of an

Figure 6-3
The GNP Gap

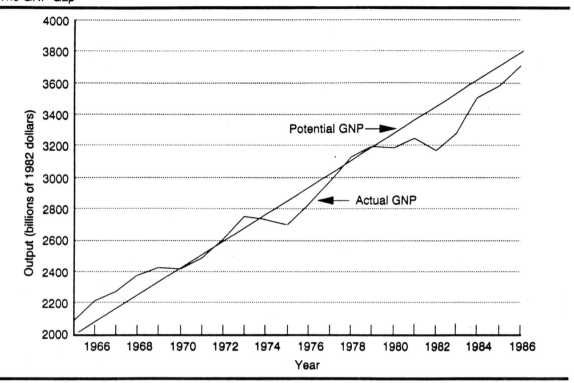

The straight line represents potential GNP; the jagged line is actual performance of the economy; the distance between the lines as you read GNP for any given year is the GNP gap.

Source: Economic Report of the President, 1987

individual who lost his job and shot himself or of another individual who hung himself in the steel mill from which he had become unemployed.

In addition to mental anguish, prolonged unemployment causes insecurities about one's self-worth. It creates family strain that goes beyond economic privation. In the past, and even more so today, prolonged unemployment has placed the individual psychologically, as well as economically, beyond the pale of normal society.

High levels of unemployment also put social and political stress on society at large. In a very real sense, a less affluent group may become pitted against a more affluent group. To paraphrase Abraham Lincoln, a society that is half affluent, half deprived, cannot long endure, or, at least, cannot expect to have social tranquility.

Prices and the Problem of Inflation

During various phases of a business cycle, the level of employment changes. Thus, a nation must not only maintain economic growth

Inflation
A general rise in the level of prices.

but also try to maintain full employment. Another problem is **inflation**, or a general rise in the level of prices. During various phases of a business cycle, the level of prices changes. Since World War II, prices have primarily been rising. This, as we all know, is inflation.

As prices of goods and services increase, the amount of them that a dollar will buy naturally decreases. Thus, inflation causes a decrease in the purchasing power of the dollar. Figure 6-4 shows the rates of unemployment and inflation in the U.S. between 1915 and 1985.

Figure 6-4
Rates of Unemployment and Inflation, 1915-1985

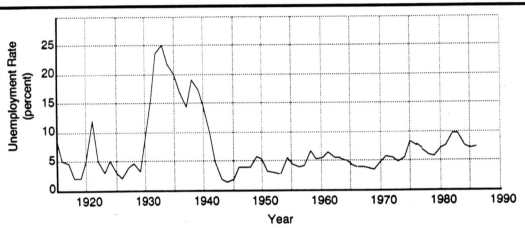

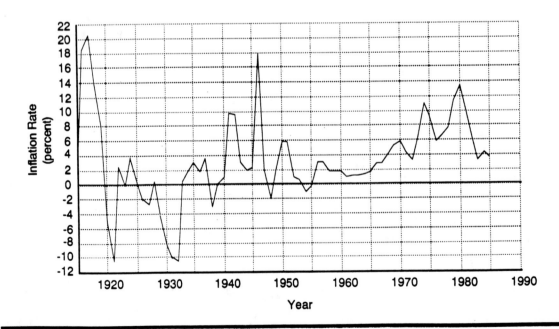

Source: U.S. Department of Labor

Kinds of Inflation

There are three kinds of inflation, which economists classify according to their source or cause.

Demand-pull inflation. Remember that in our discussion of supply and demand, we said that when demand increases (for a given supply of a good), the price of that good will increase. The same sort of phenomenon occurs for the entire economy. When the economy is at full employment, output, over a short period of time, cannot increase because there are no resources (especially labor) available to increase it. When demand for goods and services increases, there are not enough productive facilities to increase output in order to meet this increased demand. Consequently, markets ration out their goods or services, causing increased prices and eventually forcing decreases in the quantity the public demands. Thus, the economy brings back into equilibrium the quantity of a good or service demanded, and the economy's ability to supply.

Let's look at an example of a demand-pull situation: In 1966, President Johnson escalated the war in Vietnam by increasing our troops there to more than 500,000 men. To maintain these troops in combat half a world away, the U.S. government had to buy billions of dollars worth of equipment and supplies. The government had also sharply increased its expenditures on anti-poverty programs, and there had been tax cuts in 1964 and 1965. As a result of this combination of events, the economy had reached full employment. Unemployment had dropped below 4 percent. Thus, the economy was able to meet the increased demand for armaments only by drawing resources away from the production of other commodities. It did this by increasing the prices of resources used to make nonmilitary goods. Then prices of resources used to make armaments increased, which increased the price of the finished products. At the same time, the supply of resources to other markets declined, decreasing supply and increasing prices. That is what we mean when we say that the marked inflation of 1967-1969 was primarily due to demand-pull inflation.

In brief, then, demand-pull inflation occurs when an economy's demand exceeds the ability of that economy to supply at existing prices. Too many dollars are chasing too few goods. The effect is to force prices up.

Cost-push inflation. When the suppliers of resources increase their prices faster than their productive efficiency increases, cost-push inflation occurs. When resource costs go up faster than increases in productivity, a company's production costs per unit increase. These increased production costs are ultimately reflected, at least in part, in higher prices.

The usual example people give of cost-push inflation is this: When unions force industry to give workers wage increases and the workers do not produce correspondingly more output, cost-push inflation occurs. Suppose that workers in the carpet industry increased their productivity 3 percent and the union obtained wage increases of 4 percent. You can see that the carpet manufacturer's

Demand-Pull Inflation
The rise in aggregate prices that occurs when demand increases more rapidly than supply.

Cost-Push Inflation
The rise in aggregate prices that occurs when resource prices and costs increase more rapidly than factor productivity.

labor costs per yard of carpet go up. (Increased productivity reduces labor costs per unit by 3 percent, while wage increases raise costs per unit 4 percent; net cost increase is 1 percent.) Right after the war (between 1945 and 1949), labor unions staged a real drive to increase wages. They argued that wage rates had stayed at about the same level during the war, while both productivity and company profits had risen dramatically.

The labor unions naturally wanted workers' wages to catch up. On the whole, industry leaders did not fight this move to increase wage rates, because a strong demand-pull inflation was already under way because of depression and war-postponed consumption. It was easy to pass the wage hikes on to the consumer in the form of higher prices.

In the 1970s, the whole world experienced two singularly agonizing cases of cost-push inflation. At the beginning of the 1970s, the world's major oil-producing and oil-exporting countries formed an association: OPEC. Among them, the OPEC countries control the bulk of the world's oil. And between 1971 and 1974, they quintupled the price of their crude oil. The industrialized world is heavily dependent on oil. It is primarily oil that keeps the wheels of industry turning, that generates electricity for our power plants, that gets most of us to work. Therefore, the OPEC countries' two increases in oil prices quickly increased the costs of

"You've no idea what's happened to prices—you'll have to pull a really big job the first thing when you get out!"

Administered-Price Inflation
The rise in aggregate prices that occurs because non-competitive firms can raise prices to achieve target rates of profit.

production generally and set off a worldwide inflation and economic crisis.

Administered-price inflation. This might be called *profit-push inflation*, or *seller's inflation*. Monopolistic firms have considerable influence over supply and therefore over price. Companies big enough to influence prices decide on a pricing policy, thus setting prices becomes an administrative rather than a market function.

Such companies may decide that it is easier to increase their profits by just increasing prices rather than by increasing their efficiency and lowering their costs. During periods of prosperity, when demand is at a high level, these firms can easily exercise their power to increase prices, and price increases from such a source are hard to detect. During a period of recession, when demand is falling, these firms may again decide to increase prices in order to maintain their profits. They have a certain target rate of return on their investment that they seem to try to maintain by raising prices.

However, during these periods of falling demand one can most readily spot administered-price increases. In the recessions of 1958 and of 1970-1971, and in the recessions of 1974 as well as 1981-1982, prices of certain goods rose, while employment and real GNP fell. As you can see, one can trace some of the inflation during a recession back to the fact that monopolistic corporations increase their prices even though demand is falling, because they attempt to maintain profit levels.

Remember, though, that administered-price inflation takes place during both rising and falling phases of the business cycle, so we are never entirely safe from this kind of danger.

Both cost-push and administered-price inflation exist whenever there is not enough competition to keep prices under control. For example, in cost-push inflation, the people who supply the resources have enough monopoly control over the supply of their resources to give them economic power to force prices up. (Remember that this resource may be labor itself.) In administered-price inflation, the reason certain firms have so much power over prices is that they control, to an extent, the supply of finished products for which there are no good substitutes. Cost-push and administered-price inflation can interact, causing prices to spiral upward.

What Effect Do Price Changes Have?

When prices go up or down, this movement has a financial effect on all of us. It affects the economy in three ways: (1) by redistributing real income, (2) by redistributing real wealth, and (3) by changing the level of output.

Money Income
The current flows of money incomes to individuals.

1. *Redistribution of real income.* First, we should make a distinction between *money* and *real* income. **Money income** is the number of dollars a person receives in income, or the number of

Real Income
The current flows of money incomes to individuals expressed in terms of purchasing power.

dollars in the paycheck, for most people. **Real income** is what can be bought with money income. You can see that your real income can change when there is either (a) a change in your money income, or (b) a change in the general level of prices and the purchasing power of the dollar. In the following discussion, we shall assume that the total pie (the level of output) remains constant; that is, that the total level of output is unaffected by changes in prices.

In terms of income, there are two broad classes of people: people whose incomes are fixed, or semifixed, and those whose incomes are variable. When there is inflation, the people with fixed or semifixed incomes suffer because their money income does not increase as fast as prices do; their real income, therefore, declines. People with fixed incomes are usually nonunion workers, those living on welfare or pensions, and those with income based on interest; that is, the widows and orphans, the elderly and the poor, and the unorganized.

The money incomes of people with varied incomes, though, often increase faster than prices go up, for example, the incomes of the people whose earnings come from the profits of a business. Some elements of cost for the business may tend not to increase as fast as prices. In industries where this occurs, profit margins increase. In general, (although there are exceptions), the money incomes of those who obtain their incomes from profits tends to increase faster than prices increase.

Organized labor generally has enough clout to increase wages at least as fast as prices rise, and often more so, so organized labor usually can enjoy increased real income—at least for a time. This is particularly true when unions make their contracts for short periods and adjust them quickly to inflation rates.

Deflation
A general fall in the level of prices.

During a **deflation**, when prices fall, those with fixed incomes temporarily enjoy increases in their real income, because a dollar buys a little more. This does not apply to unorganized labor, because unorganized labor does not have enough economic power to prevent wage cuts. ("Times are hard. You will just have to take less per hour.")

What happens to people with variable incomes during a deflation? Those with income from profits tend to suffer losses in real income. Suppose you are living on the income from stock you own in one company. The company has to lower its prices because of the deflation. But the company still has to pay for resources (labor and materials), and the costs of these resources lag behind the fall in prices. Thus, the margin of profit gets narrower and narrower, and presently the company is unable to pay dividends to its stockholders.

As for organized labor in a deflation, it has the economic power to keep employers from cutting back wages, (though not jobs) in spite of falling prices.

2. *Redistribution of real wealth.* In terms of real wealth, there are three categories: debtors (who borrow money), creditors (who lend it), and savers (who save it).

During an inflation, debtors benefit. But creditors and savers lose real wealth; that is, their wealth does not buy as much as it used to. Suppose you are the debtor. Let's say that you borrowed $100 from your brother a year ago, and suppose that there has been a 10 percent inflation during the year. Prices in general were 10 percent lower a year ago, and thus purchasing power of each dollar was 10 percent higher. If you repay the loan today, you're 10 percent richer, assuming that you didn't pay interest. But your brother, the creditor, is 10 percent poorer. He lent you the money when prices were lower and purchasing power higher. If he spends that $100 today, he'll get 10 percent less for it than he would have a year ago.

Now suppose that your brother had saved the $100 instead of lending it to you. Unless he earned interest on it, he would still have lost 10 percent, because a year ago when he saved the money, its purchasing power was 10 percent higher than it is today. (The creditor and saver would not be hurt by inflation if the rate of interest increased enough to compensate for the inflation and to pay them back for the risk, for the loss of liquidity, for the fact that they could not use the money themselves, and for all the other sacrifices people make in order to earn interest on their money.)

During a deflation, just the reverse holds true: Creditors and savers benefit, and debtors lose real wealth. Creditors lent money when prices were higher and each dollar was worth less, but they are paid back when prices are lower and thus the dollar's purchasing power is greater. Savers, too, are better off. They saved money when prices were higher and each dollar bought less. But now that prices have come down, their savings have higher purchasing power. Debtors, on the other hand, are hurt, because they borrowed money when prices were higher and purchasing power lower, but now they have to pay it back when prices are lower and dollars have greater purchasing power.

3. *Changed level of output due to changed prices.* We have been assuming that the economy's output was unchanged as prices changed and that as prices changed, some groups gained at the expense of others. What happens if the total output changes? Relative redistribution of wealth still takes place, but its adverse effects may be lessened or accentuated. Let us see why.

A strong inflation can lead to recession and unemployment for a number of reasons: (a) Since all prices do not increase at the same rate, a sharp inflation may quickly cause structural distortions. Some firms' costs rise faster than they can raise prices of their output, so their profits are reduced. They may even take losses. They reduce their output, they lay off workers, and they may even go bankrupt. (b) Rapidly rising prices confuse both producers and consumers, so that people hesitate to make decisions. This causes a decrease in demand for output. On the other hand, rapidly rising prices may lead to **inflationary expectations**, or the belief that prices will continue to rise and cause decreases in

Inflationary Expectations
The belief that inflation is inbuilt and will continue, thus, leading to falling real income.

real income. This may lead to increased current demanded and further inflationary pressure. (c) Consumers may revolt against rising prices and refuse to buy. This again causes a decrease in demand. (d) People who are hurt by the redistributive effect of higher prices have to cut back on their buying, again decreasing the demand for output. The lucky ones who actually benefit from higher prices may step up *their* buying, but their increased demand may not compensate for the decreased demand on the part of those who are caught in the squeeze of higher prices.

The net effect of all this is a decrease in total demand for the economy's output, which means that output falls off and so does employment. The result is *recession*.

We have been discussing sharp increases in prices. But moderate increases in prices can actually be beneficial to output, for the following reasons: (a) When inflation is slight, business and industries can see in advance that the costs of their resources (labor and materials) are going to go up by a certain amount next year, so they can raise their own prices slightly and thus counter the structural effects of varying rates of price changes. (b) The prices of products may increase faster than the prices of resources, so that the profits of business and industry increase. When business people are making high profits, they are more inclined to invest. Thus, more jobs open up, employment rates rise, and the rate of economic growth increases.

However, if a moderate inflation continues for a long time, it can accelerate and become built in or what is called *creeping inflation*. And this may become a threat to the economy, for three reasons: (a) Creeping inflation can accelerate until it becomes a severe inflation, with all its potential for causing recession. (b) Creeping inflation can generate inflationary expectations and lead to a wage-price spiral, resulting in serious inflation. Unions demand wage increases to compensate for past inflation and often add an extra margin for anticipated future inflation. During a prosperous period, business people are reluctant to face a strike, so they agree to grant the unions their wage hikes, which in turn increase the costs of production. Businesses pass these higher costs on to consumers through higher prices, which often reflect an extra profit margin for the firms. (c) In due course, creeping inflation results in redistribution of wealth and puts serious economic strain on disadvantaged groups. The result is *recession*.

A moderate deflation, bringing about a gradual fall in prices, may also contribute to increases in output. Deflations, however, are quite rare, especially since World War II. During the prosperous part of the 1920s (1922 to 1929), prices sloped gently downward because of increases in productivity without corresponding increases in workers' wages. (The unions had a hard time surviving during the 1920s.) The general population enjoyed increases in their real income as prices fell. At the same time, businesses had larger profits, since productivity increased faster than prices fell. Both factors kept the demand for consumer and capital goods high. There was a moderate deflation in 1982-1983, when, in the face of restrictive monetary policy, prices moved downward.

But deflation, too, can create problems. When the decrease in prices is very rapid, it tends to reduce the level of output. The following sequence occurs: (a) Retail prices fall faster than prices of *factor inputs* (the resources an industry uses to manufacture things). This squeezes out profits and introduces losses. (b) Since prices do not fall uniformly, the structure of prices becomes distorted. Some firms have their profits wiped out entirely. (c) Business people, when faced with falling prices, become very pessimistic and tend to withhold further investment. All these conditions lead to decreases in output. The result is *recession*.

Employment and Prices

To prevent the economy from continually plunging down and climbing up, governments try to initiate policies of stabilization, aimed at maintaining full employment and stable prices. It is difficult to attain both objectives at the same time, since they are often contradictory.

Figure 6-5 shows that as output increases, more people get jobs, so unemployment is reduced and prices remain stable. At this stage, there is still some unused space and unemployed labor that industry can use without raising its prices. However, as output reaches point A, industry can achieve further increases in output only by raising its prices. Although point A is reached before there is full employment of all labor, certain categories of skilled labor and other resources may be in short supply. Beyond point A, the ever expanding output creates an ever greater demand for resources, which means that the prices of these resources will increase still further and inevitably the general level of prices will

Figure 6-5
Prices and Employment

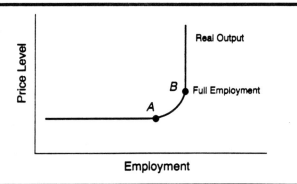

As output increase, industry starts using resources that were formerly unemployed, and prices remain stable. At point A, some resources start to be in short supply; this forces prices up. At point B, there is full employment. Further increases in demand only result in still higher prices.

also rise. At point *B* (full employment), any further effort to increase output will result in continued demand-pull inflation; prices increase but real output cannot. In other words, demand-pull inflation occurs before the economy reaches full employment because some forms of labor and resources are in shorter supply than others. More expensive resources force up the prices of products before full employment is achieved.

From this we can see that there is a tradeoff between employment and prices. Beyond some point of resource use, if you want to reduce unemployment you have to accept some increases in prices. We can diagram this tradeoff between employment and prices. The resulting curve, called a **Phillips curve** after A. W. Phillips, a British economist, looks like the one in Figure 6-6.

Phillips Curve
A function that depicts the trade-offs between unemployment and inflation.

When we examine Figure 6-6, which covers the period since World War II, we see a Phillips curve representing a relationship that many considered politically acceptable until the 1970s. Unemployment at 4 to 4.5 percent, inflation at 4 to 5 percent. If the government then had tried to force the unemployment rate below 4.5 percent, prices would have increased too much. The point of this Phillips curve is that, before the 1970s, the tradeoff between inflation and unemployment was a politically acceptable one.

Now look at what has been happening to the Phillips curve since 1970. During the recession of 1970-71, unemployment of about 6 percent was coupled with an inflation rate of about 7 percent, making the government's policy of economic stabilization much harder to carry out and the economy seemed to be in a period of **stagflation**, or a combination of inflation and economic stagnation. In other words, the economy seemed unable to move down the

Stagflation
A combination of inflation and economic stagnation.

Figure 6-6
A Phillips Curve

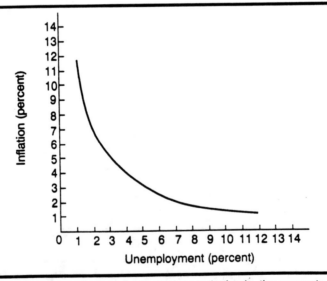

The horizontal axis is the percentage of unemployment; the vertical axis, the percentage rate of inflation. The Phillips curve shows the relationship between the two.

Phillips curve. In the recession of 1974-75, the tradeoff was even less acceptable. In 1974 unemployment reached 9 percent, while inflation exceeded 12 percent. Our experience with unemployment-inflation in the late 1970s and early 1980s hardly invites optimism about the prospects of achieving low rates of unemployment and inflation at the same time. While the period since 1982 has seen relatively low rates of inflation and declining unemployment, some continue to worry about a resumption of stagflation.

If stagflation resumes, whenever the government tries to reduce unemployment, it will have to stimulate output, which increases demand, which in turn increases prices. On the other hand, whenever the government tries to reduce inflation, it will have to somehow or other reduce demand, which reduces output, which in turn increases unemployment. When the tradeoff between inflation and unemployment is politically unacceptable, any effort the government makes to reduce unemployment just increases an already politically unacceptable level of inflation; and vice versa. We will examine these problems in more detail in the upcoming application which deals with the short-run instability of inflation-unemployment trade-offs.

SUMMING UP

1. There are four types of economic fluctuations: (a) The *secular trend*, which is the expansion or contraction of the economy over very long periods of time; (b) *business cycles*, which are repetitive but not regular variations in general economic activity; (c) *seasonal variations*, which happen regularly at the same time each year; and (d) *random variations*, which have no regular pattern or recurring cause.

2. The two phases of the business cycle are: (a) the *contraction phase*, when unemployment and unused capacity are high and investment and consumption are low; and (b) the *expansion phase*, when investment, consumption, and employment are high and prices may be rising.

3. In business cycles, there is no regularity in the length of the cycle or any of its phases, nor is there regularity in the intensity of activity. Many consider the term *business fluctuation* more descriptive than *business cycle*.

4. Prices in durable-goods industries tend to be more stable over a given business cycle than prices in nondurable-goods industries. (a) During a contraction in economic activity, people postpone buying new durable goods such as automobiles and washing machines; they tend to repair and keep using them. But they must continue to buy nondurable goods, such as food and clothing. (b) Nondurable-goods industries are more competitive than durable-goods industries; thus individual firms cannot limit the drop in their own prices.

5. *Leading economic indicators* are measures of economic activity that point the way to coming increases or decreases in economic activity shortly before there is an actual rise or fall. Economists use these leading indicators (stock-market prices, building permits, average work week, and so on) as tools with which to forecast economic activity.

6. There are three kinds of unemployment: (a) *Frictional unemployment* includes people who are unemployed only for short periods of time as they move from one job to another. (b) *Unemployment due to lack of demand* occurs when there is not enough total demand for industry's output for full employment to be attained. (c) *Structural unemployment* is due to structural changes in the economy, which take place because of changes in technology and the composition of output, with resulting changes in the pattern of demand for labor.

7. The *GNP gap* reveals the economic costs of unemployment by showing the difference between potential and actual GNP. The cost of unemployment in economic terms may be high, but the individual psychological and social costs, plus social and political tensions, may be even higher.

8. There are three types of inflation according to cause: (a) *Demand-pull inflation*, in which total demand for an economy's output exceeds the ability of the economy to supply at existing prices, and prices rise to ration the scarce supply; (b) *Cost-push inflation*, in which suppliers of resources increase their prices faster than workers increase their productivity, which pushes cost of production up, forcing companies to increase their prices; (c) *Administered-price inflation*, in which firms, exercising monopoly power, increase prices to either augment or maintain profits.

9. Cost-push inflation and administered-price inflation exist because of the dearth of competition in certain industries and can interact to cause an upward spiraling of prices.

10. During periods of inflation, redistribution of *real income* occurs, because those with fixed or semifixed incomes cannot increase their *money income* to compensate for rising prices. Those with variable incomes can usually increase their real incomes, since their money incomes go up faster than prices do. The reverse occurs during a period of *deflation* when prices fall.

11. There is also redistribution of real wealth during a period of inflation, as debtors benefit from inflation because they borrow high-purchasing-power dollars and pay back low-purchasing-power dollars. Creditors and savers lose in an inflation because they lend (or save) high-purchasing-power dollars and are paid back low-purchasing-power dollars. The opposite occurs during a deflation, when prices fall.

12. A strong inflation can lead to recession, as cost distortions put pressure on some firms, confuse both producers and consumers, and weaken the consumer's willingness and ability to buy. Moderate inflation may increase output and income by stimulating investment. *Creeping inflation* (or moderate nflation over a fairly long period) may eventually have bad effects on the economy.

13. A government cannot readily achieve both full employment and stable prices at the same time, especially in a noncompetitive economy. As the economy increases its output, some resources run out before full employment is attained. The prices of these resources will increase, and prices in general will increase, before full employment is reached.

14. A diagram of the tradeoff between more employmen and higher prices is called a *Phillips curve*. The Phillips curve for the pre-1970 period appeared to be stable and had politically acceptable levels of tradeoff between unemployment and inflation. But since 1970, the Phillips curve has reflected levels of tradeoff between unemployment and rising prices have become higher. In addition, the problem of stagflation which has at times existed since 1970, has been less acceptable.

15. This change in the Phillips curve trade-offs has made the government's economic stabilization policy more difficult and complex. The tradeoff that exists now between unemployment and inflation is politically unacceptable. Any effort to rectify one seems only to worsen the already politically unacceptable level of the other.

KEY TERMS

Secular trend
Business cycle
Seasonal variations
Random variations
Contraction phase
Expansion phase
Leading indicators
Full employment
Frictional unemployment
Structural unemployment
GNP gap
Inflation
Cost-push inflation
Demand-pull inflation
Administered price inflation
Deflation
Stagflation
Inflationary expectations

QUESTIONS

1. Some economists have said that the term *business cycle* is not accurate, and they advocate using such terms as *business fluctuation* or *economic instability*. What is the basis of their objection? Do you agree with them?

2. Define the following terms:
   a. Secular trend
   b. Concentrated industries
   c. Leading indicators (ILI)
   d. Frictional unemployment
   e. Structural unemployment
   f. The GNP gap
   g. Inflation
   h. Demand-pull inflation
   i. Cost-push inflation
   j. Administered-price inflation
   k. Stagflation
   l. Inflationary expectations

3. Compared to clothing prices, washing machine prices tend to be stable, although there are wide variations in production over a given business cycle. Why is that?

4. Unemployment due to the public's lack of demand for industry's output fluctuates as business activity fluctuates, while structural unemployment may not. Why is this so?

5. How does the existence of monopoly power affect the level of prices?

6. How does the level of prices affect the distribution of real income? the distribution of real wealth?

7. In a market economy, some argue that it is difficult to have full employment and stable prices at the same time. What is the argument?

8. The Phillips curve seems to have less favorable trade-offs between inflation and unemployment than previously. What implications does this have for an economic policy that will stabilize the economy? Why did this change occur?

9. You are a member of the President's Council of Economic Advisers in 1990. You have just told the President that the country cannot have full employment and stable prices at the same time. Furthermore, inflation in 1990 is 7 percent and unemployment is

just over 6 percent. The President charges you to advise him which should be decreased: inflation or unemployment. Which would you counter with government policy: inflation or unemployment? Give *economic* justification for the one you've chosen. Since some groups are hurt by inflation and others by unemployment, your decision hurts some and helps others. Give ethical and moral justifications for your decision.

Chapter 7:
Aggregate Demand and Aggregate Supply

We have seen that price levels, employment-unemployment rates, and real income levels have varied greatly in uneven cycles of American history. In this and succeeding chapters we will build a framework for determining what creates not only price levels, employment levels, and growth rates but also how we may understand and explain variations in those key macroeconomic variables.

Let us begin with an explanation of the price level and changing levels of price. In individual markets for commodities and services, prices are established by equilibrium forces that clear markets at levels that equate quantity demanded and quantity supplied. If we could establish a single aggregate demand curve as well as a single aggregate supply curve for the economy, we should be able to understand the resulting aggregate price level expressed as an index of prices. We see such a set of relationships in Figure 7-1.

Aggregate demand and aggregate supply determine in equilibrium the level of prices and the level of real income for the economy. Aggregate demand is negatively sloped; as the price level falls, quantity demanded increases. Aggregate supply is positively sloped; as the price level rises, quantity supplied increases.

Equilibrium national income and the equilibrium price level are established where aggregate quantity demanded = aggregate quantity supplied or at income Q_e and price level P_e. We should note that this equilibrium real income is simply the level toward which the economy tends given the underlying AD and AS schedules. It is not a target or even necessarily a desirable level of real income. Q_e might be a level associated with severe recession and high unemployment or it might be associated with over-full employment and a high rate of inflation.

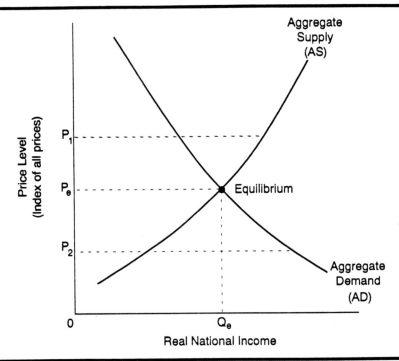

AD and AS determine in equilibrium the level of prices and the level of real income for the economy. AD is negatively sloped; as the price level falls, quantity demanded increases. AS is positively sloped; as the price level rises. Quantity supplied increases. Equilibrium national income and the equilibrium price level are where aggregate quantity demanded = aggregate quantity supplied or at equilibrium quantity, Q_e, and price level, P_e. At any disequilibrium price level, (P_1 or P_2), there would be excess supply or excess demand forcing prices downward or upward to eliminate shortages or gluts.

At any disequilibrium price level (P_1 or P_2) there would be excess supply or excess demand causing producers to adjust prices downward or upward to eliminate shortages or gluts.

In Figure 7-1, we show such an aggregate demand curve and an aggregate supply curve. Measured on the vertical axis are different levels of prices for the entire economy (measured by a price index). Real national income is measured on the horizontal axis.

Equilibrium Level of Prices and Real Income
A level that is established where aggregate quantity demanded equals aggregate quantity supplied.

The equilibrium level of prices and the equilibrium level of real national income is established where the aggregate quantity demanded equals the aggregate quantity supplied.

Only at P_e, the equilibrium level of prices, are the plans of producers to offer commodities and services for sale made equal to the plans of buyers to purchase commodities and services.

Aggregate Demand: Its Definition and Determinants

Aggregate Demand
A measure of the entire planned spending on final goods and services at each level of prices and real income.

Aggregate demand (AD) is a measure of the entire desired or planned spending on final goods and services at each level of prices and real income. As there are four sources of such planned spending, there are four corresponding determinants of AD. When we examine the "Keynesian" model of income determination, we will see that managing or influencing AD involves influencing one or more of these four components.

Consumption Expenditures
The largest element of AD, consumption spending is subject to determination and variation from many things that influence consumer behavior. Economists believe that the major elements which influence that behavior are disposable income, the availability and cost of credit, and expectations.

Disposable Income
Disposable income may be used for consumption or saving. From our individual gross incomes, what we may dispose of in these ways depends on taxes, and private and public transfer payments. If, for example, social security payments are taxed, disposable incomes of retired persons will decline and so will the contributions of such households to AD.

Cost and Availability of Credit
Durable, often expensive, consumer goods are usually purchased with loans. The cost of this credit and its availability heavily influence consumer expenditures on automobiles, housing and other such goods. If the (interest rate) cost rises, the availability of such credit diminishes and this important component of AD will fall.

Expectations
All of us have expectations about future economic events that will affect us. Will we have a job? If so, will our incomes rise? These expectations are influenced by both public and private actions. If our expectations worsen, if we expect declining income or even unemployment, our purchases of many goods will decline.

Investment Expenditures
The most volatile element of AD is investment spending on plant and equipment, inventories, research and development. Firms' investment decisions appear to be influenced by interest rates, government policy, and also by expectations.

Interest Rates
Whether investments are financed by borrowing in capital markets or by the use of retained earnings, firms use interest rates as the benchmarks against which to measure the expected profitability of an investment. Thus, if interest rates rise, the profitability of an investment must be higher to induce a firm to make the investment, and fewer investments will be made.

Government Policy

Present government policies as well as expected future policies influence investment choices. Will there be investment tax credits? Will tax breaks be given to firms that locate in a particular area? These and many other aspects of government policies affect the profitability of an investment strategy.

Expectations

Many investments have long-term payoffs. While the future is uncertain for firms as well as for consumers, both groups must establish expectations about future market conditions as well as future public policies. Present investment decisions, therefore, are partly a function of expected future events.

Government Expenditures

The second largest element of AD in the U.S., government spending is obviously variable but difficult to ascribe to a simple set of influences since it is the result of a complex political process. There are various levels of government and various factors that seem to influence their expenditure policies. Among the factors which may be influential are efforts to secure re-election by public officials, automatic stabilizer programs which are tied to varying economic conditions, changes in political philosophy (the proper role of government), and national emergencies such as war and depression.

Net Exports (Exports Minus Imports)

The smallest element of AD; this element has nonetheless become increasingly important in recent years. Net exports can be positive or negative. If positive, net exports add to AD. If negative, net exports decrease AD. Net exports are influenced by trade policy, exchange rate changes, and by politics.

Trade Policy

If Japan "voluntarily" limits its exports of cars to the U.S., Americans will probably spend less on Japanese cars and the net exports of the U.S. will tend to rise. If nations impose or raise tariffs on U.S. goods, our net exports will tend to decrease as a result of the decrease in the quantity demanded of our exports.

Exchange Rate Changes

If, for example, the dollar buys fewer yen, Japanese imports tend to cost more in the U.S., and U.S. exports to Japan tend to become cheaper. Rising U.S. sales to Japan and decreasing Japanese sales to the U.S. tend to increase our net exports.

Politics

Politics always plays an important role in trade between nations. If the government of Japan will not allow U.S. firms to bid for construction contracts in Japan, then our net exports tend to decrease. If Japan opens its markets to free trade, our net exports will tend to grow.

Summing Up

AD is the sum of intended spending on consumption expenditure, investment expenditure, government expenditure, and net exports at each overall price level. AD may thus be expressed as the sum of consumption expenditure (C) + investment expenditure (I) + government expenditure (G) + net exports (Xn).

$$AD = C + I + G + Xn$$

Why Does the Aggregate Demand Curve Slope Downward?

The AD curve shown in Figure 7-1 has a negative slope. That is the lower the price level, the higher the quantity demanded, the higher the price level, the lower the quantity demanded. It may be tempting to think that this is simply a restatement of the law of demand. That is, however, not so! Recall that the law of demand dealt with the effects of a change in the price of a good, holding other prices (and income, taste, etc.) constant. Clearly such a *ceteris paribus* assumption cannot be made in the case of the AD curve which deals with changes in the (weighted average) prices of all goods on real national income. If the aggregate price level falls, substitution effects will explain nothing for there are no substitutes for all goods and services (including savings).

Basically, there are three reasons why AD in Figure 7-1 has a negative slope, let us summarize these three causes:

1. *Effects of interest rate changes* on aggregate spending. Consider what happens when the price level rises. Households and firms need to hold more money to cover their transactions between receipts of income, thus increasing the demand for money. The increased money demand will cause interest rates to rise. As these rates rise, the demand for both consumer goods and non-consumer goods decreases, causing a decline in the quantity demanded of the economy's output.

2. *Wealth's effect* on aggregate spending. Asset values are expressed in monetary (dollar) forms. When the price level changes, the real purchasing power of these assets such as bonds and balances in banks moves in the opposite direction. If prices double, for instance, the value of a $10,000 bond is halved. Therefore, if prices go up, individuals will have to save more to restore their real wealth positions. The increase in savings will tend to reduce the quantity demanded of current output.

3. *Relative price changes between foreign and domestic goods.* An AD curve includes all sources of demand for domestically produced goods, including foreign sources. When the price level in the U.S. increases (*ceteris paribus*), American goods become more expensive relative to foreign goods. Americans substitute foreign goods for those domestically produced and foreigners substitute

their own domestically made goods for American goods. Both substitution effects tend to decrease the quantity demanded of U.S.-made commodities and services.

For all three reasons, we may assume the following:

As the aggregate price level rises, the quantity demanded of the output of an economy decreases; as the price level falls, the quantity demanded of the output of an economy increases. (AD curves slope downward.)

Aggregate Supply: Its Definition and Determinants

Aggregate Supply
A measure of the entire desired output of final goods and services at each level of prices and real income.

Aggregate supply (AS) is a measure of the entire desired output of final goods and services at each level of prices and real income. All of the things that may influence business decisions about production rates are potential determinants of AS. Included in such a list would be: (1) cost and availability of resources, (2) capacity and investment plans, (3) technology, (4) productivity, (5) expectations, and (6) government policy.

Cost and Availability of Resources
Firms making profitable supply decisions consider not only revenue but also cost in deciding what and how much to produce. If resource prices rise, their costs do as well and as tends to Decrease. in this chapter's application, we will look at what sharp increases and decreases in oil prices in the 1970s and 1980s did to output decisions as well as real income and price levels. We should remember that increases in resource prices work their way through the economy and its supply of goods quickly in comparison with other determinants of AS.

Capacity and Investment Plans
In any short-run period, an economy has only so much *capacity*; its stock of plant and equipment, skilled laborers, and other resources. Naturally, the economy cannot produce beyond the limits imposed by this stock. Investment spending, however, will in the long run result in a shift of, or increase in, this capacity and a greater AS. Since investment also creates jobs and income, it will stimulate AD.

Most investment spending is undertaken by private firms. Government spending, however, may directly or indirectly raise the capacity of the economy. In wartime, governments may actually build plant and equipment. Ordinarily, though, the effects are indirect; government spending on activities such as roads, and port and airport facilities increases the productivity of private investment and results in a larger capacity.

Technology
Technological change raises the productivity of all resources. When the U.S. automobile industry found itself threatened by the

inroads of Japanese cars in recent times, it invested billions of dollars in developing and implementing new technology including robotics.

Technological changes not only result from investments, they also cause new investments. While much technological change is gradual, the big changes, such as microchips in the 1970s, came from intensive processes of research and development. These changes occur with significant time lags before implementation and are often subsidized by government.

Productivity

The *productivity* of resources, the output produced by each unit used as an input, depends on many things. The productivity of labor, for example, depends on the productivity of the capital with which it is employed. Labor's productivity also depends heavily on training, education and on increasing skills. Economists refer to these three factors as **investment in human capital**.

Investment in Human Capital Expenditures made on training, education, and increasing the skill levels of individuals.

Productivity growth has become a major issue in the U.S. in recent years, particularly since it has been growing at a faster rate in some other industrial nations than in this country. There have been calls for more investment in human capital as well as in new plant and equipment to raise the joint productivity of labor and capital.

Expectations

Payout on investment is often long-term. In making investment and production decisions, firms must form expectations about prices for their products as well as expectations of future overall price levels in order to assess the present value of such decisions. If expectations change, we would expect firms to re-evaluate their decisions and alter both the mix and amount of investments and planned production rates.

Government Policy

Government policies affect AS decisions in numerous ways. Such policies affect the availability and cost of resources. Will the U.S. allow exploration for oil in offshore sites? The policy decision will likely affect the price of oil and energy costs of firms. Will government policy tend toward deregulation of transportation? The result will certainly affect the transport costs of firms in producing and distributing goods and services.

Why Does the (Short Run) Aggregate Supply Curve Slope Upward?

The AS curve in Figure 7-1 is positively sloped. Indeed, we will assume the following:

As the aggregate price level rises, the quantity supplied or produced will rise; as the aggregate price level falls, the quantity supplied or produced will decrease. (Short-run AS curves slope upward).

We assume that the supply curve of a firm is based on cost and that in the short run, rising costs associated with ultimately diminishing productivity result in firms offering more for sale only at higher prices. The AS curve for the entire economy in Figure 7-1 is based on the same assumption. In the short run, it is reasonable to assume that input prices (wages, interest rates, etc.) are constant and that it is rising real cost that explains the upward-sloping (short-run) AS curve. Of course, the process works in reverse. If private firms reduce output rates, they will lay off less efficient resources, and their (unit) costs will fall, making them willing to offer smaller rates of output for sale at lower prices.

It will be obvious to the reader that if the overall price level rises, there will ultimately be pressure to increase factor prices, including wage and salary rates as well as interest rates.

Equilibrium and Full Employment May Not be the Same

There is a potential or capacity GNP that a nation is capable of producing if it fully employs its resources, especially its labor force. We also saw that the full employment level, though rarely reached, does not correspond to zero unemployment. The actual level of employment is the one that economy produces. The natural rate is the one at which inflation tends neither to accelerate or decelerate. (Explained by frictional unemployment or people seeking to move to new jobs.) In recent decades, this natural rate has been thought to be between 5 and 6 percent of the labor force.

Equilibrium income, therefore, may be greater than full employment, less than full employment, or correspond to full-employment income. We see all three of these possibilities represented in Figure 7-2. In *(a)*, the equilibrium level of income, E_y is less than the potential or full employment level, E_p. The GNP gap, $E_p - E_y$ is positive and the economy is operating with an unemployment rate above the natural rate. In *(b)*, the equilibrium level of income corresponds to the potential or full employment level ($E_y = E_p$). The economy is reaching its potential and operating at its natural rate of unemployment. In *(c)*, the equilibrium level of income, is above the potential level ($E_y > E_p$), and the GNP gap is less than zero. The economy is operating at less than its natural rate of unemployment.

When Real Income and the Price Level Change

What we have seen is that AD and AS determine in equilibrium the level of real income together with the level of prices. Now let's see what happens when either AD or AS changes.

Figure 7-2
Equilibrium Income, Actual Income, and the GNP Gap

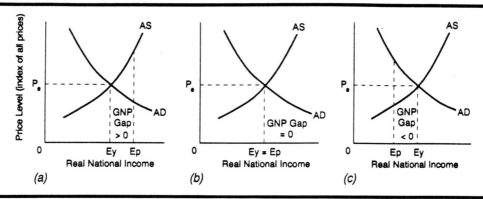

(a)   *(b)*   *(c)*

In *(a)*, the equilibrium level of income, Ey, is less than the potential or full employment level of income, Ep. The GNP gap Ep – Ey is positive. In *(b)*, the equilibrium level of income, Ey, equals the potential or full employment level of income and employment, EP. The GNP gap is zero, the economy is producing at potential with only the natural rate of unemployment. In *(c)*, the equilibrium level of income, Ey is greater than the potential or full employment level of income, Ep. The GNP gap Ey – Ep is negative.

Shifts In Aggregate Demand and Aggregate Supply

Aggregate Demand Shock
The term used to describe a shift of AD.

Aggregate Supply Shock
The term used to describe a shift of AS.

Aggregate demand shock is the term used to describe a shift in AD. A shift to the right is called an increase in AD and means that more real income will be demanded at each price level. A shift to the left is called a decrease in AD and means that less real income will be demanded at each level of prices.

      Aggregate supply shock is the term used to describe a shift in AS and means that more real product will be supplied at any price level. A shift to the left, on the other hand, means that less real product will be supplied at any price level.

      The most important point to remember from this is:

When either an AD or an AS shock occurs, there will be a change in the equilibrium level of income and product for an economy as well as a change in its level of prices.

Aggregate Demand Shocks:
Their Effects and Some Causes

We see in Figure 7-3 the effects of AD shocks. If AD increases, as from AD_1 to AD_2, both income and the price level increase as well (from $E_y{}^0$ to $E_y{}^1$ and from P_0 to P_1). If ad decreases, as from AD_2 to AD_1, both income and the price level decrease (from $E_y{}^1$ to $E_y{}^0$ and from P_1 to P_0). Both directions of change involve a movement along the short-run ggregate supply curve. For example, in the early 1980s, the U.S. faced "double-digit" inflation which was perceived to be a serious problem threatening the growth and

Figure 7-3
The Effects of Aggregate Demand Shocks

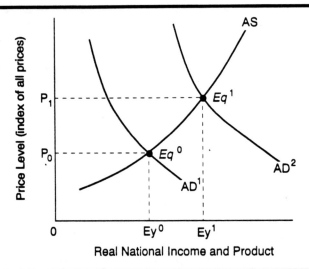

An increase in AD shifts the AD curve to the right from AD_1 to AD_2,. Equilibrium income increases from Ey^0 to Ey^1 in a movement along the upward sloping short-run AS, as prices rise from P_0 to P_1. The reverse occurs with a decrease in AD, decreasing equilibrium income to Ey^0 and prices to P_0.

stability of the economy. In response, the monetary authorities contracted the money supply sharply, reducing AD_1 and creating a severe recession with almost 10 percent unemployment and sharply falling inflation rates. In 1982-1983, AD increased in the face of tax cuts, budget deficits, and increased confidence. This resulted in growing income and falling unemployment, which has stabilized at less than 6 percent since 1987. Anything which causes households and firms to spend more at all price levels can shift AD to the right. Conversely, anything that causes households and consumers to spend less at all price levels can shift AD to the left.

Aggregate Supply Shocks: Their Effects and a Cause

In Figure 7-4, we can see the effects of AS shocks. If AS decreases, as from AS_0 to AS_1, equilibrium income decreases from E_y^0 to E_y^1 and the price level rises from P_0 to P_1. If AS increases, as from AS_1 to AS_0, equilibrium income rises from E_y^1 to E_y^0 and the price level declines from P_1 to P_0. Both directions of change in AS result in movements along the AD curve, AD. There are many things that can cause changes in AS as we have seen.

In the early- to mid-1970s, there was a dramatic and largely unexpected increase in energy prices, especially in the price of exported crude oil. As a result, the costs of producing virtually all commodities and services increased. This supply shock shifted AS to the left and contributed to reduced income, rising unemployment, and rising prices, a condition that came to be known as

Figure 7-4
The Effects of Aggregate Supply Shocks

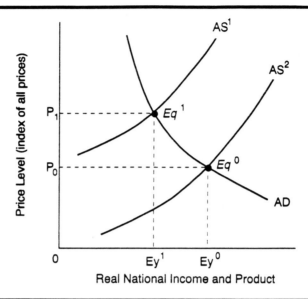

A decreasing AS shifts the AS curve to the left as from AS_0 to AS_1. Equilibrium income decreases from Ey^0 to Ey^1 and the level of prices increases from P_0 to P_1. The movement from Equilibrium to Equilibrium$_1$ is movement along the AD curve, AD. An increasing AS shifts the AS curve to the right as from AS_1 to AS_0. Equilibrium income increases from Ey^1 to Ey^0 and the level of prices decreases from P_1 to P_0. The movement from Equilibrium (Ey^1) to Equilibrium (Ey^0) is a movement along AD.

stagflation. We will look at this in more detail in the application to this chapter.

By the early- to mid-1980s, oil export prices began to grow more slowly and then to decline in absolute terms. Falling energy prices reduced the costs of supplying commodities and services, shifting AS to the right and contributing to rising real income and a declining price level. (Inflation rates actually became negative for a short period in 1987.)

Ranges of Aggregate Supply

The AS curves seen in Figures 7-1 through 7-4 were all upward sloping, showing that increasing quantities of commodities and services were associated with rising levels of prices. Clearly, however, the general state of the economy will determine whether production costs rise and how sharply they rise as output expands. We can identify three possible ranges of AS price-level relations. These three sections of AS we shall call (a) unemployment—an economy with large quantities of unemployed resources, (b) bottle-necks—the economy approaching full employment, and (c) full employment—the economy at capacity. We see all three conditions represented in Figure 7-5.

Figure 7-5
Ranges of Aggregate Supply

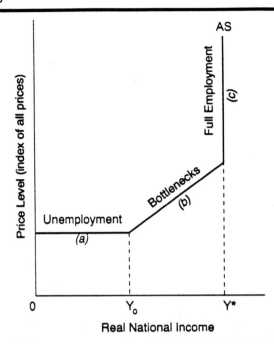

Range *(a)* represents an economy with large quantities of unemployed resources, an economy in recession or even depression. Range *(b)* represents an economy moving toward full employment and bidding less efficient resources into use as output grows; i.e., an economy with bottlenecks in supply responses. Range *(c)* represents an economy at full employment income (Y*); i.e., an economy that cannot increase real output, only prices.

Note: Ranges of AS are: (1) unemployment with many unemployed resources, (2) bottlenecks with fewer unemployed resources and a movement toward full employment, and (3) full employment, in which real output cannot rise.

In Figure 7-5, we see that in range *(a)*, the economy's real income can grow in response to changes in AD, and this growing income can be accomplished without an increase in overall prices. This stable price level growth can be maintained up to income level Y_0. In range *(b)*, the economy's real income can grow but presumably only with the rising costs associated with bottlenecks and drawing less productive resources into use. This growth with rising prices can be maintained up to income level Y*. In range *(c)*, at full employment, Y*, the economy can respond to further increases we demand only with rising prices. The economy at Y* has reached its production-possibilities frontier and until that frontier shifts outward from increasing endowments of resources or from improvements in technology, real output cannot grow.

The most important implication of these ranges is that efforts to increase real output, reduce unemployment and maintain stable price levels through changes in AD are crucially influenced by AS responses. If, for example, taxes are cut and disposable incomes increase, we would expect AD to increase. If the responding economy is in range *(a)*, real income will grow with stable prices. In range *(b)*, real income will grow but there will also be rising prices. In range *(c)*, real output cannot grow and the consequence of an AD increase will be inflation.

Supply-Side Economics

From the end of World War II to the early 1980s, national policies, including monetary and fiscal policies, focused on trying to change AD in the appropriate direction and amount necessary to create acceptable levels of employment and real income in the U.S. Such efforts were designed to create growing real income at relatively stable price levels. All such efforts seemed to grow, at least in part, from the commitments in the Employment Act of 1946, but stopped short of a commitment to full employment such as that in the (1978) Humphrey-Hawkins Act. The implicit assumption in all these efforts seemed to be that changes in aggregate quantities supplied would adjust to whatever level was required to create stable prices in the face of growing AD. In other words, the assumption seemed to be that the economy's supply responses would occur in range *(a)*.

In the 1980s, we have begun to hear from "supply-siders" who say that tax cuts and other incentives to increase AS are the recipe for economic growth with acceptable price stability. Some have even argued that cutting tax rates cannot only shift AS to the right and increase income at lower prices levels but even produce increases in tax revenues with which to deal with budget deficit problems. Supply-side advocates and supply-side skeptics are far from resolving their differences.

SUMMING UP

1. Rarely has the U.S. economy reached its potential in terms of real income at stable price levels. We have witnessed movements about this "target." Aggregate price levels and levels of income are established by the interaction of AD and AS. The equilibrium price level and the equilibrium level of income are established where aggregate quantity demanded equals aggregate quantity supplied. Equilibrium real income does not, however, necessarily correspond to desired real income.

2. Aggregate demand is measure of the entire desired spending on final goods and services at each level of prices. The four factors that make up and determine AD are (a) consumption expenditures (b) investment expenditures (c) government expenditures, and (d) net exports. Consumption expenditures depend on disposable incomes, cost and availability of credit and expectations. Investment expenditures depend on interest rates, the expectations of

producers, and government policy. Government expenditures are complex in determination but depend on such things as varying economic conditions, political philosophies, national emergencies and efforts to secure re-election. Net exports (exports minus imports) can be either negative or positive and depend on exchange rate changes, trade policy, and politics. AD, thus, is equal to consumption expenditures (C) + investment expenditures (I) + government expenditures (G) + net exports (X_m).

3. AD curves slope downward. The lower the price level, the greater the aggregate quantity demanded. The higher the price level, the lower the aggregate quantity demanded. The reason for the negative slope is not the same as with individual demand curves. Instead, the effects of interest rate changes, the effects of wealth changes, and the effects of relative price changes between domestic and foreign goods explain why AD slopes downward.

4. AS is a measure of the entire desired output of final goods and services at each level of prices and real income. The factors which affect AS are (a) cost and availability of resources, (b) capacity and investment plans, (c) technology, (d) productivity, and (e) government policy. Firms observe and act on increases in resource prices quickly as their total costs and profitability are affected. Any economy's AS is constrained in the short run by its capacity stock of plant and equipment and other productive resources. In the long run, this capacity is increased by investment. Technological change increases the productivity of all resources and both results from and causes investment. Productivity, output per unit of input, depends on many things, including investment in human capital. Concerns have been raised about slower productivity growth in the U.S. than in other industrial nations. Expectations play a role in all decision making including supply plans, and changes in these expectations may importantly affect such plans. Government policy has many influences on supply plans. Tariffs, tax rates, environmental decisions all affect costs and profitability and, thereby, supply.

5. AS curves slope upward. As the price level rises, aggregate quantity supplied rises. As the price level falls, aggregate quantity supplied falls. The explanation for the positive slope appears to lie in the ultimately rising real cost of production from using resources of diminishing productivity as aggregate income rises. Thus, short-run AS curves slope upward on the assumption that productivity diminishes but factor prices in the short run are constant as aggregate prices rise. This assumption has to be modified to examine long-run aggregate-supply conditions.

6. Equilibrium (actual) levels of real income and prices may or may not be equal to potential (full employment) levels. At full employment, an economy operates at its natural rate of unemployment or that corresponding to frictional unemployment with

inflation that neither tends to increase or decrease. Thus, equilibrium income and prices may create a GNP gap that is positive; i.e., an economy may operate with an unemployment rate greater than the natural rate. Alternatively, the economy may operate with an unemployment rate below the natural rate. Finally, equilibrium (actual) and potential (full employment) may be equal in which case the economy operates with its natural rate of unemployment, thought for the U.S. to be between 5 and 6 percent.

7. Equilibrium, real income, and price levels are subject to changes from demand shocks (changes in AD), as well as from supply shocks (changes in AS). Both AD and AS may increase or decrease. Either change will produce a change in the equilibrium level of income for the economy as well as a change in the level of prices.

8. An increase in AD will increase equilibrium real income and the price level and will cause a movement along the AS curve. A decrease in AD will decrease equilibrium real income and the price level and also cause a movement along the AS curve. Many factors including changes in the money supply and changes in government expenditure and taxation can cause such AD shocks.

9. An increase in AS will increase equilibrium real income and the price level and will cause a movement along the AD curve. A decrease in AS will decrease equilibrium income and increase the price level and will also cause a movement along the AD curve. Many factors, including all factors that change input prices and the costs of production, can cause such AS shocks.

10. General economic conditions determine whether and how much production costs change as output (supply) changes. The three ranges or possibilities of AS response are (a) unemployment—the economy has large quantities of unemployed resources, (b) bottlenecks—the economy is approaching full employment, and (c) full employment—the economy is operating at capacity. In range (a), AD growth will cause rising real income at a stable level of prices. In range (b), AD growth will cause rising real income but with rising levels of price. In range (c), AD growth in the short run can only result in rising prices since an increase in real income is unattainable.

11. For decades, public economic policy has focused on adjusting AD to accomplish macroeconomic objectives of income, employment, and price stability. By the 1980s, "supply-side" advocates voiced the view that public policy should center more on adjusting AS through enhanced incentives to production. The debate between the two groups continues.

KEY TERMS

Equilibrium level of prices and real income
Aggregate demand
Aggregate supply
nvestment in human capital
Aggregate demand shock
Aggregate supply shock
Ranges of aggregate supply

QUESTIONS

1. How are individual market prices for commodities and services established?

2. How do aggregate demand and aggregate supply interact to create an actual level of real income as well as a price level in an economy?

3. What is aggregate demand? What four components make up aggregate demand? What factors influence each component?

4. Which of the components of aggregate demand are largest and which are most volatile?

5. What are the three explanations for the negatively sloped aggregate demand curve? Is the reason for a negatively sloped aggregate demand curve the same as the reason for a negatively sloped demand curve for an individual good? If not, why not?

6. Upward sloping aggregate supply curves are based on what explanation? On what assumption about input prices is the short-run aggregate supply curve based? Would such an assumption be warranted in the long run?

7. How is aggregate supply defined? What influences determine aggregate supply?

8. What is the difference between the actual level of unemployment and the level of unemployment at full employment with a stable inflation rate called? Can this difference be zero? Why not?

9. Can the equilibrium level of income exceed the potential (full employment) level? If so, what is the relation between the natural and actual rates of unemployment?

10. If the equilibrium, (actual) national income and the potential (full employment) income are equal, with what rate of unemployment is the economy operating?

11. What is a demand shock? What is a supply shock? What affects will such shocks have on an economy's equilibrium income and price level?

12. What is meant by saying that "changes in aggregate demand cause movements along aggregate supply?" What may cause such changes in aggregate demand (demand shocks)?

13. What is meant by saying that "changes in aggregate supply cause movements along aggregate demand?" What may cause such changes in aggregate supply (supply shocks)?

14. "When aggregate demand changes, its effects on the price level depend on the range of aggregate supply in which the economy is operating." Explain.

15. What is the heart of the disagreement between "supply-siders" and "demand-siders" over achieving macroeconomic objectives?

16. Answer the questions below based on the information about aggregate demand (AD) and aggregate supply (AS) contained in the figure below.

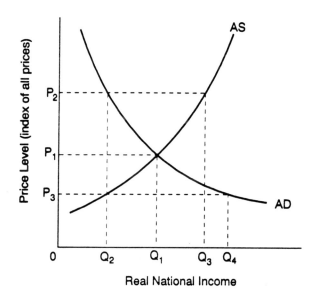

    a. The equilibrium level of income is (Q_2), (Q_3), or (Q_1)?
    b. The equilibrium level of prices is (P_2), (P_3), or (P_1)?
    c. At what price level $(P_3$, P_1, or $P_2)$ is their excess aggregate supply? Aggregate demand?

SUGGESTED READINGS

Bisignano, Joseph. "Impervious Behavior." Federal Reserve Bank of San Francisco Weekly Letter. September 23, 1984.

Hailstones, Thomas J. *A Guide to Supply-Side Economics*. Richmond, VA; Robert F. Dane, Inc., 1982.

Hailstones, Thomas J. (Ed.). *Viewpoints on Supply-Side Economics*. Richmond, VA; Robert F. Dane, Inc., 1982.

Hotson, John H. *Stagflation and the Bastard Keynesians*. Waterloo, Canada. University of Waterloo Press, 1976.

Juster, F. Thomas. "The Economics and Politics of the Supply-Side View" in McClelland, Peter D. (Ed.). *Introduction to Macroeconomics*. New York; McGraw-Hill, 1987.

Kimzey, Bruce W., *Reaganomics*. St. Paul: West Publishing Co., 1983.

Rasky, Susan F. "A New Generation of Non-Savers." New York Times, November 2, 1986.

Wanniski, Jude. *The Way the World Works*. New York; Simon and Schuster, 1978.

Application to Chapter 7: Supply Shocks: OPEC and Oil Prices in the 1970s

We have seen in the preceding chapter that the equilibrium value of real income and the aggregate price level associated with that income are determined by AD and AS. For an economy operating "normally" with some but not "depression level" excess capacity, AS slopes upward. This is so because of rising costs associated with larger quantities supplied. What happens though when the existing set of production costs are "shocked," shifted to a new higher level?

There is probably no clearer illustration of the answer to the above question than that which is found in the dramatic increases in oil prices in 1973-74 (OPEC I) and in 1979-80 (OPEC II). In a little more than 5 years, the real (discounted for inflation) price of oil increased by 600 percent. To appreciate the significance of these "shocks," recall that AS curves are based on costs of production and that they slope upward because of rising costs of larger quantities supplied from existing plant and equipment.

We saw in Figure 7-4 that supply shocks that raise the costs of production shift the AS curve upward or to the left. When this happens, we expect the equilibrium level of real national income to decrease and the price level (index of all prices) to rise. How great these effects will be depends in large measure on how much production costs have been raised. In the case of oil prices, the two shifts appear to have been quite significant. By one estimate, almost 5 percent of the world's gross product is composed of the value of oil production.[1] Putting this in perspective, it is likely that no other energy price, indeed no other resource price, reaches that level of significance. Thus, the shift in AS costs from a major change in such a price should be expected to be large.

We see the outlines of such a process in Figure A7-1. The very large increases in oil prices from OPEC II increased short-run production costs and shifted AS from AS (1979) to AS (1980). With a smaller supply, aggregate quantity demanded decreased and real income (GNP) declined with the economy spiraling into a major recession. The recession was accompanied by a strong inflationary pressure with consumer prices (including the price of gasoline and heating oil) rising from 217.4 to 246.8 or by 13.5 percent. America experienced "double digit" inflation for only the second time in its modern history. With a smaller AS, the demand for labor decreased and the unemployment rate among civilian laborers rose from 5.8 percent to 7.1 percent.

---

[1]Fried, Edward R., "World Oil Markets New Benefits, Old Concerns," in McClelland, Peter D., *Readings in Introductory Macroeconomics.* New York: McGraw Hill, 1988.

Figure A7-1
Aggregate Supply Shifts Resulting From Cost Shocks of Oil Prices in 1979-1980

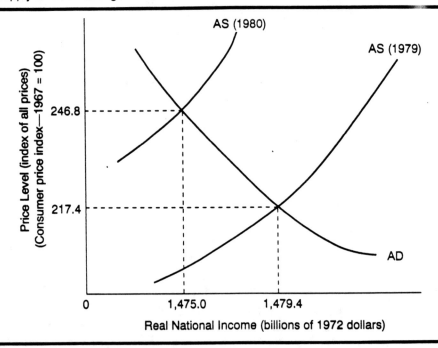

In 1979 OPEC announced major increases in oil export prices. The AS costs shifted upward from AS (1979) to AS (1980). As a result, real national income declined from 1,479.4 billion to 1,475.0 billion and the consumer price index rose from 217.4 to 246.8.

Was the entire set of macroeconomic effects attributable to the supply shock? Probably not, but most of the independent causality appears traceable to this major price-cost-supply shift. The main point is that employment, price levels, and real income can be affected dramatically not only by changes in AD, but also by changes in AS. This introduces a very troublesome element in national economic policy when such supply changes may be caused by forces difficult or impossible to effect with domestic policy measures.

We have chosen the 1979-1980 supply shock because it was a "pure price effect," one unaccompanied by other types of external shocks. The same effects might have been shown through OPEC I (the oil price change in 1974). In that instance, though, there was also an embargo with its own price and other supply effects.

Minimizing the Supply Shock

Many economists were surprised that income and price effects of OPEC II were not more dramatically adverse than they were. On reflection though, this should not be so surprising. Naturally, when the price of something as basic as energy increases sharply, consumers, including nations and firms, look for ways to minimize the costs to themselves. As Edward Fried has shown, in the case of OPEC II, the 1980s witnessed the following:

1. Energy use efficiency increased after the 1973-1974 shock. Energy was conserved as an input in production as well as in households.

2. Oil became less important as a source of energy. Oil became the relatively expensive source of energy; as a result, it declined from 55 percent to 45 percent of primary energy use.

3. At higher oil prices, many non-OPEC producers expanded output. For example, the fields in Mexico, the North Sea, and the coast of Alaska expanded output.

4. OPEC, as a cartel, found it increasingly difficult to maintain its monopoly prices. Lacking an effective means to discipline its members, it tried production quotas but the incentive to cheat on prices and quotas was intense.

5. Saudia Arabia, the lowest cost producer and holding 40 percent of the worlds reserves found its ability to maintain prices through adjusting its output increasing untenable.

As a consequence of the above, the quantities demanded of (OPEC and non-OPEC) oil proved to be smaller than anticipated. Quantities supplied, on the other hand, proved much larger. As a result, by the mid-1980s, downward pressures on oil prices became irresistible.

A Reverse Supply Shock: Oil Prices in the Late 1980s? The 1990s?

Between late 1985 and April 1986, average oil prices fell from $28 to $14 a barrel (a kind of *unintended* OPEC III). Go back to Figure A7-1, but reverse the direction of change in AS. Even though oil had become less influential as a source of energy, it was and remains very important in that regard. A major reduction in costs and a shift downward or to the right of AS occurred tending to reduce the consumer price index or at least its rate of growth. From 1985 to 1987, consumer prices rose by less than 6 percent. At the same time, the aggregate quantity demanded rose as price pressures diminished and real GNP rose by 6.2 percent. It would be wrong to think that both events were caused entirely by the reverse (positive) supply shock of dramatically falling oil prices. Indeed, other things (e.g., budget deficits) were happening to stimulate AD. The point, though, is that supply shocks can have positive as well as negative effects on inflationary pressures and growth in real income. They can, in other words, help to solve problems as well as create them.

SUMMING UP

1. When production costs are raised sharply by an event such as oil price increases, there is a shift upward or to the left of AS. This occurred twice (1973-1974, 1979-1980) (OPEC I, OPEC II).

2. According to economic principles, an upward shift in AS will cause a decline in the equilibrium level of real national income as well as an increase in the price level. Where the AS effect is large, the effects on income and prices will also be large.

3. In the case of OPEC II, the 1979-1980 oil prices increases were very large. As a result, prices rose by 13.5 percent and unemployment rose from 5.8 percent to 7.1 percent. Real income declined. Although it is unlikely that the entire set of effects can be traced to the supply shock, it was clearly a major factor.

4. Supply shocks, since they are often unpredictable and difficult, if not impossible to control, introduce an element of instability into national economic policy.

5. Supply shocks can be and tend to be minimized. In the case of OPEC II, efforts to minimize the effects led to increasing efficiency in energy use, a diminishing importance for oil as a primary energy source, increased output by non-OPEC suppliers, and, finally, decreasing stability of the oil cartel and reduced ability of Saudia Arabia to support oil prices.

6. By the mid-1980s, reductions in quantities demanded of oil and increases in quantities supplied made downward pressures on oil prices irresistible.

7. Average oil prices fell by 50 percent between late-1985 and April 1986. This helped set in motion a reverse or positive supply shock for the economy. The shift downward of AS helped to diminish price increases and to increase the equilibrium level of real income.

8. Supply shocks can have both negative and positive effects on the economy. They can help to solve economic problems as well as cause them.

QUESTIONS

1. What effect did the oil price increases of 1973-1974 (OPEC I) and 1979-1980 (OPEC II) have on aggregate supply?

2. According to economic principles, what macroeconomic effects will result from a decline in aggregate supply?

3. How important were the price, employment, and output effects of OPEC II?

4. Why is achieving national economic policy objectives more difficult in the face of supply shocks?

5. The price increases from OPEC II led to efforts to minimize their adverse effects. What things were done in these respects?

6. Oil prices fell dramatically in 1985-1986. From what did this seem to result? What happened to real income and employment as a result of "OPEC III"?

7. What should we expect to happen, in macroeconomic terms, as a result of "positive" supply shocks such as oil price decreases?

SUGGESTED READINGS

Armentano, D.T. "How to Create an Energy Crisis." World Research, Inc., San Diego, 1981. Reprinted in *Annual Editions, '82/83.* The Dushkin Publishing Group, Inc., Sluice Dock, Guilford, CT, 1982.

Fried, Edward R. "World Oil Markets: New Benefits, Old Concerns" in *Readings in Introductory Macroeconomics.* Peter D. McClelland. New York: McGraw-Hill, 1988.

Hall, Robert E. and Robert S. Pindyck. "The Conflicting Goals of National Energy Policy. *The Public Interest,* No. 47. Spring, 1977.

North, Douglass C. and Roger LeRoy Miller. "International Cartels" in *Economics of Public Issues,* 8th ed. New York: Harper and Row, 1990.

Thomas, Robert Paul. "Cartels: OPEC" in *Microeconomic Applications.* Belmont CA: Wadsworth, 1981.

Chapter 8:
Income and Employment:
The Keynesian Beginnings

I have called this book *The General Theory of Employment, Interest and Money,* placing the emphasis on the prefix *general.* The object of such a title is to contrast the character of my arguments and conclusions with those of the *classical* theory of the subject, upon which I was brought up and which dominates the economic thought, both practical and theoretical, of the governing and academic classes of this generation, as it has for a hundred years past. I shall argue that the postulates of the classical theory are applicable to a special case only and not to the general case, the situation which it assumes being a limiting point of the possible positions of equilibrium. Moreover, the characteristics of the special case assumed by the classical theory happen not to be those of the economic society in which we actually live, with the result that its teaching is misleading and disastrous if we attempt to apply it to the fact of experience.

Thus wrote John Maynard Keynes (rhymes with *gains*) in 1936, beginning the book that shook up the school of economics that had been dominant for over a hundred years. This book launched the "Keynesian revolution" in economics. Because of Keynes, many governments ultimately changed their policies. World leaders changed their minds about how various forces interact to determine the equilibrium level of income and employment and about how to control that level. It was, in short, a book that forced a lot of rethinking about economic issues.

A central problem of any economy is to control the destructive forces of unemployment and inflation. The Keynesian model has become a widely accepted economic theory by which people hope to understand, and ultimately solve, these urgent problems. Keynesian theory is not a cure-all and has indeed been subjected to much criticism, but it has many strengths.

In this chapter we will examine the foundations of the Keynesian model. This theory exercises great power over your money and your standard of living, and even the laws that govern you.

THE NEOCLASSICAL THEORY

Neoclassical Economics
A body of theories advanced in the 19th century. Among its arguments was the idea of a self-correcting economy that tended toward full employment.

Before Keyneswrote *The General Theory of Employment, Interest, and Money* in 1936, most economists belonged to the school of **neoclassical economics**, so-called to distinguish it from classical economics, a body of theories supported by economists who wrote prior to 1872. Many aspects of neoclassical economics are still accepted by most economists today. However, in this chapter we are analyzing only the neoclassical theory of income and employment. Keynes challenged some of the basic tenets of that theory. But many economists maintain that Keynes's changes lay within the general framework of neoclassical theory, and they continue to call Keynes a neoclassical economist.

Before 1936 neoclassical economists said that a market-oriented economy had enough built-in self-corrective mechanisms that if left to its own devices, its income would move to that level at which its labor force would be fully employed. They also claimed that if unemployment occurred (1) it would be due to temporary overproduction and would be quickly corrected by market forces, or (2) it would be due either to interference by the government or to insufficient degrees of competitions, or (3) it would be due to the unwillingness of workers to adjust their wage demands downward to market forces.

Three theories led economists to this conclusion that income would of its own accord move toward the level at which full employment exists: (1) Say's law; (2) the abstinence theory of interest; and (3) the theory of wage and price flexibility.

Say's Law

Say's Law
In its simple form, the law states that supply creates its own demand.

Jean Baptiste Say (1767-1832) was a French historian writing around 1800. Economists know him mainly for **Say's Law**. The simple version of that law is: *Supply creates its own demand.* We can best illustrate Say's law by the simple circular-flow model (Figure 8-1). Recall its basic premise that households provide all the resources—labor, land, capital, and entrepreneurship—to firms, and firms pay households for these resources. Using these resources, firms produce goods for consumption by households. In

Figure 8-1
Say's Law and the Simple Circular-Flow Model

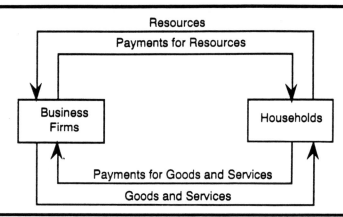

turn, households pay for these goods and services with the income they get from selling their resources to firms.

In terms of the simple circular-flow model, "supply creates its own demand" means that firms, while they are in the process of turning out all the goods and services that constitute supply, are at the same time acting as the sources of the income that households need to buy the firms' output. The level of that income is stabilized at the point of full employment because when firms employ all the labor available, households receive enough income to buy all the firms' output produced by that labor.

Say's law is stunning in its simplicity. Unfortunately, it does not hold up in real life, at least not in its simple form.

The Abstinence Theory of Interest

Neoclassical economists readily agreed that the simple circular-flow model illustrating Say's law was not adequate for an industrialized twentieth-century economy. However, they maintained that even a more complex circular-flow model (Figure 8-2) showed that income, left to itself, would move toward the level at which full employment would exist.

This is the neoclassical reasoning. Households must use some of their money for savings and taxes, which means that savings and taxes siphon off some income that they would otherwise spend on consumption. Firms get most of their support—that is, demand for their output—from households. But firms *also* derive support from two other sources: government expenditures and investment. Economists of the neoclassical school used to maintain that these four factors—taxes, savings, government expenditures and investment—could be linked so as not to disturb the basic theory that income would adjust itself to the level at which full employment existed.

Figure 8-2
The Complex Circular-Flow Model

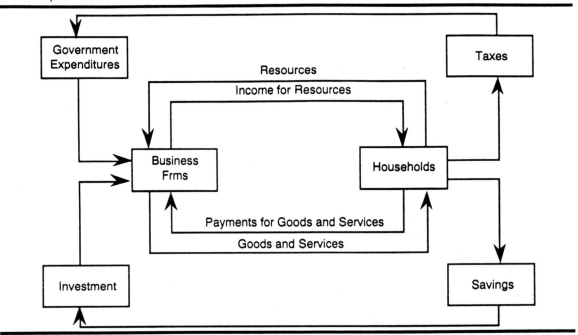

When people worried that these taxes and government expenditures would have a disturbing effect on this finely balanced model, the neoclassicists had an answer: Just see to it that government expenditures and taxes are *equal*, and keep them both at the lowest possible levels. They'll balance each other off, and this will keep the effects of government fiscal activity to a minimum.

What about savings and investment? Would *they* balance each other off? Or would they create an imbalance and perhaps cause instability and nudge income to a level that would mean less full employment?

Abstinence Theory of Interest
An argument that people will save because interest payments induce them to obstain from current consumption.

The neoclassical economists said that savings and investment would be coordinated through the medium of the interest rate. They explained this link by using the **abstinence theory of interest**. People prefer to consume goods and services now, rather than later, because present consumption yields greater satisfaction than future consumption. If people are to be induced to save—that is, to abstain from consumption—they must be given a reward. This reward is called *interest*. Given interest, the consumer is willing to abstain from present consumption, in other words, save. Then in the future the consumer will be able to consume more because he or she will have more money (savings plus interest) with which to do so. The higher the interest rate (the reward for saving), the larger the quantity saved. Thus, the abstinence theory of interest provides the link between savings and investment.

The amount of money saved determines the *supply of loanable funds*. As Figure 8-3 shows, the curve for the supply of

Figure 8-3
Supply of and Demand for Loanable Funds

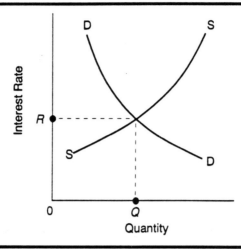

The supply of loanable funds (S) slopes up to the right because the higher the interest rate, the more people wish to save. The demand for loanable funds (D) slopes down to the right because the lower the interest rate, the more investment there is that yields a rate of return equal to or greater than the interest rate.

loanable funds slopes up to the right because the higher the interest rate, the larger the quantity saved. Therefore, the abstinence theory of interest explains why the supply of loanable funds slopes up to the right.

The decisions of businesses to expand their productive capacity by building new plant and equipment are what determine the *demand for loanable funds*. A person will make an investment when the return realized from that investment is at least equal to the cost of the interest on the money borrowed to make it. In other words, people make investments that have a rate of return equal to or greater than the interest rate. Neoclassical economists said that the rate of return on an investment was determined by its productivity and thus, in the long run, by the state of the economy's technology. The demand curve for loanable funds in Figure 8-3 slopes down to the right because falling interest rates make profitable greater amounts of investment. One could say that the interest rate is like rent paid on money. More investment is profitable at a 6 percent interest rate than at a 10 percent one, because the 6 percent rate also includes all investment that has a rate of return between 6 and 10 percent.

Thus, the interest rate links investment and savings. And the intersection between the supply of loanable funds (amount of money saved at different levels of interest) and the demand for loanable funds (amount of money invested at different rates of return) determines the equilibrium interest rate. The interest rate causes the savings that people wish to withhold from the demand for consumption to become equal to the investment that businessmen wish to add to the demand for consumption. The equality always becomes evident; demand always uses up the supply. The level of employment of resources still determines the level of income. The level of income still moves to full employment.

Wage-Price Flexibility

Neoclassical economists recognized that there can be temporary overproduction in certain areas, because of either errors in estimating consumer demand or a failure of the interest rate to bring what people are willing to save into line with what businesses are willing to invest. Fluctuations in the market prices of labor and of products, however, quickly wipe out these temporary states of overproduction. As overproduction develops, workers lose their jobs and start to compete with workers who are still employed. This has the effect of reducing wages. As wages fall, competition between firms forces prices down. Declining wages and declining prices together eliminate overproduction.

Elimination of overproduction is brought about by two effects of falling wages plus falling prices: (1) Total demand by workers is maintained, even though the money volume of spending declines, because prices of products fall in the same proportion as wages. Competition forces down wages, but also forces down prices. The neoclassicists assume that, because of competition, the decline in prices will be proportional to the decline in wages. The worker is no worse off, in effect, when wages fall 10 percent if prices also fall 10 percent. (2) The fall in prices causes those with savings to demand more goods, which eliminates excess supply. As prices fall, people with savings have greater wealth or purchasing power, their savings can buy more at the new lower prices. Feeling richer, savers buy more, and save less. This increase in savers' consumption, as prices in general fall, is called the **Pigou effect**, after its neoclassical originator, Arthur Pigou.

Pigou Effect
The argument that falling prices increase people's wealth or purchasing power and cause them to consume more.

To review: if the nation's budget is balanced (and balanced at a low level) so that government does not affect the market, and if there is enough competition in both the labor market and the product market, then the level of the nation's income automatically adjusts itself to the point at which there is full employment.

In the early-1930s the British government, in the throes of the Great Depression, sought answers from various neoclassical economists. Surely these economists could work some magical cure that would revive the economy so that the level of income would rise to the point of full employment. Obviously the mechanism that ordinarily achieved this state of affairs did not seem to be working (or quickly enough). Something was interfering with it.

Government fiscal activity was the culprit, said the neoclassicists. Let the government balance its budget and reduce its expenditures as much as possible, they ordered. So the British government in the early-1930s slashed its expenditures and raised its taxes. That will do for a start, said the neoclassical economists, but in addition, because wage-price flexibility is not working, you must counter the influence of labor unions by forcing down wages;

when the cost of wages falls, prices will fall, too, and demand will then increase.

John Maynard Keynes, pondering the situation from his chair at Cambridge University, disagreed with these recommendations. He believed that they would worsen rather than help the depression. Keynes's ideas had been anticipated by his fellow economists, and many of them were being discussed by his contemporaries. However, it was Keynes who finally put these ideas together.

THE KEYNESIAN CRITIQUE

Keynes, who died in 1946, has been rightly called the most influential economist of the twentieth century. His *general theory* refuted the neoclassical income-determination theory, that held that the level of income would automatically move toward a position in which there was full employment. His argument largely replaced neoclassical income theory for several decades. Lyndon Johnson was a Keynesian; Richard Nixon said, "We are all Keynesians," as did economist Milton Friedman. Today most, though not all, economists are Keynesians, in the sense that they at least accept certain of his basic ideas and use his framework of analysis. Some economists today even regard the Keynesian system of analysis and its policy recommendations as outdated.

What About Say's Law?

Keynes said that Say's law did not apply to a modern industrial society. In Say's eighteenth-century French world, production was small-scale and craft-oriented. People worked with simple machines, mostly made of wood. It did not take huge amounts of capital to repair them or replace them. Investment was therefore modest, and so was the need for savings. Households and firms (as viewed in the simple circular-flow model) were correspondingly small. Cottage industry abounded, and very often products were made to order. However, Say's law was an oversimplification even in his own day, because much of the French economy, and even more of the British, was taken over by larger-scale industries, as the Industrial Revolution accelerated during the latter part of the eighteenth century.

Neoclassical economists replied that they recognized the oversimplification of Say's law and came up with the complex circular-flow model, which made adjustments for the more complex world.

The Abstinence Theory of Interest: Not True

A major feature of the neoclassical theory of income was the *abstinence theory of interest*, which linked the desired level of savings (remember that savings always means decreased consumption) to the desired level of investment (which always means increased demand) through the interest rate. With government expenditures and taxes balanced, at the lowest possible levels, the neoclassical idea of the economic world seemed to be fairly valid.

But Keynes questioned the neoclassical theory that desired or planned savings and desired or planned investment are always linked. He sought to invalidate the abstinence theory of interest, as follows:

1. *Savers and investors are different groups and are differently motivated.* Business groups make all the investment decisions and base them on comparative costs and on returns on investment. Profitability is the main reason for investment. Households are the main savers. They outsave businesses, even though large corporations do save great amounts in the form of undistributed profits. But in a wealthy society, households also save great amounts. Their motivation for saving, however, naturally differs from that of the business investors. But the simple fact of these differences in motivation is not important. The important point is: *Why should the interest rate link savings and investment?*

2. *The interest rate does not determine the level of savings.* People who save are going to save regardless of the level of the interest rate, and their motives vary. Some save because of custom or morality. Some save to provide security in old age; some to pay for a large purchase, such as a house or automobile. Some save to provide a fund for emergencies; some save to send their children to college. In sum, *people's motivations for savings are varied and are not merely influenced by the level of the interest rate.* Therefore, a certain rate of interest is not necessarily required to make people save. Many people would probably set aside money each month even if no interest rate existed.

3. Not only did Keynes seek to break the tie between planned investment and savings, by showing that the interest rate did not solely determine the amount of savings, but he also weakened the tie between investment and the interest rate. He said that businesses, in computing the probable returns on their investments, had to estimate future business conditions. Therefore, if you want to analyze why businesses invest, you must take into account their expectations of future conditions. This inclusion of expectations—a psychological factor that the neoclassical economist failed to give any weight to—weakened the relationship between planned investment and the level of interest rates.

So economists, according to Keynes, were left without the comforting mechanism of the interest rate that coordinated savings and investment at full employment. Without this, the economy could experience declining demand and unemployment, or increasing demand with resulting rises in employment, and possibly inflation. Let us see why.

Look at Figure 8-2 again. If planned savings are greater than planned investment, consumer demand for the firms' output of consumer goods shrinks, and investment demand does not take up all the slack. So total demand falls, and along with it, output, income, and employment fall.

Now suppose the reverse occurs. Suppose that savings are less than planned investment. This means that savings do not cause consumer demand for the output of firms to decrease as much as investment causes the firms' output to increase. As total demand increases, so does output, income, and employment. Eventually, when full employment exists, further increases in demand only generate increases in prices.

Lack of Wage-Price Flexibility

What did Keynes have to say about the neoclassical economists' reliance on wage and price flexibility to correct any excess supply that might lead to unemployment? Remember that the neoclassicists said that a temporary oversupply of goods would cause unemployment, which would cause workers to compete harder for jobs, and that this would push wages down, which in turn would force prices down. Proportionate declines in wages and prices would leave real income unchanged, and thus real levels of demand for goods. People with savings would increase their level of consumption, and this would stimulate demand, and so on. Keynes said there were three factors that weakened this theory:

1. The flexibility of wages and prices is not great enough to generate these movements. Many corporations have so much monopoly power in product markets that they can keep prices from moving downward. Many labor unions also exercise monopoly power in factor markets in the same way; the unions are able to keep wages from moving downward. To Keynes's arguments, one can add that since 1936, governments have interfered more and more in the workings of the market, rendering it more inflexible. This has been true especially in the areas of minimum-wage laws and price-support systems for agriculture.

2. Even if wages and prices were both to decline, it is unlikely that real spending for goods and services would remain unchanged. After all, prices and wages never fall uniformly. Therefore, some groups would be hurt and some helped. And the two groups would never exactly offset each other. Furthermore, the burden of debt of workers would siphon away a large percentage of their incomes, thus cutting down on their spending. Finally, people are psychologically conditioned to plan their spending on the basis of money in hand rather than real income.

3. Even if one could overcome the obstacles generated by both factor 1 and factor 2, in order for the economy to expand very

much as a result of increased real savings brought about by a decline in prices, there would have to be sharp drops in prices, and prices would have to stay low for a long time. There are easier ways to stimulate demand during periods of excess supply.

To summarize the Keynesian view: (1) Wage-price flexibility does not exist in sufficient amounts. (2) If it did, real spending would drop anyway. (3) Even leaving aside factor 1 and factor 2, there are easier ways to eliminate a generalized excess supply in the economy.

Aggregate Supply: The Keynesian Assumptions

The Keynesian theory focuses on AD and its role in determining the level of real income and employment. The model treats price levels as constants in order to center on income and employment effects of AD and changes in demand.

What kind of supply behavior would be consistent with this simple Keynesian model of demand-determined real income at stable prices? The answer can be seen in Figure 8-4. Notice that short-run AS (SRAS) is horizontal; planned or desired output responds to all changes in AD at a constant level of prices (up to capacity levels of output). The economic conditions that would explain this are those in the range of AS in which there is substantial unemployment or excess capacity. This supply-price

Figure 8-4
Determination of Real Income with a Keynesian Short-Run Aggregate Supply Function

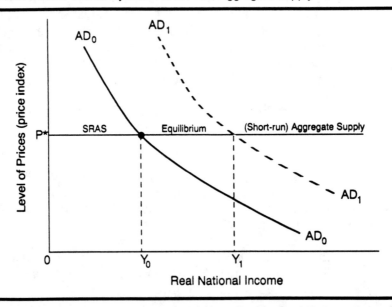

In a simple short-run Keynesian model, real income is determined by the location or amount of AD. Y_0 here is the equilibrium real income. A stable level of prices (P^*) is consistent with a growing real income up to the point at which bottlenecks appear.

relationship may be a reasonable assumption about firms offering to sell more at existing prices as long as they have idle or under utilized plant and equipment. In effect, firms have horizontal supply curves and the AS curve, as a result, is also horizontal at P*, the constant level of prices.

Note that in Figure 8-4, a change (shift) in AD, from AD_0 to AD_1, results in an increase in real income from Y_0 to Y_1. Both real incomes are consistent with the same level of prices, P*. The key point here is that:

Given the Keynesian assumption about SRAS, AD determines real income, and that demand can e adjusted to any level required to accomplish income and employment goals with stable prices.

THE KEYNESIAN CONCLUSIONS

Neoclassical economists, according to the Keynesian critique, were at least partially mistaken when they said that income would automatically move toward a level that would ensure full employment. Of course, the level of national income may arrive at a position at which there is full employment and relatively stable prices, but there are no mechanisms that ensure that if this occurs, it will do so in an acceptable period of time. Therefore, it is more likely that the level of income will be either at a position at which there is unemployment or at which there is inflation. Both states are undesirable. So let's ask ourselves, what factors determine the level of income?

In the Keynesian view, as we noted earlier, it is the level of *aggregate demand*, the total demand for commodities and services, that determines an economy's level of income. A business will produce only if it can expect profits. It can sell its goods only if there is demand for the product. In this case, what's true for one business is true for the entire economy: Output, and therefore income, will move in the same direction as AD. Increased income and employment will follow from increases in AD. Reduce demand and income and employment will suffer. But remember, according to Keynes, *there are no automatic market mechanisms that can force AD to the level at which there is full employment.*

Mercantilism
A school of economic thought that held that government should take the responsibility for maintaining economic welfare.

This being so, the implication of Keynes' theory is that to achieve full employment, the government must manipulate AD. Not since the days of **mercantilism**, from the sixteenth through the eighteenth centuries, has economic theory made it the responsibility of the government to maintain economic welfare. That is why some economists have called Keynes a modern-day mercantilist.

Incidentally, when we talk about the level of income here, we mean the *equilibrium income*. Recall from Figure 8-4 that equilibrium real income is established where aggregate quantity supplied equal to aggregate quantity demanded. It is the central tendency of real income that equates the plans of consumers with those of producers. It is the income we have after all the forces in the model have worked themselves out. It is a stable level of income, so long as the various factors in the model *do not* change.

There are five factors that determine the level of AD: (1) intended consumption, (2) intended savings, (3) intended investment, (4) government expenditures, and (5) taxes.

Three of these—consumption, investment, and government expenditures—make up *effective demand*. Increases in these items increase demand; decreases in any of them reduce demand. Savings and taxes siphon off the purchasing power of people and prevent them from using this money to satisfy their consumption demands.

Because these five factors determine demand, they also determine income and employment. So let's analyze the nature of the first three—consumption, savings, and investment—and show how they relate to changes in the level of income.

The Consumption Function

Consumption Function
A schedule showing the relationships between levels of income and quantities consumed during a particular period of time.

Savings Function
A schedule showing the amounts people save at different levels of income in a particular period of time.

Investment Function
A schedule showing the amounts people invest at different levels of income in a particular period of time.

You are already familiar with the idea of a function or curve. In the analysis of demand and supply, you saw that demand is not a relationship between a specific price and a specific quantity of a good or service, but between various quantities at various prices. When you draw a diagram of the demand schedule, it becomes a demand curve, which shows the functional relationships between prices and quantities demanded. The same thing is true for the **consumption function**. It is not a specific quantity consumed by people at some given income level; it is a schedule, showing the relationships between levels of income and quantities consumed during a particular period of time. A diagram of this schedule shows the functional relationship between income levels and quantities consumed.

The *consumption schedule*—or *function*—relates quantities consumed to levels of income. One must understand it in order to identify all the factors that influence the level of employment and income. Therefore, one must relate the various factors involved to income. So we shall deal not only with the consumption function—with how much people *consume* at different levels of income. We shall also deal with the **savings function**, the schedule showing amounts people *save* at different levels of income during a particular period of time, and with the **investment function**, the schedule showing amounts people *invest* at different levels of income during a given period of time.

Let's build our income model in steps, just as we did our supply-and-demand model. First we show consumption schedules for individuals; then we add individual schedules to get an economy-wide consumption schedule. We diagram this and have a consumption function or curve for the whole economy. Again, as before, we assume that income is the only thing that changes. All other factors affecting the quantity of goods and services that people consume are fixed.

One could construct a consumption schedule for an individual in much the same way as one constructs a demand schedule for an individual. Ask each individual how much she or he would spend on consumption at each level of income and how much he or she would save. Table 8-1 shows consumption schedules for 3 individuals, A, B, and C. Note that each differs from the other. However, each shows that quantity consumed increases with income—but *not as rapidly as income increases*. When one adds the consumption schedules and the income schedules of all the individuals, one obtains an economy-wide consumption schedule.

Table 8-2 is an example of a consumption schedule for an entire economy. It shows that at low levels of income, people live beyond their means by consuming more than income (income levels 210, 240, and 270). At income level 300, consumption just equals income and savings are zero. Above income level 300, consumption is less than income, so the economy can save as well as consume. Figure 8-5 is a diagram of the data in Table 8-2.

To bring our analysis into focus, we have drawn, in Figure 8-5, a line from the origin upward, at an angle of 45 degrees. We shall call that line the 45° line.

Note that 0A = AB = BC = C0. In other words, any point on the 45° line is equal to whatever is measured on the vertical axis.

There is argument about the exact shape of the consumption function. However, for our purposes, we make the simplifying assumption that the consumption function, C_f, is a straight line, slopes up to the right, and crosses the 45° line. Where the consumption function crosses the 45° line (at 300), quantity consumed is equal to income. Whenever the economy drops below income level 300, consumption is greater than income. For example, note in Table 8-2 that at level 210, consumption is 240, which leaves the economy 30 in the hole (negative savings). At that point, note in Figure 8-5 that the consumption function lies above the 45° line. When that happens, economists have a word for it: **dissavings**—the

Dissavings
The term used to describe negative savings by people in a society.

Table 8-1
Consumption Schedules for Individuals

A		B		C	
Income	Consumption	Income	Consumption	Income	Consumption
$2,000	$3,500	$2,000	$3,000	$2,000	$3,000
4,000	5,000	4,000	4,000	4,000	4,800
8,000	8,000	8,000	6,000	8,000	8,400
12,000	11,000	12,000	8,000	12,000	12,000
16,000	14,000	16,000	10,000	16,000	15,600
20,000	17,000	20,000	12,000	20,000	19,200
24,000	20,000	24,000	14,000	24,000	22,800
28,000	23,000	28,000	16,000	28,000	26,400

Table 8-2
Consumption and Savings Schedule

Income (billions of dollars)	Consumption (billions of dollars)	Savings (billions of dollars)
210	240	-30
240	260	-20
270	280	-10
300	300	0
330	320	10
360	340	20
390	360	30
420	380	40
450	400	50

Figure 8-5
The Relationship Between Income and Consumption

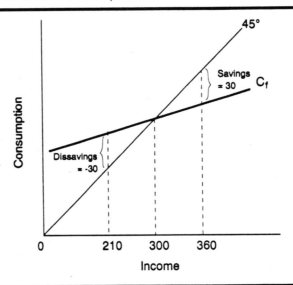

The distance from the income axis to the 45° line is the same as the distance from the 45° line to the consumption axis. Each point on the 45° line shows where income (the distance right on the axis) is equal to consumption (the distance up to the 45° line). Where the consumption function C_f crosses the 45° line, (at income 300) consumption is equal to income. Where the consumption function lies above the 45° line (income level 210) the distance from the 45° line to C represents dissaving (30). Where the consumption function lies below the 45° line (e.g., income = 360), the distance from C_f to the 45° line represents savings (30).

opposite of savings. Dissavings means that more is being consumed than is being produced within the economy.

On the other hand, if the income level is above 300 (e.g., at 360 in Figure 8-5), consumption for the economy is less than income, and the consumption function lies below the 45° line. The distance from the consumption function to the 45° line measures savings (30).

To sum up, if the economy's C_f is *below* the 45° line (income levels over 300), positive savings take place. If the C_f lies *above* the 45° line (income less than 300), negative savings, or dissavings, take place.

Everyone knows how easy it is for private citizens to consume more than their income and wind up dissaving. They perhaps start out by drawing on their savings, until the savings are gone; then they borrow or perhaps apply for public assistance. In a fairly similar way, an entire economy can consume more than it produces, and experience overall dissavings. An economy can draw on its accumulated savings, its capital stock, by the mere fact that it does not produce enough capital to replace worn-out and obsolete capital; its net investment becomes negative, and it comes face to face with dissavings. The economy can borrow from other countries, which means that foreigners' money gets invested in one's own country. Or it can obtain foreign aid, in the form of gifts or international charity. The last two options, borrowing or accepting charity, mean that more is imported than is exported. In other words, the economy is consuming more than it is producing.

The depression of the 1930s was so severe that in the U.S. and several other countries net investment was negative and consumption exceeded income. So the U.S. had dissavings. Israel, several times during its brief existence, has been forced into dissavings by the necessity of maintaining a strong military stance and the need to absorb a constant flood of new immigrants. Israel has financed its excess of consumption over income in part by international borrowing, but primarily by gifts from the world Jewish community, and especially by aid from friendly nations such as the U.S.

The Savings Function

Out of any given income, people either consume or save. So once you know the consumption schedule (see Table 8-2) or the consumption function (Figure 8-5), you can find the savings schedule and savings function, since savings is the act of *not* consuming. In brief:

$$income = consumption + savings.$$

In Table 8-2, the third column, the savings schedule, is the difference between income and consumption.

Figure 8-6, expresses this savings function graphically. However, you could have used the consumption function in Figure 8-6 to derive the savings function. The distance from the consumption function to the 45° line represents savings, either positive (incomes above 300) or negative (incomes below 300). If you measured off those distances on the income axis, with negative savings (dissavings) lying below the income axis, you would also have a savings function.

Figure 8-6
The Savings Function

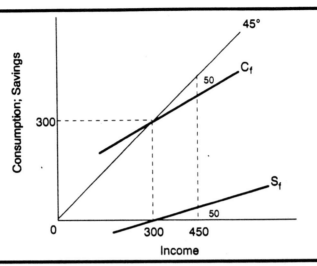

One can plot the savings function (S_f) from Table 8-2 or derive it from the consumption function (C_f). The distance from C_f to the 45° line measures savings. These distances should be marked off from the income axis to the savings function.

A Change in Consumption and Savings

When we talked about demand and supply, we stressed the distinction between a change in *quantity demanded* and a change in *demand*. The same distinction applies to other functions. A change in quantity consumed or quantity saved is a movement along a specific C_f (consumption function) or S_f (savings function) caused by a change in income. When a *non*income factor changes, it changes the entire schedule of consumption and savings and results in a shift of these functions. This constitutes a change in consumption and in savings. Let us look at the factors that can cause such shifts in consumption and savings.

Figure 8-7 shows a *change in quantity consumed* as a movement along C_1 from *A* to *B* because of a change in income. A *change in consumption* itself is a shift from C_1 to another consumption function, C_2, because of a change in one of the five *non*income factors listed below:

1. *Changes in social customs, mores, or attitudes toward savings.* Everyone knows about the Protestant ethic: hard work, thrift, rational investment. The stronger people's feelings about thrift, the higher the savings function. Today's young people seem to be less concerned with personal savings, since institutional programs, such as pension funds and insurance programs, have apparently reduced the perceived need for individual saving.

2. *Changes in assets of consumers.* There are three ways of looking at people's asset positions: (a) What are their liquid assets?

Figure 8-7
Change in Consumption and Change in Quantity Consumed

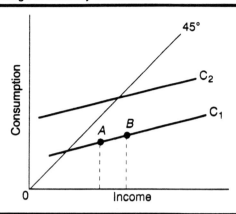

Liquid Assets
Assets such as savings accounts or government bonds that may be quickly converted into money.

(b) What is their debt level? (c) What is their stock of goods (especially durable goods)?

First, **liquid assets** are assets in the form of money or something that can be quickly converted into money, such as savings accounts and government bonds. People like to have some assets in liquid form for several reasons, mainly, being prepared for an emergency. Once people have accumulated comfortable amounts of liquid assets, they can use their incomes for consumption. Second, paying off debt reduces income available for consumption over a period of time. When people accumulate debt quickly, this temporarily increases their consumption. However, when people are paying off debt, they consume less, of necessity.

Since the level of debt affects consumption, the terms of consumer debts are important factors in determining consumption. What is the interest rate? How long a time will it take for repayment? These and other conditions of consumer loans encourage (or discourage) consumers from borrowing, and thus affect their level of consumption.

When you accumulate durable goods (cars, refrigerators, and so on), your consumption in the immediate future usually drops off sharply. If today you go on a spree and buy a washer, dryer, and color television set, you will probably not need new ones for several years, and this will surely lower your spending rate.

3. *Changes in expectations about future earnings.* If people expect that their earnings will increase in the future, and if they feel secure, they are inclined to consume more now than they would if things were otherwise. Young couples just starting a family borrow heavily to establish a home, expecting that their income will increase over the years. However, if there is a recession and they start to feel insecure about their jobs, or if inflation is cutting into their real income, people cut present consumption and increase their savings, to hedge against future want.

4. *Changes in taxes.* When taxes go up, the amount people have to spend on daily consumable items naturally becomes smaller, no matter what their income is. Households pay part of their taxes out of income that they would otherwise spend for consumption, and part out of income that they would save. The effect of increased taxes is to decrease both consumption (increased taxes shift the C_f down) and savings (taxes shift the S_f down).

5. *Changes in the distribution of income; changes in demographic (population) factors.* Changes in the way income is distributed have a strong effect on the consumption function. Poor people have to consume a much larger proportion of their incomes than rich people do. Therefore, if something happens to redistribute the wealth so that the poor get a larger portion of it, the consumption function will shift upward and slope upward at the same time. Changes in the age distribution of the population also affect the position of the consumption function. The larger the percentage of people in age groups that are not income earning, the more people there are who are consuming without working to finance that consumption (for instance, children and the elderly). The baby boom that lasted from 1945 through 1955 was a strong element in keeping consumption high. But the large drop in the birthrate over the period from 1955 to 1975 has reduced aggregate consumption in the succeeding period.

The five factors listed above can be divided into two broad categories: objective (or economic) factors and psychological factors. We consider changes in assets of consumers, changes in taxes, and changes in distribution of income and demographic factors to be objective or economic factors. We consider the psychological factors to be changes in social customs, mores, or attitudes toward savings, and changes in expectations about future earnings.

The Intended Investment Function

Autonomous Investment
Those investments not affected by changes in people's incomes and consumption.

Induced Investment
Those investments induced or generated by changes in income and consumption.

There are two kinds of investment: *autonomous* and *induced*. **Autonomous investment** is *not* affected by changes in people's incomes and consumption. It is affected by factors outside the model. In other words, the level of autonomous investment is independent of the factors within the model. **Induced investment**, on the other hand, is induced or generated by changes within the model— specifically by changes in income and consumption. For example, if the level of income increases, the quantity consumed also increases. This increases the need for plant and equipment (that is, for capacity) to produce the increased quantity of consumer goods demanded. This increased investment needed to expand capacity to take care of increased consumption is *induced* investment. For purposes of our model here, we shall assume that induced investment is zero and that we are dealing only with autonomous investment. Later, when we have completed our model, we shall add induced investment.

What Determines Autonomous Investment?

Businesses keep on investing—that is, creating capital—just as long as they expect that the returns from an investment are going to be at least equal to the cost of that investment. There are two factors that determine how much they invest. These factors are: (1) the cost of investing and (2) the expected rate of return.

1. *The interest rate.* When you invest your money in something, such as a machine or a building, and you put down some cash and borrow the rest. The cost of investing is not the price of the machine or building since you get this purchase price back by the device of *depreciation*, which is a legitimate cost of producing the product. Depreciation is built into the final price of any product. The *cost* of the investment is the interest that you must pay on the money you borrow to buy the something *or* the interest you forego by using your funds instead of lending them out. In other words, if you had not bought that something, you would have had an *opportunity* to lend your cash to somebody else and have interest payments flowing back to you.

Marginal Efficiency of Capital (MEC) The expected rate of return on capital.

2. *Marginal efficiency of capital (MEC).* The MEC is the expected rate of return on capital. In other words, it is the stream of income that businesses expect to get over the life of the capital relative to its price. Two main things, plus a number of smaller factors, determine the marginal efficiency of capital:

a. *Productivity of capital.* The more productive the capital, the greater the profit one can expect to get back from an investment. The productivity of capital changes with the development of new machines that reduce the costs of labor or capital, or with the development of a new process, a new product, or new markets. So it can be said that any growth in productivity means greater potential profits to investors.

b. *Expectations.* Since the MEC deals with future returns, it is bound to be influenced by the future economic activity investors expect. This introduces a psychological and potentially irrational element. A President may have a heart attack, a new kind of plane may crash, or meteorologists may predict a severe winter—and people in business may overreact. They may become more pessimistic, or more optimistic, than economic conditions warrant, and their attitudes may change almost overnight.

c. *Other factors.* Some of the other factors that affect the MEC are the price of capital itself (for example, the sale price of a machine); the risks connected with the investment; taxation (especially in the case of taxes such as investment tax credits, that are directly tied to the investment); and in the case of house construction, population growth and migration.

How Much Investment Will People Make?

Figure 8-8 shows how to go about figuring how much autonomous investment is likely to be made. The MEC curve shows the quantity of investment likely to yield an expected rate of return equal to, or greater than, the interest rate. The MEC curve slopes down to the right. This is so because as the interest rate falls, larger amounts of investment (capital instruments) will yield an expected return equal to or greater than the interest rate.

Instability of Investment

In good times and bad, over the years consumption and savings have shown amazing stability. Gross private domestic investment, on the other hand, has varied greatly as Figure 8-9 shows. You can understand this pattern of investment if you just stop to think of the instability of the factors that determine the quantity invested. Interest rates fluctuate widely. The influences on people's expectations about the future are both rational and irrational. The flow of technological innovations is not even, so that industry improves its production techniques in fits and starts. Furthermore, the government itself may inject instability into the investment scene through changes in its economic policies and through loss of public confidence due to scandals.

However, since World War II, a number of changes have tended to increase the stability of investment. For one thing, the Employment Act of 1946 committed the government to economic stabilization. This has probably given business people greater confidence than they formerly had and reduced the likelihood of short-term variations in investment. Corporate retained earnings increased, so that corporations have not had to depend so heavily

Figure 8-8
Factors That Determine Autonomous Investment

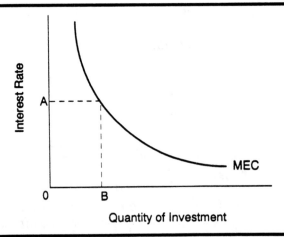

The marginal efficiency of capital (MEC) curve shows the quantity of investment at various interest rates. Investments must yield a rate of return equal to or greater than the interest rate. To find out how much investment is likely to take place, one must know the rate of interest that an investor is going to have to pay in order to borrow the money to make the investment.

Figure 8-9
Annual Changes in Real Gross Private Investment and GNP, 1950-1989

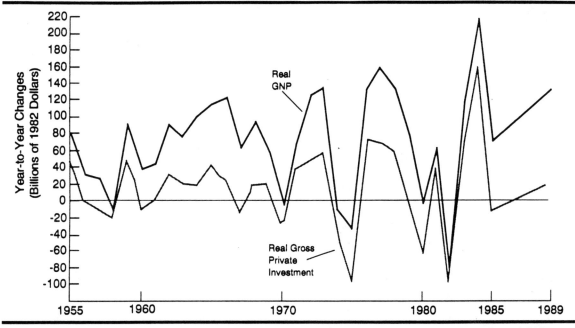

Variations in real gross private domestic investment are much larger and sharper than those in real GNP.

Source: Economic Report of the President, 1990.

on the capital markets for investment funds. However, investment is still the most unstable component in the AD model of income.

How Does Investment Fit Into Our Model?

We have made a number of assumptions: (1) We have assumed that the consumption function is a straight line that slopes up to the right. This means that as people's income increase, they spend more on consumer goods, but they spend lower *percentages* of their incomes on these goods. (2) We are including in our category of intended investment only autonomous investment. (To review, *autonomous* investment is investment that is not affected by people's levels of income.)

Now look at Figure 8-10, which takes two different approaches to the matter of intended investment as it relates to the equilibrium level of income. (Note that II in Figure 8-10 stands for intended investment, *not* roman numeral two!) Remember that the equilibrium level of income is the one that will not change unless one of the factors in the model changes.

Savings-Equals-Intended-Investment Approach
The determination of equilibrium income by equating savings and intended investment.

One approach—called the **savings-equals-intended-investment approach**—is the bottom of the diagram. This shows the relation of savings (which *reduces* consumer demand) to investment (which *adds* to consumer demand). Note that the intended

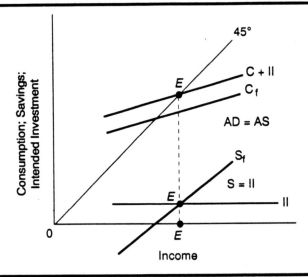

The bottom of the diagram shows intended investment in relation to savings. To find equilibrium income (E), one assumes that savings equals intended investment. Or one can add intended investment to the consumption function, so that AD equals AS. Both approaches give the same equilibrium income (E).

intended investment function that intersects the savings function is parallel to the income axis. Since the vertical distance from the income axis to the II function measures intended investment, and since it must be the same at all levels of income if it is to be consistent with the fact that investment is not affected by income, the two lines are parallel.

Aggregate-Demand-Equals-Aggregate-Supply Approach
The determination of equilibrium income by equating aggregate demand and aggregate supply.

The second approach—called the **aggregate-demand-equals-aggregate-supply approach**—adds the intended investment function to the consumption function. Putting the II function here points up the relation of AD to AS. Note again that C + II is parallel to the consumption function (C_f). The vertical distance from C_f to C + II measures intended investment. Since intended investment must be the same at all levels of income if it is to be consistent with the fact that autonomous investment is not affected by income, the two lines are parallel.

SUMMING UP

1. *Neoclassical economics* theorized that in a market-oriented economy the level of income would automatically move to a position at which there would be full employment. Three theories supported this conclusion: (a) Say's law, (b) the abstinence theory of interest, and (c) the theory of wage and price flexibility.

2. *Say's law* states in its simple form that supply creates its own demand. In terms of the simple circular-flow model, owners of

resources receive incomes generated by producing supply and use those incomes to buy the total supply of goods and services that the economy produces.

3. In terms of the complex circular-flow model, the neoclassicists said that taxes and government expenditures need not have disturbing effects if both factors were kept equal and balanced at as low a level as possible. The way to get rid of the disturbing effects of savings and investment is through the rate of interest, as analyzed in the abstinence theory of interest.

4. The *abstinence theory of interest* states that people would rather consume now than save now and consume later. Therefore, people need a reward—interest on savings—to make them save. The higher the reward, the larger the quantity saved. Thus, the curve showing quantities of loanable funds saved slopes up to the right when measured against the interest rate.

5. How much people invest depends on the rate of return, which in turn depends on the productivity of technology. Thus, the curve showing the quantities of loanable funds demanded at various interest rates slopes down to the right. More investment yields returns equal to (or greater than) the interest rate at a lower interest rate than at higher interest rates.

6. The equilibrium interest rate is the rate at which the *quantity supplied* of loanable funds is equal to the quantity *demand* for the loanable funds. Therefore, the interest rate is the stabilizer that causes the amount of savings people wish to accrue (decreasing demand) to equal the amount of investment people wish to make (increasing demand).

7. If industry produces a temporary surplus, this surplus is quickly eliminated, because industry lays off workers, and the unemployed then compete for jobs, so wages fall. Also, as firms compete to sell off excess goods, prices fall. However, the worker's real income, and in general real demand, do not fall, since wages and prices fall proportionately. Because lower prices mean that the purchasing power of each dollar is greater, people with savings feel wealthier and thus increase the quantity of goods and services they demand (the *Pigou effect*).

8. John M. Keynes, in his 1936 book, *The General Theory of Employment, Interest, and Money*, rejected the neoclassical conclusion that income always tends toward a position at which there is full employment.

9. Keynes said that Say's law was a gross oversimplification not only of the twentieth-century industrial world but also of Say's own eighteenth-century French world.

10. Keynes felt that the abstinence theory of interest was not valid because the interest rate does not correlate intended savings with intended investment, for these reasons: (a) The people who save are different from the people who invest and have different motivations. (b) The interest rate does not determine the level of savings, since the reasons why people save are largely unrelated to the level of the interest rate. (c) Business groups' expectations of the future are not strongly affected by the interest rate. Expectations are largely a psychological factor. Yet they have a strong influence on the rate of investment. These criticisms by Keynes weakened the traditional belief in the relationship between investment and the interest rate.

11. Since the interest rate does not correlate savings and investment, desired savings can exceed desired investment. This reduces demand, and, eventually, income. On the other hand, desired savings can be *less* than desired investment. People can spend too freely. This increases demand and income.

12. Keynes attacked the remaining support of the neoclassical income theory—wage and price flexibility—by making the following arguments: (a) Wages and prices are not flexible enough because there is not enough competition. (b) Even if wages and prices were to be flexible enough, real spending would drop anyway. (c) Leaving (a) and (b) out of the picture, there are easier and faster ways to get rid of a general excess supply of goods and services in the economy.

13. In the Keynesian model, it is AD that determines the level of income and employment. At least in the short run, price levels are considered constants since AS is in the range in which prices do not rise as AD increases.

14. The AS behavior that is consistent with the Keynesian assumption about constant price levels is one in which the AS curve is horizontal to the real income axis. Desired output responds to all changes in AD at a constant level of prices. Firms offer more for sale at existing prices, at least up to capacity rates of output.

15. Keynes concludes: (a) There is no market mechanism to make the actual level of income coincide with the preferred level of income at full employment. The actual level may exist at full employment, at less-than-full employment, or at full employment with inflation. (b) The level of income is determined by the level of *AD*, in other words, by the total spending in the economy.

16. Five factors determine the level of AD: intended consumption, intended investment, government expenditures (these three add to effective demand), intended savings, and taxes (these two detract from effective demand.)

17. The *consumption function* shows the functional relationship between quantities consumed and various levels of income. One assumes two things: (a) that all *non*income factors affecting the quantity consumed are fixed, and (b) that the consumption function is a straight line that crosses the 45° line (consumption is equal to income at that point) and slopes upward.

18. One can derive the *savings function* from the consumption function, since income is equal to consumption plus savings. Therefore, the difference between consumption and income is savings. The savings function is a straight line that crosses the horizontal axis and slopes upward. The distance from the savings function to the horizontal axis is equal to the distance from the consumption function to the 45° line.

19. A change in the quantity consumed or saved is due to a change in income, which causes a movement along the curve of the consumption or savings function. A change in both consumption and savings is due to a change in a *non*income factor, which causes the whole consumption and savings functions to shift.

20. Nonincome factors that may cause a change in consumption and savings are (a) changes in social customs, mores, or attitudes toward savings, (b) changes in assets of consumers (both quantity and composition), (c) changes in expectations about future earnings, (d) changes in taxes, and (e) changes in distribution of income and changes in demography (the distribution and density of population).

21. There are two kinds of investment: autonomous and induced. *Autonomous investment* is influenced only by factors other than income and consumption. *Induced investment* is determined by changes in income and in quantity consumed. To keep our model simple, we assume here that induced investment is zero.

22. People make that amount of investment for which they can expect a rate of return equal to or greater than the cost of the investment. The cost of an investment is equal to the interest paid for the funds needed to finance it. The expected rate of return is the *marginal efficiency of capital*, and it is determined primarily by increases in productivity and by expectations of future economic activity.

23. Of the three components that increase effective demand, investment is the most variable. The reason is that there are fluctuations in the three main factors determining the volume of investment: interest rates, expectations of the future, and the flow of technological improvements.

24. If one is making a diagram of the relation between consumption, savings, and intended investment, one can put the intended

investment function above the horizontal axis, and it will intersect the savings function. This emphasizes the relation of savings (which reduce the demand for consumption) to investment (which adds to it). This is called the *savings-equals-intended-investment approach*.

25. Alternatively, one can add the intended investment function to the consumption function; this is called AD. This function emphasizes the effect of total demand on income and is called the *aggregate-demand-equals-aggregate-supply approach*.

KEY TERMS

Neoclassical economics
Say's law
Abstinence theory of interest
Pigou effect
Mercantilism
Consumption function
Savings function
Investment function
Dissavings
Liquid assets
Autonomous investment
Induced investment
Marginal efficiency of capital
Savings-equals-intended-investment approach
Aggregate-demand-equals-aggregate supply approach

QUESTIONS

1. Explain how a neoclassical economist would defend the conclusion that the level of income always tends to move toward a point at which there is full employment. Include the role of Say's law, the abstinence theory of interest, and wage-price flexibility.

2. How did Keynes refute the neoclassical conclusion about income and employment, especially as it referred to the three foundations of neoclassical theory: Say's law, the abstinence theory of interest, and wage-price flexibility?

3. What was Keynes' conclusion about the relationship between income and full employment? How is the level of income determined, according to Keynes? What is the Keynesian assumption about aggregate supply?

4. What are the five factors that determine aggregate demand? How do changes in each of the five affect effective demand?

5. Which of the following factors change the quantity people consume or save, and in what direction? Why?

  a. An increase in the holding of consumer durables.

  b. A decrease in taxes.

  c. An increased desire for security in old age.

  d. An increase in income.

  e. A decrease in the amount of money that people hold.

6. Answer the following questions based on the figure below:

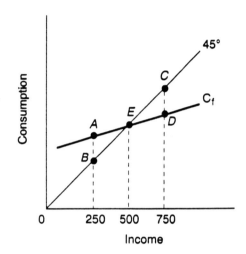

  a. The equilibrium level of income in the figure above is (1) 250, (2) 500, or (3) 750?

  b. Dissavings in the figure above is represented by the distance (1) *CD*, or (2) *AB*?

  c. Savings in the figure above is represented by the distance (1) *CD*, or (2) *AB*?

7. Distinguish between autonomous and induced investment.

8. Does autonomous investment increase or decrease when the following things happen? Why?

  a. The interest rate increases.

  b. A new breakthrough in science opens up new areas of technological innovation for industry.

  c. The stock market collapses and the general feeling is one of pessimism.

Chapter 9:
Income and Employment Without Government

Before we go any further, let's review the conclusions drawn from the Keynesian model.

1. The neoclassical theory that income will automatically move to a position at which there is full employment does not hold true. The abstinence theory of interest is also wrong, in that the interest rate does not link savings to investment. Also, the flexibility of wages and prices is not great enough to quickly correct an oversupply of an economy's goods and services.

2. The factor that determines an economy's level of real income is the volume of aggregate demand in the economy. This conclusion is based on the assumption that aggregate supply will adjust to any level of aggregate demand at a constant level of prices (up to capacity).

3. This real income level set by the total volume of spending is not necessarily the desired level for employment and prices. Our system may not be capable of automatically bringing about full employment and an acceptable level of prices, because of the problems cited above in conclusion 1. That, according to this argument, is why the U.S. often has unemployment and/or inflation.

4. Five factors determine the level of aggregate demand (and thus of income): consumption, savings, investment, government expenditures, and taxes.

Note: The market system in the U.S. creates a level of income that frequently does not lead itself to full employment and stable prices. The economy, if left to its own devices, may—and in fact often *does*—embody unacceptable amounts of unemployment and/or inflation. This has lead some, especially Keynesians, to argue that the U.S. system of private capitalism may simply have a tendency toward less than full employment and/or higher than desired levels of inflation.

In Application to this chapter, we will explore this question about whether there is inherent instability of the market economy of the U.S., by looking at the history of business cycles since 1920.

Now we will again build a simple model to enable us to approach a hard subject. Let's leave government out of the model for now and say that government expenditures and taxes are both zero. This leaves us with only three factors to deal with: consumption, savings, and investment. Now let's see what happens.

THE SIMPLE MODEL

Savings Equals Intended Investment

Figure 9-1 shows the intended investment function (II) parallel to the horizontal axis and intersecting the savings function (S_f). This placement, which emphasizes the relation of investment to savings, is called the *savings-equals-intended-investment approach*. It shows the relation of savings, which diverts people's money away from their demand for goods and services, to investment, which

Figure 9-1
Simple Model: Savings Equals Intended Investment

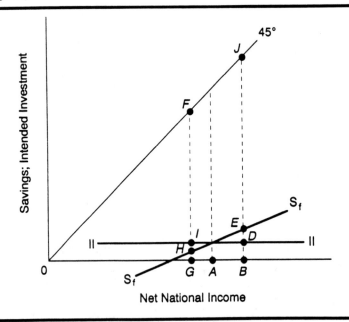

Equilibrium income is that amount of income at which savings equals investment: income *A* (360). Income levels above it (*B* = 420) yield involuntary (unplanned) additions to inventory (*DE* = 20). Income levels below it (*G* = 330) yield involuntary decreases in inventory (*HI* = 10).

supplements or adds to consumption demand. For example, you save money for a down payment on a house by denying yourself many things you would like to have. Then, when you buy the house, you invest, by paying out the capital you have created to buy the house. You increase demand for output from many firms—output needed to build the house.

What is the equilibrium level of income? And what does it take to maintain it? We have defined equilibrium income, but let's review it. Equilibrium *price* is the central tendency of the market, a price that doesn't change as long as supply and demand doesn't change. Furthermore, any price other than the equilibrium price automatically triggers forces that push the price toward the equilibrium point. In the same way, the equilibrium level of *income* is the central tendency of the economy. That level of income will not change so long as the factors in the model (consumption, savings, and investment) do not change. Any other level of income would be unstable and would trigger economic forces that push the level of income toward equilibrium.

Now look at Table 9-1. Note that investment is constant at 20, because we include only autonomous investment, which does not change when income changes. In the savings-equals-intended-investment approach, the equilibrium level of income is 360 (the same as income A in Figure 9-1).

When an economy's consumption, savings, and investment are as shown in Figure 9-1 and Table 9-1, the equilibrium level of income is the level at which savings equals investment (income level A in Figure 9-1 and 360 in Table 9-1.) To prove this, one must first show that the economy cannot maintain income levels above A (or 360) and then show that it similarly cannot maintain income levels below A (360).

From here on, we will cite Figure 9-1 only, and after each reference to Figure 9-1, there will be numbers in parentheses that refer to corresponding points in Table 9-1. If you follow the discussion on both the diagram and the table, you will understand the explanation better.

Table 9-1
Savings Equals Intended Investment (billions of dollars)

Income	Consumption	Savings	Intended Investment
210	240	−30	20
240	260	−20	20
270	280	−10	20
300	300	0	20
330	320	10	20
360	340	20	20
390	360	30	20
420	380	40	20
450	400	50	20

Now bear in mind that businesses produce most of their goods and services with the intention of selling them to consumers. However, they do set aside a portion of their output for investment. Let's say that at income B (420), which is above the equilibrium level, businesses produce BD (20) for investment (BD is the distance from the horizontal axis to the intended investment function, II). This leaves DF (400) remaining for the public to consume.

But the public has its own ideas. Let's say that people plan to save BE (40), which is the distance from point B to the savings function (S_f). This leaves a gap here, because businesses produce DF (400) for consumption, and people consume only EF (380). Business firms are left with the remainder, DE (20), as unsold output, which must be added to their inventory. This is called **unplanned** or **involuntary additions to inventory** (because inventories are defined as business investment).

Unplanned or Involuntary Additions to Inventory
The excess of what businesses plan to produce over what households plan to consume.

Business firms that have this unwanted inventory stashed in their warehouses or on the shelves of their stores must reduce orders to the companies that supply them with raw materials. Manufacturers cut production, which reduces their income, so they must lay off workers. Gradually, the economy takes a turn downward, moving from income level B (420) back toward the equilibrium income level A (360). This happens because at any level above A (360), what businesses produce for consumption is greater than what consumers wish to consume. Note that the savings function lies above the intended investment function. Business firms are forced to hold these unwanted additions in their inventories. They react by reducing inventories—and income.

Now, at any level below the equilibrium income, which for our purposes is G (330), businesses produce GI (20) for investment, which is more than the amount people save, GH (10). They also produce IJ (310) for consumption, which is less than what the public wants to consume, HJ (320). Now people are consuming more than businesses produce for consumption. When they do this, they reduce business inventories. Thus there are **unplanned** or **involuntary reductions in inventories** equal to HI (10).

Unplanned or Involuntary Reductions in Inventory
The excess of what households plan to consume over what businesses plan to produce.

When businesses find that their inventories are slipping below what they want them to be, they order more from their suppliers to replenish the inventories. Manufacturers then increase output, which increases their income, so they hire more workers. The economy moves from income level G (330) toward the equilibrium level of income A (360). Any lower income would result in unplanned decreases in inventories.

Income level A (360) is an equilibrium level because, at that level, what businesses plan to produce for investment is equal to what the public plans to save, and what businesses plan to produce for consumption is equal to what the public plans to consume. The plans of businesses mesh with the plans of the public.

In this state of balance, businesses have neither *involuntary accumulation* of inventories (in which businesses produce *more* than people consume, and their savings function lies above the intended investment function) nor *involuntary reduction* in inventories (in which businesses produce *less* than people consume, and the savings function lies below the intended investment function). What they plan in the way of inventory is what they get.

To summarize: At equilibrium income, people's savings equal business firms' intended investment. At income levels *above* equilibrium, businesses want to invest *less* than what people want to save. As a result, consumers demand less than what businesses produce for consumption. (Bear in mind that businesses *must* produce at a certain level of output just to maintain a given level of income.) So when cost-conscious citizens, intent on saving money, buy fewer consumer goods and services than businesses offer for sale, company executives watch gloomily as their warehouses fill with unwanted inventory. They must somehow dispose of this inventory. First they reduce orders to the manufacturers; then they may offer the goods for sale at lower prices.

At income levels *below* the equilibrium, the reverse occurs. Businesses want to invest *more* than the amount people want to save. As a result, consumers are willing to buy more than businesses have for sale. So inventories fall to such a point that businesses increase their volume of new orders. Business output increases, and so does business income.

Ex-ante and Ex-post Investment

By now you can see that there is a strong relationship between savings and investment. The key aspect of this relationship is that *savings reduce demand* (by lowering the level of people's consumption), while *investment adds to demand* (that is, adds investment demand to consumer demand for the output of business). In order to arrive at an equilibrium level of income, savings and investment must balance off at a level that both businesses and consumers want. The demand of businesses for investment has to equal the demand of consumers for a given amount of savings. When these two factors are not equal—when the balance is out of kilter—businesses take steps to remedy the situation, by changing their incomes and their number of employees.

It is this important relation of savings to investment that calls attention to the distinction between ex-ante and ex-post investment.

Ex-ante Investment
Planned investments by firms.

Ex-post Investment
Actual investments by firms.

Ex-ante investment is the amount of investment that businesses plan to make.

Ex-post investment is the amount of investment that they actually do make.

(A device to help you remember: *ante* means before and *post* means after.)

To get a clear idea of this relation, look again at Figure 9-1 and Table 9-1. We are going to use the same letters and numbers we used before. (Again, after the letters from Figure 9-1, we will include the corresponding figures from Table 9-1, in parentheses.)

In Figure 9-1, at income level *B* (420), ex-ante or planned investment is equal to *BD* (20), while ex-post or actual investment is equal to *BE* (40). This is because unplanned accumulations to inventory *DE* (20) are added to ex-ante (planned) inventories, and inventories are considered investment. This means that businesses are in an uncomfortable position. Their actual investment is twice what they planned.

At income level *G* (330), businesses are again in a bad spot, because their ex-ante (planned) investment is *GI* (20), while their ex-post (actual) investment is *GH* (10)—only half of what they planned. This is because unplanned reductions in inventory *HI* (10) are deducted from ex-ante (planned) inventories.

In both cases, business firms' ex-post (actual) investment is equal to consumers' ex-post (actual) savings. This equality is due either to unplanned additions to inventories or to unplanned subtractions from them. One has to take into account the fact that *inventories*—whether planned or unplanned—*are part of investment.*

However, an economy does not achieve equilibrium income simply because it arrives at a point at which actual investment equals actual savings. Unplanned (involuntary) changes in inventory cause businesses to either reduce or increase their orders to manufacturers. These changes in orders naturally cause the level of output to either rise or fall, and with it, the level of income and employment. Each factor affects each other factor. Only at the equilibrium level does ex-ante (planned) investment by business equal ex-post (actual) savings by consumers. At that point, all expectations are met. There are neither increases nor decreases in planned inventory. The level of income is in equilibrium.

Aggregate Demand Equals Aggregate Supply

Now let's approach the subject of the equilibrium level of income from another angle: Suppose we look at aggregate demand and aggregate supply (Figure 9-2). In this simple model, aggregate (in other words, total) demand is composed of (1) consumption demand plus (2) investment demand, which is represented by the line C + II in Figure 9-2; the letters stand for "consumption plus intended investment." (Remember that to simplify things we are leaving government out of the picture. There are no government expenditures and no taxes.)

In our analysis of the national economic accounts we concluded that the income generated in an economy is equal to the value of the economy's output. So in Figure 9-2, we could say that the 45° line that represents income also represents output. In effect, then, we are assuming that the vertical distance from the horizontal axis to the 45° line—the aggregate supply function—is the output that businesses think they can sell at that level of income. ("Small cars are moving pretty well. Let's make twenty thousand Dustrats, and see how they sell.")

Figure 9-2
Simple model: Aggregate Demand Equals Aggregate Supply

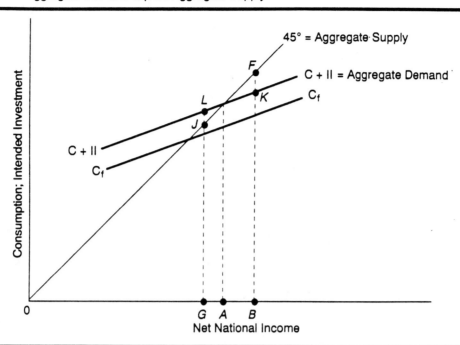

At income *A* (360), equilibrium income is at the level at which aggregate demand (C + II) equals aggregate supply (45° line). At income *B* (420), aggregate supply exceeds aggregate demand, and excess inventories *KF* (20) pile up. At income *G* (330), aggregate demand exceeds aggregate supply, and there is an inventory deficit of *JL* (10).

Figure 9-2 shows that, at income *A*, aggregate demand equals aggregate supply. This is the equilibrium level of income. To establish this, one has to show that any other level of income would *not* be an equilibrium.

Look at Figure 9-2. Again, we will use Table 9-1's figures in parentheses. Note that, at any income above the equilibrium level, aggregate supply (the 45° line) is greater than aggregate demand (C + II). In other words, businesses plan to supply more than consumers plan to demand. In Figure 9-2, at income *B* (420), aggregate supply is *BF* (420), while aggregate demand is only *BK* (400, or C + II). Supply exceeds demand by *KF* (20), which reflects unplanned additions to inventory. ("How can we ever unload two thousand tons of chicken feathers when we've ordered more than people want to buy? Cancel our order for more.") Output, income, and employment—go down. Income shrinks in the direction of *A* (360), the equilibrium level.

At any income below the equilibrium level, aggregate demand (C$_f$ + II) is greater than aggregate supply (the 45° line). Consumers demand more than businesses can supply, and inventories gradually dwindle away. ("Hey, listen to this! Insomnia Motels have increased their order by ten thousand chicken-feather pillows. Phone around and see if you can locate ten thousand yards of heavy striped ticking for pillow covers.") Output, income and employment go up. At income G (330) in Figure 9-2, aggregate demand is GL (340) (C_f + II), while aggregate supply is only GJ (330). Demand exceeds supply by JL (10), which reflects unexpected reduction in businesses' inventories. When this happens, income expands in the direction of A (360), the equilibrium level.

So you see, our economy really *must* seek equilibriu. Any unsettlement on either side of A sends the income level moving back toward that equilibrium.

Note that Figure 9-3 includes both intended investment (II) and savings (S_f). Thus we can compare the savings-equals-intended-investment and the aggregate-supply-equals-aggregate-demand approaches. Both wind up with the same equilibrium level of income: A (360).

THE MULTIPLIER

Average and Marginal Propensities to Consume and Save

At this point let's inject a modest amount of mathematics to help you understand a few new concepts: (1) the *average* propensities to

Figure 9-3
Simple Model: Aggregate Demand Equals Aggregate Supply, Plus Savings Equals Intended Investment

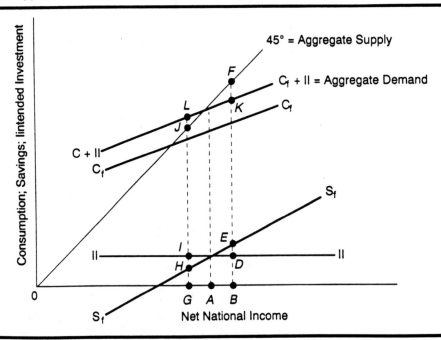

When both approaches are included in the same diagram, the same equilibrium level of income applies to both: A (360).

Average Propensity to Consume (APC)
The percentage of a given income that people tend to consume.

Average Propensity to Save (APS)
The percentage of a given income that people tend to save.

Marginal Propensity to Consume (MPC)
The change in consumption associated with a change in income.

Marginal Propensity to Save (MPS)
The change in saving associated with a change in income.

consume and save, (2) the *marginal* propensities to consume and save.

The **average propensity to consume (APC)** is the percentage of a given income that people tend to consume (or spend for consumer goods). The formula is:

$$APC = \frac{C}{Y}$$

where Y is the level of income and C is consumption. The **average propensity to save (APS)** is the percentage of a given income that people tend to save. The formula is:

$$APS = \frac{S}{Y}$$

where S is savings. Since income equals consumption plus savings, the APC plus the APS equals 1, or in other words, 100 percent of income.

The **marginal propensity to consume (MPC)** is the *change* in consumption associated with a change in income. The formula is:

$$MPC = \frac{\Delta C}{\Delta Y}$$

where ΔC means the *change* in consumption and ΔY means the *change* in income. (The triangle symbol is the Greek letter delta. It means a small change in some quantity.) The **marginal propensity to save (MPS)** is the *change* in saving associated with a change in income. The formula is:

$$MPS = \frac{\Delta S}{\Delta Y}$$

Again, the MPC plus the MPS equals 1, or in other words, 100 percent of the increase in income.

Remember that APC + APS = 1 and MPC + MPS = 1.

The key thing to remember here is that the *average* propensities to consume and save have to do with the *percentage* people consume and save out of a specific level of income, while the *marginal* propensities to consume and save have to do with the percentages people consume and save out of *changes* in income.

For example, suppose that the level of income in the economy is $400 billion and the level of consumption is $300 billion. Then the *APC* is:

$$\frac{C}{Y} \quad \text{or} \quad \frac{300}{400} \quad \text{or} \quad \frac{3}{4} \quad \text{or} \quad .75.$$

Savings equal $100 billion (Y - C = S). The *APS* is:

$$\frac{S}{Y} \quad \text{or} \quad \frac{100}{400} \quad \text{or} \quad \frac{1}{4} \quad \text{or} \quad .25.$$

Now suppose that the level of income in the economy increases by $50 billion, the level of consumption increases by $40 billion, and the level of savings increases by $10 billion. Then the *MPC* is:

$$\frac{\Delta C}{\Delta Y} \quad \text{or} \quad \frac{40}{50} \quad \text{or} \quad \frac{4}{5} \quad \text{or} \quad .80.$$

The *MPS* is:

$$\frac{\Delta S}{\Delta Y} \quad \text{or} \quad \frac{10}{50} \quad \text{or} \quad \frac{1}{5} \quad \text{or} \quad .20.$$

For a picture of the MPC, see Figure 9-4, which shows a section of the consumption function. Income increases (ΔY) from 150 to 200 (shown by arrows from A to B). Consumption increases (ΔC) from 175 to 200, shown by arrows from B to E. Income increases by 50 and consumption by 25. The MPC equals:

$$\frac{25}{50} \quad \text{or} \quad \frac{1}{2} \quad \text{or} \quad .50.$$

Now look at Table 9-2. We arrived at these figures by taking the data on income, consumption, and savings from Table 9-1 and computing the MPC and MPS. Try this yourself to see how it works.

Figure 9-4
The Marginal Propensity to Consume (MPC)

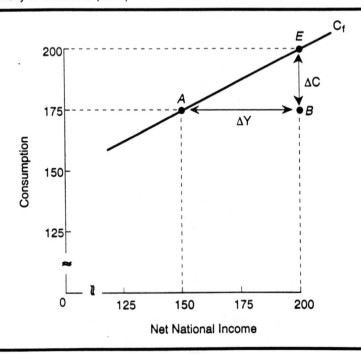

Table 9-2
The Average and Marginal Propensities to Consume and Save

Income	Consumption	Savings	APC	APS	MPC	MPS	II_1	II_2
210	240	–30	1.14	–.14	.67	.33	20	30
240	260	–20	1.08	–.08	.67	.33	20	30
270	280	–10	1.04	–.04	.67	.33	20	30
300	300	0	1	0	.67	.33	20	30
330	320	10	.97	.03	.67	.33	20	30
360	340	20	.94	.06	.67	.33	20	30
390	360	30	.92	.08	.67	.33	20	30
420	380	40	.90	.10	.67	.33	20	30
450	400	50	.89	.11	.67	.33	20	30

How Changes In Aggregate Demand Affect Changes In Income: The Multiplier Effect

Whenever aggregate demand shifts—as evidenced by a shift in investment or a shift in consumption, or both—it is a sure sign that the equilibrium level of income has also changed, because the additional money people are spending or investing must be coming from *somewhere*.

Figure 9-5 shows a case of aggregate demand (the sum of consumption plus investment) shifting up by 10, from AD_1 to AD_2. Perhaps this shift is due to an increase in autonomous investment or to an upward shift in the consumption function. Whatever the

Figure 9-5
The Multiplier Effect

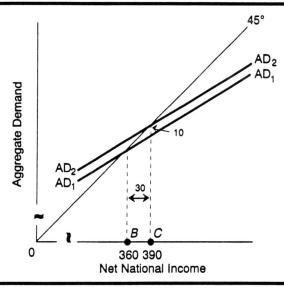

Aggregate demand shifts up from AD_1 to AD_2, an initial increase of 10, which increases equilibrium income *B* to *C*, an increase of 30. An initial change in aggregate demand changes equilibrium income by an amount larger than the initial change in aggregate demand. Since the change in income is a *multiple* of the initial change in aggregate demand, this is called the *multiplier effect*.

reason for it, this upward shift causes the equilibrium level of income to rise from *B* to *C*, or an increase of 30. Note that this figure of 30 is 3 times as big as 10, which is the upward shift in aggregate demand.

Multiplier Effect
The effect of change in aggregate demand on income.

The point we are trying to make is that income always changes by *more* than the initial shift in aggregate demand. This phenomenon is called the **multiplier effect**, because the amount of change in the equilibrium level of income is a multiple of the initial amount of change in aggregate demand. To define a multiplier, think backward, like this:

The change in income due to a given initial change in aggregate demand is a multiple of that change in demand. This multiple is called the multiplier.

There are two important points to keep in mind: (1) In order for a new level of income to be permanent, the initial upward shift of aggregate demand must be permanent. (2) The amount of increase in income is related to the amount of the initial upward shift of aggregate demand. As income increases, there is a movement up AD_2, so that in the end AD_2 is equal to income *C*.

In Figure 9-5, in which income changes by 30 and aggregate demand initially changes by 10, the multiplier is 3.

Why a Multiple?

The reason why income changes by a multiple of the initial change in aggregate demand is that people's *MPC* is greater than zero. Or, put another way, their *MPS* is less than 1. In other words, the MPC and MPS are the keys to the multiplier concept. Table 9-3 explains why this is so. It shows that the public will spend ⅔ of any increase in income on consumer goods and services.

Suppose a savings bank invests $1 million in a new bank building. Even before construction starts, many people begin to

Table 9-3
How the Multiplier Effect Works, Given that the MPC Equals ⅔.

	Initial Amount of Capital
Autonomous investment ⟶	$1,000,000
Second round of spending	666,666
Third round of spending	444,444
Fourth round of spending	296,296
Fifth round of spending	197,530
Sixth round of spending	—
Seventh round of spending	—
Eighth round of spending	—
	$3,000,000

earn incomes from this project, so aggregate demand increases. Workers, manufacturers, and many suppliers of goods and services start to benefit. Given that these people have an MPC of ⅔, they will spend ⅔ of this new income and save ⅓. This generates more new income, so a second round of spending begins. The people in round 2, in their turn, also spend ⅔ of what they get and save ⅓. This income generation continues, and on each round of spending, people spend ⅔ and save ⅓. So during each round, ⅓ becomes savings. Finally all the original $1 million *winds up as savings*. But the total increase in income that has been generated by all this spending is $3 million or 3 times the bank's original investment. The multiplier here is, of course, 3.

The Multiplier Formula

Multiplier Formula
The formula for determining the multiple change in income associated with a change in aggregate demand: $\frac{1}{1\text{-MPC}}$ or $\frac{1}{\text{MPS}}$.

There is a simple and useful formula for computing the multiplier (M), the change in equilibrium real income from a change in aggregate demand. You would do well to memorize the **multiplier formula**:

$$M = \frac{1}{1\text{-MPC}} \text{ or, since } 1 - \text{MPC} = \text{MPS}, \; M = \frac{1}{\text{MPS}}$$

The multiplier is the reciprocal of the MPS. Here, with a little simple arithmetic, is how the formula works when MPC equals ⅔:

$$M = \frac{1}{1\text{-MPC}}, \; M = \frac{1}{1\text{-}⅔}, \; M = \frac{1}{⅓}, \; M = 1 \times \frac{3}{1}, \; M = 3$$

Remember that in order for this increase in income to be permanent, the increase in autonomous investment must remain at the new higher level. This means that more new investment has to be made to replace the $1 million that originally came from the bank.

Instantaneous Multipliers Versus Periodic Multipliers

Instantaneous Multiplier
A multiplier effect that takes effect instantaneously.

You may have the impression that the multiplier process takes place very quickly. That is, strictly speaking, not true. However, the concept of the **instantaneous multiplier** (a multiplier effect that takes place instantaneously) is useful to us at this stage, so we will use it for the time being, unless we say we are using another concept.

However, you must recognize that the process of generating and regenerating demand, output, and income takes *time*. Those people and businesses in Table 9-3 who received income as a result of the savings bank's initial investment of $1 million had to have *time* to make the necessary decisions about spending their new incomes ("Should we pay Junior's college bills, or buy a new Dustrat?"). And then they had to have time to act on these decisions ("Goodbye, Junior, and don't forget to give this check to the bursar.") And when the money filtered down to the people in round 2, they also had to have time to make decisions and to spend their new incomes. (Though they had less money to make decisions about, because the people in round 1 had saved ⅓ of theirs.)

Periodic Multiplier
A multiplier effect that occurs over several periods of time.

So you can see that it would be much more realistic to visualize a **periodic multiplier**, a multiplier effect that takes place over several periods of time, as the money from the original investment passes down the line, from one round of expenditures to the next. It is true that an economy feels the biggest impact of a multiplier within the first few time periods (usually about 18 months) after the initial investment, but the long-range effects of a multiplier are spread over several time periods. These long-range effects create difficulties for the people who are trying to formulate government economic policy. A government policy maker who is trying to figure out how much money the government should pump into the economy in order to stimulate demand must be aware of previous changes in demand and their continuing impact on the economy's income.

THE ACCELERATOR PRINCIPLE

When we discussed the two kinds of investment (autonomous and induced), we assumed that induced investment was zero, in order to simplify our model. We left out induced investment. Now we are going to look at it.

Whenever the equilibrium level of income increases, people consume more goods and services, and this increase in consumption brings on, or induces, new investment. If you look at Figure 9-5, you see a higher income level (C) that would intersect the consumption curve just as before, but higher up; in other words, at a point indicating a greater quantity consumed. The level of quantity demanded is higher. This increase in quantity consumed means that industry has to have an increased capacity to produce goods and services, and this in turn requires larger amounts of investment. That is what we mean by *induced* investment. Additional investment naturally follows increased consumption. Table 9-4 shows this chain of events, using the shoe industry as an example.

Let us say that you are a shoe magnate, and you own a factory that makes shoes. Each of your 100 shoe-making machines produces 1,000 pairs of shoes a year, and has a life span of 10 years. In period 1 (imagine that each period equals 1 year), your 100 machines are equally divided as to age, so you act as you usually do, and order 10 new machines to replace 10 that wore out. In period 2, however, the demand for shoes picks up by 1 percent, so you order an additional machine that year: 10 for replacement and 1 for expansion (that 1 machine is induced investment). You want to take advantage of that demand for 1,000 extra pairs of shoes, since you naturally want all the business you can get.

Table 9-4
Induced Investment and the Accelerator Principle in the Shoe Industry

Time Period	Percentage Increase in Demand for Shoes	Number of Pairs of Shoes Demanded	Total Number of Shoe Machines	Demand for New Machines
1		100,000	100	10
2	1	101,000	101	11
3	2	103,020	103	12
4	3	106,110	106	13
5	3	109,293	109	13
6	2	111,479	111	12
7	0	111,479	111	10

Accelerator Principle
The argument that induced investment is related to the rate of change in demand or output.

In period 3, the demand for shoes increases by 2 percent (more than the 1 percent increase in period 2). Now you need 103 machines to meet demand. So you order 12 new machines: 10 for replacement and 2 for expansion (those 2 machines represent induced investment). In period 4, demand increases at an increased rate: 3 percent. Now you need 106 machines. You order 13 new ones—still 10 for replacement, plus 3 for expansion. Induced investment continues to increase. In period 5, although demand continues to increase, the rate of increase remains the same: 3 percent. You now need 109 machines. You order 13 new ones: 10 for replacement and 3 for expansion. Note that this year your induced investment did not increase. In period 6, demand still increases, but at a lower rate, only 2 percent. Now you need 111 machines, but you order only 12 new ones: 10 for replacement and only 2 for expansion. Your induced investment has decreased.

This example shows that your demand for extra new machines (your induced investment) does not depend upon the absolute level of demand for shoes. It depends on the *percentage increase in demand* for shoes. If you're going to increase your induced investment and keep expanding your plant's capacity to produce shoes, you must be able to see that there is an increasing rate of increase in demand for shoes. If the percentage increase in demand falls off, you are going to cut back your induced investment. And this also has a multiplier effect on the economy's income—only in a downward direction.

This cause-and-effect situation is called the **accelerator principle**. You can see that a small increase (1 percent) in the amount of consumer demand causes a much larger increase in induced investment. And this, in turn, has its multiplier effect on income. Higher incomes bring about an increase in demand for consumer goods and services, which has an accelerator effect on the economy.

However, this same accelerator factor introduces a strong unstable element into the growth of an economy's income. The reason is that whenever there is a decrease in the rate of growth of consumers' demands, the acceleration starts to go in the opposite direction—down. The accelerator becomes a negative one, and this causes declines in income.

Economists often use this interaction between the multiplier and the accelerator to explain business cycles. As an economy climbs up out of a recession, the increases in consumer demand bring the positive accelerator into play. This causes a rapid upswing in the economy. Gradually, though, the rate of growth embodied in that upswing slows down. Then the negative accelerator takes over and begins to pull the economy down.

Also, the accelerator does not work in the earliest phases of recovery from a recession, because there is still a lot of unused capacity (that is, idle machines and empty plant space). Until that ideal capacity is used up, one hardly notices that times are getting better. Only when an economy's recovery has reached the stage at which all machines and plant space are fully utilized, does it begin to feel the effects of the accelerator.

In Figure 9-6, you see that when the accelerator is positive (that is, when induced investment is rising and both income and consumption are also rising), the curve depicting intended investment (II) slopes upward. The opposite occurs when the accelerator is negative; then the II curve slopes downward.

Bear in mind that *the multiplier relates autonomous investment* (plus any other change in aggregate demand) *to changes in income,* whereas *the accelerator relates induced investment to changes in income or output.*

The Paradox of Thrift

During a recession, when income is falling and the newspapers are full of stories about rising unemployment, people begin to feel insecure and uncertain about their futures. Perhaps they retrench and reduce their consumption, so that they can save more. They may sleep more peacefully, knowing that their savings account is

Figure 9-6
Induced Investment

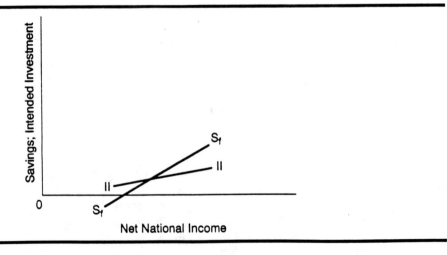

fatter. But if *everyone* does the same thing, if everyone cuts back and scrimps and saves, it may be disastrous for the economy. Eventually what happens is not an increase in savings, but a *decrease* in the quantity actually saved. This effect is know as the **paradox of thrift**.

Figure 9-7 shows this peculiar reverse effect. Suppose there is a recession, with its accompanying fall in aggregate demand and income and its accompanying increase in unemployment. The people who still have jobs nervously begin to cut back their spending so that they can save more. The line marked S_1 is the initial level of savings, before the recession. Income then stands at B, and quantity saved at C.

What happens when people begin to save more? Just the opposite of what you would expect. When everybody's savings increase, the savings function shifts upward to level S_2. Intended investment is now equal to savings only at income A. This indicates that income has fallen from B to A, and that the actual quantity people are saving has decreased to D.

The moral of all this is that when an entire economy tightens its belt, consumer demand falls and income decreases. This conclusion rests on the assumption that the increase in intended savings is not offset by an increase in intended investment. At the least, there is no assurance that the increased investment, which results from lower interest rates associated with larger savings, will offset the larger planned savings. The quantity actually saved may decrease.

Therefore, paradoxically, during a recession if everybody is trying hard to save more, the *amount* of savings may become less. Note, though, that this argument does not negate the fact that in a period of growth, or in order to have growth, an adequate supply of savings and its associated low interest rates are necessary.

Figure 9-7
The Paradox of Thrift

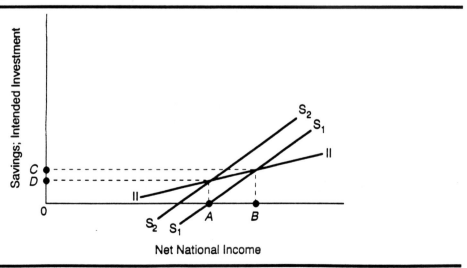

Net National Income

SUMMING UP

1. When one builds a model of an economy, omitting the factors of government and taxes and using only consumption, savings, and investment, the equilibrium level of income is the level at which savings equal intended investment. At income levels above equilibrium, people consume less than businesses produce for consumption. Businesses must endure *unplanned* or *involuntary additions to inventories*, which means that they then have to cut their orders to manufacturers. The results are reductions in output, employment, and income.

2. At income levels below equilibrium, people consume more than businesses produce for consumption. Businesses experience *unplanned* or *involuntary reductions in inventories*, which cause them to increase their orders to manufacturers. The results are increased output, employment, and income.

3. *Ex-ante investment* is investment that is desired or planned. *Ex-post investment* is investment that actually takes place. Ex-post (actual) investment always equals savings, because involuntary additions to or subtractions from inventories cause these two factors to be equal. An equilibrium income occurs only when ex-ante and ex-post investment and ex-ante and ex-post savings are all equal. At that point, all expectations or plans of businesses and the public are satisfied.

4. In our simple, *non*government model, aggregate *demand* is consumption plus intended investment, and aggregate *supply* is the 45° line in our diagram. An economy reaches equilibrium income when aggregate supply and aggregate demand intersect. When the income level is above equilibrium, aggregate quantity supplied is greater than aggregate quantity demanded, and unplanned increases in business inventory push the level of income back toward equilibrium. At income levels below equilibrium, aggregate quantity demanded is greater than aggregate quantity supplied, and unplanned decreases in business inventory push the level of income up toward equilibrium.

5. The two approaches—(a) savings equals intended investment, and (b) aggregate demand equals aggregate supply—produce the same result: the same level of income.

6. The *average propensity to consume* (APC) is the percentage of a specific level of income that people tend to consume:

$$APC = \frac{C}{Y}$$

The *average propensity to save* (APS) is the percentage of a specific level of income that people tend to save:

$$APS = \frac{S}{Y}$$

The *marginal propensity to consume* (MPC) is the percentage of any *change* in income that people tend to spend on consumption:

$$MPC = \frac{\Delta C}{\Delta Y}$$

The *marginal propensity to save* (MPS) is the percentage of any *change* in income that people tend to save:

$$MPS = \frac{\Delta S}{\Delta Y}$$

7. When aggregate demand shifts, income changes. However, a given change in aggregate demand causes income to change by an amount larger than the initial change in demand, an effect called the *multiplier effect*. The degree to which the change in income is greater than the initial change in aggregate demand is called the *multiplier*.

8. The multiplier effect is due to the fact that the MPC is greater than zero. When people have an increase in income, from whatever source, they do not save all of it. They spend part of it, which generates demand for more goods, thus creating more income.

9. The *multiplier formula* is

$$M = \frac{1}{1\text{-}MPC} \quad \text{or} \quad M = \frac{1}{MPS}$$

The multiplier is the reciprocal of the MPS.

10. *Induced investment* is investment brought on by increases in income, which cause people to consume a greater quantity of goods and services. In turn, this increases the demand for more capacity (capital) to produce the greater quantity of goods and services.

11. By means of the *accelerator principle*, one can analyze the ups and downs of induced investment over time. An increase in the rate of growth of consumer demand causes a much larger increase in the demand for additional capacity. However, any decrease in the rate of growth of consumer demand causes a much larger decrease in the demand for additional capacity.

12. The accelerator principle introduces an element of economic instability, in that, after an economy reaches full capacity during a recovery, increases in the rate of growth of consumer demand

generate large increases in induced investment. This causes income to expand rapidly. At some point, the rate of growth in consumer demand begins to slow down, and a negative accelerator (due to declining induced investment) pulls the level of income and the economy down.

13. Induced investment causes the intended investment (II) function to slope upward, so that economies with higher levels of investment have higher levels of income. (We are assuming a positive accelerator here.)

14. The *paradox of thrift* is that during a recession, when the savings function shifts upward because everyone wishes to save more, income falls because of a fall in aggregate demand. This causes the quantity saved to decline. The paradox of thrift is based on the presumption that increased investment will not offset the increases in planned savings. The argument does *not* mean that a supply of savings and low interest rates are unimportant to economic growth.

KEY TERMS

Unplanned or involuntary additions to inventory
Unplanned or involuntary reductions in inventory
Ex-ante investment
Ex-post investment
Average propensity to consume
Marginal propensity to consume
Average propensity to save
Marginal propensity to save
Multiplier effect
Multiplier formula
Instantaneous multiplier
Periodic multiplier
Accelerator principle

QUESTIONS

1. Answer the questions below based on the following figure:
   a. The 45° line represents (1) aggregate demand or (2) aggregate supply?
   b. The C + II represents (1) aggregate demand or (2) aggregate supply?
   c. The equilibrium level of net national income is (1) 500, (2) 400, or (3) 300?
   d. The distance *HI* at income 500 represents (1) excess inventory accumulation or (2) an inventory deficit?
   e. The distance *BJ* at income 300 represents (1) excess intended saving or (2) excess intended investment?

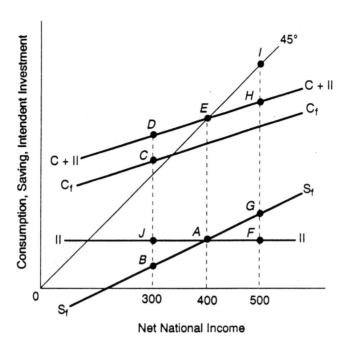

Net National Income

2. Assume that the MPC = ⅔ and the APC = ⅔.

a. Suppose that the equilibrium level of income equals 300. What are the equilibrium levels of consumption, investment, and savings? Assume that government expenditures and taxes are both zero.

b. Suppose that for the situation in part a, investment increases by 10. What are the new equilibrium levels of income, consumption, savings, and investment? Explain your answers.

3. Show how one may use a multiplier-accelerator model to explain business cycles.

4. During a recession, would it be in an individual's self-interest to increase her or his savings? Would it be in the interest of the whole economy if everybody increased savings during the recession? Why?

5. One economist said, "Savings always equals investment, whether the economy is at equilibrium or not." What makes that condition true? If an economy is not at equilibrium, what will occur to bring it toward the equilibrium point?

Application to Chapter 9:
The U.S. Economy: Ups and Downs

We have talked about the Keynesian system of income determination in a private-enterprise, market-oriented economy. We saw that the multiplier effect and the accelerator principle lead to expansion and contraction. According to the Keynesian argument, a market economy such as that of the U.S. has no in-built tendency toward full employment. How does the experience of America's market economy compare with this model? Let's look into this and discuss economic stability in our economy. We shall explore, in brief, the history of business fluctuations in the U.S. since 1920, in order to gain a better insight into the factors that cause business cycles.

The Depression of 1921

The 1921 depression was short, a little more than a year, but very severe. Money GNP fell from $91.6 billion to $70 billion, a drop of nearly 24 percent. Prices fell by more than 12 percent, and unemployment increased by more than 4 million people (to about 12 percent of the labor force).

The most significant characteristic of the 1921 depression was its sharp drop in prices. Prices of agricultural products fell even more steeply than prices of manufactured goods, leaving the agricultural sector in a precarious profit position throughout the 1920s. The steeper decline in prices of what farmers sold (relative to what they bought) narrowed their profit margins. Yet farmers had to accept these low agricultural prices and use the money to pay off the large mortgages they had taken when they expanded production during and just after World War I.

The Prosperity of the 1920s

From 1922 to 1929, the economy expanded rapidly from a low of $70 billion in money GNP in 1921 to a high of $104.4 billion in 1929. This expansion was marred by two mild recessions, one in 1924 and the other in 1927. Even so, there was less than 5 percent unemployment in these downturns. Prices declined somewhat between 1921 and 1929, from a price index of 52.8 in 1921 to an index of 51.3 in 1929. (1967 is used as a base year. In other words, in 1967 the index was 100.)

The two main props of the prosperity of the 1920s were (1) the expansion of the construction industry and (2) the increase in output of a number of "new" industries, especially the automotive industry. Both residential and business construction expanded through 1926, but then residential construction began to fall off. Further expansion in business construction, however, maintained the increases into 1927, at which time they began to decline.

This development of new industries in the 1920s was a main cause of high aggregate demand. Radios, electric power, chemicals, telephones, motion pictures, durable consumer appliances, and cars—especially cars—contributed to the boom. Although most of these industries were not new in the 1920s, they grew up in that decade. **Primary demand** (that is, demand by those who had never owned certain goods before) was large. Automobile production went from 2.2 million per year in 1920 to 5.5 million by 1929—more than double in 9 years.

Primary Demand
Demand for products created by first-time buyers.

The direct effect of this expansion was that people began to demand these new products in increasing numbers. ("I'd give anything to have a refrigerator. You never have to empty the drip pan, and you don't have to stay home to let the ice man in.") The indirect effect on maintaining demand was even greater. Car makers had to have vast quantities of raw materials and semifinished parts. Their needs stimulated booms in the steel, rubber, glass, textile, and petroleum industries and created a new service industry: gasoline retailing. Governments (mainly local and state) had to build $10 billion worth of roads for these new machines. But most important were the capital investments that auto makers had to make for plant and equipment to expand their production capacity. Although the impact on total demand by the other "new" industries was not as great as the automobile's impact, it was substantial and also had both direct and indirect effects.

Despite the general prosperity, there were some weak spots in the economy. The agricultural sector was semidepressed throughout the decade due to many factors. Another casualty was the coal industry, which suffered from chronic overproduction and underemployment because of the overexpansion during the war.

A problem that soon became more serious than the rest was developing over the international means of payments. After World War I, the German government owed huge sums of money (reparations) to the Allies. The U.S. treasury encouraged private individuals and institutions to lend more to the German government, so that Germany might pay war reparations to England, France, and Italy—so that in turn these countries could pay to the U.S. the money they borrowed during World War I. This was a very circular process and in the long run dangerous to the economy. (We shall say more about this later.)

The Depression of 1929-1933

In 1929 the U.S. economy—and for that matter, the world economy—entered the worst depression in history. Money GNP in the U.S. fell from about $104 billion in 1929 to about $56 billion by 1933. Unemployment increased to the highest level ever: 25 percent of the labor force was unemployed and another 25 percent was partially employed. Prices dropped by about 24 percent. Oddly enough, the very factors that led to the prosperity of the 1920s laid the foundations for the depression.

The large primary demand for automobiles (demand by those who had never had cars before), and for the products of the other new industries, was beginning to drop off by 1929. There was a time lag before the onset of **secondary (replacement) demand** (demand for products to replace consumer goods), which was needed to prop up demand to the levels of 1929.

. To see this, look at Figure A9–1, which is an idealized version of the life cycle of the automotive industry. During Stage 1 (1895-1920), people invented the automobile and worked to improve it. This stage is referred to as *the perfection of the innovation.* Note that the rate of growth of demand is relatively slow. In Stage 2 (1920-1929) the perfected innovation enters the primary market, and it catches on quickly. In Stage 3 (beginning in 1929) primary demand has become saturated. While the shift to replacement demand is going on, excess capacity develops. Output falls from its 1929 high.

As the demand for the products of the new industries fell, a negative accelerator effect appeared, and there was a fall in induced investment, both in the new industries themselves and in those industries that had been stimulated by them. By June of 1929, there was excess capacity, so people decreased their investing. Manufacturing output declined.

The construction industry, the second major stimulator of the 1920s economy, had been hit by excess capacity and falling

Secondary (Replacement) Demand
Demand that is created when consumers replace products.

Figure A9-1
Growth Curve of the Automobile Industry

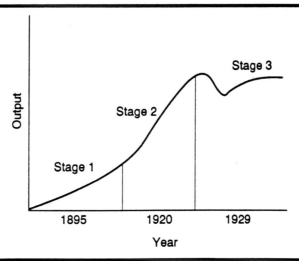

output as early as the middle of 1927. By the end of 1929, it had collapsed.

To put it in Keynesian terms: As demand fell toward the end of 1929, investment fell also. The large savings caused by the widening of the profit margins reduced consumption demand. Aggregate demand fell, and so did income.

Agriculture, textiles, and coal mining were already in trouble. The depression in 1929 made their bad situations worse. At the same time, the decline in both the construction industry and the new industries (especially automobiles) resulted in large amounts of excess capacity, a sure trigger to economic contraction. There were also additional aggravating factors that helped push an already weak economy over the brink to disaster.

For a year the stock market had been going up. Prices of stocks rose rapidly in relation to potential earnings. In October of 1929 the market simply collapsed. Another key function of the stock market is to mirror the psychological view of investors and during the year before the crash, it mirrored such optimism that few noted the signs of decline. After the crash, pessimism ruled and many people felt there was no hope.

From 1929 to 1933, the U.S. banking system also came close to complete collapse. Before the crash, banks had made some risky loans. They made large loans to people who gave them stocks to hold as security. When the stock market crashed, it crashed so quickly that banks were left holding large amounts of corporate stock—a huge capital loss. In addition, banks owned large numbers of mortgages. When mortgage holders could no longer make their monthly payments and real estate values plummeted, the banks were left holding innumerable chunks of illiquid property. All these factors eroded their asset position, and banks began to fail. People panicked. Long queues of frantic people lined up outside banks, waiting to withdraw deposits. This caused even secure banks to fail. By 1933, when Roosevelt took office, the banking system was in a desperate position.

Furthermore, between 1929 and 1933, the supply of money shrank from $26.4 billion to 18.8 billion. This sharply reduced the volume of spending in the 1930s and the sharp decline in aggregate demand caused prices to fall by about 24 percent.

As the U.S. banking system deteriorated, so did international trade, and quickly, too. The shift from government ownership to private ownership of war debts meant that private means of international payments became linked to reparations and war-debt payments. When the market collapsed in 1929, the structure of repayment of war debts crumbled also, bringing down the private system of international payments. A further blow to international trade came in 1931, when the U.S. started a round of retaliatory tariff increases that further reduced exports and put a damper on world production. These and other factors so weakened international banking that most of the leading industrial states—including Austria, Germany, England, and the U.S.—abandoned the gold standard (for a while).

Weak Recovery: 1933-1937

Franklin Delanor Roosevelt was a charismatic leader. But he was also a man of moods and contradictions. In July of 1932, when he was campaigning for the presidency, he said in a radio speech, "Any government, like any family, can for a year spend a little more than it earns. But you and I know that a continuance of that habit means the poorhouse."

And then he was elected. In 1933, when he became president, Roosevelt set about building a fire under the economy by increasing government expenditures. This government spending had the effect of creating what were, for that time, large deficits. Congress also passed a series of laws aimed at correcting weaknesses in the economy, though some, by encouraging monopoly, may have been counterproductive.

The national debt jumped from $19.5 billion in 1932 to $36.5 billion by 1937, an increase of $17 billion in 5 years. This stimulated an increase in GNP of $35 billion between 1933 and 1937. Private investment remained low, however. (In 1929 net private domestic investment was $8.3 billion. By 1933 it had dropped to *minus* $5.6 billion, and in 1937 it was still only $4.6 billion.) Therefore, America's initial recovery from the Great Depression was significantly affected by deficit spending on the part of the government.

The Recession of 1937-1938

President Roosevelt, concerned about the increasing federal deficits, decided that private investment should shoulder more of the task of coping with the continued depression. So in 1937 the federal government reduced deficit expenditures. At the same time, monetary policy was tightened. In the face of higher interest rates and weak demand, private investment, however, failed to take up the slack and continue the expansion. As a result, output declined and unemployment increased from about 14 percent to 18 percent. For the first time in the history of U.S. business cycles, a second recession came along before the economy had recovered from the first. In 1938, the government went back to its policy of increasing government expenditures (as well as the money supply) and private investment began to increase. Under this joint stimulus the economy again began its slow expansion.

The Early Forties and World War II

During 1940 and 1941, as the U.S. increased its military expenditures and its exports to its allies, who were already at war, the recovery began to quicken. Observers could see the multiplier and accelerator effects of this increased output in the form of increases in both consumption and investment.

When the U.S. entered the war, on December 7, 1941, the economy went all out in the war effort. However, because there was so much unemployment left over from the depression of the 1930s (unemployment was still at 10 percent in 1941), the economy did not reach full employment until the beginning of the third quarter of 1942. Until then, there had been sharp increases in output of military goods, consumer goods, and investment goods. Once full employment was achieved, the economy, which was now on the production-possibility curve, had to cut back on the production of investment and consumer goods in order to continue to increase output of goods needed by the military.

Since there was full employment and plenty of overtime work, people had higher personal incomes. Yet the nation's need for more and more military goods reduced the availability of consumer goods, so demand pressed on supply. The government prevented excess demand by imposing higher taxes and price controls and by encouraging people to save and to buy government bonds. Fighters against inflation included Kate Smith singing "God Bless America" in a tear-jerking performance that sold millions of war bonds.

Thus, large amounts of personal savings—plus price and wage controls and rationing—kept inflation within reasonable bounds. In the 4 war years from 1941 to 1945, the consumer price index increased only from 44.1 to 53.9.

The Postwar Boom: 1945-1948

At the end of the war, there was a slight dip in the economy as the U.S. shifted from military production to civilian production. Then, despite many people's fears that there would be a repeat of the 1930s, the economy began to expand rapidly. Even though the government cut back its military spending by more that $55 billion, the demand for consumer goods, investment, and export goods created a boom.

Because of the depression and then the war, both business investment and consumer demand had been kept low for 15 years. After the war ended, businesses rushed to invest in plant and equipment, because of depreciation, obsolescence, and the need to reconvert to peacetime production. And because residential construction had been in the doldrums since 1928, there was a serious shortage of housing. All through the depression and war years, people had postponed buying new durable goods, such as cars and refrigerators—the so-called consumer durables. Now that the war was over, everybody rushed to buy them. As late as the summer of 1947, people who wanted refrigerators had to put their names on numbered waiting lists and wait for delivery anywhere from 6 weeks to 3 months. The same wait was required for cars.

Americans were not alone in their headlong rush to achieve the good life, to gratify demands they had postponed for so long.

They were joined by the rest of the world. Exports rose to new highs as a war-ravaged world turned to the U.S. for consumer goods and for investment to rebuild the world's economy. The U.S. government did a lot to help. Through the foreign-aid system known as the Marshall Plan, the U.S. provided more than $8 billion to finance exports to countries in need.

Unfortunately, under the impact of all this demand, inflation developed. Between 1945 and 1948, the consumer price index rose from about 54 to 72 (1967 is still the base year). Although much of this increase was due to demand-pull inflation, cost-push inflation also played a part. During this postwar period there were many strikes, as labor unions, in an effort to catch up after the wartime freeze on wages, sought large wage increases.

The Recession of 1949 and the Expansion of 1950-1953

In late-1948, the economy had its first postwar recession, a short, mild downturn caused primarily by excess inventory that businesses accumulated as output temporarily outstripped demand. Money GNP dropped by about $1 billion, while real GNP increased by $0.5 billion. Unemployment went from 3.8 percent (1948) to 5.9 percent (1949). However, by the beginning of 1950, the economy began to recover.

In June of 1950, war broke out in Korea, and the recovery from the 1949 slump accelerated and became another boom. Consumers, fearing another round of inflation and also fearing that the government would again put on controls, increased their purchases. As the Cold War became hotter, the government increased its military expenditures, both to fight the war and to increase U.S. military strength in general. Real GNP rose from about $256 billion in 1949 to about $365 billion in 1953. Prices, however, followed suit. The consumer price index rose from 71.4 in 1949 to 80.1 in 1953 (using 1967 as a base). Predictably, unemployment fell from 5.9 percent in 1949 to 2.9 percent in 1953, or to just about half.

The Recession of 1954 and the Expansion of 1955-1957

When the Korean War ended, consumers stopped buying so much, and so did the government; inventories piled up. In 1954 along came a recession. This too was mild and short, however, because the government took prompt fiscal and monetary steps to ease the situation. A tax cut plus an easy money policy softened the downturn.

In 1955 a boom in residential construction and in demand for consumer durable goods, especially cars, caused U.S. national output to expand quickly. (Auto production reached heights in 1955 not duplicated until the mid-1960s.) But in 1956 and 1957, the market for consumer durables, saturated by the sales of 1955, again sagged. However, the economy held steady because of increases in producer durable goods and in nonresidential construction. Real GNP increased from about $365 billion in 1954 to $441 billion in 1957. Inflation surged again too: the consumer price index increased from 80.5 in 1954 to 84.3 in 1957 (1967 = 100). Although the unemployment rate dropped below 5 percent, it held stubbornly at 4.3 percent, in spite of the expansion, and there was a renewal of concern for inflation among policy workers.

The Recession of 1958

By the end of 1957 the investment boom slacked off. Demand for consumer durables was still as a low point after the saturation of the 1955 boom. And the government further restricted demand, both by cutting its expenditures and by following what many people considered a too tight money policy. The result was the most severe recession to come along since the war. Real GNP fell by more than $5 billion, and unemployment rose to 6.8 percent. For the first time, inflation accompanied the fall in output, and the consumer price index rose from 84.3 in 1957 to 86.6 in 1958 (with 1967 = 100 as the base).

Weak Recovery in 1960-1961 Followed by the Expansion of 1962-1969

Although the recession of 1958 was severe, it was short—less than 1 year. Business recovered, consumer demand picked up, and so did government demand, so that 1959 saw a renewed expansion. However, this recovery was not strong enough, and the economy went through another recession in 1960 and 1961, a mild one this time.

Between 1962 and 1969 the economy expanded without interruption—the longest expansion in U.S. history until the 1980s. Yet, early in the 60s, Presidents Kennedy and Johnson were both concerned about the slowness of growth, the high unemployment rates (between 5 and 6 percent between 1962 and 1964), and the perception of a problem of chronic poverty.

The government used deliberate economic policy to combat these problems. To attack chronic poverty, there was Johnson's (largely unsuccessful) "War on Poverty." The government stepped up its expenditures, which gave some stimulation to the economy. The real stimuli, however, were the Johnson tax cuts in 1964 and 1965. The 1964 tax cut alone amounted to $11 billion, which had a marked effect on the economy: Unemployment fell from 5.2 percent in 1964 to 4.5 percent in 1965. As the tax cut worked, the economy moved toward full employment.

The 1965 escalation in Vietnam compounded our problems, as defense expenditures increased from $50 billion in 1965 to $80 billion by 1968. Government—all levels of government—increased spending during this period, pouring out money, especially on schools and highways. Then, too, people's demand for consumer goods continued to be enormous, which caused a spurt in the growth of the GNP. Unemployment fell to 3.5 percent by 1969.

Excess aggregate demand, however, soon lead to substantial inflation. The consumer price index rose from 92.9 in 1964 to 109.8 in 1969—17 points in only 5 years—in large measure caused by the overheating of the economy; that is, by demand-pull inflation.

Inflation and Unemployment in 1970-1971, Wage and Price Controls in 1971-1973

Stagflation
A term used to describe the combination of high unemployment and the high rate of inflation.

Toward the end of the 60s there was such a high rate of inflation that in 1969 the government, in alarm, adopted some restrictive policies. The effect was only to increase unemployment. The fact that prices kept going up and up in 1968 and 1969 probably also cut back demand. Unemployment crept upward, from 3.5 percent to 4.9 percent in 1970 to 5.9 percent in 1971. Real GNP fell by $2.6 billion in 1970. The consumer price index rose from 109.8 in 1969 to 116.3 in 1970 and 121.3 in 1971. It was a repetition of 1958. The economy suffered from the worst of conditions, **stagflation**: high unemployment and high inflation.

In 1971, although the economy was beginning to recover and GNP was expanding, prices were still rising. The balance of payments was worsening, and unemployment was still high. Existing fiscal and monetary policy seemed inadequate to policy makers to deal with all these problems at the same time. So in August of 1971, President Nixon took several steps, announcing fiscal programs designed to increase demand and employment, a 90-day wage and price freeze, and the first of a number of "phases" to control prices. Also, to help the balance of payments, Nixon floated the dollar in international exchange markets. All this took everybody by surprise. A few weeks before, Nixon had said that he did not believe in controls and that he would never devalue the American dollar.

In 1972 price increases were noticeably less, and so was unemployment. Our balance of payments improved, and GNP increased sharply. As a result, in Phase II and Phase III, Nixon loosened price controls. But in 1973 prices went up again, by about 8 percent, and the dollar depreciated by 12 percent on the international market. So one might say that Nixon's medicine worked, but not for long.

Inflation and Unemployment Again: 1974 to 1976

From 1974 to 1976 unemployment rose rapidly to more than 8 percent. Inflation passed 12 percent, for 1974, and real GNP rose

Light Ahead

very slowly after first falling. Stagflation seemed to many to have become built into the economy.

In the mid-1970s, the central problem seemed to be how an economy could combat at the same time high unemployment, falling or very slowly growing real GNP, and significant inflation. Simply using fiscal and monetary policy to expand the economy, to reduce unemployment, and to contract the economy in order to control inflation was not feasible.

Recovery: 1977 to 1979

The stagflation concerns subsided somewhat as favorable monetary policies and continuing federal deficits stimulated the economy. As unemployment fell from 7.1 percent to 5.8 percent, real GNP grew by about 8 percent. A continuing high rate of inflation (almost 20 percent growth in the CPI) led many to conclude that productivity and supply were not growing rapidly enough in the U.S.

Recession Followed by Growth and Deficits: 1980-1989

The supply shocks of sharp energy price increases from OPEC II led to rising costs, declining aggregate supply and rising unemployment. Unemployment reached almost 10 percent and the economy entered double digit inflation (13.5 percent from 1979 to 1980). A change of administration in 1981 led to tax cuts and efforts to stimulate both aggregate demand and aggregate supply. To combat inflation, restrictive monetary policies were pursued with a sharp recession resulting in 1982-1983, and unemployment peaking at 9.7 percent in 1982. Thereafter, the stimulative effects of easier monetary policies, tax cuts, investment tax credits and large federal budget deficits combined to reduce unemployment (5 percent in late-1989) and cut inflation rates (the CPI rose only about 2 percent from 1985 to 1986 and at rates of 3 to 4 percent from 1986 through 1989). Large trade deficits to be financed and very large budget deficits remained key problems. Nonetheless, the period from 1982 through 1989 became the longest period of sustained economic growth for America in the twentieth century.

A Judgment About Stability

Is American capitalism inherently unstable? You can see from this short record of the past 60 years that the U.S. economy is subject to oscillations in levels of output, employment, and prices. We have even seen that many combinations of these three can exist at the same time.

The U.S. economy can experience severe drops in prices, income, and employment (the recessions and depressions prior to 1945). It can also have stable or near-stable prices, low unemployment, and expanding output (as in the 1920s and the mid- to late-1980s). It can have expansions accompanied by substantial inflation (1945-1948, 1950-1953, 1955-1957, 1965-1969, 1972-1973, 1977-1979). Finally, recession, with falling real incomes and high unemployment, can occur at the same time as sharp increases in prices (1958, 1970-1971, and 1974 to late 1975).

The American economy clearly is growth oriented. Its long-term trend in terms of real income and employment has been upward. Standards of living have risen secularly and in the late-1980s, a larger percentage than ever of the potential labor force was employed. Yet, the nation, historically, has been plagued by cyclical variations that sometimes have been sharp. Is there a way to have long-term growth without these cycles? Unfortunately, at this point in time, economic theory provides no clear answer to this question.

SUMMING UP

Table A9-1
History of Business Cycles

Year	Description	Current GNP (billions of dollars)	Percentage of Unemployment	Consumer Price Index (1967 = 100)
1921	Depression; severe, but short, contraction.	70	12	52.8
1922 to 1929	Prosperity of the 1920s, with only two short, mild recessions. Based on expansion of the construction industry and especially on the growth of certain "new" industries: most important, the auto industry.	74.3 104.4	4.0 3.2	50.5 51.3
1929 to 1933	The Great Depression, directly caused by slump of demand in the construction industry and the new industries. Made worse by the stock market crash of 1929, the near collapse of the U.S. banking system, the sharp decrease in the supply of money, and a sharp contraction in international trade.	104.4 55.6	3.2 24.9	51.3 38.8
1933 to 1937	Deliberate, but inadequate, deficit spending by the Roosevelt administration. A slow, weak recovery.	55.6 90.4	24.9 14.3	38.8 43.3
1937 to 1938	In 1937, Roosevelt cut government expenditures, but private investment did not take up the slack. For the first time the economy suffered a recession before it had recovered from a prior contraction.	90.4	14.3 18	43.3
1939 to 1945	Huge military expenditures both in the U.S. and in Europe before and after U.S. entry into World War II. Rapidly expanding GNP. Until the labor force was fully employed in late-1942, there were expansions in military, consumer and investment output. After full employment, output for investment and consumption shrank while military production expanded. Higher taxes, personal savings, and price controls with rationing restrained inflation.	90.5 211.9	17.2 1.9	41.6 53.9
1945 to 1948	Postwar boom, fueled by demand for consumer goods and investment, deferred for 15 years. Supplemented by increased exports to feed and help rebuild war-torn countries. Domestic investment and consumption demand were financed by savings from the war, tax cuts, government transfers to discharged servicemen, and consumer debt. Substantial inflation.	211.9 257.6	1.9 3.8	53.9 72.1
1949	First postwar recession, caused primarily by excess inventory, as output temporarily outstripped demand.	256.5	5.9	71.4

Year	Description	Current GNP (billions of dollars)	Percentage of Unemployment	Consumer Price Index (1967 = 100)
1954	Post-Korean War recession, caused by decreases in consumption and cuts in government military expenditures, kept mild by appropriate fiscal and monetary policy.	364.8	5.6	80.5
1955 to 1957	Boom, sparked by high levels of demand in 1955 for consumer durables and houses; maintained through 1957 by high levels of demand for producer durable goods. Continued serious inflation.	398 441.1	4.4 4.3	80.2 84.3
1958	The most severe of the postwar recessions, caused by a drop in government expenditures and investments, plus low demand for consumer goods. First recession in history to exhibit marked inflation along with rising unemployment.	447.3	6.8	86.6
1959 to 1961	Recovery in 1959, but not a strong one, followed by a mild recession in 1960-1961. Some people say the steel strike of 1959 was the main cause.	483.7 520.1	5.5 6.7	87.3 89.6
1962 to 1965 to 1969	Continued expansion from 1962 through 1969. In early-1960s growth was slow and unemployment high, while prices went up only slightly. The tax cut of 1964 increased output, but the Vietnam escalation of 1965 increased government expenditures and overheated the economy. Unemployment fell; inflation increased.	560.3 684.9 929.1	5.6 4.5 3.5	90.6 94.5 109.8
1970 to 1971	Inflation at end of 1960s set the stage for recession of 1970-1971. Government efforts to decrease inflation cut back demand and income. Consumers held back buying as inflation redistributed real income and wealth. Small competitive firms suffered profit squeezes. As unemployment increased, there was, unexpectedly, also substantial inflation.	976.4 1,155.1	4.9 5.9	116.3 121.3
1972 to 1973	Price and wage controls began in August 1971 when President Nixon—to expand employment, control inflation, and reduce deficit in the balance of payments—used expansionary fiscal policy, floated the dollar on the international exchange, and froze wages and prices for 90 days. Nixon's policies were only temporarily successful. In 1973 prices increased by 8 percent and the dollar depreciated by 12 percent in exchange markets.	1,155.2 1,289.1	5.6 4.9	125.3 133.1
1974 to 1976	Worst recession since the 1930s began in 1974. Inflation of over 12 percent; unemployment 8.5 percent by the end of 1975. Real GNP rose by only 3 percent. Number one policy problem was how to combat unemployment and inflation at the same time.	1,397 1,782.8	5.6 7.7	147.7

Year	Description	Current GNP (billions of dollars)	Percentage of Unemployment	Consumer Price Index (1967 = 100)
1980 to 1988	OPEC II led to rise in unemployment (9.7 percent in 1982), and double digit inflation (13.5 percent from '79 to '80). A severe recession followed from monetary policy changes. Tax reductions and large budget deficits led to falling unemployment and reduced inflation rates. Serious problems remained in financing budget deficits and deficits in trade balances.	1,732.6 4,488	7.1 6	246.8 340.4

KEY TERMS

Primary demand
Secondary (replacement) demand
Stagflation

QUESTIONS

1. What factors that contributed to the expansion of the 1920s laid the foundations for the Great Depression of the 1930s?

2. What were the major factors contributing to economic expansion during the 1960s? What problems did they create?

3. Trace the origins of the recession-inflation of 1974 to 1976. What economic policy do you think would have been appropriate to handle the situation? Explain your reasoning.

4. What seems to have been the state of the economy from 1977 to 1979?

5. What effects did OPEC II have on the economy in 1979-1980?

6. From 1980 to 1981 what happened to unemployment, inflation and GNP growth?

7. What factors seem to have contributed to the prolonged expansion of the economy between 1982 and 1990?

SUGGESTED READINGS

Aaron, Henry, Harvey Galper, Joseph Peckman, George Perry, Alice Revlin, Charles Schultze. *Economic Choices, 1987: Overview*. Brookings Institution, 1987. Reprinted in *Introduction to Macroeconomics*. Peter D. McClelland, ed. New York: McGraw-Hill, 1988.

Bailey, Martin N., Gary Burtless, Malcolm R. Lovell, Jr., and Roger D. Semerod. "Unemployment." *The Brookings Review*. Fall, 1983.

Cagan, Philip, et al. *Economic Policy and Inflation in the Sixties.* American Enterprise Institute for Public Policy Research, Washington, D.C.; 1972.

Gordon, Robert A. *Economic Instability and Growth: The American Record.* Harper & Row, New York, 1974.

Mitchell, Broadus. *The Depression Decade.* Rinehart, New York, 1947.

Soule, George. *Prosperity Decade 1917-1929.* Harper Torchbooks, New York, 1947.

Stein, Herbert, "Inflation, Disinflation, and the State of the Macro-economy," Some Second Opinions A.E.I. Economist, March, 1986. Reprinted in *Introduction to Macroeconomics.* Peter D. McClelland, ed. New York: McGraw-Hill, 1988.

Chapter 10:
Completing the Keynesian Model: Adding Government Expenditures and Fiscal Policy

---

Before Keynes, the neoclassical economists' creed was "Let government affect the economy as little as possible. Balance the budget. A competitive market economy will correct itself." After Keynes, many economists changed their tune to "The government must involve itself with the economy, because the economy's self-correcting mechanism is too slow and unsure. The level of income is rarely the socially preferred one."

To the simple model we will add the *government sector* (taxes and government expenditures) to see what happens when the government becomes involved. How can a government change an economy's level of income?

Adding Government Expenditures to the Simple Model

We can add government expenditures to our model in the same way we added intended investment to it; by seeing them in relation to (1) the savings function, and (2) the consumption function.

How do government expenditures affect savings and consumption? Recall our discussion of determining the equilibrium level of income. We spoke of the two approaches to the subject: the savings-equals-intended-investment approach, and the aggregate-demand-equals-aggregate-supply approach. When we consider government expenditures in relation to the *savings* function, they become part of the savings-equals-intended-investment approach. But considered in relation to the *consumption* function, government expenditures become part of the aggregate-demand-equals-aggregate-supply approach.

One Approach: Savings Equals Intended Investment Plus Government Expenditures

Figure 10-1 shows the savings-equals-intended-investment approach with government expenditures added. Savings, you recall, has a depressing effect on demand for output. But government expenditures, along with investment, add to consumer demand for the total output of firms. So government expenditures increase the demand for output. The point of equilibrium is now the point at which savings equals intended investment *plus government expenditures*. (Remember that without the existence of taxes, all these expenditures must be financed by borrowing.)

In Figure 10-1, the II + GX (intended investment plus government expenditures) function is parallel to the II function, and also parallel to the horizontal axis. We are assuming here that government expenditures are determined only by political factors and are not affected by the level of income of the economy. This is, of course, not a realistic assumption, but the real factors involved *are* largely political, and this assumption is useful for simplifying our model. If you understand this simple model, you can experiment with your own assumptions about how government expenditures vary with the level of national income.

To repeat, with government expenditures included, a nation's equilibrium income is the income at which *savings equals intended investment plus government expenditures*. This is income *A* in Figure 10-1, and 390 in Table 10-1. (*Note:* Our discussion will

Figure 10-1
Savings Equals Intended Investment Plus Government Expenditures

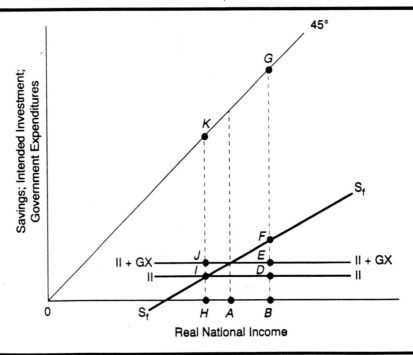

Table 10-1
Savings Equals Intended Investment Plus Government Expenditures

Income	Consumption	Savings (S)	Intended Investment (II)	Government Expenditures (GX)
210	240	−30	20	10
240	260	−20	20	10
270	280	−10	20	10
300	300	0	20	10
330	320	10	20	10
360	340	20	20	10
390	360	30	20	10
420	380	40	20	10
450	400	50	20	10

Note: The equilibrium level of income (S = II + GX) is 390 and is equal to *A* in Figure 10-1. Income *B* in Figure 10-1 equals 450, and income *H* equals 360.

rely mainly on Figure 10-1, but you can also follow it in Table 10-1. We have inserted number values after the letter symbols from Figure 10-1.)

Let's assume a level of income that is above *A* (390)—say, the high income level of *B* (450). Businesses produce for investment *BD* (20), for government demand *DE* (10), and the rest for consumption *EG* (420). The public, however, cautiously insists on saving *BF* (50) and consumes only *FG* (400). So business is producing more for consumption (*EG* = 420) than the public is consuming (*FG* = 400), creating involuntary (unplanned) additions to inventory, in the amount of *EF* (20). Businesses cut orders to manufacturers, and try to decrease the unwanted stockpile of goods. Manufacturers suffer dwindling output and income, so they lay off workers. Income moves to the equilibrium level *A* (390).

At any income below this, say at *H* (360), businesses produce for investment *HI* (20), for government demand *IJ* (10), and for consumption *JK* (330). The public saves *HI* (20), and consumes the remainder, *IK* (340). This means that businesses are producing less for consumption (*JK* = 330) than the public demands (*IK* = 340). The results are involuntary (unplanned) reductions in inventory, equal to *IJ* (10). Businesses increase their orders to manufacturers. Manufacturers increase their output, have a welcome surge of income, and hire more workers. Income again moves toward *A* (390), the equilibrium level.

It is only at the equilibrium level of income that production for investment plus government expenditures equals savings, and that the amount produced for consumption equals the amount consumed. At that level, there are neither involuntary increases nor involuntary decreases in inventory. Income stays at a particular equilibrium level, however, only as long as the various functions in the model are constant.

Another Approach: Aggregate Quantity Demanded Equals Aggregate Quantity Supplied

Now let's consider government expenditures and the consumption function, and how they fit into the aggregate-quantity-demanded-equals-aggregate-quantity-supplied approach to equilibrium income.

Figure 10-2 shows government expenditures added to consumption plus intended investment: C + II + GX, which all now add up to aggregate demand. (Aggregate supply is still the 45° line.) The equilibrium level of income is *A* (390), where aggregate quantity demanded and aggregate quantity supplied are equal. When income is *B* (450), *above* the equilibrium level, quantity demanded is less than quantity supplied. Businesses produce more than the public demands and inventories begin to pile up, so businesses cut their orders to suppliers. The results are losses in income, drops in output, rises in unemployment. The level of income moves down toward *A* (390)—the equilibrium level.

When income is *H* (360), *below* the equilibrium level, quantity demanded exceeds quantity supplied. Businesses produce less than the public demands, and inventories melt away, so businesses rush new orders to suppliers. The results are gains in

Figure 10-2
Aggregate Demand (C + II + GX) Equals Aggregate Supply

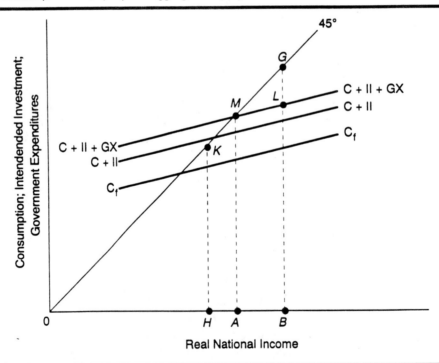

Aggregate demand becomes consumption plus intended investment plus government expenditures (C + II + GX). Equilibrium income is again at the level at which aggregate quantity demanded equals aggregate quantity supplied (45° line).

income and in output and rises in employment. Income moves up, toward the equilibrium level *A* (390).

Now we combine Figure 10-1 with Figure 10-2 to get Figure 10-3. You can see that *both* approaches—savings equals intended investment, and aggregate quantity demanded equals aggregate quantity supplied—generate the *same equilibrium level of income, A* (390).

Adding Taxes to the Simple Model

Consumption, investment, and government expenditures together make up aggregate demand. Savings *reduce* aggregate demand (because savings decrease consumption).

Now let's add taxes to our model. Taxes affect two components of the model: consumption and savings. You pay taxes out of income that you would have chosen to spend on consumption, or perhaps to use partly for savings.

Suppose that there were no taxes. How much of that income would you have spent on consumption and how much would you have saved? That would depend on your marginal propensities to consume (MPC) and to save (MPS). Since taxes change our disposable income, this means that the MPC concept applies. Suppose taxes are levied at $30 billion (see Table 10-2). This

Figure 10-3
Savings Equals Intended Investment Plus Aggregate Quantity Demanded Equals Aggregate Quantity Supplied

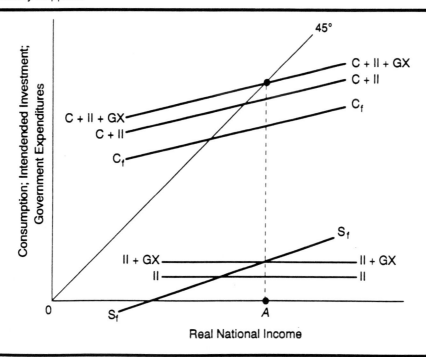

Table 10-2
The Complete Model of a Nation's Economy, Including Government Expenditures and Taxes

Income	Consumption Before Taxes	Consumption After Taxes	Savings Before Taxes	Savings After Taxes	II	GX	Taxes
210	240	220	–30	–40	20	10	30
240	260	240	–20	–30	20	10	30
270	280	260	–10	–20	20	10	30
300	300	280	0	–10	20	10	30
330	320	300	10	0	20	10	30
360	340	320	20	10	20	10	30
390	360	340	30	20	20	10	30
420	380	360	40	30	20	10	30
450	400	380	50	40	20	10	30

would cause disposable income to shrink by $30 billion, and it would affect people at all levels of income. If our MPC were ⅔ (as it is in Table 10-2), our consumption function would shift downward by ⅔ of $30 billion, or by $20 billion. At the same time, since our MPS is ⅓, our savings function would shift downward by $10 billion. Figures 10-4, 10-5, and 10-6, plus Table 10-2, show what happens when taxes are included in the model.

Figure 10-4
Another Addition to the Simple Model:
Savings Plus Taxes Equals Intended Investment Plus Government Expenditures

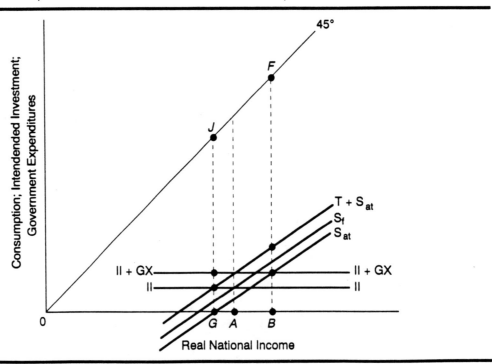

When taxes are included, the savings function drops to S_{at} (savings after taxes). S = II + GX becomes S + T = II + GX. Equilibrium income is now A.

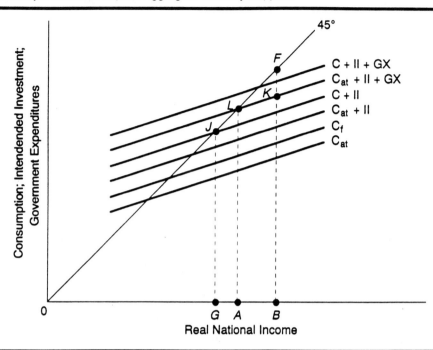

When taxes are included, the consumption function drops to C_{at} (consumption after taxes), bringing aggregate demand down to $C_{at} + II + GX$. Equilibrium income is now A, at which level aggregate quantity demanded equals aggregate quantity supplied.

Note that including taxes shifts both consumption and savings functions down proportionately, so that the new functions are parallel to the old. We are assuming that all the taxes are proportional taxes. If taxes are proportional, there is no change in the distribution of income or in the MPC and to MPS; thus, C_f and C_{at} are parallel in the figures, as are S_f and S_{at}.

One Approach: Savings Plus Taxes Equals Intended Investment Plus Government Expenditures

You can see in Figure 10-4 that introducing taxes into the model causes the savings function (S_f) to shift downward. Taxes are measured by the vertical distance from savings after taxes (S_{at}) to taxes plus savings after taxes ($T + S_{at}$).

Now that we have added taxes and government expenditures to the model, the savings-equals-intended-investment approach becomes the *taxes*-plus-savings-equal-intended-investment-plus-government-expenditures approach. Now two main factors reduce consumption demand: taxes and savings. That elusive equilibrium level of income is now the level at which these two main factors—savings and taxes—are offset by two supple

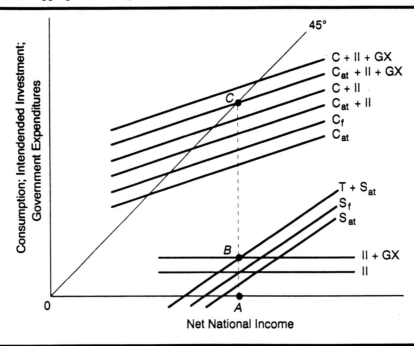

One obtains the same equilibrium level of income whether one uses savings plus taxes equals intended investment plus government expenditures, or aggregate quantity demanded equals aggregate quantity supplied.

mental elements of demand: intended investment and government expenditures.

The process can be expressed algebraically:

$$C + S + T = \text{aggregate supply (income)},$$

$$C + II + GX = \text{aggregate demand (for products)}.$$

In an equilibrium situation:

$$C + S + T = C + II + GX.$$

When you subtract C from both sides:

$$S + T = II + GX \ (A \text{ in Figure 10-4, or 330 in Table 10-2}).$$

Those who prefer graphic illustrations may look at Figure 10-4. The equilibrium level of income is *A* (330 in Table 10-2).

How does it happen that equilibrium income is only 330 now that we have added the effects of taxes? In Figure 10-1 and Table 10-1 the equilibrium level was 390. But that was when we were counting only government expenditures. Add taxes, and the level goes down by 60 points, to 330. Why? Income *B* (390) is now *above* the equilibrium. At that level businesses produce *BD* (30) for investment and the government, and the rest (*DF*, or 360) for consumption. The public wishes to consume only *EF* (340) and use the rest (*BE*, or 50) for savings and taxes. This lowers the quantity of goods that businesses sell. Inventories pile up (*DE*, or 20), so firms cut their orders to suppliers. Manufacturers cut output, lay off workers, and lose money. The national level of income drifts downward, toward *A* (330).

The reverse happens at income level *G* (300), because that's *below* the equilibrium level. So businesses produce only *IJ* (270) for consumption, plus *GI* (30) for investment and the government. But the public consumes *HJ* (280), and uses the rest (*GH*, or 20) for savings and taxes. So they're consuming more than business is producing, with the usual results: unplanned reduction of inventories (*HI*, or 10). Businesses increase their orders, manufacturers increase their output, hire more workers, and earn more money. The national level of income drifts upward, toward *A* (330).

Another Approach: Aggregate Quantity Demanded Equals Aggregate Quantity Supplied

Now let's try a different approach—aggregate quantity demanded equals aggregate quantity supplied—and see if the same formula for equilibrium income holds, now that we have added taxes to the picture. People pay part of their taxes with money they would have spent on consumption and part out of money that they would otherwise have saved. In Figure 10-5, consumption shifts down from C_f to C_{at}. As it does so, aggregate demand also shifts down, to C_{at} + II + GX. This means that equilibrium income is again at the level at which aggregate quantity demanded equals aggregate quantity supplied-income level *A* (330).

At income *B* (390), aggregate demand (*BK*, or 370) is less than aggregate supply (*BF*, or 390). The excess supply of *KF* (20) causes business firms to cut orders to manufacturers, who in turn cut output, lose income, and then must lay off workers. National income drifts downward, toward *A* (330), as it did when we used the approach of savings plus taxes equal investment plus government expenditures.

At income *G*, or 300, aggregate quantity demanded, *GL* (310), is greater than aggregate quantity supplied, *GJ* (300). This excess demand, *JL* (10), causes businesses to increase orders to manufacturers, who in turn increase output, income, and number of workers. National income drifts upward, toward the equilibrium level *A* (330).

By now the process should be clear. In Figure 10-6, the same equilibrium level of income (*A*) is reached by approaching the problem from the standpoint of savings plus taxes equal investment plus government expenditures (equilibrium point *B*), or by approaching it from the standpoint of aggregate quantity demanded equals aggregate quantity supplied (equilibrium point *C*).

Deflationary and Inflationary Gaps

John Maynard Keynes came to the conclusion that a nation's economy does not always move toward a full-employment equilibrium level of income. A country could be at an equilibrium level of income and still have unemployment. *Or* it could have full employment. *Or* it could have inflation. There were no automatic market mechanisms that could bring income to any one level that might be socially preferred.

The Deflationary Gap

Deflationary Gap
The amount by which aggregate demand would have to increase to move NNP to its full-employment level.

Look at Figure 10-7. Suppose that there is full employment at *B*, but that the equilibrium level of income is only *A*. Let us suppose also that the economy's producers would respond to an increase in demand by offering larger quantities supplied at existing prices. It is obvious there is unemployment. To do away with this unemployment, income would have to increase by *AB*. However, it is apparent that the economy could not maintain an income of *B*. The reason is that at point *B*, aggregate supply would exceed aggregate demand by *DE*, and inventory changes would then cause income to drop back to *A*. An increase in demand of *DE* would be needed in order to achieve full employment. This gap, *DE*, is called the **deflationary gap**. To get rid of it and to push income up to the level *B*, aggregate demand would have to shift to *E*. How could this be achieved? There are several ways: by increasing consumption,

Figure 10-7
A Deflationary Gap

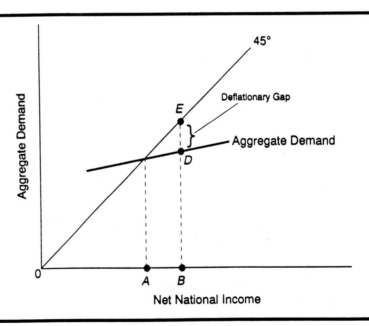

Although equilibrium income is *A*, the income that will achieve full employment is *B*. The deficit between actual demand and demand necessary to obtain full employment is *DE*, called the deflationary gap.

by increasing investment, or by increasing government expenditures. It can also be done by reducing taxes and savings. In the 1980s, a combination of tax cuts and investment tax credits together with federal budget deficits increased aggregate demand. This expansionary influence was also accompanied, however, by an increase in aggregate supply which reduced any inflationary pressures that might otherwise have existed.

The Inflationary Gap

Figure 10-8 shows another situation, in which equilibrium income is again A, but this time the level at which there is full employment is F. If you look at that aggregate demand curve, you will see that the economy cannot maintain the F level, because of excess demand. This excess demand will cause money incomes to go up to A. But there was already full employment at F. Manufacturers cannot hire more workers (there are none to hire), so they cannot increase output. How would you go about moving money income from F to A? If you increase prices, the result is inflation. Clearly, the economy is operating in the capacity range of aggregate supply and the gap can only result in price increases with no increase in real output. This excess demand (GH in Figure 10-8) is called the **inflationary gap**. To keep prices from increasing, you would have to decrease aggregate demand: lower consumption, cut down investment, or cut down government expenditures. In the inflationary year of 1981, consumption and investment spending were sharply

Inflationary Gap
The amount by which aggregate demand would have to decrease to move NNP to its full-employment (non-inflationary) level.

Figure 10-8
An Inflationary Gap

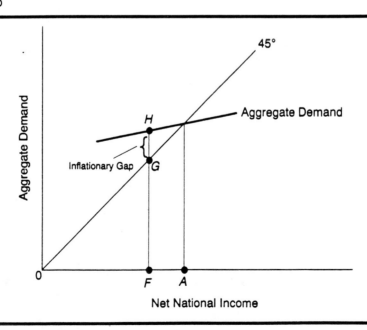

Although equilibrium income is *A*, the income that will achieve full employment and relatively stable prices is *F*. The excess demand, which causes inflation, is *GH*, called the *inflationary gap*.

curtailed by the higher interest rates resulting from a tightened monetary policy.

In brief, the *de*flationary gap is the deficit in demand that leads to unemployment, and the *in*flationary gap is the excess of demand that leads to inflation.

The Balanced-Budget Multiplier

Balanced-Budget Multiplier
The change in NNP that results when both government expenditures and taxes change in the same direction and by the same amount.

The government sector includes (1) government expenditures and (2) taxes. Suppose the government decides it must increase its *expenditures* by $10 billion this year. It also decides to increase *taxes* by $10 billion at the same time. When both GX and T increase by the same amount, the equilibrium level of income also increases by the same amount. When both decrease by the same amount, what happens? The opposite is true. When a government makes a balanced-budget decrease in taxes and in expenditures, equilibrium income falls by the amount of the decrease. The **balanced-budget multiplier** is 1.

We can explain this best through an example. Suppose that government expenditures and taxes both increase by 10 and that the MPC is ¾, or .75. An increase in government expenditures of 10 means that aggregate demand goes up by 10. Now comes the difficult part. When *taxes* go up by 10, only 75 percent of that increase (remember that MPC = .75) has a depressing effect on consumption. It is assumed that people take the extra 25 percent of the tax increase out of their savings. In other words, consumption drops by 75 percent of 10, or 7.5. So government expenditures add 10 to aggregate demand, but taxes reduce aggregate demand by 7.5. The net effect on aggregate demand is thus an increase of only 2.5. Yet we have just said that equilibrium income will rise by 10. This happens because 2.5 is ¼ of 10, so when the MPC is .75, the multiplier is 4. If you multiply 2.5 by 4 you get 10. It looks like this:

$$M = \frac{1}{1\text{-MPC}} = \frac{1}{.25} = 4 \times 2.5 = 10.$$

(Remember that the multiplier applies to changes in aggregate demand and that the balanced-budget multiplier applies to equal and same-direction changes in taxes and government expenditures.) With aggregate demand increased by 2.5 and with a multiplier of 4, total income increases by 10. In brief, when the government makes a balanced-budget increase of 10 (that means increasing both expenditures and taxes by 10), the equilibrium level of income also increases by 10. No matter what the MPC, the results are the same. You can test this by choosing a different MPC and using the same $10 for government spending and taxes.

The existence of the balanced-budget multiplier emphasizes the fact that changes in the federal budget are not neutral, they affect the level of income even when the changes are of a balanced-budget nature.

Fiscal Policy

In the days before Keynes, the neoclassical economists favored little government involvement in business affairs, a balanced national budget, and a government that used as few resources as possible. These tenets were based on the idea that when a market economy developed problems, it would automatically adjust itself so that the problems disappeared.

Is There a Self-Correcting Mechanism for the Economy?

We do not wish to leave you with the impression that economists since Keynes have concluded that market economies have no self-correcting mechanisms. While Keynes argued that such mechanisms could not be relied on to create full employment, evidence for the period since 1930 clearly indicates their existence. Wages and prices, in other words, are not completely inflexible. In the 1930s, for instance, wages and prices fell and this undoubtedly contributed to the recovery of 1937. The deep recession of 1981-1982, in another example, saw the economy operating at an estimated $265 billion below its GNP potential or capacity. Again, wages and prices fell, at least their rates of increase fell sharply. This point can be seen in Figure 10-9. Both wages and prices were

Figure 10-9
Rates of Growth in the U.S.: Wages and Prices, 1981–1986

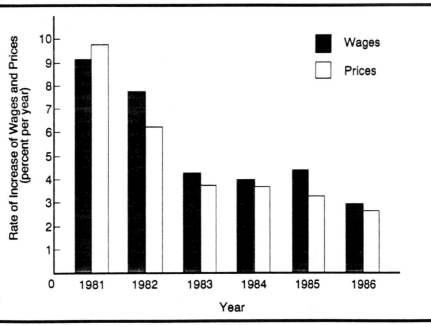

In the face of a large inflationary gap in 1981-1982, wage and price growth slowly declined over a 6-year period.

Source: Economic Report of the President, 1987.

growing at rates in excess of 9 percent in 1981. By 1986, their rates had been cut to 3 to 4 percent.

Most economists since Keynes, however, seem to argue that it would be unwise to simply wait for the workings of this wage-cost-price mechanism to correct either deflationary or inflationary gaps, though there are some who think all government intervention through fiscal or monetary policy or wage-price controls distorts and delays the self-correcting mechanism. The preponderance of view, however, seems to be that intervention appropriately timed and in the appropriate amounts is called for to reduce the delays in the self-correcting mechanism.

The makers of government economic policy have three aggregate demand-based approaches they can use to try to make the situation better:

1. *Fiscal policy.* Raise or lower government expenditures and taxes (as in the tax cuts of the 1960s and again in the early-1980s).

2. *Monetary policy.* Vary the supply of money and the rate of interest (as in the restrictive monetary policy of 1981 and 1982).

3. *Incomes policy.* Fix wages, prices, and profits (as in the Nixon wage and price freeze of the early-1970s).

The rest of this chapter will explore the various aspects of fiscal policy. We will have to wait to discuss monetary policy until we have analyzed money itself, and have seen how it can be increased or decreased. Only after the discussion of monetary policy will we examine incomes policy. We will end with a discussion of the various ways government tries to maintain full employment and still keep prices at some satisfactory level.

Discretionary Fiscal Policy

Discretionary Fiscal Policy
Changes in government expenditures and taxes that involve discretionary decisions about coping with changing economic conditions.

There are, as we have seen, factors in an economy that do tend to "automatically" offset economic instability. These stabilizers are not, however, powerful enough to prevent business fluctuations. Nor are these stabilizers completely automatic. Federal policy makers who seek to influence income and employment must make discretionary decisions. When we say **discretionary fiscal policy**, we mean a fiscal policy that has to be watched and changed, at the discretion of those who are doing the watching, on an ongoing basis to cope with changing economic conditions.

Functional Finance
Functional finance (or, as some call it, compensatory fiscal policy) aims at compensating for changes in aggregate demand in an economy's private sector by varying the public sector: government expenditures and taxes. When there is a recession, with increased

unemployment and a deflationary gap, fiscal policy should aim at eliminating this gap by increasing aggregate demand. When there is a business boom, with increased prices and an inflationary gap, fiscal policy should aim at eliminating the gap by decreasing aggregate demand. Only the government has the power to achieve such goals. While most economists have rejected the idea of "fine tuning" an economy through fiscal policy, many continue to regard discretionary changes in taxes and expenditures as important policy tools.

How Functional-Finance Economists Handle Recession
Suppose you are a follower of the functional-finance school of thought and your country is in the midst of a recession, with income falling, unemployment rising, and a wide deflationary gap. You want to increase aggregate demand. How do you handle the situation? One direct way is to increase government expenditures, since government expenditures are a large component of aggregate demand. On the other hand, you could cut taxes, which would shift

"I don't care what your economics professor told you in college—we're not going to base *our* fiscal policy on deficit financing."

the consumption function upward, again increasing aggregate demand. The decrease in taxes also increases investment.

Rising Deficits in the 1980s

Increasing government expenditures and decreasing taxes makes sense, in terms of the Keynesian view of a deflationary gap, but this policy has one big drawback. It creates a deficit in the federal budget; that is, expenditures are larger than income from taxes. Functional finance proponents have tended to minimize or ignore the effects of budget deficits, regarding them merely as tools to help accomplish employment objectives. As we see in Table 10-3, however, the deficits in the 1980s have been quite large and, in large measure, attributable to fiscal policy decisions. Two things are noteworthy in Table 10-3. First, the increasing deficits (111 billion in 1982 to 208 billion in 1985) were associated with declining levels of unemployment (9.5 percent in 1982 to 7.0 percent in 1985). Second, the *cyclical deficits component,* that part which arises from the automatic stabilizers (unemployment compensation, etc.) is now a relatively small part of the deficit. The *structural deficit component,* that part that arises from discretionary changes in tax and expenditure policy has grown in importance.

How Can Deficits Be Financed?

1. A *government can simply print currency to pay for the deficit.* It has been done several times. The Continental Congress printed currency during the American Revolution. Both the North and the South printed large amounts of currency during the Civil War. In 1922-1923, the Weimar Republic in Germany printed currency to cover World War I reparation payments. However, printing currency to cover deficits is considered highly risky because of its inflationary impact on an economy. (The hyperinflation in Germany in 1922-1924 under the Weimar Republic is a frightening example of chaos caused by printing money to cover government deficits. Inflation was so bad that a wheelbarrow full of marks was needed to buy a loaf of bread.) In Bolivia, in the mid-1980s, inflation reached 25,000 percent per year!

Table 10-3
Budget Deficits:
Cyclical and Structural Components 1981-1985

Fiscal Year	Unemployment Rate (%)	Total Deficit ($ billions)	Cyclical Deficit ($ billions)	Structural Deficit ($ billions)
1980	7.0	60	4	55
1981	7.5	58	19	39
1982	9.5	111	62	48
1983	9.5	195	95	101
1984	7.4	187	49	138
1985	7.0	208	44	163

Source: Economic Report of the President, 1985.

2. *The government can issue interest-bearing debt instruments (bonds and notes) for sale to private individuals and nonbanking corporations.* The U.S. government did this with Liberty Bonds during World War I and War Bonds during World War II. When people buy government bonds, their purchasing power is siphoned off. They cannot consume as much or invest as much, so these government bonds tend to counteract the expansionary effects of the deficit. Much of the federal budget deficits seen in Table 10-3 for the 1980s were financed through the sale of federal debt (short-term and long-term government bonds). Indeed the federal debt doubled between 1981 and 1987 (from less than $1 trillion to over $2 trillion).

3. *The government can issue bonds and aim their sale at banks.* The Federal Reserve helps banks keep their reserves high by buying government bonds from the banks, thus increasing their reserves. There are still enough loanable funds to loan to the public for consumption and investment and to loan to the government.

Note that in both the second and third methods of deficit financing, the government, through the sale of these bonds, is tapping private domestic and foreign savings.

How Functional-Finance Economists Handle Inflation
Suppose you are a follower of the functional-finance school of thought and your country is in the midst of an inflation, with rising prices, excess demand, and a serious inflationary gap. You want to decrease aggregate demand. How do you handle the situation? One direct way is to cut government expenditures. You could also increase taxes, thereby reducing consumption and probably investment. Decreasing government expenditures and increasing taxes may make sense, but this policy has two problems. One, it is more difficult to cut expenditures and raise taxes than to do the reverse. Two, it creates a budget surplus, which simply means that the government is taking in more money from taxes than it is spending.
The government can use this surplus in three possible ways:

1. *The government can use the surplus to pay off the national debt owed to individuals and nonbanking institutions.* However, this increases the purchasing power of these groups, and tends to increase consumption and/or funds for investment.

2. *The government can use the surplus to pay off the national debt owed to banks.* However, this increases the banks' liquid assets and can increase the supply of funds that they have to loan to the public for consumption and investment borrowing.

3. *The government may deposit the surplus in Treasury vaults or in Federal Reserve Banks, to be used to cover future budget deficits.* The first two possibilities generate expansive forces that tend partially to counteract the contracting or shrinking effect of the

original budget surplus. The third possibility removes the surplus funds from circulation and keeps them from counteracting the effects of initial efforts to decrease aggregate demand.

Government Expenditures

In the face of large deficits, functional finance no longer seems simple. Advocates continue to argue as follows: (1) Government expenditures have a greater impact on the economy because each government dollar spent increases aggregate demand, while only part of a change in taxes affects aggregate demand. (2) When the government spends money, taxpayers get more that a simple increase in aggregate demand. They get highways, schools, and hospitals; bureaucrats and bombers; and many other goods and services.

There are a number of problems associated with using government expenditures to counter variations in private spending. One of the most difficult is *timing*. How can the government time its expenditures in such a way that they offset the fluctuations in the private sector? Economic forecasting is far from being an exact science. For one thing, a group of economists cannot analyze the nation's economy and come up with a unanimous opinion. Then, too, statistical information about the economy is often not current because it takes so long to collect such information and process it. Forecasters generally have to work with economic statistics that are 1 to 3 months old.

Once a recession has hit and the economic forecasters in Washington realize it, the government hurries to bolster the economy with expenditures. But it takes *time* to design a program of expenditures, more time to get Congress to approve the program, then still more time to set up the administrative machinery and to begin the project. Often, the recession may already be over and the country may be in the midst of an inflation before these projects are really under way. Now, in the new inflationary period, how can the government immediately cut off expenditures? Can it leave highways ending in the middle of nowhere or schools and hospitals half completed?

Since the timing of government expenditures to offset business fluctuations is such a thorny problem, some people advocate that the government use transfer payments to achieve its stabilization goals. At least a government can shuffle these payments around in a hurry. *Transfer payments* are monies the government spends on such things as social security, pensions to disabled persons, welfare, veterans' benefits, subsidies to businesses, and so forth.

One can stimulate the economy by manipulating transfer payments. That is, when a recession develops, the government might stimulate the economy quickly by increasing welfare, social security, school lunch programs, farm subsidies, and the like. It sounds feasible, doesn't it?

But there is a catch. What happens when an inflation comes along? Can Congress reduce transfer payments at the very time that rising prices are creating serious problems for many of those who receive these payments? This would mean not only political problems for incumbent politicians but also that the poor who benefit from many of the transfer programs, would have to bear the brunt of the anti-inflationary measures. What Congressman wants to take milk away from babies? Would any senator or representative be willing even to introduce such a bill?

Clearly, it is easier for the government to introduce expenditures than to cut them out. Relying on expenditures to counteract economic instability encourages growth of a larger and larger government. Furthermore, special interest groups, such as farmers and defense contractors, rush forward each time there is a rumor of a cut and try to protect their own areas of government expenditure. Thus government expenditures carry within them a hidden trigger that may touch off inflation. Therefore, should government expenditures simply be set at levels needed to carry out useful projects? Or should they be determined primarily by variations in the nation's economic activity?

Taxes

Because of the flaws that economists find in a system of using expenditures to counter business cycles, some people feel that Congress ought to set government spending at whatever level is appropriate to fund essential programs and then use variations in *taxes* to speed up or slow down the economy.

But this approach also has its problems. During a recession, the government can certainly aim its expenditures directly at those people who need help. But if the government cuts taxes, it is not directly helping the people without jobs, though it is helping them indirectly, by stimulating consumer demand. The government is increasing taxpayers' income and, thus, the money they have for consumption as well as saving and investment. All this eventually should create new jobs. But the structurally unemployed are not helped even *in*directly by a cut in taxes. (Remember that structural unemployment means unemployment due to changes in technology and/or in the composition of demand.)

Furthermore, people take money for taxes only partly out of money they would otherwise have used for consumption, so it is only this part that affects aggregate demand. Therefore, larger variations are needed in taxes than would be needed in government expenditures to achieve the same relative effect. When the MPC is .75, a $12.25 billion decrease in taxes would be needed to create a $10 billion initial increase in aggregate demand, in order to increase income by $40 billion. But only a $10 billion increase in government expenditure would generate the needed multiplier effect to increase income by the desired $40 billion.

"Which way to the confessional?"

Of course, there are other aspects to this argument. An important consideration is that of economic philosophy. For example, who is going to decide what the billions will be spent on? If the government cuts taxes, then private individuals and firms will make most of the spending decisions. If the government increases expenditures, the spending decisions are made publicly, by lawmakers and cabinet members. Who *should* make the decisions? This question of economic philosophy, is one you will have to answer for yourself. Your perspective on it will, we hope, be broader as a result of taking a course in economics.

Just as special-interest groups affect the level and composition of expenditures, they also affect the composition, incidence, and level of taxation. Whenever taxes are to be changed, lobbyists for special interests descend upon Washington. Obviously, groups that are politically strong obtain tax concessions.

Balanced Budget

We discussed earlier the effect of the balanced-budget multiplier being 1. If the government increases both expenditures and taxes by the same amount, the equilibrium level of income increases by the same amount. In the case of a balanced decrease in the budget, the reverse applies. People who are concerned about the level of the national debt favor using a fiscal policy whereby the government makes balanced-budget changes sufficient to change aggregate demand as needed. Such a course of action does not affect the level of the national debt. Proposals to require a balanced budget have been advanced by many including former President Reagan who advocates a constitutional amendment to require it.

There are two problems associated with this balanced-budget idea. First, to achieve stability, the government would have to vary both taxes and expenditures by larger amounts. For example, assume that the MPC is .75 and that in order to achieve full employment national income must increase by $40 billion. The multiplier is 4. If the government increased expenditures only, it would have to increase them by $10 billion. If the government decreased taxes only, it would have to decrease them by $12.25 billion. If the government followed the balanced-budget policy, it would have to increase both expenditures and taxes by $40 billion.

Second, if the government followed a balanced-budget policy, it would have to increase taxes along with government expenditures, even during a recession. And a recession is a very hard time, politically or economically, to squeeze more taxes out of people.

There is one other problem connected with using government expenditures to stabilize an economy: would doing so increase the size of the government and the portion of resources used in the "public sector"? The federal government keeps getting bigger and bigger. For example, in the years between 1950 and 1971, the federal payroll quadrupled and the number of employees rose from 2.1 million to 2.9 million.

Some Flaws in the Keynesian System

People have been arguing about the Keynesian system ever since 1936. One does not need to hear all sides of this debate to understand Keynes's economic theory. However, there have been changes in the structure of the economy itself that have reduced the relevance of the simple Keynesian model. Let's look at some.

Writing in 1936, Keynes assumed that there was a close correlation between employment and the level of income. If the level of income increased, employment would also; the reverse would happen when income declined. Keynes felt that unemployment (except for frictional unemployment) was due to the fact that an economy did not have enough aggregate demand to achieve the desired level of income. But when we talked about business fluctuations, we said that a third variety of unemployment had made itself felt since World War II: structural unemployment. In structural unemployment, changes in technology and patterns of demand render groups of workers with certain kinds of skills irrelevant or unneeded. Since these skills are no longer needed, increasing effective demand does not help create jobs for structurally unemployed people. This is one problem Keynes did not take into account.

A second weakness involves the Keynesian model's usefulness as a tool for analyzing inflation. One can use the model to analyze the effects of demand-pull inflation, since the inflationary gap is essentially demand-pull inflation. (Excess aggregate demand forces prices up, and this has the effect of rationing the short supply.) However, we mentioned two other kinds of inflation: cost-push inflation and administered-price inflation. These inflationary forces stem from the exercise of monopoly power either by the suppliers of resources or by manufacturing firms. The monopolists may increase prices not only during periods when the level of demand is high, but also during times when demand is falling. Keynes did not take into account these last two kinds of inflation.

By the late-1980s, many economists saw the major weakness in the (simplified) Keynesian system presented in this chapter as being its sole focus on the role of aggregate demand in influencing employment and real income.

SUMMING UP

1. When one includes government expenditures in the simple model, and diagrams the GX curve so that it intersects savings, the equilibrium level of income is where savings equals intended investment plus government expenditures. At incomes *above* the equilibrium level, businesses produce more for consumption than the public consumes, and therefore have involuntary additions to inventories. At incomes *below* the equilibrium level, businesses produce less for consumption than the public consumes, and therefore have involuntary reductions in inventory.

2. When one includes government expenditures in the simple model, aggregate demand becomes consumption plus investment plus government expenditures. The equilibrium level of income is still the point at which aggregate quantity demanded equals aggregate quantity supplied (the 45° line). At incomes above that, businesses supply more goods and services than the public demands, and thus have unplanned additions to inventory. Therefore, income moves down toward equilibrium. At incomes below the equilibrium level, aggregate quantity demanded is greater than quantity supplied, and businesses have unplanned reductions in inventory. Thus, income also moves up, toward equilibrium.

3. People pay their taxes in part from money they would have spent on consumption and in part from income they would have saved. So taxes shift both the consumption function and the savings function downward. How great the shift is depends on the MPC and to MPS.

4. When one includes taxes in the simple model, the equilibrium level of income becomes the level at which taxes plus savings equals intended investment plus government expenditures. At incomes above the equilibrium level, businesses produce less for investment and for the government than people save and pay out in taxes, so that businesses produce more than the public consumes. Thus, businesses have involuntary accumulation of inventories, and income moves toward the equilibrium level. The reverse occurs at incomes below the equilibrium level.

5. For equilibrium to exist, aggregate quantity demanded must still equal aggregate quantity supplied, even after taxes and government expenditures are added. Now, however, taxes push down the C_f, and thus the rest of aggregate demand. At incomes above the equilibrium level, aggregate quantity supplied exceeds aggregate quantity demanded. This excess supply causes income to fall. When incomes are below the equilibrium level, the reverse occurs.

6. When an economy does not have enough demand to achieve an income that engenders full employment, this deficiency in demand creates a *deflationary gap*. When an economy has full employment, an excess of demand creates an *inflationary gap*.

7. When there is a balanced-budget change (a change in which government expenditures and taxes move in the same direction and by the same amount), the equilibrium level of income changes by the same amount and in the same direction. The *balanced-budget multiplier* is equal to one. Income changes because any change in expenditures affects aggregate demand by the full amount, while a change in taxes affects *only* aggregate demand by that portion the public takes away from consumption to pay taxes. The public dips into savings to pay part of the tax increase.

8. The experience of the 1980s suggests that there is a self-correcting mechanism in the economy, at least in the case of inflationary gaps. Wage and price growth slowed in the face of high unemployment rates. Most economists, though, would regard it as unwise to rely solely on this slow self-corrective mechanism to deal with inflationary and deflationary gaps.

9. *Discretionary fiscal policy* involves the conscious manipulation of government expenditures and taxes to move aggregate demand toward a preferred level of employment and prices as needed to cope with changing economic conditions.

10. *Functional finance,* or compensatory fiscal policy, is a policy by which the government compensates for changes in aggregate demand in the private sector. To stimulate employment during a recession, the government should increase expenditures and decrease taxes. This strategy will lead to a budget deficit. To curb price increases during an inflation, the government should cut

expenditures and increase taxes. This strategy will lead to a budget surplus.

11. Functional finance supporters have minimized or ignored the budget deficit, effects of expenditure increases, or tax cuts. Although the large federal deficits of the 1980s have been associated with reductions in unemployment, the *structural component* of the deficit, that associated with discretionary fiscal policy, has grown. Many have expressed concerns that budget deficits are not merely tools of functional finance but may have adverse effects as well.

12. The *advantages* of a government's varying its expenditures instead of varying taxes are as follows: (a) All of a government's expenditures stimulate aggregate demand, while only part of its taxes do. (b) The public gets goods and services in return for the government's expenditures. (c) The government can aim its expenditures directly at those it wishes to benefit; tax cuts aid specific groups only indirectly, by stimulating general demand.

13. The *disadvantages* of a government's varying expenditures instead of varying taxes are as follows: (a) It is hard to mesh government expenditures with the vagaries of business fluctuations. (b) It is politically very uncomfortable to cut off government programs once they have begun. Restricting variations in expenditures to variations in *transfer payments* (welfare, for example) means that the public does not receive any goods or services in return for the government expenditures. Another difficulty is that when the government cuts down on transfer payments during inflation, it is the underprivileged who bear the brunt of the anti-inflationary measures.

14. Relying on the balanced-budget multiplier to increase or decrease aggregate demand without changing the size of the national debt creates problems for these reasons: (a) To achieve the desired objective, the government must vary both expenditures and taxes by larger amounts than is necessary when it varies them and leaves the budget *un*balanced, (b) The political and practical problems of varying expenditures and taxes.

15. The simple Keynesian model of income and employment has become less relevant of late because of the increased importance of (a) structural unemployment, which does not respond readily to changes in aggregate demand, and (b) cost-push and administered-price inflation, which tend not to respond readily to declines in aggregate demand, and (c) it focuses solely on the role of aggregate demand rather than both aggregate demand and aggregate supply in achieving economic goals of employment and price stability.

KEY TERMS

Deflationary gap
Inflationary gap
Balanced-budget multiplier
Discretionary fiscal policy

QUESTIONS

1. Using the figure below, answer the following questions:

a. Equilibrium net national income using the intended investment + government expenditure approach is (a) 400, (b) 375, (c) 200, or (d) 300?

b. Equilibrium net national income using the aggregate quantity demanded equals aggregate quantity supplied approach would be (a) 400, (b) 375, (c) 200, or (d) 300?

c. The line labelled C + ?, in the figure above, represents aggregate demand including government expenditures and taxes. What should the line be labelled (a) C + II, (b) C_{at} (c) C + II + GX, or (d) C_{at} + II + GX?

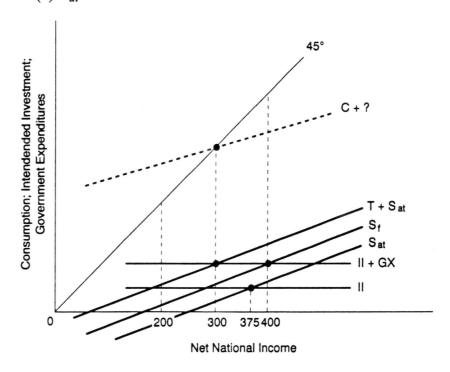

2. Assume that the MPC = $^2/_3$, the APC = $^2/_3$, and the equilibrium level of income is 300.

a. Government expenditures increase by 10. What is the new equilibrium level of income, consumption, savings, investment, and government expenditures? Explain your answers.

b. Assume that taxes increase by 10, in addition to the increase in government expenditures in part a. What is the new equilibrium level of income, consumption, savings, investment, government expenditures, and taxes?

3. Parts a and b of question 2 depict a balanced-budget increase; you should show an increase in income of 10 by the end of part b. Use a different MPC, and recompute a and b. With different MPCs, is the balanced-budget multiplier still 1?

4. How can one use a multiplier-accelerator model to explain business cycles?

5. How can one get rid of a deflationary gap? an inflationary gap?

6. If one wishes to stimulate aggregate demand by increasing government expenditures, the form in which the government makes these expenditures makes no difference. A dollar of expenditures is a dollar of expenditures! Do you agree? Explain (and be complete).

7. You are a member of the Joint Economic Committee of the Congress. The committee must formulate a plan for implementing functional finance during a recession with significant amounts of unemployment. They must decide whether to increase government expenditures for goods and services, or to increase transfer payments, or to decrease taxes, or some combination thereof. What would you recommend? Since the plan the committee adopts would benefit some people more than others, what *economic* justifications can you give for your choice over any alternative? What philosophical justification underlies your choice over any alternative?

8. Do you think it wise to wait for self-correcting mechanisms to solve problems of inflationary and deflation gaps? Why or why not?

Chapter 11:
Automatic Stabilizers and the National Debt

We have noted the huge increase in federal debt that has occurred since 1981. It is clear from that discussion that most of the build up resulted from *discretionary fiscal policy* decisions, those relating to changes in taxes and expenditures. President Reagan, riding the crest of a tremendous election victory in 1980, persuaded the congress to cut income taxes, enact investment tax credits for firms and begin a long-term build up in U.S. defense capability. Although it was argued that this fiscal policy stimulus would result in productivity growth and an expanding tax base, productivity growth in the 1980s (less than 2 percent per annum), though close to historic averages, actually was less than in the 1970s (3.2 percent per annum). The result has been the already noted budget deficits financed through growth in the national debt.

We also noted that there are *automatic stabilizers*, variations in tax revenues and federal expenditures that are timed automatically to variations in income and employment. These include such things as unemployment compensation and income tax rates that vary with people's incomes. In the first part of this chapter, we are going to look at these automatic stabilizers, to assess how influential they have been and can be in moderating both deflationary and inflationary gaps and, thus, the cyclical variations of the economy.

In the latter part of this chapter, we will turn to the federal debt and examine not only how it is created but also who bears its burdens. Finally, we will discuss some of the current controversies surrounding the federal debt including the push by some to mandate reductions in its size and by others to require a balanced federal budget.

AUTOMATIC STABILIZERS

Automatic Stabilizers
Non-discretionary
factors that increase
economic activity in
recessions and
decrease economic
activity in inflationary
periods.

Prior to World War II there were some business slumps that were relatively mild. However, occasionally the economy suffered severe depressions: 1907, 1921, 1929, and 1937. Until 1974-1975, U.S. recessions had been mild ones since World War II: 1949, 1954, 1958, 1960, 1969-1970. One explanation for the mildness of the contractions after the war, in comparison with many of those before it, is the postwar appearance of a number of new stabilizing characteristics in the economy. People refer to them as **automatic stabilizers**; non-discretionary factors that move against business cycles or increase economic activity in recessions and decrease economic activity in inflationary periods.

Automatic stabilizers tend to lessen a recession. They also tend to lessen an inflation, but, as we noted earlier, they have not proved strong enough to prevent business fluctuations. These stabilizers are not varied by deliberate manipulation, as are changes resulting from the government's discretionary policy, and they were not created by the government to function as stabilizers.

The inflation-recession of 1974-1975, one of the worst since the 1930s, presented a special problem. The existence of both recession and inflation at the same time brought into question whether automatic stabilizers are able to function under such conditions.

In the following section we shall discuss the functioning of the stabilizers until the 1974-1975 recession. Then we shall discuss the way they function during an inflation-recession such as that in 1981-1982.

The Employment Act of 1946

At the end of World War II, many people worried that the severe unemployment of the 1930s would reappear. Partly in response to those fears, Congress passed the Employment Act of 1946 which provided for the following:

1. This act made the federal government responsible for "promoting maximum employment, production and purchasing power." It formally made the government responsible for policies of economic stabilization.

2. The act created a Council of Economic Advisers to advise the President on stabilization and other economic problems. It also required the President to make an economic report each year, which is published under the title of *The Economic Report of the President.*

3. The act decreed that Congress was to participate in formulating economic policy, and to this end, it established a joint congressional committee, called the Joint Economic Committee.

A Longer Horizon

When the Employment Act of 1946 became law and the business community realized that from now on the government was going to take an active role in promoting employment and output, businesses changed their economic expectations. They were less subject to the fear of another Great Depression and this new freedom encouraged businesses to plan further into the future. That is, they could plan their investments for longer periods of time.

This longer *horizon* (or planning period) itself stabilized aggregate demand. Businesses felt that when times got bad, they could count on the contractions being short. So they did not shy away as much as before from new planned long-term investments. From 1946 to the present, the U.S. has had a relatively more stable climate for investment. That by itself has been a boom to the economy's stability, since investment is the most variable component of aggregate demand.

Increased Size of Government Expenditures

Prior to the Great Depression of the 1930s, the share of aggregate demand attributable to government expenditures was no more than 10 percent. Today this share has risen to between 25 and 30 percent. In other words, the federal government—plus state and local governments—buys at least ¼ of the nation's goods and services. This growth introduces a large stable element into aggregate demand, because government expenditures are not as readily influenced as private expenditures by variations in national income. Indeed, government expenditures can be *contracyclical*, that is rise when income is falling and, at least theoretically, decline when income is rising too rapidly.

However, despite the overall stabilizing effect of large government demand, variations in the *composition* of this demand can seriously affect local areas. For example, during and after the 1966 Johnson build-up in Vietnam, the military shifted its emphasis to more conventional weapons. This reduced the demand for engineers in the aerospace industry. Massachusetts alone lost 125,000 jobs. The closing of military installations after Vietnam created pockets of hardship throughout the nation, as did the canceling of certain projects, like the SST (supersonic transport plane), which affected Seattle and other areas. With the improvement of American-Soviet relations, there are plans to close military bases and reduce defense expenditures in the 1990s. These may well have effects similar to those of the 1960s.

Progressive Taxes

The post-World War II period has seen the rise of a number of structural features that have tended automatically to vary the tax

"I hope you'll bear in mind this is for a government that has everything."

Marginal Tax Rates
The percentage of tax paid on *additional* income.

rate and government expenditures in the way recommended by functional-finance economists.

Income taxes in the U.S. are progressive. Not only do tax obligations increase with income but also **marginal tax rates**, those on additional income rise, thus tax obligations vary at a greater rate than income. These taxes do have a stabilizing effect, even though they were not specifically designed to act as stabilizers. For example, during a recession, money incomes fall. Many people move into lower tax brackets. Thus, the absolute amount the government collects in taxes declines, and also a lower general tax rate applies. During an inflation, the reverse occurs. Money incomes rise. Many people move into higher income brackets, where higher tax rates apply.

As you can see, a progressive tax structure means lower tax rates during a recession, and higher ones during an inflation. At both extremes, tax collections nudge the level of disposable income in a direction that counteracts recession or inflation.

Taxes and Stability: The Near Future

The broad revision in the federal income tax that went into effect in 1987 has narrowed the number of marginal tax rates. Although it is too early to know the impact of this change on the stabilization role of income taxation, it is likely that this will reduce its impact. This is especially true since the inflation of the early-1980s lead in 1981 to indexing tax rates to overall price movements. Tax rates rise for individuals only as their *real income* grows. Although, "bracket creep," the movement upward of tax rates for individuals with growing incomes may have been stabilizing from the standpoint of the business cycle, it was widely regarded as inequitable since the income growth was often, in the face of inflation, nominal rather than real.

Expenditures That Stabilize

Certain forms of federal expenditure also change in a contra-cyclical manner; that is, they increase during a recession and decrease during an inflation, like unemployment compensation, for example. Social security payments also increase during a recession because, as jobs get scarce, more eligible people apply for social security. During an inflation, as the job picture gets brighter, the trend reverses, and people postpone retirement. Welfare payments rise more rapidly during a recession (jobs are scarce) than during an inflation (jobs are plentiful). Agricultural subsidies increase during a recession, as farm profits are falling. But subsidies fall during an inflation, when farm profits are rising.

Automatic Stabilizers: A Final Word

Whether from the structure of taxes or from the structure of government expenditures, the key point of the automatic stabilizers is that they cause disposable incomes to vary less than GNP over the course of business cycles. The stronger the automatic stabilizers are, the less sharp the variations in consumer spending will be and, thereby, the movements in income and employment. It follows, then that the stronger the automatic stabilizers are, the less the need for discretionary fiscal policy changes.

The Full-Employment Budget

We have presented two factors that determine the balance of the federal budget. The first one—discretionary fiscal policy. Functional finance is the keynote of this policy, by which the government deliberately creates a deficit to combat recessions (unemployment) and a surplus to combat inflation (rising prices). The second factor involves automatic stabilizers. During a recession, tax receipts fall and government expenditures tend to rise, generating a deficit. During an inflation the reverse occurs, at least in theory, which tips the scale toward a budget surplus.

Because of these two factors—discretionary, or deliberate, fiscal policy and automatic stabilizers—it is hard to measure the impact of budget policy. It cannot be done by simply looking at projected budget balances, or even actual balances. In 1958, President Eisenhower projected a near-balanced budget. But this balance meant cutting back federal expenditures. Unfortunately, there were, at the same time, decreases in private investment. So the country entered the recession of 1958, and the actual deficit in the federal budget was $12 billion. Sometimes the error is in the other direction: in 1972, the projected deficit was $33.9 billion, while the actual deficit was only $15.9 billion. The economy had expanded more rapidly than anticipated, which increased tax receipts.

Full-Employment Budget
A budget that balances government expenditures against the level of tax receipts that *would* exist if the economy were at full employment.

Comparing projected and actual budget balances is not very informative. One cannot see the impact of the federal budget on the economy because that impact depends on the state of the economy. For this reason, economists developed the concept of the **full-employment budget**. Instead of balancing government expenditures against actual tax receipts, the full-employment budget balances government expenditures against the level of tax receipts that *would* exist if the economy were at full employment.

For example, the 1972 full-employment balance was a $7.7 billion deficit, while the 1973 full-employment balance was a $5.8 billion surplus. This indicates that the level of expenditures in 1972 was more expansionary than in 1973. The full-employment deficit of 1972 (during a period of close-to-full employment) had an inflationary effect. The 1973 full-employment surplus had a contracting effect.

Structural and Actual Deficits

Actual Deficit
In the federal budget the difference between actual federal expenditures and actual federal revenues.

Structural Deficit
In the federal budget, the deficit that would exist if the economy were operating at full employment.

It is worth mentioning again that just as projected and actual balances in the federal budget are difficult to project, so, by extension, are projected and actual deficits in that budget. The **actual deficit** is, of course, the difference between actual federal revenues and actual federal expenditures. The **structural deficit**, on the other hand, is a measure of what the deficit would be if the economy were operating at full employment. If the actual deficit is far larger than the structural deficit, the economy is operating far below its potential. From mid-1982 until 1984, the American economy was in this position. From mid-1984 to 1989, the actual and structural deficits have been nearly the same indicating that the economy is operating at a level close to its potential.

THE NATIONAL DEBT

In our discussion of functional finance, we mentioned the national debt only briefly. We did not fully discuss its size or how fast it is growing. Then we were mainly concerned with how to maintain economic stability and how to minimize the economic and social costs of unemployment and inflation. We assumed that when the government increased the national debt, it was for a worthwhile purpose. While this may be, we must recognize the fact that many people are worried about the national debt and its unprecedented peace-time increase in the 1980s. Let's look at some facts about it. Table 11-1 lists the figures for the national debt from 1929 to 1986 and Figure 11-1 presents them in graphical form.

The Size of the Debt

Back in 1929, the federal debt was about $16 billion. In 1989 it was over $2.8 trillion—a rise of more than 3,100 percent in 60 years (see Table 11-1). To understand what this increase means, you have to bear in mind a number of points:

1. Until the Reagan presidency, most of the increases occurred during wars, to pay for the huge expenditures by the military. Table 11-1 shows that the expenditures during World War II (1940 to 1946) increased the debt by about $200 billion. That alone

Table 11-1
National Debt, GNP, and Interest (in current dollars), 1929-1989

1	2	3	4	5	6	7	8
Year	National Debt (billions)	GNP (billions)	Interest Payme nts (billions)	National Debt as Percentage of GNP (2 + 3)	Interest as Percentage of GNP (4 + 3)	Per Capita National Debt	Current Per Capita Disposable Income
1929	16.3	103.1	0.7	16	0.7	134	
1940	50.9	99.7	1.1	51	1.1	382	573
1946	259.5	208.5	4.2	124	2.0	1,827	1,100
1950	256.7	284.8	4.5	90	1.6	1,689	1,364
1954	278.8	364.8	5.0	76	1.4	1,404	1,600
1960	290.4	503.7	7.1	58	1.4	1,604	1,937
1964	318.7	632.4	8.3	50	1.3	1,651	2,280
1970	389.2	976.5	18.3	40	1.9	1,895	3,376
1974	493	1,397	31.3	35	2.2	2,324	4,621
1975	544.1	1,598.4	18.8	34	1.1	3,591	5,291
1976	631.9	1,782.8	23.2	35	1.3	4,061	5,744
1977	709.1	1,990.5	25.1	35	1.3	4,477	6,262
1978	780.4	2,249.7	28.2	35	1.2	4,867	6,968
1979	833.8	2,508.2	30.8	33	1.2	5,170	7,682
1980	914.3	2,732.0	36.3	33	1.3	5,518	8,421
1981	1,003.9	3,052.0	52.2	33	1.7	6,038	9,243
1982	1,147.0	3,166.0	60.1	36	1.9	6,849	9,724
1983	1,381.9	3,405.7	68.1	40	2.0	7,848	10,340
1984	1,576.7	3,765.0	87.1	42	2.3	8,815	11,265
1985	1,827.2	4,010.3	92.3	46	2.4	9,256	11,986
1986	2,132.9	4,235.0	107.1	50	2.6	10,644	12,705
1987	2,345.6	4,524.3	138.6	52	3.1	9,617	13,140
1988	2,600.8	4,880.6	151.7	53	3.1	10,555	14,116
1989	2,866.2	5,233.2	169.1	55	3.2	11,520	15,191

Source: *Economic Report of the President*, 1987 1990; *Statistical Abstract of the United States*, 1987.

Figure 11-1
Graphical Representation of National Debt and GNP from Table 11-1 (billions of dollars)

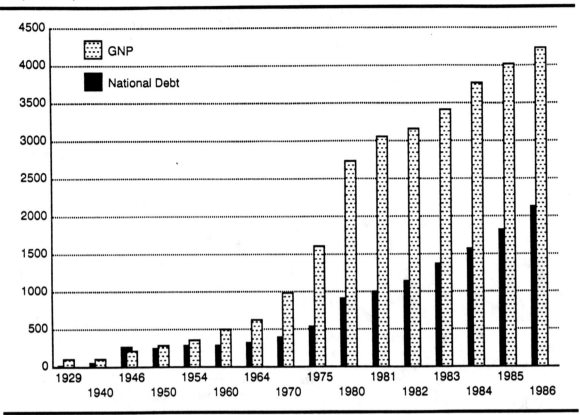

accounted for almost half the total debt in 1974. After a slight fall between 1946 and 1950, the debt rose sharply again during the Korean War (1950 to 1954). From 1964 to 1972, during the Vietnam War, debt went up by more than $100 billion. The doubling (in nominal terms) of the debt since 1981 has come during peace-time. To some, it has raised questions about the basic fiscal process of the U.S. and about congressional-presidential relationships within that process.

2. To assess the significance of the national debt, one must compare it with other measures of economic activity. To do so makes the size of the figures less frightening in some respects but troublesome in terms of current trends. For example, columns 2 and 4 of Table 11-1 show the size of the debt and the size of interest payments. But now look at columns 5 and 6. For many years, there seemed to be a long-term trend downward after 1946 in the percentage that the debt was of the GNP (from 124 percent in 1946 to 33 percent in 1981). Since 1981, however, the trend has sharply reversed. By 1986, the debt had risen to more than 50 percent of GNP.

How Significant is the Debt?

There is increasing concern about the federal deficit and the outstanding debt. A distinguished economist, Robert Eisner, concludes, however, that the debt is overstated. He suggests that we treat the federal government as a firm and develop a capital budget for it (subtracting from its liabilities, its financial assets). Doing so leaves us with the government's "net debt." The main liabilities are the government's securities (bonds, etc.). Its assets include cash, taxes due, loans made and real assets (property such as land and including even the White House). For 1980, Eisner figures the liabilities at about $1.1 trillion. The financial assets he calculates at about $700 billion. This leaves a net debt of about $450 billion. Adding in the value of the real assets though (over $700 billion), Eisner concludes that the "net worth" of the federal government is positive, about $280 billion!

At the very least, Eisner's calculations remind us that the "Feds" do indeed own a lot of real assets. It is interesting to note that the 1988 budget agreement between the President and the Congress calls for selling some of those assets to reduce the deficit.

The figures for interest payments as a percentage of GNP fell, too, until the period between 1964 and 1974, when they rose to 2.2 percent of GNP. There was a reason for this rise. The government was trying to put the brakes on the post-1966 Vietnam inflation, so it increased the interest rates. When interest rates go up, the government has to pay more too. Since 1981, the interest payments as a percentage of GNP have gone from 1.3 percent to 2.6 in 1986.

Another figure that fell between 1946 and 1960 was per capita national debt (column 7 in Table 11-1). After 1960 it rose again rising sharply in the 1980s.

All this goes to show that increases in the national debt show up whenever our country is involved in a war and when its discretionary fiscal policies lack restraint.

Qualitative Significance

There is a big difference between government debt and individual debt. When you borrow money, you increase your purchasing power in the present. You can buy that car or piano you want. The pinch comes in the future, when you must use part of each month's paycheck to repay the loan. For the next 36 months you will be in debt to the bank. This will inevitably reduce your future purchasing power and cut down the number of things you will buy. Thus, one effect of borrowing by an individual is to reduce that person's purchasing power over a period of time. Some people get so deeply in debt that their incomes cannot cover repayment and they become insolvent.

Debt owed by the government and to be repaid in its own currency is different. Federal borrowing *transfers* purchasing power from one group to another—from those who buy government bonds to those who receive the income from government expenditures. The country's purchasing power continues at the same level. When the government eventually pays off the bonds, this again transfers purchasing power from one group to another—from taxpayers, whose taxes go to pay the debt, to the bond holders.

When the government pays interest on the national debt, the same thing happens. The citizens pay their taxes, which go to pay the interest. The people to whom the government owes the debt receive the interest payments. The net result is no change in total purchasing power.

If the national debt were to be evenly distributed among the entire population, according to the amount of taxes each person paid, each citizen would own a little of the debt. The government would owe a little to you, a little to me. When you paid your taxes, you would know that your tax money would return to you in the form of interest payments. Your right hand would pay your left.

However, the national debt is *not* evenly distributed, and so income is redistributed from some groups to others. This does have some effect, but it is quite different from what most people worry about when they think of the national debt.

Clearly there are major differences between private debt and the national debt. All debt issued by the federal government is denominated and repayable in U.S. dollars. Since these dollars are either printed by the U.S. government or created through its monetary system, there is no limit on the ability of the federal government to finance its debt through creating dollars other than the consequences of inflation and other undesirable results that might occur. While the U.S. has become a net debtor nation in the late-1980s, its federal debt is, in these respects, quite unlike that of Mexico, Brazil and other debtor nations whose debt is also repayable in dollars. Those nations, unlike Congress and the President cannot print or otherwise create U.S. dollars.

A troublesome element of the growing national debt in the 1980s is that a growing proportion of it is foreign held. Unlike the internal redistribution we referred to earlier, these repayments and interest payments do involve a burden since they transfer resources (via claims to dollars) to individuals and institutions abroad.

Debt Burdens and Future Generations

An economist at the University of Rochester, Robert Barro, doubts that deficits in the federal budget are nearly as stimulative to the economy as functional finance proponents argue. "Individual consumers," says Barro, "are interested not only in their own consumption but also that of their children who in turn, will be interested in the consumption of their children." When the federal government engages in deficit spending, it keeps current taxes lower than they would be if it financed its spending out of current tax revenues.

Individuals realize that in the future taxes must be raised to pay for the current deficit-financed outlays by government. In order not to burden their children with higher taxes in the future, they will consume less and save more in order to leave bequests to their children. Tax payers, thus, form expectations about future tax increases and, as a result, may offset the stimulative effects of the deficit spending by (rationally) saving more and reducing aggregate demand. The Barro view that deficit spending has only limited effects in stimulating the economy is controversial though it has received some empirical support. It is interesting in that in contrast to the Keynesian view, it takes a much longer-term look at deficits.

Distortive Effects of Debt: Crowding Out

What happens when the federal government chooses to expend large sums but does not finance these expenditures through tax revenues? Suppose, for example, that Congress and the President decide to spend $50 billion on a new anti-missile defense system and to finance it entirely through new U.S. Treasury bonds. Some economists who are highly critical of the huge increase in federal debt argue that such debt when sold in financial markets, "crowds out" some other more interest sensitive private spending by raising interest rates.

Those who are unpersuaded by the crowding out argument concede that there may be some distortion which is akin to the government imposing its tastes on the private sector with respect to the uses of financial capital. Those who continue to view deficits as functional finance tools reply that crowding out is minimal and simply a result of all interest rate increases, not only those caused by debt financed government deficits. Functional finance proponents say that the net effects of the deficits are stimulative, they create greater aggregate demand and multiplier effects that expand real income and employment. The stimulus to the economy, say proponents of deficit spending is more likely to "crowd in" than "crowd out" investors as the economy expands.

Why the Deficits of the 1980s?
Where Do We Go from Here?

Prior to the 1980s, deficits seemed, as we noted earlier, to be connected with national emergencies, especially wars and depressions. No such explanation will suffice for recent years. Why do we seem to be unable now to control the revenue-expenditure relationships of the federal government?

One explanation that has come to enjoy increased currency is that of *public choice*, an attempt to explain governmental decisions with accepted economic theory. Let us suppose, say public choice theorists, that public officials have as a primary objective their reelection. To maximize the chances of success, they must broaden their appeal to as many influential groups as possible, especially those who are the most likely voters and whose political action committees may contribute to campaigns.

How does an elected official broaden appeal? By supporting expenditure programs (or tax benefit programs) that provide benefits to the likely voters and contributors. This creates an incentive for such officials to vote for such expenditures as well as trade votes (called "logrolling") with other officials who have their own special interests to appeal to. All well and good, say public choice advocates until payment for these programs must be provided. As citizens, we enjoy the benefits of public expenditures, but we resist paying the increased taxes to pay for them. This asymmetry between support for benefits and resistance to taxes, tied with the efforts of elected officials to secure reelection is ripe for the creation of deficits.

Why, you may say, have we witnessed this tendency toward deficits only since the 1930s, especially since the 1960s? One explanation is that offered by James Buchanan, a Nobel laureate and founder of public choice. Before the 1930s, there was a kind of Victorian ethic that commonly held that budget deficits were bad. While they might be tolerated for short periods of public emergency, they were not to be the norm in public finance. After Lord Keynes' *General Theory* in 1936, and particularly with its wide spread acceptance in the 1960s, this restraint no longer was binding. It was no longer moral to practice fiscal restraint; it was, indeed, immoral to do so in a world of deflationary gaps and real income multipliers and accelerators.

Now we are hearing a renewed cry to impose the morality and discipline of a balanced federal budget. Buchanan thinks it might substitute for the victorian morality of an earlier era. Former President Reagan among others supports the idea. Some economists say it is unattainable if not undesirable because it would rob us of the tools of functional finance or merely shift expenditures to other levels of government. The controversy continues as the national debt and federal budget deficits gain growing attention.

SUMMING UP

1. Business fluctuations after World War II (1945) were much milder than before the war, in part because of certain new characteristics in the U.S. economy that tended to create greater stability. These are called *automatic stabilizers* or tax and expenditure programs that vary inversely with changes in income and employment.

2. The automatic stabilizers contributed to economic stability in the following ways: (a) The Employment Act of 1946 committed the

federal government to work toward maximum employment and stable prices. (b) The government's assumption of responsibility for economic stabilization gave businesses the confidence to plan their investments for longer periods of time in the future. They extended their economic horizons, which created greater investment stability. (c) Government expenditures, which are not readily influenced by business fluctuations, increased from 9 percent of GNP in 1929 from 25 to 30 percent of GNP in the 1980s. This buying by the government created a larger and more stable element in aggregate demand. (d) Progressive income taxes cause an automatic increase in tax rates during inflation (as incomes go up) and an automatic cut in tax rates during a recession (as incomes decline). (e) Certain forms of government expenditures (unemployment compensation, social security, welfare, and agricultural subsidies), which rise during recessions and fall during inflations, counteract business fluctuations.

3. Both federal tax and expenditure structures cause disposable incomes to vary less than GNP. The stronger are these stabilizers, the less need there is for discretionary fiscal policy.

4. The best concept to use in measuring the impact of the federal budget on the economy is the *full-employment budget*. According to this concept, actual government expenditures are compared with theoretical tax receipts that the government would have received if the economy had been at full employment. The *actual deficit* in the budget is compared with the *structural deficit*, that which would exist at full employment to determine how close the economy is to full employment.

5. Between 1929 and 1986 (57 years) the federal debt rose from $16 billion to more than $2 trillion. Of this, $322 billion piled up during World War II, the Korean War, and the Vietnam War. Almost half of the debt has been created since 1981.

6. For many years after 1946, the debt was shrinking as a percentage of GNP, falling from 124 percent in 1946 to 33 percent in 1981. Since 1981, the debt has grown more rapidly than GNP and by 1986 had reached more than 50 percent of GNP. This rapid increase in the 1980s has caused the national debt to be increasingly regarded as a source of problems.

7. A significant effect of the national debt is in income redistribution. Money is transferred from taxpayers to the government, which uses the money to pay the interest on the debt. The people who receive the interest on the debt are the holders of government bonds. In this respect, the increasing foreign ownership of the debt in the 1980s represents a potential burden and problem.

8. Some critics of the national debt argue that it causes "crowding out" in financial markets, that is it distorts private uses of financial

capital by raising interest rates and crowding interest sensitive private investments out. Advocates of functional finance say that the stimulative effects of the deficits that give rise to the debt, (the increase in investment real income and jobs), more than offset the crowding out and even result in "crowding in" investments.

9. Robert Barro argues that deficits have very limited effects in stimulating the economy because individuals, expecting tax increases in the future and not wishing to burden their children, will save more in order to leave bequests to their descendents. As a result, the stimulative effect of public spending may be offset by the contractive effect of decreased private spending.

10. Much concern has been directed to an explanation for the growing gap between federal expenditures and revenues. One explanation that has received increasing attention is *public choice*. This school of thought says that deficits can be traced to efforts of elected officials to gain reelection. To do so, officials cater to groups likely to vote and to contribute to campaigns by offering the benefits of expenditure programs. Because voters enjoy benefits but resist tax increases, officials are unlikely to finance expenditures with current tax revenues.

11. The public choice explanation for the recent timing of (non-war and emergency) related deficits is that the morality of deficits changed after Keynes and functional finance. Since 1936, according to public choice theorists, it has been immoral not to run budgetary deficits with their stimulative effects on the economy.

12. In the 1980s, we witness a call for a return to balanced budgets and eliminating or narrowing deficits.

KEY TERMS

Automatic stabilizers
Marginal tax rates
Full-employment budget
Actual deficit
tructural deficit

QUESTIONS

1. The automatic stabilizers are not strong enough to prevent business fluctuations. How do you think they could be strengthened? What new ones might be invented?

2. Are private and public debts the same? If not, in what ways do they differ?

3. Under what conditions would you start to worry about the size of the national debt?

4. Should General Motors pay off all its bonds as quickly as possible and maintain a balanced budget? Does the same reasoning apply to the federal debt?

5. You are the economic adviser to the President and you need to help him formulate a position on discretionary fiscal policy and automatic stabilizers. Let's suppose that inflation is 12 percent and unemployment is nine percent. What strategy will you recommend to the President? Are you going to emphasize discretionary fiscal policy or automatic stabilizers? How and why? Remember that policy recommendations are never cost free. Most often, policies benefit some and not others. In your recommendations be sure you establish the positions' *economic* justifications. Also be sure you establish your *moral* or *ethical* justifications.

SUGGESTED READINGS

Bowen, William G., Richard G. Davis, and David H. Kopf. "The Public Debt: A Burden on Future Generations?" *American Economic Review*. September 1960, pp. 701-706.

Browning, Edgar K. and Jacqueline M. Browning. *Public Finance and the Price System*. New York: MacMillan, 1983.

Cargill, Thomas F. and Gillian G. Garcia. *Financial Reform in the 1980s*. Stanford: Hoover Institution, 1985.

Economic Report of the President. G.P.O., Washington, D.C., published annually.

Eisner, Robert. *How Real is the Federal Deficit?* New York: Free Press, 1986.

Heller, Walter W. *New Dimensions of Political Economy*. Norton, New York, 1967.

McClelland, Peter D. (ed.) "The Burgeoning Federal Deficit," Part VII, Articles 32 through 38 in *Introduction to Macroeconomics*. McGraw-Hill, 1988.

North, Douglass C. and Roger LeRoy Miller. "More Taxes and Less Work" in *The Economics of Public Issues*, Eighth Edition. New York: Harper and Row, 1990.

Okun, Arthur. *The Political Economy of Prosperity*. Norton, New York, 1969.

Pechman, Joseph A. *Federal Tax Policy,* 4th Ed. Washington, D.C. Brookings Institution, 1983. Esp. Chs 1, 2, 3.

Rasche, Robert H. "Deficit Projections vs. Deficit Forecasts." Federal Reserve Bank of San Francisco, *Weekly Letter*. July 5, 1985. Reprinted in Peter D. McClelland, *Introduction to Macroeconomics*. New York: McGraw-Hill, 1988.

Sobato, Larry J. *PAC Power*. New York: W. W. Norton, 1985.

Application to Chapter 11:
The "Share Economy":
Would it Create Full Employment?

As we have seen the percentage of people unemployed (those who did not work last week and have been looking for work for at least 4 weeks) has been up and down in a near roller coaster fashion for the last 60 years. The "Keynesian revolution" ascribed this tendency to instability to a lack of wage and price flexibility in the economy. The Keynesian recipe for dealing with that flaw in a modern market economy was government management of aggregate demand; i.e., expenditure and tax programs to push the economy toward full employment at stable prices.

By the 1980s, there seemed to be appreciably less enthusiasm for this type of macroeconomic policy. Faced with an escalating federal debt and seemingly intractable budget deficits, "Keynesian" demand management would be difficult to pursue even if it enjoyed widespread political support. A number of economists have undertaken to identify ways to create a tendency toward full employment without major fiscal policy involvement by government. The most prominent of such efforts is that of Martin Weitzman, an economist at MIT. In a book entitled *The Share Economy*, Weitzman argues that both inflation and unemployment problems can be solved by making wages more flexible and by tying the pay of workers at least partly to the profitability of the firms that employ them.

Share Economy
A proposal under which some of the wage earnings of labor would be tied to the profitability of firms.

A Two-Wage System

Weitzman would separate wages into two components, a base pay that does not vary with firms' profits and a second component that would fall as profits diminish and rise as profits increase. The current wage system in the U.S. results in lay-off of workers in a recession as firms' cut back production. The result is an increase in unemployment. Under the "share economy" proposals, the (1) non-base component of wages would fall as firms revenues decline, (2) costs of production will decrease, (3) prices will be cut to increase sales, and (4) the work force will be maintained (a scenario similar to the classical one that Keynes sought to disprove). Weitzman thus believes that full employment can be maintained even in the face of a recession.

Weitzman argues that even if only 15 to 25 percent of workers' wages were in the form of profit sharing, this stabilizing influence on unemployment would be effective. This would happen in a "share economy" without sacrificing the resource mobility essential to any capitalist system. Workers would not be laid off when there was a declining demand for a firm's products. If the decline continued though, the firm's profitability and the wages it would offer workers would fall relative to those in growing industries. When the wage gap grew large enough, thus, labor would relocate to higher wage areas of the economy, where consumer's apparently prefer those labor resources to be used (in view of the higher prices they are willing to pay for the growing industry's output).

When, asked if this "share economy" proposal has been tried elsewhere, Weitzman points to Asia. "Japanese workers receive 25 percent of their pay as a bonus. In Korea and Taiwan about 15 percent of pay comes as a bonus. Even government workers in Korea have their pay tied to profitability." The proposal would of course, cause workers to assume some of the risks of business; in other words, workers would become partly venture capitalists. Because of this, Weitzman expects the greatest opposition to his proposal to come from unions whose senior member's are least vulnerable to lay off and who through seniority, command the highest wage premiums. Such workers would be asked to accept more wage variability in order to assure a higher and more stable level of employment.

Critiques of the Share Economy

It might be reasonable to suppose that "Keynesian" economists would oppose Weitzman's proposal for it would seem to diminish the role of demand-management macroeconomic policy. In fact, some of the most prominent "Keynesians," while expressing doubts about the proposal, have urged that it be seriously investigated. Lawrence Summers of Harvard says: (1) in view of the widely held belief that a natural rate of unemployment precludes effective long-run trade-offs between inflation and unemployment, and (2) that the gains achievable by increasing the average level of employment" make other macroeconomic goals seem trivial. Summers believes that the system deserves study and that it would not necessarily have an inflationary bias because the tight labor markets resulting from its low rate of unemployment would not cause upward pressure on wages. Indeed, he states that, "with profit-sharing, taut labor markets and stable prices can coexist."

Nonetheless, Summers argues that there is no free lunch offered by the share economy. Negative effects could come about from two sources: (1) fellow worker problems, and (2) investment problems. The fellow worker problem derives from the incentives of workers faced with a declining revenue pie to resist hiring additional workers and an incentive to let the least productive workers go. Workers, concludes Summers, would be in competition with each other which would be exactly the opposite of the Japanese system. The investment problem comes from fixing the profit share of the revenue pie while allowing the wage component to vary. This, according to Summers, seems likely to reduce incentives to investment.

Another prominent macroeconomist, Alan Blinder of Princeton University, says the Weitzman plan may be seen in two somewhat different ways. As a device for ending unemployment, it is a "bottle half full"; as an intrusion on the business cycle (with its elimination of less productive enterprises) it is a "bottle half empty". Blinder, who sees unemployment elimination as *very* important, believes the bottle "three quarters full". In addition, he says, by giving workers greater job security and a greater stake in the companies they work for, there might be higher productivity and less resistance for labor-saving technical change.

Blinder refuses to reject the Keynesian idea that "shorter and shallower" recessions are better, and continues to argue that the externalities of firms' actions (affects on consumers' incomes) "justifies government intervention to smooth business cycles."

What Is the Status of the Share Economy?

Clearly, the wage-price system of the American economy continues to be different from the share economy. Indeed, as Blinder notes, even if the Weitzman plan is socially optimal, it will not be adopted unless it is also seen as privately optimal. To this end Weitzman has argued for a tax subsidy to firms that would cause them to adopt the plan. Blinder says that there are numerous other practical problems that would have to be solved as well. Many economists, Keynesians and non-Keynesians alike, feel that the proposal is worth serious study.

SUMMING UP

1. The Keynesian arguments for government intervention to manage aggregate demand and reduce the severity of business cycles were less well received in the 1980s. One of the proposals to replace this demand management is contained in the idea of a "share economy" advanced by Martin Weitzman.

2. Under the share economy proposal, there would be two components of the wage payment to workers. Most of the payment would be in the present contract form which guarantees a wage but not permanent employment. The second component would be tied to the profitability of firms, with that share rising as profits increase and falling as profits diminish.

3. Under the share economy proposal, wages would fall in a recession. This would result from falling demand and reduced profits of firms. Thus, firms, will not lay off workers but will cut prices to restore sales.

4. Weitzman's plan would still retain the desirable feature of labor mobility. Declining industries would still lose labor to growing industries because of increasing wage differentials between the two.

5. Weitzman believes his plan would be akin to the systems of successful economies such as Japan, Taiwan, and Korea. Workers would assume some of the risks of business in order to obtain job security. Unions who protect senior members from lay offs may be the strongest opponents of the plan.

6. Keynesians such as Lawrence Summers and Alan Blinder believe that the plan, while not perfect or a "free lunch" deserves to be studied. Given the view that there is a natural rate of unemployment below which the economy cannot be pushed in the long run, this may be an attainable way to achieve full employment.

7. Summers concludes that the plan may not have an inflationary bias. However, workers would be in competition with each other and the least productive workers might be let go as a result of the "fellow worker" problem. There might also be a discentive to investment as a result of a decreasing profit share.

8. Alan Blinder regards the proposal as worthy of serious study. Not only does it help solve the *very* serious problems associated with unemployment it gives greater job security and a greater stake in the company to workers. Both things might raise productivity and lessen resistance to labor-saving technical change.

9. The share economy will not be adopted unless it is seen as *privately* optimal. Weitzman argues for tax subsidies to firms to induce their acceptance of the system. There are, no doubt, other practical problems to be solved as well.

KEY TERM

Share Economy

QUESTIONS

1. What is the "Keynesian" solution to the problem of the business cycle?

2. What would be the system of wage payment in a "share economy." How does this differ from the present wage-price system?

3. Would there be labor immobility in a share economy? Explain.

4. What nations have wage systems similar to that in the "share economy?"

5. Who would you expect to strongly oppose a share economy? Why?

6. Why has the acceptance of a natural rate of unemployment heightened interest in the "share economy?"

7. What does Summer's mean by fellow worker problems and investment problems associated with a share economy?

8. What might the share economy do to worker job security, labor productivity and implementation of labor-saving technological changes?

9. Identify some of the problems in getting agreement to create a "share economy."

SUGGESTED READINGS

Blinder, Alan S. "The Share Economy: A Bottle Half Full." *Challenge.* November-December, 1986.

Summers, Lawrence H. "On the share Economy: Prospects and Problems." *Challenge.* November-December, 1986.

Weitzman, Martin. "The Share Economy—Can It Solve Our Economic Ills?" *U.S. News and world Report.* August 26, 1985.

Lee, Susan. "High Wages Versus Unemployment—A Way to Break the Impasse." *Forbes.* March 11, 1985.

Readings in Introductory Macroeconomics. Peter D. Editor. 1987-1988 Annual Edition. "Proposal for a Share Economy." (Contains reprints of the Blinder, Summers, Weitzman articles).

Levinson, Marc. "Economic Policy: The Old Tools Won't Work." *Dun's Business Month.* January, 1987.

Judd, John P. and Bharat Techan. "Unemployment and Inflation." Federal Reserve Bank of San Francisco, *Weekly Letter.* March 9, 1990.

Chapter 12:
Money in the Modern Economy

Money is an important part of an economy. Yet the factors of production, the resources essential to producing things (land, labor, capital, entrepreneurship) do not contain money. Money does not directly produce anything although resources are required to produce money. In view of this, how does money contribute to turning out automobiles or typewriters or haircuts?

Before we can trace a clear relationship between the supply of money and the production of goods and services, there are some questions we must answer in this chapter about money itself: What is money? What are its functions? How is it increased or decreased, and how is this process controlled? How does the system of banks and non-bank financial institutions work? How does money affect the level of economic activity and prices? Most important, how can the government influence the supply of money in order to bring about a desired level of income, employment, and prices?

A Barter System of Exchange

Barter
A system in which goods are exchanged for other goods.

People can produce goods and services without the existence of money; where there is no money, goods must be exchanged for other goods. When this happens, the system of exchange is called **barter**.

For example, Farmer Nielson needs 100 bushels of wheat and a pair of shoes, size 11. He looks around his farm to see what he can barter and decides that his 250-pound pig is surely worth 100 bushels of wheat and a pair of size-11 shoes. He takes his pig to his nearest neighbor, Farmer Gomez, a wheat farmer, and offers to barter the pig for the wheat and the shoes. Farmer Gomez agrees that it's a fair exchange, but although he has the wheat, he doesn't have the size-11 shoes. So Farmer Nielson goes down the road to

Camilla McGrath. Her father died recently and left a closet full of size-11 shoes, but she has no wheat. Her brother on the next farm also has some of their late father's size-11 shoes, and he has plenty of wheat, but he doesn't want the pig. Farmer Nielson will probably make his trade eventually, but it may cost him a lot of time and effort.

Double Coincidence of Demand
A situation in which there is a mutuality of needs and in which one individual is willing to exchange goods with another.

The central requirement of the barter system is what is called a **double coincidence of demand**, or of wants. Not only must Farmer Nielson want what the other person has, but also the other person in the exchange must want what Nielson has. Establishing mutuality of needs is usually time consuming and therefore inefficient. How much easier it would be for Nielson to take the pig to the butcher in town, sell it for money, buy the wheat from the miller, and then drop by the shoemaker's and pick up a pair of size-11 shoes.

A Money System of Exchange

The more complex economies become, the greater the necessity to replace barter with a system of *money exchange*. As a society specializes its labor and other resources, it must also specialize the means by which exchanges are made.

Your instructor is not only a teacher, not only a college teacher, but, even more specialized than that, an economics instructor, producing a service called education. How should he or she be paid? In a society without money, would one student barter potatoes, another mow the instructor's lawn, or another clean the classroom? Although barter was used in the early days of our country, it is too cumbersome today. The existence of money makes possible efficiency, a smooth flow of goods and resources, and a more highly developed economy.

But what is money? What is the essential ingredient that makes a thing money?

Money
Anything that people accept in exchange for goods and services.

A thing becomes **money** when people accept that thing in exchange for goods and services in general. *Money is money because people say it is money* and accept it in exchange for almost anything else. Governments may decree that something be accepted as payment for all debts, public or private. Although this *encourages* acceptance of that thing as a medium of exchange, it does not guarantee it. In the past, money consisted of gold and silver or paper backed by gold and silver. You could exchange a paper $5 bill for a $5 gold piece. This increased its acceptability as money. Today if you take a $5 bill to a bank, you will get in return only a new $5 bill. And yet you can still exchange it for goods and services.

In the long run, it is just the *acceptance* of the thing called money in exchange for goods and services that makes it money.

The Functions of Money

There are four functions that money performs:

1. Money acts as a *medium of exchange*. The central ingredient of money is its acceptability by others. When money is exchanged for goods and services, it is functioning as a medium of exchange.

2. Money is a *standard of value or unit of account*. Money serves as a measure by which a value can be set on goods and services. In a barter economy, if Farmer Nielson wanted to know the value of his pig, he compared it with the value of other goods. The pig might be worth 100 bushels of oats and the extraction of an aching tooth, and so on.

   In a money economy, the pig's value is set in terms of the monetary unit of the country. The monetary unit of the U.S. is the dollar, so here the pig is valued in dollars. Although other nations have differing standard units (pounds, francs, and so on), in each country money functions as a standard of value or unit of account and makes it possible for people to place a value on goods and services.

3. Money acts as a *store of value*. In a barter economy, how can Farmer Nielson *save*? He can do so only by storing goods. He can stash away wheat or preserve the products of the pig (bacon, ham, sausages), or he can accumulate larger numbers of things. But it costs a lot to store these things, and such products can deteriorate over a period of time. It would be simpler if Nielson could sell his output and save the accumulated *money*. (Money occupies little space; it doesn't rot or breed weevils. It just sits there.)

   But money *does* fluctuate in value, because of increases or decreases in prices. Inflation reduces the purchasing power of money and therefore reduces its value. Deflation causes the reverse to happen. This variation reduces the efficiency of money as a store of value.

4. Money is a *means of deferred payment*. Money facilitates lending and the repayment of loans. In a barter economy, borrowing is a most cumbersome affair. Suppose that Nielson's land is next to the river, and 1 year the river floods and destroys his wheat crop. He goes to Farmer Gomez, who lives in the unaffected uplands, and borrows wheat so he can plant a new crop. But because of the flood, wheat is now relatively scarce—that is, in short supply—with a high relative exchange value. The following year the weather is fine, and there is a bumper crop. Nielson, with plenty of wheat today, pays Gomez back for the wheat he borrowed last year. But with this year's abundance of wheat, the scarcity value of wheat has declined markedly, compared with last year, and wheat has a low relative exchange value.

   It is more efficient to base credit on a general medium of exchange: money. One expects money and its scarcity value (in simple language, its purchasing power) to be less subject than barter items to variations outside people's control.

However, the value of money—its purchasing power—does vary as prices vary, and this reduces the usefulness of money. There have been times in history when the supply of money increased so rapidly that it led to monetary disaster. During the American Revolution, for example, the Continental Congress issued so much currency with no backing that the people lost confidence in it. The purchasing power of that money dropped so low that the expression "not worth a Continental" became popular.

Characteristics of a "Good" Money

Many things have performed the function of money. During the American Revolution, in Massachusetts wheat served as money, and in Virginia tobacco was legally defined as money. American Indians used strings of colored beads called wampum as money; some African tribes have used cattle and cowry shells, and some groups in the South Sea Islands have used large stones. Even human slaves have functioned as money in some parts of the world. Apart from paper currency, gold, silver, and copper are the materials that most commonly serve as money.

What characteristics should one look for in a good money? (1) It should be portable, or easy to carry. (2) It should be easy to recognize, but hard to counterfeit or duplicate illegally. (3) It should be easily subdivided, to allow for small as well as large purchases. (4) The cost of storing it, that is, physically storing it in a safe place, or storing it in an accounting sense, should be low. (5) It should be durable, and not wear out or rot quickly. (6) The relative supply should not vary so greatly that large variations in relative scarcity value occur, since purchasing power changes as prices vary.

The Supply of Money: How to Define and Measure It

Defining and identifying the supply of money in the U.S. has become more difficult in the past decade or two. Ideally, we would like the definition to include all financial instruments that may readily be used in the short-term exchange of goods and services. Because of institutional and legal changes in our monetary system since the early-1970s, the exact identification and measurement of those instruments has become more complex for reasons we will look at in this and the succeeding chapter. As a first approximation, however, let's define money in the following way:

Money consists of all liabilities in commercial banks and other financial institutions that are subject to demand plus currency and coin in circulation.

Demand Deposits
Accounts that are
subject to withdrawal
by means of a check.

Demand deposits are what you know as *checking accounts.* They are called demand deposits because you can withdraw these deposits "on demand," by presenting a check.

A *check* is merely an order to a financial institution from the holder of a demand deposit to transfer some money from the deposit and pay it to someone else. The deposit is the money, not the check. If there is no deposit, the check is worthless.

Table 12-1 indicates that about 40 percent of our money supply, as defined was in the form of demand deposits in 1987 and another 33 percent in other checkable accounts. However, the economic importance of "checkbook money" is even greater than that, since about 90 percent (by value) of all economic transactions are accomplished by means of demand deposits.

Depository
Institutions
Those institutions that
hold demand deposits.

The keepers of demand deposits are **depository institutions.** Commercial banks are the largest part of the institutions that hold our demand deposits. Since demand deposits comprise the bulk of the U.S. money supply, commercial banks hold most of the supply of money in the U.S. (As we shall see later, however, many other institutions in the U.S. now hold and create money.)

The second largest component of our narrowly defined money supply is *currency in circulation,* which means currency that is in use rather than in the vaults of banks or of the Federal Reserve. Currency is the paper money in the U.S. economy. It is issued by the Federal Reserve, not by the U.S. Treasury.

Coins are the smallest part of the supply of money, but a very vital part of it. These metal tokens are minted by the Treasury and issued through the Federal Reserve Banks.

Fiat Money
Monetary instruments
that have less value as
commodities than as
money.

Legal Tender
All forms of money
that, by law, must be
accepted in payment
of private or public
debt.

Today both currency and coin are called **fiat money.** Their value as monetary instruments is greater than their value as commodities. The $5 bill as a monetary instrument is worth $5 in goods and services. As a *commodity* (waste paper or perhaps a wall decoration) it is worth very little. The 25¢ coin, if it were melted down and sold as metal, would be worth far less than 25¢. Currency and coin are also defined as **legal tender,** which is any money the law says must be accepted as payment for all debt, public (owed to or owed by the government), or private (owed by one individual to another).

Table 12-1
One Measure of the U.S. Supply of Money:
Demand Deposits, Currency and Coins, 1987.

Kind of Money	Amount (billions of dollars)	Percent of Total
Demand deposits	292	40
Currency and coins	200	27
Other checkable deposits*	255	33
Totals	745	100

*Includes ATS and loan balances at all depository institutions including credit unions.

Source: *The Federal Reserve Bulletin*, Apr. 1988.

"I'm holding onto my cash, I think money is going to come back."

Each of the three different kinds of money—demand deposits, currency, and coin—has its own advantages and disadvantages. The convenience of paying for things through the medium of checks that transfer demand deposits is fairly obvious. One does not have to carry large sums in currency. Most people use demand deposits most of the time to pay for all larger bills or expenses.

However, checks have two disadvantages: (1) Not everyone is willing to accept a check in economic exchange. The fear of fraud or of inadequate funds in the check payer's demand deposits, plus the trouble of collecting on bad checks, reduces the acceptability of checks as money. (2) For small purchases, a check ordering a transfer of a demand deposit is a very inefficient form of money. Imagine a child in a candy store pulling out a checkbook to pay for a 10¢ purchase. Coins and currency are better in such cases.

Money Is Debt

Demand deposits are liabilities of institutions that create them. Currency is a liability of the Federal Reserve banks. Both are non-interest-bearing debt. In effect, the supply of money is the monetization of certain forms of debt. The commercial bank or other institution that holds your demand deposit promises to pay you in money the amount of your account when you demand it. If you go into the bank and demand the deposit, the bank will give you currency. But what is currency? A $10 bill says on the face of it that it is a Federal Reserve Note. The Federal Reserve promises to pay you $10 for it. Like the demand deposit, the $10 bill is a promise to pay. But if you go to the Federal Reserve bank and demand payment, you will receive only a new bill or change for the old one.

Since government will not exchange anything tangible for currency, like gold or silver, what is currency good for? What are demand deposits good for? Their worth lies in the fact that people are willing to exchange goods and services for them. Thus, by definition, currency is money. The value of money is not the gold or silver that backs it up (there is today no gold or silver backing the U.S. supply of money), but the goods and services that the money can buy. That value depends on the *prices* of the goods and services to be bought in relationship to the supply of money. The lower the prices, the more a given amount of money can buy, and thus the higher the value of money.

Other Measures of the Money Supply

M1
A measure of money supply that includes currency and coin plus all deposits that are subject to checks.

The money supply we have talked about above, demand deposits and coin and currency, is a measure of money that focuses on those things that serve as a medium of exchange. That measure is referred to as **M1** money.

M1 = Currency, Coin and all Checkable Deposits

Remember though, that money also serves as a standard of value, a store of value, and a means of deferred payment. To focus on these functions of money and to correlate the money supply more closely with changes in GNP, we shall define the money supply two other ways.

M2
A measure of the money supply that includes all M1 money plus small time deposits and money market mutual funds.

M2 = M1 + Savings Deposits + Small Time Deposits + Money Market Mutual Funds

M2 includes all of the components of M1 plus savings deposits, small time deposits and money market mutual funds. These last three elements are called **near monies**, assets that have all the characteristics of money (particularly as a store of value) except that they do not circulate as a medium of exchange. To get some idea of the relative importance of M1 and M2 in 1986, M1 amounted to $713.4 billion while M2 was equal to $2.78 trillion.

Near Monies
Assets with all of the characteristics of money except that they do not circulate as a medium of exchange.

M3
A measure of the money supply that includes all M1 + M2 money + large value certificates of deposits (CDs).

M3 = M2 + Large Value Certificates of Deposit

A third, and still broader, definition of the money supply is also possible. **M3** consists of all the components of M2 plus negotiable certificates of deposit (CDs). This is the broadest of the three money supply measures. In 1986, its value was $3.46 trillion.

Summing Up the Money Supply

For many purposes, the money supply can no longer be defined simply as currency, coins and checkable deposits (M1). There are so many new (and ever changing) near monies in America's financial markets that we must take account of these if we are to have an adequate measure not only of the things that serve as a medium of exchange but also serve to store value, serve as a standard of value and as a means for deferred payments. The near monies we have looked at are:

1. *Savings Deposits*, those that earn interest but do not mature at a specific date. These deposits are found not only in commercial banks but also in savings and loan associations, mutual savings banks and credit unions. They are not subject to routine checking demands and thus, are not included in M1.

2. *Time Deposits*, those that have a specific maturity date that typically is as short as 30 days and range up to several years. Some financial institutions offer similar non-negotiable CDs with fixed interest rates. They are not included in M1 because they cannot be resold and must (subject to large penalties) be held to maturity.

3. *Money Market Fund Accounts*. First introduced by Merrill Lynch in 1971, they exist in large amounts but are not included in M1 because of restrictions on checking against them and also because minimums are established for these checks. They are, in other words, not sufficiently flexible to be included as a medium of exchange.

4. *Negotiable CDs*. Certificates that have some of the characteristics of money but are usually denominated in large sums ($100,000+) and are not subject to checking. For these reasons, they are included neither in M1 nor M2.

Near Monies, Liquidity, and Credit Cards
When an economy has a large amount of near money (that is, is in a highly liquid state), the average and marginal propensities to consume tend to increase. If the economy is already in an inflationary gap, high liquidity may worsen the inflation. However, if the economy is in a recession, with a deflationary gap, high liquidity may soften or cushion the contraction.

Credit Cards
Credit Cards: Where do they fit? Are they substitutes for money? The credit card is only a quick and convenient way to *borrow* money. At the end of the month, the borrower gets a statement of purchases made with the credit card during the month and must pay in *money* for what was charged. All a credit card does is reduce the inconvenience and risk of carrying around a large amount of money. It is not a substitute for money. But credit cards do enable

people to increase their purchasing power temporarily. This can affect total demand, and thus, the level of income, employment, and prices. Furthermore, the public's ability to vary purchasing power temporarily by using credit cards can make it harder for the government to carry out a stabilization policy.

The Origins of Commercial Banking: Goldsmith Banking

To understand how M1 is created, we must understand the original depository institutions and their role in creating demand. The origins of today's commercial bank lie with the goldsmiths of seventeenth-century England.

In the early-1600s in England, the safest places to store valuables were the vaults and safes of the goldsmiths of London, who made useful items out of gold. Wealthy people put their gold and silver in these vaults for safekeeping; the goldsmiths charged a fee for this watchdog service. At first, the goldsmiths had to return the same gold and silver that people had entrusted to their care. However, after a while, people said the goldsmith did not have to return the piece of gold that was deposited, just an amount of gold of equivalent value. This relaxing of the rules began a series of developments that eventually led to the modern commercial bank.

The depositor—the person who left gold with the goldsmith—received a document stating the value of the gold deposited. (This document was equivalent to your bankbook, which shows how much you have deposited.) When Lady Upton-Chase found that she needed money or wanted to buy something, she could take this document and transfer ownership of all (or any part) of the gold to a third party. She would write, "I order you, the goldsmith, to pay to the third party so-and-so much of the gold on deposit."

Thus, the modern check was born. Since the goldsmiths were internationally known, these endorsements of deposits to another person were widely accepted as a means of payment. Thus, they functioned as money. Deposits of gold at goldsmiths eventually became today's demand deposits. But the story does not end there.

The goldsmith became known as a person with money to lend, and people who needed money began borrowing from the goldsmith. At first goldsmiths lent their own gold. In time, they realized that people who stored gold with them would not want that gold back for a while. There was always a certain amount of stored gold in their vaults, so they began to lend some of it. After a while the borrowers, instead of taking the gold, accepted documents stating that they had gold on deposit with the goldsmith. The borrowers would *endorse* these documents of deposit (write checks) over to those people they wished to make payments to.

The goldsmiths were soon creating documents of deposits in amounts much larger than the amounts of gold they actually had in their vaults. Since these documents attesting to deposits were accepted as payment, they functioned as money. Thus, the goldsmiths, by making loans and creating deposits (attested to by documents), were creating and increasing the supply of money.

The goldsmiths, however, had to be prepared to give gold back when people presented these documents transferring deposits (checks). Not all of these documents were presented at the same time, fortunately. Thus, the goldsmiths were able to keep a reasonable supply of gold—enough to meet these demands—on hand at all times. This was the origin of the **fractional reserve principle**, that is, the need to have on hand an amount of reserves (in this case gold) smaller than the total amount of deposits, to meet possible demands for withdrawal of deposits in gold.

So one sees in seventeenth-century English banking the *origins* of our modern commercial banking system: (1) deposits that can be withdrawn on demand; (2) the check as a means of transferring these deposits and the functioning of these deposits as money; (3) the practice of lending money by creating a deposit and increasing the supply of money; and (4) the need to keep reserves of gold in amounts that are fractions of total deposits, which make possible the lending and creation of new deposits, and thus a larger supply of money.

Fractional Reserve Principle
The need to maintain on hand a reserve less than the amount of total deposits.

The Future of Money, or Can the Computer Replace Currency and Coin?

Today, as we have seen, their are many forms of money and near money. It is possible to create a scenario in which M1 money or at least coin and currency may lose most if not all of its importance as a medium of exchange.

Imagine an economy without currency and coin, and also without checks as you know them. Imagine a great central computer. In its memory banks are entered all expenditures and all receipts of money. All receipts of income are fed directly into the computer and added to each individual's account. No more depositing of paychecks, no more lugging around dirty, germ-covered currency and coin.

Everyone has an account. Everyone has her or his own card, perhaps keyed to the thumbprint. Every place that sells things, every place at which people make payments has terminals connected to the computer. When you buy something, you take your card, slip it into the terminal, and it types out the deduction to be made from your account at the computer.

No more bad checks. If you overdraw your account, lights will instantly flash, and a recorded voice from the computer terminal will say, "You're overdrawn." No more hours spent figuring your bank balance. You can obtain it on request from the computer. No more hiding income from the Internal Revenue Service. The computer knows all. Big Daddy will indeed have become a machine.

Have we not already begun to see this process in the 1990s? Want to buy gasoline? No need for cash, your automatic teller machine card is used instead and the amount automatically deducted from your bank balance.

The Economy and the Supply of Money

How do changes in the supply of money affect the level of economic activity? Two major factors are (1) the absolute size of the supply of money and (2) the rapidity with which the supply of money changes hands in a given period of time.

For example, there are three people in the economy: Farmer Martinez, Mo Courington the shoemaker, and Vee Jackson the baker. The supply of money in the economy is $20. Vee Jackson buys $20 worth of sausages from Farmer Martinez. Therefore, Farmer Martinez exchanges $20 worth of output for $20 in money. Farmer Martinez buys $20 worth of shoes from Mo Courington, and again exchanges $20 in output for $20 in money. Finally, Mo Courington, buys $20 worth of bread from Vee Jackson, and there is a further exchange of $20 in output for the same $20 in money. Although the supply of money is only $20, this $20 has changed hands 3 times, and the total output supported through this process is $60. Figure 12-1 shows the circular-flow diagram.

Equation of Exchange (MV = PQ). The supply of money times its velocity equals the price level times the amount of net goods and services.

The Equation of Exchange

One can express the circular-flow process in Figure 12-1 in the form of an equation, called the **equation of exchange**:

$$MV = PQ.$$

Figure 12-1
The Circular Flow of Money and Output

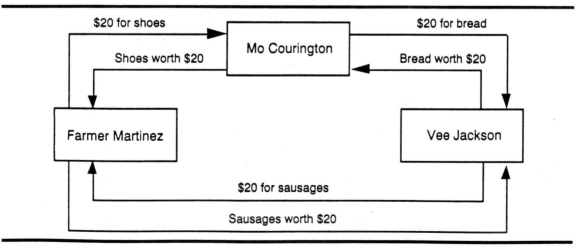

M stands for the supply of money and V is the *velocity of exchange*, or the number of times the supply of money changes hands in a given period. One might call MV the *effective supply of money*. Also, if P is the average price level of the goods sold, and Q is transactions in physical terms and can be restricted to include only the output of net final goods and services, then PQ (the money value of that output) is *net national product (NNP)*.

$$MV = PQ = NNP.$$

Let's make an equation from our example: M, the supply of money, is $20; V, the velocity of exchange, is 3 (since the money changed hands 3 times); and Q, physical output, is the sausages, shoes, and bread. It can be seen that MV equals PQ, since 20 x 3 = 20 x 3.

So the equation of exchange works perfectly in this extremely simple model. Although the gigantic economy of the U.S., with its 245 million people and its multitude of transactions and output, is vastly more complex, it operates the same way.

(We have considered PQ as being NNP and V as being essentially the velocity of income. Now we can define Q as including *all* economic transactions. We can say that Q includes the buying and selling of intermediary products, financial instruments, and even used items. When one defines transactions, Q, that way, velocity, V, is much higher. One can call it the velocity of transactions. Here, in order to keep our analysis simple, we shall consider only the velocity of income.)

The Velocity of Exchange (V)

You now see that the dollar value of output PQ is determined by changes in the supply of money, and also by changes in the velocity of exchange (the number of times the money supply, M, changes hands). The supply of money is controlled by the monetary authority responsible for doing so. (In the U.S., it is the Federal Reserve.) The velocity of exchange cannot be controlled. It depends on the structure of the financial system and on the actions of the public. One can easily measure velocity by dividing the NNP by the supply of money. Table 12-2 shows the velocity of exchange between 1960 and 1985.

Note in Table 12-2 that money is moved faster and faster until the mid-1980s. NNP grew faster than the supply of money, the increase in velocity of money offset this differential. The velocity of exchange rose over the years because the public was able to use the supply of money more and more efficiently— for three reasons: (1) Financial institutions and financial markets grew both more complex and more available to the public. The increased use of savings accounts, money market accounts, stocks and bonds, government securities, and various forms of private short-term commercial credit moved money more rapidly from one use to

Table 12-2
The Velocity of Exchange

	M1 (billions of dollars)	NNP (billions of dollars)	V
1960	141.8	468.9	3.3
1965	169.5	647.4	3.8
1970	216.6	926.6	4.3
1975	291.1	1,436.6	4.9
1980	414.2	2,428.1	5.9
1985	626.6	3,560.9	5.7

Source: *Economic Report of the President*, 1987, G.P.O. Washington D.C.

another. (2) The public greatly increased its use of credit cards, which cut down its need to hold money. (3) The public increased its use of institutions such as banks and other financial intermediaries, which has reduced its need to hold money for longer periods of time. We should also note that there may be a problem with M1 as the money supply here. Other assets may be so liquid that the appropriate measure of money to correlate with NNP growth is not, any longer, M1. This is a subject of great controversy among monetary economists.

One must be wary about accepting this long-run increase in velocity without qualification. Not only is there a problem with the M1 measure, but also the dates used in Table 12-2 are mostly good years; the table does not show the contraction of velocity during recessions. When people see hard times ahead, they tend to retrench and hold onto their money longer. Businesses and consumers seek the safety of greater liquidity, that is, larger holdings of M1 money itself especially cash.

Output, Prices, and Money *(M)*: A Simple First Look

To examine the way changes in the supply of money affect output of goods and services and their prices, we must make a simplifying assumption: We will assume that V (the velocity of exchange) is constant.

Given the equation of exchange, $MV = PQ$, when M (some measure of the supply of money) increases and V (the velocity of exchange) is constant, then PQ (the value of output) must increase. The important question is: Will P (prices) increase, or will Q (output) increase? The clue to the answer lies in the discussion of aggregate demand and supply. There we pointed out that during a recession, when there is high unemployment and excess capacity in factories, output can increase without much increase in prices. This is because an increase in aggregate supply can occur without increases in prices from private producers. Therefore, if the U.S. has a recession, and the supply of money (M) increases, prices (P) will remain relatively stable and output (Q) will increase. As an economy approaches full employment, some resources will be in shorter supply than others, and prices will begin to increase. This is because aggregate supply under these conditions is upward sloping. An increase in aggregate quantity supplied in response to an increase in the money supply occurs only with rising costs and prices. Therefore, as money (M) increases and the economy approaches full employment, prices (P) begin to rise, along with output (Q). Obviously, when the economy is at *full* employment, any increase in the supply of money (M) will only result in an increase in prices (P). Output (Q) cannot increase any further, because all resources are fully employed.

If an economy wants to increase output and employment, the appropriate policy is to increase its supply of money. On the other hand, if it wants to decrease inflation, the appropriate policy is to decrease its supply of money.

But remember, we are assuming that the velocity of exchange (V) is constant. When V changes, it may either reinforce or counteract the effects of changes in the supply of money.

The Demand for Money: An Alternative

There is another way of looking at the way the supply of money affects output and prices. For many reasons, people need to hold part of their assets in the form of money (opposed to real estate, etc.). People do not receive income at the same time that they have to pay for the goods and services they buy. For example, professors are paid once a month. Although they pay the usual recurring bills on the first of the month, they must keep some money on hand to buy food, gasoline, haircuts, and so forth, for the rest of the month. This is called holding money for *transaction purposes*. People also need to hold money for emergencies: The car breaks down, the water heater springs a leak, or someone gets sick. This is called holding money for *precautionary purposes*. In addition, people hold money to take advantage of economic opportunities. Stock prices may be low, or there may be a sale on coats. One needs money on hand to take advantage of these opportunities. This is called holding money for *speculative purposes*.

Whatever the reason, people want to hold certain amounts of money. How much they hold depends on their incomes, the amounts and kinds of assets they have accumulated (durable goods, liquid assets, and so on), and their personal lifestyles. If the supply of money increases, people find themselves holding more cash than they wish, and they may invest all or part of it, or they may spend all or part of it on more consumer goods and services. Therefore, when money increases, both investment and consumption demand increase.

Suppose the supply of money decreases. Then people have less cash on hand than they want, so they have to either decrease their consumption (an uncomfortable solution) or convert other assets into cash. That is why investment and consumption demand both fluctuate with the supply of money.

Because people want to hold a certain amount of their assets in the form of money, they react when what they actually hold is not what they want to hold. If they have more assets in the form of money than they want when the supply of money increases, they increase their investments. They also buy more consumer goods. This expands the economy. Income increases, which has the effect of increasing the amount of money that people wish to hold. This process continues until what people wish to hold becomes equal to the increased supply of money. When the supply of money decreases, the reverse occurs.

Thus, the two monetary approaches (the equation of exchange and the demand for money) lead to the same conclusions put in Keynesian terms. An increase in the supply of money increases aggregate demand and expands the economy. A decrease in the supply of money decreases aggregate demand and contracts the economy.

SUMMING UP

1. When people use the *barter* system, they exchange goods for goods and do not use money. The most serious flaw in the barter system is the need for *double coincidence of demand*. That is, the person you wish to trade with must have what you want, and also want what you have.

2. When people use a *money exchange* system, they exchange goods for money and then money for goods. This is a much more efficient way to carry out the four functions money performs: (a) It is a *medium of exchange*. (b) It is a *standard of value or unit of account*. (c) It is a *store of value*. (d) It is a *means of deferred payment*.

3. The characteristics of a good money are the following: (a) It is portable, or easily carried. (b) It is easily recognized, but hard to counterfeit or duplicate. (c) It is easily subdivided. (d) It costs little to store. (e) It is durable. (f) The supply of it is relatively stable.

4. The *supply of money* in the United States has become more difficult to define and measure. One definition is that it consists of all *demand deposits* and all currency and coin in circulation. About 75 percent of the supply of money, thus defined, is in the form of demand and other checkable deposits *(checking accounts)*. *Depository institutions* are those financial firms that hold demand deposits and honor checks written against them. *Currency* is issued by the Federal Reserve, while *coins* are minted and issued by the Treasury. *Fiat money* is any money that has greater value as a monetary instrument than as a commodity. *Legal tender* is any

money that the government says is to be accepted for all debts, public and private.

5. Money is debt. *Demand deposits* are debts (liabilities) of commercial banks. *Currency* is a debt (liability) of the Federal Reserve.

6. Measuring the money supply as demand deposits, currency and coin is known as M1, a measure of the highly liquid financial instruments that are quickly used as a medium of exchange.

M1 = Currency, Coin and Checking Deposits

7. Since money also serves as a standard and store of value as well as a means of deferred payment, we can broaden the money supply measurement to include those financial instruments that serve these additional purposes. This measure is known as M2 and adds near monies, things that have all the characteristics of money except that they do not readily serve as a medium of exchange. Included in M2 are the components of M1 plus savings deposits, small time deposits and money market mutual funds.

M2 = M1 + Savings Deposits + Small Time Deposits + Money Market Mutual Funds

8. The broadest conventional measure of the Money supply, M3 adds long-term negotiable financial instruments, especially large denomination certificates of deposit.

M3 = M2+ Large Value Certificates of Deposit

9. Credit cards are not money. They are simply instruments that permit individuals to borrow against future income. As such, they may affect short-term variations in demand but serve none of the four functions of money; neither are they near money.

10. Goldsmith banking in seventeenth-century England established the basic structures of modern commercial banking including the *fractional reserve principle*.

11. One can use the *equation of exchange,* MV = PQ, to describe how changes in the supply of money affect economic activity. In this equation, M is the supply of money, V is the velocity of exchange, P is the price level, and Q is actual output.

12. Assuming *velocity of exchange* (V) to be constant, when the supply of money (M) increases, PQ increases. If there is unemployment and unused plant capacity as M increases, output (Q) increases and price (P) is relatively stable. As the economy approaches full employment, price (P) begins to increase while M is still increasing, and when the economy reaches full employment, only prices increase.

13. An alternate approach to how changes in the money supply affect economic activity examines why people hold money. They hold it for purposes of *transactions, precaution,* and *speculation.* The amounts they want to hold depend on their incomes, the quantities and kinds of assets they have, and their lifestyles.

14. When the supply of money increases, people have more money on hand than they want, and they try to convert it to other assets (invest it) or they spend it on more consumption. If the supply of money decreases, people have less money on hand than they want, and they try to increase their cash on hand by cutting back on their consumption or by reducing their investments (or both).

KEY TERMS

Barter
Double coincidence of demand
Money
Medium of exchange, standard of value, store of value, means of
    deferred payment
Demand deposits
Depository institutions
Fiat money
Legal tender
M1 money
M2 money
M3 money
Near monies
Fractional reserve principle
Equation of exchange

QUESTIONS

1. What are the four basic functions of money? How does rapid inflation affect the performance of these functions?

2. "Money is the root of all evil." Why don't we do away with it?

3. Suppose that our government suddenly printed up enough money to give everyone a new $50 bill. What would happen to output and prices? State clearly the assumptions you are making about employment and velocity of exchange.

4. Why are near monies not included in M1?

5. How does M3 differ from M2?

6. What characteristics of goldsmith banking make it like the present commercial banking system?

7. What are the characteristics of a good money? Pick three commodities, and analyze their favorable and unfavorable characteristics as a good money.

8. "Money is money because people say it's money." Do you agree? Why?

9. What effect do credit cards have on the supply of money?

SUGGESTED READINGS

Friedman, Milton. "Quantity Theory of Money." *The International Encyclopedia of the Social Sciences,* Vol. 10. Free Press, New York, 1968. Pp. 432-446.

Goldfield, Stephen M. and Lester V. Chandler. *The Economics of Money and Banking,* 9th ed. Harper & Row, New York, 1986.

Johnson, Ivan C. and William W. Roberts. *Money and Banking—A Market Oriented Approach.* Chicago: The Dryden Press, 1988.

Mayer, Thomas, James S. Duesenberry, and Robert Alber. *Money, Banking and the Economy.* New York: WW Norton, 1987.

Nadler, Paul S. *Commercial Banking in the Economy.* Random House, New York, 1973.

Chapter 13:
Commercial Banking and the
Creation of M1 Money

We have discussed the functions, the characteristics, and a little of the history of money. We mentioned that the bulk of the M1 money supply is in the form of demand and other checkable deposits, which are held primarily by commercial banks but also by other financial institutions. So in analyzing how the supply of money is increased or decreased, and how it is controlled, we must look again at commercial banking.

The Simple Economy: Four Assumptions About a Simple Model

The U.S. banking system is so complex that the best way to approach it is to set up a simple model. We will call it the Simple Economy and make four assumptions about its banking system to enable us to analyze the process of increasing and decreasing the supply of money in simple terms. Then we will drop these assumptions, one by one, so that the analysis will gradually become more complex and realistic. Finally, we will examine that giant jigsaw puzzle, the U.S. banking system.

Here are the four simplifying assumptions:

1. There is only one bank in the Simple Economy's banking system. That bank, the First National Bank, is a monopoly bank, or in other words, it is the Simple Economy's banking system.

2. The government has no control over the First National Bank, so there are no regulations that restrict its banking activities.

3. There is no paper currency or coin. The Simple Economy's entire money supply consists of the demand deposits (checking accounts) in the First National Bank.

4. There is no international trade. This last assumption is the only one we will not drop later in the discussion. If we were to take international trade into account, we would make our discussion of banking transactions unnecessarily complex at this stage.

First we will analyze the process of increasing and decreasing the supply of money in the simplest model. Then we will drop assumption 3 and show what effects currency and coin have on the money supply. Then we will drop assumption 2 and show what happens when the government regulates the supply of money. Finally we will drop the assumption that there is only one bank and analyze the functioning of the multibank system with many separately incorporated banks. At that point we will analyze the U.S. banking system in relation to the supply of money.

Now let's consider the First National Bank, an established and ongoing commercial bank (Table 13-1 shows its balance sheet), with *liabilities* of $1 million, all in demand deposits. In other words, the First National owes its depositors $1 million. It also has $500,000 in *net worth*, which represents the equity or ownership of the stockholders in the bank. Last, it has $1.5 million in assets, $1 million in the form of loans. The First National has loaned that $1 million to the citizens of the Simple Economy. The other $500,000 in assets is in the form of the bank's buildings and equipment. Remember that for the First National's books to balance, the bank's assets and liabilities plus net worth have to be equal, just as they must in any company's accounting balance sheet.

The following short tables will show only *changes* in the balance sheet. This will help us focus on the effects of banking transactions on the supply of money. Note that there is only $1 million in money in the Simple Economy, and remember that all of the Simple Economy's money is in the form of demand deposits (no currency and no coin).

Money Creation in the Simple Model

Joe Bloggs, one of Simple Economy's more ambitious citizens, has made a discovery which he hopes will make him rich. He has

Table 13-1
The First National Bank's Balance Sheet

Assets		Liabilities and Net Worth	
Loans	$1,000,000	Demand deposits	$1,000,000
Buildings and equipment	500,000	Net worth	500,000

invented mottled-gray bubble gum that will blend into sidewalks. He goes to see Elvira Snodgrass, president of the First National Bank, to tell her of his discovery. "Wonderful!" says Snodgrass. "No more of those unsightly pink blobs on our sidewalks. You'll make a pile out of this invention, son!"

When Bloggs asks to borrow $10,000 to set up a bubble-gum factory, Snodgrass approves the loan. Table 13-2 shows what happens then.

First, Bloggs signs a promissory note, stating that he will pay the bank $10,000 in 6 months' time. To the bank, this promissory note is an asset, since Joe Bloggs now owes the First National Bank $10,000. The category "Loans" increases by $10,000. But now the First National must pay Bloggs that money he has borrowed. It does this by increasing his demand deposits at the bank by $10,000; by this act, it increases the supply of money in the Simple Economy by $10,000.

"But," you may say, "where did the First National Bank get the $10,000 to give Joe Bloggs?" The answer is simple. The bank created that demand deposit by simply writing on Bloggs' account, "plus $10,000." *The bank creates demand deposits to pay for the loans that it makes.* It cannot just take the demand deposit from somebody else's account, because what would *that* person do if he or she wanted to use that demand deposit? Nor can the bank take it from accounts in its own name, because that would mean that the bank owed money to itself, which is an absurdity. The point we are trying to make is that commercial banks create demand deposits when they make loans.

With that $10,000 demand deposit, Bloggs first hires a contractor to build his factory and pays the contractor $2,500. He makes this payment by writing a check on his account. So Bloggs' account goes down by $2,500 and the account of the contractor goes up by $2,500. There is no change in the Simple Economy's supply of money, for accounts are only transferred. Bloggs then buys machinery for $2,500, and writes another check to pay for it. Again his account shrinks by $2,500, while the machinery seller's demand deposits increase by $2,500. Again, there is no change in the supply of money, only transfers of demand deposits. When Bloggs buys raw materials for $2,500, the same thing happens. And it happens again when he hires workers and starts producing bubble gum.

In effect then, as Bloggs spends his demand deposit, his account is slowly transferred to those to whom he makes payments by writing checks. The supply of money changes hands as the

Table 13-2
The Effect of a Loan on the First National Bank's Balance Sheet

Assets		Liabilities	
Loans	+$10,000	Demand deposits	+$10,000

demand deposit at the bank is transferred. (Isn't this like your own experience with commercial banks?)

Now Bloggs starts selling bubble gum to retail stores, which the store owners pay for by writing checks drawn on their own demand deposits. Bloggs deposits those checks, so his account increases while the accounts of the store owners decrease. Still no change in the *supply* of money. Joe makes profits, and eventually his demand deposits increase to $10,000.

Now Bloggs can pay off his promissory note to the bank. He goes to the office of President Snodgrass and writes a check for $10,000. Snodgrass writes "Paid" on the promissory note and deducts the amount from Bloggs's account. (In effect, Bloggs has received and paid off an interest-free loan. To keep our analysis simple, we have avoided the subject of interest on loans.)

Table 13-3 shows the transactions on the books of the First National Bank. Note that the account called "Loans" decreases by $10,000 as Bloggs pays off the note. The First National Bank's demand deposits are also decreased by $10,000 as the bank deducts the check from Bloggs' demand deposits. The Simple Economy's supply of money actually decreases by $10,000, for Bloggs's check to the bank decreases only his own demand deposit and is not transferred to any other account.

What has this analysis shown us? (1) When a commercial bank (First National Bank) makes a loan, and creates a demand deposit in order to make the loan, the supply of money is increased. (2) When a loan is paid off by means of a check that decreases demand deposits, the supply of money is decreased.

Enter Currency and Coin

We are about to drop assumption 3 because there are two basic weaknesses in this simple model: (1) For small purchases, it is very inefficient to write checks transferring demand deposits; one needs paper currency and coin. (2) The existence of currency and coin provides an automatic check on the ability of the First National Bank to expand the supply of money.

The first weakness (no currency or coin) is apparent. When a supply of money consists only of demand deposits, all transactions, no matter how small, have to be made by checks and

Table 13-3
Decrease in the Supply of Money

Assets		Liabilities	
Loans	-$10,000	Demand deposits	-$10,000

transferring demand deposits. When you buy a newspaper, you would have to write a check for twenty-five cents. The cost of handling checks for these small amounts is greater than the value of the transactions. Therefore, one important function of currency and coin is to provide a more efficient form of money for small-value transactions.

The second weakness is that in this simple model without currency or coin, the bank (by lending) can expand the supply of money without limit. When we introduce currency and coin, you will see that they provide an automatic check on the ability of the bank to expand loans and thus to expand the supply of money.

People in the U.S. find it most comfortable to hold about 25 percent of the M1 supply of money in the form of currency and coin. (This percentage varies somewhat from place to place and from one month to another.) We will assume that the Simple Economy people are like Americans. They also want to hold 25 percent of the supply of money to be used for exchange purposes in the form of currency and coin. And we will also assume that this percentage does not vary.

Let's introduce currency and coin into the economy. The Simple Economy's government wants to spend $1 million more than it receives in taxes. To cover this deficit, it issues $1 million in currency and coin. What happens when the government deposits the currency in the First National Bank? Table 13-4 shows the effect on the First National's balance sheet.

The bank now has an asset of $1 million called "Cash in vault," and also a liability of $1 million, which is the demand deposit held by the government that represents the deposit of currency. The Simple Economy's supply of money has increased by $1 million, the demand deposit owned by the government. Remember that the actual cash in the First National Bank's vault is not yet part of the supply of money, because it is not yet in circulation.

The government spends the $1 million for various goods and services, like roads, bombers, and education. This spending transfers the demand deposit from the government to the individuals who sell these goods to the government. Remember, though, that people want 25 percent of their supply of money in the form of currency and coin. Therefore, they withdraw from their demand deposits $250,000 in cash.

Table 13-5 shows the results. Only $750,000 remains in the vault in cash, and demand deposits are only $750,000. The supply of money, however, is still $1 million consisting of $750,000 in

Table 13-4
The Effect of the Government's $1 Million Deposit of Currency and Coin on the Balance Sheet of the First National Bank

Assets		Liabilities	
Loans	+$1,000,000	Demand deposits	+$1,000,000

Table 13-5

The Effect on the First National Bank of a Withdrawal by Depositors of $250,000 in Cash from Their Demand Deposits

Assets		Liabilities	
Loans	$750,000	Demand deposits	$750,000

demand deposits and $250,000 in currency and coin in circulation, in people's pockets.

Now the First National Bank has assets in a form that does not earn it any income (the $750,000 cash in its vault). The bank's officers want to put those assets to work earning income. So they lend out $1 million, which, as you already know, creates demand deposits of $1 million.

Remember that the bank can lend more money than the amount of cash it holds in its vault because the depositors want to keep only 25 percent of the supply of money in the form of currency and coin.

Now the demand deposits are $1 million fatter. What happens? Well, the people still want to keep 25 percent of the country's money in the form of currency and coin, so they withdraw *another* $250,000 in cash. Table 13-6 shows the net results. "cash in vault" is down to $500,000 and the total of demand deposits is $1.5 million. The supply of money is now $2 million— $1.5 million in demand deposits and $500,000 in currency and coin in circulation.

The First National Bank still has assets in a form that does not earn them any income (the $500,000 "cash in vault"). The bank's officers want to put the assets to work, so they extend *more* loans. Let's say they loan $2 million, and thereby create demand deposits of an additional $2 million. The citizens of the Simple Economy still wish to keep 25 percent of their M1 money in the form of currency and coin. To do this they withdraw $500,000 in cash, reducing demand deposits by a like amount.

Table 13-7 shows the net results. The First National Bank's vault no longer has any cash at all. Loans and discounts are $3 million and demand deposits are $3 million. The country's supply of money is now $4 million; that is, $3 million in demand deposits and $1 million in currency and coin in circulation. If the bank extends still more loans, and thereby creates still more demand deposits, the depositors, to get the 25 percent of the total money

Table 13-6

The Effect on the First National Bank's Balance Sheet of a Second Withdrawal of $250,000 by Depositors

Assets		Liabilities	
Cash in vault	$ 500,000	Demand deposits	$1,500,000
Loans	1,000,000		

Table 13-7
The First National Bank's Balance Sheet When It Increases Loans to $3 Million

Assets		Liabilities	
Cash in vault	0	Demand deposits	$3,000,000
Loans	3,000,000		

supply in currency and coin that they want, will demand more currency than the bank has.

In effect, *the amount of currency and coin in the vaults of the bank places a limit on the amount that the bank can lend.* Since the people want to hold 25 percent of the money supply in the form of currency and coin, the country's total supply of money is limited to 4 times the amount of currency and coin available, or $1 in cash for every $3 in demand deposits. In order to increase its lending, and thus, the supply of money (demand deposits), the First National Bank would have to get more currency and coin from the government.

To summarize, currency and coin perform two functions: (1) For purchases that have small value, they are a more efficient form of money than demand deposits. (2) They provide an automatic check on the ability of the bank to make loans, create demand deposits, and increase the supply of money.

Enter the Government

Let us now drop our second assumption—that there is no government regulation. The Simple Economy's government creates a Federal Reserve Bank for the purpose of controlling lending by the First National Bank. The government requires that the First National Bank keep assets in the form of reserves equal to a specific percentage of its demand deposits, and gives the Federal Reserve Bank the power to increase or decrease these reserves. (Bear in mind that the Federal Reserve is only a banker's bank. It does not engage in banking activities involving the public.)

Reserve Requirements

Remember that a bank's reserves are not demand deposits, but some form of assets that the banking authority defines as reserves. The U.S. government defines *reserves* as all deposits by *depository institutions* in the Federal Reserve, plus currency and coin held in the vaults of these institutions.

Let's say that the Simple Economy's Federal Reserve Bank defines reserves as the U.S. Federal Reserve does. This means that the First National Bank may count as reserves all First National Bank deposits at the Federal Reserve Bank, plus all currency and coin the First National Bank holds. The law says that the First

Enter the Federal Reserve (Courtesy Federal Reserve System)

Required Reserve Ratio
The minimum ratio of reserves to deposits that depository institutions are required to maintain.

National Bank must keep a minimum quantity of reserves equal to a certain percentage of its demand deposits. This percentage is called the **required reserve ratio**. For example, suppose that the required reserve ratio is 20 percent and that the First National Bank has $1 million in demand deposits. According to law, the First National Bank must have $200,000 in reserves (20 percent of $1 million) or $200,000 in deposits at the Federal Reserve Bank, and/or in currency and coin.

Table 13-8 shows that the First National Bank has $1 million in reserves and also $1 million in demand deposits. Since there is only a 20 percent required reserve ratio, to comply with the law, the First National Bank is required to hold only $200,000 of those reserves. The other $800,000 of its reserves are not required, and are called **excess reserves**. A bank's required reserves plus its excess reserves equal its *total reserves*.

Excess Reserves
Reserves of depository institutions that are above the required reserve ratio.

Now consider the excess reserves of the First National Bank—assets it is not required to have and that are not earning income for it. What can the First National Bank do to remedy this?

Table 13-8
Reserves Versus Demand Deposits for the First National Bank

Assets		Liabilities	
Required reserves	$ 200,000	Demand deposits	$1,000,000
Excess reserves	800,000		
Total reserves	$1,000,000		

Table 13-9 shows the First National Bank's accounts after it lends out $1 million, which is turn creates (or increases demand deposits by) $1 million (the payment of the loan). The First National Bank's total reserves are still $1 million, because there has been no change in deposits at the Federal Reserve Bank and no change in currency and coin. All that the First National Bank has done is to create a loan, and therefore to create a demand deposit. However, demand deposits are now $2 million, and the amount of reserves that are required (which must be 20 percent of demand deposits) increases to $400,000. Excess reserves decrease, to $600,000, since some of those excess reserves now become part of required reserves.

The First National Bank still has $600,000 worth of non-income-earning assets (the remaining excess reserves of $600,000). Table 13-10 shows that the bank's officers finally increase their loans by $3 million, which increases demand deposits by the same amount, to $5 million. Nothing has happened to the First National Bank's total reserves because there has been no change in either its deposits at the Federal Reserve or its holdings of currency and coin. However, required reserves (20 percent of demand deposits) now equal total reserves, and there are no excess reserves left in the bank. So the First National Bank cannot lend another penny to anyone.

Each time a bank extends loans and creates demand deposits, its required reserves must increase by 20 percent of the increase in demand deposits. Since the act of lending and creating demand deposits does not affect total reserves, this increase in required reserves must come out of excess reserves. Now the First National Bank has reached the position (see Table 13-10) of zero excess reserves. It cannot lend any more money, because, if it tried to, the law would require it to hold more reserves than it has, and it would be violating the banking laws. The bank must have excess reserves before it can lend more and increase its demand deposits further. These excess reserves can then quickly become required reserves to comply with the law that specifies 20 percent required reserves.

In comparing Tables 13-8, 13-9, and 13-10, one can see that $800,000 in excess reserves enables the bank to create 5 times that amount in demand deposits. Because the required reserve ratio is 20 percent, the First National Bank can expand the supply of money by 5 times its excess reserves. This means that it needs only $1 of reserves for every $5 of demand deposits. This is the bank's

Table 13-9
The First National Bank's Accounts After it Lends $1 Million
(thus increasing demand deposits by $1 million)

Assets		Liabilities	
Required reserves	$ 400,000	Demand deposits	$1,000,000
Excess reserves	600,000		
Total reserves	$1,000,000		
Loans	$1,000,000		

Table 13-10
The First National Bank's Accounts After it Lends $3 Million More and Reduces its Excess Reserves to Zero

Assets		Liabilities	
Required reserves	$1,000,000	Demand deposits	$5,000,000
Excess reserves	0		
Total reserves	$1,000,000		
Loans	$4,000,000		

Fractional Reserve Requirement
The minimum percentage of reserves against demand deposits that depository institutions must legally maintain.

fractional reserve requirement. If the required reserve ratio were to be increased to 50 percent, the bank would need $1 of reserves to create $2 of demand deposits. If the required reserves were to be increased still further, to 100 percent, the bank would have to hold $1 for every dollar it loaned. In other words, required reserves and demand deposits would have to be equal.

Enter Many Other Banks

Now remember the first assumption that the First National Bank is the only commercial bank in Simple Economy. It is a *monopoly* bank; it is, in fact, the entire commercial banking system. A monopoly bank can lend money and create demand deposits (money) that are a multiple of its excess reserves. The First National Bank can do this because depositors cannot write checks and deposit them in other banks. There *are* no other banks.

The behavior of an individual commercial bank in a multibank system differs from that of a monopoly bank with respect to its excess reserves, lending, and creation of demand deposits.

Now we will drop the assumption that there is only one bank, a monopoly bank, in the economy. Let's assume that there are more than 15,000 separately incorporated, privately owned, commercial banks, and that the economy being discussed is the U.S. economy. Now we can begin to analyze the U.S. banking system.

The Federal Reserve and Clearing Checks

In the U.S., there are 12 Federal Reserve (Fed) Banks, each of which serves one large district. And a Fed Bank performs an important function not previously discussed: It serves as a national clearinghouse for checks. Now what does that mean?

In our system, with its many commercial banks, you can write a check on your account in one bank and have it deposited in an account in another bank. How do banks collect or receive payment for such checks from other banks? They do it through the Fed collection process.

Table 13-11 shows what changes take place in this collection process. You write a check for $1,000 on a demand deposit in the Bank of America in California, and this check is deposited in the First National Bank of Boston. The demand deposits in the First National Bank of Boston are increased by $1,000. To collect its money, the First National Bank sends the check to the Fed, which increases the First National Bank's deposits with the Fed. In other words, the reserves of the First National Bank increase by $1,000. Meanwhile, back at the Bank of America, the situation is the opposite. The Fed reduces the Bank of America's deposits with the Fed by $1,000. In other words, the reserves of the Bank of America decrease by $1,000. The Fed then sends the canceled check to the Bank of America, which reduces *your* demand deposits by $1,000.

In brief, at a multibank system, when a check is drawn on an account in Alpha Bank and deposited in Bravo Bank, there is a transfer of both demand deposits and reserves (deposits at the Fed). The Fed acts as the third party, the go-between.

Lending by Individual Banks: A Little Goes a Long Way

Now we are going to deal with a number of independent banks in the Fed system. Let's call our 4 representative banks Alpha, Bravo, Charlie, and Delta.

An individual bank in a multibank system can lose both demand deposits and reserves overnight to other banks, through a flow of checks. Therefore, Alpha Bank—an individual bank in a multibank system—cannot lend money and create demand deposits that are a multiple of its excess reserves. Alpha Bank, following a conservative rule, lends an amount *equal only to its own excess reserves*. If it lends more, it runs the risk of losing (through a flow of checks) so much of its reserves that it cannot meet the law's reserve requirements.

Table 13-12 shows the changes in the relevant accounts for Alpha Bank as it applies this rule. Part (a) shows that Alpha Bank, before it lends $800,000, has $1 million of established demand

Table 13-11
The Effect of One Check on the Federal Reserve and Two of its Member Banks

Bank of America		Federal Reserve Deposits	First National Bank of Boston	
Assets	**Liabilities**		**Assets**	**Liabilities**
Reserves −$1,000	Demand deposits −$1,000	First National Bank of Boston +$1,000 Bank of America −$1,000	Reserves +$1,000	Demand deposits +$1,000

Table 13-12

(a) Alpha Bank Before It Lends $800,000		(b) Alpha Bank After It Lends $800,000	
Assets	**Liabilities**	**Assets**	**Liabilities**
Required reserves $200,000 Excess reserves $800,000 Total reserves $1,000,000	Demand deposits $1,000,000	Reserves $1,000,000 Loans $800,000	Demand deposits $1,800,000
(c) Alpha Bank After Checks Have Cleared		**(d) Bravo Bank After Receiving Checks**	
Assets	**Liabilities**	**Assets**	**Liabilities**
Reserves $200,000 Loans $800,000	Demand deposits $1,000,000	Reserves $800,000	Demand deposits $800,000

deposits. On the basis of its past experience, Alpha Bank estimates that these deposits will remain with the bank. Alpha Bank also has $1 million in reserves, of which $200,000 are required and $800,000 are excess, since the required reserve ratio is 20 percent.

Part (b) of Table 13-12 shows Alpha Bank lending only an amount equal to its excess reserves. Suppose, however, that the worst occurs, part (c), and that all these new demand deposits flow out as checks to other banks, for example, to Bravo Bank.

Bravo Bank now has an increase in demand deposits of $800,000, part (d). It sends these checks to the Fed, which promptly increases Bravo's deposits there by $800,000 and at the same time reduces Alpha's deposits there by $800,000. The Fed then sends the canceled checks to Alpha Bank, which duly notes the fact that its demand deposits have shrunk by $800,000.

Part (c) shows us, however, that even though Alpha Bank has lost $800,000 in reserves and demand deposits, it can still meet its obligations. It still has its required reserves ($200,000 in reserves is adequate because the bank has $1 million in demand deposits and the required reserve ratio is 20 percent).

In Table 13-13, part (a) shows that Bravo Bank now has excess reserves of $640,000. Part (b) shows Bravo lending up to its limit of $640,000, thereby creating demand deposits of $640,000.

Now suppose the worst happens, part (c). All the checks drawn on Bravo Bank's newly created demand deposits flow to Charlie Bank. Charlie Bank now has an increase in its demand deposits of $640,000. Charlie Bank sends these checks to the Fed, which increases Charlie Bank's deposits with the Fed (and its own reserves) by $640,000, part (d). At the same time, the Fed deducts $640,000 from Bravo Bank's deposits at the Fed (and lowers Bravo's reserves by that amount). When Bravo gets these canceled

Table 13-13

(a) Bravo Bank Before It Lends $640,000		(b) Bravo Bank After It Lends $640,000	
Assets	**Liabilities**	**Assets**	**Liabilities**
Required reserves $160,000 Excess reserves $640,000 Total reserves $800,000	Demand deposits $800,000	Reserves $800,000 Loans $640,000	Demand deposits $1,440,000
(c) Bravo Bank After Checks Have Cleared		**(d) Charlie Bank After Receiving Checks**	
Assets	**Liabilities**	**Assets**	**Liabilities**
Reserves $160,000 Loans $640,000	Demand deposits $800,000	Reserves $640,000	Demand deposits $640,000

checks back, it records the information that it has $640,000 less in demand deposits.

Bravo Bank has followed the rule and lent only as much as it held in excess reserves. Even though it has lost the newly created demand deposits and equivalent reserves, it can still satisfy the legal reserve requirement.

We could continue to analyze this process at great length. At each round of lending, the excess reserves diminish (as excess reserves are reclassified as required reserves), so that excess reserves decrease as only to the limit of its excess reserves, creating demand deposits (money) to pay for the loans. However, as excess reserves filter through all the banks, the whole banking system makes loans and creates demand deposits that are a multiple of the original excess reserves in Alpha Bank.

Table 13-14 shows what happens. Alpha Bank created $800,000 in demand deposits. This money, by means of checks, was transferred to Bravo Bank. Bravo Bank took this $800,000 and created $640,000 in demand deposits. If we had continued our

Table 13-14
Demand Deposits Created

Bank	Amount
Alpha Bank	$ 800,000
Bravo Bank	640,000
Charlie Bank	512,000
Delta Bank	409,600
Rest of the banks	<u>1,638,400</u>
	$4,000,000

analysis, you would have seen that Charlie Bank then created $512,000 in demand deposits. And when that money got over to Delta Bank, Delta Bank created $409,600. As the money went further and further, the other banks in the system created $1,638,400. Because the required reserve ratio is 20 percent, the whole banking system could create $4 million in new demand deposits, even though each bank made loans and generated new demand deposits only up to the amount of its excess reserves. If each bank lends an amount equal to its excess reserves and uses only demand deposits to pay out money for the loans, the formula for the multiple that demand deposits may be of the required reserve ratio **deposit multiplier** (DM) is:

$$DM = \frac{1}{R},$$

where R is the required reserve ratio. In our example, R is 20 percent. The deposit multiplier equals:

$$\frac{1}{.20} \quad \text{or} \quad 5.$$

Deposit Multiplier
The formula for determining the multiple that demand deposits may be of required reserves.

$$DM = \frac{1}{R}$$

But there are Leakages

We have seen that it is technically possible, with a 20 percent required reserve ratio, for banks to have a maximum potential of creating new demand deposits 5 times the original excess reserves. However, the full multiple creation of demand deposits rarely takes place. There are what are called **leakages**, factors in the creation of demand deposits in the process, which reduce the ability of the depository institutions to expand demand deposits.

Leakages
Factors in the creation of demand deposits which reduce the ability of depository institutions to expand demand deposits.

1. Suppose that people who borrow from the bank withdraw currency and coin from their demand deposits. This has the effect of withdrawing reserves from the banking system, thus reducing the amount of demand deposits that can be created. For example, suppose that when Alpha Bank lends out the original $800,000, one of the borrowers demands $100,000 in currency as payment, instead of a demand deposit. So, instead of $800,000 in checks being transferred from Alpha Bank to Bravo Bank, only $700,000 in checks is transferred. Reserves (deposits at the Fed) shifted from Alpha to Bravo are $700,000 (not $800,000). Bravo's excess reserves are thus $560,000, not $640,000. Bravo Bank cannot make as many new loans or create as large demand deposits, and this effect is passed on through the rest of the system. The $100,000 taken as currency in payment of loans at Alpha Bank reduces the original excess reserves in the banking system, and thus the total of new loans and demand deposits.

2. We have assumed so far that each independent bank lends up to the limit of its excess reserves, that it lends every penny it can,

provided it can maintain enough reserves to meet the legal minimum. In practice, bankers are often much more conservative and want to keep a cushion or extra reserve in case checks are drawn against them in amounts greater than the amounts of the new demand deposits. What if some depositors write checks against Alpha Bank's original deposits and this money flows into other banks? If Alpha has not kept some of its excess reserves on hand, it will not be able to meet these unexpected transfers of demand deposits and reserves. However, if banks do lend out amounts less than their excess reserves, then the amount of the demand deposits created in the system is much less.

3. The fact that the banking system has excess reserves (the ability to make loans) does not mean that there are always good opportunities to lend. During a business slump, bankers may fear that some potential borrowers will not be able to repay loans. So when times are bad, bankers may not lend up to the maximum. Also, at times there may not be much demand for loans even when interest rates are low.

When we take these leakages into consideration, the formula for the deposit multiplier becomes more complex:

$$DM = \frac{1}{R+E+C},$$

where R is the required reserve ratio, E is excess reserves, those *not* used by the banking system to create loans, and C is the currency withdrawn by those receiving loans.

The Role of Excess Reserves

In our analysis of the way money is created under government regulation, we have pointed out the crucial role of excess reserves. Without excess reserves, banks cannot extend loans and create demand deposits. Therefore, control over the amounts of reserves in the banking system means control over the amount of lending that is done, and, by extension, control over the supply of M1 money itself. As the supply of the many near monies we looked at earlier has grown, the Fed's ability to control all forms of money has been somewhat diminished. As we saw with the sharply restrictive monetary policy of the Fed in 1981-1982, however, its power to control money and economic activity remains very great and its authority over reserve requirements has been extended to all depository institutions, not simply commercial banks. Only the Fed has the power to increase or decrease the required amount of excess reserves in the system. If it wishes to increase economic activity it can lower deposits creating reserve requirements. If, on the other hand, it wishes to restrict the growth of economic activity, it can raise reserve requirements.

A Final Word About Excess Reserves

Federal Funds Market
The market in which banks, through inter-bank transfers, lend their excess reserves to other banks.

Excess reserves can be used to create earnings for financial institutions. Though cautious, bankers naturally tend therefore, to minimize the amount of excess reserves they hold. One important way they do this is to turn them into very-short-term earning assets by lending them to other banks that are short of required or desired reserves. A market has been created in which such transfers occur. That market, the **federal funds market**, handles billions of dollars of such inter-bank transfers through brokers. If Alpha Bank is short of reserves, it contacts a broker who arranges a short-term (often overnight) transfer of excess reserves from Bravo Bank. The interest rate at which such reserve loans is made is known as the *Federal funds rate*. A key point, in other words, is that excess reserves do not just sit around idly in the American financial system.

SUMMING UP

1. Our analysis of the banking system of the imaginary Simple Economy is based on four assumptions: (a) There is only one bank in the system, the First National Bank. (b) There are no government regulations. (c) There is no currency or coin. The economy's supply of money is limited to the amount of demand deposits in the First National Bank. (d) There is no international trade.

2. The First National Bank increases the supply of M1 money by extending loans, which are paid to the borrower by creating new demand deposits. The borrowers pay off the loans by checks drawn on their demand deposits. This decreases the supply of M1 money in the economy.

3. The Simple Economy banking system, limited by our four assumptions, has the following weaknesses: (a) For purchases of small value, demand deposits are a very inefficient form of money. (b) The First National Bank's ability to expand the supply of M1 money through lending is unlimited. But we can counter these weaknesses by dropping our third assumption and introducing currency and coin.

4. People like to hold a certain percentage of a nation's money in the form of currency and coin. The amount of currency and coin can provide an automatic check on the bank's ability to extend loans and increase demand deposits. As the bank lends out money, it creates more demand deposits, and demand deposits are money. Then people withdraw more currency and coin from the bank in order to maintain that desired percentage of the money supply in the form of currency and coin. When the bank no longer has any currency and coin left in its vaults, it can no longer lend, and create demand deposits.

5. Varying the quantity of currency and coin is not an efficient way to regulate the total money supply. A more efficient system is to (a) establish a central bank, such as the Fed system, (b) require commercial banks to keep assets in the form of reserves equal to a certain percentage of demand deposits, and (c) empower the central bank (the Fed in the case of the U.S.) to vary the amount of reserves. In the U.S. financial system, *reserves* are defined as deposits of depository institutions at the Fed plus cash in the vaults of those institutions.

6. In a one-bank (monopoly) system, loaning money creates demand deposits, but does not affect total reserves. However, in a system that has a government-imposed *required reserve ratio,* an increase in demand deposits raises the figure for required reserves. Banks must then count their *excess reserves* as part of their required reserves. When all its reserves come under the heading of "required," a commercial bank cannot extend loans, because it has no more excess reserves that it can reclassify as equired reserves when demand deposits increase.

7. Because the required-reserve ratio is less than 100 percent—that is, it is *fractional*—depository institutions can create demand deposits that are a multiple of their reserves.

8. In our simple model of the banking system in the Simple Economy, the monopoly bank need not be concerned about a flow of checks and reserves to other banks because there is only one bank in the system. Therefore, a monopoly bank can expand the supply of money (create demand deposits) by lending out money equal to a multiple of its reserves. The size of the multiplier depends on the size of the required reserve ratio.

9. When we drop the assumption that there is only one bank and assume that there are 15,000 banks, with the Fed controlling all of them, we are approximating a model of the U.S. banking system. The Fed acts as a national clearinghouse for checks. When Alpha Bank receives a check from Bravo Bank, Alpha sends it to the Fed. The Fed increases Alpha's deposits (reserves) with the Fed and reduces Bravo's deposits (reserves) with the Fed. When Bravo Bank receives the check, it reduces the demand-deposit account on which it is drawn.

10. When checks flow from one bank to another, both reserves and demand deposits are transferred. To avoid letting its reserves fall below the required level, an individual bank in a multibank system makes loans (and thus creates demand deposits) only up to the level of its excess reserves. But as these excess reserves gradually filter through the banking system, the banking system creates demand deposits (money) that are a multiple of the original excess reserves.

11. In the real world, the banking system does not increase the supply of M1 money by the full multiple of its excess reserves because of the following *leakage* effects: (a) Some borrowers want currency instead of demand deposits in payment for their loans, which has the effect of withdrawing reserves from the banking system, thus reducing the amount of demand deposits that can be created. (b) Some banks will not lend up to the limit of their excess reserves because they fear that an unexpected flow of checks to another bank might drain off reserves not only from their new demand deposits, but also from old demand deposits. (c) If there is a business slump, some banks will not lend money up to the limit of their excess reserves, because they fear that some loans will not be repaid. Sometimes, too, there is not enough demand for loans, even when interest rates are low.

12. Banks minimize excess reserves held. Banks that have excess reserves lend them, for very short periods, to banks that need reserves. This is done through the Federal funds market at a rate of interest known as the Federal funds rate.

KEY TERMS

Required reserve ratio
Excess reserves
Fractional reserve requirement
Deposit multiplier
Leakages
Federal funds market

QUESTIONS

1. What effects do the following transactions have on the demand deposits and reserves of Alpha Bank? On the whole commercial banking system? Why? (The required reserve ratio is 20 percent.)
   a. Ernie Jones withdraws $100 from his demand deposit account in Alpha Bank.
   b. Susan Smith borrows $500 from Alpha Bank, but puts the proceeds into Bravo Bank.
   c. Betty Cohen deposits $200 in her account at Alpha Bank by a check drawn on someone else's account at Alpha Bank.
   d. Susan Smith pays off her loan at Alpha Bank by a check drawn on her account at Alpha Bank.

2. What effects do these four transactions have on the supply of money? Why?

3. Why must a commercial bank maintain a certain level of reserves under the U.S. banking system? What are excess reserves, and what is their significance?

4. In a commercial banking system, how is the supply of money increased and decreased?

5. In a multibank system, an individual bank makes loans only up to the level of its excess reserves, while the whole commercial banking system can lend out money that is a multiple of the original bank's excess reserves. Why is there this difference?

6. What leakages can prevent a commercial banking system from lending at the full multiple of its original excess reserves?

7. What is the Federal funds market? What is the Federal funds rate?

SUGGESTED READINGS

McCarty, Marilu Hurt. *Money and Banking.* Financial Institutions and Economic Policy. Longman, 1988.

Annual Editions, 87/88. John Pisciotta, ed. Section IV, "Money, Banking and Monetary Policy." Pp 68-105. Sluice Dock, CT, 1987.

McClelland, Peter D. ed. Introduction to Macroeconomics. Section IV, "Monetary and Fiscal Policy." Especially Articles 20, 21, 22. New York McGraw-Hill, 1988.

Application to Chapter 13:
First Steps in Banking

The following selection from *Punch,* the British humor magazine, requires no introduction.

Q. What are banks for?

A. To make money.

Q. For the customers?

A. For the banks.

Q. Why doesn't bank advertising mention this?

A. It would not be in good taste. But it is mentioned by implication in references to Reserves of £249,000,000 or thereabouts. That is the money they have made.

Q. Out of the customers?

A. I suppose so.

Q. They also mention Assets of £500,000,000 or thereabouts. Have they made that too?

A. Not exactly. That is the money they use to make money.

Q. I see. And they keep it in a safe somewhere?

A. Not at all. They lend it to customers.

Q. Then they haven't got it?

A. No.

Q. Then how is it Assets?

A. They maintain that it would be if they got it back.

Q. But they must have some money in a safe somewhere?

A. Yes, usually £500,000,000 or thereabouts. This is called Liabilities.

Q. But if they've got it, how can they be liable for it?

A. Because it isn't theirs.

Q. Then why do they have it?

A. It has been lent to them by customers.

Q. You mean customers lend banks money?

A. In effect. They put money into their accounts, so it is really lent to the banks.

Q. And what do the banks do with it?

A. Lend it to other customers.

Q. But you said that money they lent to other people was Assets?

A. Yes.

Q. Then Assets and Liabilities must be the same thing?

A. You can't really say that.

Q. But you've just said it. If I put £100 into my account the bank is liable to have to pay it back, so it's Liabilities. But they go and lend it to someone else, and he is liable to have to pay it back, so it's Assets. It's the same £100, isn't it?

A. Yes, But ....

Q. Then it cancels out. It means, doesn't it, that banks haven't really any money at all?

A. Theoretically....

Q. Never mind theoretically. And if they haven't any money where do they get their Reserves of £249,000,000 or thereabouts?

A. I told you. That is the money they have made.

Q. How?

A. Well, when they lend your £100 to someone they charge him interest.

Q. How much?

A. It depends on the Bank Rate. Say five and a half per cent. That's their profit.

Q. Why isn't it my profit? Isn't it my money?

A. It's the theory of banking practice that....

Q. When I lend them my £100 why don't I charge them interest?

A. You do.

Q. You don't say. How much?

A. It depends on the Bank Rate. Say half a per cent.

Q. Grasping of me, rather?

A. But that's only if you're not going to draw the money out again.

Q. But of course, I'm going to draw it out again. If I hadn't wanted to draw it out again I could have buried it in the garden, couldn't I?

A. They wouldn't like you to draw it out again.

Q. Why not? If I keep it there you say it's a Liability. Wouldn't they be glad if I reduced their Liabilities by removing it?

A. No. Because if you remove it they can't lend it to anyone else.

Q. But if I wanted to remove it they'd have to let me?

A. Certainly.

Q. But suppose they've already lent it to another customer?

A. Then they'll let you have someone else's money.

Q. But suppose he wants his too...and they've let me have it?

A. You're being purposely obtuse.

Q. I think I'm being acute. What if everyone wanted their money at once?

A. It's the theory of banking practice that they never would.

Q. So what banks bank on is not having to meet their commitments?

A. I wouldn't say that.

Q. Naturally. Well, if there's nothing else you think you can tell me...?

A. Quite so. Now you can go off and open a banking account.

Q. Just one last question.

A. Of course.

Q. Wouldn't I do better to go off and open a bank?

Chapter 14:
Monetary Policy: Central Banking in
Deregulated Financial Markets

Money, as we have seen, plays a vital role in the economic life of people. The money supply and changes in the money supply affect the decisions of every consumer and producer, as well as the activities of the government. Because of the important link between money and the levels of income, employment, and prices, all modern governments exercise some degree of control over their system of financial institutions. In the U.S., these controls began taking their modern form with the creation of the Federal Reserve (Fed) System in 1914.

Control by the Fed generally increased from its inception to the 1980s. This was especially true with the banking reforms of the 1930s. By the 1970s, it became clear to many that regulation of monetary institutions had, in some respects, gone too far. As a result, substantial deregulation has occurred in response to rapidly evolving financial markets. At the same time, in recognition of the macroeconomic importance of controlling the money supply, some regulatory powers of the Fed were broadened in the 1980s.

How to control as well as measure the money supply remains an area filled with controversy. After we have examined the workings of the Fed, America's central bank, we will in the application following this chapter, assay some of the controversies between Keynesians and Monetarists as well as arguments about how effective, if at all, are discretionary macroeconomic policy changes.

The Structure of the Federal Reserve

Where do *banks* go when they want to go to the bank? They go to a Fed bank, which is a banker's bank.

When Congress passed the Federal Reserve Act of 1914, it did not create just one bank. It divided the country into 12 Fed districts, with a Fed bank in each. Figure 14-1 shows the 12 districts and the location of the 12 Fed banks. For example, the first Fed district takes in all of New England. Its Fed bank is in Boston. The twelfth district consists of 7 western states plus Alaska and Hawaii. Its bank is in San Francisco.

Figure 14-1
Boundaries of Federal Reserve Districts and Their Branch Territories

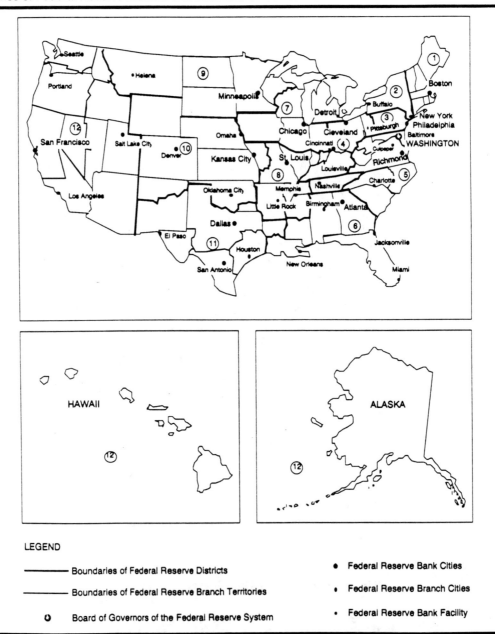

LEGEND

—————— Boundaries of Federal Reserve Districts

—————— Boundaries of Federal Reserve Branch Territories

○ Board of Governors of the Federal Reserve System

● Federal Reserve Bank Cities

▪ Federal Reserve Branch Cities

▪ Federal Reserve Bank Facility

Source: *Federal Reserve Bulletin.* Reproduced by permission of the Board of Governors of the Federal Reserve System.

National Banks
Commercial banks
chartered by the
federal government.

State Banks
Banks chartered by
state governments.

All **national banks** (commercial banks chartered by the federal government) are required to be members of the Fed system. **State banks** (commercial banks chartered by the various state governments) can join it if they wish. Not all commercial banks are members of the Fed system. Those that are, however, comprise the larger commercial banks in the U.S., and control more than 70 percent of U.S. banking assets. It is important to note that the Depository Institutions Deregulation and Monetary Control Act of 1980 imposed uniform reserve requirements on all depository institutions, bank and non-bank alike. The distinction between members and non-members has, thus, become much less important.

Each Fed bank is technically owned by the commercial member banks in its district. On becoming a member, each commercial bank must buy stock in its district Fed bank, the amount depending on the size of its capital surplus. It receives a fixed annual dividend on these shares.

The main policy-making body of the Fed is the board of governors, in Washington, D.C. There are 7 governors including the chairman, who are appointed for terms of 14 years by the President, with the advice and consent of the Senate. Like the Supreme Court, the Board of Governors of the Fed is substantially independent of the executive branch of government. Only rarely has a President had the chance to appoint a majority of the board of governors, since a President ordinarily appoints a new member only once every 2 years. Therefore, a President who wanted to try to play God with the nation's money supply would not be able to do so unless all seven members of the Board of Governors of the Fed died or resigned at the same time. Some regard this as a nice built-in safety valve.

There are 2 main committees that help the board of governors formulate policy:

1. *The Federal Open Market Committee (FOMC)* controls decision making about the most important weapon the Fed has in controlling excess reserves, lending, and the supply of money: open market operations, which we will say more about later. In addition to the 7 governors, the committee consists of certain others appointed by the board, who do the day-by-day work.

2. *The Federal Advisory Council* consists of 12 people, one from each of the 12 boards of directors of the Fed banks. They advise the governors about problems in the various districts of the system.

Each of the 12 Fed banks has a 9-member board of directors. Three are appointed by the board of governors in Washington, to represent the national interest. Three are elected by the member commercial banks—1 from the large banks, 1 from the medium-size banks, and one from the small banks; they represent banking interests in the particular district. These 6 appoint the remaining 3, who represent the general economic community.

So we see a mixture of both private and public elements in the Fed system. The national board of governors, with its 2 main support committees and its 3 appointed members on each board of directors of the 12 Fed banks, is the public element. The ownership of the 12 district Fed banks by the commercial banks in that district, plus the fact that the commercial banks appoint 3 members to the board of directors of their district Fed bank, is the private element. Unquestionably, however, the public element is the dominant influence in monetary decision making.

General Powers of the Federal Reserve

Commercial banks must have excess reserves in order to make loans and create demand deposits, and that as a bank increases its demand deposits, it must transfer or reclassify excess reserves as required reserves. Also, in a multibank system, the individual commercial bank needs a safe margin of excess reserves in case its customers decide to write an unexpectedly large number of checks, thereby transferring demand deposits and reserves to other banks. Its ability to participate in the Federal Funds Market helps it to maintain this margin.

General Power
The authority of the central bank (Fed) to increase or decrease the required reserve ratio.

The device we used to explain the central bank was a hypothetical economy, simple economy, with one central bank that had the power to vary the amount of excess reserves held by commercial banks. This power is called the **general power** because it enables a central bank to increase or decrease the excess reserves that a commercial bank must have in order to make any kind of loan.

The U.S. Fed has 3 powers over excess reserves: open-market operations, the discount rate, and the required reserve ratio.

Open-Market Operations
What is for sale in the open market? Debt instruments that are short term (maturing in 90 days to 1 year), highly liquid (easily sold for a cash return), and relatively free of risk. Examples are *prime commercial paper* (promissory notes of large secure corporations), *banker's acceptances* (short-term debt of banks), and *Treasury bills* (short-term debt of the federal government).

In the open market, the Fed (FOMC) is an important customer. It buys and sells already issued federal government debt (primarily Treasury bills), which has the effect of increasing or decreasing excess reserves in the commercial banking system. This effect makes open-market operations the most important of the Fed's three weapons. The added advantage of this weapon is that it can be applied selectively. Remember that in open-market operations, the bonds are not bought directly from the Treasury.

1. *Increasing reserves.* To increase a depository institution's excess reserves, the Fed buys government-debt securities on the open market, as shown in Figure 14-2.

Figure 14-2
Changes in Assets and Liabilities of both the Federal Reserve Bank and the Commercial Bank When the Commercial Bank Sells Government Securities to the Federal Reserve

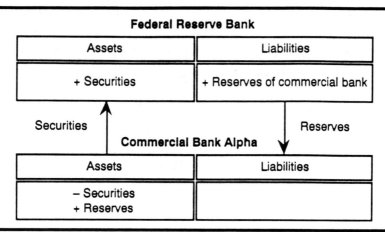

Let's say that a certain commercial bank, Alpha Bank, has customers begging for loans, but Alpha does not have enough excess reserves to lend any more money or to create any more demand deposits. Instead of going to the Federal Funds Market, let's suppose that the Fed comes along and buys some assets—government securities—from Alpha Bank. To pay for these assets, the Fed increases Alpha Bank's deposits with the Fed. This means that the Fed is taking on a liability. Alpha Bank is exchanging its government securities for a deposit at the Fed bank. So Alpha's total reserves increase, and thus, its excess reserves also increase.

But what happens when the Fed buys government securities from private individuals? (See Figure 14-3.) Along comes an ordinary citizen, Joe Reed. The Fed buys a government security from him and gives him a check in return. Reed deposits the check in his account at his commercial bank, Alpha Bank. Alpha sends the check to the Fed, which increases Alpha's deposit with the Fed. That is, it increases Alpha Bank's reserves. The Fed has an increase in its assets (the government security it bought from Joe Reed) and an equal increase in its liabilities (the deposits of the commercial bank at the Fed). Joe Reed's total assets are unchanged. The decrease in his holdings of government securities is exactly equal to the increase in his demand deposits. The effect of all this on Alpha Bank is an increase in assets (its reserves increase because its deposits with the Fed increase), and an increase in liabilities (Reed's demand deposit account). Thus, Alpha Bank's total reserves have increased and, therefore, so have its excess reserves.

2. *Decreasing reserves.* To decrease depository institutions' excess reserves, and also to decrease their total reserves, the Fed sells government securities. Figure 14-4 shows how this works.

Figure 14-3
Changes in Assets and Liabilities of the Federal Reserve Bank, Plain Citizen Joe Reed, and Commercial Bank Alpha When the Federal Reserve Bank Buys Government Securities from a Private Citizen

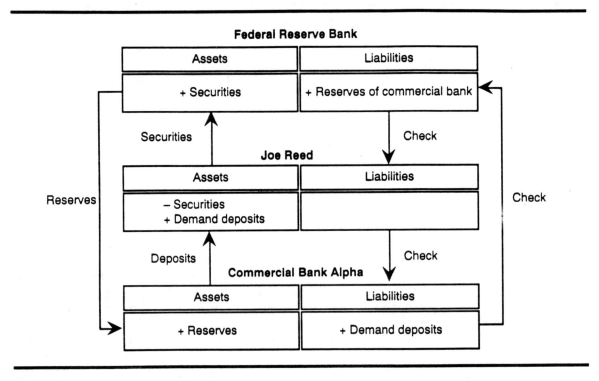

Figure 14-4
What Happens to Assets and Liabilities of the Federal Reserve Bank and Commercial Bank Bravo When the Fed Sells Government Securities to Commercial Bank Bravo

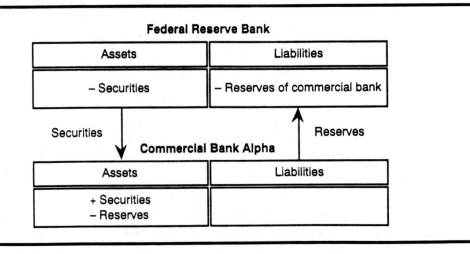

First, lets say that the Fed sells the government security to a commercial bank (Bravo Bank). When Bravo Bank buys a government security from the Fed, it pays for it by accepting a reduction in its deposits with the Fed. The Fed's assets decrease (by the amount of the securities sold to Bravo Bank). Its liabilities also decrease, because Bravo Bank's deposits with the Fed decrease. This means that Bravo Bank's total reserves decline. Therefore, Bravo Bank's excess reserves decline.

How does it affect excess reserves and the supply of money when the Fed sells government securities to *non*-commercial banking institutions, or to private individuals? Figure 14-5 shows what happens.

Here is Maria Deluca, citizen, who buys a government security from the Fed and gives a check in return. The Fed collects on the check by reducing the deposits with the Fed of Charlie Bank, the commercial bank that holds Deluca's demand deposits. The Fed sends Deluca's check to Charlie Bank, which reduces the amount of demand deposits in her account. The Fed's assets decrease by the amount of the securities sold to Deluca. There is an offsetting decrease in the Fed's liabilities (Charlie Bank's deposits with the Fed). The total assets of Maria Deluca are unchanged. Her holdings of government securities increase and her demand deposits decrease by equal amounts. Charlie Bank's assets decrease

Figure 14-5
What Happens to Assets and Liabilities of the Federal Reserve Bank, Maria Deluca, and Commercial Bank Charlie When the Fed Sells Government Securities to a Private Citizen

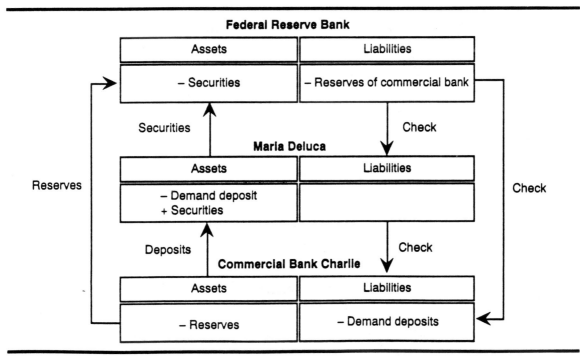

(its reserves—that is, its deposits at the Fed—are less) and there is an equal decrease in its liabilities (the demand deposits of Maria Deluca).

Therefore, when the Fed sells government securities, the effect is to reduce total reserves, and thus to reduce excess reserves of the whole commercial banking system. Because of this decrease in the excess reserves of commercial banks, their lending ability decreases, and so does their power to increase demand deposits (the supply of money).

The Discount Rate

The Fed bank, as we have said, is a banker's bank to depository institutions: It holds deposits for them and helps collect or clear checks between institutions. The Fed also makes loans to member commercial banks by buying either their promissory notes or by buying from the banks IOUs of nonbanking corporations or individuals defined as acceptable by the Fed. When the Fed buys such promissory notes, it deposits the proceeds in the commercial bank's Fed account, increasing the bank's total reserves, and thus increasing its excess reserves.

Depository institutions do not get all these services free. The Fed bank charges interest for making these loans. It is called a *discount* rather than interest, because the Fed collects the interest charge when it makes the loan.

Discount Rate
The rate of interest charged by the Fed when it makes loans to member banks.

For example, a commercial bank, Delta Bank, sells the Fed a $1,000 promissory note that matures in 3 months. The **discount rate** (interest rate) is 8 percent per year, a 2-percent discount for the 3-month period. Delta Bank actually receives from the Fed only $980, or $1,000 less 2 percent. Delta's deposits at the Fed increase by $980. In other words, Delta pays the Fed $20 for the privilege of using $1,000 for 3 months.

If the Fed wants to encourage depository institutions to increase their reserves this way (that is, to increase their deposits with the Fed), it can reduce the cost of borrowing by *lowering the discount rate*. If the Fed wants to discourage institutions from increasing reserves this way, it can increase the cost of borrowing by *increasing* the discount rate.

Note: The Fed cannot reduce the reserves of depository institutions by this device. It can only use the discount rate to *encourage* or *discourage* the increasing of reserves. In addition, the Fed in recent years has restricted its lending through discounting to situations in which depository institutions are in temporary need of reserves. Remember, though, institutions can borrow each other's excess reserves through the Federal Funds Market.

Note: There is a difference between discount-rate policy and discount policy. *Discount-rate policy* has to do with variations in the discount rate and their effects. The *discount policy* has to do with the availability of discounts. As a means of power over excess reserves, the Fed's ability to manipulate the discount rate is not as important as its operations in the open market.

However, through the responses of the depository institutions, the Fed discount rate controls interest rates on loans of all sorts: mortgage loans, car loans, and so forth. When the Fed raises its discount rate, this is a sequence of repercussions in the economy: (1) Everybody knows the higher rate is a signal that the Fed is tightening credit. (2) The higher rate discourages institutions from increasing their reserves, and thus keeps them from making as many loans. (3) The higher discount rate pushes up all other interest rates.

The Required Reserve Ratio

Required Reserve Ratio
The percentage of reserves against deposits that financial institutions must maintain.

When a depository institution makes a loan, as you know, the essential ingredient is excess reserves. The institution cannot loan more money and create more demand deposits once it reaches the bottom of its excess-reserve barrel, because it might risk dropping below its required reserves. The final and most powerful weapon by which the Fed can affect the banking system is that it can change the **required reserve ratio**, the percentage of reserves against deposits that financed institutions are required to maintain.

Varying the required reserve ratio does not change the total reserves of a depository institution, just the proportion of total reserves that the bank must have on hand, that are *required*. Therefore, it changes the proportion that is counted as excess.

For example, a commercial bank has $100,000 in demand deposits and $25,000 in total reserves. If the required reserve ratio is 20 percent, its required reserves would be 20 percent of $100,000 (the amount of demand deposits) or $20,000. Its excess reserves would be $5,000 ($25,000 minus $20,000). If the Fed were to reduce the required reserve ratio to 10 percent, the commercial bank's required reserves would be $10,000 (10 percent of $100,000) and its excess reserves would be $15,000 ($25,000 minus $10,000). In other words, if the Fed lowers the required reserve ratio, the commercial bank's excess reserves increase.

If the Fed were to increase the required reserve ratio from 20 percent to 25 percent, the commercial bank's required reserves would increase to $25,000 (25 percent of $100,000) and its excess reserves would decrease to zero ($25,000 total reserves minus $25,000 required reserves). In other words, if the Fed increases the required reserve ratio, the commercial bank's excess reserves decrease.

Clearly, the Fed's ability to vary the required reserve ratio is a very powerful weapon, since it means that the Fed can readily change the excess reserves of the whole commercial banking system. The problem is that it is *too* powerful to be used often. Small percentage changes in the reserve ratio can have enormous effects on the reserve position of depository institutions. That is why the Fed varies its activity on the open market on an ongoing basis, giving the economy the ongoing changes in M1 money that are needed to carry out its monetary policy. Only rarely and cautiously does it tamper with the reserve ratio. Changes in the reserve ratio usually signify major shifts in Fed policy.

A Review: How the Fed Nudges the Banking System

If the Fed wishes to *increase* the excess reserves of commercial banks to enable them to increase loans and create more demand deposits (the supply of money), it can do the following: (1) *buy* government securities on the open market, (2) *lower* the discount rate, or (3) *lower* the required reserve ratio.

If the Fed wishes to *decrease* banks' excess reserves, to reduce commercial banks' ability to make loans and create more demand deposits, it can do the following: (1) *sell* government securities on the open market, (2) *raise* the discount rate, or (3) *raise* the required reserve ratio.

Specific Powers of the Federal Reserve

Specific Powers
Additional authority of the Fed beyond the general power to control lending and credit.

No sooner had Congress passed the Federal Reserve Act of 1914, which brought the Fed bank into existence, than people came forth with ideas to improve it. So, over the years Congress has passed amendments giving the Fed additional powers, especially in the areas of lending and credit. Powers added to the Fed over specific areas of lending are called **specific powers.**

Margin Requirements on Stocks

Margin Requirement
The percentage of cash required as a down payment on stock purchases.

The **margin requirement** is the percentage of cash required as a down payment on the purchase of a share of stock. The Bank Act of 1933 gave the Fed power to set the *margin* that buyers of stock in the various stock exchanges must pay when they buy corporate stock. The purpose of the margin requirement is to control speculation on the stock market.

If the Fed wants to reduce speculation on the stock exchange, it can increase the margin requirement. Let's say that the Fed increases the margin from 50 percent to 75 percent. This means that a person buying stock must pay cash equal to 75 percent of the value of the stock and can borrow only 25 percent of its purchase price. It works in reverse too. For example, in 1974 the stock market fell drastically from the high 900s to below 600. (These figures are from the Dow Jones Industrial Index, which measures changes in the prices of stock on the New York Stock Exchange.) To stimulate demand for securities, the Fed dropped margin requirements to 50 percent. It did not do so in October, 1987, however, because the market recovered rather quickly and steadily.

The Fed's responsibility for watchdogging speculation in the stock market does not clash with its responsibilities for controlling excess reserves. Variations in stock-market margin requirements do not affect the total or excess reserves of commercial banks.

Regulation X
Empowered the Fed to control loans on consumer goods.

Regulation W
Empowered the Fed to control real estate loans.

Regulation Q
Empowered the Fed to set maximum interest rates commercial banks could pay on savings accounts.

Regulations X and W

Beginning in World War II, Congress gave the Fed the power to regulate consumer and real estate loans. **Regulation X** concerned loans on consumer goods, while **Regulation W** involved real estate loans. These regulations made the Fed responsible for determining the minimum down payment on a loan and the maximum length of time in which a loan could be repaid.

Regulation Q

Regulation Q empowered the Fed to set the maximum interest rates that commercial banks could pay on savings accounts (time deposits) and on demand deposits. The Fed would not let banks pay interest on demand deposits and set the maximum interest rates payable on savings accounts.

Deregulation and Financial Markets: The 1980s

A movement to reverse some of the regulatory controls established or expanded in the 1930s took hold in the U.S. in the late-1970s. Although deregulation began with the airline industry, financial markets, including commercial banking, were not far behind. Regulation Q had placed controls over banks regarding interest rates, the kinds of assets they could invest in, and the kinds of financial instruments they could issue. By the late-1970s, this regulation seemed to many, including many in the banking industry, to be anachronistic. Banks, by then, were only an (important) part of a much larger financial industry comprised also of savings and loan associations, mutual savings banks, brokerage houses and other thrift institutions. It seemed inequitable and inefficient to many that banks should be subject to regulations that did not apply to the other institutions. Perhaps more importantly, it seemed that the American economy and its people would benefit from allowing all the players in these markets to compete on an equal footing.

The "Deregulation Act" of 1980

The Depository Institutions Deregulation and Monetary Control Reform Act of 1980, which repealed Regulation Q, was seen by many as a move toward a more competitive set of financial institutions. The law provided that:

1. Controls over interest rates on deposits were phased out over 5 years.

2. All deposit-taking institutions could issue checking accounts

3. Thrift institutions could make a wider range of loans.

4. Reserve requirements were extended uniformly to all depository institutions.

5. All depository institutions would be able to avail themselves of the services of the Fed (clearinghouse, etc.).

All in all, the 1980 Act went a long way toward creating a competitive, though not necessarily stable, environment in American financial markets.

Further Concerns About American Financial Institutions

In many respects, the 1980s were more turbulent for American financial institutions than any period since the 1930s. Major U.S. banks (including Continental Illinois) failed or were "bailed out." Others saw much of their loan portfolios (to underdeveloped nations, to farmers, etc.) on the verge of becoming non-performing or written off as bad debts. The Savings and Loan Associations had an even more rocky period with 17 percent of them disappearing in the first 2 years of the 1980s and continued failures with a massive "bail-out" of these institutions agreed to in the late 1980s. Partly in response to the perceived instability in the industry (more a threat to shareholders than to depositors who are insured), the Garn-St. Germain Act was passed in 1982. The legislation was designed primarily to increase the borrowing authority of savings and loan associations and thereby to avoid a wave of bankruptcies in that industry. At the same time the act authorized all depository institutions to sell money market mutual funds, adding further to the competitiveness of financial markets.

A Further Movement Toward Competition? Nationwide Banking

Bank Holding Companies
Corporations that may own several banks, even in different states.

Throughout American history, the number of banks has been large relative to that of other industrial nations such as Canada and Great Britain. The reason for the disparity has lain in the tradition and often legal insistence on branch banking. Some states have even insisted on unit banking, the practice that a bank have one location and no branches even within the same state. Interstate branches are forbidden by Federal law, though permitting the practice would probably increase the competitiveness of the industry. Resistance to changing the restrictions on interstate banking has led to the formation of **bank holding companies**, corporations that may own several banks, even banks in different states. Nearly all big banks in the U.S. today are owned by holding companies who not only offer diversified banking services but also such collateral activities as leasing and credit cards.

Financial Institutions: A Summing Up

We have witnessed a number of fundamental changes in American financial institutions in the 1980s, and it seems likely that process of evolution will continue into the 1990s. It has become easier to enter financial markets, and they have become more broadly defined. At the same time, it has also become easier to fail. Many questions remain to be resolved. Does deposit insurance encourage depository institutions to take excessive risks? Are regulatory functions adequate to protect society's interests? How do we measure the money supply so that, once defined, a supply exists that can be closely correlated with changes in income and unemployment. As Keynes wrote, "We can draw the line between 'money' and 'debt' at whatever point is most convenient for handling a particular problem." Even in the 1990s, we will still be trying to draw that line.

The Powerful Fed: A Summary of Its Functions

We have seen that the Fed is a powerful agency and that its authority over the financial institutions of America in many respects, grew in the 1980s. Although we have mentioned some of its powers before, let's summarize them.

The Fed Regulates the Supply of Money

Through its control over the excess reserves of depository institutions, the Fed regulates the supply of M1 money. By means of its operations in the open market, and its variations in the discount rate and in the required reserve ratio, the Fed may increase or decrease excess reserves. Depository institutions must have excess reserves in order to make loans and create new demand deposits, which are the main form of money.

A great economist, Joseph Schumpeter, once said that whoever controls credit or access to financial capital is akin to the judges (ephors) of ancient Egypt who had power of life or death over all that nation's citizens except for pharaoh. To Schumpeter, bankers who controlled access to credit exercised this power in a modern capitalist society. If Schumpeter is right, is the Fed their pharaoh? After all it controls the ephors (bankers and lenders at all depository institutions) in the U.S.

The Fed Acts as a National Clearinghouse for Checks

When a depository institution receives a check written against an account in another financial institution, it gets paid by sending the check to the Fed bank. The Fed bank, when it receives the check, increases the deposits with the Fed of the institution sending the check and reduces the deposits of the bank on which the check is drawn. The Fed institution then sends the check to the depository institution on which it is drawn. *That* institution reduces the amount of demand deposits in the account of the person who wrote the check.

The Fed Issues Paper Currency
The Fed issues all the paper money in circulation. The Fed does not use the issuance of currency as a device to control the overall supply of money, but it must make certain that there is enough currency around to meet the economy's needs. For instance, the need for currency varies from season to season.

Before Christmas, people want to hold cash to buy Christmas presents so demand for paper currency increases. As people withdraw currency from their demand-deposit accounts, depository institutions run low on cash in their vaults. They therefore order more currency from the Fed, which fills their currency order and reduces their deposits with the Fed by an equal amount. In this way the Fed increases the supply of currency in the economy each Christmas season.

After Christmas, business falls off and people become uneasy about holding more currency than they actually need, so they deposit the excess in their demand-deposit accounts. The depository institutions now have more cash in their vaults than they want, so they send the excess back to the Fed, which stashes away the cash and increases the banks' deposits with the Fed. In this way the Fed withdraws currency from circulation. This high elasticity in the supply of currency helps take care of seasonal changes in the volume of business.

The Fed Regulates and Examines Member Banks
Congress has given the Fed the power to regulate many of the activities of depository institutions. To check whether these institutions are obeying the rules, the Fed periodically examines their books. Not much escapes the Fed's notice, which helps to keep the member banks honest and in good fiscal condition.

The Fed Acts as a Banker's Bank
When depository institutions want to go to the bank, they go to the Fed, which loans them money by accepting—at a discount, to be sure—their short-term debt instruments. The Fed also holds deposits of depository institutions, deposits that form part of their total reserves.

The Fed is a Fiscal Agent and Bank for the U.S. Treasury
The U.S. Treasury itself keeps deposits at the Fed and writes checks on them. Furthermore, the Fed handles the national debt for the government. When the Treasury issues the federal debt, the Fed sells the debt instruments and collects the proceeds for the Treasury. When this debt *matures* (is due for payment), the Fed pays what is owed out of the Treasury's account.

The Fed is a Fiscal Agent for Foreign Central Banks and Treasuries

A number of foreign central banks and treasuries use the Fed as their bank in the U.S. The Fed treats them as impartially as it does its own member banks or the U.S. Treasury. It loans money, buys and sells debt instruments, and in general acts as their fiscal agent.

Monetary Policy

Monetary Policy
Decisions of the Fed regarding changes in the money supply and interest rates.

Monetary policy consists of the decisions of the Fed regarding changes in the money supply and interest rates to achieve economic goals. The most important goal is to reach acceptable levels of growth, employment and price stability. Therefore, in order to understand monetary policy, one needs to know how changes in the money supply affect interest rates and influence income, employment, and prices.

Varying the Supply of Money

You have looked at the effects of changes in the money supply on employment and prices. You've learned that increases in the supply of money expand effective demand, while contractions reduce it. Therefore, to counter unemployment, a nation's monetary policy should be to expand the money supply. On the other hand, to counter inflation, a nation's monetary policy should be to cut back the money supply.

Varying Interest Rates

What happens to an economy when interest rates vary? When interest rates go up, people do not want to borrow as much to buy consumer goods, because the cost of borrowing money has risen. Businesses do not want to buy as much new plant and equipment, for the same reason. So investment decreases. (Remember that investments need to have an expected rate of return equal to or greater than the interest rate.) Also, when interest rates go up, government expenditures at the state and local levels that are financed by borrowing tend to go down. State and local governments must be concerned about their taxpayers moving to other locales, with lower tax rates. So state and local governments are more sensitive than the federal government about raising taxes to pay increased interest costs on borrowed money. (You knew, didn't you, that state and local governments have to borrow heavily in order to see themselves through the fiscal year?)

All in all, raising interest rates decreases aggregate demand by decreasing consumption based on consumer borrowing as well as investment, and debt-financed expenditures by state and local governments.

What happens when interest rates go down? Just the reverse of what happens when they go up. People more readily borrow money to buy consumer goods because credit is cheaper.

Businesses increase their investment spending because there are more investments that yield a return equal to or greater than the cost of the interest. And state and local governments increase their deficit-financed expenditures, too, because the price of money is low.

Some Recommendations on Monetary Policy

During a recession, when there is a lot of unemploymen, monetary policy, if used, should aim at expanding total spending by increasing the supply of money and decreasing the interest rate. During an inflation, monetary policy should aim at decreasing total spending and discouraging price increases by reducing the supply of money and increasing the interest rate. Table 14-1 outlines the methods the Fed can use to combat unemployment or inflation.

What to Do When Recession Hits

Suppose there is a recession. Aggregate demand is low, unemployment is high and nobody is buying much. What can be done? The monetary policies that increase the supply of money also lower the interest rate and combat unemployment.

During a period of high unemployment, the Fed should follow policies that increase excess reserves. In the discussion of the Fed, you learned how this can be done. The Fed should do one or more of the following:

1. *Buy government securities on the open market.* The proceeds are used to increase the deposits of commercial banks with the Fed that is, the commercial banks' total and excess reserves rise, so that they can lend out more money.

2. *Lower the discount rate.* This encourages commercial banks to discount acceptable short-term debt and increase their total and excess reserves.

3. *Lower the required reserve ratio.* This does not change commercial banks' total reserves, but it does lower the percentage of reserves that are required, and thus, it creates more excess reserves.

Table 14-1
The Federal Reserve's Monetary Policy

What should the Fed do about unemployment?	What should the Fed do about inflation?

Increase excess reserves
    Buy government securities
    Lower the discount rate
    Lower the required reserve ratio
	Decrease excess reserves
	    Sell government securities
	    Raise the discount rate
	    Raise the required reserve ratio

The Monetary Transmission Mechanism: Credit Markets in a Recession

Let's suppose the monetary policy task is to increase real income and reduce unemployment while minimizing upward inflationary pressures on prices. Whichever of the three "tools" or combination of them it employs, the effects of Fed action will be felt in credit markets. Let's trace through how those effects occur.

In Figure 14-6, we see the workings of a credit market. Remember that most of our money is in the form of credit (interest bearing loans), created by depository institutions. There are, thus, many credit markets. For convenience, however, let's aggregate them into a hypothetical credit market as in Figure 14-6. The supply of credit (S_c) slopes upward (holding everything else but interest rates constant); as interest rates rise more credit is offered because savings move from non-interest bearing form (e.g., stocks) into interest bearing deposits at banks, savings and loan associations and the like. The demand for credit (D_c) is downward sloping

Figure 14-6
Credit Market Equilibrium

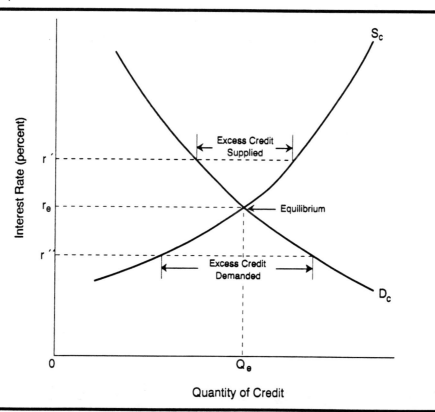

The Supply of Credit (S_c) is upward sloping, and the demand for credit is downward sloping as functions of interest rates. Equilibrium is established at interest rate r_e, where quantity demanded = quantity supplied. Other interest rates (such as r' and r'' are disequilibrium rates associated with excess supply or excess demand.

(holding everything else but interest rates constant). The quantity demanded rises because firms, consumers, and even governments borrow more at lower interest rates. Equilibrium is established where the quantity demanded equals the quantity supplied of credit at interest rate r_e. Any other interest rate than r_e would lead to other excess quantity supplied (at r´) or excess quantity demanded (at r´´).

A Recession: Enter the Fed

Let's suppose that credit markets are in equilibrium with market clearing interest rates but that the economy is in recession. The Fed (FOMC, Board of Governors) decides to fight the recession with an "easier" monetary policy. Through whatever means (discount rate, reserve requirements, open market purchases of government securities, etc.), the Fed, acting through depository institutions, creates an increase in the supply of credit as in the shift of supply from S_c to $S_c´$ in Figure 14-7. As a result interest rates fall from r_e to $r_e´$.

Short-run Effects

As the above happens, we see in Figure 14-8 that short-run equilibrium real income is affected. As depository institutions expanded credit in Figure 14-7, interest rates fell. In 14-8 that leads to investment increases that shift aggregate demand in the short run

Figure 14-7
Credit Market Response to an Increased Supply of Credit

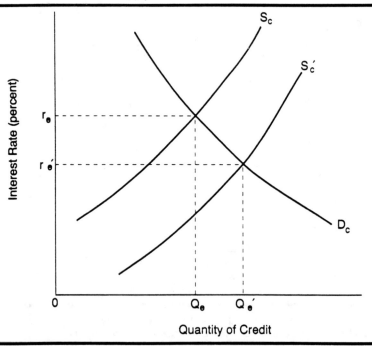

The Fed follows an "easier" monetary policy and the supply of credit (S_c) increases to $S_c´$). The equilibrium interest rate rises and the quantity of credit demanded (borrowing) rises from Q_e to $Q_e´$

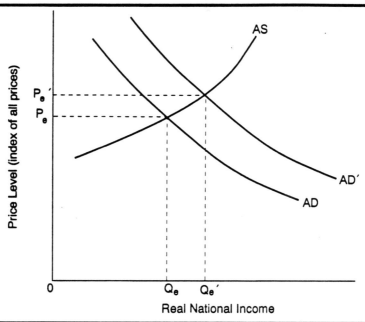

As interest rates fall with an easing of monetary policy, investment increases cause a growth of Aggregate demand (AD to AD'). Real income rises from Q_e to Q_e' and prices rise modestly from P_e to P_e'.

from AD to AD' Real income grows from Q_e to Q_e' and prices rise modestly from P_e to P_e'.

Note: There would have been no upward pressure on prices if aggregate supply had been horizontal at price level P_0. That aggregate supply assumption is the Keynesian assumption. Monetarists do not necessarily agree with the idea that resource idleness is so widespread that increases in aggregate demand that cause real income growth always occur with no short-run upward pressure on prices.

Long-run Effects
What about the long-run effects of easing monetary policy? We see these in Figure 14-9. What we have seen so far is a monetary policy transmission mechanism that looks like this when put in Keynesian terms.

Easing of Monetary Policy → Increase in Supply of Credit → Decrease in Interest Rates → Increase in Investment → Increase in Aggregate Demand in Short Run → Increase in Real Income and Prices

Now we must factor in the long-run supply effects of the investment increases resulting from lower interest rates. In Figure 14-9, we see that in the long run, further shifts that occur in

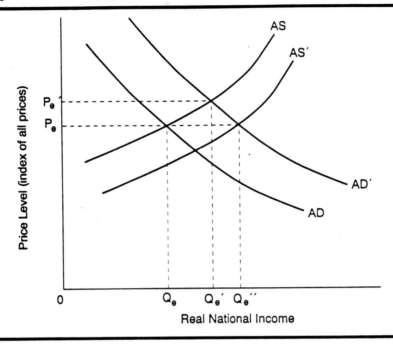

The short-run increase in real income (Q_e to Q_e') and increase in prices (P_e to P_e') leads to the long-term increase in aggregate supply (AS to AS') that restores price equilibrium at P_e and further increases real income (Q_e' to Q_e'').

aggregate supply from AS to AS' resulting in a growth in real income from Q_e' to Q_e''. Note that the supply increase results in lowering prices from P_e' back to P_e. Note also that it is not necessarily a monetarist assumption.that money supply growth is price neutral in the long run. Rather, the important point is that increasing aggregate supply in the long run will reduce the upward pressures on prices from increased spending or increased aggregate demand. Completing the transmission mechanism (in Keynesian terms), it becomes:

Easing of Monetary Policy → Increase in Supply of Credit → Decrease in Interest Rates → Increase in Investment → Increase in Aggregate Demand in Short Run → Short-run Increase in Real Income and Prices → Long-run Increase in Aggregate Supply → Further Growth in Real Income and Reduced Pressure on Prices.

What to Do When Inflation Hits

Suppose there is an inflation. Aggregate demand is high, and prices are rising fast. What can be done? During a period of rising prices, the Fed should follow policies that decrease the supply of money and increase interest rates. From the discussion of the Fed, you know how this can be done. The Fed should do one or more of the following:

1. *Sell government securities on the open market.* This has the effect of reducing the financial institutions' deposits at the Fed, which means that their excess reserves go down by a like amount, and they have fewer loanable funds.

2. *Raise the discount rate.* This makes it more expensive for financial institutions to borrow from the Fed, and, therefore, discourages them from increasing their reserves by means of short-term debt.

3. *Raise the required reserve ratio.* This leaves financial institutions' total reserves untouched, but makes them hold a higher percentage of their total reserves as required reserves, which leaves a smaller percentage of excess reserves.

Remember that each of these general powers has different effects. Open-market operations can increase excess reserves or decrease them, and they are also more selective than the other powers. For ordinary monetary policy operations, the Fed uses mainly open-market operations. Varying the discount rate cannot decrease excess reserves, but it does have a strong immediate impact on interest rates. It causes the interest rates for various kinds of debt instruments (mortgages, personal loans) to fluctuate readily. Varying the required reserve ratio, as we noted before, is too strong and unselective a weapon for the Fed to use often. The use of this weapon generally signals a major change in Fed policy.

The Monetary Transmission Mechanism: Credit Markets in Inflation

Let us suppose now the economy we are looking at has a serious (demand-pull) inflationary problem. Imagine that it is like the American economy in 1981-1982 with double-digit inflation. The job of the Fed, using any of the above "tools" is to "cool-off" the economy with a restrictive monetary policy. Go back to Figure 14-6 and imagine that equilibrium interest rates are too low, that is they are creating inflationary levels of aggregate demand. How can the Fed get interest rates up? Go back to Figure 14-7, but let's have the Fed decrease the supply of credit (S_c' to S_c in 14-7), which reduces the quantity demanded of credit (Q_e'' to Q_e) and causes interest rates to increase from r_e' to r_e. Put again in Keynesian terms, the transmission mechanism in the short run is:

A "Tightening" of Monetary Policy → Decrease in Supply of Credit → Increase Interest Rates → Decrease in

Investment → Decrease in Aggregate Demand → Lower
Level of Prices

The effects of the decrease in investment can be seen in a reduction of aggregate demand such as from AD´ to AD in Figure 14-8. As AD falls, price levels diminish as from $P_e´$ to P_e, and real income will fall. Of course, if the inflation is pure demand pull, aggregate supply may have a vertical (capacity range) look as in Figure 14-10. Here the economy has reached its maximum (capacity) real income at Q_e and is operating with its natural rate of unemployment. Increasing aggregate demand cannot cause a growth in real income so, instead, with "too many dollars chasing an unchanged quantity supplied of goods" prices are pushed up from P_e to $P_e´$. The Fed decreases the supply of credit by the proper amount, interest rates rise and aggregate demand decreases from AD´ to AD. The economy in the short run then enjoys both full employment and price stability (established as a target level of prices).

What happens in the long run? The higher interest rates would be expected to lead to a short-run decrease in investment

Figure 14-10
The Effects of Restrictive Monetary Policy on Aggregate Demand, Real Income, and the Price Level When the Economy is Operating at Capacity

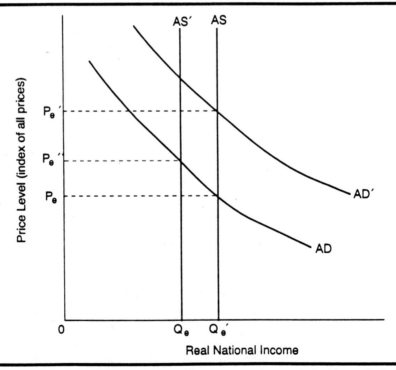

The inflationary economy is operating at capacity with an aggregate supply that is vertical at real income Q_e. Increasing AD is causing demand-pull price pressures that raise prices from P_e to $P_e´$. The Fed reduces the supply of credit, interest rates rise and aggregate demand decreases from AD´ to AD. Prices are stabilized at P_e and real income maintained at capacity, Q_e.

and a long-run decrease in aggregate supply (as from *A* _____
Figure 14-10). The consequence of the supply effects _____
monetary policy might be full employment with lower _____
$(Q_e - Q_e')$ and higher prices (P_e to P_e'). A falling l_____
income and rising prices would probably be seen as _____
productivity growth and a call, as we witnessed in the 1980s, for
stimulating the supply side of markets. To do that, of course, the
Fed would have to reverse course, ease up in credit markets, and let
interest rates drift downward.

The Main Point

The main point of the preceding discussion is to emphasize the
complexity of the cause-and-effect relationships in monetary
policy. These depend on: (1) credit markets, (2) interest rates as
signals to borrowers and lenders, (3) investment effects of
changing interest rates, (4) demand effects of investment decisions
and, in the long run, (5) the supply effects of investment decisions.

There are some who say that in view of all these complexities, discretionary monetary policy is a job for a "philosopher
king," not a Fed chairman. In this regard, some would argue for a
simple monetary rule (increase the supply of credit by X percent
per year) as opposed to discretionary changes from week to week.
It is no easy job being Chairman of the Fed. If you are right about
direction and magnitude of choice, you may get some credit (Paul
Volker in the 1980s). If you are wrong about direction and amount,
you may be blamed for a recession or depression (ironically, the
same Paul Volker for the 1981-1982 recession).

Weaknesses of Monetary Policy

The monetary policy we have outlined does not contain all the
solutions to economic problems. Here are five weaknesses in it:

1. *Inadequate demand for credit.* During a serious recession or a
depression, monetary policy may be quite ineffective in stimulating
the economy. Depository institutions may already have all the
excess reserves they need. (a) As business goes into a slump,
people may shy away from borrowing to such an extent that more
loans are paid off than are made. So excess reserves increase
without the help of the Fed. (b) With the economic outlook so
gloomy, lending institutions are often unwilling to run the risk of
lending. So no matter what the Fed does to increase excess
reserves, lending institutions refuse to increase loans and the
supply of money. (This is what the commercial banks did during
the Great Depression of the 1930s.) (c) The depository institutions
may have money they are willing to lend, but people are just not
borrowing. During a mild recession, however, monetary policy
aimed at increasing excess reserves may work well, as it did in the

recession of 1954. That recession was caused by the decline of defense expenditures at the end of the Korean War. At that time, people's confidence in the economy was strong. There was a tax cut; and an easy-money policy increased excess reserves, thus stimulating bank lending, increasing the supply of money, and reducing interest rates.

2. *Non-demand-pull inflation.* Monetary policy may curb inflation, provided that it is a demand-pull inflation of the type in Figure 14-10. The Fed can dry up excess reserves so much that depository institutions cannot make loans. Then people cannot get money to buy things with. However, if the inflation is caused by factors *not* susceptible to control by the lowering of aggregate demand cost-push and administered-price inflation), monetary policy may not be the cure. For example, the inflation of 1973-1974 was caused in part by the raising of oil prices by OPEC (Organization of Petroleum Exporting Countries) and the rise in agricultural prices. The Fed tried to use monetary policy to decrease prices. But its tight-money policy, that is charging very high interest rates on the money it lent, only led to commercial banks raising *their* interest rates to 12 percent. A liquidity crisis (that is, a shortage of assets that could be easily converted into money) in the banking system was predicted. The Fed was forced to back off from its tight-money policy before the double-digit inflation could be contained. (*Double-digit inflation* means inflation at any rate of 10 percent or more per year.)

3. *Recognition and Implementation Lag.* Only a philosopher king has perfect foresight. A Fed chairman (and board) rely on data that is always lagged and that may or may not be an accurate measure of current economic activity. Monetary policy changes, thus, may be a reaction to an incorrect perception of problems, akin to giving someone a dose of medicine for an ailment that the patient no longer has!

Even a philosopher-king cannot have orders carried out instantly. While some Fed policies can be changed quickly (open-market operations) others take 30 months or more to fully implement. Lower interest rates may find a few firms with invest-ment plans on the shelf waiting for the right present value; many other firms will only *begin* planning new investments as interest rates fall. Implementation lags can seriously slow the workings even of correct monetary policy.

4. *Distributive effects.* During inflation, a tight-money policy of raising interest rates does not affect the economy *evenly*. It hits some groups harder than others. For instance, in the construction industry, high interest rates cause the demand for new houses to plummet. Each time there has been a period of tight-money policy and high interest rates, the construction industry has experienced serious cutbacks, with consequent layoffs of workers.

Depository institutions, as their excess reserves dwindle, do not lend their reduced supply of money evenly. Safe customers get loans, but risky ones do not. The more risky firms (generally smaller-scale, new firms) not only face higher interest rates, but also have difficulty getting loans. Larger corporations do not have this problem. They are isolated from the tight-money situation because, when *they* want money, they can dip into their own retained earnings and depreciation funds.

5. *Changes in Velocity.* As the Fed increases the money supply during a recession and decreases it during an inflation, changes in the velocity of exchange may partially counteract these trends. During a recession, the velocity of exchange may decrease, which reduces the impact of an increased supply of money. Pessimistic consumers and businesses try to hold on to their money. During an inflation, the velocity of exchange, V, may increase, which reduces the impact of a decreased supply of money. Optimistic consumers and businesses, expecting that prices will go up still higher, continue to buy at an ever greater rate.

6. *Changes in Inflationary Expectations.* To execute its monetary policies through credit markets, the Fed must set up equilibrium interest rate targets. Suppose, for example, that the Fed wants to expand the economy and decides to try to get interest rates down from an average of 9 percent to 7 percent. To do this, it uses some set of policy tools to increase the supply of credit as in Figure 14-11 from S_c to S_c'. With demand D_c, the Fed's target would be achieved. The public, however, expecting this increase in the quantity demanded of credit to cause a higher rate of inflation, tries to lock in the seven percent rate and increases its demand for credit from D_c to D_c'. In the new credit market equilibrium, the interest rate effect of the Fed's action is not to lower interest rates to seven percent but to raise them to 13 percent!

Monetarism

Monetarism
An approach to macroeconomic policy in which the supply of monetary is the dominant factor.

Monetarism is an approach to macroeconomic policy in which the supply of money plays the dominant role. Nobel Laureate Milton Friedman, the economist who founded the monetarist school, maintains that both fiscal policy and monetary policy based on Keynesian analysis are wrong. He and other monetarists charge that the Keynesians underestimate the effects of the supply of money on the economy. Friedman, as well as newer monetary theorists, says that people have a stable and predictable demand for money, a demand related to the size of the economy. Therefore, the supply of money and its relationship to national income should be the key to government policy, both fiscal and monetary. To control unemployment and inflation, the monetarists say, the government should follow a policy of increasing the supply of money at a proper and constant rate.

Figure 14-11
Expectations Effects on the Demand for Credit Result in perverse effects of Monetary Policy

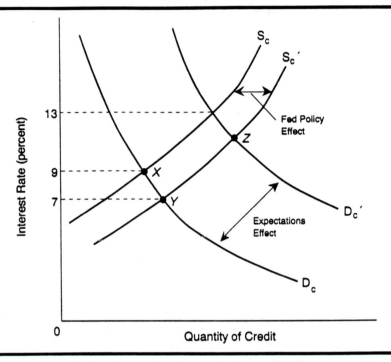

The Fed seeks to lower interest rates from their initial equilibrium at X (D_c intersects S_c) and 9 percent. The target interest rate is 7 percent, which can be attained by increasing the supply of credit from S_c to S_c' (S_c' intersects D_c) at point Y. The public, expecting higher inflation to result, attempts to lock in the lower interest rate and increases its demand for credit from D_c to D_c'. At the new equilibrium, point Z, (D_c' intersects S_c') interest rates rise to 13 percent.

This monetarist attack on Keynesian fiscal and monetary policy deserves full treatment. So in the following application we will explore this controversy.

SUMMING UP

1. The Federal Reserve (Fed) System is organized as follows: (a) There are 12 Fed banks in 12 districts. (b) All *national* commercial banks must be members of the system, while *state banks* may join if they wish. (c) Each member bank must buy some stock in its particular district Fed bank. (d) A 7-member board of governors in Washington controls the system. Its members are appointed by the President, with the advice and consent of the Senate, for terms of 14 years. (e) The Open Market Committee and the Federal Advisory Council are the two main committees under the board of governors. (f) Each Fed bank has 9 people on its board of directors: 3 appointed by the board of governors, 3 elected by the member banks, and 3 from the local community.

2. The so-called "general powers" of the Fed, including those granted in the Deregulatory Act of 1980, entitle it to control the excess reserves of all depository institutions, bank and non-bank alike by the following devices: (a) *Open-market operations.* To increase all institutions' excess reserves, the Fed buys government securities in the open market; it buys them from the commercial banks and pays for them by increasing deposits with the Fed. To reduce excess reserves, the Fed sells government securities on the open market to the depository institutions and deducts the amount of the sale from their deposits (reserves). (b) *Varying the discount rate.* When the Fed wants to encourage an increase in excess reserves, it lowers the *discount rate,* so that money becomes cheaper for the depository institutions to borrow. The institutions therefore borrow more, which increases their deposits with the Fed and increases their excess reserves. When the Fed wants to discourage the discounting, it increases the discount rate. (c) *Varying the required reserve ratio.* The Fed can lower or raise the percentage of a depository institution's total reserves that are considered "required," which in turn raises or lowers the reserves that are counted as "excess."

3. The Fed has *specific powers* over certain aspects of lending. (a) The Fed sets the *margin requirement* for stock purchases. The *margin* is the percentage of cash required as a down payment on a purchase of corporate stock. The balance may be borrowed. (b) Regulation Q, the authority of the Fed to set maximum interest rates, was repealed in 1980. The act made all depository institutions subject to uniform reserve requirements and gave all such institutions access to the Fed's services. In general, it created a much more competitive American financial industry.

4. The functions of the Fed are the following: (a) It regulates the supply of money. (b) It acts as a national clearinghouse for checks. (c) It issues all paper currency. (d) It regulates and examines member banks. (e) It acts as a banker's bank. (f) It acts as a fiscal agent and bank for the U.S. Treasury. (g) It acts as a fiscal agent for certain foreign central banks and treasuries.

5. Monetary policy works through credit markets that are controlled by interest rates. Using any one or a combination of its powers, the Fed can increase or decrease the supply of credit in these markets and, thereby, cause interest rates to rise or fall. As they rise, the quantity demanded of credit falls. As they fall, the quantity demanded of credit rises.

6. A lowering of interest rates, seen in Keynesian terms, leads to an increase in investment. As investment increases, aggregate demand grows, leading to an increase in real income and prices in the short run. In the long run, there is also an increase in aggregate supply

that will cause further growth in real income and may partially or entirely offset the short-run price increase.

7. Increasing interest rates leads to a reduction in investment. Seen in Keynesian terms, as investment decreases, aggregate demand falls, leading to a decline in the short run in real income and prices. In the long run, the decline in investment may lead to a decline in aggregate supply and a reduction in real income.

8. Discretionary monetary policy is based on complex relationships involving credit markets and interest rate targets. Some argue that it is so easy to be wrong about direction and magnitude of policy change that it would be better to have a monetary rule or fixed rate of increase in the supply of money and credit.

9. *Monetary policy* involves manipulating the supply of credit and interest rates so as to achieve low unemployment and only slight price increases. The Board of Governors of the Fed is the group responsible for administering monetary policy.

10. To overcome unemployment, one should increase the supply of credit and decrease interest rates in order to increase investment, aggregate demand, and income. In the long run, this should increase aggregate supply and further increase real income. To increase excess reserves, and thereby increase the money supply, the Fed should: (a) buy government securities on the open market, (b) lower the discount rate, or (c) lower the required reserve ratio.

11. To overcome inflation, one should decrease the supply of credit and increase interest rates; this should decrease aggregate demand and reduce prices. To decrease excess reserves, and thereby decrease the money supply, the Fed should: (a) sell government securities on the open market, (b) raise the discount rate and (c) raise the required reserve ratio.

12. The weaknesses of monetary policy are: (a) Inadequate demand for credit. During a severe recession, the policy may not work. People are afraid to invest, so they pay off loans and shy away from further borrowing. As a result, excess reserves increase without Fed interference. (b) Non-demand-pull inflation. During an inflation, monetary policy may be ineffective in dealing with kinds of inflation that are not susceptible to the lowering of aggregate demand (cost-push and administered-price inflation). (c) Monetary policy becomes ineffectual when inflation accompanies high unemployment. (d) Lags of recognition and implementation. (e) Changes in inflationary expectations may offset the plans of the Fed about interest rate changes.

13. Milton Friedman and some other economists of the monetarist school of thought reject discretionary fiscal and monetary policy aimed at stabilizing aggregate demand. They believe that a constant and proper level of increase in the supply of money is the key to containing both inflation and unemployment.

KEY TERMS

General power
National banks
State banks
Discount rate
Required reserve ratio
Specific powers
Margin requirement
Regulation X
Regulation W
Regulation Q
Bank holding companies
Monetary policy
Monetarism

QUESTIONS

1. Which is more important, the public or the private element of the structure of the Fed?

2. Given that the required reserve ratio is 20 percent, describe the way the following transactions would affect the following accounts: Required Reserves, Excess Reserves, Total Reserves, and Supply of Money.

   a. A commercial bank *buys* $10,000 in government securities from the Fed bank.

   b. A commercial bank *sells* $10,000 in government securities to the Fed bank.

   c. A commercial bank discounts a $1,000 note at 8 percent for 90 days at the Fed.

   d. The Fed raises the required reserve ratio to 25 percent.

   e. The Fed lowers the required reserve ratio to 15 percent.

3. What are the general powers of the Fed? How do they work? Why are they called general powers?

4. How do federal reserve policies affect credit markets?

5. What would you advise the board of governors of the Fed to do in case of an inflation? of a recession? What would you have advised them to do in the 1981-1982 inflationary situation?

6. When the Fed practices a policy of tight money in order to combat inflation, who pays the cost? Give reasons.

7. How does non-demand-pull inflation complicate monetary policy?

8. You have just been appointed to the Board of Governors of the Federal Reserve System. The chairman has asked you to review monetary policy and present your recommendations on:
    a. Fed policy to counter inflation or unemployment.
    b. the groups in the economy that obtain advantages or disadvantages from your recommendations.
    c. the economic justification for your recommendations.
    d. how you would deal with significant amounts of inflation and unemployment at the same time.

9. How may changes in inflationary expectations complicate reaching Fed policy objectives?

10. What were the major changes in the 1980s in American financial institutions? What is the present role of the Fed vis-a-vis these institutions?

SUGGESTED READINGS

Annual Editions Macroeconomics. Section IV. "Money, Banking and Monetary Policy." John Pisciotta, ed. Sluice Dock: Dushkin, 1987.

Cargill, Thomas F. and Gillian G. Garcia. *Financial Reform in the 1980s.* Stanford: Hoover Institution, 1985.

Federal Reserve Bank of Chicago. "The Garn-St. Germain Depository Institutions Act of 1982." *Economic Perspectives.* Chicago: Federal Reserve Bank of Chicago, March/April, 1983.

Federal Reserve Bank of Kansas City. *Restructuring the Financial System.* Kansas City: Federal Reserve Bank of Kansas City, 1987.

Federal Reserve Bank of Kansas City. *Issues in Monetary Policy.* "Section I: Principles of Monetary Analysis." Kansas City: 1980.

Keynes, J. M. *The General Theory of Employment, Interest and Money.* New York: MacMillian, 1936.

McCarthy, Marilu Hurt. *Money and Banking.* 2nd ed. Chicago: Longman, 1988.

McClelland, Peter D. *Introduction to Macroeconomics,* Sections IV, V. "Monetary and Fiscal Policy." Pp 51-95. New York: McGraw-Hill, 1988.

"The Politics and Economics of Monetary Policy" in *Contemporary Policy Issues,* Vol III, No. 5. Fall, 1985.

West, Robert. "The Depository Institutions Deregulation Act of 1980: A Historical Perspective." *Economic Review.* February, 1982.

Application to Chapter 14:
*How **Much** Does Money Matter?*
Monetarists Versus Keynesians

The most serious challenge to Keynesian theories of economics—
especially to the monetary and fiscal policies—has come from
Nobel laureate Milton Friedman and the monetarist school of
economics. These economists say that monetary policy is more
important than fiscal policy, and that in order to stabilize an
economy, a steady rate of growth in the supply of money must be
ensured. The monetarists do not simply say that money matters, as
would Keynesians, they go further, and say that money supply
policy matters more than anything else.

The Monetarists Position

The basic tenet of the monetarists is that the biggest single factor in
determining money income, real income, and the level of prices is
the *rate of growth of the money supply*. They contend that people
want to keep a fixed percentage of their assets in the form of
money, a percentage that depends on their real incomes, their
standards of consumption, and the composition of their other
assets. As you know, if the supply of money increases too quickly,
people find themselves holding more money than they wish. They
try to re-establish the old equilibrium, by demanding more
nonconsumption assets, such as land, machinery, stocks, and
bonds; and/or more consumer goods—either of which causes the
economy to expand. If the supply of money shrinks, the reverse
happens, and the economy contracts.

This variation in the supply of money also affects prices.
Monetarists, as we noted, do not accept the Keynesian view that an
economy with growing expenditures can expand with stable prices.
Beyond some point, as the economy expands, demand-pull inflation sets in. Conversely, as the supply of money and the economy
contract, excess capacity and excess inventory drive prices down.

Some but not all monetarists are critical of discretionary
policy. They recommend that the Fed concentrate on monetary
rules maintaining a steady increase in the money supply, at about 2
to 4 percent per year. This, they say, would force the economy into
a stable growth with low inflation.

The 4-percent growth in the money supply would provide
enough expansion to accommodate the 3 percent increase in
productivity that some economists feel is historically what can be
sustained. It would also provide enough flexibility to reinforce
sectors of the economy that have less capacity than others, so that
inflation would be mild.

Friedman challenges the assumption that by means of continuous adjustments in fiscal policy and monetary policy, one can cause the economy to grow with relative stability. He says that changes in fiscal policy are ineffective and that the monetary policy of changing the interest rate also accomplishes little, since it is the *percentage rate of change in the supply of money* that is most closely correlated with changes in levels of income and employment. Furthermore, because nobody can accurately predict future business trends, it is dangerous to use changes in the rate of growth of the money supply for fine-tuning purposes.

Thus, monetarists who support decision by rule make simple and direct recommendations for government economic policy: Let the monetary authority (the Fed) increase the supply of money at a fixed rate of 2 to 4 percent per year and the economy will adjust itself. Although this will not eliminate all economic instability, it will avoid extreme variations. As Friedman notes: "We do not know enough to avoid minor fluctuations. The attempt to do more than we can will itself be a disturbance that may increase rather than reduce instability."

Discretionary monetary policy has at times seemed to complicate stabilization rather than solve the problems of economic fluctuations. After World War II the Fed used its open-market operations to peg the price of government securities, and neglected the postwar inflation. In 1957, the Fed enforced such a tight policy, in an attempt to fight inflation, that it contributed to the 1958 recession. Often just before or during an inflation, the Fed has increased the supply of money by greater amounts than the 4 percent recommended by Friedman. This has fed the inflation; 1973 is a good example.

It is somewhat ironic that the sharply restrictive monetary policy practiced by the Fed in 1981-1982 has been both hailed as a triumph of correctly timed monetary restraint and pointed to as an example of overreaction by some monetarists. While the decrease in money supply growth did, as we have already seen, lead to a reduction in inflation, it also caused a fall in real GNP and a sharp increase in unemployment.

The Keynesian Defense

While Keynesians do not deny the importance of the money supply, they regard it as a complementary tool to fiscal policy. Commenting on the rapid growth in income and jobs in the mid-1980s, a leading Keynesian and Nobel Laureate James Tobin remarked that "the patent success of fiscal stimulus in promoting recovery in the U.S. in 1983-1984 reinforces the Keynesian side of this old debate."

A flaw in the monetarists' theory is the implied assumption that velocity of exchange remains constant. (The monetarists say that V is constant in the short run, but not in the long run.) As you have seen, V does not remain constant. Not only has the velocity of exchange increased in the past few years, but it varies greatly over short-run periods. These variations indicate the economy's responses to changes in many factors, including fiscal policy (taxes and government expenditures). Variation in the supply of money, say the Keynesians, is not the main stimulus that brings about changes in money income and real income. It is only one of a number of factors, including variations in fiscal policy and interest rates, that cause such changes. Critics of monetarism claim that the rigid link that the monetarists would forge between money and economic activity just does not exist.

A leading economist and former chairman of the Council of Economic Advisers, Martin Feldstein, says, however, that perfectly stable or predictable trends in velocity are not necessary, merely that "controlling monetary aggregates is better than the alternative bases for guiding monetary policy."

The monetarists' demand for a rigid monetary rule opens up several areas of debate. What money are they talking about? Is it to be just demand deposits plus all currency and coin in circulation (M1)? Or does it also include various forms of near money (M2)? If near money is excluded, don't variations in these highly liquid assets affect the situation?

Debates about whether to include M2 elements of near monies and which to include explain some theoretical differences. This explains also some of the conflict in policy recommendations.

Also, how much time elapses between an increase in the supply of money (however one defines it) and the effect of that increase in the form of improved economic activity? The data that Friedman presents show great variability in time lags.

If, as is questionable, there is any validity to the Phillips curve, and if there is some tradeoff between inflation and unemployment, what clue does one get from the monetarists that can be used to decide at what level the tradeoff should be with this fixed growth in the money supply? If the Fed should increase the money supply at a certain fixed annual rate, this would force into the open certain changes in the economy. There might be fluctuations in interest rates that might be too large for comfort.

A Conclusion

Milton Friedman and the monetarist school of economists have affected the thinking of many economists and public policy makers. People have begun to pay a lot more attention to the role of the money supply and monetary policy. These factors have assumed greater importance in government economic policy. Nearly everyone agrees that money does matter. However, many economists are unwilling to concede that money is the only—or even the only major—thing that matters. Nor are they willing to completely abandon discretionary fiscal policy as a tool to affect the economy, although its use is much more restricted today than in earlier decades. Many continue to espouse correcting for ups and downs in economic activity by making periodic adjustments in fiscal and monetary policy—a little of this and a dash of that—and prefer this on-the-spot approach to the measured-recipe method of following the rigid monetary rule and adding 4 percent to the money supply each year.

Keynesian and Monetarist Views: A Summary of Differences

The Keynesian-Monetarist debate is far from over. Both see the growth of the 1980s as providing supporting evidence for their views. Table A14-1 gives a summary of their contrasting views.

Monetary practitioners (e.g., Paul Volker at the Fed in the 1980s) see discretionary monetary policy as a powerful and effective force. Milton Friedman sees the problem with discretionary policy as being people inadequate to a task. (Friedman: "Clearly the problem is not the person who happens to be chairman, but the system.") Thus, the crux of the debate *among* monetarists

Keynesians see both views as too narrow, believing that discretionary fiscal and monetary policies can be linked together to achieve macroeconomic targets of growing real income and stable price levels. James Tobin regards the pure monetarist view as an "ebbing tide: which enjoyed its heyday in the 1960s and 1970s." The debate, in other words, is far from over.

Table A14-1
Keynesian Versus Monetarist Views

Item	Keynesian View	Monetarist View
Demand for Money	Determined by people's incomes, (opportunity) cost of holding money, interest rates.	Determined by inflationary expectations, people's incomes, the level of prices, rates of returns on various forms of wealth and institutional factors.
How Money Affects the Economy	Increases in money supply lower interest rates, increase investment, and raise aggregate demand.	Increases in money supply cause increases in consumer spending as well as investment, which raise real income.
Discretionary Fiscal Policy	Very important as a tool to raise aggregate demand, lower unemployment, and raise real income.	Ineffective if not counterproductive in reaching real income targets because deficits lead to crowding out and politicians are short sighted.
Discretionary Monetary Policy	Useful, but not as potent a tool as discretionary fiscal policy.	Seen as very powerful and important by many monetarists while other prefer a fixed monetary rule.

Monetary Policy and International Markets

Whatever the eventual outcome of the Keynesian-Monetarist debate, its importance may diminish from a policy standpoint. As we have seen, aggregate demand management, however effective or ineffective it might be, is severely constrained by the reality of the large federal debt together with the acceptance of the view that a natural rate of unemployment makes demand management ineffective or even counterproductive in the long run. That same debt and the necessity to finance it, together with the extreme ease with which capital funds move internationally, seems also to be making discretionary monetary policy more difficult to administer.

Much of the federal debt (about $400 billion) is held by foreigners. The Japanese alone buy about 40 percent of U.S. government bonds. In order to attract foreign capital in these amounts, U.S. long-term interest rates have to be competitive with those in other major capital markets, such as Germany and Japan. When those rates rise, U.S. rates have to be kept high also even if domestic concern for a recession might otherwise cause the Fed to move toward monetary ease.

An article in *The Wall Street Journal* in March, 1990 relates a case in which the Fed acted in December 1989 to increase the money supply (buying treasury bills) to act against a possible recession: Although long-term interest rates fell briefly, they quickly moved upward and were soon *above* the rate existing before the easing of the money supply.

Fed Chairman Alan Greenspan, asked whether the powerful Central Bank could still do its job of managing the money supply in a contracyclical manner, responded to a congressional committee: "To what extent have we lost control over our economic destiny? The Fed can still do its job but it's more difficult." Former New York Fed Chairman Anthony Solomon compares the difficult with trying to juggle 3 balls at the same time: (1) economic growth, (2) inflationary pressures, and (3) foreign holdings of U.S. debt together with the need to attract long-term capital from abroad. At this point, few doubt that the Fed *can* do so, but it will almost certainly be a more difficult task in the 1990s.

SUMMING UP

1. The monetarists claim that the rate of growth of the money supply is the primary factor that influences the level of economic activity (employment and prices). Some argue that deliberate (discretionary) monetary policy that changes the money supply may have a perverse effect on economic activity. This, plus the fact that no one can accurately predict future business affairs, makes discretionary, monetary, and fiscal policy ineffective and dangerous. Some monetarists therefore advocate a simple monetary rule: Let the government increase the supply of money by a fixed

rate of 2 to 4 percent per year. Other monetarists regard discretionary monetary policy as effective and important in achieving economic growth and stability objectives.

2. The Keynesians point to the following weaknesses in the monetarist position: (a) The velocity of exchange is not constant, either in the short or long run. Therefore, there is no rigid link between the economy and the supply of money. (b) The monetarists leave a number of questions unanswered: What do they define as being money? What about variations in time between changes in the supply of money and changes in the economy?

3. Keynesians believe that discretionary monetary and fiscal policies can be devised to achieve real income and price-level goals.

4. The debate between Keynesian and monetarist views continues. All economists, nonetheless, regard the supply of money as an important macroeconomic variable.

QUESTIONS

1. What are the basic elements of the monetarists' position? Do they seem justified? Why?

2. What are the basic elements of the Keynesians' position regarding the importance of money? Do they seem justified? Why?

3. Are there some things in the Keynesian-Monetarist debate on which the two sides agree? If so, what?

4. Why may both monetary policy and demand management policy be more difficult in the 1990s?

SUGGESTED READINGS

Tobin, James. "Monetarism, an Ebbing Tide?" *The Economist.* April 27, 1985. Reprinted in *Annual Editions 87/88.* John Pisciotta, Ed. Sluice Dock, Ct: Dushkin, 1987.

Friedman, Milton. "The Case For Overhauling the Federal Reserve." *Challenge.* July/August, 1985. Reprinted in *Annual Editions 87/88.* John Pisciotta, Ed. Sluice, Dock, Ct: Dushkin, 1987.

Walters, Alan. "Monetarism: The Right Stuff." *The Economist.* May 4, 1985.

Modigliani, Franco. "The Monetarist Controversy or Should We Forsake Stabilization Policies?" *American Economic Review.* March, 1977.

McClelland, Peter D. "A Layman's Guide to the Keynesian Monetarist Dispute" in *Introduction to Macroeconomics.* Peter McClelland, Ed. New York: McGraw-Hill, 1988.

Brunner, Karl. "Monetarism Isn't Dead." *Fortune.* June 9, 1985. Reprinted in *Introduction to Macroeconomics.* Peter D. McClelland, Ed, New York: McGraw-Hill, 1988.

Feldstein, Martin. "Monetarism: Open-Eyed Pragmatism." *The Economist.* May, 1985.

Chapter 15:
Aggregate Supply, Supply-Side Economics,
and the Role of Expectations

As America entered the 1980s, its economy seemed to face some unprecedented challenges. Having survived the supply shocks of the early- to mid-1970s, (OPEC I) and the late-1970s (OPEC II), it found itself in 1981 with an inflation rate of almost 9 percent (briefly over 10 percent), an unemployment rate rising to almost 10 percent (in 1982) and a growth in real GNP declining sharply through much of the early-1980s. As often happens in periods of economic difficulty, the nation looked for new ideas or old ideas re-expressed to fit the times.

In electing Ronald Reagan as President, the country, at least in part responded to his promise to reinvigorate the American economy. Prominent among Reagan's arguments and those of his advisers was that of using **supply-side economics**, arguments about efforts and incentives to stimulate growth in aggregate supply. These efforts were designed to ensure real income growth at stable prices. Growth was to occur rapidly enough to create jobs at a rate that would bring down unemploymen. In this chapter we are going to look at some of these supply-side arguments and the evidence regarding policies undertaken in their support. Finally, we will look at some of the reservations expressed by those who argue that such discretionary government policies can have little or no macroeconomic effect.

Supply-Side Economics
Arguments about efforts and incentives to stimulate growth in aggregate supply.

Aggregate Supply and Aggregate Demand: A Review

Recall that equilibrium real income and the price level are established where aggregate quantity demanded equals aggregate quantity supplied (the level of output and prices at which the plans of those making expenditure decisions are made equal to the plans of those making production decisions). The initial equilibrium in

Figure 15-1 is at real income, Q_e, and price level, P_e, where AD equals AS. Now suppose that aggregate demand grows to AD´ as the result of stimulative fiscal (tax cuts, etc.) or monetary policy. With aggregate supply unchanged, real income grows to Q_e´ but prices rise to P_e´. In the interest of price stability, an increase in aggregate supply is called for such as from AS to AS´. It would then be possible to establish a new higher level of real income at Q_e´´ (AD´ = AS´) and for prices to stabilize at the old level P_e.

How Do We Stimulate Aggregate Supply?

The shift of aggregate supply in Figure 15-1 could be a reaction to long-run investments that occur because of the larger aggregate demand. That simple Keynesian view of aggregate supply changes as responses to changes in aggregate demand is disputed by "supply-side" economists. These economists assign aggregate supply a much more important and autonomous role in achieving the macroeconomic objectives of real income growth and price stability. Let's look, then, at the foundations of supply-side economics.

Figure 15-1
Changes in Aggregate Demand, Aggregate Supply and Prices

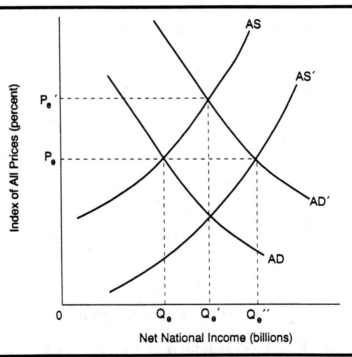

The initial equilibrium real income is Q_e with price level P_e (AD = AS). If aggregate demand is increased through fiscal or monetary policy, the short-run effect is to shift AD to AD´. The new equilibrium real income (AD´ = AS) is Q_e´ with price level P_e´. In the long run, if aggregate supply grows, AS shifts to AS´ and prices reequilibriate at P_e with real income Q_e´´.

Fundamentals of Supply-Side Views

Writing in 1981, F. Thomas Juster argued that supply-side economics is based on four elements or hypotheses:

1. Entitlement programs (unemployment compensation, social security payments, etc.) have lowered work incentives; reducing such programs will restore incentives and cut the tax burden on tax payers and investors.

2. America's system of taxes is biased against effort, saving, and investment. Lowering taxes will increase labor supplies and savings and investment.

3. Public regulation designed to protect consumers and employees raises costs and reduces investment. Many such activities offer few benefits relative to their costs.

4. The long use of monetary and fiscal programs to stimulate aggregate demand has created a climate of inflationary expectations. Changing those expectations (through, for example, a commitment to balanced budgets) will help to reduce inflationary pressures.

While Juster expresses sympathy for some of these four propositions, he expresses serious doubt about the linkage between tax reductions, labor supplies and the volume of savings. One should not forget, though, that supply-side policies are founded not only in economic theory but also in political philosophy. As President Reagan said in his *Economic Report* of 1987: "Government should play a limited role in the economy, it should encourage a stable economy in which people can make informed decisions. It should not make those decisions for them or arbitrarily distort economic choices..."

The Tax Cuts of 1981: How Well Did They Work?

We have witnessed numerous changes in Federal taxation in the 1980s. The 1981 changes reduced the highest marginal income tax rate from 70 percent to 50 percent (by 1984). Income taxes were indexed to prevent "bracket creep," rising marginal tax rates associated with growth in nominal but not real income. In line with article (b) of the supply-side propositions, this was expected to increase savings and investment as well as to encourage a larger supply of labor. It might also be added that it would encourage legal transactions as opposed to the **underground economy**, those transactions that give rise to taxable income but are not reported for tax purposes. In 1985, Reagan proposed a further reduction in the highest marginal tax rate to 35 percent; a proposal that went into effect in 1987.

Underground Economy
Economic transactions that give rise to taxable income but are not reported for tax purposes.

It is still difficult to assess the long-term aggregate supply effects of the 1981 tax cuts. It is, of course, still too early to forecast the long-run effects of the 1987 tax law. President Reagan, in his 1987 *Economic Report*, regarded the 1981 cuts as a clear success, reporting that "businesses fixed investment set records as a share of real GNP in 1984 and 1985 and remains high by historical standards." Some economists have criticized the correlation saying that increased investment rates were merely a reaction to the extraordinarily low investment rates during the severe recession of 1981-1982 rather than a long-term improvement in savings and investment. Benjamin Friedman, a Harvard economist, says that attacking the deficits will be necessary before such a long-term change in savings and investment rates can occur.

Supply-Side Economics: Why So Controversial?

That there was a significant recovery of the American economy between 1982 and 1990 is unquestionable. That it constitutes the longest sustained recovery in the economy's peacetime history is also correct, as is the statement that relatively stable prices (inflation rates of 2 to 4 percent) and declining unemployment (5.2 percent in early-1990) have accompanied the expansion. In many respects, this would seem to validate the idea that proper coordination between changes in aggregate demand and changes in aggregate supply can produce sustained real income growth *and* relative price stability. Why, then, the controversy over supply-side economics? In substantial measure, the controversy (at least at the macroeconomic level) derives from the large budget deficits of the 1980s. Many supply-siders had argued that real income growth could occur with no need to incur such deficits because federal revenues would grow in spite of tax cuts as the economy expanded.

The Laffer Curve: Too Much Taxation Reduces Revenue

Laffer Curve
A theoretical association between various tax rates and the tax revenues collected at each rate.

An early precept upon which supply-side economic arguments were founded was the validity of a proposition named for economist Arthur Laffer and called the **Laffer curve**. This is a theoretical association between various tax rates and the tax revenues collected at each rate. We see a (hypothetical) Laffer curve in Figure 15-2. Note that as tax rates rise from point *0* to point *B*, tax revenues rise and reach a maximum of $1,000 billion ($1 trillion) at point *B*. As rates rise above 40 percent, revenues decline. Cutting tax rates from 75 percent to 40 percent could, thus, increase revenues (from $500 billion to $1 trillion). It follows from the curve that there is more than one rate that will generate a specific amount of revenue. Notice that points *A* and *C* correspond to the same revenue ($500 billion) but to very different tax rates

Figure 15-2
A Hypothetical Laffer Curve for an Economy

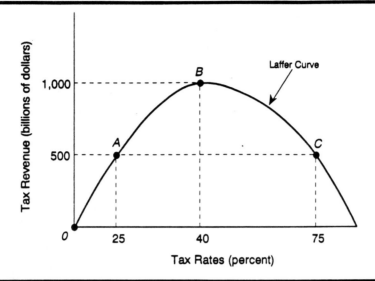

As tax rates rise, tax revenues rise. At *A*, a tax rate of 25 percent yields revenues of $500 billion. That same revenue would be yielded however at point *C* with a tax rate of 75 percent. Tax revenues are at a maximum ($1,000 billion) at point *B*.

(25 percent and 75 percent). The reasoning underlying the Laffer curve is that of point (b) in our supply-side elements: taxes are biased against effort, saving and investment. Beyond some point, as they rise, they lead to reduced effort (or diversion of resources to the underground economy) as well as reduced saving and investment. As they are cut, the supply of effort increases as does savings, investment, income, and the tax base.

The major problem with the Laffer curve is in making it operationally testable. How can we know where point *B* lies in reality? If we want to produce a certain amount of tax revenue, how can we structure taxes in advance and in the proper way to avoid the disincentives of proceeding past point *B*? President Reagan and others were apparently persuaded of the validity of the Laffer argument in the case of the 1981 tax cuts. Although there may be some who say investment lags have simply postponed the revenue inflow, many others point to the deficits and question the Laffer curve concept itself.

Can Discretionary Policy Changes Alter Growth Anyway? Rational Versus Adaptive Expectations

Economists of whatever view agree that expectations play an important role in private economic decision making. Consumers must form expectations about the future including such things as incomes, prices, taxes, interest rates, and inflation rates. Firms

*Adaptive
Expectations
Hypothesis*
The argument that
decision makers form
their view of the
future on the basis of
actual events that have
occurred in the recent
past.

*Rational
Expectations
Hypothesis*
The argument that
decision makers form
their view of the
future partly on the
basis of events in the
recent past but also on
the basis of present
events.

must form expectations about future events including many of the same things. Neither group can make informed present decisions without some perspective on the future.

Differences exist among economists as to how expectations are formed. A traditional idea is that called the **adaptive expectations hypothesis**, which holds that decision makers form their view of the future on the basis of actual events that have occurred in the recent past. Consider the question of inflation rates. As we noted earlier, inflation since 1983 has ranged from 2 to 4 percent. Adaptive expectationists would argue that this range is probably the prevailing view that we have of the immediate future. Suppose now that the monetary authority increases the supply of credit and inflation rises to 10 percent. Wage demands of labor (and other costs) will not likely rise immediately to offset the difference between expected and actual inflation rates. As a result, firms (real) costs fall, profits rise and investments are likely to increase. In the long run, of course, resource suppliers will adapt to the new inflation rate and adjust their resource price demands upward to offset the change in inflationary expectation. In the short run, though, monetary (or fiscal) policies could work to stimulate the economy.

A more recent view associated in particular with Robert Lucas, Jr. and Thomas Sargent of the University of Minnesota, is called the **rational expectations hypothesis**. This hypothesis is that private decision makers form their inflationary expectations partly on the basis of events in the recent past but also on the basis of present events. People not only learn from what *has* happened but from what *is* happening. Combining the two sources of information, they anticipate future events including inflation rates and changes in inflation rates. Suppose that this view is accepted. If the monetary authority increases the supply of credit, private decision makers quickly build this information into their view of the future. If they now expect (without the lag of adaptive expectations) that inflation rates will rise, they adjust their wage and other price demands upward, raising costs, reducing the profitability of investment, and offsetting the investment effects of the macroeconomic efforts to stimulate the economy.

Rational expectationists would argue, thus, that discretionary macroeconomic policy, especially monetary policy, is not only ineffective but even destabilizing. Only if the macroeconomic policy change was greater than expected by firms and consumers would it work. If one accepts this idea, it would seem almost impossible to fool all private decision makers in some systematic way. Discretionary macroeconomic policy would seem to be ruled out, and that macroeconomic policy by rule would be called for.

How Influential Is Rational Expectations Theory?

There is no doubt that rational expectations theory is influential. It has forced many economists to rethink and even question some of their beliefs about the degree of effectiveness of various macro-economic policy tools (money supply changes, tax cuts, etc.). There are many economists, nonetheless, who are not prepared to abandon their view that the macroeconomy can successfully be nudged toward more rapid growth or price stability through selectively applied policy changes. As recently as 1981-1982, a powerful dose of monetary restraint did moderate inflation as well as impel the economy into recession. Policy changes, in other words, may work; they just may not work as well as adaptive expectations conclude, but not as poorly as rational expectationists conclude.

SUMMING UP

1 As America entered the 1980s, it had high inflation, rising unemployment and a declining rate of growth in real GNP.

2. Macroeconomic policy under the Reagan administration was partly based on *supply-side economics*, policies designed to stimulate growth in aggregate supply at stable price levels.

3. The equilibrium level of real income and prices is established where aggregate quantity demanded equals aggregate quantity supplied. In the face of growing aggregate demand, price stability requires incentives to increase aggregate supply through savings and investment.

4. "Supply-siders" have argued that macroeconomic growth and stabilization policy, which had long focused on aggregate demand changes, should shift emphasis to treat changing aggregate supply as an autonomous variable.

5. Supply-side views seem to be founded in four ideas: (a) entitlement programs reduce incentives; their reduction will raise incentives and cut tax burdens, (b) taxes are biased against saving and investment: lower taxes will mean more effort as well as savings and investments, (c) much public regulation to protect consumers and employees has high costs and relatively few benefits, (d) stimulating aggregate demand through monetary and fiscal policies has created high inflationary expectations and there is a need to lower these expectations.

6. The tax cuts of 1981 were intended to stimulate saving and investment and to redirect resources away from the underground economy of non-taxed transactions. Marginal tax rates were cut in 1982 and again in 1987.

7. There was an increase in investment rates after 1982; it is unclear how much of that increase is attributable to the tax cuts.

8. The main controversy over supply-side economic policies is not in the post-1981 sustained growth or relative price stability but rather in the large federal deficits that have resulted.

9. According to the *Laffer curve*, tax rates can be so high that disincentives to work, save and invest set in and actually reduce tax revenues as rates rise beyond some level. The Laffer curve apparently had some influence in the 1981 tax cuts.

10. The principal problem with the Laffer curve is implementing it. We do not know whether the cuts in 1981 raised tax revenues through incentive effects. What we have observed is that revenues did not rise as rapidly as expenditures and large deficits resulted.

11. Expectations play an important role in private decisions by consumers and by firms. *Adaptive expectations* are those formed by people on the basis of recent events. Macroeconomic policy changes can be influential in affecting saving and investment in the short run according to this hypothesis because resource prices that are based on current expectations are not immediately adjusted upward in the face of rising rates of inflation.

12. Expectations, say some economists, are formed according to the *rational expectations hypothesis*, that is, on the basis not only of recent events but also current events. Combining both sets of information, private decision makers anticipate the consequences of current macroeconomic policy changes such as the higher inflation that may result from a growing money supply. Thus, resource prices adjust quickly and negate any stimulative effect from the policy change. Discretionary policy does not work; policy by rule is called for.

13. Rational expectations theory has been influential but it still appears to many economists that discretionary policy changes such as the 1981 curtailment of the money supply can work.

KEY TERMS

Supply-side economics
Underground economy
Laffer curve
Adaptive expectations hypothesis
Rational expectations hypothesis

QUESTIONS

1. Describe the general macroeconomic conditions of the American economy in the early-1980s.

2. What is meant by the term "supply-side economics"?

3. In the face of growing aggregate demand, what is necessary to ensure price stability?

4. On what four propositions are supply-side economic views founded?

5. What were the intended effects of the 1981 tax cuts?

6. Were the 1981 tax cuts successful? If so, in what sense?

7. What is the source of the major controversies surrounding the supply-side policies of the 1980s?

8. In the figure below a hypothetical Laffer curve is drawn. Answer the following questions about the curve.

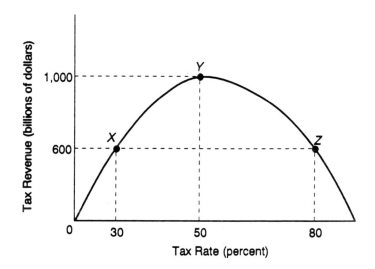

a. What is the Laffer curve argument about the association between tax rates and tax revenues?
b. At what tax rate do revenues reach a maximum?
c. Why are there two tax rates (30 percent, 80 percent) that yield the same revenue?
d. What causes tax revenues to decline beyond point Y?
e. What is the principal problem with using the Laffer curve as a basis for tax policy?

9. Explain the difference between the rational expectations hypothesis and the adaptive expectations hypothesis? Under which of the two may short-run charges in discretionary macroeconomic policy be successful?

SUGGESTED READINGS

Baily, Martin Neil. "Are the New Economic Models the Answer?" *Brookings Review*. Fall, 1982. Reprinted in Peter D. McClelland, *Readings in Introductory Macroeconomics*. 1987-1988. New York: McGraw-Hill, 1988.

Economic Report of the President. Published Annually. G.P.O. Washington, D.C.

Forman, Leonard. "Rational Expectations and the Real World." *Challenge*. November/December, 1980.

Friedman, Benjamin M. "Did Reagan's 1981 Tax Incentives Work? The Vaunted Investment Boom is a Bust." *New York Times*. July 7, 1985. Reprinted in *Readings in Introductory Macroeconomics*. Peter D. McClelland, Ed. New York: McGraw-Hill, 1988.

Holland, A. Steven. "Rational Expectations and the Effects of Monetary Policy: A Guide to the Unitiated." *Economic Review*. May, 1985. Federal Reserve Bank of St. Louis.

Juster, F. Thomas. "The Economics and Politics of the Supply-Side View." *Economic Outlook USA*. Autumn, 1981. Reprinted in *Readings in Introductory Macroeconomics*. Peter D. McClelland, Ed. New York: McGraw-Hill, 1988.

McCallum, Bennett. "The Significance of Rational Expectations Theory." *Challenge*. November/December, 1980.

Pisciotta, John. "Conservative and Liberal Economic Philosophies" in *Annual Editions*. 1987-88. John Piscotta, Ed., Dushkin: Sluice Dock, Ct., 1987.

Readings in Introductory Macroeconomics, Section VII. "The Burgeoning Federal Deficit." Peter D. McClelland, Ed. New York: McGraw-Hill, 1988.

Sargent, Thomas J. *Rational Expectations and Inflation*. New York: Harper and Row, 1986.

Chapter 16:
Expansion and Growth

Until now, we have dealt with macroeconomic and microeconomic principles that are primarily *static*. That is, they are like a snapshot of a situation at a point in time, rather than like a motion picture showing the situation changing with the passage of time. Static principles of economics, such as supply and demand and national income determination, have helped us analyze problems as diverse as how to view the effects of rent control laws, and whether monetary policy is an effective tool against inflation.

Dynamic Framework
A framework that explains how things change over time.

We are about to explore some problems that—at least in some of their aspects—require a **dynamic framework**, one that explains how things change over a period of time. We will examine, for example, the growth record of the U.S. economy and its prospects for the future. In this chapter we will discuss several theoretical explanations of economic growth, and in Application 2 to this chapter, we will present the following related problem: Do we have to choose between more growth and a clean environment?

Expansion
The extensive process by which the output of an economy grows.

Let's begin by making a distinction between expansion and growth. We'll use **expansion** to refer to the extensive process by which the output of an economy grows as it uses more and more resources. **Growth** refers to the intensive process by which productivity, output per hour of labor (or income per capita), increases.

Growth
The intensive process by which productivity, output per hour of labor increases.

Sources of Expansion

An economy can achieve expansion by using more resources. First, it might achieve expansion because of an increase in the *supply* of total resources (land, labor, and capital). Let's look at each of those resources to see how—and how much—each might contribute to expansion.

Land represents all the natural resources of a nation, not only the surface soil but the subsoil minerals, the timber, and the water. It is tempting to think of all resources as being fixed: so many acres of land, so many acre-feet of water, tons of minerals, and so forth. Although it is useful to know (or estimate) the economy's resources at a particular time, you should realize that they can change as time and technology change the ways of producing things as well as the things that can be produced.

Consider the case of offshore oil, under the continental shelf: A few decades ago no one was even sure it was there. After geologic surveys confirmed its existence, it was still only a potential resource that might be tapped someday. Now, technology, has made a difference. With new oil-drilling technology, and with world oil prices much higher than in 1971, offshore oil has become a resource, something available to use.

Another example of technology creating a resource occurred in iron mining. In the Mesabi iron range, the richest iron ore was mined and the second-grade ore, called *taconite*, was thrown aside because it was too expensive to refine. Now, with new technology, the mining companies are working the Mesabi range again, this time getting iron from the taconite. The price of iron makes it economical, definitely worth the trouble.

We should note here that technology and changes in technology affect not only expansion, through making resources out of previously unusable potential resources. They also, as you shall see shortly, increase the productivity of resources that are employed and, thereby, are a major source of growth.

Labor represents the human resources of a society. In a sense, labor is the most basic of all resources. Without labor, nothing happens. The whole process of expansion and growth depends on human motivations, work, aspirations, and skills. An increase in population or an increase in participation in the labor force (for example, women during and since World War II) increases a society's total output (that is, it creates expansion).

Capital is the physical result of investment. Capital consists of the plant and equipment and tools with which people work. There is also human capital. Capital's productivity rises with specialization, and specialization is limited by the size of the market. In a small town in a largely rural (perhaps low-income) area of the U.S., there's not much specialization of either labor or capital. If you get sick, you go to the town doctor, who is almost certainly a general practitioner. If you have a leaky roof, you go to the town's general handyman, a jack-of-all-trades. If your car's engine is idling badly, you take it to the town mechanic, no matter whether the car is a Chevy or a Nissan.

Now, what happens if you live in a city and have the same problems? If your medical problem is a skin rash, you go directly to a dermatologist or you are referred to one. If you have a roof leak, you call in a firm of roof specialists. If you have car trouble, you probably find a garage that specializes in that particular make of car.

Whether in small town or city, the kind and amount of capital that people have to work with has a lot to do with their productivity. The more capital, and the more sophisticated the capital available to workers, the greater their output.

The difference in these two situations is due to *different market sizes*. The small (poor) town has few consumers and relatively little aggregate demand. The city has many consumers and a lot more aggregate demand. In the city there are enough people with enough purchasing power to warrant the investment that results in specialized tools, machines, and plant facilities. Without this capital, jobs for those in the (increasing) labor force will not be created and the society will not be able to use its (potential) natural resources.

Increasing Productivity and Growth

There is a link between productivity and growth. As more and more resources are used in production, growth may occur because as productivity increases the cost per unit of output goes down. As the economy uses existing plants, or builds more plants, and as it employs more people and uses more land (natural resources), output may increase more rapidly than input. In other words, a 5 percent increase in the use of inputs may generate more than a 5 percent increase in output. Let's examine the reasons for this.

According to Adam Smith and other classical economists, *specialization* is a major reason for such increases in output. In an economy whose market size is growing, there is more and more specialized use of labor and capital, which leads to more and more output. In fact, large market size, as we mentioned a bit earlier, is necessary if specialization is to exist in a community.

Technological Change
The growth in knowledge or advances in techniques that result in more productive capital goods and more efficient organization.

Technological change, the growth in knowledge or advances in techniques that result in more productive capital goods and more efficient organization, is perhaps the main thing that holds out hope for future growth. If all our prospects for growth depended on specialization, the future might prove as gloomy as the classical economists (Adam Smith, David Ricardo, Karl Marx, and others) predicted. Their dismal view prevailed through much of our industrial history. To see why, examine Figure 16-1.

Let's suppose that the economy shown in Figure 16-1 has met various preconditions for growth: attitudes favorable to growth, financial institutions to receive and channel savings into productive investments, a government to establish and enforce commercial rules, people drawn into the market system—all the things we have discussed in previous chapters. Suppose also that it has at least one industry that has a high growth potential whose effects seem likely to spread throughout the economy.

What will happen first as the economy starts to grow and expand? In the early years, its productivity and per capita income may rise rapidly. The part of the growth path (Y/P) from zero up to

Figure 16-1
Growth Paths of an Economy

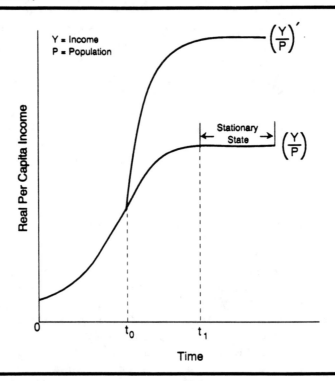

time t_0 represents this period. As the size of its market gets larger (as reflected in its growing per capita income), it begins to enjoy all the efficiencies of increased specialization. The slope—rate of change—of (Y/P) increases, indicating that real per capita income is growing faster and faster.

Then, after time t_0, the slope of (Y/P) becomes less steep, which means that if the economy remains on this growth path (even at full employment), growth will be slower. (As time passes, the increments in growth will get smaller and smaller.) This implies that there are barriers or resistances to rapid growth. What are they? Why can't the economy simply keep on growing at the same rate?

Decreasing Productivity and Growth

Let's answer the question of why there is a slow-down in the growth rate:

1. In the short term, some resources may be relatively fixed in usage. For example, the Atlas Company makes stereo sets, for which plant and equipment are the fixed inputs. Now it naturally takes longer to put new plant and equipment into use than it does to vary the use of other inputs (labor, land, and materials). So if Atlas

wants to make more stereos, and if it starts using more labor and land without increasing its use of capital (plant and equipment), then its productivity (output of stereos per unit of additional input) will, in the long run, decline. Why? Basically, because of over-crowding. With a fixed number of machines and a fixed amount of plant space, workers may start having to wait to use machines. They may finally get in each other's way and disrupt the specialized routines of the plant.

2. As an economy begins to suffer diminishing productivity growth, the rate at which per capita income grows slacks off. At some point (t_0 in Figure 16-1), diminishing efficiency (due to the slowness of increase in plant and equipment) begins to more than offset the increased amount of efficiency resulting from specialization. The slope of the (Y/P) curve becomes less and less steep. When it reaches zero (past t_1), the society is in a *stationary state*. Real per capita income is at a maximum and will not grow further until something in the economy changes.

The Classical View

The classical economists (Adam Smith, et al.) who talked about the stationary state disagreed about how high the upper limit to (Y/P) might be. Smith was among the most optimistic. Unlike others, Smith refused to look upon technology as containing a fixed number of choices. Some classical economists gloomily predicted that a society would use techniques that added less and less to productivity as time went on and that it would finally run out of new technological choices. They felt that this gradual disappearance of new technology—combined with the need to produce more and more food for a growing population on a fixed supply of land—would ultimately produce the stationary state at a fairly low level of real per capita income. But Smith had slightly more optimistic hopes for the future. He believed that population growth might be held in check because as people become accustomed to more and goods and services, they might develop a taste for goods rather than children.

Malthusian Specter
The view of Thomas Malthus that because of slower growth in food supplies than in population, starvation, wars, plagues, and famines would result.

The most pessimistic of the classicists was the English economist, Thomas R. Malthus. Parson Malthus (he was a preacher) originated what has become known as the **Malthusian specter**. His grim view of the future derived from two influences: the supply of people and the supply of food to maintain them. Malthus argued that the supply of people (the population) will increase at a geometric rate (1, 2, 4, 8, 16, and so on), that is, double each generation, or every 25 years. On the other hand, the food supply will increase only at an arithmetic rate (1, 2, 3, 4, 5, and so on). Finally, widespread starvation will result unless people are able to restrict the population. According to Malthus, there will be wars, plagues, and famines that ultimately will bring population into line with the means of sustaining people.

Hawker

"Now will you have the vasectomy?"

Has the Malthusian Nightmare Occurred in Some Places?

We have said that one-fourth of the world's population lives in high-income countries. For this lucky minority, the ominous predictions of the classical economists have obviously not come to pass. For the other three-fourths, however, the scenario, especially Malthus's version, has real meaning. Everyone reads about starvation, plague, famine, and war in such countries as Ethiopia. The photographs from those areas are heart-rending. Real per capita income in such countries is extremely low. For example, in India, each year population growth presses ever harder on the means of sustaining India's 725 million people. In spite of the green revolution (that is, the growth in agricultural productivity), countries such as Bangladish and Ethiopia need foreign relief in the form of massive shipments of grain and other foodstuffs to prevent widespread starvation. For such countries, the low-level stationary state is a grim reality.

But what about that one-fourth to one-third of the world's people who live in Europe, North America, Australia, Japan, and the newly industrializing nations such as Taiwan and Korea? Why have they escaped? Look again at Figure 16-1, and let's use the U.S. as an example. The U.S. has experienced, at least over the last 150 years, a continuous shifting of Y/P, our growth path. Each time, before the economy actually reached a point of declining growth (such as t_0), it has moved into a higher growth path, such as $(Y/P)'$. A series of such shifts has kept the U.S. economy from entering a stationary state. A study of our industrial history suggests that there are two major reasons for this: technological change and population increase.

Technological Change
A large part of U.S. productivity growth and increase in real income is due to the fact that U.S. industry has constantly changed the techniques by which it produces things. There is an old story about the clerk in the U.S. Patent Office who resigned, in the early-nineteenth century, because he was sure that most of the important inventions had already been made. But Americans as a rule are optimistic about the future and count on technological change to increase their incomes and their productivity. To a great extent, their optimism is justified. Except for cyclical variations in investment in new forms of technology (such as the depression of the 1930s), U.S. industry has kept pushing ahead, using new methods as fast as people invent them. Beginning with the cotton gin in the late-eighteenth century and continuing through the glamorous devices made possible by the aerospace technology and computer technology of the 1960s, 1970s, and 1980s, U.S. industry has employed better and better machinery and tools, which have raised the productivity of American laborers. The U.S. has also made larger and larger investments in people themselves, spending billions on such things as education, health programs, parks, and slum clearance—all of which have helped raise the productivity of the American worker.

Population Increase
In 1930 there were 123 million Americans. In 1989 there were more than 245 million—about double! This increase in population has been favorable to growth in the U.S. Until people began to question the idea in recent years, Americans believed that growth in numbers would make them better off in the long run, which naturally influenced their willingness to have children. During the nineteenth century, when we were an agricultural society, large families were like money in the bank. Children started working on the farms at an early age and were active producers.

Likewise, when the U.S. was becoming an urban industrial society, in the late-nineteenth and early-twentieth centuries, large families (together with waves of immigrants) were a good thing because they produced the labor force needed to build and operate mass-production factories.

But now that the U.S. is a mature industrial, or post-industrial, society, large families are no longer an *economic* asset (at least to individuals), although we continue to benefit from a large influx of immigrants. Children are consumers, not producers. So now, in the second half of the twentieth century, Americans are trying to halt the population explosion. Though controversial to many, birth-control information is free in most states, and the advent of the Pill, plus the passing of laws to legalize abortion (which are even more controversial) have combined to reduce the number of births from 27.7 live births per 1,000 in 1920 to 12 live births per 1,000 in 1985—a drop of more than 50 percent in 55 years. America appears to be close to zero population growth.

Instead of trying to expand its labor force, the U.S. is trying to expand its capital. This means that industry produces things through techniques that are ever more **capital-intensive** (using relatively more capital than labor or land) rather than through techniques that are **labor-intensive** (using relatively more labor than capital or land). As this is done generally, **capita-deepening** occurs, that is, relatively more and more capital is used (raising the capital-to-labor ratio for the economy).

By contrast, **capital-broadening** occurs when capital instruments (tools, plant, and the like) grow at the same rate that labor grows.

There is a lesson to be learned from U.S. economic history: The Malthusian nightmare need not come true at all. Technological change can rapidly increase a nation's ability to produce food. Population increase need not be a drag on industrial growth. In fact, an educated populace *can* slow the population growth to zero.

But the extent to which the experience of the U.S. (and other industrial nations) will be repeated in other nations as they attempt to industrialize, or whether the grim Malthusian scenario will indeed come to pass for some of the world's poorer countries, remains to be seen.

Slowing Productivity Growth in the United States?

Edward Denison, a leading authority on productivity in the American economy found that the growth of potential output (shifting of the American production-possibilities frontier) declined between 1948 and 1983. For the period 1948-1973 this potential grew at an annual rate of 3.9 percent per year. Between 1973 and 1979, this rate fell to 3.0 percent. From 1979 to 1983, it fell dramatically to 1.8 percent, less than half of the 1948-1973 rate. Growth in output per worker fell over the same period from 2.3 percent per year to zero or less. Why the dramatic slow-down or virtual elimination of the shifting of the production-possibilities curve? At least five basic explanations have been offered:

1. *A change in the composition of the American labor force.* People who have had years of on-the-job experience have higher levels of productivity than new entrants. As the proportion of the labor force made up of new entrants has risen, productivity growth has slowed. This change, however, does not appear to be a major explanatory factor.

2. *The composition of output in the American economy has changed.* As America's demand for output shifts more and more to

Capital-Intensive
Techniques that use relatively more capital than labor or land.

Labor-Intensive
Techniques that use relatively more labor than capital or land.

Capital-Deepening
When the capital/labor ratio rises for the economy.

Capital-Broadening
When capital grows at the same rate as labor and the capital/labor ratio remains constant.

labor-intensive services, productivity will grow more slowly than it did when a larger part of the GNP was produced by more capital-intensive manufacturing industries. Almost all students of the productivity growth problem agree that this factor has contributed to the slow down. Some say it has had little effect, others say almost half of the slow down can be explained by this change.

3. *Growth in government regulation.* Resources are required not only to regulate industries but also to meet standards of compliance with regulations. Neither of these resource usages is directly productive. While such diversions may improve our quality of life or standard of living, as in the case of much environmental regulation, they reduce the (full-employment) growth of our productive potential.

4. *Rising resource prices.* Some have particularly suggested that OPEC I and OPEC II made fuel inefficient capital less productive to use and encouraged the substitution of labor for capital. Denison found, however, that rising prices for energy in the 1970s accounted for only about $\frac{1}{10}$ of 1 percent of the reduction in productivity growth. If so, we may expect little positive effect in this regard from the falling energy prices of 1987-1988.

5. *A decline in the rate of capital formation.* Capital formation and productivity growth are closely related. Economies that use relatively more capital have higher levels of productivity. Imagine a choice between solving data processing problems with (a) pen and paper, (b) mechanical calculators, (c) modern computers. Obviously (c) is the most capital-intensive and also the most productive. Denison found, however, that only a small part of the productivity growth slow-down could be explained this way.

What Is the Implication: A Contrary View

A leading American economist, William Baumol of Princeton, argues that the U.S. economy is *not* losing its productivity edge. Writing in the *Wall Street Journal* in March, 1990, Baumol cites the following: (1) Although the productivity growth rate has fallen, it has simply adjusted back to its historic rate, (2) the productivity growth rate has slowed in all industrial nations (That of Japan has decreased as much as that of the U.S.), and (3) the "absolute productivity level of U.S. labor in general, and manufacturing in particular continues to be the highest in the world."

U.S. domination of manufacturing output, says Baumol, is growing along with that of Japan and in contrast to the European economies. Service sector employment ("flipping the hamburgers") has grown because of rapid population growth between 1962 and 1985. U.S. labor is moving into services less rapidly than that of any U.S. trading partner except New Zealand. That the U.S. has become increasingly a service economy has resulted from "the outstanding productivity achievements of both industrial and agricultural section—there is nothing disturbing about the U.S. record."

While conceding that some U.S. industries have lost their competitive edge (including consumer electronics, automobiles, and such), and that this has created tragedies, especially for older workers, this process of rise and decline in industries, has been, according to Baumol, a "hallmark of technological progress accompanied by international competition." Views to the contrary, he says, are "a melange of half-truths" and the implications drawn from them false.

Technological Change Again: The Answer to Faster Growth?

A Nobel Laureate, Simon Kuznets, said that about 90 percent of growth came from a qualitative improvement in resources or from technological change. For this reason, many feel that more should be done in America to stimulate research and development activities (R&D). While R&D by private firms has been fairly constant since the 1960s, government support fell although it has been partially recovered in the 1980s. The repeal of investment tax credits in the 1987 law is regarded as unwise by some economists who believe that government subsidization is warranted in view of the declining rate of growth in productivity.

SUMMING UP

1. In order to be able to analyze many economic problems, one needs a *dynamic* rather than a *static* framework, that is, a structure that shows change through time.

2. *Expansion*, a process by which total output increases, comes about through the use of more resources, land, labor, and capital. *Growth* is a process by which productivity, output per hour of labor (or income per capita), increases and becomes more complex.

3. According to Adam Smith and other classical economists, growth takes place because of the increased productivity that accompanies specialization in the uses of resources. This specialization is limited by the size of the market. As the market grows, more and more specialization takes place. But because of limited supplies of land and, ultimately, diminishing efficiency, an economy's growth will diminish beyond some point and will ultimately reach a *stationary state*.

4. The stationary state may be high or low in terms of real per capita income. Smith envisioned it as becoming high, since with

the development of better technology, people might prefer more goods to more children. Malthus thought it was likely to be low, since population increase would outstrip the food supply, and famine, plagues, and the like would result.

5. The classical scenario (the Malthusian version in some cases) has come true in many poor countries, whose growth has been very slow, or nonexistent, and whose investment in education has been slight.

6. Industrial nations and newly industrializing nations have escaped the stationary state, for two reasons: (a) Technological change has shifted their growth paths upward and overcome the long-term tendencies toward stagnation. (b) As growth has occurred, the rate of growth of their populations has tapered off.

7. Even a growing economy's growth is not necessarily accompanied by full employment. Therefore, a society's *actual growth path*—the change in its real per capita income as time goes by—may be less than its full-employment potential.

8. The *aggregate production function* is the relationship between total output and the labor force employed. It tells us how much output an economy produces at various levels of employment.

9. According to Edward Denison productivity growth in the U.S. slowed over the period from 1948 to 1983, especially from 1979 to 1983. Some of the reasons for this slowing appear to be: (a) a change in the composition of the American labor force, (b) a change in the composition of the output of the economy, (c) growth in government regulation, (d) rising resource prices, (e) a decline in the rate of capital formation.

10. Most productivity growth is due to improvements in the quality of resources or to technological change. There are calls in the U.S. to create greater incentives to research and development and the resulting improvements in applied technology.

11. The U.S. has a long record of growth. Over the last 100 years its output has increased at a compound annual rate of 2.1 percent. But it has had long periods of less than full employment, and therefore its growth path has often been below the full-employment level. Thus, the U.S. has lost a great deal of per capita income.

12. According to William Baumol a slowing rate of growth in productivity is not a reflection of economic failure. For the U.S. this slowing reflects what has happened in most industrial nations. Growth in services was caused by rapid population growth and, though severe dislocation have resulted in some industries, this has been so throughout modern U.S. history.

KEY TERMS

Dynamic framework
Expansion
Growth
Technological change
Malthusian specter
Capital intensive
Labor intensive
Capital deepening
Capital broadening

QUESTIONS

1. Why is a dynamic framework more useful than a static one for analyzing growth relationships and problems?

2. Is expansion or growth more important to improving the material well-being of people? Why?

3. What explanations are offered for the slowing of productivity growth in the U.S.?

4. If you were asked to recommend ways to increase the amount of savings and investment in the U.S., what would you propose?

5. Do you think the U.S. should devote more of its GNP to research and development? Why?

6. What does William Baumol conclude about the causes and effects of a slowing rate of growth in productivity?

SUGGESTED READINGS

Adelman, Irma. *Theories of Economic Development.* Stanford University Press, Stanford, CA, 1961 (for those who know some mathematics).

Baumol, William J. "U.S. Industry's Lead Gets Bigger." *Wall Street Journal.* March 21, 1990.

Baumol, William J. "America's Productivity "Crisis": A Modest Decline isn't all that Bad." *New York Times,* February 15, 1987. Reprinted in *Readings in Introductory Macroeconomics.* Peter D. McClelland, Ed. New York: McGraw-Hill, 1988.

Harberger, Arnold (Ed.) *World Economic Growth.* San Francisco: Institute for Contemporary Studies, 1984.

Little, Ian M. *Economic Development Theory Policy and International Relations*. New York: Basic Books, 1982.

Olson, Mancur. *The Rise and Decline of Nations*. New Haven: Yale University Press, 1982.

Slichter, Sumner H. *Economic Growth in the United States*. Free Press, New York, 1966.

"The Oil Uncrisis." *Gallons and Sense*. May, 1986. Reprinted in annual Editions 87/88. John Pisciotta, Ed. Dishken: Sluice Dock, Ct., 1987.

Application 1 to Chapter 16:
Can We Have Growth Without Massive
Military Spending?

Do Wars Keep the Economy Healthy?

Must the American economy have heavy injections of government spending for war and defense in order to achieve full-employment, full-capacity growth? Opinions vary greatly. Let's look at two contrasting views.

Writing about the period since World War II, Douglas Dowd, an economist critical of many aspects of the American economy, says, "The key to this process of sustained growth—i.e., the absence of even a serious recession, let alone a depression—is to be found in the record of federal purchases, and in that category, the key factor is purchases geared to the military." Dowd says that between 1946 and 1971, 80 percent of the $1.4 trillion of federal expenditures was in some way connected with defense. This, he argues, is the primary reason for the stability and growth of our post-World War II economy.

Other observers claim that the connection between defense spending and the growth of the American economy is not at all clear. It is true, they say, that defense spending has helped to create jobs and stimulate consumption and investment spending, and that massive war expenditures beginning in 1941 had a lot to do with reducing unemployment from 14.6 percent in 1940 to 1.2 percent in 1944. It is also true that unemployment reached its lowest postwar point (2.9 percent) in 1953 when Korean War expenditures were at their peak. Yet the unemployment rate swung up and down widely between 1946 and 1986, and defense spending was probably only one of several factors affecting employment and growth.

To put these two positions in perspective, see Table A(1)16-1. From the mid-1940s to the end of the 1960s, unemployment varied from 2.9 percent to 6.8 percent of the civilian labor force. The high points in unemployment (1949-1950, 1958-1963) reflect downturns in the economy. Notice, however, that they do not correspond to downturns in military spending either in absolute terms or in terms of a percentage of GNP. (Military spending includes military purchases and military salaries, but not interest on the national debt associated with deficits attributable to war or defense spending.) The low points in unemployment (1946-1948, 1951-1953, 1955-1957, 1965-1969, the late-1980s) also reflect upturns in the economy, not upturns in defense spending. These conclusions generally follow even if one introduces a time lag of a year or so between changes in defense spending and changes in the rate of unemployment.

Table A(1)16-1
The Federal Government's Purchases of Goods and Services for the Military and Their Relation to GNP, 1945-1989

Year	Amount of Military Spending (billions of dollars)	Percentage of GNP	Unemployment as a Percentage of Civilian Labor Force
1945	73.7	34.5	1.9
1946	16.4	7.7	3.9
1947	10.0	4.2	3.9
1948	11.3	4.3	3.8
1949	13.9	5.3	5.9
1950	14.3	5.0	5.3
1951	33.8	10.1	3.3
1952	46.2	13.1	3.0
1953	49.0	13.2	2.9
1954	41.6	11.2	5.5
1955	39.0	9.6	4.4
1956	40.7	9.5	4.1
1957	44.6	10.0	4.3
1958	46.3	10.1	6.8
1959	46.4	9.4	5.5
1960	45.3	8.8	5.5
1961	47.9	9.0	6.7
1962	52.1	9.1	5.5
1963	51.5	8.5	5.7
1964	50.4	7.8	5.2
1965	51.0	7.2	4.5
1966	62.0	8.1	3.8
1967	73.4	9.0	3.8
1968	79.1	8.9	3.6
1969	78.9	8.2	3.5
1970	76.8	7.6	4.9
1971	74.1	6.7	5.9
1972	77.4	6.4	5.6
1973	77.5	5.7	4.9
1974	82.6	5.6	5.6
1975	89.6	5.6	8.5
1976	93.4	5.2	7.7
1977	100.9	5.1	7.1
1978	108.9	4.8	6.1
1979	121.9	4.9	5.8
1980	142.7	5.2	7.1
1981	167.5	5.5	7.6
1982	193.8	6.1	9.7
1983	215.7	6.3	9.6
1984	237.0	6.3	7.5
1985	262.0	6.6	7.2
1986	273.4	6.5	7.0
1987	282.0	6.2	6.2
1988	290.4	6.0	5.5
1989	303.6	5.8	5.3

Source: *Economic Report of the President, 1986, 1990.*

The single exception appears to be 1953-1954, when the percentage of the GNP consumed by national defense fell from 13.5 percent to 11.3 percent (in absolute terms, it fell by about $8 billion) and unemployment rose from 2.9 percent to 5.6 percent. Even if the income (and employment) multiplier was large, say 2 or 3, a decline of $8 billion in defense spending in 1954 should not by itself have produced a near doubling of unemployment. In fact, GNP rose in 1954, and it appears that a rise in people's spending for personal consumption, together with a rise in net exports, more than offset the decline in defense spending. The rise in unemployment was probably largely due to industry's having to make a transition from producing military to producing civilian goods.

On the basis of these data and the relationship between defense spending and employment, we can say two things with a fair amount of confidence:

1. The U.S. was apparently not used *variations* in defense spending as a strategic weapon to combat unemployment.

2. Military spending constituted a large, relatively stable portion of GNP (aggregate demand).

If there had been no military spending in the U.S. since 1946, unemployment would have been much higher. The same thing could be said, however, about *other* federal expenditures. As Arthur Okun, a former chairman of the Council of Economic Advisers in the Johnson administration, put it, "Ever since Keynes, economists had recognized that the federal government could stimulate economic activity by increasing the injection of federal expenditures into the income stream or by reducing the withdrawal of federal tax receipts." If any net increase in GX or decrease in T in the $C + I + GX = C + S + T$ equilibrium is stimulative, then there is nothing unique about defense spending. Lord Keynes himself expressed it well in 1936, when he wrote about societies that lower unemployment by engaging in government spending:

> Ancient Egypt was doubly fortunate, and doubtless owed to this its fabled wealth, in that it possessed *two* activities, namely, pyramid-building as well as the search for precious metals, the fruits of which, since they could not serve the needs of man by being consumed, did not stale with abundance. The middle ages built cathedrals and sang dirges. Two pyramids, two masses for the dead, are twice as good as one.

In other words, the government might have spent the same amount of money on developing the world's best system of mass transit or on some income-maintenance scheme to supplement the earnings of the nation's poorest citizens, and achieved the same aggregate demand effect on the economy.

What About Reaching Potential?

In the 1980s, the government began to shy away from using fiscal policy (both expenditures and tax cuts) as a "fireman's tool" to cure unemployment fires already burning. The emphasis turned instead to stimulating the economy toward its productive potential (with only frictional or transitional unemployment). People believed that, in the long run, and especially if the economy could move toward full capacity as well as full employment, this would bring forth the continued investment (aggregate supply) needed to increase productivity and create new jobs as well.

To see how close the U.S. has come to reaching its potential GNP, examine Figure A(1)16-1. Since 1955, the performance has been uneven. In the late-1950s, the gap between actual and potential GNP widened. Yet during this period, defense spending was growing, though slowly, and it remained nearly constant as a percentage of GNP. Beginning in the early-1960s, the U.S. moved toward reaching its potential GNP, with the pace quickening after the tax cut of 1964. By 1966, the economy was running just about

Figure A(1)16-1
Actual and Potential Gross National Product

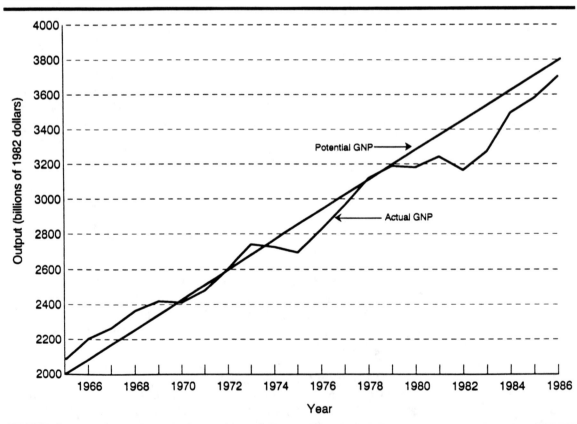

Source: *Economic Report of the President*, 1987.

at or slightly above potential, and continued to do so through 1969. Note in Table A(1)16-1 that in this period there was no significant change in the percentage of GNP spent on defense.

So you can see that the following occurred: (1) Defense spending from 1951 to 1970 was a stable component of government spending and therefore provided a floor under aggregate demand, income, and employment. (2) Movement toward full-potential growth in the 1960s was caused by fiscal (tax) policy, not change in defense spending. (3) Defense spending since 1975 has varied only between 5.6 percent and 6.6 percent.

Defense Spending: Does It Encourage or Retard Technological Change?

Some economists argue that large defense expenditures actually reduce our full capacity rate of growth. They feel that research and development skills and resources which are put to military uses do little to increase the nation's industrial capacity. As a result, the U.S. gives up larger increases in capacity that could be used to help solve not only employment problems but also income-distribution problems, such as problems of the cities, of racial minorities, and of poverty.

"All right, suppose we abolish war, and the entire
world is at peace—then what?"

There is another way of looking at this. A good many people feel that the government's expenditures for defense (and space exploration) have helped increase our full capacity growth through fostering technological change (in communications equipment and in many other things).

Who is right? It's hard to say; both viewpoints may be right. The unanswered question is: What is the net effect, the relation between what the economy gives up in technological change in the private sector versus what is gained? One cannot estimate this at present.

What About the 1990s?

With the end, or at least the dramatic decline in importance of the "cold war," there are many calls for large scale reductions in defense expenditures, a call has been intensified by the large deficits of the 1980s. Will such reductions trigger a recession or other undesirable economic effects? While there is no clear answer, the evidence we have examined suggests that the unfavorable results need not follow from such cutbacks. Whether the economic growth of the 1980s continues would appear to depend on a set of factors far more complex than simply defense spending.

SUMMING UP

1. Some economists, including Douglas Dowd have argued that defense spending since World War II has been the key to growth and stability in the American economy. Other economists, however, dispute that connection.

2. The economic record for the 1950s and 1960s seems to show that (a) *variations* in defense spending were not used to reduce unemployment, and (b) that military spending was a large but stable portion of aggregate demand.

3. Military spending, like other federal expenditures, adds to aggregate demand and, thereby, to the stimulation of economic activity and to a reduction in unemployment.

4. In the 1960s there was a movement away from using fiscal policy (including defense expenditures) to reduce unemployment.

5. The 1980s saw a major increase in defense expenditures. While there was a decline in unemployment after 1983, increased defense spending was only one of several factors including tax reductions that may have contributed to a lower rate of joblessness.

6. Anticipated reductions in defense expenditures will not necessarily raise unemployment. Unemployment trends, as well as growth will depend on many factors.

QUESTION

Suppose that you are chairman of a special task force on employment. The President of the U.S. calls you in and says that he is going to propose an extraordinary increase of $20 billion in federal spending in order to create 1 million new jobs. He can't decide, though, whether to increase the spending of the Defense Department (which maintains that it needs a manned bomber system) or the Department of Health, Education, and Welfare (which wants to expand educational benefits, medical care benefits, and other such programs). The President wants to know whether there will be different economic effects from the two types with expenditures of equal size. What would you tell the President?

Application 2 to Chapter 16: More Growth Versus a Clean Environment

More than a century has passed since the era of the "dismal science" and its grim Malthusian predictions. Optimism about the material future of human beings has grown. Improved technology and better organization, plus growing supplies of resources (including labor), have caused more and more countries to follow Britain and the U.S. toward ever higher levels of real income and better standards of living. Evidently the economist's assumption about growing output chasing rising aspirations was correct.

In the 1970s, however, the optimists began to qualify their optimism. (As Don Marquis said, "An optimist is a guy who has never had much experience.") Some argued that growth was inconsistent with environmental quality.

The Economists' View

Economists in general will not concede that pollution of the environment is the result of economic growth *per se*. Many also believe that the market system can offer solutions to the problems of pollution. In addition, many economists believe that continued growth is necessary, not as an end in itself, but as a means of solving a Pandora's box full of economic problems. Walter Heller (chairman of the council of Economic Advisors during the Kennedy and Johnson administrations) summarized these views as follows:

> In the starkest terms, the ecologist confronts us with an environmental imperative that requires an end to economic growth—or a sharp curtailment of it—as the price of biological survival. In contrast, the economist counters with a socioeconomic imperative that requires the continuation of growth as the price of social survival....Like it or not, economic growth seems destined to continue.

Heller goes on to say the following: (1) Ecologists disagree with economists about whether real growth (improvement in the quality of life) has occurred, considering negative externalities. (2) Ecologists envision absolute bans and absolute limits to growth: economists envision marginal tradeoffs and cost-benefit relations. (3) Ecologists want to rely on government to solve ecological problems; economists would rely on the price system to create solutions. Walter Heller says that growth could be checked, but that this "would throw the fragile ecology of our economic system so out of kilter as to threaten its breakdown."

Most economists would probably agree with Heller that it is the *pattern* of growth of the U.S. economy, not growth itself, that has created environmental pollution. Heller makes the point that scares about the environment (based on a static view of resources) occur periodically. He also says that our attempts to solve problems such as adequate defense, poverty, discrimination, and pollution have so mortgaged future GNP growth that there is no choice left; the economy *has* to grow.

Economists generally agree that good environmental quality is a scarce commodity. Most of them acknowledge that the market system does not adequately incorporate externalities, such as pollution of the nation's water supply by industry, into its pricing system. However, this problem cannot be solved by limiting growth or by eliminating it.

Let's examine the problem of water. The world is running short of clean water, yet our need for it is growing with each passing year. Industries use millions of gallons of it hourly—for quenching steel ingots, for washing paper pulp, for cooling nuclear power plants, for cleaning newly slaughtered animals being readied for market, for washing away the chemicals from textile mills, and for thousands of other uses. The *effluent*—that is, the used water that flows out of factories—is usually dumped into nearby rivers or streams. The water itself is not used up in this process. Rather, we have to clean it so that we can use it again, for bathing, swimming, cooking, and drinking.

To solve this problem, we could do three things: (1) *set minimum standards for industrial effluents* (though this would circumvent the market, and create large bureaucratic costs), (2) *tax industrial effluents* (this would make firms—and ultimately consumers—internalize the costs of pollution) or (3) Sell the rights to pollute water and raise the revenues to clean it up.

How Population Enters the Picture

Both economists and ecologists point out that the problems of economic growth are inextricably tied in with the problems of population growth. However, as industrialization and urbanization take place, population growth tends to level off—even to decline. Families that live in urban, industrial societies acquire education and realize that children are consumers, not producers. Also, since a pollution-free environment is a "luxury" good, demand for it rises with income. As the economy continues to grow, people may be expected to demand more of this luxury (income superior) good and substitute it for the relatively less desirable (income inferior) good, in other words, more children.

It is mainly ecologists who present the anti-growth view, but some economists join in. Fundamentally, the arguments are founded on the belief that it is nature that imposes the limits to growth. As the distinguished historian Arnold Toynbee put it:

More and more people are coming to realize that the growth of material wealth, which the British industrial revolution set going, and which the modern British-made ideology has presented as being mankind's proper paramount objective, cannot in truth be the "wave of the future." Nature is going to compel posterity to revert to a stable state on the material plane and to turn to the realm of the spirit for satisfying man's hunger for infinity.

Economist Kenneth Boulding has argued that we must move from viewing the economy as an open system, with unlimited resources and growth (the "cowboy economy"), to a "spaceship earth" closed economy (the "spaceman economy"). Boulding says that in the latter system, consumption and production that use up finite (nonreproducible) resources is not "good." Society must distinguish between reproducible and nonreproducible resources.

As Some Ecologists Have Seen It

Zero Economic Growth (ZEG)
The argument that GNP growth should be stopped.

Zero Population Growth (ZPG)
The argument that population growth should be stopped.

Others, such as Herman Daly, argued for many years that "growthmania"—the insistence that growth is the solution to economic problems—had outlived its usefulness. This view was reinforced by certain famous computer studies (the 1971 Club of Rome study is the most famous one) that predicted disaster unless growth trends were reversed. Daly and others argued not only for **zero economic growth (ZEG)**, *no* increase in GNP, but also **zero population growth (ZPG)**, no increase in population. To alleviate any hardships that this reversal of industrial history would cause, they wanted to see constant controls on physical wealth and distribution of income.

Such ecologists reject the market solution, which would entail forcing industries to internalize the externalities. Two observers, Richard England and Barry Bluestone, maintained, however, that this would require *total recycling* of wastes, with an accompanying "astronomical cost."

As Many Economists Have Seen It

Economists in favor of ZEG have argued that using selective means, such as tax cuts, to stimulate consumer spending is *not* necessary to maintain full employment. They say that a guaranteed annual income can maintain a full-employment level of spending just as well, and accomplish many of the same objectives.

In rebuttal, economists who opposed ZEG generally (1) attacked the idea (which is implicit in the computer models) that the supply of resources is static—that the world will soon run out of oil, coal, and other essentials; (2) argued that leaving resources unused so that future generations may use them may not be as important as the capital and technology that would result from using them in the present; (3) felt that the ZEG and ZPG groups underestimate the ability of the price system to ensure efficient use of resources, to cause substitutes to be developed, and to force industry (when required to) to internalize the externalities that may have been ignored in the past.

Growth and the Environment: A New Consensus?

As America enters the 1990s, concerns for achieving an acceptable level of environmental quality seem to be growing. At the same time, few people now seem inclined to advocate stopping economic growth to solve problems such as acid rain or the greenhouse effect. Indeed, as political scientist Robert Slavins has argued: "A new environmentalism has now emerged that embraces market-oriented environmental-protection policies." In 1989, the nation elected a president who calls himself the "environment president." Both economists and ecologists now see that there are major environmental problems and, unlike the earlier era, many ecologists now believe market forces can be harnessed to help solve these problems in ways consistent with maintaining economic growth.

Cartoon Feature Syndicate

SUMMING UP

1. Until recently, twentieth-century economists, unlike their nineteenth-century forerunners, generally held an optimistic view of economic growth and its potential for solving economic problems. In the late-1980s, optimism is tempered by the need to maintain environmental quality.

2. Certainly it is not economic growth alone that is responsible for polluting the environment. In fact, many economists believe that economic growth and the free market can solve the problems of the environment in the future.

3. Walter Heller said that economic growth seems destined to continue and that (a) economists and ecologists disagree over whether the quality of life has improved in recent years; (b) ecologists see absolute limits to growth and to resources, while economists do not; and (c) ecologists want government to solve environmental problems, while economists rely heavily on the market system.

4. The market system does not incorporate externalities, such as pollution of the nation's water supply by industry, into its pricing system. The solutions to this might be (a) to set minimum standards for industrial effluents, or (b) to tax industrial effluents so that producers (and ultimately consumers) would have to pay the full social costs of polluting the water.

5. Economic growth is inextricably intertwined with population growth. However, population growth declines with economic growth, since children in an urban, industrial society are nonproducers and people begin to prefer higher *per capita* income as well as environmental improvement to more children.

6. Arnold Toynbee argued that growth is not the wave of the future, but that natural forces will force the world's people to revert to a stable state, that is, no growth.

7. Some economists and ecologists have decried "growthmania" and argued for both *zero economic growth (ZEG)* and *zero population growth (ZPG)*. They argued that obtaining these would necessitate government controls over physical wealth and distribution of income.

8. Some ecologists rejected for many years the idea of the free market offering the solution to environmental pollution, on the grounds that the cost of total recycling of wastes would be astronomical.

9. Economists in favor of ZEG said that a guaranteed annual income (with its income redistribution effect) would be a good

substitute for economic growth. A guaranteed annual income, they said, would sustain consumption demand and thereby keep employment at an acceptable level.

10. In rebutting the gloomy arguments of the ecologists, most economists oppose ZEG on the grounds that (a) resources are not static, (b) it is better to leave capital and technology to posterity than to leave unused resources to posterity, (c) proponents of ZEG and ZPG underestimate the ability of the price system to change patterns of resource use and to induce people to use and find substitutes for nonreproducible resources.

11. In the early-1990s, there appears to be a growing consensus among economists and ecologists that environmental problems are severe and that market solutions to many of these problems are possible without sacrificing economic growth.

KEY TERMS

Zero economic growth (ZEG)
Zero population growth (ZPG)

QUESTIONS

1. What is the relationship between economic growth and the solutions to such ills as poverty, discrimination, and the welfare situation?

2. Is pollution of the environment *necessarily* the result of economic growth? If not, what else might it result from?

3. How may the market system—either with or without additional government control—develop solutions to problems of pollution?

4. What does Boulding mean by the "spaceship earth" concept?

5. State what you think of the arguments for and against ZEG.

SUGGESTED READINGS

Boulding, Kenneth E. "The Economics of the Coming Spaceship Earth," in *Environmental Quality in a Growing Economy*. Johns Hopkins, Baltimore, 1966.

Brown, Lester R., Christopher Flavin, and Sandra Pastel. "No Time to Waste: A Global Environmental Agenda for the Bush Administration." *Shared Watch*. January/February, 1989.

Daly, Herman E. "The Steady-State Economy: Toward a Political Economy of Biophysical Equilibrium and Moral Growth," in *Toward a Steady-State Economy.* Edited by Herman E. Daly. Freeman, San Francisco, 1973.

Drayton, William. "Economic Law Enforcement." *Harvard Environmental Law Review,* 4, No. 1. 1980.

Hailstones, Thomas J. and Frank V. Mastrianna. *Contemporary Economic Problems and Issues.* Cincinnati South Western Publishing Co., 1988. Chapter 10, "Clean Air—Are We Willing to Pay the Price?"

Heller, Walter W. "Economic Growth and Ecology, an Economist's View," in *Economics, Mainstream, Reading and Radical Critiques,* 2nd ed. Edited by David Mermelstein. Random House, New York, 1973.

Krupp, Frederic D. "New Environmentalism Factors in Economic Needs." *Wall Street Journal.* 20 November, 1986.

Meadows, D. H. et al. *The Limits to Growth.* Universe Books, New York, 1972.

Stavins, Robert N. "Harnessing Market Forces to Protect the Environment." *Environment.* January/February, 1989. Reprinted in Annual Edition Economics 90/91. Don Cole, Editor. Hince Dock, Guilford, Conn., 1990.

Tietenberg, Tom. *Emissions Trading: An Exercise in Reforming Pollution Policy.* Washington, D.C. Resources for the Future, 1985.

Chapter 17:
Patterns of International Trade

We have analyzed the many aspects of a single market. The society we looked at was a *closed economy,* one that did not trade with other nations. Most of our discussions began with abstract ideas; then we added the complexities of reality. We introduced each topic this way because it is easier to see a tree without the forest around it. Then we put in the forest, a little at a time. Finally, by the end of each discussion, we had built principles that were applicable to a wide range of problems.

Now we will remove the last, and most significant, of the simplifying assumptions: that the U.S. is an economic island unto itself. In other words, we will now look at America as an *open economy,* one that trades with the rest of the world and that must finance that trade. Everyone is aware that the U.S. does indeed trade with other nations and, indeed, has the largest volume of international trade of any nation. In 1986, U.S. merchandise imports and exports together totaled $591.3 billion.

What Is Trade?

Visible Items
Those physical commodities that are exported or imported by a nation.

Invisible Items
The services including financial services associated with exports and imports by a nation.

Trade consists of *exports*—commodities and services sold to other nations—and *imports*—commodities and services bought from other nations. Suppose that a dealer in San Francisco imports a Toyota. The price the importer pays (plus any shipping charges paid to foreign shippers) is added to the total of U.S. imports. Similarly, when a Japanese grain dealer imports American wheat, the payments that U.S. wheat sellers receive (plus any payments to our own shippers) are added to the total of our exports.

Thus, international trade is made up of both **visible items** and **invisible items**. The visible items are the commodities (cars, wheat, television sets, petroleum, machinery, and so on) that are exported and imported. Invisible items are the services, including financial services (services of exporters and importers, ship rentals, cost of financing, and so on) which are exported and imported.

How Important Is Trade to America?

Only a few years ago, you might have said: "Look, the U.S. is a big nation; it produces a great variety of goods and services and has vast natural resources. Surely, trade with other nations isn't all that important to us. Why devote a whole chapter to it?" Now, hardly a day passes without reference in the media to the importance of foreign trade to our economy and to the jobs of its people. Deficits in trade (imports > exports) are front page news to which stock markets react. Negotiations between the U.S. and Japan over further opening of Japanese markets to American exports are both economically and politically sensitive. Arguments about what the dollar-yen exchange rate should be are not mere academic issues. International trade and the financing of that trade had, by the late-1980s, become vital issues and seem likely to increase in importance as the nation progresses into the 1990s.

Trade and the American Economy

Balance of Trade
The difference between a nation's exports of goods and services and its imports of goods and services (also called net foreign trade).

A nation's exports constitute sales of its goods and services to other economies; its imports, of course, constitute purchases from other economies. The difference between exports (X) and imports (M) is known as the **balance of trade** (or *net foreign trade (NFT)*).

Balance of Trade = X − M

When the balance of trade is positive (X > M), a nation is selling more of its goods and services abroad than it is purchasing from other nations. This positive NFT is commonly referred to as "favorable" balance of trade. When the balance of trade is negative (X < M), the nation is purchasing more goods and services from abroad than it is selling to other economies; the negative NFT is commonly referred to as an "unfavorable" balance of trade. While one should be cautious about reading too much into the terms "favorable" and "unfavorable," it is well to remember that differences between exports and imports (sales and purchases) must be financed each year by every nation.

What has been the record of the American economy in recent years regarding NFT? From Table 17-1, you can see that from 1960 to the 1980s there were years in which X − M was very small and reflected an occasional surplus (X > M) and often a small deficit (X < M). Throughout the period, however, the effect was relatively small. After 1980, and especially after 1983, the pattern changed both qualitatively and quantitatively. During the period from 1983 to 1987, X − M was consistently negative and growing. The dramatic growth of the NFT deficit (from $19.6

Table 17-1
U.S. Exports, Imports,* and Net Foreign Trade, 1960-1986 (billions of dollars)

Year	Merchandise + Service Exports (X)	Merchandise + Service Imports (M)	Net Foreign Trade (X-M)
1960	98.4	102.4	-4.0
1965	132.0	134.7	-2.7
1970	178.3	208.3	-30.0
1975	259.7	240.8	18.9
1980	388.9	332.0	-56.9
1981	392.7	343.4	-49.3
1982	361.9	335.6	26.3
1983	349.4	368.8	-19.6
1984	370.9	455.9	-85.0
1985	359.9	468.3	-108.4
1986	368.4	498.6	-130.2

*Merchandise plus Services

Source: *Economic Report of the President,* 1987.

billion in 1983 to $130.2 billion in 1986) seems to have come about because of:

1. *Changes in exchange rates.* Between 1980 and mid-1985, U.S. dollar/foreign currency exchange rates soared. Against the currencies of America's major trading partners, the dollar increased in value almost 70 percent. Goods imported into the U.S. became relatively cheaper while Americans exports became relatively more expensive. Our rising quantity demanded of imports and the declining quantity demanded of our exports pushed X – M to ever larger negative figures.

2. In the face of the tax changes and other stimulative actions from 1982 on, the American economy and the real incomes of its citizens grew. Since Colonial days, Americans have had a strong (income-related) taste for imported goods. A growing demand for imports, combined with declining prices added fuel to the large NFT deficits.

But is Trade as Important to Us as to Others?

Perhaps you are saying, "All right, granted that foreign trade *can* have an effect on the U.S. economy, and will continue to do so in the 1990s, is the effect really important compared to the other factors that influence jobs, and the welfare of Americans?" One way to answer the question is to look at how large a part exports or sales abroad are of the GNP or final value of all goods and services produced in America. Table 17-2 shows that for the U.S., exports make up a smaller percentage of GNP than they do for the other nations listed. Trade constitutes only 7 percent of U.S. GNP, but for the other nations, which account for a large part of the world's trade, the figure ranges up to almost 75 percent (Belgium).

Do these figures mean that trade is relatively unimportant to the U.S.? The answer is, emphatically, *no*—for the following reasons:

1. The 7 percent represents an important part of the demand for U.S. output and thus the derived demand for labor (jobs) and other resources. If this foreign market for U.S. goods were to disappear, it would mean not just an 7 percent reduction in GNP, but a much larger reduction.

2. The additional demand created by trade enables American firms to operate more efficiently and to achieve economies of scale that might not otherwise be possible. Because of this international trade, manufacturers are able to lower their costs. This means not only potentially lower prices to consumers (both for exported goods and for goods produced in the U.S. from exported inputs), but also more profitable investment opportunities and demand for labor (jobs).

3. In recent years, the percentage-of-GNP figure for foreign trade has grown, as we see in Table 17-2. Early in U.S. history, trade was very important to the economy of the U.S. Then, as the U.S. came of age, the importance of foreign trade declined. Now, there seems to be a resurgence of international trade as a mainstay of the U.S. economy.

4. One big reason for the increased importance of trade is the growing dependence of the U.S. on imports of raw materials. The U.S. now imports over 40 percent of the petroleum it uses (even in the 1950s it was an exporter of oil). And although the U.S. has huge mineral resources, it must import 100 percent of the chromium and tin it uses, as well as between 90 percent and 100 percent of such minerals as cobalt, manganese, platinum, and

Table 17-2
Exports as a Percentage of GNP for Some Industrialized Nation

Nation	1960	1985
Belgium	33.3	74.5
Italy	12.9	23.7
United Kingdom	20.0	28.8
Mexico	10.6	20.8
West Germany	20.0	35.5
Japan	11.5	16.5
United States	4.9	7.0

Source: International Monetary Fund, International Financial Statistics, 1986, International Financial Statistics, 1987

nickel. In other words, the U.S. *needs* foreign trade for the sake of our industrial economy.

Of course, the U.S. must, as we noted earlier, pay the countries from which it imports in their own currencies. Japanese business firms want yen, not dollars, so that they can pay their workers and other costs. In turn, to earn these foreign currencies, the U.S. must export its own goods and services as well as import capital.

The Gains from Trade

Earlier in our history, there were those who argued for isolationism, both politically and economically. Even today, there might be some who would say: "Apart from those needed minerals (and we can probably find substitutes even for many of them in the long run), I fail to see that we are necessarily better off because of trading. After all, we can use macroeconomic policy to achieve full employment, even without trade. Surely if we made the effort, we could produce just about everything we want. Where is the advantage to be had from trade?"

The answer to the above question is not obvious. The U.S. is among a few fortunate nations that probably could—from a technical point of view—achieve *autarky*, economic self-sufficiency. Most food can be grown in the U.S.—even tropical fruits. The nation could achieve self-sufficiency in energy, too, if it chose to do so. But is complete self-sufficiency necessarily desirable—for the U.S. or for any nation? Virtually all economists say no, for reasons we shall now examine.

Trade and Comparative Advantage

In discussing the reasons for trade among nations, one immediately encounters two terms: the *absolute advantage* and the *comparative advantage* that each nation has in producing things. We can best define these terms by example.

Let's say that you are a graduate engineer, and you set up a personal, if hypothetical, small business of your own. You have an assistant named Pat Bloggs, who does the filing and other routine jobs in your office. You pay Bloggs $30 a day to perform these tasks, while you, as a professional engineer, earn $100 a day. After a particularly hellish week, in which drawings have gone to the wrong firm and correspondence has been mislaid in the wrong folders, you review the operation of the office. You realize that you can do these routine chores much more efficiently than Bloggs. Thus you have an *absolute advantage* over Bloggs. Should you fire Bloggs and do the job yourself? No! The $100 a day you earn as an engineer reflects your marginal revenue productivity (MRP); the $30 reflects Bloggs' *MRP*. Therefore, you should stick to your specialty of engineering, because in this you have a *comparative advantage*. In other words, you are relatively more productive as an engineer than as an office assistant. There is a lesson to be learned here. Even a person with an absolute advantage in doing *every* task should specialize in that field in which her or his comparative advantage lies.

We demonstrated how this principle works when we were discussing the market system of a single country: for efficiency's sake, resources should move to their most productive alternative uses. A city could hire engineers to sweep the streets, and they would probably do a great job. But it would be foolish for a society to employ its engineers in this way, since their comparative efficiency is greater when they are building roads, bridges, and offshore drilling rigs.

Now let's apply this idea of comparative advantage to trade between nations. In the real word, international trade involves many nations and thousands of commodities and services. To keep things simple in this illustration, though, we shall deal with only two nations, the U.S. and Honduras. We will examine the trade in only 2 commodities that each country can produce—tractors and bananas. Discussing additional goods and countries would not change the basic principles; it would just make the relationships more complex.

Table 17-3 shows the production-possibilities schedules for the U.S. and Honduras. Each country is capable of producing both bananas and tractors. However, note that the rate at which tractors can be traded off for bananas (that is, the rate at which the output of tractors decreases as the output of bananas increases) is very different for the two countries. The reason is that there are different resource endowments in the two countries including climate and human capital.

Figure 17-1 illustrates the production possibilities for the two countries. Unlike the production-possibilities curves we saw earlier, these "curves" are straight lines. That is, they reflect a constant rate of exchange of tractors for bananas (we are assuming

Table 17-3
Production-Possibilities Schedules, United States and Honduras (Hypothetical)

United States		Honduras	
Units of Tractors	Units of Bananas	Units of Tractors	Units of Bananas
50	0	0	100
40	5	5	80
30	10	10	60
20	15	15	40
10	20	20	20
0	25	25	0

Figure 17-1
Production Possibilities for (a) the United States and (b) Honduras

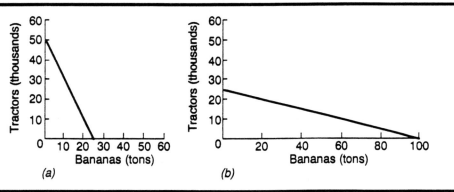

that the cost of producing each item is constant). Later in this chapter we will discuss production-possibilities curves that are concave to the origin and reflect increasing real cost.

The Terms of Trade

Terms of Trade
The ratio for a nation at which its exports exchange for its imports.

Now that we have established that the U.S. should specialize in producing tractors, and Honduras should specialize in bananas, the real **terms of trade** (the relation for a nation between at which its exports exchange for imports) must be decided. That is, a ratio must be determined at which Honduran bananas will be exchanged for U.S. tractors. There must be an advantage for each country. The Americans must get more than ½ unit of bananas for each unit of their tractors, and the Hondurans more than 1 unit of tractors for 4 units of their bananas.

Each country must get more for its products in the world market than it would if it had sold them domestically. If both countries are to benefit, the actual exchange rate must lie between 1T = ½B (preferred by Honduras) and 1T = 4B (preferred by the U.S.).

The exact terms of trade will depend on the market demand for both products. Market demand depends on the degree to which one can substitute other products for either commodity, and on the relationship of demand to supply. If there are no good substitutes for tractors, and if demand for them is large relative to supply, the exchange rate (terms of trade) will be in favor of the U.S. If conditions are reversed, the terms of trade will be favorable to Honduras.

Suppose that the exchange rate moves to 1T = 2B. Figure 17-2 shows what happens to production and consumption in both countries. Look at the replotted production-possibilities curves of both countries. The dark lines (called consumption-possibilities curves), indicating consumption after trade, show what each country can consume if it specializes in the good in which it has a

Figure 17-2
Production-Consumption Possibilities for (a) the United States and (b) Honduras (after trade)

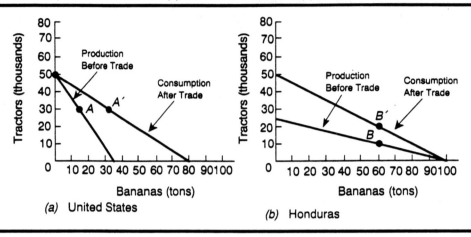

(a) United States

(b) Honduras

comparative advantage and exports part of its output. For example, at point A´, if the U.S. consumes 30,000 of its tractors and exports 20,000 to Honduras, it can import 40,000 tons of bananas in exchange. Thus, it can have 40 units of tractors plus 20 units of bananas, as opposed to 30 units of tractors and 10 units of bananas before trade (point A).

Likewise, at point B, Honduras, before exchange, can produce and consume 10 units of tractors and 60 units of bananas. With trade, it has 60 units of bananas and exports its remaining 40 units of bananas for 20 units of tractors, a combination that is much better (point B´).

The important result that Figure 17-2 enables us to visualize is:

As long as a nation has a comparative advantage in producing some things, it should specialize in producing those things. It should then export part of the goods for which it has a comparative advantage and import goods in which it has a comparative disadvantage. By so doing, it will have more to consume.

This is true even if the nation has an absolute advantage in producing everything it consumes.

What Determines Comparative Advantage?

Since we have shown that comparative advantage is a mutually advantageous basis for trade, we need to identify the factors that determine a nation's comparative advantage. Also we want to ask the question: Are nations locked into a particular comparative-advantage position, or do their positions change?

First, *nations have differing comparative advantages*, for the following reasons:

1. Different nations have different endowments of natural resources, both in quantity and quality. For example, nations such as the U.S., Canada, the Soviet Union, and the People's Republic of China have large quantities (although different proportions) of relatively high-grade resources (petroleum, mineral deposits, topsoil, and so on).

2. Different nations have different physical features (mild or extreme climate, many or few natural harbors).

3. Different nations are at different stages of development of markets. For example, the U.S., Japan, and the countries in Western Europe have well-developed capital markets, reflecting large supplies of savings that can be transformed through investment into capital, including human capital (skills and abilities resulting from investment in education). In other countries, markets may be either rudimentary or nonexistent.

4. Different nations have different supplies of factors of production, including labor. For example, China and many other less developed countries have large supplies of labor relative to capital.
A country tends to specialize in products (or services) that intensively use those resources in which it is relatively rich.
Second, *the comparative advantages of nations change.* Nations are not locked into a position with respect to comparative advantage. For example, the U.S. began as a nation rich in land and short of capital and labor. Today, it is relatively rich in capital and land, and relatively short of labor. (This has nothing to do with our unemployment rate. It means that, as the U.S. presently produces things—even at full employment —capital and land are abundant relative to labor.) Up until the Civil War, the U.S. specialized in land-intensive agricultural exports (cotton, tobacco, rice, and so on). Today, it specializes in exports that are capital-intensive and land-intensive. For example, in 1984, more than 50 percent of U.S. exports were comprised of machinery, transportation, services, equipment, chemicals, goods manufactured of iron and steel, and nonferrous metals—all fairly capital-intensive. Another 10 percent were grains and cereals, which are land-intensive. Thus, more than 60 percent, nearly two-thirds of U.S. exports, were derived from processes that were capital- and land-intensive. On the other hand, the U.S. mainly imports things (coffee, cocoa, inexpensive textiles, handicrafts) that are relatively labor-intensive.

Demand Considerations

Domestic economic trade is, as we have seen, based on the benefits of voluntary exchange.

International trade whether between nations or as is most often the case, between individuals, is also based on expected benefits of voluntary exchange. We saw in Figure 17-2 that supply (cost based) considerations make it possible for nations, through exchange, to consume more with trade. There are also important benefits to trade that derive from demand considerations. The structure of demand differs greatly from one country to another as well as from one part of the world to another. The primary reason for these differences lies in the diversity of tastes and preferences that exists among individuals within countries as well as between different nations. Consider tastes in food and clothing. Americans (both North Americans and Latin Americans) prefer coffee; the English and many Asians prefer tea. The Japanese prefer fish; Americans have a much stronger taste for beef, pork and chicken. Out of these differences arises a willingness to pay prices for goods and services that differs substantially from one area to another and, thus, gains to be had in exporting.

There are many arguments about changing the comparative advantages of countries, especially about whether comparative-advantage trade tends to help the poor trading nations to develop. In the application which follows this chapter, we will examine some of these arguments.

Increasing Costs and Other Cautions

In the case involving the U.S. and Honduras, we concluded that each would produce only its most advantageous good, tractors or bananas. We showed that bilateral exchange between the two nations would make both better off in terms of the quantities of the two goods available for consumption. There are some qualifications to the argument, however.

1. As each country reallocates its resources from the disadvantageous good to the advantageous one, it will run into *increasing costs*. For example, as the U.S. produces more tractors, the cost (in bananas not produced) may rise, until it reaches a point at which it would be better off if it produced some bananas of its own rather than always exchanging tractors for Honduran bananas. Honduras, whose costs of producing bananas also rise, may be better off producing some of its own tractors. The point is that increasing costs cause international specialization to be less than complete.

2. When two countries specialize in making things in which they have a comparative advantage and then trade with each other, achieving the greatest possible production, we assume that there is full employment in the trading nations. However, at times this trade means reallocating resources, and when this results in unemployment, the countries' output may fall below the production-possibilities curve. So there are some possible undesirable effects for a country from trade. But there are various macroeconomic

(fiscal and monetary) tools that a nation can use to achieve its employment goals, and there are microeconomic tools that can be used to reallocate resources in efficient resource markets (job retraining, for example). Thus, many economists feel that the risk of creating temporary unemployment is not a compelling reason to forego trade.

3. The principle of comparative advantage depends heavily on *competition* in international trade. If the tractors are produced by a monopolistic firm but the bananas are exported by competitive firms, Honduras may not fully reap the benefits of trade. If monopolistic export boards (perhaps government ones) negotiate the terms of trade (American wheat for Russian oil, for example), one cannot tell what the outcome will be. This is also true of bilateral monopoly. The end result depends on the relative skills and bargaining strengths of the participants.

4. If there are *externalities*, the terms of trade may not reflect the real costs of production. The countries may produce and exchange either too little or too much. (Suppose that the tractor factories pollute the water and air and that their costs do not reflect the added social costs of cleaning up the environment.)

5. The principle of comparative advantage depends on the fact that relative prices (the American price of tractors and the Honduran price of bananas) reflect relative scarcities of resources in each nation. If the prices do not reflect these scarcities, an international (as well as domestic) misallocation of resources occurs. Suppose that the U.S. subsidizes the tractor industry. Then international prices of tractors (the terms of trade) would not reflect underlying relative scarcity and companies would produce more tractors than is efficient (and trade them). (Americans would, in effect, be producing tractors when they should be producing bananas.)

Protectionism
Efforts by governments to protect domestic firms and industries from the competition of imported goods.

6. The biggest obstacle to trade being conducted according to comparative advantage is **protectionism**, the efforts of governments to protect domestic firms or industries from the competition of imported goods. Consequently, there has been little completely free trade in modern times (or indeed at any time).

The Means of Protection

There are two principal means by which countries usually intervene to protect their own industries from overseas competition: tariffs and quotas.

Tariffs
Taxes on imported goods.

Tariffs
The most common means of protection are **tariffs**, which are taxes on imported goods. Figure 17-3 shows how a protective tariff

Figure 17-3
How a Protective Tariff Works

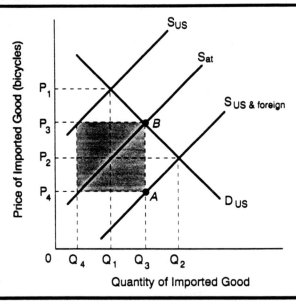

Figure 17-3 illustrates the effects of a protective tariff. The domestic supply of the good is S_{US} and the domestic demand, D_{US}. Without trade equilibrium price is P_1 and Q_1 of the good is sold. If free trade in the good occurs, imports increase the domestic supply to $S_{US \& foreign}$. As a result of trade, price declines to P_2 and Q_2 of the good is sold. Both the decline in price and the increased consumption of the good ($Q_2 - Q_1$) are benefits to consumers attributable to trade. If a protective tariff of AB supply declines to S_{at}, with the tariff, price rises to P_3 and quantity sold declines to Q_3. Both the increase in price (P_2 to P_3) and the decrease in consumption of the good ($Q_2 - Q_3$) are costs to consumers attributable to protectionism.

works and also shows its effects on trade and prices. Before trade begins, the U.S. demand for bicycles is D_{US} and the supply is S_{US}. Equilibrium price is P_1 ($Q_1 D_{US} = Q_1 S_{US}$). At this price, Q_1 of bicycles are sold. (Presumably, bicycles are goods in which this country has a comparative *dis*advantage.) Now trade opens up. The U.S. begins to import foreign bicycles (from Japan, Italy, and France). The supply of bicycles increases to $S_{US \& foreign}$. Equilibrium price falls to P_2, and Q_1 bicycles are sold. The supply increases until the price of bicycles in the U.S. is equal to the price of bicycles abroad (not including transportation costs). As long as the American price is higher, foreign producers will continue to export bicycles in order to sell in the more profitable American market.

Now suppose that the bicycle manufacturers complain to Congress, as the Bicycle Manufacturers' Association did in the 1970s. They argued as follows:

> A deluge of imported bicycles into the U.S. has increased imports from 19.8 percent of our market in 1964 to 37.1 percent in 1972. We don't feel our business should go down the drain. Standards must be established that would automatically impose restrictions on imports competing with American products.... This is not protectionism.

"He wasn't even warm—was he, Mom?"

Let's say that the bicycle lobby convinces Congress that this argument is valid, so that Congress levies a tax—a tariff—on imported bicycles. The tax which is equal to AB in Figure 17-3 increases the cost of importing bicycles and reduces the supply to S_{at} (supply after tariff). The new equilibrium price is P_3, which is higher than the pre-tariff price (by $P_3 - P_2$). The number of bicycles sold goes down (by $Q_2 - Q_3$). Note that part of the gain to consumers from all the foreign bicycles coming into the country is eliminated. If the tariff had been higher, imports might have ceased altogether, and supply might have fallen back to S_{US}. Then price would have gone back up to P_1 (with only Q_1 sold).

So the tariff hurts consumers, because now they must buy bicycles at a price higher than the international price, and they are getting fewer bicycles. The tariff also hurts foreign bicycle manufacturers, because the net price they receive (after paying the tariff) is P_4. In addition, the tariff hurts U.S. firms that may use the product as an input (messenger services and the like). The total revenue to the U.S. government from the tariff is shown by the shaded area. This is the unit tariff per bicycles ($P_3 - P_4$) times the number of bicycles imported ($Q_3 - Q_4$). (At price P_3, American manufacturers supply Q_4.)

Elasticity and the Burden of the Tariff

You probably recognize that the burden of the tariff (either the higher price to consumers or the lower net price to sellers) is distributed on the basis of the price elasticity of demand for the imported good. We see in Figures 17-4 and 17-5 how the distributive burden of the tariff is related to elasticity. There may be both a *consumer burden*, the portion of a tariff paid by consumers in higher prices and a *producer burden*, the portion of a tariff paid by importers in a lower net price and reduced sales of the imported good.

In Figure 17-4 the demand for the imported good is price inelastic, implying that poor substitutes exist for the good or that consumers spend relatively little of their incomes on it. With unrestricted trade, the bicycle market clears at Q_{wt} (quantity without tariff) and at price, P_{wt} (price without tariff). After tariff AB is levied, supply is reduced from $S_{US \& foreign}$ to S_{at} (supply after tariff). Now the market is cleared at Q_{at} and P_{at} (quantity and

Figure 17-4
The Burden of a Tariff With Inelastic Demand

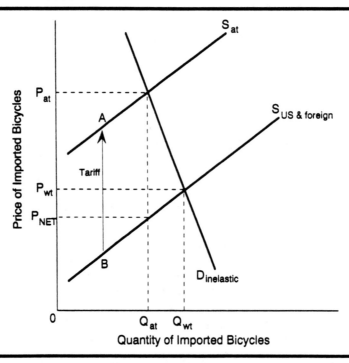

The burden of a tariff is related to the elasticity of demand for the imported good. Figure 17-4 illustrates the relationship for the case in which demand is price *inelastic*. Without a tariff supply is $S_{US \& foreign}$ and price with tariff is P_{wt} and quantity sold before the tariff Q_{wt}. A tariff of AB on the imported good decreases supply after tariff to S_{at}. As a result, price rises to P_{at} and quantity sold declines to Q_{at}. There is a large increase in price (P_{wt} to P_{at}) relative to the decline in sales ($Q_{wt} - Q_{at}$). Most of the burden of the tariff is borne by consumers in the form of higher prices though foreign producers also are burdened by the lower net price (P_{NET} as opposed to P_{wt}).

Figure 17-5
The Burden of a Tariff With Elastic Demand

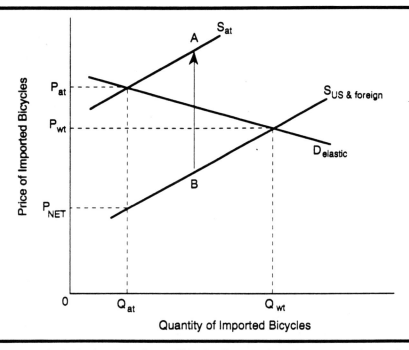

We see in Figure 17-5 how the burden of a tariff is distributed when the demand for the imported good is price elastic. Before the tariff, with elastic demand, $D_{elastic}$, and supply, $S_{U.S. \& foreign}$, price is P_{wt} and the quantity sold of the good is Q_{wt}. When tariff AB is imposed, costs of importing the good rise, and supply declines to S_{at} resulting in a higher price (P_{wt} to P_{at}) and a decrease in the quantity of the good sold (Q_{wt} to Q_{at}) and a lower net price (P_{NET}) to foreign producers. There is a large decrease in quantity sold relative to the increase in price and most of the burden of the tariff falls on firms importing the good.

price after tariff). Most of the market burden ($P_{at} - P_{wt}$) is borne by consumers in the form of higher prices but part, $Q_w - Q_{at}$ is borne by producers in the form of reduced sales and a lower net price (P_{NET}). Clearly, however, consumers absorb most of the burden.

In Figure 17-5, we see the reverse. The demand for the imported good is price elastic; implying that relatively good substitutes for the imported good exist or that consumers spend a significant part of their income on it. With unrestricted trade, the market clears at Q_{wt} and P_{wt}. After tariff AB is imposed, supply falls from $S_{US \& foreign}$ to S_{at} and the market clears at Q_{at} and price P_{at}. The consumer burden $P_{at} - P_{wt}$ is relatively small while the producer burden, $Q_{wt} - Q_{at}$ and the lower net price ($P_{wt} - P_{NET}$) is relatively large. Clearly, when demand is elastic, most of the burden falls on producers in the form of reduced sales and lower net prices

Is anyone better off as a result of the tariff? Yes, the American bicycle manufacturers are. They do not have to pay the tariff, so they keep the full price (P_{at}) of their product. This is higher than P_{NET}, which is the price foreign makers have after they pay the tariff. The federal government is better off by the amount of revenue. The tariff, in other words, represents a loss in income by consumers, which is transferred to the government and protected domestic firms.

Beyond the burden, two points about tariffs should be emphasized: (1) When the government imposes a tariff, it makes a *net addition to domestic monopoly power.* In our example, bicycle manufacturers had been getting a competitively set international price for their product. Now they are getting a more monopolistically established price instead. (Though in this case the government, rather than private business, is the agent that creates the monopoly influence.) Thus, tariffs defeat our objective of having a competitive market system. (2) When the government imposes a general tariff (or other trade restriction), it *reduces the number of good substitutes that consumers have for domestically produced goods.* This, in turn, may make the demand *more price inelastic* and (because it increases monopoly power) may cause prices in the long run to rise by an even greater amount than the amount of the tariff itself.

Import Quotas

Import Quotas
Restrictions imposed by governments on the quantity of a good that may be imported.

The second major means governments' use to protect their industries against competition from abroad is **import quotas,** that is, restrictions on the quantity of goods that may be imported. In one way, the effects of quotas are much like those of tariffs. Look again at Figure 17-3. Suppose that Congress, instead of enacting a tariff, had said that only $Q_3 - Q_4$ bicycles could come into the U.S. Supply would still have dropped to S_{at} (or S_{aq} to stand for "supply after quota"). Total supply (Q_3) would have been domestic supply (Q_4) plus foreign supply ($Q_3 - Q_4$). Consumers would be affected just as adversely and U.S. bicycle makers would still get the higher price, P_3. The difference is that *a quota is not a revenue-producing device* (the shaded area would not exist), so the government would not get any extra tax revenue. Foreign bicycle makers would get the same price as domestic makers, P_3 (less transportation costs, of course), and domestic consumers would carry the burden of the quota.

Import Embargo
A prohibition on the importation of a good imposed by government.

The most extreme form of a quota is an **import embargo,** which is an absolute prohibition against importing a good. If Congress had imposed an embargo on foreign bicycles, supply would have reverted to S_{US}. Price would have risen to P_1 (domestic producers would have been restored to whatever monopoly power they originally had).

Embargoes are relatively rare in American history. In 1808, during the Napoleonic wars, President Jefferson imposed one. After 1962, the U.S. government embargoed trade with Cuba (no Cuban cigars, sugar, or rum). Until the 1970s, there was a U.S. embargo on trade with the People's Republic of China. It is worth noting that when embargoes are lifted, they are usually lifted in the interest of political expediency (détente, for example) rather than in the interests of free trade. Embargoes are usually short-term political penalties against antagonistic nations.

Export Quotas: Rational Ignorance by Consumers?

As we have seen, quotas have effects similar to tariffs except that they do not generate revenues for governments. In protecting domestic producers, governments sometimes assign shares of their domestic markets to foreign exporters. Examples of this in the U.S. include imports of textiles, apparel, and sugar. The American government assigns quotas to foreign governments (Dominican Republic, Taiwan, etc.), and those governments, recall, assign the quotas to their own producers. In all cases, of course, American consumers pay prices above the world price (for example, more than twice the world price of sugar). Clearly, American sugar producers have benefitted as well as foreign producers who are able to obtain quota shares. By one estimate, the value of these monopoly rights (rents) to foreign producers in 1987 was over $7 billion.

Why, you may ask, do such clear and obvious impediments to free trade exist when millions of consumers are harmed and a few thousand (domestic and foreign) producers reap the benefits. Why should consumers ignore these added costs rather than inform themselves fully and attempt to resist efforts by government to impose such costs? Many economists believe that the explanation lies in the concept of *rational ignorance*, the rationality of consumers in ignoring many proposals of government in view of the large costs of informing themselves about such proposals and the small individual benefits of doing so. It is worth reminding ourselves of this idea. Would you, for example, as a consumer of sugar, bother to inform yourself about monopoly sugar prices in the U.S. and lead a campaign to overturn the public decision to impose a quota system? Even if you were successful in eliminating quotas (a very unlikely result for one voter), the benefit/cost ratio of this activity to you would be unfavorable. Notice, though, that the same calculus would not apply to most private consumption decisions. Would you inform yourself about the private choice between a Chevrolet Corvette and a Nissan 300-ZX? In the latter instance, the benefits and costs would be quite different and almost certainly would make it irrational to ignore the information needed to be fully informed.

Many economists would argue that quotas are clearly less preferred to tariffs where governments intend to restrict international trade. Notice that tariffs create tax revenues whereas quotas generate benefits only to private producers. At least with tariffs, the revenues *could* be used to reduce other taxes as well as to fund public expenditure programs. It is for this reason that some economists have proposed auctioning the rights to export quotas. Presumably, the rights would bring something close to the $7 billion referred to earlier.

Arguments In Favor of Protection

As already noted, the U.S. has rarely if ever practiced completely free trade. (Neither have other countries.) Americans frequently say they believe in competition. But many, including many of their elected representatives, seem to argue against it when it is to their financial advantage. Economists in general—most U.S. economists, that is—sing the praises of free trade. But apparently, the economists who make public policy cannot completely convince the government. In the late-1980s, we again saw efforts to impose new restrictions on trade between the U.S. and other nations. In view of this continuing push for protectionism, let's examine the arguments most commonly advanced in favor of restricting trade.

The Infant-Industry Argument

The infant-industry argument is as follows: Industries that are just starting cannot meet the pressures of competition by similar, already established industries located in other, more industrially mature countries. Such infant industries deserve the protection of a tariff or other protective device, and they must be sheltered until they have become big enough to take advantage of economies of scale.

This argument may seem reasonable. However, there are opposing arguments: (1) Tariffs and other forms of protection, once enacted, are extremely hard to abolish. For example, the bicycle industry still enjoys tariff protection. So do the automobile and steel industries and many other U.S. industries that are hardly infants. (2) If an industry needs to be protected before it is mature, direct government subsidies are preferable, since they make the costs of such protection explicit. (3) The logic of the infant-industry argument is difficult to apply, since it is hard to know (in either a developed or underdeveloped nation) *which* infant industries will (and should) survive. Short of pursuing a goal of autarky, a nation must choose, without any clear guidelines, *which* infant industries to put into its protective and expensive incubator. The protecting nation runs the risk not only of distorting its uses of resources but even of ending up with an industry that fails anyway, especially if the protection is finally withdrawn.

The National-Security Argument

The national-security argument is as follows: The U.S. can never really be certain of the supply of a good produced in a foreign country. The nation cannot even depend on its present friends to help in a tight spot. This means that, when it comes to defense goods, U.S. security must take precedence over U.S. economic efficiency.

This argument is difficult for economists to judge, since there are no objective criteria by which to evaluate the tradeoff between increased national security and decreased industrial efficiency. Economists can only identify the costs involved in (1) levying tariffs or (2) directly subsidizing firms that make defense goods. Almost all economists would say that direct subsidies are preferable, because they identify the costs involved.

The Cheap-Foreign-Labor Argument
The cheap-foreign-labor argument can best be summed up in an example. The American textile industry, say proponents of protection, must be protected from imported textiles from nations such as Korea, Taiwan, and Malaysia. Wages in Korea and other such nations are so low that American firms cannot price their textiles low enough to compete. Although this argument is persuasive to many people, it is irrelevant to economists because (1) the higher wages of Americans presumably reflect higher marginal productivity; (2) it is socially inefficient to have an American firm that cannot compete with labor-intensive imports try to do so; and (3) it is less costly to retrain labor and reallocate resources to more efficient uses than it is to protect an inefficient industry. (However, remember the exception: the national-security argument.), and (4) wage costs are only part of the costs of production. Costs per unit of product produced depend not only on prices paid for labor but on labor's productivity. Much of the seeming advantage of low wage countries seems to be disappearing in the late-1980s. Much of this advantage has been in "blue collar" labor cost, which is declining and will continue to decline as a portion of total cost in the 1990s. Already, as Peter Drucker has observed, this no longer provides a competitive edge to low wage countries, and, as a result, we are witnessing a return of industries to the U.S. to take advantage of lower transport costs.

The Macroeconomic-Employment Argument
The macroeconomic-employment argument is that during hard times the U.S. can "export" some of its unemployment. (This is sometimes called a *beggar-thy-neighbor* argument.) Large segments of the business community (except big importers) and of labor often support this idea. The principle is to create more jobs at home by excluding, or sharply restricting, imports. Such an increase in domestic demand for formerly imported goods causes the U.S. to move toward full employment.

Has the U.S. followed the beggar-thy-neighbor principle? Figure 17-6 shows what has happened to tariffs during our "hard-times" periods. You can see that tariffs have been high during most recession and depression periods, such as the mid-1870s, 1890s, early-1900s (though they were falling then), and 1921. They were especially high in the early years of the Great Depression (the Hawley-Smoot tariffs, in 1930, were the highest in modern American history). The purpose of the so-called Tariff of Abominations (1828) was to protect U.S. infant industries such as textiles and iron. Tariffs have from time to time protected American makers of every sort of commodity. Cheese, watches, cameras, musical instruments, and machinery are some that come to mind.

Figure 17-6
History of American Tariffs

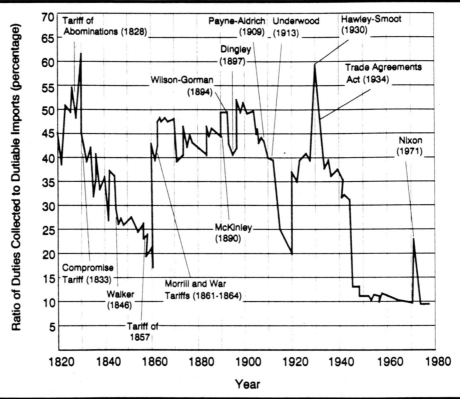

Source: U.S. Department of Commerce, Historical Statistics of the U.S. and Statistical Abstract of the U.S., 1982.

Economists usually feel that a beggar-thy-neighbor action is not likely to succeed. Even if it does work initially, the cost is great because such actions invite retaliation in the long run by other countries. (If the U.S. raises its tariff on bananas, Honduras will raise *its* tariff on tractors.) A trade war is likely to result and every nation will be hurt. The reason is that as tariff walls go up, governments try to stimulate domestic demand, through tax cuts, increased government spending, and lowered interest rates. Assuming that previous international trade has reflected a comparative advantage, the U.S. will increase its domestic output, substituting homemade products for imported ones, at the expense of efficiency. Without trade, even if the U.S. reaches full employment, there will be relative inefficiency in the industries producing these products. Thus, the level of U.S. production of goods and services will be lower than if the tariff had not been introduced.

Retaliation for "Unfair" Trade Practices

Proposals to restrict trade are often based on the view that they are necessary to punish unfair trading practices by other nations. Such proposals frequently include the following reasoning: "Since free trade does not, and perhaps cannot exist, trade restrictions can be used as leverage against unfair traders to create a system of fair trade." In part, this rationale is found in the provisions of the Trade Agreement Act of 1979. Among the provisions of the Act is one prohibiting foreign firms from dumping or selling products in the U.S. at prices lower than those in their own domestic markets. The act provides that, on a finding of dumping by the International Trade Commission, the President may impose penalties against foreign producers.

Economists are divided on the question of penalizing dumping. Some say that dumping is merely a subsidization of domestic consumers by foreign producers. Why turn down a gift? Others say that dumping may be predatory, an attempt to suppress competition or prevent its development through entry into an industry. The problem with this rationale for trade restrictions is that it supposes that dumping may create monopoly. Many economists would say that if it does, the monopoly profits will serve as a stimulus to entry anyway, and tend to eliminate the benefits of dumping.

The Rustbelt: Protecting Declining Industries

Many of the arguments for trade restriction in the 1980s came from elected officials of areas with declining industries or industries containing antiquated plants and equipment. An argument was advanced that is the reverse of the infant-industry argument. Such industries, it is said, need temporary protection while they phase out or cut back production and during the period in which jobs are found for workers in other industries. While plausible, the argument suffers from many of the same problems as the infant-industry argument. Which industries should be protected? How much cost is reasonable? An illustration will suffice. About 75 percent of all shoes sold in the U.S. are imported (mainly from Brazil, Taiwan, and The Republic of South Korea). In an effort to protect this declining industry, Congress, in 1985, studied imposing import restrictions that would have saved more than 30,000 jobs in the industry, The cost *per job*, however, in terms of higher prices and other costs, would have been about $68,000! Publicity about the costs led to the demise of the proposal.

An equally serious problem is in choosing the industries that are declining and face ultimate elimination. Only a few years ago. the American steel industry seemed a candidate with the closing of much of its older plants and equipment and the consequent loss of jobs in the Mid-west. With the exchange rate changes of 1987-1988, however, the steel industry is again fully competitive and operating at high levels of capacity. The "rustbelt" now is prospering and has low unemployment rates. Would protection have been either necessary or wise?

Tariffs Since World War II: GATT

As we have seen, tariff levels have fluctuated greatly since World War II. After the War, the U.S. was instrumental in creating the General Agreement on Tariffs and Trade (GATT) in 1947. From 23 original members, it has grown to more than 90 nations and soon may include much of Eastern Europe and even such nations as the People's Republic of China and the Soviet Union. Dedicating itself to fostering trade and lowering tariffs, GATT has held a series of meetings, which have culminated in freer trade.

Free Trade: A Reprise

In general, then, a nation that is trying to get the greatest output out of the full-employment use of its resources is better off if it lets trade remain free. When a nation, for national defense or other reasons, puts up a protective wall, the form of this protection should be clear and explicit (for example, direct subsidies) so that the costs of protection will be evident to all.

SUMMING UP

1. International trade is the final link in the chain of principles related to the market system. Nations that trade with other nations are open rather than closed economies.

2. Trade consists of *exports*—commodities and services sold to other nations —and *imports*—commodities and services purchased from other nations. Exports and imports consist of both *visible items* (commodities) and *invisible items* (services).

3. *Net foreign trade (NFT)* or *the balance of trade* is the difference between exports (X) and imports (M); it is a part of aggregate demand. Thus

$$NFT = X - M$$

Foreign trade is important, even to a diversified economy such as that of the U.S.

4. NFT can exert a significant macroeconomic influence on the level of income and employment, the demand for goods, services and the creation of jobs. This is so even in the U.S., in which exports (and NFT) form a smaller percentage of GNP than they do in many other major trading nations. (However, in dollar volume, the U.S. is by far the largest international trader.)

5. Between 1960 and 1980, the U.S. usually ran a small trade surplus or trade deficit (X < M). After 1983, the U.S. ran up

increasingly large trade deficits that seemed to be due to exchange rate changes and the income taste of Americans for imported goods.

6. Trade is important to the U.S. for these reasons: (a) Trade constitutes an important part of demand for U.S. output, and hence demand for labor (that means more jobs) and other resources. (b) Demand that results from trade enables many U.S. industries to operate more efficiently and on a larger scale. (c) The percentage of U.S. GNP represented by trade has grown in recent years. This reflects a greater interdependence with other nations. (d) The U.S. needs imports of raw materials, such as certain key minerals, in order to operate many industries.

7. *Autarky* (economic self-sufficiency), although it may be technologically possible for the U.S., is economically unwise, because the U.S., by specializing in items in which it has a comparative advantage, can realize gains from trade.

8. *Absolute advantage* refers to a nation's ability to produce all of a good it consumes more efficiently than any other nation. (Some nations may have an absolute advantage in all goods.) *Comparative advantage* refers to a nation's being more efficient in producing some good or goods than in producing others (even though the nation may also be absolutely more efficient than its neighbors in producing everything).

9. At any given time, nations have certain production possibilities. These are reflected in their production-possibilities curves (assuming full employment and given technology). So long as any two nations have different internal rates of exchange (tradeoffs) between producing the same two goods, it is mutually beneficial for each to specialize in producing the good in which it has a comparative advantage.

10. By specializing in producing those things in which it has a comparative advantage, and by trading what it does not consume to other nations for goods in which *they* have a comparative advantage, a trading nation can have more goods to consume (the consumption-possibilities curves will be above the domestic production-possibilities curve). Differences in tastes and preferences of consumers in different countries also create gains from trade.

11. Comparative advantage derives from (a) different endowments of natural resources, (b) different physical features (climate, harbors, and so on), (c) different states of development of markets (for example, some nations have well-developed capital markets), and (d) different supplies of labor.

12. Comparative advantages change, sometimes dramatically. The U.S. began with a comparative advantage in land-intensive

commodities, which it exported. Today it has a comparative advantage in capital-intensive as well as land-intensive goods.

13. If nations run into increasing costs as they specialize, the specialization will not be complete. They will produce a wider variety of goods. (For example, Honduras will produce some of its own tractors, the United States will produce some of its own bananas.)

14. Some people disapprove of foreign trade because of the unemployment that occurs when resources (especially labor) must be reallocated as a result of that trade. To economists, this is not a compelling argument against an open economy. They point to the macroeconomic tools that can be used to increase employment, and the microeconomic tools that can be used to reallocate resources (for example, job retraining).

15. Comparative advantage depends on competition. When competition does not exist, or when nations with equal advantage do not trade competitively with each other, some of the benefits of comparative-advantage trade are lost.

16. Trading nations that are burdened by *externalities* may produce and trade too much or too little for comparative advantage to work. Prices for goods exported must accurately reflect relative scarcity of resources.

17. The theory of comparative advantage depends on relative prices reflecting relative scarcities of resources in each nation. If prices do not reflect these scarcities, an international misallocation of resources occurs.

18. The biggest obstacle to free trade is *protectionism,* the effort to protect farmers and industries from the competition from lower-priced goods imported from foreign countries when there is free international trade.

19. The two major means of protectionism are (a) *tariffs,* which are taxes on imported goods, and (b) *quotas,* which are limitations on the quantity of imports.

20. Tariffs and other trade restrictions reduce the supply of goods and raise the prices charged consumers. They also add to the monopoly power of domestic producers, and they may reduce the number of good substitutes available to consumers, making domestic demand for a good more inelastic. One thing in their favor is that they produce revenue for governments.

21. The burden of a tariff consists of a *consumer burden,* that part of the tariff paid by consumers in a higher price, and the *producer burden,* that part paid by sellers in a lower net price and reduced sales. The more inelastic is the demand for the imported good, the

greater is the consumer burden. The more elastic is the demand for the imported good, the greater is the producer burden.

22. Quotas do not produce revenue for governments. Otherwise the effects of quotas are similar to those of tariffs. They reduce supply, raise prices to consumers, and enhance the monopolistic position of domestic producers. The most extreme form of quota is an *embargo,* an absolute prohibition against importing a certain good or trading with a certain country. Export quotas are sometimes assigned not only to protect domestic firms but to favor foreign countries and firms. Voters (consumers) may not resist the higher prices of these quotas because of rational ignorance.

23. Arguments in favor of protectionism are as follows: (a) the *infant-industry argument* (firms that are new and small need to be protected until they are large enough to compete with more established firms in foreign industries); (b) the *national-security argument* (uncertainty of foreign supply, plus need for a reliable source of military hardware, means that domestic producers must be protected, even if they are inefficient); (c) the *cheap-foreign-labor argument* (domestic firms that must pay high wages should be protected against imports from countries in which wages are low); (d) the *macroeconomic-employment argument* (recessions and depressions can be "exported" if a nation puts up barriers to trade that reduce imports without reducing exports); (e) retaliation for "unfair" trading practices (make them trade fairly) and; (f) protection of declining industries (help such industries temporarily) during phasing out.

24. Economists generally reject these arguments that favor protectionism, with the exception of the national-security argument, for which there is no objective basis for evaluation. However, even in the case of protection given to industries producing goods needed for national security, economists feel that there should be direct subsidies instead of tariffs, so that the costs of protection are clearly identified.

25. Beggar-thy-neighbor tariffs are likely to be ineffective, even counterproductive. When one nation sets up high tariffs, other nations retaliate. As a result, without specialized trade, nations have fewer goods and services to consume, even when they have full employment.

26. Free trade is in the best interests of a nation that wishes to have maximum production *and consumption,* with the full employment of its resources and technological capability. The creation of GATT, the General Agreement on Tariffs and Trade laws, since 1947, has led to a general lowering of tariffs and other forms of protection.

KEY TERMS

Exports, imports
Visible items, invisible items of trade
Net foreign trade or balance of trade
Comparative advantage, absolute advantage
Terms of trade
Tariffs, quotas, embargoes
Burden of a tariff (consumer burden, producer burden)
Infant-industry argument
National security argument
Cheap foreign labor argument
"Beggar-thy-neighbor" argument
Rational ignorance
GATT

QUESTIONS

1. What imported goods do you often buy? How would you be affected if the U.S. restricted international trade or stopped trading with other nations entirely?

2. Why are most production-possibilities curves *not* straight lines? What happens to international specialization when such curves are truly curves?

3. Consider the following hypothetical production-possibilities schedules for the U.S. and Honduras:

United States		Honduras	
Units of Tractors	Units of Bananas	Units of Tractors	Units of Bananas
50	0	0	100
40	5	5	80
30	10	10	60
20	15	15	40
10	20	20	20
0	25	25	0

    a. Plot the production-possibilities curves.
    b. Is there a basis for mutually beneficial trade between the two countries?
    c. What will determine the terms of trade that are established between the two countries?

4. Based on the arguments advanced in this chapter, why, in your opinion, did the beggar-thy-neighbor tariff (Smoot-Hawley tariff) of 1930 fail to stimulate American recovery between 1930 and 1934?

5. What happens to the trade from either developed or under-developed nations when monopoly export and import agencies are set up? Why?

6. Evaluate the following statements:
    a. "Free trade forces domestic producers to pay attention to consumer tastes and needs."
    b. "Free trade would be desirable, but we can't afford to rely on the Soviets, or the French, or even the British, for our military hardware."
    c. "High tariffs to create more jobs will work for the U.S. because other, less powerful nations wouldn't dare retaliate."
    d. "In several recent years, the U.S. has run a large trade deficit. What we should do to counteract this is to buy less from abroad."
    e. "In several recent years, the U.S. has run a large trade deficit. We don't need to worry, though, because exchange rate changes will eliminate the deficit."

7. In the graph below, we see the demand for and supply of an imported good. D_d is the domestic demand, S_d the domestic supply. S_{ft} is the supply with free trade of both domestic producers and imports, and S_{at}, the supply after a tariff is imposed.

    a. What is the price and quantity of the good without trade? With free trade? After a tariff is imposed?
    b. Who bears most of the burden of the tariff, consumers or importing firms? What is the burden of each?
    c. Who benefits from the tariff? What is the price benefit?

SUGGESTED READINGS

Baldwin, Robert E. "The Political Economy of Postwar United States Trade." Reprinted in Baldwin, Robert E. and J. David Richardson (Eds.). *International Trade and Financial Readings*, 2nd. ed. Boston: Little Brown, 1981.

Bergsten, C. Fred. "Reform Trade Policy with Auction Quotas." *Challenge*. May/June, 1987.

Council of Economic Advisers. "International Economic Report of the President." 1987. G.P.O., Washington, D.C., 1987.

Culbertson, John M. "The Folly of Free Trade." *Harvard Business Review*. September/October, 1986. Reprinted in *Economics 88/89*. Don Cole, Editor, The Dushkin Publishing Group, Inc., Guilford, Ct., 1989.

Dolan, Edwin G. and John C. Goodman. *Economics of Public Policy*, Fourth Edition. St. Paul, West Publishing Co., 1989. "Restricting Automobile Imports," Chapter 13.

Drucker, Peter J. "Low Wages No Longer Give Competitive Edge." *The Wall Street Journal*. March 16, 1988.

Friedman, Milton. "Outdoing Smoot-Hawley." *The Wall Street Journal*. April 20, 1987.

Lindert, Peter H. and Charles P. Kindleberger. *International Economics*, 8th ed. Homewood, Ill., Richard D. Irwin, 1987.

Meier, Gerald M. *Problems of Trade Policy*. New York: Oxford University Press, 1973.

Rezvin, Philip. "As Trade Gap Closes, Partners of U.S. Face End of Gravy Train." *The Wall Street Journal*. March 20, 1988.

Safire, William. "Smoot-Hawley Lives." *The New York Times*. March 17, 1983.

Application to Chapter 17: Does Trade Create Development?

During the 1960s and 1970s, it became apparent that nations such as Mexico, Brazil, Korea, Taiwan and Singapore were developing major manufacturing sectors and that international trade was playing a key role in this process. Indeed, these nations came to be known as the newly industrializing countries (NICs), in contrast with the less developed countries (LDCs). The emergence of the NICs seemed to reignite a long-standing debate among economists and others, not only about the future course of economic development but also about the role of international trade in fostering such development.

In the 1980s, the "debt crisis" of some of the NICs and many of the LDCs further complicated efforts to assay the relationship between trade and development. That the issues will continue to be important to all nations, rich, poor and in between, seems nearly certain. Development cannot begin or continue without capital and other imports, and importing cannot occur unless nations have export earnings with which to finance imports. Likewise, debt cannot be serviced, much less repaid except out of export-derived revenues. In an increasingly interdependent international economy, few issues take on more importance than the relationship between trade and development.

The Relation Between Trade and Development

To establish this relationship, we must find a relation between exporting-importing and the increase in productivity that is the key to development. Opinions are divided about whether trade—especially trade based on comparative advantage—enhances economic development. In this application we will examine some of the controversies surrounding this subject.

The Classical View

Early economists, including Adam Smith and David Ricardo, believed that trade was essential to economic development, or to what Smith called "the wealth of nations." Writing about the country's efforts to produce things that it could import more cheaply, Smith said, "The value of its annual produce is certainly more or less diminished, when it is thus turned away from producing commodities evidently of more value than the commodity which it is directed to produce."

This idea of maximizing the wealth of a nation through trade, however, is based on a static situation (*static* meaning timeless). Much of the argument over its validity arises from the distinction between the static economic position of a country at a point in time, and the improvement (or deterioration) in the country's position that occurs over time. Let's illustrate the difference between these two perspectives.

The U.S., early in its history, started out with a certain endowment of land, labor, capital, and entrepreneurship. For simplicity, assume that all its resources were integrated into the market system. Now ask yourself the following questions: (1) In any given year—for instance, 1940—would the per capita national income be higher if the U.S. followed a policy of free trade? Or would it be higher if it imposed restrictions on trade? (2) Which policy—restricted trade or unrestricted trade—would cause income to grow faster from one date to another (for instance, from 1940 to 1990)?

Figure A17-1 will help you visualize the answer. It shows that in 1940 the U.S. could have two levels of per capita income: $1,400 or $1,450. The $1,400 figure corresponds to the level if the government enforced protective practices (such as tariffs or quotas). It represents many possible levels of income resulting from different combinations of trade restrictions. Each of the combinations causes resources to be used in ways that are *less* productive than would be the case if there were free trade, or if there were comparative-advantage trade. The $1,450 represents the *free*-trade (comparative advantage) case.

Therefore, the answer to question 1 is that at any point its process of development, a nation will have a higher income if it

Figure A17-1
Growth Paths of the United States: Free Trade and Protectionism

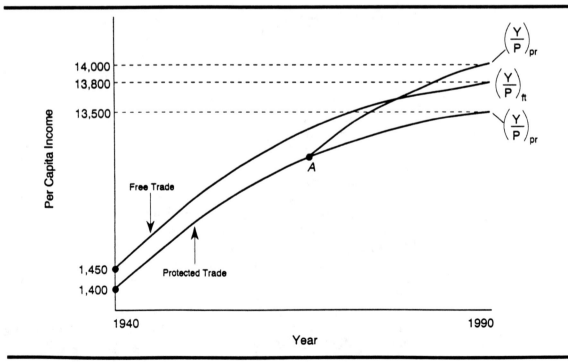

engages in free trade and utilizes all its resources on the basis of comparative advantage.

Now what about *growth* as it relates to international trade? Which policy—comparative-advantage (free) trade or some sort of protective tariffs or quotas—would yield the U.S. the greater growth in income during the period from 1940 to 1990? Adherents of the classical economic view say that comparative-advantage trade would give the greatest growth, because a nation that trades according to the principle of comparative advantage allocates its resources to their most productive uses. Thus, the nation is maximizing its productivity. With free trade, as income grows over time (along $(Y/P)_{ft}$ in Figure A17-1), the size of the nation's market grows. There is specialization and division of labor. Capital increases and productivity increases as well.

The growth path with protected trade $(Y/P)_{pr}$, begins at a lower level ($1,400) in 1940 and in 1990 results in a lower level of per capita income ($13,500) as well. This is because even with full employment of its resources, allocation is less efficient and productive with protection than with (comparative advantage) free trade. This is the traditional view of the relationship between trade and development and the reason why many economists espouse free trade as the desired policy objective of developing nations.

Reservations About the Traditional View
There are objections to the above scenario. Some economists feel that a policy of comparative-advantage trade is not, in the long run, the best policy for developing nations. They feel that one cannot prove an explicit relationship between growth and free international trade. Economist Hollis Chenery has been one of the doubters. Chenery, for a long time an official of the United States Agency For International Development (USAID), has argued that there are five reservations that point to the wisdom of modifying comparative advantage as a policy, to enhance economic development for NICs and LDCs:

1. *Factor costs.* The benefits of comparative advantage depend on factor markets producing equilibrium prices of resources. This means that the prices reflect "true" relative costs of production. Consider the imperfections in labor or capital markets that one sees in developing countries (for example, the U.S. in the nineteenth century or in virtually all LDCs today). As development takes place, markets perform more efficiently. There are often dramatic changes in factor costs, and thus in comparative advantage.

2. *Export markets.* Comparative-advantage trade gives rise to specialization. NICs and LDCs frequently come to specialize in producing—and exporting—just one, or a very few, raw materials. Then they must import food and raw materials that they do not produce along with manufactured (and semimanufactured) products. The result is an unstable economy, which is tied to the fluctuating prices of raw materials. (For example, the world price

of copper plunged 65 percent in the early 1970s. Chile, which produces one-eighth of the world's copper, suffered acutely.) You can see that following a policy of comparative-advantage trade makes it hard for an underdeveloped nation to keep its economy stable. In addition, price and income elasticities of demand for these countries' raw materials are low, though data are conflicting. (When the price of copper falls on the world market, and a country's chief export is copper, it cannot make up in export earnings for the drop in price by selling a greater quantity to its industrialized neighbors.) So the terms of trade, the ratio of export prices to import prices may turn against the exporter of the raw material. The reason is that the poor nation—for example, Chile—must continue to import manufactured goods, whose prices (compared to the price of the exported copper) are now relatively much higher.

Many economists fail to see factors 1 and 2 as being necessarily valid arguments against a developing country's specializing in its comparative advantage raw-material exports. In their view, a developing nation's rate of return on investment in its raw material is greater than the rate of return it *would* get if it tried to build up other internal projects, such as factories, even after correcting for factor costs and fluctuating world prices.

3. *Productivity changes.* Manufacturing, by its very nature, may enhance the skills of labor and management more than agriculture does. So some economic advisers urge a developing nation to stress manufacturing, even at the expense of comparative-advantage exports. Some of the NICs appear to have done so. Others disagree, asking whether such an advantage exists. Perhaps, they say, the developing nation could make as much headway by concentrating on agriculture as by concentrating on manufacturing. Some of the LDCs are attempting to reemphasize agriculture. All agree, however, that the nation must make allowances for productivity changes in allocating its resources—even if it does not, in the long run, opt for manufacturing as the area of concentration.

4. *Dynamic external economies.* As an industry grows, its costs fall. Or demand for its output increases. As a result, the costs of other industries may also fall. There may, in fact, be a whole group of investments that are profitable *only if they are undertaken together*. Comparative advantage, manifested in market signals such as equilibrium prices, does not under these conditions indicate to a nation how it should allocate its resources. Suppose, for example, that the underdeveloped nation increases its investment in industry and realizes certain of these external economies. This will reduce the costs of more than one industry. But, some economists say, perhaps it would have realized even more external economies if it had allocated its capital to comparative-advantage agriculture. For example, it could have built fabricating plants, including expanding the production of the raw material.

5. *Uncertainty and flexibility.* Some economists feel that changes in the market can happen so quickly, and are so hard for policy makers to foresee, that a diversified economy—one that can quickly adjust to changes in supply and demand—is better (and certainly more flexible) than one that relies on a single product, or only a few products. Economist C. P. Kindleberger has argued that the terms of trade now discriminate against the raw-material-exporting nations and favor the industrialized nations, because the raw-material-exporting nations lack flexibility. So it seems that a developing nation might be well advised to sacrifice some short-term efficiency in the interests of longer-term flexibility, and a capacity to adjust more rapidly to changes in world supply and demand.

A serious problem with this, though, is that inefficiency often involves creating monopoly privileges and rents that are very difficult to eliminate in the long run. Many examples can be found in some of the NICs and LDCs of this problem. A report in the *Wall Street Journal* in November 1986 indicated that in Indonesia, a country possessed of many exportable natural resources including oil, export revenues have done little to finance broadly based economic development programs. Principal among the reasons for this has been the substitution of bureaucratic import controls and corruption for free trade. A small oligarchy, including the Presidents' family, has received monopoly rights over imports and control over access to import quotas along with (monopoly) distribution rights to products within the country. Such monopoly pricing might ordinarily attract investors into these industries but investment licensing has prevented that. Higher monopoly prices make Indonesian exports less competitive and reduce export earnings, thereby reducing the ability to finance developmental imports. It is not surprising that bureaucratization and corruption have made the export position of many LDCs less competitive. Indeed, their share of world exports has been falling since the 1950s.

Those With Reservations: Modify Free Trade

Those who have reservations about comparative advantage trade and its ability to insure or accelerate growth argue for modifications in trade policy. Such modifications may involve significant departures from free trade. Some of the measures adopted include (1) rationing of trade (foreign exchange) earnings either direct controls or through multiple pricing (exchange rate) controls, (2) providing direct subsidies or tax incentives to firms that produce import substitute products, and (3) creating import-export monopoly agencies to obtain lower prices for imports and capture revenue from domestic producers for governmentally determined development uses. To the extent that these noncompetitive market interventions are effective, proponents say that the growth path with protection, $(Y/P)_{pr}$, in Figure A17-1 can accelerate at some point (point A in Figure A17-1), utilizing dynamic externalities and other advantages to propel the nation onto a new path that will generate higher real income at the end of the period ($14,000 versus $13,800) than would be the case with free trade.

Debt Problems of the LDCs and NICs

With the dramatic exception of the "Asian Tigers" (South Korea, Taiwan, Hong Kong, Singapore, Malaysia, and, recently, Thailand), the trade positions of the LDCs and NICs have deteriorated in the 1970s and 1980s. Most of the LDCs exports consist of primary commodities. For most of them (Indonesia and Venezuela excepted), agricultural primary commodities dominate their exports. Such products have declined in value from more than one-third in 1955 to less than 14 percent in 1986. While those that export fuels have benefitted (until the mid-1980s) from rising prices, this added, ironically, to the financial problems of others. The dramatic increase in manufactured engineering products has benefitted some NICs (especially the "Asian Tigers") while it has had little effect on many LDCs whose manufactured products are not competitive in world markets.

Faced with rising import prices (especially fuels) and softening primary commodity export prices, many NICs and LDCs turned to international capital markets and borrowed heavily in the 1970s. In some instances, the long-term investment credits were wisely invested and resulted in dramatic productivity growth and growth in exports (e.g., South Korea). In other instances, the long-term credits appear to have been less wisely employed, often in the bureaucratic controls and corruption to which we referred earlier. Some countries, especially in Latin America (Brazil, Argentina, Peru) appeared to be on the verge of inability to even service the interest payments on their debts (often 50 percent or more of their GNPs) and as we begin the 1990s, there are frequent fears of default.

Implications for Trade Policies

For many years, representatives of the LDCs and, to a lesser extent, the NICs argued for creating a special system of trading and financial preferences for the "developing nations." At times, especially at the United Nations Conference on Trade and Development (UNCTAD) they lobbied for a system under which there would be guaranteed export prices for primary commodities, easier access to markets in industrial nations and long-term capital flows to LDCs and NICs at preferential interest rates. Those pressures, however, seemed to abate until the debt crisis of the 1980s.

In the 1980s, we hear again arguments for trade preferences. One NIC (Brazil) temporarily suspended interest payment on its debt. An LDC (Peru) announced it would pay no more than

15 percent of its GNP in interest payments on its external debt. Two American Secretaries of the Treasury have argued for more public and private capital flows to LDCs and NICs at below market interest rates. Which shall it be in the future, free trade in commodities services and capital or a "new (non-free trade) order" of trading relationships? Economists are not of one mind about which trade policies are consistent with sustained growth and development. Many would agree with Arnold Harberger (*World Economic Growth: Cases of Developed and Developing Nations*, San Francisco: Institute for Contemporary Studies, 1984) that free trade, and a minimum of government involvement in domestic and international economic affairs is preferable. Other economists would agree with Chenery that free (comparative-advantage-based) trade may be stacked against the LDCs and NICs. For them, government action is called for to encourage the real and financial trading relationships that will permit more and more LDCs to become NICs and for the NICs to become major industrial countries.

SUMMING UP

1. Policy makers today must face a major question: Can international trade provide the primary basis for the economic development of poor nations? In the 1980s and 1970s, newly industrialized countries (NICs) seemed to suggest yes.

2. Views differ as to the relation between trade and development. Classical economists (Adam Smith, David Ricardo) felt that comparative-advantage trade was essential to increasing output and maximizing the wealth of a nation.

3. Much of the debate over the relation between trade and development involves the distinction between the static principles of comparative-advantage and the dynamic principles of growth.

4. One can show that, in a static sense (that is, at a point in time), a nation can maximize its output if it allocates all its resources to their most productive uses. However, there is no certainty that if a nation does this, the growth of its output over a period of time will be greater than it would have been if it had departed, selectively, from comparative-advantage trade.

5. Those who argue for restricting comparative advantage, as the basis for trade, argue on the basis of: (a) *Factor costs*. Imperfections in the factor markets of underdeveloped nations cause their factor costs not to reflect their real relative cost. (b) *Export markets*. Comparative-advantage specialization on the part of the poor nations may result in unstable economies. Low income and price elasticities of demand for raw-material exports may turn the terms of trade against the nation that specializes. (c) *Productivity*

changes. In an economy based on manufacturing, the skills of labor and management increase and diversify more rapidly than they do in an economy based on agriculture. (d) *Dynamic external economies.* Several investments—a whole package of them—may have to be made simultaneously in order to make them succeed, or pay off. This is more likely to happen in an industry-based economy than in an agriculture-based economy. (e) *Uncertainty and flexibility.* A diversified economy is more flexible, and can adjust more readily to changes in supply and demand, than an economy that specializes in a few raw-material exports. Thus, it can better resist the effects of worsening terms of trade.

6. Economists generally discount points a and b as reasons to abandon comparative-advantage trade. However, they must take into account factors c, d, and e when they are working out trade policy.

7. Deviations from free trade seem often to give rise to bureaucratic red tape in LDCs and to monopoly grants and corruption. These impediments to productivity growth raise prices and make LDC exports less competitive in world markets

8. Faced with rising import (especially fuel) prices in the 1970s and falling primary commodity prices, LDCs and some NICs borrowed heavily in world capital markets. Where the capital was not wisely invested, a "debt crisis" has arisen in which threats to default or limit payments have created serious problems in financial markets.

9. For years LDCs and NICs have argued for a "new international economic order" with restrictions on free trade involving guaranteed export prices, easier access to markets, and below market interest rates for capital.

10. Economists are divided about the wisdom of diverging from free trade. Many, probably most American economists, argue that free trade is preferable in creating productivity growth and minimizing distortions of bureaucracy and corruption. Others argue that free trade is stacked against LDCs and NICs and that trade preferences should be considered.

QUESTIONS

1. What are the differences between the static view of comparative advantage and the dynamic view of growth?

2. If you were recommending economic policy to a developing low-income country, at what point would you recommend that it follow a policy of comparative-advantage trade, and at what point would you recommend that it sacrifice a certain amount of efficiency in the use of its resources in order to achieve more growth?

3. Consider an underdeveloped country (for example, Chile), and suppose that it primarily exports one raw material (for example, copper). How can low price and income elasticities of demand for copper affect Chile's export earnings, its ability to import other, necessary goods, and its terms of trade?

SUGGESTED READINGS

Baldwin, Robert E. and David Richardson, Jr. (eds.). *International Trade and Finance Readings*, 2nd edition. Boston: Little Brown, 1981.

Brandt, Willy, et al. *North-South: A Program for Survival.* Cambridge: MIT Press, 1980.

Cameron, Rondo. "Some Lessons of History for Developing Nations." Reprinted in *Economics: Readings in Analysis and Policy*. Edited by Dennis R. Starleaf. Scott, Foresman, Glenview, Ill., 1969.

Caves, Richard E. and Ronald W. Jones. *World Trade and Payments, An Introduction,* 4th edition. Boston: Little Brown, 1985.

Chenery, Hollis B. "Comparative Advantage and Development Policy." *American Economic Review,* 51:1. (March 1961). Reprinted in *Economic Development: Readings in Theory and Practice*. Edited by Theodore Morgan and George W. Betz. Wadsworth, Belmont, Calif., 1970.

Cline, William R. (ed.). *Trade Policy in the 1980s.* Cambridge: MIT Press, 1983.

Council of Economic Advisers. International Economic Report of the President. G.P.O., 1987.

Dornbusch, Rudiger and Jacob A. Frenkel, (eds.). *International Economic Policy, Theory and Evidence.* Baltimore: Johns Hopkins Press, 1979.

Harberger, Arnold C. (ed). *World Economic Growth: Case Studies of Developed and Developing Nations.* San Francisco: Institute for Contemporary Studies, 1984.

Hirschman, A. O. *The Strategy of Economic Development.* Yale, New Haven, Conn., 1958.

Johnson, Harry J. *Economic Policies Toward Less Developed Countries.* Brookins Institution, Washington, D.C., 1967.

Jones, Steven and Ralph Pura. "Indonesian Decrees Help Suharto's Friends and Relatives Prosper." *The Wall Street Journal.* November 24, 1986.

Myrdal, Gunnar. "Asian Drama: An Inquiry into the Poverty of Nations." London: Penguin, 1968.

Pincus, John. "Trade Preferences for Underdeveloped Countries." Reprinted in *Economics in Action* by Shelley M. Mark, 4th ed. Belmont, Calif: Wadsworth, 1969.

Singer, Hans W. "The Distribution of Gains Between Investing and Borrowing Countries." Reprinted in *Economic Development: Readings in Theory and Practice.* Edited by Theodore Morgan and George W. Betz. Belmont, Calif: Wadsworth, 1970.

Smith, Adam. "Restraints on Foreign Imports" in *The Wealth of Nations*, vol. I. Reprinted in *Readings in Introductory Economics.* Edited by John R. McKean and Ronald A. Wykstra. New York: Harper & Row, 1971.

Chapter 18:
Paying for International Trade

In the previous chapter we dealt with the theory of international trade in general terms. We examined the bases for trade between nations: (1) comparative advantage and (2) protectionism. Trade based on barter *is* possible; for example, the U.S. once exchanged destroyers with the British for military bases. Barter, though, is very rare among modern economies, and virtually all international trade today requires that money change hands. Let us see how international money flows or exchanges take place to finance purchases of commodities and services.

An Example of Money Exchange

The American Steel Company agrees to sell $500,000 worth of rolled steel to the Japanese Automobile Company. Suppose also that the *rate of exchange*, the price at which Japanese yen can be exchanged for American dollars, is 120 yen per dollar. (Later we will see how this rate is established.) The Japanese importer, in other words, owes 60 million yen to the American Steel Company. Let's follow this transaction through the banking system in both countries:

1. Japanese Auto writes a check on its Tokyo bank for 60 million yen, and mails the check to American Steel.

2. American Steel cannot pay its workers and creditors in Japanese yen; it needs dollars. Therefore, it sells the check to a New York bank that has a correspondent relation with a Japanese bank.

3. Now American Steel has a $500,000 deposit in the New York bank. The New York bank deposits the check from Japanese Auto in its correspondent bank in Tokyo and becomes the owner of a claim to Japanese yen.

Note. Nearly all of this is now accomplished by electronic transfers.

In other words, an American company's exports of a commodity create a demand for dollars. When this demand is fulfilled, more foreign currency is available to people in the U.S. who will demand it to pay for their own (Japanese) imports.

When a U.S. company imports something, the process is reversed. The American company must obtain a supply of the currency of the country from which it is buying the goods. The supply comes from foreign currencies that American firms have earned through their exports. Thus, Japanese yen are available to pay for U.S. imports of Toyotas because Americans have exported wheat (and many other commodities) to Japan. In other words, *in order to be able to pay for its imports, a country must also export or sell its goods to other countries.*

A Good International Monetary System

This two-country illustration, although it is correct, makes the financing of international trade seem simpler than it is. Financing trade is quite complex, and involves intricate relationships between the domestic economies of more than a hundred independent nations that exchange goods and services. In short, it involves an elaborate international monetary system.

Let's examine the characteristics of a good money system in an *international* economy. One feature that is absolutely essential is that the system expedite the trading of goods and services. (After all, barter, as we noted earlier, is no more feasible in international trade than it is in domestic trade.) By what criteria is a system of payments judged?

1. *The system must strike a reasonable balance between stability and growth in international trade and stability and growth in the individual nations that engage in it.* The economy of the U.S. (or Britain, or any other nation) should not have to absorb large shocks to its own employment and investment situation in order to accommodate changes in its international trade position, or that of other nations. (Later in this chapter, we will discuss the gold standard, which forces exactly such adjustments.) The present set of monetary arrangements, although it is a great improvement over the gold standard in these respects, may still force some countries, especially those with large external debts denominated in other currencies, to make drastic adjustments in their internal economies in order to handle their international payments.This is a problem for many LDCs and NICs, as we have seen.

Essential to this requirement of reasonable balance is consistency of action. Once the rules for international financial transactions have been made, all the participating nations must play by the rules. The system may force a nation to make adjustments that conflict with its political and economic objectives, or even threaten the political survival of its government. (For example, it may have to raise interest rates, lower investment, and create unemployment.) If the system demands too many adjustments of this sort, nations will probably not adhere to it consistently. Then the system will become unstable.

2. *The system of payments must be seen to be equitable.* It is hard for nations to agree on how the costs and benefits of a system are to be distributed so that there is equity for all. Many nations, especially the underdeveloped ones, feel that present international financial arrangements are inequitable. They claim that they do not have enough control over decisions about the availability of capital and credit, and about who is to bear the costs of financing. At the same time, the system must facilitate the repayment of capital whose movement is essential to the finance of exports and imports. Proposals for further capital flows to the LDCs and even some NICs must incorporate this principle.

3. *The system of payments must be efficient,* just as any other system of markets must. The efficiency of an international system of payments is measured in terms of the effect of that system on the cost of trade. An efficient system encourages trade by making the means of financing exports and imports readily available, and by reducing the risks of trade (unanticipated changes in exchange rates, for example).

Determining Equilibrium Exchange Rates

Equilibrium Exchange Rates
Rates of exchange between currencies that clears currency markets or that eliminate excess supply or excess demand.

Freely Floating Exchange Rate
A competitive rate of exchange, one that is free to move to any equilibrium level that will clear currency markets.

An **equilibrium exchange rate** is the rate of exchange between two currencies that clears the market or eliminates excess supply or demand. This rate will change only as the supply of or demand for the currencies changes. Like any other price, the exchange rate may be established in one of two ways: (1) It may be freely floating, that is established by impersonal market forces (competition). (2) It may be fixed, that is, administered (determined by certain individuals or agencies). Here are some of the ways exchange rates are determined and export-import equilibrium established:

Freely Floating Exchange Rates

Let's take as an example the exchange rate between the dollar and the deutsche mark. With a **freely floating exchange rate**, the exchange rate is established through the interplay of supply and demand. Figure 18-1 illustrates this interplay.

The curve D_0 is the American demand for marks. It slopes downward because as the dollar price of marks falls (as a dollar buys more marks), German goods (Volkswagens, Rhine wine, cameras, binoculars, and so on) become cheaper for Americans to buy. When that happens, the quantity demanded by Americans of German goods increases and Americans demand more marks, so

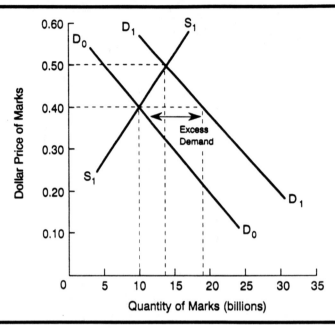

they can pay for those goods.The demand for marks, in other words, is a *derived demand*, a demand derived from the demand for German imports. The curve S_1 is the supply of marks. It slopes upward because as the dollar price of marks rises (as marks buy more dollars), American exports become cheaper for Germans to buy. When that happens, Germans increase the quantity demanded of imported American goods and demand more dollars, so they can pay for those goods (cars, computers, wheat, and so on). The Germans pay for their purchases with checks drawn on German banks.

Since the exchange rate is free to seek its market level, the equilibrium level is the one at which quantity supplied equals quantity demanded.We see in Figure 18-1 a foreign exchange market, the market in which exchange rates and exchange rate charges are established. Here, equilibrium is established at .40, which is 2.5 marks to the dollar ($\frac{1}{.40} = 2.5$). In other words, a mark will buy four-tenths of a dollar. The equilibrium quantity of marks in Figure 18-1 is 10 billion.

Now what if a disequilibrium—a variation in supply or demand that throws things off balance—develops in this market? Suppose that Detroit auto makers, in a surprise move, announce a big increase in prices. (If the price increase had been anticipated, it would have been reflected in D_0—the original demand for marks.) Higher prices for Detroit-made cars mean that German cars are now cheaper by comparison. As a result, the demand for marks shifts upward (people want to buy more Volkswagens and Mercedes Benzes). But now there is disequilibrium. At the present exchange rate (.40), only 10 billion marks are supplied, but foreign-exchange buyers now want nearly 20 billion.

When the exchange rate is freely floating, the excess demand of 10 million marks is taken care of by dealers in foreign exchange markets who bid up the dollar price of the mark. (There are foreign exchange markets and dealers in nearly every major city in the world.) The mark then costs more to buy. When the rate of exchange rises to .50 ($1/.50 = 2$ marks to the dollar), excess demand is eliminated. Remember that the additional quantity of marks supplied is forthcoming because, as the mark appreciates in value, Germans buy more of relatively cheaper American goods (ironically, they even buy more of the now relatively cheaper American cars if exchange rate changes more than offset the original price increases), thus creating claims to marks by American exporters.

Let's look at the advantages and disadvantages of allowing the value of currencies to float freely. The *advantages* are those of a competitive market: (1) The system responds quickly to changes in supply and demand. (2) Disequilibria in payments are readily resolved; for example, the excess demand that appeared when Americans wanted to buy more German goods (Figure 18-1).

The *disadvantages* of the system are as follows: (1) The rate of exchange may be very unstable. This instability may inhibit trade, because a buyer who orders an imported article will soon stop buying if large changes in the exchange rate make the article cost more when it is delivered than when it is ordered. (2) Some countries depend heavily on international trade to provide jobs and investment capital (especially the LDCs and NICs, in which the foreign-trade sectors dominate the economies). In these countries, wide swings in exchange rates can cause very destabilizing changes in exports and imports. (3) A nation's financial terms of trade can change quickly and sharply. The terms of trade, recall, refer to the ratio of export prices to import prices. In a sense, they measure the value of exports a nation must have in order to maintain a given level of imports. Wide variations in the values of currencies can cause either variations in imports or disruptive efforts to adjust exports. In either case, destabilization may result.

Freely floating exchange rates have only been common since 1971 and President Nixon's decision to "float" the U.S. dollar. Some economists have reservations about such fluctuations. Arthur Burns, former chairman of the Federal Reserve Board, gave four reasons for his skepticism: (1) Freely floating rates are an academic dream that cause people to demand protection through government controls or government intervention in the money market. (2) Floating rates may lead to political friction. If other nations suspect that the rates are being manipulated, they will take retaliatory steps. (3) Floating rates increase people's uncertainty and thus inhibit both commodity trade and capital flows. (4) Floating rates make it harder for the government to implement domestic fiscal and monetary policies that are suitable.

Other economists (such as Milton Friedman) believe that fears such as these about the dangers of floating rates are exaggerated. They say the following: (1) Where the policy of floating rates has been tried, there have not been enormous swings in rates. The apparent reason for this is that speculators in foreign exchange, those who engage in *arbitrage* or who buy and sell in different markets to make profits, stabilize the market. (2) Although freely floating rates do increase business uncertainty, this is a price worth paying in exchange for the above-mentioned benefits of the system.

Fixed Exchange Rates

Fixed Exchange Rates
A system in which the rates of exchange between currencies are established by government and not allowed to vary with changing currency market conditions.

International Reserves
Assets available to central banks and other agencies that are accepted in payment of international debts.

Some rates of exchange between currencies are based on **fixed exchange rates,** a system of payments involving agreed-upon relationships between the world's currencies. Even today, some nations fix the rate at which their currencies exchange. Some have a two-tiered system with fixed rates for some transactions and flexible rates for others. For most of the post-World War II period fixed exchange rates prevailed. To see how a fixed rate system works, refer again to Figure 18-1. Suppose that at the fixed rate of 2.5 marks to the dollar, there is an excess demand of 6 billion marks. The U.S. and German governments (perhaps dealing through an international agency) are committed to maintaining the 2.5:1 rate. The additional marks come from somewhere. Since the market will not supply them at the fixed rate, governments or international agencies must. (Note that this is hypothetical: the dollar/mark exchange rate is, in fact, not fixed.)

The additional marks can come only from **international reserves,** assets available to central banks and other agencies that are acceptable in payment of international debts. (In the past it was gold.) It is possible, of course, that the German central bank, the Deutsche Bundesbank, might lend the marks to the Federal Reserve (Fed) System. The Fed, in turn, would make them available to American commercial banks. Alternatively, there might be an international agency such as the *International Monetary Fund (IMF)*, which has reserves of dollars, deutsche marks, Swiss francs, British pounds, claims to gold, and all other major currencies. The IMF makes loans to the Fed and through the Fed to our commercial banks.

Note: Fixed exchange rates require large currency reserves. In the face of growing world trade, they require *increasing reserves,* if banks are to be able to take care of fluctuations in demand for currencies.

The chief advantage of fixed exchange rates is that they lend stability to world trade. Fixed rates reduce uncertainty about international prices. If you want to buy a German car or import German machinery, and you know that the banking system is committed to a 2.5:1 exchange rate, you can plan your purchase even if the goods are not actually delivered to you until months later. This stability provides a favorable climate for the growth of trade, especially for long-term capital flows.

Even fixed exchange rates are not necessarily fixed forever. For example, the German government may decide that subsidizing German exports to the U.S. is not in Germany's best interests. The U.S. government may decide that at the 2.5:1 rate its exports to Germany are too low. The international reserves needed to finance this trade imbalance may run dangerously low. The countries, by mutual agreement, may change the rate to 2 marks to the dollar (which will equilibrate the exchange market shown in Figure 18-1).

Exchange Rate Market Intervention

Dirty Float
A system in which exchange rates are "pegged" or allowed by central banks to move within certain limits.

We have posed the exchange rate policy choice of governments as either: (1) Allow exchange rates to float freely (flexible rates) or (2) fix rates and adjust them occasionally by mutual agreement (fixed rates). For both political and economic reasons, governments, including that of the United States seem unwilling to consistently follow one path or the other. When they do not, they choose to intervene selectively in exchange markets. In doing so, they create a system of managed exchange rates on what is often called the **dirty float**. Essentially, it means that the Fed allows the dollar to float but only within certain "pegs" or limits. While these pegs are rarely clearly defined, their expectation does send a (poorly defined) signal to exchange rate dealers about the limits of rate changes.

Why, in the absence of fixed exchange rates, do governments intervene in this way? It is sometimes said that nations intervene out of national pride to keep their currency high and stable in value against other currencies. There is no evidence to support this and it seems that there are much stronger reasons that can be shown for intervention. Consider the case of the U.S. dollar, which is a key currency in international finance. Much of the reserves of America's trading partners (reserves of their central banks) consist of holdings of U.S. dollars. Thus, when the U.S. dollar declines sharply, so do the value of the assets of those banks (Bank of Japan, Deutsche Bundesbank, etc.). The Fed then, perhaps under pressure from our allies, may intervene if the dollar drops too sharply. The U.S. dollar is sometimes the only currency accepted in payment for certain international transactions. OPEC, for example, accepts only U.S. dollars in payment for its oil exports. If the U.S. dollar rises sharply against the pound sterling or French franc, those countries must spend more to buy the dollars to pay for their oil imports. Again, the Fed may intervene to moderate the growth in the exchange value of the dollar.

Market intervention by different governments may, of course, be contradictory. When the dollar falls against other currencies, U.S. exports become cheaper and the Fed may do nothing to support its currency. This was generally the case with only rare exceptions in 1987 and 1988 because stimulating export growth was U.S. national policy. Other nations such as Japan, however, see the dollar falling against their currencies and their own exports becoming more expensive. To avert a decline in its export industries, Japan may intervene to buy dollars and keep the yen from falling further against the dollar. It is not surprising in view of the potential for conflicting interventionist policies that there are numerous meetings and other efforts by central banks to agree on exchange rates.

Adjusting Economies to Fluctuations in the Exchange Rate

One can trace the origin of an exchange-rate disequilibrium (such as the excess demand in Figure 18-1) to changes in economic conditions in the exporting and importing nations. Figure 18-2 gives you the situation at a glance.

Suppose that the dollar-mark exchange market is initially in equilibrium. The demand for marks is D_0, supply is S_1, and the exchange rate is 2.5:1 (that is, the mark is equal to 0.4 dollars). Ten

Figure 18-2
Exchange-Rate Equilibrium Maintained Through Macroeconomic Adjustment

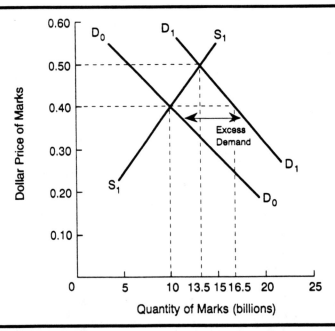

In Figure 18-2, the dollar-mark exchange rate is in equilibrium with demand, D_0, and supply, S_1. The equilibrium exchange rate is .40 dollars per mark (or it takes 2.5 marks to buy a dollar). As a result of U.S. inflation, rising domestic prices make German imports cheaper and the demand for marks increases to D_1 to finance additional imports. At the new demand, D_1, there is excess demand for marks at the old rate of .40. With a freely floating rate, the exchange rate would rise to .50 where quantity demanded of marks would equal quantity supplied. To maintain the old (fixed) exchange rate of .40, governments would (1) have to ration the exchange available (10 million marks) to prevent the excess demand (6.5 million marks) from raising the rate or (2) deflate the American economy, reducing the total demand for imports and reducing the demand for marks again to D_0.

billion marks are exchanged. Now, suppose that inflation hits the U.S. The rapidly rising prices of American goods make German imports relatively cheaper. As a result, American demand for marks to finance purchases of German goods rises to D_1. At the old exchange rate, there is an excess demand of 6.5 billion marks (16.5–10). If the dollar-mark rate is *not* freely floating, and if there is no system of international reserves to finance the payments deficit at existing exchange rates, two things may happen.

Exchange Controls
A system by which a nation rations foreign currency when there is excess demand for that currency.

1. The excess demand may be treated as a rationing problem. People demand more marks than the amount of marks available at the going exchange rate. So to "ration" marks, a nation might set up a system of **exchange controls** (perhaps an agency acting through its central bank). The agency could establish priorities to determine who should get the available marks. In effect, this would mean determining what kinds and quantities of German goods could be imported into the U.S. (perhaps Volkswagens, but no Mercedes Benzes, or perhaps machinery, but no cars at all). Presumably, these priorities would reflect certain national goals.

The main advantage of this approach to managing fluctuations in the exchange rate is that it enables countries to hold to a fixed exchange rate (with the aforementioned stability of trade), while at the same time ensuring that national import priorities are consistent with domestic economic priorities. The main disadvantages are that it does not allow the market to work, and that it imposes public tastes and preferences in place of private ones. (No matter how much you might like to import a Mercedes, you cannot, because the government regards it as more important to the country to import farm machinery.) It can also lead to corruption through granting special access to foreign exchange on the part of those favored by the government.

Neither the U.S. nor other major trading nations use exchange controls, although many less developed countries do. Low-income countries must import much of their capital. They do not have the domestic markets to provide it, and their governments do not wish to import expensive consumer goods at the same time.

Deflation
A general lowering of prices in an economy.

2. The deficit in payments (or the excess demand) shown in Figure 15-2 may be taken care of by adjustments in income and employment in the economy of the country that is demanding "too much" foreign currency.

In this case, inflation in the U.S. is causing the excess demand for marks. To counter this demand, the U.S. must use the the macroeconomic adjustment of **deflation**, which is a general lowering of prices. To accomplish this, the government may reduce aggregate demand by increasing taxes. It may also reduce government spending and raise interest rates. Or it may adopt any of the combinations of means that you will/or have already learned in your Macroeconomics course. (Of course, a tax on imports could correct the relative imbalance in prices between the two countries, but this victory would be at the price of free trade.)

If the U.S. follows a deflationary policy and aggregate demand does decrease, money incomes will certainly decrease also. Now let's assume that the demand for imports has a strongly positive income elasticity. (Americans, like most people, have a strong taste for imported goods.) Demand for imports, and for German marks, will fall. If the decline is strong enough, D_1 in Figure 18-2 may shift back to D_0, and the dollar-mark ratio may again find its equilibrium at 2.5:1.

The main advantage of tying a nation's economy to its exchange-rate position is that it practically guarantees stable rates of exchange. (Remember that stable exchange rates are desirable because they enhance trade and make possible longer-term planning for trade.) The main disadvantage of such a policy is that the nation has to pay a price for this stability of exchange rates and equilibrium of payments. Most economists believe this price is out of proportion to its worth. It is truly letting "the tail wag the dog." In the example here, the U.S. would have to deflate its economy deliberately—with all the effects it would have on income distribution, jobs, savings, and investment. Even if the U.S. had been at full employment before the government introduced the fiscal and monetary measures necessary to bring about deflation, there would soon be some significant changes in prices, incomes, and employment. But suppose that the U.S. had been suffering significant unemployment coupled with inflation, as it did in the early-1980s, and the government came along and put through these measures. Then, deflating the economy would just add to the unemployment problem, thus curing an external problem by worsening an internal one. Few countries would be willing to pay such a price for stability of exchange rates, though some LDCs and NICs have done so as part of a program to lower inflation and refinance external debts.

The Gold Standard

Gold Standard
An international system under which currencies are valued in terms of gold content. Nations are obligated to exchange their currencies for that amount of gold.

In the past, the system of fixed exchange rates was tied to the **gold standard**. The gold standard provided for the rates of exchange of most of the world's currencies for about 50 years before World War I, and in varying degrees up until the Great Depression of the 1930s. Under the freely convertible gold standard, nations could be sure of two things:

1. Each trading nation permitted unrestricted exports and imports of gold.

2. Each nation defined its own currency in terms of a specific quantity of gold, and guaranteed to convert any claims to that currency into gold at the defined rate.

Under the gold standard, each currency was defined to be worth so many grains of gold. For example, the German mark might be defined as 10 grains of gold and the American dollar as 25 grains of gold. Therefore, the dollar would be worth 2.5 marks. No one would pay more than 2.5 marks to get a dollar, or sell a mark for less than 40 cents, because the dollars (or marks) could always be converted into gold at the official rate. People could take their dollars or marks down to the bank and get gold for them. (Here we are ignoring the cost of moving gold—actually physically moving it—from one nation to another: transporting, insuring, and handling it.)

Suppose that the U.S. was operating on the gold standard with an initial equilibrium at demand, D_0, and supply, S_1, and a dollar price of marks of 0.40 (point A in Figure 18-3). A disequilibrium of payments (see Figure 18-3). Demand increases first to D_1 and then to D_2. The U.S. is committed to exchanging dollars for gold at 25 grains of gold per dollar. But it is *not* bound to keep the dollar-mark exchange rate constant. At first, therefore, the excess demand for marks at 40 cents apiece (distance AB, or 10.5 billion

Figure 18-3
Exchange-Rate Equilibrium Under the Gold Standard

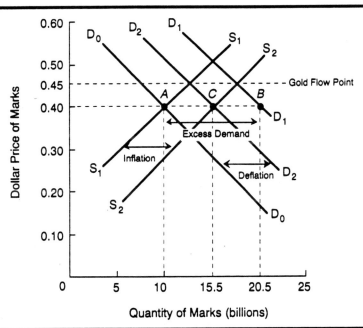

Under the gold standard, gold may move if an exchange rate is significantly different from the official (gold determined) rate. In Figure 18-3, there is an initial equilibrium at point A where demand, D_0 and supply, S_1, intersect. Because of demand increases (D_0 to D_1, D_1 to D_2) there is ultimately a disequilibrium or excess demand for marks at the old exchange rate (.40) of 10.5 billion marks (AB). At some exchange rate (.45) the gold-flow point is reached and gold moves to Germany from the U.S. As this happens, the U.S., with less gold to back to its currency, must reduce the money supply and *deflate* the economy. This in turn reduces the demand for marks. The influx of gold into Germany increases the supply of marks and *inflates* the German economy, enlarging the demand for U.S. goods and shifting the supply of marks to S_2. In a new equilibrium with demand for marks, D_2, and supply of marks, S_2, the old equilibrium of .40 is established at B.

marks) causes the dollar price of marks to be bid upward (depreciating the dollar). At some price—let's say 40 cents per mark plus the cost of transferring gold (shown arbitrarily as 45 cents to the mark)—it becomes cheaper to buy gold in the U.S., at the fixed price, and ship it to Germany to pay for imports than to buy marks with dollars to pay for the imports. This price is called the **gold-flow point.**

Let's suppose that the dollar price of the mark (Figure 18-3) rises beyond the gold-flow point. Gold begins to flow from the U.S. to Germany. Under the gold standard, the U.S. government backs its dollars by gold and must redeem them for gold. Since there is now less gold to back the currency, the money supply in the U.S. must be reduced.

The contraction in the money supply leads to a decline in the volume of transactions. Banks call in their loans, refuse to renew loans, and tighten credit. In effect, there is a deflation. Assuming a positive income elasticity of demand for German goods, the demand for imports (and German marks to pay for them) diminishes. The American demand for marks, D_1, will shift to the left, to D_2.

Now let's switch to Germany, where the gold is flowing in. More gold means a larger supply of money, M. Either prices (P) will rise, or quantities of goods sold (Q) will rise, or both. In either case, the German economy is inflated toward full employment. This will increase German demand for American imports, and thereby increase the supply of marks available to the U.S. The supply of marks, S_1, shifts to the right, to S_2 in Figure 18-3.

In the long run, equilibrium is restored. The changed supply of marks again intersects the demand, at the previous exchange rate of 40 cents to the mark. The equilibrium quantity of marks exchanged must be between A and C: in this instance at B (15.5 billion marks).

The U.S. and other leading trading nations have not used the gold standard since the 1930s. Yet there are still those, including some economists, who advocate its return. In the 1970s, the government of France came out in favor of it. The gold standard thus remains a source of controversy.

The advantages of the gold standard are the following: (1) It is automatic; any imbalance in relations between currencies sets in motion corrective gold flows. (2) It stabilizes exchange rates, and thereby makes possible long-term planning for trade. (3) Some economists maintain that gold flows make a nation practice economic self-discipline, live within its own (gold-determined) means, and refrain from forcing other nations to subsidize its consumption of goods.

The disadvantages of the gold standard are the following: (1) It causes domestic economic policy to be tied to international trade (the tail-wagging-the-dog argument). (2) It causes the volume of trade to be tied to the supply of an exhaustible resource, gold, which is in inelastic supply.

Postwar International Exchange Arrangements

The International Monetary Fund (IMF)
An international agency designed to administer the adjustable peg system of post-World War II monetary relationships. It makes loans to nations with problems of exchange rate disequilibrium.

Most present-day arrangements for financing trade stem from a meeting that the allied nations (the U.S., Britain, and France) held at Bretton Woods, New Hampshire, in 1944. There were many other nations present as well, however, Britain and the U.S. dominated the meeting. The Bretton Woods conference set up two basic trade features: (1) a system of adjustable pegs for exchange of currencies, a system that lasted until the 1970s, and (2) the **International Monetary Fund (IMF)**, an intergovernmental agency designed to administer the post-World War II monetary system and enhance its stability. It administers the operation of the *adjustable-peg system*, a system of exchange in which currencies are pegged, or are not allowed to change in value by more than a specific percentage. It can use its capital to make bridge loans to nations experiencing exchange rate disequilibrium problems.

The nations that met at Bretton Woods sought to create relatively fixed exchange rates, which could be maintained. Each currency was to be valued in terms of both gold *and* U.S. dollars. Currencies could vary from these parities by no more than 1 percent. Exchange rates could be changed, however, when countries found that there was a "fundamental disequilibrium" in their payments position. But the Bretton Woods conference failed to define the term *fundamental disequilibrium.*

So, beginning in the 1950s, countries such as the U.S. began to run long-term deficits in payments, with no changes in exchange rates. They did this by drawing on gold reserves—reserves held by the IMF—and by borrowing from the central banks of other countries. Thus, they were without the automatic, self-correcting, adjustment mechanism that had existed under the gold standard (a good feature, for all its other flaws). This went on until 1971, when President Nixon devalued the dollar and set it free from the pegged rate.

During the 1960s, pressure for change in the international money system began to develop. The countries that had to absorb the excess dollars created by U.S. balance-of-payments deficits began to be dissatisfied with the terms of the Bretton Woods agreement—and with good reason: Speculators in the late-1960s were moving huge amounts of money out of dollars and into strong currencies such as German marks.

Special Drawing Rights (SDRs)
A kind of "paper gold" or lines of credit that nations may borrow from the IMF to cover exchange rate disequilibrium.

One modification of the system was the creation by the IMF of **special drawing rights (SDRs)**. By using SDRs, countries with deficits could borrow so-called paper gold from the IMF to finance their imbalances of payments. This made it possible for the exchange system itself to finance trade. But it did nothing to establish equilibrium relations between the world's major currencies.

A second modification was to allow currencies to establish a supply-demand equilibrium through freely floating against each other. The dollar, as you know, led the way in doing this, in 1971.

The system of freely floating rates even if it is accompanied by the "dirty float" that is presently in force seems to work reasonably well. It does not satisfy those who want more stability in the exchange rate for dollars. Other people, who want a competitive exchange rate system, praise the system.

The Managed (Dirty) Float: Whither the Future?

There are some economists who say the Bretton Woods exchange rate system with its fixed but adjustable pegs died in late-1971 with the floating of the dollar against other major trading currencies. That assessment is warranted at least to the extent that there is no longer a governmental or intergovernmental agreement on the ratios at which (or even within which) international currencies will be allowed to trade.

The present international monetary system is a hybrid version of those (gold standard and fixed exchange rates with adjustable pegs) that preceded it. SDRs in some measure have provided the liquidity that might have been supplied by gold flows. The managed (dirty) float seems to be workable in the face of multi-country central bank cooperation. Dissatisfied with a dollar subject to wide swings in price, efforts have been made to create alternatives to it as *the* international currency. Some European nations have formed the European monetary system under which they value their currencies against each other. This group has also created a new unit of money called ECU (European currency unit), which the countries hope will become a rival to the U.S. dollar in international trade and finance.

For the near-term future, it seems unlikely that there will be major changes in the present system of international finance. The "dirty float" seems likely to continue. What effect the integration of Europe in 1992 will have on the system of international payments is, at this juncture, impossible to assay. The IMF seems likely to increase in importance as industrial nations, LDCs, and NICs alike attempt to come to grips with debt crises, threats of repudiation, and balance of payments problems that, for some nations, threaten domestic economic growth.

The Balance of Payments

Balance-of-Payments Statement
An annual monetary statement by a nation of its exports, imports, and reconciliation and payments.

Up to now, we have dealt with trade as a process of exporting and importing goods and services and paying for them directly with currency, but there is more to international trade. Not only goods and services move between nations. There are capital flows as well as other movements.

Each nation puts together an annual accounting of all its trade transactions (including trade in goods and services). This is called its **balance-of-payments statement**. This national statement is like a firm's profit-and-loss statement. It reveals not only what is bought and what is sold, but also how any difference between the two is financed. Table 18-1 shows a recent balance-of-payments statement for the U.S.

By definition, the balance of payments must balance. A nation, like a firm or a person, must somehow find a means to pay for everything it buys. Let's look at these accounts to see how the U.S. paid for all the things it bought (imported) in 1986.

The Balance-of-Payments Statement

A. Current account. The current account is like a family's calculation of current income and expenses. It includes both visible items (exports and imports of merchandise) and invisible items (services, including financial services). The biggest item, a visible item, is (1) merchandise exports and imports. In 1986, the U.S. exported $221.8 billion and imported $369.5 billion worth of merchandise. This means that imports of merchandise were greater than exports by $147.7 billion. Thus, the U.S. had a large *balance-of-trade deficit.* (2) (Remember, though, that this is only a part of the balance of payments.)

Other items in the current account include service exports (3) and service imports (4) Since we sold more export services than we bought, but imported more goods and services than we exported, the goods and services balances (5), like the trade balance is negative (-$125.5 billion). Net unilateral transfers consist of dollar claims transferred to foreigners by governments (foreign aid), by individuals (e.g., social security payments to

Table 18-1
The United States Balance of Payments, 1986 (billions of dollars)

Item	Debits (-)	Credits (+)	Balance
A. Current Account			
1. Merchandise Exports		+221.8	
2. Merchandise Imports	-369.5		
3. Trade Balance (1+2)			-147.7
4. Service Exports		+149.0	
5. Service Imports	-126.8		
6. Goods and Services Balance (3+4+5)			-125.5
7. Net Unilateral Transfers	-15.1		
8. Current Account Balance (6+7)			-140.6
B. Capital Account			
9. Outflow of U.S. Capital	-100.1		
10. Inflow of Foreign Capital		+179.9	
11. Statistical Discrepancy		+27.1	
12. Capital Account Balance (9+10+11)			+106.9
C. Basic Balance (A-B)			-33.7
D. Official Reserve Transactions Account			
13. Decrease in U.S. Official Assets Abroad		+0.3	
14. Increase in Foreign Official Assets in U.S.		+33.4	
15. Official Reserve Balance (13+14)		+33.7	
United States Net Total (Balance) (8+12+15)			0.0

Sources: *Federal Reserve Bulletin,* July, 1987, International Financial Statistics, International Monetary Fund, June, 1987.

Current Account Balance
A statement for a nation of its annual balance of exports of goods and services minus its imports of goods and services together with net unilateral transfers.

Americans retired abroad), and charitable donations. As in every year since World War II, these transfers were negative (Americans earned fewer such transfers than we transferred abroad), by $15.1 billion. The **current account balance** (6) is obtained by adding exports of goods and services minus imports of goods and services plus net unilateral transfers. The current account balance need not balance (be zero) and for 1986, the U.S. had a deficit on the current account balance of $140.6 billion.

The deficit on the current account must, of course, be paid for, and we see how the U.S. financed that deficit in item B which reflects capital flows.

B. Capital account. Note that slightly more than $100 billion of capital flowed out of the U.S. in 1986. We are referring here to financial capital flows, purchases of assets abroad such as stocks and bonds. In the same year, almost $180 billion of foreign capital flowed into the U.S. in the form of purchases of U.S. assets by foreigners. For most of the 1980s, America enjoyed this net inflow or surplus in its capital account. There are two major reasons why this has happened. First, interest rates were relatively high in the U.S., resulting in investors buying U.S. assets for interest returns. Second, in contrast with many countries, the U.S. is a relatively "safe" place to invest without threat of nationalization, exchange controls to limit repatriation of funds, and other constraints that raise the risk of owning assets, especially in the LDCs. The statistical discrepancy of $27.1 billion in 1986 is an entry to ensure that debits and credits balance as they must in the balance of payments. It is thought that much of this statistical discrepancy is due to secret or unreported movements of capital into the U.S., especially from countries where such movements are either limited or prohibited on an official basis.

C. Basic balance. The combination of a nation's current account and its capital account is often referred to as its **basic balance**. In 1986, the basic balance of the U.S. showed a deficit of $33.7 billion. This amount had to be financed.

D. Official reserve transactions account. The account labeled **official reserve transactions account** shows how the U.S. met its payments to the rest of the world that remained on its basic balance. For 1986, this difference (A + B = -140.6 + 106.9 = $33.7 billion). Mainly, it did so by borrowing from official agencies (usually central banks), by persuading them to hold more dollars ($33.4 billion more). Also, the U.S. sold some government debt ($0.3 billion).

Basic Balance
The balance shown in the nation's current account (A) plus its capital account (B).

Official Reserve Transactions Account
An account of those sources such as borrowing from other official agencies that finance the basic balance.

The Balance of Payments in Summary
As you can see, there is a lot of detail in the balance of payments. For an overview of it, let's put it in capsule form (Table 18-2). The four major accounts are shown again, without the previous detail. A, the current account, shows a deficit of $140.6 billion. To this is added B, the capital account, which has a surplus of $106.9 billion. Together (A + B) they form the basic balance, which shows a

Table 18-2
The United States Balance of Payments, 1986, Summary Form
(billions of dollars)

Item	Credits (+) Debits (−)
A. Current account	−140.6
B. Capital account	+106.9
C. Basic balance (A + B)	−33.7
D. Official reserve transactions balance	+33.7
Balance of payments (B + C)	.00

deficit of $33.7 billion. The balance to be financed is C or $33.7 billion. The balance (again, there *must* be one) comes from the official reserve transactions balance (D). The balance of payments (C + D) equals zero. In other words, the U.S., in 1986, as in every other year, financed all its international trade.

The U.S. Balance-of-Payments Deficits

Figure 18-4 shows that since 1960 the U.S. has had deficits (amounts to be financed) in the balance of payments for most

Figure 18-4
The United States Trade Balances, 1965-1985 (billions of dollars)

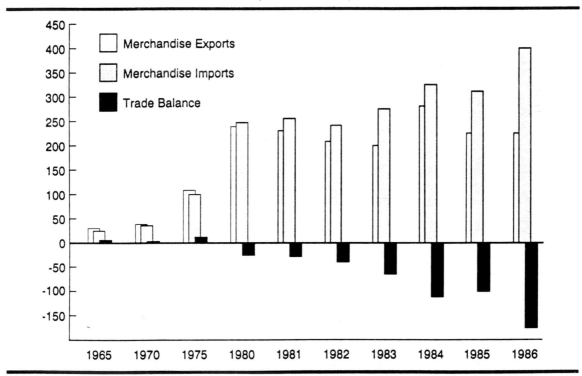

As late as 1975, the U.S. had a small surplus on its trade balance (exports > imports). Since 1980, exports have grown much less rapidly than imports with the result that now exports < imports.

years. The exceptions were 1959, 1971, and 1975 when there were surpluses. The problem in recent years seems to be primarily in the merchandise export-import position, Because the dollar's exchange rate is free to float (at least a "dirty" float), and because American goods in the 1980s became relatively more expensive and difficult to export (at least until 1987), the trade (merchandise) deficits from 1980 to 1987 grew rapidly. Since 1988, however, the dollar has fallen against the yen and other currencies, and America's exports have grown substantially. Because imports have also grown rapidly, there remain large deficits to be financed as we enter the 1990s.

The deficits to be financed in the 1980s were largely accommodated, as we have seen, through capital inflows into the U.S. While some people have seen this as the "buying of America," these inflows of capital have not only financed America's taste for imports but also, through enlarging the supply of financial capital, have permitted credit markets to be equilibriated at what otherwise might have been higher interest rates. In this sense, they have stimulated the domestic American economy through encouraging domestic investment.

If the dollar falls against other currencies and the deficits to be financed decline, there are some who forecast an end to the "trade" deficits within 5 years. This will require major readjustments in trade patterns and flows of capital. Financing trade deficits with the United States will again become a problem for many nations. At this juncture, such forecasts are difficult to make with confidence. Whether the deficits are eliminated and whether trading relationships will continue to be essentially free are political as well as economic questions as we will see in the application "Politics and the Balance of Payments" that follows this chapter.

SUMMING UP

1. Very little international trade is carried out by means of barter. Nearly all of it requires a means of monetary payment, a money exchange system.

2. The conversion of currency of one nation to that of another is carried out by the international banking system and by specialized dealers. For example, a person importing a pair of shoes from Italy can mail a check to the Italian exporter. The exporter deposits it in a bank in Italy and gets a certain amount of lire for it. The Italian bank gets a claim to dollars from its correspondent bank in the U.S.

3. The money exchange system enables exporters and importers to end up with the kind of national currency (dollars, marks, yen, and so on) that they need.

4. Exports by the U.S. create a demand overseas for dollars to pay for them. When a French firm imports American goods, for example, it creates a supply of claims to francs with which Americans may pay for their imports from France. In other words, *a country that wishes to export must import, in order to create the claims to currency necessary for it to trade.*

5. A good international monetary system has the following characteristics: (a) It establishes a balance between stability and growth in international trade and stability and growth in each of the trading nations. (b) It is equitable and ensures that each nation will have access to foreign exchange, and that each will help bear the costs of operating the exchange system. (c) It is efficient and thus enhances the growth of international trade.

6. Exchange rates are established in foreign exchange markets. There are two basic exchange rate systems: (a) freely floating and (b) fixed.

7. A *freely floating exchange rate* is determined by the supply of a currency and the demand for it. The *equilibrium exchange rate* is the rate at which quantity supplied and quantity demanded are equal. This means that there is no excess demand or excess supply.

8. The advantages of a freely floating rate are that (a) the rate responds quickly to changes in supply and demand, and (b) imbalances or disequilibria in payments are readily resolved. The disadvantages are that (a) there can be great instability in rates; (b) there can be great instability in savings, investment, and prices in countries that depend heavily on foreign trade; and (c) there can be sudden changes in *terms of trade,* requiring a country to make a reallocation of resources so that it can export more, in order to continue to import.

9. Economists differ on the merits of freely floating exchange rates. For the time being, however, the U.S. seems committed to letting the dollar continue to float within certain ill defined limits.

10. *Fixed exchange rates* mean that the currency of a country keeps the same value with respect to the currencies of other countries. The main advantage of fixed rates is stability; they permit longer-term planning for trade. The main disadvantage is that supply and demand are not allowed to work freely. Also, fixed exchange rates require a system of *international reserves* to fill excess demands.

11. Most governments do not consistently follow the principle of freely floating or that of fixed exchange rates. They intervene selectively in what is called a "dirty float" or managed exchange rate system.

12. Fluctuations of exchange rates derive from changes in economic conditions in the exporting and importing nations. Excess demand can be handled by (a) introducing *exchange controls* (rationing of currencies) or (b) by adjusting the economy of the country suffering the disequilibrium so that the domestic cause is eliminated.

13. LDCs often use exchange controls. They determine who shall have access to the limited foreign exchange available. The advantage is a stable exchange rate; the disadvantage is that exchange controls impose a set of public tastes on what would be the private tastes for imports. The government decides what is best for the country to import. Such controls may also give rise to corruption or favoritism in access to foreign exchange.

14. Adjusting a country's domestic economy to eliminate excess demand for foreign exchange means adjusting domestic prices, incomes, and employment. Although a nation may use such means to establish exchange-rate equilibrium, it is a drastic solution. Most economists feel that it creates a major problem (unemployment) in order to solve a lesser problem for which other solutions exist.

15. Under the freely convertible *gold standard,* which has not been used since the 1930s, currencies are valued in terms of grains of gold. Each currency has a value in terms of gold as well as in terms of other currencies. In order for the gold standard to work, the exchange value cannot deviate much from the gold value. If it does, people buy gold and ship it overseas to pay for traded goods, rather than using currencies to pay for them.

16. The *gold-flow point* is the exchange rate at which it is cheaper to ship gold in payment for traded goods than to buy currency.

17. The *advantages* claimed for the gold standard are that (a) it operates automatically, (b) it stabilizes exchange rates, and (c) gold flows impose an economic self-discipline on nations. The *disadvantages* claimed for the gold standard are that (a) it ties a nation's internal economic policy to the balance of its foreign payments (the tail wags the dog), and (b) it ties the world's volume of trade to the inelastic supply of an exhaustible resource.

18. The Bretton Woods Conference in 1944 established (a) an *adjustable-peg system* for international currencies, and (b) and *International Monetary Fund (IMF)* to administer the system.

19. The system of pegging currencies meant that they could change in value by no more than 1 percent. The world no longer uses this currency-pegging system. However, the IMF still exists. It administers a system of *special drawing rights (SDRs), (or "paper gold")* through which countries with balance-of-payments problems can borrow from the IMF.

20. The freely floating exchange rates now in use appear to work reasonably well. Actions of private speculators, who buy and sell currency (arbitrage), may have helped to prevent exaggerated fluctuations.

21. Each nation annually prepares a *balance-of-payments statement,* an accounting of its international purchases and sales, plus an explanation of how it has financed any deficit payments.

22. A balance-of-payments statement lists (a) current account (visible and invisible items of trade), (b) current account balance (balance on current account including unilateral transfers), (c) capital account which shows both capital outflows and capital inflows (d) balance to be financed, and (e) *official reserve transactions balance* (what the nation borrows from other nations, changes in its gold holdings, and so on). A nations' official reserves change when it has a payments deficit or surplus. The balance of payments *must* balance.

23. Since the late-1960s, the U.S. has usually had a deficit to be financed in its balance of payments. Recently, this deficit has been due mainly to a *balance-of-trade deficit* (merchandise exports minus imports), and partly to military commitments abroad and our foreign aid program. Our trade position in the late-1980s improved somewhat. Prices of things we exported fell relative to prices of other nations' export items. Even so, the deficit in our balance of payments continues. Some, however, forecast an end to the deficits within five years but such forecasts are extremely difficult to be made precise.

KEY TERMS

Freely floating exchange rates
Equilibrium exchange rates
Fixed exchange rates
International reserves
Dirty float
International Monetary Fund (IMF)
Exchange controls
Deflation
Gold standard
Gold flow point
Special drawing rights
Balance-of-payments statement
Current account balance
Basic balance
Official reserves transactions account

QUESTIONS

1. Do you think the U.S. should continue to let the American dollar float against other currencies, or should it go back to some sort of pegged or fixed exchange rate system? Why?

2. Evaluate the following statement: "A nation cannot for long export (sell its goods to others) unless it imports (buys from others)."

3. What were the problems associated with the gold standard? What were its advantages?

4. Why is it correct to say that a nation's balance of payments *must* balance? What are the main balancing items?

5. What is the "dirty float"? Why do nations try to manage their exchange rates?

6. In the figure below, the exchange rate between the U.S. dollar and the Japanese yen is initially in equilibrium with demand for yen, D_0 and supply of yen, S_0 at 120 yen = 1 dollar. An increase in the demand for yen D_1 occurs to finance imports from Japan:

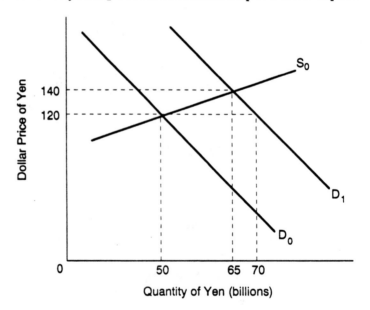

a. If the exchange rate of the dollar to the yen is freely floating, what will be the new equilibrium exchange rate?

b. If the U.S. and Japan want to restore the old equilibrium rate (120), how many yen will have to be supplied to eliminate excess demand?

c. If the excess demand is treated as a rationing problem, what might be the solution?

d. If the U.S. sought to reduce demand for yen by deflating the economy, what might it do?

7. What are the advantages and disadvantages of (a) fixed exchange rates? (b) freely floating exchange rates?

8. Suppose that the Secretary of the Treasury calls you in and says, "I have to go before the Joint Economic Committee of Congress and present a good argument for why the dollar should not be allowed to float on world currency markets. What's the best argument I can make?" What would your response be?

SUGGESTED READINGS

Adams, John (ed). *The Contemporary International Economy.* New York: St Martins Press, 1985.

Cline, William R. (ed). *Trade Policy in the 1980s.* Cambridge: MIT Press, 1983.

Williamson, John. *The Open Economy and the World Economy.* New York: Basic Books, 1983.

Caves, Richard E. and Ronald W. Jones. *World Trade and Payments, An Introduction,* 4th edition. Boston: Little Brown, 1985.

Lindert, Peter H. and Charles P. Kindleberger *International Economics*, 8th edition. Homewood, Ill. Richard D. Irwin Co., 1987.

Rezvin, Philip. "As Trade Gap Closes, Partners of U.S. Face End of the Gravy Train." *Wall Street Journal.* April 3, 1988.

Stone, Charles F. and Isabel V. Sawhill. "Trade's Impact on U.S. Jobs." *Challenge.* September/October, 1987. Reprinted in Annual Editions: *Economics 88/89.* Don Cole, Editor. Guilford, CT: The Dushkin Publishing Group, 1989.

Application to Chapter 18:
Politics and the Balance-of-Payments
Problem

Reasons Behind Import Restraints

Whenever the U.S. buys more goods and services from other countries than they buy from us there is a deficit in our balance of trade, (current account or goods and service's balance) and a resulting cry to "buy American!" Various people, union leaders and business executives alike, exhort the citizenry to either buy products made in the U.S. or to impose restrictions on imports. In fact, firms or industries may urge this at any juncture, whenever foreign producers begin to take away any sizable share of domestic sales from American industry. In the mid-1980s for instance, lobbyists for both the steel and automobile industries worked hard in Washington, trying to get Congress to impose import restrictions on European and Japanese steel and cars. (Detroit watches with gloom the import figures on Toyotas and Nissans, Volvos and Saabs, Renaults and Peugeots, Hyundais and Hondas.)

Up until the Great Depression of the 1930s, there was rarely much attention paid to the buy-American slogan. A country's nervousness about excessive imports usually comes out when some if not most of its industries are enduring hard times. But as we have seen in the 1980s, there were large deficits in the U.S. goods and services and U.S. current account (including U.S. government grants). The U.S. has had such continuing deficits in its balance of trade only twice since 1893 (also in the early-1970s).

In the early-1980s, the cries for protectionism, which had been muted since the mid-1970s, again became loud. In apparent response to the threat of protective legislation, the executive branch of the government negotiated "voluntary" export agreements with some foreign manufacturers, especially with Japanese auto makers. Like quotas, these restraints limited imports but, unlike quotas, were imposed or at least agreed to by foreign manufacturers. While such firms (Nissan, Toyota, etc) may have agreed to the export limitations to prevent more restrictive action by the U.S. Congress, they may also have agreed because they benefit from the higher net price on automobiles in the American market that resulted from the reduced supply.

Voluntary export agreements, alone, did not seem to satisfy the proponents of protectionism including those who believed that America should work more aggressively to open the markets of other nations to its exports. Many argued that the U.S. should retaliate against those who engaged in "unfair" trading practices including dumping goods in its markets. The Trade and Tariff Act of 1984 did little to allay the fears of those who have argued for "fair" as opposed to "free" trade. The act extended the Generalized System of Preferences (GSP) adopted in 1974, which provides duty-free access to U.S. markets for many "non-import sensitive" items from the LDCs and NICs. In a policy statement in 1985, the AFL-CIO argued that such preferences, especially for many of the successful NICs (Korea, Taiwan, Singapore, Hong Kong) are no longer necessary, and argued as well that they have even been extended to some Communist countries. The 1984 act authorized the President to negotiate bilateral free-trade agreements with other nations, with the recent free trade agreement with Canada being the first major fruit of that activity.

The trade-offs between trade policy and policy toward the LDCs and NICs promise to be difficult. As distinguished economist Bela Belassa has recently argued: "The more advanced developing economies would, thus benefit from liberalizing their imports in exchange for reductions in the trade barriers of the developed countries." Perhaps such bilateral "free trade" agreements will become a more prominent feature of U.S. policy. The 1984 act also extended the authority of the President to negotiate further voluntary export agreements, especially with foreign steel producers and these, too, may become a more prominent feature of our trade policy.

Protectionism: Costs and Benefits

Restrictions in the form of tariffs or quotas have usually been imposed for the purpose of saving the jobs of workers in the U.S. In 1985 the AFL-CIO put it this way:

> "...positive governmental action is needed to reverse the erosion of America's industrial base—(between 1982 and 1985) it is estimated that more than 3 million jobs have been lost or not created due to America's continued trade decline."

In the mid-1970s, a major labor leader in the U.S. argued that the costs of free trade ("low-wage imports") were borne by American workers but that "international operators" not U.S. consumers got the benefits. Economists, on the other hand, have estimated that the cost of both tariff and nontariff restrictions (including voluntary export controls) is between $20 billion and $45 billion per year. This figure reflects the consumer burden of higher prices resulting from import duties (for example, there is a 12 percent import tax on cars). It also reflects the higher prices resulting from a lowered supply and a less competitive market in the U.S. for cars, steel, cattle, meat, dairy products—and all the other goods protected by high tariffs. For example, economist William Albrecht says:

Between 1969, when the quota system was first introduced, and 1972, steel companies increased their prices 5 times as much as they had in the preceding 8-year period, despite the fact the industry was experiencing declining demand and had unused capacity of 25 to 50 percent.

To the extent that this heightened price structure may be generalized to apply to many industries, one could say that it is indeed the American consumer who suffers as a result of import restrictions. Even a consumer who has lost a job because of competition from cheap imports is worse off. After all, the jobless consumer, who very much needs bargains, cannot buy cheap shirts made in Taiwan or cheap shoes made in Korea or low-price beef from Argentina.

America's Trade Problem: The Myths

Murray Weidenbaum, a former chairman of the Council of Economic Advisers, says that much of the rhetoric surrounding our trade problems is based on misconception. Weidenbaum identifies five myths that he believes are fairly common:

1. *Japan is the problem*, and if it would only open its markets, much of the problem would disappear. As Weidenbaum points out, our trade deficit extends to Canada, Mexico, Europe, and almost every non-communist nation in the world. It must be "our problem," not a "Japanese problem."

2. *The U.S. is alone in practicing free trade.* In fact, says Weidenbaum, we have an elaborate system of preferences, even apart from quotas (sugar, beef, etc); only 30 percent of our imports are allowed in duty free.

3. *Imports depress the American economy*, especially in terms of manufacturing jobs. Imports, says Weidenbaum, have little to do with the structural decline in relative importance of manufacturing; services have been larger than manufacturing in the U.S. since 1929. Manufacturing production, in an absolute sense, has never been as high as it is today.

4. *The way to save American jobs is through trade protection.* On the contrary, says Weidenbaum, "protectionism is the most inefficient welfare program ever devised." Saving a job in the steel industry, for example, may cost 3 to 4 jobs in steel using industries (due to higher costs).

5. *Workers in import-sensitive industries deserve better treatment than other workers.* As Weidenbaum says, "I know of no reason why the one group is more meritorious than the other."

Protectionism: Will It Triumph or Fail?

It is not difficult to imagine some form of protectionism triumphing in the political arena. If it does, a likely explanation is that offered by Weidenbaum who says that "Protectionism is a politician's delight because it delivers visible benefits to the protected parties while imposing the costs as a hidden tax on the public." This public choice explanation, seems compelling. After all, a higher tariff or a quota on automobiles, for example, will clearly and significantly benefit a particular industry (its owners and manager's) as well as a particular groups of American workers (the members of the United Automobile Workers Union). The costs, on the other hand, will be spread over many millions of would-be automobile buyers in the form of higher automobile prices. Which group has the more intense and intensely expressed preferences: The protectionists or the free traders?

Before we too hurriedly proclaim the likely demise of freer trade, however, let us remember the following:

1. For more than 50 years, America has moved toward lower tariffs and freer trade as reflected in Reciprocal Trade Agreements Acts and other forms of legislation as well as through bilateral agreements. Many industries and workers in this country are well served by lower priced imported goods and services. In addition, many industries and jobs depend on American exports and would surely suffer in the retaliation that American protectionism would engender. Resistance to protectionism may be strong from those with preferences for freer trade.

2. The push for increased protectionism has stemmed in large measure from U.S. trade deficits in the 1980s. If the dollar continues to decline against the currencies of its major trading partners in the 1990s, we are likely to see a growth of American exports, and decline in imports; some even predict, trade surpluses in the 1990s. Historically, when this has happened, the push for protectionism has abated, and we may see this happen again in the near future.

The Lesson to Be Learned

There are several things one can learn from the recent unusual balance-of-trade situation. First the U.S. should not formulate foreign economic policy on the basis of short-term variations in its trade position. This position can change so quickly, and the changes are so hard to forecast, much less control, that the situation may change by the time the policy is implemented. Second, protectionism is nearly always self-defeating. If the U.S. enacts a drastic import-quota system, Western Europe and Japan assuredly will retaliate. They will put import quotas of their own on the things the U.S. wants to sell to *them*. U.S. exports will decline and the projected balance-of-trade turnabout will never take place. Tariffs and quotas have a way of boomeranging.

In general, then, economists rarely espouse the cause of protectionism. When industries find that they can no longer maintain a competitive cost position with respect to foreign suppliers, economists' advice is usually "Retrain labor! Reallocate resources!"

SUMMING UP

1. When any nation experiences a deficit in its balance of trade (that is, when it exports less than it imports), citizens are urged to buy locally made products, and people call on the government to impose either voluntary or mandatory controls in order to limit imports of foreign goods.

2. A strong push for protectionism reemerged in the 1980s. To head off protective legislation, "voluntary" export agreements to limit foreign sales, especially of Japanese autos, were negotiated. The AFL-CIO, however, argued for a new trade policy including the elimination of many of the preferences given to the LDCs and NICs. The Trade and Tariff Act of 1984, however, authorized more voluntary export agreements and other bilateral trade agreements which may become an increasing feature of American trade policy.

3. Labor leaders maintain that protectionism is necessary to guard American workers against competition from low-wage areas of the world. They also claim that low-priced foreign imports do not benefit American consumers; they benefit international (multinational) manufacturers. Economists, however, estimate that direct and indirect controls cost American consumers between $20 and $45 billion per year. They maintain that such import controls not only add to the costs of goods, but also enhance the monopoly power of domestic producers.

4. Support for protectionism seems in part to be based on some myths about America's trade problem. These include: (a) Japan and its protectionism are the problem. (b) Only the U.S. practices free trade. (c) Imports have caused the decline of manufacturing industry in the U.S. (d) American jobs can be saved through protectionism. (e) Workers in import-sensitive industries deserve better treatment than other U.S. workers.

5. One can learn two things from the recent U.S. balance-of-trade experience: (a) The U.S. should not base its foreign economic policy on short-term changes in its trade position, because its trade position can change dramatically and is difficult to predict. (b) Protectionism is almost bound to be self-defeating, since it invites retaliation by foreign customers for U.S. exports.

6. Economists rarely support protectionism. Most feel that retraining of labor, plus reallocation of resources, is the way out for an industry that cannot compete with cheaper imports from low-wage areas of the world.

QUESTIONS

1. From the standpoint of value, the U.S. has a greater volume of international trade than any other nation. In the face of this, why would a protectionist policy with respect to imports almost certainly cause other nations to retaliate?

2. Evaluate this statement: "American workers earn high wages. The government must protect them against the imports of goods that are from low-wage countries."

3. What groups are likely to pay the bill for protectionism?

4. In what ways is a policy of retraining workers and reallocating resources preferable to a policy of protecting (by tariffs and quotas) a firm or an industry that is inefficient, relative to foreign firms or industries?

5. What are some of the myths about America's trade problems?

SUGGESTED READINGS

Balassa, Bela. "The Importance of Trade for Developing Countries." *Banca Nazionale Del Lavoro Quarterly Review*, No 163. Rome, December, 1987.

Baldwin, Robert E. and J. David Richardson (eds). *International Trade and Finance Readings,* 2nd ed. Boston: Little Brown, 1981.

Battles, Deborah. "Trade Theory and Comparative Advantage: Is the Real World *Really* Like That?" *The Margin*. March/April, 1989.

"Car Wars: Protectionism Battle Over Imports May Head for Congress." *Wall Street Journal*. February 15, 1980.

Erceg, John J. and Theodore G. Bernard. "Productivity Costs and International Competition." *Economic Commentary*. Federal Reserve Bank of Cleveland. November 15, 1989.

Gordon, David M. "Do We Need to Be No. 1?" *The Atlantic Monthly*. April, 1986. Reprinted in Annual Editions 87/88, John Pisciotta, ed. Dushkin, Sluice Dock, CT, 1987.

"International Trade and Investment." *The National Economy and Trade.* Report of the Executive Council of the AFL-CIO. October, 1985. Reprinted in *Introduction to Macroeconomics.* 1986-1987. Peter D. McClelland, Ed. New York: McGraw-Hill, 1986.

Lindert, Peter H. and Charles P. Kindleberger. *International Economics*, 8th edition. Homewood, IL: D. Richard, C. Irwin, 1987.

Maskus, Keith E. "Rising Protectionism and U.S. International Trade Policy." *Economic Review,* Federal Reserve Bank of Kansas. July/August, 1984. Reprinted in *Annual Editions 87/88.* John Pisciotta, ed. Sluice Dock, CT: Dushkin, 1987.

Stein, Herbert. "Don't Worry About the Trade Deficit." *The Wall Street Journal.* May 16, 1989.

"The Politics of Trade: Five Ways to Choke off Imports." *Business Week.* October 7, 1985. Reprinted in *Annual Editions 87/88.* John Pisciotta, ed. Sluice Dock, CT: Dushkin, 1987.

Weidenbaum, Murray L. *Foreign Trade and the U.S. Economy: Dispelling the Myths.* CATO Policy Report. January/February, 1986. Reprinted in *Introduction to Macroeconomics, 1986-1987.* Peter D. McClelland, Ed. New York: McGraw-Hill, 1986.

Yeutter, Clayton. "Protectionism. Competition in the World Marketplace." *Readings in Introductory Macroeconomics.* Peter D. McClelland (ed). New York: McGraw-Hill, 1988.

Chapter 19:
Other Economic Systems in Theory

Economic System
The institutions a
society establishes
to deal with the
choices imposed on
it by scarcity.

Throughout this book we have looked at the operation of an **economic system**, the institutions that a society establishes to deal with the choices imposed upon it by scarcity. To this point, we have almost entirely confined our view to the system characteristic of the U.S.: *capitalism*. To put this view of a capitalist economy in perspective, let's conclude our introduction to economics by examining and comparing capitalism with other economic systems.

Economic systems are as diverse as the institutional arrangements that can be created to make economic choices. We are going to concentrate on the major systems found in societies in the twentieth century: capitalism, planned socialism, market socialism, and fascism. Before we can look at each, however, it is necessary to set forth the criteria by which systems are evaluated as well as to remind ourselves of the basic choices all societies must make.

Basic Economic Choices: A Reminder

Economic systems, as indicated above, are created out of the necessity to make choices. Such choices are imposed by scarcity, the existence of unlimited wants and limited resources. Regardless of the philosophical or ideological preferences of a society, there are certain questions about using resources that *must* be answered. By way of quick review, those choices are:

1. *What* shall be the composition of output? Since everything that is desirable cannot be produced in the quantities desired, difficult choices must somehow be made about allocating resources to produce one good as opposed to another. Shall these choices be made by individual consumers or shall government planners make

the decisions? Whose tastes and preferences, in other words, shall dominate the choice about output?

2. *How* shall goods be produced? At any particular time, there is a menu of choices about producing goods. Shall we, for example, produce steel with a lot of capital (oxygen furnaces and continuous rolling mills) or with less capital and more labor (even charcoal fired furnaces)? An answer to this question is necessary; shall it come from individual managers and entrepreneurs or from central planners?

3. *Who* shall receive the output (real income) of the society? This question of distribution is perhaps the most difficult and potentially divisive one for all nations. Shall markets, responding to productivity signals, ration output on the basis of (market-earned) incomes and tastes or shall planners set prices and factor incomes according to some set of "social" objectives? What is equitable or fair? Since, as we have noted at various points, there is no unique definition of distributive equity, each society must not only find a means or process to distribute income, but must also agree on the results of that process.

Evaluating an Economic System

There are many dimensions to the evaluation of an economic system and economic, along with moral and political criteria may be used. An economic criterion that inevitably is used is that of efficiency in resource usage. Rich society or poor, socialist, capitalist or any other, the ability to provide solutions to economic problems now and in the future depends heavily on efficiency. We shall look at efficiency questions in two dimensions.

Static Efficiency
At a point in time, using resources in ways that produce the most desired mix of output.

Static Efficiency
Since resources are scarce, they must, to be used efficiently, be allocated to produce that mix of goods and services that the society prefers. While the answer to what is preferred depends on whose preferences are considered, no society in a static (timeless) sense is efficient if it produces one good (for example, pet rocks) where doing so causes it to produce less of another good (microcomputers for example) that is more preferred.

Dynamic Efficiency
Over a period of time, using resources in ways that maximize the long-term benefits from their employment.

Dynamic Efficiency
Dynamics involves looking at a process over time. Present uses of resources will have consequences for the future and for future consumers. Efficiency over time requires that scarce resources be used in ways that maximize the stream of long-term benefits from their employment.

Property Rights:
Should They be Vested in Individuals or in the State?

Property Rights
The rights to own, control, and profit from the use of resources.

Property rights, the rights to own, control, and profit from the use of resources, must be vested somewhere in any society. Without property rights and the control they carry with them, choices about resource usage would be impossible. There are two basic ways these rights may be assigned in any economic system:

Private Property Rights

Property rights in resources may be assigned exclusively to individuals who not only control their use but also have the right to transfer control to others through a process of exchange. In such a system, the individual owns not only his own labor, but also any other real or financial assets to which title is held. Homes and land, for example, are owned by individuals and families who are free to sell them, rent them, or make any other lawful use of them.

Public Property Rights

Public property rights are not assigned to individuals but are held in some kind of communal ownership. Though individuals own their own labor, other resources including land and housing are not individually owned and cannot, therefore, be sold or rented to others by their occupants. Collective ownership of resources implies that the state through some means must decide who shall have access to a society's resources.

There is no society today in which property rights are assigned entirely in one way or the other. In the U.S. there are some goods such as parks and many schools that are collectively owned. There are also public goods that have indivisible benefits. In the former Soviet Union, there were some goods, such as automobiles, that were privately owned and proposals to expand private ownership rights in the commonwealth that succeeded the Soviet Union continue to be made in the 1990s. Still, each present society has a *emphasis* about the location of property rights.

Why Do Property Rights Matter?

Property rights are important to an economy in two separate but interrelated ways. To begin with, such rights or their lack, create incentives or disincentives on the part of individuals to supply effort and to create innovations. If I do not own the home in which I live, what incentive have I to keep it up or improve it? If I cannot patent a new process, what incentive have I to develop it? A society with widespread private property rights is, therefore, one in which individuals will be likely to supply effort voluntarily and one in which innovation is likely to be forthcoming.

Property rights also heavily influence the distribution of income in a society. Those who own more resources or more productive kinds of resources will be likely to receive a greater part of the income and real product of the economy. If individuals such as inventors or innovators are given exclusive use to their new processes, they will enjoy monopoly returns and incomes. If, on the other hand, individuals are completely denied such ownership rights, disincentives to effort and innovation are created. Trade-offs, thus, are created in all societies when property rights choices are made.

Housing may well be one of the best examples of these trade-offs. If privately owned, incentives exist to maintain and improve it. At the same time, the best housing will go to those with the most income and some others may actually be homeless. If housing is publicly owned, disincentives exist for individuals to maintain and improve it but there may be more widespread access to it (assuming enough of it is produced).

With this background in mind, let us turn to look at each of the four major benchmark economic systems in turn. First, we will examine capitalism, a system whose detail has been examined throughout this book. Now, however, we want to examine its systemic fundamentals.

CAPITALISM

Capitalism
An economic system characterized by (1) private assignment of property rights and (2) decision making about uses of resources expressed through a system of product and factor markets.

A system of **capitalism** has two *essential criteria*:

1. Most of the means of production are privately owned. Property rights are vested in individuals. As a result, economic decision making is relatively decentralized, and

2. Economic decisions about uses of resources are expressed through a system of interrelated product and factor markets.

By private ownership of the means of production, we mean that the legal owners of real capital (machines, buildings, and so on) used to produce goods and services in an economy are *individuals* in that society. This definition allows for the existence of corporations, since they are owned by stockholders. In addition, it allows for some government ownership. But the amount of capital owned by the government is a small percentage of the total means of production. The fact that in the U.S. governments own schools, hospitals, parks, and so on does not, therefore, mean the U.S. economy is not *capitalist.*

We have seen that markets in a capitalist economy may be organized in many ways ranging from highly competitive to mono-polistic in structure. The key feature of capitalism, though, is not the structure of these markets, but the fact that *markets exist.* Capitalism is not necessarily the same thing as a competitive-free-enterprise market system. Nor, in the political realm, does capitalism *necessarily* translate into a representative; democratic system of government.

*Necessary Legal
Features of
Capitalism:*
(1) right of private
ownership, (2) legal
enforceability of
contracts.

To make it possible for the two **necessary legal features
of capitalism** to exist, a society must establish a legal framework
to support them. Two basic elements in this legal framework are
(1) *the right of private ownership* and (2) *the legal enforceability
of contracts.*

Economic Advantages of Capitalism

Because choices about what to produce and what to buy are made
by private individuals, choice making under capitalism, as we
noted, is relatively decentralized. This is true even in a capitalist
economy in which significant elements of monopoly may exist in
product and factor markets. Voluntary exchange based upon
mutual advantage is the distinguishing characteristic of capitalism.
The role of government in such an economic system, while
significant, is relatively limited.

A principal advantage of a capitalist economy lies in the
incentives to efficiency created by private property rights. Because
private owners of resources keep the gains of their use and have the
right to sell their property, there is a strong incentive to maximize
the value of those rights by using resources efficiently. Those who
take risks receive whatever profit is created; to use the term
economists prefer, there are no **"free riders,"** individuals who can
lay claim to the benefits from resource usage for which they bore
none of the costs.

Free Riders
Individuals who can
lay claim to the
benefits of using
resources while
bearing none of the
costs of their usage.

A second advantage of capitalism is that the costs of
decision making are likely to be low relative to societies without
private property rights. The administrative costs of firms and
private decision makers in general may be sizable but there is an
incentive to minimize them since profit is the residual after
subtracting those costs from revenue flows. In a centrally planned
economy, on the other hand, the planning mechanism must be
relatively large and costly. Those who manage it have less clear
incentives to minimize its costs since they have no property rights
in the resources and must share any productive gains with
numerous "free riders."

Economic Disadvantages of Capitalism

Even though a capitalistic system allocates resources with efficiency, there are still two drawbacks:

1. The tastes of some consumers, those with greater incomes; are
given more weight than those of others in determining what to
produce. Output is rationed, therefore, on the basis of how much
money each consumer has to spend. For those in poverty, who have
needs but less purchasing power, the market does not readily
supply goods. These output results trouble those who regard them
as inequitable and frequently lead to arguments in capitalist
societies "for income transfer programs."

2. Business firms, in setting output and prices, fail to include in their calculations the external costs (and benefits) that result from production but that are not part of the private costs of production or consumption. The most notable of these external costs are pollution and other forms of damage to the environment. *Note:* Socialist countries are by no means untarnished in this respect. The same kinds of externalities appear to occur in socialist economies such as the Soviet Union as was seen in the nuclear plant disaster at Chernobyl in 1987 and in the pollution of many of that nation's major lakes and waterways.

In order to deal with the problems of poverty and ecological damage, governments must devise means of interfering with or supplementing market decisions. Inevitably, such interferences involve abridgments of private property rights.

SOCIALISM

Socialism
Economic systems with a common belief that resources other than labor should be subject to social ownership with few if any private property rights in their use.

Because of the diversity of socialist theory, it is difficult to give a precise definition of **socialism** that can encompass all its forms. Here we will describe the most important ones: Planned socialism and market socialism. One feature common to both is the belief that resources other than labor should be under some form of social ownership or control, the control to be in the hands of either the government or cooperative groups. The principal difference between the two forms of socialism is that in planned socialism, moral and other incentives are substituted for the gains of private property rights, while in market socialism, markets are employed to allocate resources and economic incentives are more heavily emphasized.

Marx and Socialism

Just as Adam Smith created much of the foundation for capitalist thought, Karl Marx is responsible for the foundation of both planned and market socialism. Marx's theory of history sought to explain the evolution of socialism and, for that reason, we will briefly examine the principles he set forth. This is true even though Marx wrote mostly about Capitalism rather than socialism. Indeed, his most important work, *Das Kapital*, is an analysis of capitalism and a forecast by Marx of its ultimate demise.

Dialectical Materialism
A view that material things are the subject of all change and that technology, and the natural environment are the causes of that change.

Dialectical Materialism

The philosophical foundation of Marxism is **dialectical materialism**, a philosophy that views material things as the subject of all change and technology, and the natural environment as the main forces that cause human society to change continually. Let's examine this philosophy one step at a time.

Dialectics emphasizes that all phenomena, natural and human, involve processes of development. The seed grows into the plant. The infant grows into the child, the child into the youth, the youth into the adult. (Darwin's theory of evolution is another example of this dialectical process of reasoning.)

Marx analyzed this process of development of human society, and used it, as he came to understand it, as the scientific basis for socialism. The first law of this argument is that the foundation of society is materialistic. Technology and the natural environment (climate, resources, geography) are the dominant forces in society's development. The rest (culture, institutions, social classes, and the relations between them) are linked to the economic (materialist) base, and are shaped by that base.

Historical Materialism
The view that human society undergoes a continual process of change from one form to another.

Dialectical materialism is the basic idea behind Marx's concept of **historical materialism**, which holds that human society throughout history has undergone a continual process of change, or development from one form to another: this change results from conflict between classes in a society. In ancient times, there was slavery; in medieval times, serfdom; then came handicraft and cottage industry, which gave way to factory-oriented capitalism. The guiding factors in this process are changing technology and the natural environment.

Figure 19-1 illustrates this process of social change or class conflict for the transition from feudalism to the beginnings of capitalism. The *thesis* (the class system that is dominant at a given time) is feudalism, in which the ruling class is the landed aristocracy. The *antithesis* (the class that is the main force in changing the thesis) is the emerging commercial class. The *synthesis* (the system that evolves after the antithesis has forced

Figure 19-1
An Example of Marxian Analysis

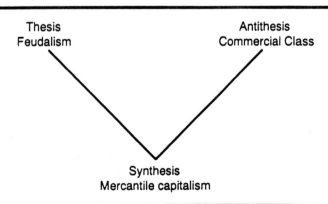

Thesis
Feudalism

Antithesis
Commercial Class

Synthesis
Mercantile capitalism

Another example would be: thesis = industrial capitalism; antithesis = the proletariat, or laboring class; synthesis (what Marx predicted would occur) = communism.

changes) is mercantile capitalism, in which the commercial class replaces the landed aristocracy as the dominant class.

Class Conflict

Marx, as we indicated before, believed that the most dramatic feature of this process of change was the conflict of classes at each stage of development. In ancient Rome, the slaves were in conflict with their masters. In medieval Europe, the serfs and the emerging merchant class were in conflict with the landed aristocracy. With the development of factories, a new class, the *proletariat* (the workers in the factories), came into conflict with the capitalists, the owners of the factories. The basis of these conflicts is the effort of one class to dominate and exploit other classes. A basic tenet of Marxism is that as long as there are private property rights classes will continue to exist, and conflict will result. Marx argued that all value is created by labor, but that wages under capitalism tend toward a subsistence level. The difference between the value of products created by labor and the wage payments to labor constituted what Marx called **surplus value**.

Surplus Value
In Marxist theory, the difference between the value created by labor and its wage payments.

Falling Profits and the Reserve Army of the Unemployed

According to Marx, competition between firms and the increasing scarcity of profitable investment opportunities would cause profits in a capitalist economy to fall. Capitalists could counter this fall in two ways: (1) They could get employees to work longer hours, and in this way increase surplus value and the degree of exploitation of labor. But the opportunity to do this was limited. (2) They could invest more and improve technology further, thus increasing output per worker and surplus value. However, improving technology meant that more and more machines replaced more and more workers, and this increased unemployment.

Reserve Army of the Unemployed
Marxist idea that capitalist societies displace labor in favor of capital and create a growing number of unemployed workers.

The rising number of unemployed caused by increased use of capital and improved technology was called the **reserve army of the unemployed**. This reserve army, Marx said, competed with the employed workers, and this competition had the effect of keeping wages down.

Recurring Business Cycles

Marx also maintained that as capitalists increase investment to ward off falling profits, the productive capacity of the economy expands and output increases. But because wages are kept low, workers do not have the ability to buy this expanded output. So, although the economy expands for a while, eventually industry's ability to produce output far outstrips consumers' ability to buy that growing output. (If you tool up your factory with all the latest equipment, so that you can make 10,000 washing machines a month, but the public has enough purchasing power to buy only 5,000 of them, you will eventually go broke.) Excess capacity is generated, which causes economic crisis and then collapse. Along comes a depression, and firms are forced out of business. Eventually, enough firms are forced out of business so that capacity contracts to a point at which expansion can be renewed, and the process repeats itself. Marx identified the business cycle and the exploitation of labor as the two hallmarks of the capitalist system. Marx was one of the first to introduce the idea of recurring business cycles, and his theory of them constituted a significant contribution to economic theory.

Marx's Gloomy Prediction: The Collapse of Capitalism

Marx concluded that capitalism (the thesis) contained within it inherent contradictions (capitalism's antithesis) that would bring about its end and a movement toward the next stage of development, socialism. He predicted that economic crises would recur, and would become progressively more serious. With more investment and continuing technological change, the reserve army of the unemployed would become larger and larger. Because of their increased investment and ever-greater need to compete against others, firms would get bigger. As this occurred, those among the bourgeoisie who owned smaller firms would be forced into the proletariat and into the reserve army of the unemployed.

Eventually, Marx predicted, economic crisis and unemployment would become so large that revolution would take place, and capitalism would be overthrown. The proletariat would come to realize that capitalism was against their self-interest; the wastes of resources due to recurring crises would become apparent. The proletariat would therefore seize political power and establish a socialist society which would ultimately evolve into a classless communist society.

What Happened to the Revolution?

Marx argued that the overthrow of capitalism would take place in the most advanced countries. To date, however, Marxist socialism has been established almost entirely in economically backward societies. In addition, in the late twentieth century, some Marxist economies have moved toward the establishment or reestablishment of capitalist economic institutions. Has history proved Marx wrong?

Whether the Marxist prediction would have ever been fulfilled had capitalist economies remained unchanged is unclear. What is evident is that since Marx's prophesy, there have been four fundamental changes in capitalist economies:

1. Contrary to the labor theory of value, labor's wage depends, in a market economy, on its productivity. As more capital is employed, labor's productivity rises as does its wage. Indeed, labor's (wage-salary) share of national income, at least in the U.S., has grown to 60 to 70 percent. The Marxist view of increasing exploitation seems unwarranted. The very (labor) theory of value on which it was based has been repudiated.

2. Since the 1930s, governments in market economies have taken an active role in trying to stabilize their economies. To many economists, this seems to have reduced the severity of recurring business crises.

3. Modern capitalist states have developed extensive social welfare programs to redistribute real income.

4. Many workers have themselves become capitalists in a small way. In the U.S., 67 percent of the population either own or are buying their own homes, and about 22 percent own stocks or bonds. In other words, larger numbers of workers are sharing in the property rights of capitalism.

Transition from Socialism to Capitalism: How Long and How Difficult?

Ironically, by the 1990s, it is planned socialist states, especially the Soviet Union, that have entered into a malaise if not into economic stagnation or decline. In Eastern Europe, there are clear signs of a reintroduction of capitalist institutions and incentives. The economies of Poland, Hungary, and Czechoslovakia are undergoing dramatic structural changes in their economic and political systems. Private assignment of property rights and the re-creation of product and factor markets to allocate resources are well underway in those and other countries of Eastern Europe. Germany has been reunited with East Germany becoming a part of the economy of West Germany. Structural economic change, however tentative, has occurred even in the Soviet Union and the People's Republic of China.

Major questions exist about how to accomplish a transition from planned socialism to capitalism and about the length of time required for such a transition. Even in Eastern Europe, which had market economies until the 1940s, major problems of transition have occurred. While it might seem relatively simple to privatize a socialist economy, in fact, it has proved complex even in Poland, whose pace of reform has been among the most rapid in the region.

What happens when the centralized economic discipline of a command economy is removed without being immediately replaced by the discipline of well organized product and factor markets? The experience of Poland in the early 1990s is instructive. In January, 1990, the country's first non-communist government since the mid-1940s decided to end price controls, freeze wages, eliminate most government subsidies, allow the currency (the zloty) to move to a market relationship with western currencies, and to reduce inflation. The short-term effects were predictable: (1) without price controls, inflation rose to an annual rate of almost 400 percent, (2) individual prices shot up dramatically, (for example, household utility bills by 400 percent, bread by 40 percent), (3) lines of people waiting to buy goods (meat, toilet paper, or the like) previously unavailable disappeared—this, at least in part, because Poles did have the income to buy all that was now being produced.

By March, 1990, inflation had decreased to about 60 percent per annum. By May, many goods were appearing in stores. Martha Martin reports that by mid-May, potatoes were in such excess supply that many were left to rot in the fields; as meat prices rose, farmers slaughtered pigs and meat supplies increased. By June, the Polish government announced that 90 percent of prices were market determined and that 30,000 private firms had been chartered.

The partial turnaround of the Polish economy in 5 months, though difficult for Polish consumers, was remarkably brief. Poland, unlike some of its East European neighbors chose to undertake decisive, almost total reform. It remains to be seen whether other nations can replicate the Polish experience, and whether Poland itself can make the full transition to capitalism.

Some of the Transitional Problems that Remain

In spite of remarkable successes several serious economic problems remain: (1) in privatizing firms, which should be reorganized and which should be liquidated? The absence of market information on the potential profitability of such organizations makes answers difficult, (2) how should other formerly state-owned resources, especially the stock of housing be transferred to private ownership?, and (3) where, in the absence of well-developed domestic capital markets, will the supply of credit needed to reenergize formerly socialist economies such as Poland's come from?

A problem made more difficult in the transition from public to private property rights is corruption. As property rights become blurred, collusion between government bureaucrats and would-be private owners becomes potentially lucrative. In an article in *The Wall Street Journal* in April, 1991, Barry Newman reported many such cases in Poland. Two are especially interesting: (1) a dairy went into business with 3 private firms started by the dairy's managers; the firms then mailed bills to the dairy for services rendered by the dairy's own staff!, (2) a textile mill contributed machines to its joint-venture partners; an inspector then tripled their value, whereupon most were decapitalized following which the partner sold the machines.

In all likelihood, privatization will ultimately run its course, and the discipline of markets including fiduciary responsibility to shareholders will be established. In the meantime, instances such as those reported by Newman are likely to remain in which privatization means "easy access to state property."

To provide background to and understand these dramatic changes in socialist economies, let's look at their nature from a theoretical point of view.

What Is Planned Socialism?

Planned Socialism
An economic system in which property rights are largely held publicly, and choices about resource usage are made by central planners.

Of the many varieties of socialism found in the late twentieth century, **planned socialism** is the one with most direct ties to Marxist thought. Property rights are largely held publicly and choices about resource usage are made centrally by a group of planners. If one created a spectrum of economic systems, this one would be at the opposite end in terms of resource decisions and rewards from the pure form of capitalism discussed earlier.

Advantages of Planned Socialism
Unlike the results of pure capitalism, planners in socialism can create any distribution of real income desired. By allocating resources and by setting prices, all distributional "inequities," at least in theory, can be eliminated. By planning, all externalities (theoretically) can be incorporated into those prices and resource allocations.

Disadvantages of Planned Socialism
The major disadvantage of planned socialism is that with public property rights, there are, as indicated earlier, disincentives to individual effort. If all laborers, for example, are to be paid the same, why would one work harder than any other? Distribution, in other words, can be made more "equitable," but there may be less to distribute since productivity differentials are not rewarded. The second major disadvantage of planned socialism is more technical. Since there are no private markets to guide the allocation of resources (no "market test"), how do the planners figure out where financial capital and other resources should go? All must be done by plan, an enormously more difficult and costly task than the "invisible hand" direction of capitalism. If to this is added the fact that managers who actually produce goods are given quotas, the incentives to quality as opposed to quantity may be low as well. Resource wasteage may be high.

Market Socialism
An economic system in which most property rights are held publicly but decentralized markets, acting on price signals from the state, are allowed to allocate resources.

What Is Market Socialism?

Market socialism is a system in which most property rights are held publicly, but in which decentralized markets are permitted to allocate resources in response to price signals created through trial and error by the state. State-owned firms are required to minimize costs and produce output at a rate that equates price and marginal cost. From microeconomics, you know that this is the same result as that created in private competitive markets. As a system, this structure was proposed by Polish-American economist Oskar Lange who argued that it would combine the distributional features of socialism with the efficiency incentives of capitalism. Lange argued that with modern computers, the equilibrium quantities and prices could be created quickly. Interestingly, though, when given political power.Lange, as Minister of Economic Affairs of Poland after World War II, opted for strict central planning. Are there examples of market socialism? Some view the economy of Yugoslavia, as an example.

Advantages of Market Socialism

The principal advantage is that through public property rights, extremes in the distribution of real income are reduced. In theory, if the state chooses "correct" equilibrium prices, decentralize markets can allocate resources efficiently. Because prices themselves, however, are not left to market determination, distortions in resource allocation and wasting of resources may remain significant.

Disadvantages of Market Socialism

Since all resources (except labor) are publicly owned, they are treated as free goods (common property resources) by those given access to them. As with all common property resources, there is a tendency to overuse them and not to maintain them or provide for their replacement. If at the same time, there are some goods that are privately owned, there is a tendency to husband them and even to divert public resources to support them. Resource distortions seem likely in such a system.

Fascism
An economic system combining private property rights with centralized choices about what to produce.

FASCISM

How Fascism Contrasts With Capitalism and Socialism

Under this system, private property rights are combined with centralized choices about what goods to produce, and even how to produce them. Hitler's Germany and Mussolini's Italy were examples of this system. Proponents of the system might argue that the state's priorities are superior to those of the individual but that individuals can carry them out more efficiently with the incentives of private ownership.

Advantage of Fascism

If the state's tastes are regarded as "socially correct," then under Fascism, those tastes are likely to guide resource usage. At the same time private property rights create many of the efficiency incentives of capitalism.

Disadvantages of Fascism

While the regulation of state planners may introduce inefficiency, the principal loss under fascism is economic freedom, the right of individuals to choose what to produce. Many economists would say also that loss of political freedom seems likely to accompany the loss of economic freedom as happened in Nazi Germany and Fascist Italy.

Mixed Economies: A Fifth System?

Mixed Economies
Economic systems that combine elements of private and public property rights and centralized as well as decentralized choices about resource usage.

There is no economy in the late-twentieth century that falls neatly into one of the four systems that we have outlined. Private property rights are dominant in some, public property rights in others; almost all have a mixture of the two assignment methods. In some economies choices about using resources are very decentralized; in others, central planning of those choices continues; in almost all there is some mixture of these levels. Nations at this time are, thus, **mixed economies**, those that combine elements of private and public property rights along with centralized as well as decentralized choice making about resources.

Many Western European economies have evolved what is known as *democratic socialism*. Sweden, Belgium and other economies come to mind. One may question whether such modern "welfare states" are really a distinct economic system. Almost all, in practice, rely on private property rights to create incentives for resource usage while permitting decentralized private markets to allocate resources. Democratic socialism, in other words, seems more a political than an economic system, one in which the state has distributional goals which it achieves through political means while relying on a decentralized market economy for the resources with which to achieve those goals.

The Twenty-First Century: The End of Socialism?

Does the end of the Cold War mean that capitalism has won out over socialism and that the latter will disappear as an economic system? The argument *has* been advanced that ideological contest and the evolution of economic systems is over. Contrary to Marx's prophecy, say proponents of this view, capitalism has proved to be the ultimately successful economic system. Others, including the well known American socialist economist, Herbert Gintis, conclude that "reports of the death of socialism are premature." Gintis concedes that "markets work because they are disciplinary devices," thus they avoid shirking, reveal price information and produce high-quality goods under the threat of losing buyers. In turn, managers have incentives to invest in profitable activities and employees incentives to work hard to avoid loss of jobs.

Nonetheless, says Gintis, Eastern Europe (including the Soviet Union) was never the socialism envisioned by its philosophical founders. Nor, according to Gintis, are modern capitalist economies, the models envisioned by Conservatives because they have "incorporated socialist goals and structures into their institutional fabric." Both systems, he argues, must continue to evolve and incorporate the features of each that have merit.

SUMMING UP

1. An economic system consists of the institutions created by a society to deal with the problems created by scarcity.

2. The basic questions that all economic systems must address because of scarcity are: (a) What to produce, (b) What shall be the technology of production, and (c) Who shall receive the real income of the society.

3. Any economic system can be evaluated in terms of its (a) static efficiency, (does it produce what is desired?), and (b) dynamic efficiency, (are resources used to maximize the long-term stream of benefits from their use?).

Cartoon Feature Syndicate

"I forget whether he calls himself a conservative radical or a radical conservative."

4. The placement of the *property rights*, rights to own, transfer and profit from the ownership of resources, may be public or private. All societies have some mix of these two assignment methods.

5. Property rights are important to societies in two ways: (a) they create incentives innovation and (b) they heavily influence the distribution of income.

6. A system based on *capitalism* has two essential criteria: (a) The means of production are privately owned and property rights are vested in individuals. (b) Economic decisions are expressed through a system of interrelated markets and are decentralized. The two legal features necessary to achieve these essentials are (a) the right of private ownership and (b) the legal enforceability of contracts.

7. The disadvantages of capitalism are: In a society in which there is pure capitalism, the needs of poor people who have less purchasing power are given less weight in establishing market demand. In addition, firms may fail to consider external costs and benefits, especially the costs to the populace of pollution and other forms of environmental damage. The economic advantages of capitalism include: (a) the efficiency that private property right incentives creates, and (b), the low costs of decision making that decentralized decision making creates.

8. *Socialism* has various forms but there is a common belief in each that resources other than labor should be socially owned and there should be few private property rights.

9. Karl Marx, the intellectual father of modern planned socialism wrote about capitalism and predicted its ultimate demise. *Dialectical materialism*, the basic principle behind Marx's concept of *historical materialism*, holds that human society throughout history has undergone a continual process of change or development. The social structure evolves from one form to another; the guiding factors in this process of evolution are changing technology and the natural environment.

10. It is basic to Marxist thought that as long as there is private ownership of the means of production, there will be differing classes. As long as classes exist, conflict will exist, as one class exploits another.

11. According to Marx, surplus value, the difference between the value of products created by labor and its wage payments will create a problem of inadequate demand for growing output under capitalism. A declining rate of profit will lead to recurrent depression according to Marx.

12. Marx argued that the falling profits would lead capitalists to increase their investment to improve technology, and this in turn would increase unemployment. The result would be a *reserve army of the unemployed,* with the effect of keeping wages down.

13. Because Marx based his theory of value on labor, he failed to see that labors' payment depends on its productivity. As more capital, and other factors are used that productivity rises and so does labor income; He also failed to foresee that (a) governments in market economies, would step into the picture and reduce the severity of business cycles by manipulating interest rates, taxes, and government spending, (b) that modern capitalist states would develop extensive social welfare programs and, (c) that many workers would themselves become capitalists, through ownership of property or stocks and bonds.

14. By the early-1990s, many long-time socialist states, especially in Eastern Europe, have begun to reinstate market incentives. This is apparently a reaction to the disincentives created by a lack of private property rights. These changes also appear, at least tentatively, to be occurring in the Soviet Union and the People's Republic of China.

15. *Planned socialism* involves public property rights with centralized choices about using resources. Theoretically, it can create any distribution of real income chosen and can incorporate externalities. However, it creates disincentives to efficiency and lacks an appropriate and low-cost way to allocate resources. It is also far from clear that planned socialism in practice leads to the incorporation of externalities.

16. *Market socialism* involves public property rights and centrally established prices but decentralized allocation of resources through markets. In theory, the system can create the results of private competitive markets. It also minimizes extremes in the distribution of income but tends to misuse resources since most are common property to which individuals hold no title.

17. *Fascism* involves private property rights and centralized choices about what to produce. Proponents may argue that the State's priorities are superior, but that private individuals can carry them out more efficiently. Its main disadvantage is that the loss of economic freedom seems likely also to lead to loss of political freedom.

18. Most economies today are mixed economies. They involve various mixes of property rights and levels of resource usage decision making. *Democratic socialism* seems to be a system in which private property rights exist but in which states intervene after decentralized choices about resource usage are made to achieve distributional goals.

19. Arguments remain about the continuing viability of socialism in the post-cold war era. Some conclude that ideological evolution has ended and that capitalism has been proved the only viable economic system. Others, such as Herbert Gintis, argue that a new socialism true to its intellectual origins will evolve and that each system will adopt the best features of the other.

KEY TERMS

Economic System
Static efficiency
Dynamic efficiency
Property rights
Capitalism
Essential Criteria of Capitalism
Free riders
Socialism
Planned Socialism
Market Socialism
Historical Materialism
Dialectical Materialism
Surplus Value
Reserve Army of the unemployed
Fascism
Mixed economies

QUESTIONS

1. What is an economic system?

2. As a reminder, what choices *must* any economic system create answers to? Why must it do so?

3. As a student of economics, what arguments would you advance for capitalism as a desirable economic system?

4. Sketch the main points of Marx's model of history and explain why Marx's prediction about the collapse of capitalism has not come true.

5. What is meant by the Marxist term, "surplus value"? What is the labor theory of value on which it was based?

6. Sketch the economic advantages and disadvantages of (a) capitalism, (b) planned socialism, (c) market socialism, and (d) fascism.

7. How is the "free rider" problem resolved in a capitalist economy?

8. Why do property rights and the level at which choices about using resources occur matter to an economic society?

9. What seems to be the explanation for the fact that most economies in the late twentieth century are "mixed economies"?

10. What seems to be the explanation for the economic changes in Eastern Europe, the Soviet Union, and the People's Republic of China that began in the 1980s?

11. What are the principal problems associated with transition from planned socialism to a market economy?

SUGGESTED READINGS

Beichman, Arnold. "The Returns Are In and Socialism Is Out." *The Wall Street Journal.* September 16, 1989.

Brainard, Lawrence. "Reform in Eastern Europe: Creating a Capital Market." *Economic Review.* Federal Reserve Bank of Kansas City. January/February, 1991.

Buchanan, James. "Socialism Is Dead; Leviathan Lives." *The Wall Street Journal.* July 18, 1990.

Engels, Friedrich. "Socialism: Utopian and Scientific." *The Marx-Engels Reader.* Edited by Robert C. Tucker. New York: Norton, 1972.

Friedman, Milton. *Capitalism and Freedom.* Chicago: University of Chicago Press, 1972.

Gintis, Herbert. "Is Socialism Dead?" *The Margin.* March/April, 1991.

Howe, Irving. *Essential Works of Socialism.* New York: Bantam, 1971.

Lange, Oscar. "The Computer and the Market." *Socialism, Capitalism and Economic Growth.* C. H. Feinstein, ed. Cambridge. Cambridge University Press, 1967.

Lange, Oskar and Taylor, Fred M. *On the Economic Theory of Socialism.* New York: McGraw-Hill, 1964.

Mann, Martha Lindberg. "Warsaw Diary: The Long Road to Capitlism." *The Margin.* March/April, 1991.

Marx, Karl. "Capital," reprinted in Charles W. Needy (ed) and Owen, Robert. "A New View of Society." In *Masterworks of Economics*, edited by Leonard D. Abbott. New York: McGraw-Hill, 1946. Volume II.

Newman, Barry. "Poland Has Plenty of One Thing: Crooks." *The Wall Street Journal.* April 9, 1991.

Newman, Barry. "Poland's Shaky Switch To a Free Market Is A Warning for Soviets." *Wall Street Journal.* September 18, 1991.

Roberts, Paul Craig. "Shatalin Plan Can Work if Privatization Comes First." *The Wall Street Journal.* September 20, 1990.

Schnitzer, Martin C. *Comparative Economic Systems.* 4th edition. Cincinnati: South-Western Publishing Co., 1987.

Seldon, Arthur. *Capitalism.* Cambridge, Mass: Basil Blackwell, Inc. 1990.

Chapter 20:
The Former Soviet Union: Is it Moving from
Planned Socialism to a Market Economy?

Emergence of the Planned Economy:
The Early Soviet Union

In the name of Marxian economics, Lenin led the Bolsheviks in the 1917 revolution that overthrew the pluralistic Russian government of Alexander Kerensky and made Marxist socialism a political reality. Karl Marx had primarily examined the development of advanced capitalist countries, such as Great Britain, and had prophesied the collapse of capitalism in those countries. But the Soviet Union that Lenin and the communists proclaimed in 1917 was an underdeveloped country that had just begun, by 1913, to enter a capitalist phase, a country, in fact, not fully emerged from feudalism.

The Communist party and the Soviet government were, from 1917 to early-1990 one and the same. Initially, the country was faced with a desperate problem of scarcity. How to achieve economic development was the number-one difficulty. Between 1917 and 1928, the new Soviet government had to make a humiliating peace with Germany, put down a long civil war and experiment with its New Economic Policy (NEP) that allowed for significant amounts of private enterprise. The government experienced vicious infighting among the Communist leaders—infighting that changed it from a nominal dictatorship of the proletariat to a dictatorship by one person, Joseph Stalin. In 1928, the Soviet Union's level of economic activity was lower than it had been in 1914. It was at this point that Stalin launched the first of many subsequent 5-year plans, and the Soviet Union became a **command economy**.

A command economy is one in which the problems generated by scarcity are dealt with by a central planning system.

Command Economy
One in which the problems created by scarcity are dealt with by a central planning system.

In this chapter we will explore the ways such centrally planned command economies organize themselves to deal with the problems imposed by scarcity. We will also examine the problems of central planning and the changes in the process that continue to take place in the Soviet Union. Finally, we will try to evaluate the economic successes and the sources of the serious current problems of the Soviet Union.

What to Produce: Central Planning

The command economy of the Soviet Union answered the question of what to produce by running it through a system of committees. These groups of bureaucrats decided on the kinds and amounts of different products the economy produces, together with wages, prices, and profits by sifting through whatever information is available. Contrast this process with that of a capitalist system that we have examined throughout this book, in which such decisions are determined largely by responses to market prices.

You are aware of how complex the allocation of resources is in a market economy. In a command economy the problem is just as complex, and, in addition, the planning process itself is centralized and more difficult. Let's look at the planning system in the Soviet Union. Figure 20-1 shows the flow of Soviet planning. Follow it as you read about the process.

Figure 20-1
The Process of Soviet Planning

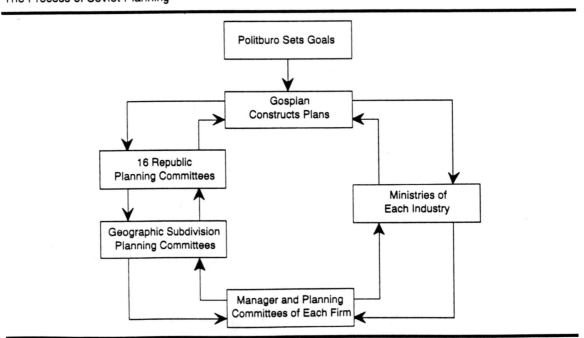

Arrows show the flow of information as the plan is composed.

Setting of Goals and Priorities

The Politburo—the highest decision-making level in the Soviet government—was responsible for the initial setting of goals for the economy during the upcoming planning period. The Soviets operated with 5-year plans. Their first 5-year plan was for 1928-1932; in 1990, the twelfth 5- year plan was completed.

Until the early-1990s, the two kinds of output with the highest priority in the Soviet Union were investment in heavy industry to increase productive capacity (tractors and turbines) and production to increase military might. Consumer goods were low on the list. But in the early-1990s, the government was being pressured to increase the production of consumer goods. So, although investment and military production have historically been given top priority, citizens of the old Soviet Union are now pressing for more consumer goods and it is the unresponsiveness of the economic system established in the 1920s to this that seems to have created some of the new commonwealth's most severe problems.

Gosplan
The Soviet government agency that administered the central plan of the USSR.

How Did the Planning Process Work?
Once the Politburo established goals and priorities in the broadest sense, a planning body called **Gosplan** translated the objectives into a consistent set of plan targets setting forth how many goods and services of each kind were to be produced and where. Gosplan used whatever information was available, and called in specialists to give further advice.

It set up a 5-year plan, broke it down into yearly plans, and then submitted these plans to various units of bureaucracy for study and criticism. Any criticisms made by these administrative units were fed back to Gosplan. Administrative units were arranged either according to geography or according to industry. A suggested 5-year plan was inspected by both kinds of units, and much haggling about the plan occurred.

Mattresses are an example. Most consumers want mattresses, but how many mattresses need to be produced, in what sizes, of what materials, in what localities, to sell at what prices? In the absence of price signals, Gosplan had to come up with an answer. The agency pondered the situation: How many extra-firms in Azerbaijan? How many crib mattresses in Kazakhstan?

Gosplan sketched a plan for each geographic unit (until 1991 the Soviet Union was divided into 16 units, called *republics)*. These plans for the republics stressed decisions about things that flow from one republic to another, and are very complex in the short term (that is, when dealing with periods of 1 year), since a given plan must spell out millions of instructions to thousands of plants, telling them what to produce, how and when to process, ship, and deliver millions of items of all sizes, materials, and types. A main weakness of the system in terms of supplying goods arose from the sheer volume of decision making that Gosplan had to carry out. Also the lack of knowledge of consumers' tastes and preferences has been a major weakness from the demand side.

After Gosplan sketched a plan, it traveled down a lengthy ladder. The planning committee of the individual republic to which the plan applied studied it and added its own ideas. Then the plan was passed still further down the chain of command, to the manager and planning committees of each individual firm, who studied the feasibility of the production targets assigned to it. If the committees or managers had objections, they were passed along the line, back up the planning ladder. The master plan set forth the goals, and the firm had to figure out what is could actually achieve.

Whose Tastes are Considered:
A Problem When Resource Priorities are Centrally Planned

Differences in the mix of consumer and producer goods between the U.S. and the former Soviet Union are startling. Russian economist Vladimir Popov estimated that the USSR devoted about 50 percent of its GNP to consumer goods while in the U.S. that percentage is 85. In contrast to the U.S., which spends 7 percent of its GNP on defense, the Soviet Union devoted 20 percent to the military (an official figure which some analysts believe may have been closer to 25 percent). This relative slighting of consumer goods in the USSR becomes even more dramatic when one considers that the Soviet GNP was no more than one-fourth to one-half that of the U.S. According to a CIA estimate in 1989, consumption per capita in the USSR was about 30 percent of that in the U.S. causing Soviet standards of living to be comparable to those of less developed nations such as Mexico.

Product Quality:
A Second Problem With Centrally Planned Priorities

Plant and industry managers assigned physical production quotas are judged and rewarded by whether they meet those quotas. This contrasts sharply with managers in private markets who are judged on the basis of whether they produce products that consumers will buy in sufficient quantities and at costs to firms that result in profits. In the absence of a market test, then, managers have an incentive to emphasize quantity rather than product quality. The dual problem that may result is (1) products produced may not be those consumers prefer, and (2) products may be of such low quality, that consumers may not buy them, or if they do, are dissatisfied with what they buy. A failure to match output and its quality with consumer tastes would ultimately result in firm failure (or reorganization) in a market economy; there is no assurance that this will happen in a planned economy.

Problems When Prices are Controlled

Even if a somewhat larger portion of Soviet resources had gone to consumer goods production, the tastes and preferences of Soviet citizens would have been, at most, only indirectly considered in establishing prices and deciding what to produce. Prices of many basic goods, including foods (bread, milk, etc.), housing, and electricity, have been set below market-clearing levels. Rents on housing, for example, were set below market clearing rates and, indeed, have not changed since 1928! While these low prices may well have been set on the grounds of equity, we already know from our discussion of supply-demand principles that a non-market-clearing price results in shortages. These shortages appear to be increasingly severe in the early-1990s.

Housing and Bread as Examples

We see in Figure 20-2 a hypothetical illustration of a housing market in the Soviet Union in which disequilibrium pricing occurs. Given the (state-determined) short-run supply of housing, S, (which is perfectly inelastic at Q_0) and the demand for housing, D, a market-clearing price would be established at P_{mc}. Soviet authorities, however, set the price lower at P_p but the quantity demanded at P_p is Q_1, rather than Q_0. A shortage of housing $(Q_1 - Q_0)$ results (there are reports that young couples in crowded Soviet cities waited as long as 4 years for an apartment). An "artificially" low price may seem equitable to some; if, however, little of the good is available at that price, is equity well served? As with any equity question, this one has no unique answer. The *distortive* effects of creating non-market-clearing prices, however, are much clearer.

Figure 20-2
A Hypothetical Housing Market in the Soviet Union

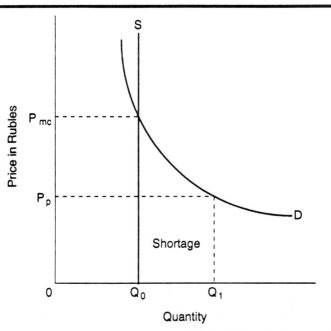

In Figure 20-2, D represents the demand for housing and S the (perfectly inelastic) supply of housing. With Q_0 housing supplied, a market clearing price of P_{MC} would be established. If central planners, instead, set price P_p, there is a shortage of housing $(Q_1 - Q_0)$ at the below equilibrium price.

Consider another case, that of a food staple, bread (whose price did not change between 1954 and 1990). Suppose the state, in the interest of equity, sets its price below equilibrium and without consideration of the real (opportunity) costs of production. At the same time, the state sets some other prices at opportunity cost levels. There will then be a tendency to substitute the subsidized good for the nonsubsidized good. Just such a case was reported in the (then) centrally planned economy of Poland in the late-1980s. Polish farmers faced with unsubsidized or less subsidized prices for animal feed and heavily subsidized prices for bread, bought bread and fed it to their animals! Both static and dynamic efficiency suffered in the process.

Why Soviet Central Planning was Technically So Difficult

Material Balance System
A planning approach in which desired output is established by planners and resources are allocated in ways designed to accomplish those output objectives.

Invisible Hand Approach
An approach to resource allocation in which profit seeking entrepreneurs and managers make choices about using resources to produce and price output.

Central planning of an economy as large and complex as that of the former Soviet Union turned out to be a daunting task. To make the job more manageable, an approach known as the **material balance system** was employed. Gosplan planned only the most important, highest priority outputs such as steel, motor vehicles and energy. At a lower level, planners decided on the output of goods, such as, clothing, household furniture and other consumer goods. Some goods, especially those produced for local consumption, were not planned at all.

In a capitalist economy, the matching of resources with output is done by markets acting on considerations of (cost-based) supply, (benefit-based) demand, and equilibrium prices. The **invisible hand approach** employs self-interest based on decisions on the part of profit-seeking entrepreneurs and managers to achieve the coordination. Soviet planning, on the other hand, involved the very visible hand of bureaucratic decision making. If the approved plan called for producing 120 million tons of steel (to be used in automobiles, tanks, etc.), for example, planners had to allocate sufficient resources to assure that the quantity demanded (by other industries and for export) equaled the quantity supplied. If, as frequently happens with output targets, the quantity supplied fell short (less than 120 million tons), planners had to change supplies to other (steel using) industries and readjust their planned output.

Input, Output, and Planning

The process involved in material balance, though somewhat decentralized, remains extremely complex. Besides the vast numbers of different finished products, there are huge numbers of intermediary products and raw materials that go into the finished products. In any developed economy there is a complex set of interrelated requirements of inputs needed for the economy to produce various combinations of output. In the Soviet Union the planning agencies that set up the master plan needed considerable amounts of information about these *input-output relationships*.

Table 20-1 shows the input-output relationships of a hypothetical economy. Note that the sectors in the horizontal row (those that consume inputs) are the same as the sectors in the vertical column (those that produce output). Each producing entity produces output and consumes input at the same time. For example, sector 1 (steel), in order to produce 51 units of output, consumes 5 units of its own output, plus 33 units of capital, 5 units of energy, 3 units of agriculture, and 5 units of labor. (We have made the simplifying assumption that all these industries are constant-cost industries.) Trace the inputs the other sectors need to produce their outputs. You can see the interdependence between all sectors even more clearly if you increase the output desired from any one sector.

For example, suppose Gosplan decided to increase shoe production by 1 million pairs per year over the succeeding 5 years. To achieve that output, the Soviet Union would need to build more machines to produce shoes and more factories to house these machines, which means more electricity to power the machines, more leather, plastic, rubber, nails, glue, shoelaces, and so forth; which in turn means more machines to produce these increased raw materials and more factories to house them. This would require expansion in agriculture (more cattle for leather) and in mining (more iron for nails), which means still more machines and buildings and equipment to produce the extra machines needed to make more shoes and the raw materials needed to produce them. In other words, there would be a resource *ripple effect* that extended throughout the economy.

Thus, you can see that each time a planned economy decides either to increase or decrease output of a given product, there is a vast, complex set of corollary decisions that must be made. Each decision brings in its wake a host of further decisions.

This set of input-output relationships between raw materials, semifinished products, and finished products is what makes planning so complex from a technical point of view.

Table 20-1
A Simplified Input-Output Table for a Hypothetical Economy

	Consumers					
	1 Steel	2 Capital	3 Energy	4 Agriculture	5 Labor	6 Output
Producers						
1. Steel	5	33	5	3	5	51
2. Capital	20	3	18	38	13	92
3. Energy	8	3	3	3	10	217
4. Agriculture	8	5	25	25	250	313
5. Labor	50	100	50	225	25	450

Efficiency of Production:
State Ownership and the Example of Agriculture

The second problem that all economic systems must deal with is *how* production is to take place. Under capitalism, productive enterprises are privately owned, and the profit motive is the driving force behind them. In a command economy, such as the Soviet Union, from the 1920s to 1991 the state owns most of the resources of production, and all productive enterprises, except for (1) a few retail and wholesale outlets, and (2) some parts of the agricultural sector.

Although the state owned and operated certain farms, the bulk of Soviet farm products came from agricultural cooperatives that were closely controlled by the state. Most of these cooperatives came into being in the early-1930s during the period of forced collectivization of agriculture, though some were formed voluntarily by their members.

However, *some* farmland was privately used (an estimated 2 percent of it), because a small amount of farm land was privately owned and on cooperatives, members were allowed to farm small private plots. Farmers tended these latter plots in their spare time, spending on them as much time as they could squeeze from their work obligations to the cooperatives, because they were allowed to sell the produce of these plots privately.

Although the Soviet Union's record as far as agriculture in general is concerned was full of failures and inefficiencies, these small plots of privately farmed land proved highly productive. By some estimates, they produced as much as 30 percent of the agricultural output of the Soviet Union. Nonetheless, Soviet agriculture was subject to the regulation of numerous ministries and bureaucratic agencies whose employees numbered 3 million—more than the entire civilian work force of the U.S. government.

This amazing productivity of the small percentage of land that was privately used in the Soviet Union seems to validate the view that private control is the most productive method—under any economic system—to induce maximum output from an agricultural population. It is worth noting that some state-owned capital has probably diverted to these private plots in which individuals have property rights and away from the communal farms. The productivity of the private plots may be somewhat distorted as a result. Clearly, however, where property rights are privately vested, productivity seems to be higher.

Who Receives Output: The Wage System

The third problem that all economic systems have to face is who is to receive the output of the economy. In both capitalist and communist states, it depends on who has the money to buy it. A big difference, however, is that goods are generally available to those who have the income to purchase them in capitalist (market) economies. In the U.S., people receive income from wages and salaries, interest on capital, rent on property and homes, and profits from businesses. In the Soviet Union, people received about 70 percent of income from wages and salaries, with the remainder coming from bonuses given to them to induce them to meet, and even exceed, their production quotas. The extra income was intended to act as an incentive.

In the Soviet Union, to a far greater degree than in the U.S., workers operated on a piece-rate system. There have been big differences between wages paid to unskilled and to skilled workers. And among skilled workers, there were considerable wage differences between different grades of skill. When it came to the managerial grades (both in industry and in government bureaus) and the highly technical or professional grade (scientists, doctors, engineers, professors), salaries were relatively high—as much as 20 times higher than salaries of unskilled workers.

The Distribution of Money Income and the Allocation of Real Goods and Services

It has been difficult to obtain concrete evidence about the distribution of income in the former Soviet Union, but the following discussion seems generally valid.

Because of the great differences between wage rates for unskilled, semiskilled, and skilled workers, and the high salaries paid to professional people, the distribution of money incomes from wages and salaries probably was more unequal in the Soviet Union than in the U.S. But when you include Americans' money income from all sources, including profits, interest, and rent, the distribution of money income was probably more equal in the Soviet Union. The distribution of money income, however, was less important in the Soviet Union than the United States because in the former, many goods were in short supply or even unavailable to most consumers except through bribery and preference. Thus, real income and consumption may well have been more equal in the U.S.

The Soviet Union: Was it a Classless Society?

Nomenklatura
A term used to describe the Soviet elite whose special entitlements increase their real incomes.

Work done by Abram Bergson concludes that the distribution of pretax income in the former Soviet Union was not very different from that in the U.S. In terms of after-tax incomes the distribution in the Soviet Union was comparable to that of Sweden.

The difficulty, however, with comparing the Soviet Union with other non-socialist societies in terms of income distribution lies in the receipt of real income by the Soviet elite or **nomenklatura**. Estimated to have comprised about 1 percent of the population, these people and their families—who were from the communist party, the arts and sciences in government and union officials, industry managers, and military officials—received subsidized prices, permission to shop in well-stocked stores, payment in coupons redeemable only in those stores, and housing, cars, and other services not readily available to the rest of the population. Bergson reports, for example, that housing was provided on the basis of status, with ordinary service workers getting 7 square feet per family member and graduating upward through a hierarchy to science academy members who are allocated spacious cottages and, finally, to senior officials with country estates or dachas. Only if value could be imputed to the (after-tax) real incomes of Soviet citizens and compared with the (after-tax and plus-transferpayment) incomes of U.S. citizens would we have an accurate comparative picture of income distribution under the two systems.

This elite tended to be self-perpetuating since most of its new members were children of existing nomenklatura members. Education and appointments to positions were strongly correlated with family connections. Another method of entry into this elite group was through bribery.

Summing Up the Problems of Soviet Planning

By way of summary, here are some of the problems with central planning that were reflected in the severe economic difficulties that beset the Soviet economy:

1. The more developed the economy became, the more complicated the planning of its output became. Since each industry (and each firm) used the products of other industries, at a given time in any economy there was a certain set of input-output relationships. In the early stages of development of its centrally planned economy, these input-output relations were simpler than they were later, when the economy became more mature.

2. Soviet planners, as indicated before, encountered a problem in deciding how to state the production goals of a firm. When stated in terms of volume of output, firms skimped on quality and frequently produced products consumers did not wish to buy.

3. Efficiency incentives were weak. Soviet planners had problems motivating managers to be efficient in the absence of profit incentives and with output goals not tied to consumers' tastes. Managers' incentives were to produce quantity, not quality and to use whatever resources are necessary to do so. Since these resources were common property they tended to be overused. There also had been widespread pilferring of state-owned property since the forced collectivization of farms in the 1920s.

4. Agriculture remained an ailing limb of the Soviet economy to its demise in late-1991. Although much land in the Soviet Union has too little annual rainfall or too short a growing season for highly productive farming, the land that *can* grow crops has been inefficiently used.

Prior to the forced collectivization in the 1920s, Soviet agriculture was characterized by small privately owned farms (especially after the breakup of the large estates of the landed gentry in 1917-1918). These small farm owners were strongly opposed to the collectivization of agriculture, and feelings ran high, so agricultural planners were faced at the outset with a resentful labor force who had no property rights in the disposal of their output. One result was that despite the mechanization of agriculture, productivity remained low. Today, about 30 percent of the population is employed on farms. In the U.S., on the other hand, less than 5 percent of the population is still employed in agriculture. This small percentage manages to feed almost 250 million Americans and have so much left over that food is the number-one U.S. export commodity.

5. Maintenance and repair was relatively poor. Tractors, for example, were produced in huge numbers (almost 2 million between 1976 and 1980) but only a few were added to the nation's stock (250,000 in the same period). Capital was scrapped, either because of lack of support to repair and maintain it, or because of lack of incentive to do so in the absence of private property rights.

Beyond the absence of incentives to maintain and repair publicly owned capital were the problems of complementary facilities. Perhaps one-fourth of Soviet crops rotted in the field because of inadequate transportation and distributional facilities and because few skilled technicians remained on the farm, but traveled instead to cities where wages were higher. As a result of all this, a nation that was once a major food exporter became the world's largest importer.

6. Innovation appears to have slowed greatly in the Soviet Union in recent years. In data processing as well as in many other areas, the USSR lagged far behind capitalist economies. Advanced technology was used—for example, in producing new, sophisticated military hardware, but such technology was not uniformly applied throughout most of the economy.

Computers present an interesting example of this failure to utilize available technology. Plant managers were reluctant to use advanced computers and some have asked why. The answer appears to lie in the incentives of managers to hide information from central planners. Faced with production quotas that may not be met, managers tended to understate their use of inputs and overstate their plant's output. Were computer-generated central accounting information available to planners, this would have been far more difficult. Also, where such computer systems are installed, the technical and other support facilities necessary to make them function properly and regularly were often absent.

Finally, personal computer use in the Soviet Union was discouraged. Few are produced (40,000 in 1987 compared with 5 million in the U.S.) because the State sought to control the flow of information.

Individual entrepreneurship is the key to innovation. Though entrepreneurship exists in the Soviet economy, its role, according to Madeleine Kalb, was "far from Gorbachev's idea of a controlled socialist market" and also "far from the reformer's dream of a smoothly running western model." Kalb reports of a Moscow cooperative created with private capital by a former research scientist, that "bought unprofitable factories from the government, offered high wages and incentives to workers" an is now a profitable enterprise. Such co-ops (210,000 in the USSR) employed more than 5 million workers or 4 percent of the work force. According to Kalb, these entrepreneurial activities were especially thriving at greater distances from Moscow. Exchanges were often based on barter, including exchanges between republics, and seem likely to continue under the commonwealth.

Structural Change In the Economy of the Former Soviet Union

Soviet leaders from Nikita Khrushchev to Mikhail Gorbachev (excepting Leonid Brezhnev) urged reform of the Soviet economy. Burdened with huge defense expenditures (the Soviet Union, as we noted earlier, spent about 3 times as much of its GNP on defense as does the U.S.) and slowing growth (real output is now apparently declining with one prediction for 1991 at 25 percent!), ways were sought to reintroduce efficiency and faster growth.

The changes in the old Soviet Union that occured in late-1991, though difficult to assay at this point, appear to have taken the following form:

1. *Decentralization:* Although the material balance system envisioned substantial decentralization of decision making, in practice a huge-centralized planning bureaucracy arose. Plans were announced in 1988 to give plant managers simpler and fewer objectives and to allow them more discretion in solving problems as well as to compete with each other. Not only are successful managers (those who meet their sales and profit targets) to receive larger bonuses, but a production and development fund was created to funnel capital to such firms. The idea was to ensure that capital for expansion went to the best managed activities in the economy. In agriculture, collective farms were given greater autonomy, and in industry, firms were allowed to enter joint ventures with foreign firms.

The central planning bureaucracy was supposed to be sharply reduced. By emphasizing quality of output and rewarding efficiency, Gorbachev hoped to reinvigorate the Soviet economy. These changes were seen by some as presaging a move toward market socialism though not necessarily to a true market economy.

2. *Perestroika*: Gorbachev who left office as President in late December, 1991, promised the people of the Soviet Union that Perestroika (reform) together with Glasnost (openness) would result in both a representative society and a healthy, growing economy. In 1989 and 1990, however, GNP apparently declined and a sharp decline, as we noted above, was forecast for 1991. Soviet citizens, accustomed to waiting in lines to buy goods (whenever available), saw the lines grow longer and the availability decline. Their pockets full of rubles (the so-called "ruble overhang"), Soviet consumers became more and more disgruntled and seemingly disillusioned with perestroika. That unrest was only heightened when in 1991, the government invalidated all the large (100 or larger) ruble notes, which had constituted much of the savings of Soviet consumers.

A major question that remained unresolved was whether the Soviet economy could be reformed (socialism modified to work as Gorbachev has said until recently that he wants) or whether, as in the case of Poland, only a massive change to a market economy would "jump start" the system.

3. *The "500-Day" or Shatalin Plan:* A 1989 plan developed by a group of reformers, including economists S. Shatalin, G. Popov, G. Yavlinsky, and N. Petrokov called for a movement within 500 days to (a) privatization, (b) debureaucratization, (c) price deregulation, (d) denationalization of land, and (e) monetary reform. The plan was initially supported by Gorbachev though he later withdrew his support. Popov argued that, "The old economic system doesn't work." Popov's forecast took on greater meaning with the popular election of Boris Yeltsin as the President of the Russian Republic in mid-1991. Yeltsin, as President of the new Russian Republic, has called for the creation of a private enterprise economy with private ownership of land as well as firms in Russia.

4. *Private Enterprise:* Some tentative steps toward private enterprise were taken as early as 1987. In that year, the Soviets reversed a course which began in the 1920s and selectively began to reintroduce private enterprise. Twenty-nine categories of services (taxis, tailoring, automobile repair, etc.) were opened to private individuals who received state licenses. While not allowed to employ other (non-family) persons, some 2 to 3 million citizens are affected. Some say that this was not a reversal of ideology so much as an acceptance of existing practice. Many of these services had been widely available for years only from the underground or second economy. The difference to the authorities was that now such activities can be monitored and taxed. A difficulty that arose, however, is that these enterprises could now charge "market" prices. Soviet consumers, used to subsidized prices of many basic

goods, resisted the change. A second problem expressed by would-be entrenpreneurs was the difficulty of securing approval for small private firms from the Soviet bureaucracy.

Aid to the Former Soviet Union: Boost or Deferrent to Reform?

Whatever the course of further economic change in the former Union of Soviet Socialist Republics, leaders of the commonwealth continue to argue that economic aid from the European Community, Japan, and the U.S. is essential to a transition to a market economy. Budget deficits in the former USSR have increased sharply. For the first *two* months of 1991, the official deficit was 31.1 billion rubles in contrast to a predicted deficit of 26.7 billion rubles for the entire year. President Bush has authorized U.S. government credits for agricultural purchases. Also, "most-favored-nation" status under which goods from some members of the commonwealth could enter the U.S. with sharply reduced tariffs, has been approved.

Apparently, though, some Russians, as well as Americans, are arguing for much more; direct aid of $100 billion has been mentioned. If that or other large scale aid is granted, there are two arguments about the consequences: (1) the aid will be a "bridge" to permit the new commonwealth economy to undertake massive structural change without further serious deterioration in living standards and the political instability that would likely follow, or (2) the aid will, like recent price hikes, according to Yuri Maltsev, "help fund the military, and entrench centralized economic control." At this juncture, both the likelihood of aid and, if granted, its consequences remain unclear.

SUMMING UP

1. Until late-1991, the Soviet Union remained a *command economy*, one in which the problems generated by scarcity were dealt with by a system of central planning. The Soviet Union's state planning authority was called *Gosplan*.

2. In the Soviet Union's command economy, the decisions about what to produce and how much to produce have been made by means of central planning. First, the Soviet government at its highest decision-making level stated certain goals and priorities. Down to the present, top priority has been given to investment in heavy industry and production of military goods.

3. After Gosplan drew up a plan, using all available data, it channeled the plan through the various administrative units, both geographic and industrial (that is, through the planning committees of the 16 different republics, and through the ministries and

planners of the various industries). Eventually, the plan reached the individual firm and its manager, who commented on the feasibility of the plan and decided whether the firm could fulfill it. The firm had the chance to negotiate the terms and objectives of the plan.

4. Soviet planning relied on a material-balance approach. Deciding output, resources were allocated so that quantity demanded and quantity supplied are made equal. If this complicated task was not fulfilled, output targets were readjusted.

5. Developing and carrying out Gosplan's plan proved to be difficult, especially because the *input-output relationships* (between raw materials, semi-finished goods, and finished goods) in any developed economy are complex. Anytime Gosplan decided to increase or decrease output in any one area, a complex set of corollary decisions had to be made.

6. Soviet resource priorities were dramatically different from those of the U.S. Far less of the GNP consisted of consumer goods and Soviet standards of living were much lower. Soviet managers assigned *output quotas* tended to emphasize quantity, not quality.

7. There are problems when resource allocation decisions are centrally controlled. Consumer tastes are not directly reflected in output and prices. While luxuries are very expensive, many basic goods have non-market clearing (low) prices. Shortages result which in turn lead to distortions in resource usage, as well as incentives to create an underground economy.

8. The command economy of the former Soviet Union solved the problem of how to produce by having the government own most of the resources of production, except for a few small retail and wholesale enterprises and cooperative farms, plus small plots of land that the state assigns to each farm family. These private plots (comprising only about 2 percent of the Soviet Union's land) accounted for about 30 percent of its total farm output, though their productivity may have been overstated or subsidized by the diversion of state resources to use on these plots. Nonetheless, Soviet agriculture remained heavily regulated.

9. In the former Soviet Union, as in the U.S., who received the output depended on who had the money to pay for it. The Soviet wage system was mainly based on piece rates, which rewarded the able worker, and on differences in the level of skill, so there have been wide differences in pay. People received income only from wages and special bonuses, not from profit, interest, and rents.

10. Despite the greater wage differentials in the former Soviet Union, the distribution of money income has tended to be more nearly equal in the Soviet Union than in the U.S. (ignoring transfer payments). People in the U.S. get income not only from wages but from profits, interest, and rent—payments that tend to go to upper-

income groups. The distribution of money income, however, was less important in the Soviet Union because of widespread shortages or unavailability of goods.

11. The comparison of real income distribution between the former Soviet Union and other countries is complicated by the existence of a Soviet elite or nomenklatura who have received access to goods not available to others and who have benefited from subsidized prices.

12. The planning process in the Soviet Union faced several major problems. As the Soviet economy became more developed, the relations between input and output became more complex and planning vastly more difficult for the following reasons: (a) As its economy developed and output increased, firms become more specialized; this increased the number and kinds of firms. (b) Improved technology brought about more complex relationships between firms. (c) The more developed its economy became, the wider the range of products it produced.

13. The agricultural sector proved troublesome to Soviet planners. The productivity of the Soviet Union's farms remained low; 30 percent of the Soviet labor force worked on farms (as compared to about 5 percent in the U.S.).

14. Soviet planners found it difficult—in the absence of profit incentives—to motivate plant managers to be efficient.

15. Maintenance and repair in Soviet enterprises was poor. For lack of motivation, such activities did not work well, and there was apparently much overuse of common property resources.

16. Reforms in the old Soviet Union focused on (a) decentralization of decision making and a reduction in the planning bureaucracy, and (b) a reintroduction of private enterprise and incentives to produce more.

17. Arguments continue about whether western aid to the commonwealth that has succeeded the Soviet Union will help it to move toward a market economy or will, instead, prevent true economic reform.

KEY TERMS

Command economy
Gosplan
Material balance approach
Invisible hand approach
Nomenklatura
Perestroika, Glasnost

QUESTIONS

1. Compare the ways that the Soviet Union's command economy solved the scarcity problems of *what to produce, how to produce,* and *how to distribute the output* with the ways that the U.S.' market economy has solved the same problems.

2. What are the technical problems with using a material balance approach to allocation resources?

3. What role did consumer tastes play in determining Soviet output?

4. What are the major problems with comparing the distribution of real income between the former Soviet Union and the U.S.?

5. What were the major problems with the planning process in the Soviet Union? What problems arise when resource priorities are centrally planned? When prices are centrally controlled?

6. What are the contrasting arguments about the role of western aid in continuing economic reform in the former Soviet Union?

SUGGESTED READINGS

Barro, Robert. "If Moscow Would Only Honor Its Debts," *The Wall Street Journal*, June 12, 1991.

Bergson, Abram and Levine, Herbert L. *The Soviet Economy: Towards the Year 2000*, London: George Allen and Unwin, Ltd., 1983.

Bergson, Abram. "Income Inequality Under Soviet Socialism" *Journal of Economic Literature*, September, 22, 1984.

Berliner, Joseph. *"Managing the Soviet Economy: Alternative Models" Problems of Communism,* January/February, 1983.

Bobrowsky, Igor. "Will the Soviet Union Survive Until 1994?" *The Wall Street Journal*, November 6, 1989.

Brady, Marjorie. "The Fascist Element in Perestroika." *The Wall Street Journal*, October 31, 1989.

Business Week. "Soviet Technology," November 7, 1988.

Dolan, Edwin G. and John C. Goodman. *Economics of Public Policy*, St. Paul, West Publishing Co., 1989. Chapter 14. "Perestroika: Restructuring the Soviet Economy."

Goldman, Marshall. "Many Soviets Find Life Worse Under Perestroika," *The Wall Street Journal*, September 27, 1989.

Hewett, Ed A. *Reforming the Soviet Economy*, Washington D.C.: Brookings Institution, 1988.

Johnson, Gale and Brooks, K. M. *Prospects for Soviet Agriculture in the 1980s*, Bloomington: University of Indiana Press, 1984.

Kalb, Madeleine G. "The Wild, Wild East: Soviet Frontier Capitalism," *The Wall Street Journal*, June 11, 1991.

Kondracke, Morton. "Soviet Democracy, Cheap at $100 Billion," *The Wall Street Journal*, June 14, 1991.

Kontorovich V. and Shlapentokh, V. "Soviet Industry Grows Its Own Potatoes," *The Wall Street Journal*, January 1, 1985.

Lane, David. *Soviet Economy and Society*, London: Basil Blackwell, 1985.

Maltsev, Yuri. "A 500-Day Failure," *The Free Market*, November, 1990.

Maltsev, Yuri. "Prices and Soviet Socialism," *The Free Market*, June 1991.

Moore, Thomas. "Managers: Russia's New Elite," *Fortune*, November 25, 1985.

Schnitzer, Martin C. *Comparative Economic Systems*, 4th edition. Cincinnati: Southwestern, 1987. Ch 13.

Seldon, Arthur. *Capitalism*, Basic Blackwell, Inc., Cambridge, Mass., 1990.

Seligman, Daniel. "The Great Soviet Computer Screw-up," *Fortune*, July 8, 1985.

Shlapentokh, Vladimir. "Soviet Ideas on Private Property Invite Abuse of Capital Stock," *The Wall Street Journal*, March 20, 1986.

Stein, Herbert. "Perestroika: Gorbachev's New Deal?" *The Wall Street Journal*, December 4, 1989.

Steinberg, David. "Reforming the Soviet Economy," *Fortune*, November 25, 1985.

Tregarthen, Timothy, "The Unsteady Pace of Soviet Reform," *The Margin*, January/February, 1991.

U.S. Congress. Joint Economic Committee. *Allocation of Resources in the Soviet Union and China*, G.P.O. 1984.

Application to Chapter 20: China, Yugoslavia, and the Convergence of Systems

China:
How Far Has it Changed from Planned Socialism?

The country one tends to think of first in connection with planned socialism is the former Soviet Union. The second and remaining colossus of the communist word is the People's Republic of China, with a land area of 3.7 million square miles and an estimated population of about 1.2 billion. Because China's economy evolved in ways different from that of the Soviet Union, it is interesting to compare the development and economic problems of these two vast, populous nations.

China became communist more than 30 years after the Soviet Union, and from 1949 to 1976, was ruled by Mao Tse-Tung, a charismatic leader whose objectives included not only creating a new economy but also creating of a new set of values in individuals. At first the Chinese sought guidance from the Russian central planning experience with land reform and the formation of mutual aid societies. By 1957 there was complete collectivization of land and state ownership or collectivization of all industrial enterprises. In the "Great Leap Forward" from 1958-1960, China attempted to effectively use its huge population, creating agricultural communes and labor intensive manufacturing enterprises. Although output rose, quality was extremely poor and real cost considerations were given no weight in allocating resources. Not surprisingly, the great leap forward was an economic disaster. Large numbers of workers were shunted from farms to jobs in industry, with the result that agriculture lagged and food production fell. Planning was poor and execution uncoordinated. Industry churned out poorly constructed and often almost useless products. The government directed millions of people for example to produce steel in backyard furnaces; an estimated 600,000 small-scale furnaces were set up. The result was a 25 percent increase in the amount of steel produced, but the quality of it was poor.

A new plan, set forth in 1961, shifted priorities and gave primary emphasis to agriculture, ordering those firms producing resources that farmers needed (for example, tractors and fertilizers) to give these items highest priority. Continuing the emphasis on agriculture, the government decreed that light consumer-good industries that made articles needed by the people who lived in the communes had next-highest priority. Much was done to increase the peoples incentives to work in farm communes. However, the disasters of the 1958-1960 period were so great that it was not until

1969 (according to some estimates), that both food and industrial production caught up and began to show gains.

In the period from 1966 to 1969 there came the *Cultural Revolution*, apparently an effort (mainly by Chinese teenagers encouraged by the government) to rid China of what were considered bourgeois influences. Bands of earnest young revolutionists traveled around China, destroying clothing and books they felt were antirevolutionary, sacking private homes, and burning property they considered unproletation. They preached the spirit of cooperation between workers and explained the character of the socialist man or woman who would create a utopian and egalitarian society. The revolutionists ousted newspaper editors, university presidents and economists. Schools and universities shut their doors in the face of this chaos, hardly what China needed at this juncture. Economic efficiency suffered; for example, 400,000 specialists could not complete their training because the schools were closed in 1967-1968.

After the Cultural Revolution 1970-1980

The end of the cultural revolution saw the return of centralized economic planning. The fourth 5-year plan (1971-1975) emphasized heavy industry, agricultural self-sufficiency, and investment in infrastructure (dams, irrigation, etc.). Toward the end of the period, political infighting to succeed the ailing Mao led to both political and economic instability. With Mao's death in September, 1976, a long struggle ensued between those who wanted to maintain the status quo of collectivization and internal development and the faction led by Deng Xiaoping which favored modernizing and rationalizing the nation's economy.

With the victory of Deng's reformers, an ambitious 10-year plan was adopted in 1978 with emphasis on importing foreign technology and simultaneous development in agriculture, industry, science, technology, and defense. Inability to easily assimilate foreign technology led to some expensive failures and to a reassessment of China's goals.

1980 to the Present

A substantial reversal of Mao's drive for ideological purity occurred between 1980 and 1989. Overly ambitious goals in the 1978 10-year plan were scaled back. In the interest of increasing productivity and more rapid growth, elements of private ownership and limited property rights in one's own work were established. Agricultural communes all but disappeared. A series of basic reforms announced in 1984 included:

1. Establishing a national system of prices. Many subsidies (meat, fish, eggs, etc.) were withdrawn, and many prices were established at market-equilibrium levels.

2. Enterprises and enterprise managers were given more autonomy and urged to compete with each other, a reform similar to the Gorbachev proposals in the Soviet Union.

3. Wages and bonus differentials were used to reward the productive and punish the inefficient or lazy. The problems created by the latter are illustrated by the story of a worker who failed to show up for work for 20 years but continued to be paid!

4. New forms of economic organization were encouraged. In some parts of China, state enterprises were even leased to private individuals. Firms were now allowed to enter into labor agreements that provided bonuses for the efficient and permited lay-offs for the inefficient.

5. Increased economic participation by foreign firms investors and technical personnel was encouraged. Joint enterprises, especially in the "Special Economic Zones" along China's coast were not only permitted, but encouraged.

6. Management, engineering, and accounting personnel were trained in modern techniques in an effort to enhance technological change.

China in Change: A Tentative Appraisal
China, in the 1980s, made some significant moves toward economic reform. Egalitarianism was clearly no longer the primary objective of its leaders. An increasing if yet small part of the economy as the nation entered the 1990s, consisted of private enterprise (small-scale farms, restaurants, repair shops, personal services) with the number of such firms rising from 2.6 million in 1982 to 5.9 million in 1984. Orville Schell estimates that such firms accounted for more than 10 percent of retail sales in 1984.

The biggest changes occurred in agriculture where 80 percent of the population remained employed. Allowed to sell their surplus in free markets, many farmers prospered with reports of a few even importing automobiles. Private plots of agricultural land, about 5 percent of cultivated land before 1980, now constitute 10 to 15 percent and are unquestionably the most productive in China in view of the individual property rights enjoyed. From the state's point of view, they are, as Martin Schnitzer has observed, "A practical way of obtaining the intensive use of peasant labor for the production of some highly valued items."

China: A Postscript
Through much of the 1980s, China experimented with new forms of organization and even some new assignments of property rights. There was considerable decentralization of planning. As the nation entered the 1990s, however, it became more difficult than ever to confidently forecast its future organization as an economic system. The political suppression of Summer, 1989, was followed by contradictory signals about a return to market central planning and reinstatement of price controls together with a call for restored economic ties to outside nations including Japan and the western industrial nations.

Yugoslavia: Is this Market Socialism?

The Soviet Union represents centrally planned socialism that may be on the verge of major reform. China represents centrally planned socialism that has undergone significant change that may or may not continue. Yugoslavia represents a brand of socialism different from either. The economic structure of Yugoslavia combines elements of central planning and a market economy.

Beginning in 1947 with central planning of the Soviet type, planning was greatly decentralized after 1951 and especially after the economic reforms of 1965. Although a national plan is created, it lacks the detail of Soviet plans; planning occurs also at the state and commune (city-county) level. Although the state owns the means of production, capital is allocated to individual firms that are worker managed. Firms establish their own prices, and compete with each other, with the (owner) employees sharing whatever profits are earned.

The proponents of Yugoslavian-style socialism argue that it combines the best features of a capitalist economy with its incentives to efficiency and the more even distribution of profits espoused by socialism. An examination of the economic growth of Yugoslavia suggests rather mixed results. In the 1970s, per capita GNP grew by more than 5 percent annually. In the 1980s, however, the economy experienced very slow (1-2 percent) growth and in 1 year (1983) negative growth. In the early-1990s, growth appears to be very slow also.

Theoretically, Yugoslavian worker-managed enterprises ought to be as efficient and as profit-oriented as those in a capitalist nation. In the absence of a detailed central plan, they produce for the market; those that are better managed should have higher profits and those that produce inefficiently or fail to satisfy consumer demand should suffer losses. Efficient, high-profit firms should grow and others should fail.

A Problem With Incentives

An essential problem with the system lies in the set of incentives it creates. The worker-managers of a successful firm have little reason to reinvest profits in the firm since there is no assurance of a return later. Investment tends therefore, to be relatively low under this system. At the same time, the consumption of capital tends to be high. Yugoslavian factories tend to use capital intensive processes; workers in such plants keep their numbers low so profits per worker will be higher. This incentive to maximize profit per worker may well prevent the maximization of total profit and the allocative efficiency of a capitalist market system. Venture capitalist behavior on the part of would-be entrepreneurs is inhibited and this may help account for the dramatic slowing of Yugoslavian growth, and the nation's high rate of inflation.

Yugoslavia and Eastern Europe: A Postscript

The dramatic political and, in many cases, economic changes, occurring in Eastern Europe, including the repudiation of central planning in Poland, Hungary, and Czechoslavakia, may well effect the organization of the Yugoslavian economy. Already, there are moves to create a multi-party political system. The slowdown of that economy in the 1980s, together with the demonstration effect occuring throughout surrounding nations (even including Albania) may portend pressures for further systemic adaptation. Perhaps second only in fascination to the unfolding drama in the former USSR is that to be played out in the region. In 1991, it appears that the Yugoslavian confederation is in danger of dissolving with the more market-oriented economy of Slovenia seceding and with Croatia and others attempting to do so.

Economic Systems:
Is Convergence the Wave of the Future?

Observers of the development of the Soviet Union, China, Yugoslavia, the U.S., and other nations in the last few decades have commented on a seeming trend for socialist and capitalist countries to converge, at least in the structure of their economic societies. Some people have even predicted that in the not-too-distant future, socialist countries will drift slowly away from the left, and that capitalist countries (faced by problems arising from the differences between the haves and the have-nots) will drift away from the right, and that the two systems will perhaps meet in the middle. In brief, some people predict that the ideological conflicts and differences between the two systems will be resolved not by the triumph of one system or another, but by changes in both economies, changes brought about by internal forces.

This convergence hypothesis, though supported by some of the events we have mentioned in this application and in the preceding chapter may be a bit too grand. It is true that all nations face the same basic economic problems; it is also true that solving them means searching for efficiency and growth. It is also true that all societies must deal with the problem of equity. In view of these commonalities, it is not surprising that structures that do not work well are abandoned or modified and that those that work well are emulated by others. This, we see happening in Eastern Europe as well as in the former USSR. Thus, the *structure* of national economies may *appear* more and more similar. It is a major leap from that view, however, to the conclusion that ideology will give way to considerations of efficiency and growth and that ideological convergence will follow in the wake of structural convergence.

QUESTIONS

1. Under Mao Tse-Tung, China's economy went through several stages between 1949 and 1976. What were these stages?

2. What have been the major changes in the Chinese economic system since 1980?

3. In what respects has Chinese agriculture moved toward a market system since 1980?

4. In what sense does the Yugoslavian economy combine features of central planning and a market economy?

5. Evaluate the argument that Yugoslavia's economy with its worker-managed enterprises combines the best features of private enterprise and socialism.

6. How may the incentives created by worker management in Yugoslavia have contributed to its slow growth and high rate of inflation?

7. What is the difference between structural convergence and ideological convergence?

SUGGESTED READINGS

Barnett, A. Roak. *China's Economy in a Global Perspective*, Washington: Brookings Institution, 1981.

Bennett, Amanda. "China Plans a Transformation of Its Economy to Unpeg Prices, Reduce State Planning Role," *Wall Street Journal*, October 11, 1984.

Cheung, Steven S. *Will China Go Capitalist?* London: The Institute of Economic Affairs, 1985.

Chow, Gregory. *The Chinese Economy*. New York: Harper and Row, 1985.

Dyker, David A. *Yugoslavia: Socialism, Development and Debt*, New York: Routledge, 1990.

Estrin, Saul. *Self-Management: Economic Theory and Yugoslav Practice*. New York: Cambridge University Press, 1984.

Johnson, D. Gale. *Progress of Economic Reforms in the People's Republic of China*. Washington: American Enterprise Institute, 1982.

Kleinberg, Robert. *China's "Opening" To The Outside World: The Experiment With Foreign Capitalism,* Boulder: Westview Press, 1990.

Lin, Wei and Chao, Arnold (eds.). *China's Economic Reforms.* Philadelphia: University of Pennsylvania Press, 1982.

McCracken, Paul W. "Maybe You Can't Get There From Here," *The Wall Street Journal,* July 24, 1989.

Myers, Ramon H. *The Chinese Economy Past and Present.* Belmont, CA: Wadsworth Publishing Co., 1981.

Schell, Orville. *To Get Rich is Glorious: China in the Eighties.* New York: Pantheon Books, 1985.

Schrenk, Martin, Ardalan, Cyrus, and Tatawy, Nawal E. *Yugoslavia: Self-Management Socialism and the Challenge of Development.* Baltimore: Johns Hopkins University Press, 1979.

Singleton, Frederick B. *The Economy of Yugoslavia.* New York: St. Martin's Press, 1982.

The Wall Street Journal, December 7, 1989. "Can the Soviet Economy Be Saved?"

Tyson, Laura D'Andrea and Eichler, Gabriel. "Continuity and Change in the Yugoslan Economy in the 1970s and 1980s," *East European Economic Assessment* Part 1, U.S. Congress, Joint Economic Committee, 97th Cong. 1st Session, 1981.

Wren, Christopher S. "China's Courtship of Capitalism," *New York Times.* November 10, 1983.

Glossary

Ability-to-pay principle A principle of taxation under which those who have a larger income are deemed capable of paying not only a larger tax but a larger percentage of their income in taxes.

Absolute advantage The ability of a given nation to produce all commodities more cheaply (that is, using up few resources per unit of output) than any other nation with which it might trade.

Abstinence theory of interest A theory that people prefer to consume goods and services now, rather than later; therefore, people will save (postpone consuming) only if they are given a reward. That reward is called interest.

Accelerator principle The general rule that changes in the rate of change of consumer demand cause much larger changes in induced investment. The accelerator is positive if a change in the increase in consumer demand causes induced investment to increase. It is negative if the change in induced investment decreases.

Accounting profit The difference between total revenue and total explicit cost.

Adaptive expectations hypothesis The view that decision makers form their inflationary expectations on the basis of events of the recent past.

Adjustable-peg system A system of exchange in which currencies are pegged, or are not allowed to change in value by more than a specific percentage. The pegs themselves, however, may be changed from time to time.

Administered-price inflation A kind of inflation that occurs when firms with some control over price use that power to raise prices more rapidly than cost increases.

Administered pricing A term used by some economists to refer to prices that are set by the administrators of firms rather than established by independent influences of supply and demand.

Age-earnings profile A profile that shows the relationship between annual incomes and age for groups with various levels of education.

Aggregate-demand-equals-aggregate-supply approach (Keynesian) An approach to the problem of finding equilibrium income in a simple economic model without government and foreign trade. According to this approach, the equilibrium is at that level at which *aggregate supply*—consumption plus savings (C + S)—is equal to *aggregate demand*—consumption plus intended investment (C + II).

Aggregate-demand-equals-aggregate-supply approach (General) An approach that holds that equilibrium real income is established where aggregate quantity demanded equals aggregate quantity supplied.

Aggregate demand shock A term used to describe a shift in aggregate demand.

Aggregate production function The relationship in physical (nonmonetary) terms between output and employment for a given economy (at a specific time). A "receipe" for output.

Aggregate supply shock A term used to describe a shift in aggregate supply.

Allocative inefficiency The tendency for monopoly firms to set prices above marginal costs and to allocate fewer resources to producing their products than consumers prefer.

Antithesis In Marxist theory, the force arising from a social contradiction that compels a change in the existing theses (or set of social arrangements).

Arbitrage The practice of buying international currencies at low prices and selling them at high prices.

At factor prices Method of computing national income using the prices paid in the factor markets. This measuring practice excludes indirect business taxes.

At market prices Method of computing national economic accounts using the prices paid in the markets for goods and services. This measuring practice must utilize all market costs incurred in production.

Autarky Economic self-sufficiency.

Automatic stabilizers Structures built into the U.S. economy that have a moderating influence on recessions and inflations. They are automatic in that they operate without being invoked by government policy makers. They are not considered strong enough to prevent, by themselves, the occurrence of business fluctuations. The progressive personal income tax is an example.

Autonomous investment Investment that is not affected by changes in the nation's overall level of income and consumption.

Average propensity to consume The percentage of their incomes that people at a given level of income tend to consume:

$$APC = \frac{C}{Y}$$

Average propensity to save The percentage of their incomes that people at a given level of income tend to save:

$$APS = \frac{S}{Y}$$

Average revenue Total revenue divided by output.

Average total cost Average fixed cost plus average variable cost.

Backward-bending labor supply curve A graphic illustration of a situation in which the quantity of labor supplied decreases as the wage increases beyond a certain level.

Balance-of-payments statement The annual accounting statement disclosing the status of a nation's foreign trade, including its capital transactions. The statement reveals what was bought and sold, and how any difference between the two was financed. (The balance-of-payments account must balance.)

Balance of trade The monetary value of exports minus imports:

$$X - M.$$

Balance to be financed In the balance-of-payments statement, the combination of the basic balance plus the short-term capital account.

Balanced-budget multiplier The multiplier that makes itself felt when a balanced-budget change in government expenditures and taxes (that is, government expenditures and taxes moving in the same direction and by the same amount) causes the level of national income to change in the same direction and by the same amount as the expenditure-tax change. *See also* Multiplier effect.

Bank holding companies Corporations that own one or more banks.

Barriers to entry Factors that prevent other firms from entering monopolist's market.

Barter A system of exchange that does not involve money; the trading of goods directly for other goods.

Basic balance In the balance-of-payments statement, the balance in the current account plus the balance in the long-term capital account.

Benefits-received principle of taxation The theory of taxation according to which people pay taxes that are commensurate with, or in line with, the benefits they receive from government services.

Bilateral monopoly A market situation in which a single seller bargains with a single buyer.

Bonds Instruments of debt, guaranteeing payment of the investment (face value) plus interest by a certain date. Interest on bonds is a cost of production to a business firm that raises capital by selling bonds.

Break-even point or price Occurs when a firm just covers its opportunity costs. A price that equals average cost and marginal cost is a break-even price.

Bretton Woods Conference International monetary conference held in 1944, which established the International Monetary Fund (IMF) and the International Bank for Reconstruction and Development (IBRD).

Budget restraint The limits on purchases of goods imposed by a consumer's income and by the prices of the goods bought.

Business cycles Variations in a nation's general economic activity; fluctuations in output, income, employment, and prices.

Capital account The account, in a nation's balance-of-payments statement, that is made up of long-term and short-term capital flows.

Capital broadening (constant capital-to-labor ratio) The situation in which capital instruments grow at the same rate as the amount of labor employed.

Capital consumption allowance *See* Depreciation.

Capital deepening The situation in which a nation's employers use more capital relative to the amount of labor used, thus raising the capital-to-labor ratio for the economy.

Capital gains tax A tax placed on the increase in the value of an asset, which is realized on sale of the asset. It is considered a tax loophole because the tax rate on such gains tends to be lower than on other forms of income.

Capital-intensive process A production process that uses relatively more capital than labor or land.

Capitalism An economic system with two essential ingredients: (1) the private ownership of the means of production, and (2) the expression of economic decisions through a system of interrelated markets.

Capture hypothesis The view that regulatory agencies are often captured by the industries they regulate and serve industry interests rather than those of the public.

Cartel A group of producers who join forces and behave like a monopoly with respect to price and output.

Ceteris paribus In economic analysis, the practice of holding certain variables constant and permitting other *key* variables to change.

Change in demand A shift in a demand curve (by which more or less of a good is bought at all prices) that results from a change in (1) income, (2) tastes, (3) prices of other goods, (4) number of consumers, or (5) consumers' expectations of future prices.

Change in quantity demanded A movement along a demand curve that results from a change in the price of that good.

Change in quantity supplied A movement along a supply curve that reflects a change in the amount of a good offered for sale as only the price of that good changes.

Change in supply A shift in a supply curve that reflects that more or less of a good is offered for sale by a firm at all prices.

Check An order to a bank from the holder of a demand deposit to transfer money from that demand-deposit account and pay it to someone else.

Checking accounts *See* Demand deposits.

Closed market economy A market economy consisting of interrelated product and factor markets that does not trade products, services, or resources with other economies.

Closed shop An employment situation in which workers *must* join a union in order to get or hold a job.

Coins Metal tokens minted by the Treasury and issued through the Federal Reserve Banks; the smallest component of the supply of money.

Command economy An economy in which the problems generated by scarcity are solved by a system of central government planning.

Commercial bank Any bank that holds demand deposits.

Common property resources Those that are open to use by everyone. They have, thus, no individual owners (also called common access resources).

Common rent *See* Quasi-rent

Common stock Instruments of ownership of a corporation. People who own shares of common stock can vote on all matters requiring stockholders' consent, and there are no limitations on the amount of dividends they can receive. However, they receive dividends only after all prior claims against the company (interest on bonds, and so on) have been paid.

Comparable worth A proposal under which wages would be based on the intellectual and physical demands of various jobs. Points would be created for each job and jobs with the same numbers of points would receive equal wages.

Comparative advantage A situation in which a nation is relatively more efficient at producing some goods than at producing others, compared with the production capabilities of other nations with which it trades.

Compensatory fiscal policy *See* Functional finance.

Competing interest laws Those in which special interest groups on both sides of a legislative issue vie for favor in order to obtain concentrated benefits.

Competition The market form in which no individual buyer or seller has influence over the price at which she or he buys or sells. *See also* Pure competition.

Complementary investment An investment that increases the productivity of other investments.

Complements Products used in conjunction with each other.

Concentration ratios A measure of the combined market shares of an industry's largest firms.

Conscious parallelism A practice in which a dominant firm sets its prices and other firms set theirs in a way that parallels those of the price leader.

Constant capital-to-labor ratio *See* Capital broadening.

Constant-cost industry An industry in which the cost curves of individual firms remain the same as the output of the industry varies.

Constant GNP *See* Real GNP.

Constant returns to scale The condition for a firm when total costs increase at a constant rate and long-run average costs are constant.

Consumer choice A theory of demand that rests on four assumptions about consumers: (1) Consumers buy competitively. (2) Consumers have limited money incomes and full information. (3) Consumers are rational. (4) Consumers maximize their utility or satisfaction.

Consumer price index An index that measures price changes for a certain market basket of goods likely to be purchased by a family of four living in an urban area. Compiled and published monthly by the Bureau of Labor Statistics.

Consumers' surplus The difference between what consumers would be willing to pay for a good and what they actually pay for it.

Consumption function Schedule of the quantities that people are willing and able to consume at different levels of income during a given time period.

Contestable market One in which there are no significant losses from entry or exit due to sunk costs.

Contraction phase That part of the business cycle in which the level of economic activity falls.

Control through the ruble Control that the Soviet Union exercises over business firms through the medium of the Gosbank (central bank). A business firm's account at the Gosbank is credited with the value of its assigned production goal. As the firm uses resources, it pays for them by checks on its account. If the firm uses up its account before it achieves its assigned goal, it fails in its assignment.

Corporate profits The return to entrepreneurship in firms that are incorporated. Corporate profits equal dividends plus retained earnings (undistributed corporate profits) plus corporate taxes.

Corporation A legal entity or form of business enterprise, created by the process of incorporation, which functions separately from its owners.

Cost-plus pricing A form of administered pricing in which a firm first computes its variable cost, then its overhead or fixed cost, and finally adds its expected profit per unit. The result is the price it charges to consumers.

Cost-push inflation The kind of inflation that occurs when suppliers of resources increase their prices faster than productivity of manufacturers increases. Costs of production then go up, which forces prices up.

Countervailing power The idea that monopoly power often exists on both sides of a market. The monopsony power of buyers is counterbalanced by the monopoly power of sellers.

Coupon economics The system by which a government rations the output of the economy by issuing ration coupons to consumers, which consumers must redeem in order to buy rationed products.

Covert collusion A situation in which representatives of various firms in the same industry meet and decide on prices, shares of the market, and other conditions of the market.

Creeping inflation A kind of inflation in which there is a moderate rise in prices that continues for an extended period of time.

Criticism and self-criticism program A program in the Soviet Union that requires individual citizens to identify and report deviations from the government's economic plan.

Cross price elasticity of demand The percentage change in the demand for one good divided by the percentage change in the price of another good.

Crowding theory A theory that explains the effects of discrimination by tracing the impact that discrimination has in forcing women, blacks, or other minorities into certain kinds of employment and out of others.

Cultural Revolution A mass social movement that took place in the People's Republic of China in 1966-1969, supported by the Chinese government and aimed at rooting out bourgeois and antirevolutionary thought and action.

Currency in circulation Currency (both paper money and coins) that is actually in use, not in the vaults of banks or in the Treasury.

Current account An account in the balance-of-payments statement that is like the income and expense statement of a nation. It includes all current transactions, but excludes short-term and long-term movements of capital.

Current account balance The balance in the interpayments accounts obtained by adding exports of goods and services minus imports of goods and services plus net unilateral transfers.

Customer discrimination Job and wage discrimination resulting from tastes of buyers (for example, diners in restaurants preferring to be served by men or whites).

Cyclical deficits component That part of the federal deficit which arises from automatic stabilizers.

Deadweight loss of monopoly A welfare loss to society of consumers' and producers' surplus that results from monopoly. It is a loss not captured by someone else.

Decreasing-cost industry An industry in which external economies cause costs of all individual firms in the industry to fall as the output of the industry as a whole increases.

Deflating current GNP The act of decreasing current GNP to take into account a rise in prices; expressing GNP in terms of dollars of constant purchasing power.

Deflation A general lowering of prices in an economy.

Deflationary gap The increase in aggregate demand necessary to make aggregate demand equal to aggregate supply at full employment.

Demand A set of relationships representing the quantities of a good that consumers will buy over a given range of prices in a given period of time.

Demand curve A graphic plotting of the demand schedule, or a set of relationships between various prices of a good and the quantities of it that the public will buy at each of those prices in a given period of time.

Demand deposits Deposits in commercial banks that can be withdrawn "on demand" by one who presents a check.

Demand-pull inflation A rise in prices that occurs when demand for goods exceeds the ability of the economy to supply these goods at existing prices. The result is that the market rations this short supply through the medium of increased prices.

Demand schedule Indicates the quantity demanded at each of several prices.

Democratic socialists Those who believe in using democratic procedures to gain political power and curtail capitalism.

Dependent variable The factor in a two-variable system that changes as a result of changes in the independent factor.

Deposit multiplier That formula for determining the multiple that demand deposits may be of the required reserve ratio.

Depreciation An account allowance for the capital that "wears out" (either through use or obsolescence) while being used to produce the final goods and services of an economy in a given period of time.

Derived demand A demand for one thing that depends on the demand for something else. (For example, the demand for labor depends on the demand for the goods produced by labor.)

Dialectical materialism A philosophy in which material things are viewed as the subject of all change, and technology and the natural environment as the main forces that cause society to change continually.

Diminishing marginal utility of income The theory that people get less and less satisfaction from each increase in their incomes.

Diminishing rate of transformation The idea that the rate at which one good may be traded off, or transformed, into another decreases.

Direct The relationship between the independent variable and the dependent variable is direct if the dependent variable changes in the same direction as the independent variable.

Direct democracy A governmental system in which citizens directly choose the rules under which they will be governed.

Dirty float A system of managed exchange rates in which exchange rates are "pegged" or allowed by central banks to move with certain limits.

Discommunication The problems that a large organization encounters in trying to communicate in order to achieve effective decision making; due in part to large size.

Discount rate The rate of interest that the Federal Reserve charges depository institutions when it discounts acceptable short-term debt at the Federal Reserve, to enable the institutions to obtain reserves.

Discretionary fiscal policy Day-to-day fiscal policies established by government officials, designed to cope with changing economic conditions.

Diseconomies of scale The disadvantage a firm may encounter when it increases the size of its plant and increases its output, only to find that the cost of each unit produced is greater than before.

Dissavings Consuming more than is produced, or consuming more than one's income.

Double coincidence of demand In a system of barter exchange the requirement for a mutuality of needs; each party to a transaction must want what the other has.

Double taxation A situation that arises when a corporation pays taxes on its gross receipts. Then it distributes its dividends from these receipts to its stockholders, who must then pay income tax on the previously taxed money.

Duopoly An industry with two interdependent major sellers, although there may be a number of fringe firms as well.

Durable goods Commodities (such as automobiles) that are used up at a very slow rate; that is, it takes a long time to use them up.

Dynamic efficiency Over a period of time, using resources in ways that maximize the long-term benefits from their employment.

Dynamic framework A concept or set of relationships by which one can explain the way certain things change through time.

Economic capacity The level of long-run production that is achieved with the lowest per-unit cost of the optimal plant.

Economic determinism Assuming that all actions are reactions to changing economic reality.

Economic development The long-term process by which the material well-being of a society's people is significantly increased.

Economic dualism The coexistence within a society of two or more different economies (frequently, one with markets and cash incomes and the other with barter).

Economic imperialism A Marxist concept according to which capitalists ward off a fall in profits and lessen the severity of economic crises by exploiting the underdeveloped countries. Supposedly, capitalists do so by using the underdeveloped countries as a source of demand for their output and supply of cheap raw material and as places to invest capital.

Economic integration The degree to which an economy's resources are employed in their most productive uses.

Economic institutions Social institutions through which economic decisions are made (for example, the Federal Reserve System).

Economic loss The excess of total costs over total revenues.

Economic loss with production A situation in which a firm's short-run total revenue is less than its total costs, but greater than its total variable costs. The firm minimizes its loss by continuing to produce.

Economic loss with shut down A situation in which a firm's short-run total revenue is less than its total costs, but greater than its total variable costs. The firm minimizes its loss by continuing to produce.

Economic loss without production A situation in which a firm's short-run total revenue is not only less than its total costs, but also less than its total variable costs. The firm loses less by closing down altogether.

Economic profit Profit that is above normal profit. When there is economic profit, total revenue is greater than total cost (including the opportunity cost of entrepreneurs).

Economic rent The payment made to a resource whose supply is perfectly inelastic.

Economics The social science that deals with the analysis of material problems, how societies allocate scarce resources to satisfy human wants.

Economies of scale Achieved by a firm when the cost of each unit produced falls as output increases with larger plant size.

Effective demand The total aggregate demand for commodities and services in an economy.

Elasticity of (product) supply A measure of the rate of change in quantity supplied divided by the rate of change in price.

Elasticity of resource demand The rate at which the quantity of a resource demanded changes as its price changes:

$$\frac{\Delta Q}{Q} \div \frac{\Delta P}{P},$$

where Q = quantity of the resource demanded, P = price of the resource, and Δ (Greek delta) = "change in."

Elasticity of resource supply The rate of change in the quantity of an input supplied as its price changes:

$$\frac{\Delta L}{L} \div \frac{\Delta W}{W},$$

where L = amount of labor, W = wage rate, and Δ (Greek delta) = "change in."

Elasticity of supply of labor The rate of change in the quantity of labor supplied divided by the rate of change in the wage or:

$$\frac{\Delta Qs}{Qs} \Big/ \frac{\Delta W}{W},$$

where W equals the wage rate.

Embargo An absolute prohibition against importing certain goods.

Employment The situation in which a unit of resource (labor, land, capital, entrepreneurship) is used in some economic activity.

Entrepreneurship The function of organizing labor, land, and capital into a firm capable of producing and marketing a commodity or service.

Entry limit pricing The practice by monopoly and oligopoly firms of setting prices below profit maximizing levels in order to deter entry of new firms.

Equation of exchange MV = PQ, where M = supply of money, V = velocity of exchange (number of times M changes hands), P = price level, and Q = number of transactions.

Equilibrium exchange rate The rate of exchange between two currencies that clears the market or eliminates excess supply and demand.

Equilibrium income The level of income that results from the central tendency of a model. This level will be maintained as long as the factors in the model (savings and investment) remain the same.

Equilibrium price The market-clearing price, or the price at which quantity demanded equals quantity supplied.

Equity stock *See* Common stock.

Ex-ante investment The amount of investment firms plan to make.

Ex-post investment The investment that firms actually undertake (not simply plan to undertake).

Excess demand The excess of quantity demanded over quantity supplied at a price lower than the equilibrium price.

Excess reserves Assets that depository institutions hold in the form of reserves, but which are over and above that required by Federal Reserve regulations.

Excess supply The excess of quantity supplied over quantity demanded at a price higher than the equilibrium price.

Exchange controls Devices governments use to ration foreign currencies or eliminate excess demand for those currencies.

Exclusive unions Bargaining agents that agree to restrict union size and maximize the wage gains of their members.

Expansion The process by which a society's output grows as it uses more and more resources.

Expansion phase That part of the business cycle in which economic activity rises.

Expenditure approach A method of computing national income accounts that is concerned with the kinds of goods people buy, with what kinds of expenditures they make.

Explicit costs Those costs of a firm that result from contracting for resources in the markets.

Exploitation In neoclassical economic theory, a payment to a resource that is less than its value of marginal product.

Exports Commodities and services sold to other nations.

External diseconomies of scale An increase in a firm's costs caused by changes in the output of the industry as a whole.

External diseconomy A cost increase originating outside of the individual firm.

External economies of scale A decrease in a firm's costs caused by increases in the output of the industry as a whole.

External economy A cost decrease originating outside of the individual firm.

Externalities The differences between privately expressed (market) costs and benefits and publicly expressed (nonmarket) costs and benefits. *See also* Spillovers.

Factor markets Those in which the prices of resources like land, labor, capital, and entrepreneurship are established and in which these resources are allocated.

Fascism An economic system combining private property rights with centralized choices about what to produce.

Featherbedding A practice in which unions require a certain number of jobs for the production of goods or services.

Federal funds market The market in which banks lend their excess reserves to each other at the federal funds rate.

Fiat money Money that has greater value as a monetary instrument than as a commodity. It is money because the government issued it and says that it is money, and because people accept it as such.

Final goods and services Goods and services sold to the ultimate user.

Final-value method Method of computing GNP that sums up the prices to final buyers of all goods and services produced by the economy. Avoids double counting by eliminating intermediate production, and leads to the same statistical result as the value-added method of computing GNP.

Financial capital Capital in the form of money; savings that are available for investment in physical capital.

Fine tuning Discretionary changes in fiscal and monetary policy leading to counterchanges in the state of the economy.

Fiscal policy Manipulation of the expenditures and taxes of the federal government to achieve certain economic goals.

Fixed costs Costs that do not vary with output.

Fixed exchange rates A system of international exchange in which the currency of each nation has a certain fixed relationship to the currencies of other nations that is established by government decision. Rates are not allowed to vary with changing market conditions.

Foreign-trade multiplier effect (FTM) The change in GNP resulting from a change in net foreign trade:

$$FTM = \frac{\Delta GNP}{\Delta(X-M)},$$

where X = exports, M = imports, and Δ (Greek delta) = "change in."

Fractional reserve requirement The percentage of demand deposits that depository institutions must hold as reserves. As a result, such institutions can lend out amounts that are a multiple of their reserves.

Free good A good with a price of zero. Supply is greater than demand at any price above zero.

Free rider problem Refers to the fact that once public goods are produced, they are available for consumption by individuals who may have contributed nothing to the cost of producing them.

Freely-floating exchange rate A competitive system of international exchange in which the currencies of the various nations are valued according to supply and demand in the international money market. The exchange rate is free to move up or down to eliminate excess supply or excess demand.

Frictional unemployment Short-term unemployment resulting from workers moving from one job to another.

Full capacity A situation in which a firm or industry is at the low point on its long-run average-cost curve.

Full economic integration When all resources of a society are employed and used in their most productive uses.

Full employment A situation in which everyone in the labor force is employed except those who are frictionally unemployed.

Full-employment budget The budget that balances government expenditures against the level of receipts (taxes) that the government would receive if the economy were at full employment.

Functional distribution of income An approach to the distribution of income that emphasizes the *sources* of income: wages, interest, rent, and profit.

Functional finance A policy that aims at compensating for changes in aggregate demand in the private sector by varying the public sector's expenditures and taxes.

General powers of the Federal Reserve System Powers that enable the Federal Reserve to increase or decrease the amounts of excess reserves that commercial banks need in order to make loans.

General price index Index construction by the Commerce Department to convert current GNP to constant GNP.

Giffen goods Those inferior goods with an income effect that moves in the same direction as price and for which the income effect is larger than the substitution effect.

GNP gap The difference between potential GNP at four percent unemployment and actual GNP achieved.

GNP implicit price deflator *See* General price index.

Gold-flow point The disequilibrium exchange rate at which it is cheaper to buy and ship gold in payment for trade than to buy currencies.

Gold standard The system of international exchange used up until the 1930s, according to which currencies were valued in terms of gold and were convertible into gold, and each nation was obligated to exchange its currency for gold.

Gold tranche position The amount of gold a member nation can borrow from the International Monetary Fund (IMF).

Gosbank The state bank in the Soviet Union, used to control and audit individual firms' activities. All firms have accounts with Gosbank, and all their purchases and sales go through the bank.

Gosplan An agency in the Soviet Union that translates overall goals into a comprehensive plan for the economy. Gosplan is the central planning committee of the Soviet Union.

Government expenditures In the national economic accounts, the measure of all government purchases of goods and services.

Great Leap Forward Second 5-year plan of the people's Republic of China (1958-1962). Execution of the plan was such a disaster that it was abandoned in 1960.

Gross national income (GNI) Total income at market prices generated in the production of all final goods and services during a specific time period. GNI = wages and salaries + rent + interest + proprietors' income + corporate profits + depreciation + indirect business taxes.

Gross national product (GNP) Total dollar value of all final goods and services produced in a given time period. GNP = consumption + gross investment + government expenditures + net foreign investment (export - imports).

Gross private domestic investment Investment including depreciation or capital consumption allowance. *Private* means counting only nongovernment investment; *domestic* means counting only investment made in the U.S.. Investment is the act of creating capital, manufactured producer goods that aid in producing consumer goods and other capital goods.

Growth The intensive process by which the productivity (output per hour of labor employed or income per capita) increases.

Hedonism A philosophical school that argues that self-satisfaction is the primary goal of individuals.

Hedonist One who argues that people act to achieve self-satisfaction.

Herfindahl index A measure of market concentration obtained by summing the squared percentage market shares of firms in an industry.

Historical materialism The view that society throughout history has undergone a continual process of change and development from one form to another. The guiding factors in this process are the natural environment and changing technology.

Historical period A period of time in which technology changes.

Homo communista Communist or communal man.

Homo economicus A term meaning "economic man."

Homogeneous product A product so standarized that buyers do not differentiate between the output of different firms.

Horizontal mergers Those between firms in the same industry.

Human capital The improvement in labor skills (marginal physical product) attributable to education or other training, innate ability and acquired skills.

Implicit costs Those costs associated with using self-owned resources.

Import duties *See* Tariffs.

Imports Commodities and services bought from other nations.

Inclusive unions Bargaining agents that seek to expand the number of jobs offered, and thus, the size of the union.

Income approach Computation of the national income accounts based on measuring the kinds of income generated in producing the output of the economy.

Income effect In demand analysis, the change in the quantity of a good that consumers demand as a result of a change in its price and thereby the consumers' purchasing power, or real income.

Income elasticity of demand An estimate of the rate at which the demand for a good varies as consumer incomes vary.

Income-inferior goods Those goods that consumers tend to buy less of as their incomes increase, and more of as their incomes fall.

Incomes policy A policy that frequently involves wage and price controls by the government. In general, a cooperative effort of labor, management, and government to find mutually agreeable goals for the economy and the means to achieve these goals.

Increasing-cost industry An industry in which individual firms experience external diseconomies (increasing costs) caused by increases in output by the industry as a whole.

Increasing marginal utility of income The assumption that people get more and more satisfaction from each additional increase in their incomes.

Increasing opportunity cost The assumption that as a nation chooses to produce more of one good, it must (ultimately) give up increasing amounts of the other good.

Incremental capital-output ratio The additional capital needed to produce additional output.

Independent variable In a set of relationships, the variable that changes first.

Indicative planning The kind of planning one finds in France, where the government draws up targets for the economy and brings together employers and unions to discuss and modify the proposals. Firms and workers, with government support, move to implement these plans.

Indirect business taxes Taxes on goods and services passed on to consumers in the form of higher prices (for example, excise and sales taxes).

Induced investment Investment generated by changes in income and in quantity consumed. An increase in income leads to greater quantities consumed. Then there is an increase in investment to expand capacity in order to satisfy the new demand.

Inferior goods A general case of goods for which there is a weak income related taste. As price rises, quantity demanded decreases because the substitution of goods outweighs the tendency to buy more with reduced real income (in contrast with Giffen goods, a special case of *very* income-inferior goods).

Inflating current GNP Increasing current GNP to take into account a fall in prices; expressing GNP in terms of dollars of constant purchasing power.

Inflationary gap The excess demand at full employment that causes prices, rather than output, to increase.

Innovation Introduction of new products or processes.

Input-output relationships The complex set of interrelated requirements for inputs needed by the economy to produce various combinations of output (arranged by industries).

Instantaneous multiplier A multiplier effect that takes place without an intervening period of time. *See also* Multiplier effect.

Interdependency A situation in which economic actions depend on each other (for example, when firms in an industry act on the assumption that their price and output policies are dependent on the actions of other firms in that industry).

Interest The return to the owners of capital. Only interest paid by businesses is included in gross national income. (Interest on the national debt or interest on consumer loans is not included.)

Interlocking directorates A practice in which individuals serve on the boards of directors of more than one firm in the same industry.

Internal economies of scale Decreasing costs from a firm's increased output in the long term.

Internalizing costs and benefits The process through which the prevention of spillovers or externalities is accomplished by having all costs, private and public included in the price of a good.

Internal rate of exchange The rate at which a nation gives up one good in order to produce another.

International monetary fund (IMF) An organization set up at the Bretton Woods Conference in 1944 to facilitate international trade, especially to assure the financing of such trade and to administer the adjustable peg system of post-World War II exchange rates.

International reserves Assets available to central banks and other agencies that are accepted in payment of international debts.

Inverse The relation between independent and dependent variables is inverse if the dependent variable changes in the opposite direction from the independent variable.

Investment function A schedule of the quantities that people are willing and able to invest at various levels of income during a given period of time.

Invisible hand argument The idea attributable to Adam Smith that self-interest based voluntary exchanges can make all those involved in the exchanges better off.

Invisible items The services, including financial services (as opposed to physical commodities), that are exported or imported by a nation. Items not normally reflected in merchandise exports and imports.

Involuntary additions to inventory *See* Unplanned additions to inventory.

Involuntary reductions to inventory *See* Unplanned reductions in inventory.

Jawboning The use of persuasion on the part of the government to get business and industry to comply with wage and price guidelines.

Job discrimination A situation in which workers are employed on the basis of some consideration other than their productivity, such as race or sex.

Kibbutz A community that operates on the principle of complete income equality. In Israel in 1973, there were 240 kibbutzim, with more than 85,000 members.

Kinked-demand curve A demand curve that is based on the assumption that firms in an oligopoly follow suit when competitors' prices decrease, but ignore other firms' price increases.

Labor-intensive process A production process that uses relatively more labor than capital or land.

Laffer curve A theoretical association between various tax rates and the tax revenues collected at each rate.

Law of demand The general rule that consumers buy more at low prices than they do at high prices; that price and quantity demanded are inversely related.

Law of diminishing marginal utility The general rule that as more of a particular good is consumed in a given time period, the additional utility of each additional unit of the good will ultimately decrease.

Law of diminishing returns *See* Law of variable proportions.

Law of supply The general rule that the quantity supplied rises as price rises, and falls as price falls; that price and quantity supplied are directly related.

Law of variable proportions (diminishing returns) The general short-run rule that as a firm uses successive equal units of a variable input in conjunction with a fixed input, additions to output (marginal output) derived from the variable input begin to diminish beyond some point.

Leading indicators Certain kinds of economic activity that lead the business cycle by increasing or decreasing before the rest do. Measurements of these indicators are "weather vanes" for the economy.

Leakages Factors in the multiple creation of demand deposits that reduce the ability of depository institutions to expand the supply of money or demand deposits.

Legal tender Anything that the law requires be accepted in payment of a debt.

Limited liability A legal term that means that those who own the corporation (stockholders) are not responsible for its debts. Stockholders' liability (or the amount stockholders are liable for if the firm goes bankrupt) is limited to the purchase price of their stock.

Liquid assets Assets, such as savings accounts or government bonds, that can be quickly converted into money with little risk of loss.

Liquidate To sell a firm or to convert its plant capacity to producing other goods.

Logrolling The practice of trading votes or trading support for one issue in order to obtain support for another.

Long-run period A planning period of a firm or industry, in which all inputs are variable. During this period, the firm can choose any plant size permitted by present technology and by its financial limitations.

Lorenz curve A curve that shows the degree of inequality in the distribution of income for a specific year. The percentage of people in different groups is shown on the horizontal axis, and the percentage of income going to each group is shown on the vertical axis.

Loss minimization *See* Profit maximization.

M1 money A measure of the money supply that consists of currency, coin and checking deposits.

M2 money A measure of the money supply that consists of all components in M1 plus savings deposits, small time deposits and money market mutual funds.

M3 money A measure of the money supply that consists of all the components of M2 plus large value certificates of deposit.

Macroeconomics The study of the forces that determine the level of income and employment in a society.

Malthusian specter The nineteenth-century view, advanced by Thomas R. Malthus, that the supply of people (increasing at a geometric rate) would outrun the supply of food (increasing at an arithmetic rate), and that widespread starvation would result.

Margin requirements Regulation by the Federal Reserve of the percentage of the selling price of stock that a purchaser must put down in cash in order to buy a stock. The purchaser may borrow the rest from a bank or a stockbroker.

Marginal cost The cost of producing an additional unit of output.

Marginal efficiency of capital The expected rate of return on capital; the stream of income a business expects to obtain over the life of a piece of capital in relation to the price of that capital.

Marginal physical product The additional amount of product that a firm can produce as a result of hiring an additional unit of input (labor, capital, and so on).

Marginal private cost or benefit Cost or benefit that individuals derive from producing or consuming an additional unit of a good.

Marginal propensity to consume The percentage of any change in income that people tend to spend:

$$MPC = \frac{\Delta C}{\Delta Y},$$

where C = consumption, Y = income and Δ (Greek delta) = "change in."

Marginal propensity to save The percentage of any change in income that people tend to save:

$$MPS = \frac{\Delta S}{\Delta Y},$$

where S = savings, Y = income and Δ (Greek delta) = "change in."

Marginal resource cost The amount it costs a firm to hire one more unit of a resource or factor.

Marginal revenue The change in total revenue due to a small or one-unit change in output.

Marginal revenue product The addition to total revenue attributable to using an additional unit of a resource. One finds it by multiplying the marginal physical product of the resource times the marginal revenue from selling the additional units of product it produces.

Marginal social cost or benefit Cost or benefit to society caused by producing and consuming an additional unit of a good.

Marginal tax rates The rates on additional taxable income.

Marginal utility The additional satisfaction derived from the consumption of the last unit (or additional unit) of a good purchased.

Marginal utility of income The change in satisfaction derived from a change in income.

Marginal utility of leisure The change in satisfaction derived from a per-unit change in leisure time.

Market period The period of time in which a firm has already produced its output. All costs are fixed costs.

Market system The set of means by which exchanges between buyer and seller are made.

Marxist socialism A system of philosophy of government and economics that grew out of the writings of Karl Marx in the nineteenth century.

Materials-balance approach An explanation of environmental problems based on the amount of input used in production and the disposal of waste products created in the consumption of that output.

Means of deferred payment The function of money that is concerned with facilitating lending and the repayment of loans.

Medium of exchange The function of money that deals with exchanging goods for money and money for goods.

Mercantilism A system of economic thought, at its peak from the sixteenth to nineteenth centuries, according to which governments were responsible for the welfare of the economy.

Microeconomics The study of disaggregated economic activities or how a market economy allocates resources through prices.

Midpoint formula A device for calculating the price elasticity of demand by dividing the average rate of change in quantity demanded by the average rate of change in price.

Mixed economies Economic systems that combine elements of private and public property rights and centralized as well as decentralized choices about resource usage.

Model A device economists use to create a systematic analogy to actual economic behavior.

Monetarism An approach to economic policy that emphasizes the dominant role of the supply of money. It calls for a fixed and appropriate increase in the money supply each year as the basic policy for economic stabilization.

Monetary policy A government's manipulation of the money supply and the rate of interest to achieve economic goals.

Money Anything that performs the functions of a medium of exchange, standard of values, store of value, and standard of deferred payment.

Money (current) GNP Output of a given year valued at the prices of that year. Data on GNP before being adjusted for price changes.

Money income The number of dollars received in income; does not reflect purchasing power.

Monopolistic competition A market situation with three main characteristics: (1) many firms, (2) differentiated products, and (3) relative ease of entry into and exit from the market.

Monopoly power A firm's ability to influence the price of its product.

Monopsony A market situation in which there is only one buyer.

Monopsony profit *See* Technical factor exploitation.

Moral suasion The use of persuasion by the Federal Reserve to get depository institutions to do what it wants.

Multinational corporations (MNCs) International firms that buy raw materials, sell finished products, and have production facilities in many countries.

Multiplier effect The multiple change in income due to a given initial change in aggregate demand. *See also* Balanced-budget multiplier.

Multiplier formula

$$M = \frac{1}{1-MPC} \quad \text{or} \quad M = \frac{1}{MPS},$$

where MPC = marginal propensity to consume and MPS = marginal propensity to save.

National banks Commercial banks chartered by the federal government.

National income (NI) Net income of a country using factor prices generated in the production of all goods and services in a given period of time. NI = wages and salaries + rent + interest + proprietors' income + corporate profits.

National income at factor prices Net income of a country obtained by using only market prices of factors rather than market prices of finished commodities or sales on the commodity markets.

Natural monopoly A market situation for an industry in which there are economies of scale up to the output rate that fills the market. A single firm is more efficient than any larger number of firms.

Natural rate of unemployment The difference between full employment and a zero level of unemployment. Explained by frictional unemployment.

Near money Assets that have all the characteristics of money except that they are not used as a medium of exchange.

Negatively sloped Sloping downward, as in a curve.

Negative net investment A situation in which gross investment is less than depreciation. In such a case, the capital stock of the economy is contracting.

Negative savings *See* Dissavings.

Negative sum game When losses exceed the winnings in a game.

Neoclassical economics School of economic thought developed during the late nineteenth century. Many aspects of this thought are considered valid today, and many others have been changed and expanded. For example, Keynesian economics (named after John Maynard Keynes) evolved from a basic change in one aspect of neoclassical economics.

Net foreign trade (NFT) The difference betwen exports and imports:

$$NFT = X - M,$$

where X = exports and M = imports.

Net national income (NNI) A nation's net income at market prices generated in the production of all final goods and services during a given period of time (excluding depreciation) NNI = wages and salaries + rent + interest + proprietors' income + corporate profits + indirect business taxes.

Net national product (NNP) The net value of all final goods and services a nation produces during a given time period (excluding depreciation), NNP = consumption + net investment + government expenditures ± net exports.

Nomenklatura The term used to describe the Soviet elite whose special entitlements increase their real incomes.

Nondurable goods Commodities, such as food, that are used up fairly quickly.

Nonprice competition Forms of competition between businesses that do not involve price. May include competition in styling, services, advertising, and quality.

Normal goods Those that consumers buy more of as their real incomes rise and less of as their real incomes fall.

Normal profit A profit just large enough to keep the firm producing in the long run. Normal profit equals the entrepreneur's opportunity cost (what entrepreneurship could earn in other uses). A normal profit is included in total cost.

Normative economics Economic discussions that make judgments about the way things should be.

Official reserve transactions account An account of those sources such as borrowing from other official agencies that finance the basic balance.

Official reserve transactions balance In a nation's balance of payments, the account showing how a payment deficit is financed.

Oligopoly An industry characterized by (1) the existence of several firms, each of which can affect the actions of others in the industry; (2) either homogeneous or differentiated products; and (3) significant barriers to entry.

Oligopsony A situation in which there are few buyers in the market.

OPEC An acronym for the Organization of Petroleum Exporting Countries, an international oil export cartel that sets the price of (most) exported oil.

Open market economy A market economy that does exchange products, services, or resources with other economies.

Open-market operations The buying and selling, by the Federal Reserve, of highly liquid, short-term, low-risk government debt.

Opportunity cost The alternative goods one gives up when one chooses to produce a certain thing.

PACs or political action committees Organizations that channel funds from special interest groups to the election campaigns of politicians.

Paradox of thrift An ironic situation in which, during a recession, if people all try to increase their savings, the equilibrium level of income of the nation and the actual quantity saved decrease.

Paradox of value That some goods have great total utility in use (e.g.; water) but little in exchange while other goods have relatively little value in use (e.g.; diamonds) but great value in exchange. The price we are willing to pay for a good is based on its value in exchange.

Pareto optimal A rule change that makes at least one person better off while making no one else worse off.

Parity A level for farm-product prices, maintained by governmental support and intended to give farmers the same purchasing power for each product sold as they had in some designated base period.

Partnership A business arrangement in which two or more individuals combine to operate an unincorporated business enterprise.

Per capital real GNP The figure obtained by dividing real GNP by the size of the population.

Per se rule A rule in law that certain acts are illegal in and of themselves, no matter what their intent.

Perfect economic integration The situation in which units of a resource are paid the same amount in all uses of that resource.

Perfect elasticity The situation in which price elasticity of demand approaches infinity. This means that as the quantity demanded changes, there is no change in price. The demand curve is horizontal.

Perfect inelasticity The situation in which price elasticity of demand equals zero. This means that as price changes, there is no change in quantity demanded. The demand curve is vertical.

Perfect integration The situation in which units of a resource are paid the same amount in all uses of that resource.

Perfect price discrimination The situation in which a firm charges the same consumer a different price for each unit sold. The price is the maximum that the consumer will pay for each unit.

Perfectly contestable market One in which there are no losses from entry or exit due to sunk costs.

Periodic multiplier A multiplier effect that takes place over time. *See also* Multiplier effect.

Personal disposable income The portion of personal income that people may either spend or save. PDI = personal income - personal taxes.

Personal income All income received by people, whether from production or from transfer payments. PI = national income + undistributed corporate profits + corporate taxes ± net transfer payments.

Phillips curve A curve that shows the tradeoff between unemployment and price changes. If employment increases, prices will increase; if unemployment increases, price increases will go down.

Physical capital Capital in the form of tools and instruments of production.

Pigou effect An economic reaction whereby, as prices fall, people with savings have greater purchasing power; therefore, savers increase their demand for goods and services.

Positive economics Economic discussions that consist of pointing out what *is*.

Positive net investment A situation in which gross investment exceeds depreciation; this means that the capital stock of the economy is expanding.

Positive sum game When winnings exceed losses in a game.

Positively sloped Sloping upward, as in a curve.

Precautionary purposes One reason why people want to hold money; they want cash in hand in case of emergencies.

Preferred stocks Stocks that have preference status when it comes to receiving dividends and assets of a given corporation, in case the corporation should have to liquidate. Preferred stocks usually do not carry voting privileges, and the amount of dividends is usually limited.

Present discriminatory activity Basing jobs and wages on goods other than productivity.

Price discrimination The charging of different prices for a good to different consumers. A situation in which the price of a unit of some good, divided by the marginal cost of that unit, is not the same for all customers. The seller of the good discriminates against some customers.

Price elastic A term describing a market situation in which the quantity of a good demanded changes at a faster rate than the price of the good:

$$\frac{\Delta Q}{Q} > \frac{\Delta P}{P},$$

where Q = quantity demanded, P = price, Δ (Greek delta) = "change in, " and > = "greater than."

Price elasticity of demand (E_d) An estimate of the rate at which the quantity demanded of a good varies in response to its price:

$$E_d = \frac{\Delta Q}{Q} / \frac{\Delta P}{P},$$

where Q = quantity demanded, P = price, Δ (Greek delta) = "change in."

Price elasticity of supply An estimate of the rate at which the quantity demanded of a god supplied changes as the price of the product changes:

$$\frac{\Delta Q}{Q} / \frac{\Delta P}{P},$$

where Q = quantity supplied, P = price, Δ (Greek delta) = "change in."

Price floor A target price, usually established by government, below which the market price is not allowed to move.

Price index A measure of changes in a price level.

Price inelastic demand A term describing a market situation in which the quantity of a good demanded changes at a slower rate than the price of the good:

$$\frac{\Delta Q}{Q} < \frac{\Delta P}{P},$$

where Q = quantity demanded, P = price, Δ (Greek delta="change in," and < = "less than."

Price leadership In an oligopoly, a form of implicit collusion in which a leader firm sets prices that are observed and followed by others in the industry.

Price rivalry The contest in which sellers watch what prices others charge and then react to those prices.

Price seeker A firm that must set the price of its product(s) as well as determine its most profitable output rate.

Price taker A firm which acts on a price that is beyond its control.

Primary demand Demand for a commodity (such as cars or refrigerators) by those who have not owned that commodity before: first-time owners.

Private equilibrium The *market* equilibrium between the buyer's privately and noncollusively determined benefits from the sale of a commodity and the seller's privately determined costs (including the profit necessary for entrepreneurship).

Private rates of return Rates of return on investment that do not take into account indirect social costs and benefits (called external costs and benefits).

Producers' surplus The difference between the actual selling price of a good and the marginal cost of producing it.

Product differentiation The preference of consumers for the products of one firm over those of other firms.

Production-possibilities curve A useful device derived from the production-possibilities function. *See also* Production-possibilities function.

Production-possibilities function A relationship expressing those combinations of goods that the full-employment use of a society's resources can produce during a particular period of time (using the best available technology).

Profit A return or payment to the entrepreneur.

Profit maximization Profit is said to be maximized or loss minimized when production is at the level at which marginal cost is equal to marginal revenue.

Profit-push inflation *See* Administered-price inflation.

Profits of unincorporated businesses. *See* Proprietors' income.

Progressive tax A tax with a rate that increases as the tax base increases.

Proletariat Workers in the factories of the industrial societies developed since the eighteenth century.

Property rights Rights of ownership to use, to transfer, and to benefit from the employment of factors of production.

Proportional tax A tax with a rate that remains the same as the tax base changes.

Proprietors' income The return to entrepreneurship in firms that are not incorporated.

Protectionism The government's effort to protect domestic firms or industries from free (competitive) international trade by imposing tariffs or quotas on imported commodities.

Public goods Goods that can be used by a person without reducing the amount available for other people to use.

Pure competition A market form that has the following characteristics: (1) No single firm can influence price. (2) There is no collusion. (3) Products are homogeneous. (4) There are no barriers to entry or exit. (5) Prices are flexible. (6) Buyers and sellers have full information.

Pure economic determinism The assumption that the actions of people and institutions are reactions to changing economic reality.

Pure economic rent The payment to a resource whose supply is perfectly inelastic.

Pure monopoly A market form in which (1) there is just one firm, and (2) the firm's product has no close substitutes.

Pure monopsony A labor market situation in which there is one employer that sets wage rates.

Pure number A number that is independent of the units of measure of the factors involved in compiling it.

Quantity adjuster A firm that has no control over the price at which it sells its product. It decides only how much to produce.

Quasi-rent or common rent The difference between the actual payment to a resource in relatively inelastic supply and its opportunity cost.

Quotas Restrictions on the quantities of goods that may be imported into, or exported from, a country.

Random variations Variations that cannot be accounted or planned for, since they do not follow any regular pattern.

Rational expectations hypothesis The view that decision makers form their inflationary expectations on the basis of current and recent past events and thus anticipate future events.

Rate of exchange The price at which one nation's currency is exchanged for that of another.

Rate of transformation The rate at which one good is traded off for another.

Rational ignorance The argument that when the benefits of a public choice are highly concentrated and its costs highly diffused, it is rational for those who bear its costs to ignore them.

Real GNP The output of a nation for a given year, adjusted for price changes between that year and given base year.

Real income The value of what one can buy with one's money income.

Regressive tax A tax with a rate that declines as the tax base increases.

Regulated monopoly A market situation in which one firm usually has a franchise from government, but a government regulatory commission sets prices and other conditions that the firm must follow.

Regulation Q A government regulation that empowered the Federal Reserve to set the maximum interest rates that commercial banks can pay on savings accounts and demand deposit (checking) accounts. This regulation was abolished in the early 1980s.

Regulations X and W Government regulations that empowered the Federal Reserve to set minimum down payments and maximum length of loans for consumer lending and real estate lending; expired in the 1960s.

Relative rent Differences in rent payments to a resource in different uses.

Rent (national income measures) In the calculation of gross national income, the payments to owners of land. Includes an estimated rent on homes occupied by their owners.

Rent (resource market payments) A payment to resource owners above that which would just induce them to employ resources in a particular use.

Rent seeking activities Those activities undertaken by special interest groups to obtain privileges from governments that will raise their return above opportunity cost.

Replacement demand *See* Secondary demand.

Representative democracies Systems of government in which voters choose elected representatives to make public choices.

Required reserve ratio The percentage of depository institutions' demand deposits that the Federal Reserve requires these banks to keep in the form of assets called reserves.

Reserve army of the unemployed A Marxist term denoting the number of people who are unemployed in capitalistic societies because of the increased use of capital and improved technology (that is, machines replacing labor).

Reserves Eligible assets (their eligibility determined by the Federal Reserve) that must be held by depository institutions.

Resource externalities Changes in the costs of resources that are not attributable to the actions of a single firm but are due to changes in the industry, or in the natural or political environment.

Resources The inputs (land, labor, capital, entrepreneurship) used to make consumer and producer goods.

Results of historical discrimination The effects on present patterns of jobs and wages attributable to previous economic discrimination.

Retained earnings Undistributed corporate profits.

Rule of reason A rule under which there is a broad judicial determination of the reasons for a firm's conduct and the effects of that conduct on restraint of trade.

Sales maximization hypothesis The argument that firms seek to maximize sales or the size of the firm rather than the firm's profit.

Satisficing A decision to seek an acceptable or satisfactory level of profit as opposed to a maximum level of profit.

Savings-equals-intended-investment approach An approach to the problem of finding equilibrium income—in a model without government and foreign trade—according to which the intended investment curve is placed above the x axis (measured income) in relation to the savings function ($S = II$).

Savings function Schedule of the quantities that people are willing and able to save at different levels of income during a given period of time.

Say's law Supply creates its own demand

Scarcity The relation between limited resources and unlimited wants which results in the inability to satisfy all human wants for goods and services.

Seasonal variations Fluctuations in employment, money supply, and cash flows that occur regularly at certain periods each year.

Second degree price discrimination The practice of charging different prices to different groups of buyers.

Secondary demand Demand by consumers for commodities to replace consumer goods.

Secular trend The expansion or contraction of an economy over very long periods of time. The long-term trend in any time series.

Services Those products of an economy (haircuts, medical attention, and so on) that are not commodities. The value of services is included when GNP is computed.

Short-run period The period of actual production, in which some resources used by a firm are fixed and at least one resource is variable.

Shut down point or price The rate of output that corresponds to a price equaling average variable cost. Total revenue equals total variable cost and the firm's loss is no greater with than without production.

Signaling The idea that employers pay higher wages to more educated workers because the education is a signal of other aspects of productivity increasing behavior.

Single-tax movement A school of thought in the late nineteenth century, led by Henry George, which proposed taxing away all land rents and using the revenues to fund governments.

Social costs Private costs plus spillovers (externalities). *See also* Externalities; Spillovers.

Socialism A social system in which there is collective or governmental ownership of the means of production and distribution of goods. There are many brands of socialism, encompassing many gradations of political and economic thought. Common to all of them is the idea that control of the means of production should be in public, not private, hands.

Sole proprietorship A form of business enterprise in which one person is the owner, and is solely responsible for that enterprise.

Special drawing rights (SDRs) A system of international reserve assets, the so-called "paper gold"; a market basket of currencies established by the International Monetary Fund (IMF). Nations that are members of the IMF may borrow these SDRs to ease currency crises.

Special interest laws Those that confer concentrated benefits but impose diffused costs on voters.

Specific powers of the Federal Reserve Powers of the Federal Reserve to regulate particular areas of lending, such as margin requirements on stock purchases; Regulation Q, W, and X were part of these powers.

Speculative purposes One reason why people wish to hold some of their assets in the form of money: they want to be able to take advantage of unforeseen opportunities to invest, to buy bargains, and so forth.

Spillovers Differences between *private* costs and benefits and *public* costs and benefits. *See also* Externalities.

Standard of value The function of money that enables people to place values on goods and services.

State banks Commercial banks chartered by the various state governments.

Static efficiency At a point in time, using resources in ways that produce the most desired mix of output.

Stationary state A condition in which a given society has reached the upper limit to its growth in per capita income.

Store of value The function of money that enables holders of money to save by a process of transferring value from the present to the future.

Structural deficits component That part of the federal deficit that arises from discretionary fiscal policy.

Structural unemployment A kind of unemployment caused by changes in the structure of the economy, either in the composition of demand or in technology. Either one of these types of changes may cause changes in the composition of the demand for labor.

Substitutes Products that may be consumed in place of each other.

Substitution effect An effect that appears when there is a change in the quantity of a good demanded resulting from a change in its price relative to other goods' prices. This effect comes to light during analysis of demand in a given market. A relatively cheaper good is substituted for relatively more expensive goods.

Sunk costs Outlays on resources that have already been made. Also called fixed costs.

Superior goods Those whose consumption varies in the same direction as but at a greater rate than real income.

Supply A set of relationships representing the quantities of a product that a firm (or all firms in an industry) will offer for sale at each possible price in a given period of time.

Supply curve A graphic plotting of the supply schedule, or a set of relationships between various prices of a good and the quantities of it that a firm supplies.

Supply of M_1 money All demand deposits in commercial banks, plus all currency and coin in circulation.

Supply of resources The quantities of a resource offered for sale at various prices in a given period of time.

Supply side economics Efforts and incentives to stimulate growth in aggregate supply.

Surplus value Marxist term for the differences between the wages paid to workers and the market value of what workers produce. Surplus value, to Marxists, measures the degree of exploitation of the proletariat (working class).

Synthesis In Marxist theory, the system that evolves after the antithesis has forced social changes.

Tariffs Taxes on imported goods.

Tax avoidance The process by which tax obligations are minimized by lawful use of the provision of tax laws.

Tax evasion The illegal process by which tax obligations are either not reported or incorrectly reported in order to evade payment.

Tax rate With respect to income, the percentage of income a citizen must pay annually in taxes. With respect to property, the percentage of the value of property the owner must pay to the government annually in taxes.

Technical factor exploitation In factor markets, the failure of a monopsonistic employers to pay resources their value of marginal product or marginal revenue product (also called monopsony profit).

Technocrats Term used by John Kenneth Galbraith to describe those who hold power in large corporations (also used to apply to those who would "manage" the economy).

Technological change Growth in knowledge or advances in techniques that result in more productive capital goods and more efficient organization.

Technostructure Term used by John Kenneth Galbraith to describe the many interlocking committees of people with technical expertise in large corporations, who make the essential corporate decisions.

Terms of trade Relationship between a nation's export prices and its import prices:

$$T = \frac{P_X}{P_I},$$

where P_X = prices of exports and P_I = prices of imports.

Thesis In Marxist theory, the set of social arrangements existing at a given time.

Tight money policy A policy of a nation's central banking authority that aims at reducing aggregate demand by decreasing the supply of money and increasing interest rates.

Time deposits Savings accounts for which depository institutions can require prior notice before the account holder can withdraw the funds.

Total cost Total fixed cost plus total variable cost.

Total utility The entire satisfaction from consuming a good.

Transactions purposes One reason for holding some assets in the form of money. People do not receive their income at exactly the same time that they need to pay out money. Thus, they want to hold money to be able to meet these day-to-day payments.

Trust An organization that controls the voting shares of an industry and thus can set output rates and prices like a multi-plant monopoly.

Turnover tax A tax on goods as they pass through the various stages of production. The Soviet Union uses turnover taxes to increase prices so that the quantities of goods available (quantity supplied) will be equal to the quantities demanded. It is also employed in some Western European countries.

UNCTAD United Nations Conference on Trade and Development.

Underemployment An employment situation in which units of resources are not employed in their most productive uses.

Unemployment A situation in which a unit of a resource is unable to find use as an input.

Underground economy Transactions that occur and give rise to taxable income but are not reported for tax purposes.

Union shop A labor market in which individuals who are employed by a firm must then join the union.

Unions Organizations formed by employees for purposes of collective bargaining with employers.

Unit elastic demand A term describing a market situation in which quantity demanded of a good changes at the same rate as its price:

$$\frac{\Delta Q}{Q} = \frac{\Delta P}{P},$$

where Q = quantity demanded, P = price, and Δ (Greek delta) = "change in."

Unit of account *See* Standard of value.

Unlimited liability A situation in which there is no differentiation between the assets of the business and the personal wealth of its proprietor. If the business suffers reverses, the owner is personally liable for all its debts.

Unlimited life A situation in which a corporation can continue to exist no matter who owns its stock.

Unplanned additions to inventory A situation in which a business firm produces more of its product than the public is willing or able to buy, which must then be added to inventory. The result is that the business acts to reduce supplies and reduce amounts produced; income moves toward equilibrium.

Unplanned reduction in inventory A situation in which a business firm does not produce as much of its product as the public is willing and able to buy. The result is that the business acts to increase its orders and increase the amounts produced; income moves toward equilibrium.

Utility theory A theory of demand that assumes that consumers buy things on the basis of their evalution of the satisfaction to be derived from various combinations of goods, and of their effort to maximize that satisfaction.

Value-added method A method of computing GNP in which one adds all additions to the value of a product made at each stage of production; the total of these additions for a given product equals the final value of that product.

Value of marginal product The value to consumers of the output produced by using an additional unit of a resources. One computes this value by multiplying the marginal physical product of the resource times the price of the good produced by the resource.

Variable costs Costs of factors of production (such as labor, raw materials, and so forth) that vary according to variations in the firm's output.

Veblen good A good whose appeal is greater at higher prices than at lower prices.

Velocity of exchange The number of times the supply of money changes hands in a given period of time.

Vertical mergers Those between firms in different industries.

Visible items Those commodities (such as cars, food, and machinery) that are exported or imported by a nation.

Wage and price controls Mandatory limits on wages and prices established by a regulatory authority and enforced by law.

Wage and price guidelines Suggested rules for levels of wages and prices. The government suggests these rules, but compliance with them is voluntary.

Wage discrimination A form of price discrimination in which employers use, as criteria to determine the wages they pay to their employees, certain characteristics that have nothing to do with the productivity of the employees, such as race or sex. They may pay lower wages to blacks than to whites, to women than to men, and so forth.

Wages and salaries The money income, including social security taxes, that is the return to labor; figured into the computation of gross national income.

Waste of monopolistic competition The failure of monopolistically competitive firms to produce at minimum long-run average cost or, in other words, the tendency to product with excess capacity.

Wholesale price index An index that measures change in wholesale prices.

Zero economic growth (ZEG) The idea or belief that an economy's GNP should not increase. ZEG is usually based on a concern for preserving or improving the physical and cultural environment.

Zero population growth (ZPG) The slogan advanced by people who feel that the birth rate should equal the death rate so that population will not increase.

Zero sum game When winnings are equal to losses in a game.

Index